THE COURSE OF LIFE

Volume I

THE COURSE OF LIFE

Volume I

Infancy

Edited by

Stanley I. Greenspan, M.D.
George H. Pollock, M.D., Ph.D.

INTERNATIONAL UNIVERSITIES PRESS, INC.
Madison   Connecticut

This is a revised and expanded version of *The Course of Life: Psychoanalytic Contributions Toward Understanding Personality Development*, edited by Stanley I. Greenspan and George H. Pollock, published by the U. S. Government Printing Office, Washington, D. C., 1980.

Library of Congress Cataloging in Publication Data

The Course of life / edited by Stanley I. Greenspan, George H. Pollock.
p. cm.
"Revised and expanded version"—T.p. verso.
Includes bibliographies and index.
Contents: v. 1. Infancy.
ISBN 0-8236-1123-X (v. 1)
1. Personality. 2. Psychoanalysis. 3. Developmental psychology.
I. Greenspan, Stanley I. II. Pollock, George H.
[DNLM: 1. Human Development. 2. Personality Development.
3. Psychoanalytic Theory. WM 460.5.P3 C861]
BF698.C68 1989
155.2'5—dc 19
DNLM/DLC   88-28465
for Library of Congress   CIP

Manufactured in the United States of America

Contents

List of Contributors

T. Berry Brazelton, M.D., Associate Professor of Pediatrics, Harvard Medical School; Chief, Child Development Unit, Children's Hospital Medical Center, Boston.

John Bowlby, Honorary Consultant Psychiatrist, Tavistock Clinic, England.

Helen Buchsbaum, Ph.D., Postdoctoral Fellow, Department of Psychiatry, University of Colorado, School of Medicine, and MacArthur Foundation on Early Childhood Transitions.

Robert N. Emde, M.D., Professor of Psychiatry, University of Colorado, School of Medicine;Adjunct Professor of Psychology,University of Denver; Faculty, Denver Institute of Psychoanalysis.

Erik H. Erikson, Psychoanalyst, Professor of Human Development and Lecturer on Psychiatry, Emeritus, Harvard University.

David A. Freedman, M.D., Professor of Psychiatry, Baylor College of Medicine; Training and Supervising Analyst, Houston-Galveston Psychoanalytic Institute.

Anna Freud, C.B.E., LL.D., Sc.D., M.D. (Hon),† Past Director, Hampstead Child Therapy Course and Clinic, now known as the Anna Freud Centre, London, England.

W. Ernest Freud, B.A., Training Psychoanalyst, Institute of Psycho-Analysis, London; Training and Research Psychoanalyst, Hampstead Child Therapy Clinic, now known as the Anna Freud Centre, London, England.

Pirkko L. Graves, Mag. Phil., Ph.D., Assistant Professor of Psychiatry; Lecturer in Medicine; Senior Research Psychologist, The Precursors Study, The Johns Hopkins Medical Institutions, Baltimore, Maryland; Associate Clinical Professor of Psychiatry, University of Maryland School of Medicine, Baltimore, Maryland.

Stanley I. Greenspan, M.D., Clinical Professor of Psychiatry and Behavioral Sciences, and Child Health and Development, George Washington University Medical Center, Washington, D.C.; Supervising Child Psychoanalyst, Washington Psychoanalytic Institute.

Alicia F. Lieberman, Ph.D., Associate Professor, University of California-San Francisco; Senior Psychologist, Infant-Parent Program, San Francisco General Hospital.

Lewis P. Lipsitt, Ph.D., Professor of Psychology and Medical Science; Director, Child Study Center, Brown University.

†Deceased.

Reginald S. Lourie, M.D., Med. Sc.D.,† Professor Emeritus, Child Health and
Development, Psychiatry and Behavioral Sciences, George Washington
University; Senior Research Scientist, NIMH; Faculty, Baltimore-Washington Institute for Psychoanalysis.

Dorian Mintzer, Ph.D., M.S.W., Private practice in psychology and social
work, Boston; Lecturer in Psychiatry, Cambridge Hospital, Harvard
Medical School.

Lois Barclay Murphy, Ph.D. (Retired), Director of Developmental Studies,
Menninger Foundation.

Robert A. Nover, M.D., Associate Clinical Professor of Psychiatry and Behavioral Studies, and Child Health and Development, George Washington University Medical Center; Teaching Analyst, Baltimore-Washington
Institute for Psychoanalysis.

Louis W. Sander, M.D., Professor of Psychiatry, Division of Child Psychiatry,
University of Colorado Medical Center, Denver.

Theodore Shapiro, M.D, Professor of Psychiatry, Professor of Psychiatry in
Pediatrics, Cornell University Medical College, New York City; Director
of Child and Adolescent Psychiatry, Payne Whitney Clinic.

Martin A. Silverman, M.D., Clinical Professor, Training and Supervising
Analyst, Child Analysis Section, The Psychoanalytic Institute, New York
University Medical Center, New York City.

Daniel Stern, M.D., Associate Professor of Psychiatry, Cornell University
Medical Center, New York.

Preface

Perhaps the most illusive aspect of human development is the nature of man's innermost wishes, thoughts, and feelings. Until relatively recently, our limited understanding of this aspect of the mind has in part stemmed from a focus on the contributions of only a few developmental phases. Now, a wealth of observational, experimental, and clinical case studies at each stage in the course of life, ranging from early infancy to advanced ages, makes it possible to formulate a truly developmental perspective on mental functioning.

Each stage of development has its own special challenges, organizing properties, and unique meanings. Yet, each new stage builds on former ones, creating a developmental progression characterized by both continuity and opportunity. To understand the unique character of each stage of development, outstanding pioneers, clinical scholars, and researchers have prepared papers on each phase of development. Authors have been given an opportunity to update their original papers from the first edition of *The Course of Life*. Many have written new sections or entirely new papers. In addition, new contributions by outstanding investigators have been added for this revised and expanded edition. These papers have been organized according to stages in the course of life: infancy, early childhood, latency, adolescence, young adulthood, midlife, and the aging process. For each stage, each group of papers will illuminate the special challenges, potentials, and, most importantly, highly personal ways experience is organized.

1

Child Analysis as the Study of Mental Growth (Normal and Abnormal)

ANNA FREUD, C.B.E., LL.D., SC.D., M.D. (HON.)

The contributions of psychoanalysis to the understanding of human development and its many deviations from the norm have been manifold from its beginnings. They have become all the more significant with the advent of child analysis, when the reconstructed picture of early mental growth was deepened and extended by direct analytic exploration of the hidden mental processes in the very young, as well as by the analytically guided direct observation of their manifest reactions and types of behavior.

Trends in Child-Analytic Work

It is well known to workers in the field that the gradual spread and intensification of child analysis produced a variety of trends, consecutive or simultaneous, permanent or transitory, with lasting or evanescent results, each direction of interest upheld by prominent representatives, and also, in some instances, disappearing from the field with them.

The Infantile Neurosis and Its Prevention

The most familiar chapter in this development is the early era devoted to the study of the infantile neurosis and its prevention, initiated by Freud's case history of Little Hans (1909) and followed on the one hand by the first child-analytic treatments in Vienna, Berlin, and London, and on the other hand by the first analytic-educational experiments in Vienna, London, and Moscow.

The Technique of Child Analysis

There followed as a permanent, still ongoing trend, the struggle for the creation of a child-analytic technique, whether dependent or independent of the classical technique for adult analysis. Such a method was meant to mitigate the effects of the child's unwillingness or inability to embark on free association, his reduced insight and sincerity, his different transference reactions, and his unreliable therapeutic alliance due to the heightened pressure for immediate wish fulfillment and resulting diminished tolerance for frustration and anxiety.

The Widening Scope of Therapeutic Effort

Intermittently, as in the mainstream of psychoanalysis, the ambition to widen the scope of therapeutic application dominated the scene and led to the experimental treatment of disorders beyond the limits of the infantile neuroses, namely to the inclusion of borderline cases, autisms, infantile psychoses, mental deficiencies, etc.

Child Analysis Versus Adult Analysis

At times, the interrelations between child analysis and adult analysis were pushed into the foreground with questions posed and answered such as the following: whether the child analyst's findings confirm, refute, or amend what adult analysis had gleaned about the individual's early history; whether, beyond this, child-analytic work can break new ground; and, more recently, whether the added developmental information gained in child analysis has repercussions for the technical approach to adult patients and helps in understanding some of their more obscure deficiencies and abnormalities.

The Search for the Onset of Pathology

Finally, in our times, these various efforts culminated in one overriding concern, namely a determined search for the starting point of pathological involvement as such, whether this manifested itself as neurotic or psychotic symptomatology, as ego distortion, as character malformation, or as social casualties of every description and severity. As the studies proceeded, pathogenic processes which were originally ascribed to the phallic-oedipal phase were traced further and further back to the very beginning of mental or even of physical life.

Specialization of Theoretical Interest

It is this last-mentioned concern which caused many child-analytic authors to move toward a specialization of interest, i.e., to select as their particular subject of study the one period of life which to them seemed outstanding in its significance for determining the future difference between function and malfunction, efficiency and deficiency, adaptation and maladaptation—in short, between normality and pathology in human growth. Some authors fasten onto the birth process itself, hold its accumulation of distress responsible for creating an imbalance within the pleasure/pain series and for reducing the individual child's later frustration tolerance. Others choose as the vital era the first year of life with the transition from primary narcissism to object-directed libidinal interests, the whole process monitored by a successful, or stunted by a deficient, mother/infant relationship. Following Margaret Mahler's lead (1971), still others select the fascinating period of separation-individuation in the second year of life as the crucial one for deciding about the individual's further healthy independence and intact sense of identity. The oral, anal, and phallic levels have each found their own protagonists, with links being forged between events at these levels and specific pathological manifestations. If less pathogenic significance is attributed to the latency period (the normality or disruption of which is seen in itself as a function of the preceding developmental processes), this is offset again by a concentration of interest and accumulation of publications on the adolescent years, which, after all, have the final say about the young person's adult sexuality and social adaptation.

The relevant child-analytic literature thus presents to its readers a multitude of phase-centered studies, basically independent of each other but almost identical in their orientation

toward the elucidation of pathology as the derivative of one or
another specific developmental stage.

The Concept of Developmental Lines

What the child-analytic literature does not as yet offer are
consecutive longitudinal lines of development which, irrespec-
tive of health or illness, are concerned with all the characteristics
which distinguish the mature from the immature human individual.

Three Examples of Developmental Lines in Psychoanalytic Theory

Not that in the main body of psychoanalytic theory we are
left without prototypes for such lines. Concerning the development of the sexual drive, this is offered by the stepwise advance from one level to another, the oral, anal, and phallic
organizations following each other in a sequence determined
on the physical side by the prominence of certain relevant body
zones, and on the libidinal side by the moves from anaclitic to
constant, from ambivalent to postambivalent relationships, both
progressions heavily influenced by the environmental responses
of the human objects toward whom the child's urges are directed.

Concerning the ego's mechanisms of defense against danger, anxiety, and unpleasure of all types, we have been given
a distinctive line leading from flight and denial (against external
dangers) to projection and introjection (against internal ones)
and from these primitive methods to the highly important, sophisticated devices of repression, reaction-formation, sublimation, etc.

As regards the phenomenon of anxiety and the reasons
for its arousal, a line has been traced, leading from the archaic
fears of darkness, noise, and loneliness (caused by the ego's
weakness and immaturity) to the fear of abandonment, object
loss, and loss of love (caused by the child's libidinal dependence),
and finally to fear of the superego's disapproval, i.e., guilt
(caused by the internalization of parental demands).

Some Child Analytic Work on Further Lines

What concerns us today are the many other characteristics expected from the average adult which, on the basis of analytic work with adults, are described as to their end products, but for which no developmental pre-stages are itemized. This omission not only leaves a gap in developmental theory; it creates also the false impression that such achievements are come by easily, in fact that they are simply the result of smooth, undisputed, i.e., nonconflictual maturation.

By now there are a number of instances where child-analytic work has been able to correct this error. Developmental lines have been traced and implemented in detail, from libidinal dependence to self-reliance; from egocentricity to peer relationships; from inability to manage the body and its functions to the child's control of them; from play to work; etc. Apart from the steps which lead up to the final achievement in each instance, three important characteristics of such advances have been elicited: (1) that they are, without exception, determined by a multiplicity of influences; (2) that, not unlike neurotic symptoms, their various stages are compromise formations, constructed to comply at one and the same time with all of these disparate determinants; (3) that they are the result of the ego's synthetic function, of the working of which they give important evidence.

Developmental Moves Under Multiple Determination

As reported above for the line of sex development, the unfolding of all the other adult characteristics also proceeds under the combined influences, stemming on the one hand from the agencies within the personality structure, and on the other from the environment. To give a few examples only:

For the step from anaclitic (need-satisfying) relationships to object constancy, the *id's* urgency for gratification needs to decrease; the *ego* needs to acquire the ability to retain memory traces of objects, regardless of their absence; the human *objects* of the child's libido need to be constantly and reliably available in the external world.

The separation/individuation process is completed under three determinants: on the *physical side* the attainment of independent motility; on the *libidinal side* a lessening of utter dependence; on the *environmental side* the mother's acquiescence with her child's growing independence.

Control of elimination proceeds under the combined influence of the *physical* maturing of the sphincters; of the *environmental* routine imposed by the mothering adult; by the *ego's* tendency to comply to avoid loss of the latter's love.

The various steps on the complex line from play to work depend on the child's need for direct (or sublimated) *drive* satisfaction; on his awakening *ego* interests; on *environmental* provision of toys and opportunities; and, finally, on the ego's maturing ability to maintain aim-directed activities *regardless of immediate pleasure gain.*

Developmental Moves as Compromises in Two Types of Conflict

To render the described developmental advances nonconflictual would presuppose that the multiple influences on them are basically united as to their purposes and essentially coordinated as to the timing of their maturation. Since neither is the case, conflicts are inevitable. As described in the theory of the neuroses, each agency within the personality structure pursues its own aims while the environmental forces insist firmly on theirs. Thus, each step on each developmental line needs to be a compromise and to respond at least partially to each determinant. For example, while acquiring sphincter control to satisfy external authority, the child manages to salvage at least some pride and interest in his anal products and to satisfy these in indirect, displaced ways. While adopting the reality principle, he develops a whole secret domain of imagination and fantasy, free of interference by external demands. While learning to work in obedience to ego and environmental pressure, he invents hobbies to replace the pleasures formerly gained from play.

Compromises of this kind are adaptive and stabilizing for development. Uncompromising advances, which serve exclusively either external or a single internal agency, prove intolerable for the individual in the long run and are apt to lead to breakdowns.

There is a second source of conflicts which impede progress

and need to be resolved. The four interacting forces are frequently in disharmony with each other as regards the time factor. Ego and superego development may reach a level of maturity far in advance of the maturing of the drives, and vice versa, progress on the side of drive development may outstrip a delayed ego-superego growth. External intervention may be either too early or too late. Such different rates of progress in the various parts of the personality structure, as well as wrongly timed environmental action, throw development into confusion. Examples of this are manifold. For instance, *archaic fears* (of darkness, noise, etc.) do not fade out and give way to the next type of anxiety at the appropriate time in cases where ego growth is delayed due to mental deficiency. *Oral-cannibalistic* fantasies that normally arise before the ego's critical function is in action become unacceptable, i.e., a source of conflict, in cases where ego functions are precocious. *Individuation* is hindered where the child's readiness to separate does not coincide in time with the mother's readiness to detach herself from symbiosis with him. *Anal satisfactions* are defended against too energetically and cause obsessive manifestations in cases where the superego is premature, etc. In short, temporal disharmony, within the structure and/or with the environment, disrupts the order of developmental lines with pathological results on all levels.

Development as the Result of Synthesis

During our therapeutic activities we are confronted routinely by psychological formations which, as the result of introjection, identification, and integration, make up the personality. Firmly embedded as they are in the adult, they put our analytic efforts to dissect and dissolve them to a severe test. It is only during our work with children that we are offered the opportunity to meet psychic structure in the making and watch the ego's synthetic function at work.

Integration serves healthy growth provided the elements synthesized by it—namely the constitutional givens, the rate of structuralization and parental influence—remain within the limits of an expectable norm. As often as not, this is not the case. Constitutional handicaps often affect the ego/id substratum. Structure building is often uneven, with defects on the id, ego, or superego side. Parents often happen to be indifferent, absent, rejecting, punitive, insensitive, or, contrariwise, over-protective, possessive, and seductive. Whatever the elements for personality building offered thus to the immature being, integration will take hold of them and forge them into a whole. It is the hallmark of the synthetic function that, while doing its work, it does not distinguish between what is suitable or un-suitable, helpful or harmful for the resulting picture. Thus, every step on a developmental line, besides being a compromise between conflicting forces, represents also an amalgam of ben-eficial and malignant ingredients. The various mixtures pro-duced thereby can be held responsible for the numerous variations, deviations, quirks, and eccentricities displayed in the final personalities.

Suggestions for Further Work

The Range of Developmental Lines

The samples of developmental lines given above must by no means be mistaken for a complete enumeration. The list of adult characteristics is vast, and none of them is exempt from stepwise, gradual evolution.

Secondary process functioning, for example, is attained very slowly, linked with speech development, but with many halts and relapses, so far uncharted, which occur whenever the urge for immediate drive gratification reinstates direct primary proc-ess action.

Distinguishing between the *inner* and *outer world* has many—not yet described—pre-stages before it reaches its final form as the adult's *reality sense*.

On the line toward *discharging mental excitation* via mental (not somatic) pathways, there are all the notable (but not yet noted) holdups, breakdowns, and exemptions which occur whenever the road to conscious psychological expression is blocked by repression.

The line toward *impulse control* needs to be studied in view of degree and extent on the one hand and its constant alternation between success and failure on the other.

Development of a *time sense* in the adult is too much taken for granted, with too little attention paid to the pre-stages when time is measured exclusively by the id via the urgency of the drives, or to the period when environmentally imposed routine begins to prepare the child for the understanding of clock and calendar.

Likewise, the intermediate steps need to be characterized on the road from the child's *egocentric* to the adult's *objective* view of external events; on the road from childish *lack of insight* into internal processes to the adult's *acknowledgment* of them; as well as on the road to many other achievements.

The Respective Importance of Developmental Lines

That progression on the various developmental lines has different value for the final personality picture needs further elaboration. What can be stated now is only that some are vital, others of contributory relevance.

Obviously, the essential lines are those toward secondary process functioning, reality sense, objectivity, and insight (with some others to be added). No individual is deemed mature before all the steps on them have been taken and before the end result is not only reached but made secure. This is different in the case of impulse control, mental discharge, peer relationships, even sex, etc. In these respects, numerous individuals achieve no more than partial results, i.e., they stop at some intermediate station on the way, which affects the qualitative performance of their personality while leaving their adult status unquestioned.

We know that, in *sex*, large numbers of people never reach the end-point of the line, namely true genitality, and being otherwise adult, function sexually on a pregenital or prephallic level.

Regarding *impulse control* by the ego, many individuals cannot maintain this securely in the face of all conditions. They are adults, but their adult status in this respect is interrupted intermittently by temper outbursts or uncontrollable irritability when aggression reverts to the former state of being dominated by the id.

Where the line from *motor* to *verbal* expression of *aggression* remains uncompleted, it produces adults with violent characteristics.

The changeover from *somatic* to *mental* discharge of excitation is rarely carried to completion (except perhaps at the price of an obsessional neurosis); in many adults affects such as anger, fear, impatience, frustration, etc., still find outlet in headaches, sleep disturbances, and digestive upsets.

Any study of the line toward *peer relationships* demonstrates how rarely, even in maturity, its final point is reached and how often the intermediate stages of rivalry, jealousy, and lack of empathy continue to be dominant.

The Interdependence of Developmental Lines

There are many open questions in this respect, beyond the obvious fact that certain lines of development cannot materialize without being preceded or at least supported by certain others.

Ego control of body functions and impulses depends on prior steps from dependence on objects to identification with them.

Secondary process functioning implies a simultaneous advance toward impulse control.

The reduction of *panic* to *signal anxiety* presupposes advances in the maturity of defense activity.

Any step from *play* to *work* needs a prior commitment to the reality principle.

More knowledge about these interrelations will benefit the upbringing as well as the treatment of children with manifest developmental difficulties. In the case of any particular trend failing to progress, it is important to determine whether the deficiency is rooted in that particular line itself or whether it is the secondary consequence of failure on another line.

It is wasted educational or therapeutic effort to urge a child toward advancing on the line of play materials if the real reason for backwardness in this developmental area is an arrest on the line of libido development (i.e., utter dependence on the mother that results in a preference for soft toys as transitional objects).

A solitary child will not develop better peer relationships by being exposed to community life if his failure to progress on this line is due not to lack of opportunity, but to a deficiency in the advance from narcissism and egocentricity to object-libidinal relationships.

A Chronology of Developmental Lines

A chronology of development will always have to restrict itself to general terms in view of the wide range of individual variation. What can be hypothesized at present is no more than a rough division into three successive periods, each characterized by the number of forces interacting within it and to some extent by the major lines of development which have their beginning in it.

The *first period*, which covers approximately the first year of life, is simple in one respect, however important it may be in others. Interaction is restricted to two agents, the infant on the one hand, the mother on the other. The infant supplies to the combination the needs and urges inherent in his id/ego matrix; the mother her care in response to them.

Provided that constitutionally and environmentally the ingredients from both sides are within the norm, three developmental lines take their departure from here: distinction between soma and psyche; between the child's own and the mother's body; between self and object. However modest these beginnings are, and how distant still from the later mental discharge phenomena, from reality testing and from true object relationships, their occurrence is vital, and their absence has disastrous results. A child who tries to rid himself of unacceptable thoughts by standing on his head to shake them out is definitely borderline. A child who does not acknowledge the extent and limits of his own body jeopardizes his later sense of identity. A child who maintains symbiosis with the mother fails to move toward the higher levels of libidinal relatedness.

The *second period*, which, roughly, extends over the remainder of the preoedipal stages, marks the interaction of three forces. Id and ego, after the onset of structuralization, act as two separate ones, with parental intervention making up the third.

The developments which are initiated and continued under these conditions are, among others, those toward the control of *motility* and other *physical functions*, and toward *impulse control, secondary process* functioning, and object *constancy*. They are vital as a basis for further growth, and their failure or serious defects in them constitutes an ominous departure from mental health. They share at this stage the characteristic that forward and backward moves on the lines, progression and regression, alternate with each other. This is due to the state of the ego, which, while immature, vacillates in its allegiance. When under pressure from the drives, it sides with the id in the interest of gratification. When under pressure from parental demands, it sides with the environment to avoid recrimination and loss of love.

Irregularity and interruption of advance in this second period are normal, provided the relapses are temporary. If, instead of being short-lived, they are prolonged or even permanent, they cause pathological manifestations which resemble neurotic symptoms but, according to their structure, are not identical with them. They are preneurotic insofar as the conflicts they are trying to solve are not yet truly internal but due in equal parts to disharmonies within the personality and with the external world. However, they represent a fertile breeding ground for the later infantile neuroses.

In the *third period*, after completed structuralization, all further steps toward maturity on all developmental lines take place under the combined and competing influence emanating from four sides: id, ego, superego, and environment. However, as the superego gains independence due to its introjections, it strengthens the ego in its attitudes on the one hand and, on the other, takes over much, or all, of the environment's role in shaping progress. Accordingly, advance becomes stabilized and the disharmonies and conflicts involved in it change from the partly external to the truly intersystemic. Their solution, reached by compromise, may be adaptive, i.e., normal; or nonadaptive, i.e., truly neurotic.

Conclusion

On the basis of the foregoing argumentation, normality of development is seen to depend largely on four factors:

1. on the constitutional and experiential element in the life of an individual that determines whether or not he departs too far from what is average and expectable
2. on the internal agencies of the individual's personality maturing at approximately the same rate of speed, none of them being either delayed or precocious compared with the others
3. on external intervention being well-timed, coming neither too early nor too late
4. on the ego's mechanisms used to achieve the necessary compromises being age-adequate, i.e., neither too primitive nor too sophisticated

Investigation of the happenings on individual developmental lines from the aspect of these four points is recommended as a next rewarding trend for child-analytic work.

References

Freud, S. (1909), Analysis of a phobia in a five-year-old boy. *Standard Edition*, 10:5–147. London: Hogarth Press, 1955.

Mahler, M.S. (1971), A study of the separation-individuation process and its possible application to borderline phenomena in the psychoanalytic situation. *The Psychoanalytic Study of the Child*, 26:403–424.

2

Elements of a Psychoanalytic Theory of Psychosocial Development

ERIK H. ERIKSON

An Historical Note on the "Outerworld"

To restate what theoretical considerations one has advanced over the years in a variety of data-filled contexts may seem to be an unrewarding task to writer and reader alike. However, when the National Institute of Mental Health asked me to summarize my psychosocial concepts for these volumes, this appeared to me at once to be a valid undertaking. For such an extension of psychoanalytic theory could have originated only in this country and in a period when psychoanalysis—against a background of growing world turbulence—found itself welcomed into medical centers as well as into intensive interdisciplinary discussion. And such discussion later proved to be fundamental to the formulation of the central theme of the Midcentury White House Conference on Children and Youth, namely, "a healthy personality for every child."

The term and concept *psychosocial*, in a psychoanalytic context, is obviously meant to complement the dominant theory of psychosexuality. To chart the beginnings of such an effort I must go back to the time of my training in Vienna—the period of ascendance of ego psychology—and briefly trace some changing conceptualizations of the ego's relation to the social

The work on this essay was in part supported by a grant from the Maurice Falk Medical Fund in Pittsburgh, Pennsylvania.

environment. True, the two basic works on the ego, namely, Anna Freud's *The Ego and the Mechanisms of Defense* and Hartmann's *Ego Psychology and the Problem of Adaptation* appeared only in 1936 and in 1939, respectively. But the observations and conclusions on which these two works were based dominated much of the discussion in the years before the completion of my training and my migration to this country in 1933. The defensive and the adaptive functions of the ego have, in the meantime, become a firm facet of psychoanalytic theory. My purpose in referring back to their origins is to indicate in what way the overall theory seemed to be working toward and yet stopping short of a systematic attention to the place of the ego in the relationship of individuality to communality.

Most interesting in retrospect and most indicative of the hidden ideological controversies which mark the advancement of a field was the original discord between A. Freud's and Hartmann's emerging ideas. Freud herself, in her straightforward and instructive way, reports that when she first submitted her conclusions regarding the defensive functions of the ego to the Vienna Society in 1936, "Hartmann showed himself appreciative on the whole, but he emphasized the point that to show the ego at war with the id was not the whole story, that there was many additional problems of ego growth and ego functioning which needed consideration. My views were more restricted at the time, and this was news to me which I was not yet ready to assimilate." For, she continues, her contribution came "from the side of the ego's defensive activity against the drives; Hartmann, in a more revolutionary manner, from the new angle of ego autonomy which until then had lain outside analytic study" (Loewenstein, Newman, Schur, and Solnit, 1966).

The last three words point to the question of self-chosen boundaries drawn at various times in the development of psychoanalytic theory. To appreciate these we would need to consider the ideological as well as the scientific implications of every advance and of every corresponding term in psychoanalytic theory, and indeed in all applications of theories of natural science to man. Freud's original position, of course, was *drive*-oriented, and my generation of men and women trained in

Middle Europe will remember that this most fundamental of all terms, *Trieb*, in its German usage had a number of nature-philosophical connotations of an ennobling as well as elemental force which (for better or for worse) are lost in its translation into either "instinct" or "drive." *"Die suessen Triebe"*—"the sweet drives"—the German poet could say, while stern physiologists could speak of the obligation in all work worthy of the name of science to find "forces of equal dignity" (Jones, 1953) to those already isolated and quantified in the natural sciences. But if Freud (1914) insisted that "all our provisional ideas in psychology will presumably some day be based on an organic substructure," he was also willing to wait for a truly reliable experimental substantiation of an all-inclusive and then still admittedly mythical *instinctual energy*. Freud's work, furthermore, had begun in the century of Darwin's search for the evolutionary origin of the species; and the new humanist ethos demanded that mankind, once so proud of the consciousness and the moral stature of its assumed civilized maturity, would have to accept the discovery of its primary roots in its animal ancestry, in its primeval prehistory, and in the infantile stages of ontogeny. All this, at any rate, was once implied in that terminology of instinctual energy which over the years has come to convey a certain ritualistic conviction rather than the persistent hope of strict scientific substantiation. In its time, however, that energetic form of thought opened up undreamt-of—or was it dreamt-of?—insights. The purpose of drawing the line there, however, was (as the recently published correspondence between Freud and Jung has again so dramatically illustrated) Freud's conviction of the prime necessity to study vigilantly that unconscious and instinctual core of man which he called the "id" (and thus something akin to an inner outerworld) and to take no chances with man's tenacious resistance, which was and is always ready to devitalize new insights by remythologizing them or, indeed, by glibly ascribing them to "surface" psychology. No wonder, then, that social reality, in relation to the inner cauldron to be explored, at first occupied something of an extraterritorial position and, more often than not, was referred to as the "outerworld" or "external reality." Thus, our proud ego, which Freud (1914) called a "frontier-creature," owes "service to three masters and [is] consequently menaced by three dangers: from the external world, from the libido of the id, and from the severity of the super-ego" (p. 46).

When first discussing the relationship of the ego to group life, Freud (1921) discussed those social authors of his time (e.g., Le Bon, McDougal) who elaborated on "artificial" group formations—that is, mobs, crowds, mere masses, or what Freud calls "primary" and "primitive" groups. He focused on the "grownup individual's *insertion* into a collection of people which has *acquired* the characteristic of a psychological group" (italics mine). Prophetically, he mused on how such groups "allow man to throw off the repression of his unconscious impulses." Freud did not, at that time, ask the fundamental question as to how the individual in turn had first acquired what he "possessed outside the primitive group," namely, "his own continuity, his self-consciousness, his traditions and his customs, his own particular functions and position." Freud's main objective in analyzing "artificial" groups (such as a church or an army) was to show that such groups are held together by "love instincts" which have been diverted from their biological aims to help form social attachments "though they do not operate with less energy on that account." This last assumption must interest us in the context of psychosocial development: by what lawfulness can "love be transferred . . . from sexual to social aims"—and this undiminished?

A. Freud (1936), in her summary of the ego's defensive measures, again delegated the otherwise acknowledged presence of social forces to an "outside world": "the ego is victorious when its defensive measures . . . enable it to restrict the development of anxiety and so to transform the instincts that, even in difficult circumstances, some measure of gratification is secured, thereby establishing the most harmonious relations possible between the id, the super-ego, and the forces of the outside world" (p. 176). In her later work this trend continued in the formulation of the *developmental lines* which "in every instance . . . trace the child's gradual outgrowing of dependent, irrational, id- and object-determined attitudes to an increasing ego mastery of his internal and external world" (A. Freud, 1965). In asking, however, "what singles out individual lines for special promotion in development," she did suggest that "we have to look to accidental environmental influences. In the analysis of older children and the reconstruction from adult analysis we have found these forces embodied in the parents' personalities, their actions and ideals, the family atmosphere, the impact of the cultural setting as a whole." Here the question remains which of these environmental influences are more or less "accidental."

Hartmann, in turn, went all out in speaking not only of the independent roots of ego development and in calling motility, perception, and memory "ego apparatuses of primary autonomy"; he also considered all these developing capacities to be in a state of adaptedness to what he called "an average expectable environment." As Rapaport put it: "By means of these concepts [Hartmann] laid the foundation for the psychoanalytic concept and theory of adaptation, and outlined the first generalized theory of *reality relations* in psychoanalytic ego psychology" (Rapaport in Erikson, 1959). But, so Rapaport adds, he "does not provide a specific and differentiated psychosocial theory." And, indeed, an "average expectable environment" seems to postulate only a minimum of environmental conditions which make survival universally possible while putting aside the enormous variations and complexities of social life which are the source of individual and communal vitality—as well as conflict. In fact, Hartmann's writings, too, continued to employ such terms as "acting in regard to reality," "action vis-à-vis reality" (1947) and "acting in the outer world" (1956), to mention some of the shortest quotable indications as to where, in a field's development, the lines are drawn at a given time.

The mechanistic and physicalistic wording of psychoanalytic theory as well as the persistent references to the "outerworld" came to puzzle me early in my training, especially in view of the general climate of the *clinical* seminars, which were alive with a new closeness to social as well as inner problems and thus were animated by a spirit which characterizes the nature of psychoanalytic training at its best. Freud (1926) once wrote to Romain Rolland that "our inborn instincts and the world around us being what they are, I could not but regard that love as no less essential for the survival of the human race than such things as technology . . ." (p. 279). And I see, indeed, a modern form of Caritas in the basic psychoanalytic acknowledgment that, in principle, all human beings are equal in their exposure to the same conflicts—this to the point where any healing contract demands that the healer exercise his "technique." These are, at any rate, the concepts and words I would use today in order to characterize the core of a new communal spirit which I perceived at times in my student years. Thus, the intense and extensive presentation and discussion of cases seemed to be in polar contrast to the terminological legacy which provided the framework for theoretical discourse: the *clinical* and the *theoretical* language seemed to celebrate two different attitudes toward human motivation, although, historically seen, they proved complementary within our training experience. Furthermore, as the treatment of adults had led to the formulation of some definite and most fateful substages of childhood, and thus to developmental assumptions which set an early pattern for the eventual study of the whole life cycle, the direct psychoanalytic observation and treatment of children had suggested itself powerfully.

In such work, the *developmental ethos* of psychoanalysis came to manifest itself most clearly, for as children offered striking symptomatic verifications of the pathographic assumptions of psychoanalysis, they often did so by outdoing all adult expectations in their directness of playful and communicative expression. Thus they revealed, along with the child's intense conflicts, a resourceful and inventive striving for experience and synthesis. At any rate, it was in seminars dealing with child patients and shared by psychoanalysts deeply involved in "progressive education" that the reductionist language of scientistic theory moved into the background, while the foreground became vivid with innumerable details illustrating the patient's mutual involvement with significant persons, even if they were said to be the "outerworld." Here, instead of the single person's inner *economics* of drive and defense, an *ecology* of mutual relations shared by a communal unit such as the family suggested itself as a future theoretical baseline.

Today I would not hesitate to designate the basic difference between the theoretical and the clinical approaches characterizing our training as that between last century's preoccupation with the economics of energy and this century's emphasis on complementarity and relativity. Without quite knowing what I was doing, I later titled the first chapter of my first book "Relevance and Relativity in the Case History" (Erikson, 1950). Whatever I said there, and however analogistic such thinking may be, I have come to consider the basic clinical attitude of psychoanalysis an experience based on the acknowledgment of multiple relativities—which, I hope, become clear in this essay.

But there was a third ingredient in the training situation in Vienna which to me could not be subordinated to either the clinical or theoretical approach: I mean the pleasure (I can only call it aesthetic) of an open, *configurational attention* to the rich interplay of form and meaning for which, above all, Freud's *Interpretation of Dreams* is the model. From there it was easily transferred to the observation of children's play behavior and permitted equal attention to what such behavior denied and distorted and to the artfulness of manifest expression, without which symbolic, ritualized, and, indeed, ritual patterns of behavior could not be understood—and without which I, as one then trained more in visual than in verbal communication, could not have found a "natural" access to such overwhelming data. (At any rate, one of my first psychoanalytic papers in Vienna was on children's picture books [1931], and my first paper in this country was to be "Configurations in Play" [1937].) I reiterate all this here because to me all these ingredients remain basic for the art and science of psychoanalysis and cannot be replaced for the purpose of "proof" by experimental and statistical investigations, suggestive and satisfying as they may be in their own right.

The 1930s were to become one of the most catastrophic periods in history, which in fact was about to threaten the very existence of those then engaged in the studies described here. Yet their efforts were (as the publication dates show) stubbornly redoubled, as if a methodical devotion to the timeless pursuits of healing and enlightenment was now needed all the more desperately. On this side of the Atlantic I found that the cautious but definite pointers toward social inquiry prepared in the development of Viennese ego psychology could be immediately continued and expanded, as we were drawn into inter-disciplinary work and shared the pioneer spirit of new psychoanalytic institutes as well as of new "schools." At Harvard there was a hospitable medical milieu invigorated by upsurging psychiatric social work. There also, Henry A. Murray was study-ing life histories rather than case histories, while at a variety of interdisciplinary meetings (under the wide influence of Law-rence K. Frank, Margaret Mead, and others), the doors between the different compartments of medical and social study were unlocked for an exchange of concerns which soon proved com-plementary. And so it happened that in the very year when *The Ego and the Mechanisms of Defense* (A. Freud, 1936) appeared in Vienna, I was privileged to accompany the anthropologist Scud-der Mekeel to the Sioux Indians' reservation in Pine Ridge in South Dakota and could make observations which proved basic to a psychoanalytic, psychosocial theory. One of the most sur-prising features in our first conversations with American In-dians was the convergence between the rationale given by the Indians for their ancient methods of child rearing and the psy-choanalytic reasoning by which we would come to consider the same data relevant and interdependent. Child training in such groups, so we soon concluded, is the method by which a group's basic ways of organizing experience (its group ethos, as we came to call it) is transmitted to the infant's early bodily experiences and, through them, to the beginnings of his ego.

The comparative reconstruction of the ancient child train-ing systems of this hunting tribe of the Great Plains and, later, of a California fishing tribe threw much light on what Spitz called the "dialogue" between the child's developmental read-iness and the pattern of maternal care readied for the child by a community—and Spitz (1963) called the dialogue "the source and origin of species-specific adaptation" (p. 174). We also learned to recognize the importance of the style of child training not only for the inner economy of the individual life cycle but also for the ecological balance of a given community under changing technological and historical conditions.

It is the concern of this essay to clarify the psychosocial theory which evolved, especially in regard to its origins in and its possible significance for psychoanalytic theory as a whole.

What, to begin with the beginning, *is* the function of pregenitality, that great distributor of developmental energy, in the healthy as well as the disturbed ecology of the individual life cycle—and in the cycle of generations? Does pregenitality exist only for genitality and ego synthesis only for the individual?

What follows is based on a great variety of observations and experiences, clinical and "applied," which are related in my publications. Here I must attempt to do without narrative. Moreover, having said it all (or most) before, I must paraphrase and, here and there, even quote myself, while I am unable here even to attempt to relate these summary thoughts to those of others who over the decades have expressed similar or opposing views. But as I said, the challenge seems to warrant such a circumscribed effort.

Pregenitality and the Cycle of Generations

Epigenesis and Pregenitality

Combined designations such as "psychosexual" and "psychosocial" are obviously meant to focus on the borderlines of established fields such as biology, social science, and psychology which have found means to isolate and classify groups of phenomena and between them have divided the study of human nature into approaches of both methodological and ideological power. But such attempts to define borderline areas to be studied by two combined approaches at the same time rarely overcome the human tendency to mistake the established techniques of divisive approaches for the true nature of things. Luckily, healing always calls for a holistic attitude which does not deny established fact but attempts to understand the way such facts are complementing each other. On the basis of clinical experience, therefore, I can only begin with the assumption that a human being's existence depends at every moment on three processes of organization which complement each other. There is, in whatever order, the biological process of the hierarchic organization of organ systems constituting a body (*soma*); there is the psychic process of organizing individual experience by ego synthesis (*psyche*); and there is the communal process of the cultural organization of the interdependence of persons (*ethos*).

To begin with, each of these processes has its own specialized methods of investigation which must in fact stay clear of each other in order to isolate and study certain elements basic to nature and to man. But in the end, all three approaches are necessary for and prove to be complementary to each other in the clarification of any intact human event.

In clinical work, of course, we come face to face with the often much more striking way in which these processes, by their very nature, are apt to fail and isolate each other, causing what by different methods can be studied as somatic tension, individual anxiety, or social panic. Yet to diagnose any failure of human behavior in terms of one of these processes always means to find oneself involved in the others, for each item that proves relevant in one process is seen to give significance to, as it receives significance from, items in the others. One may—as Freud did in his clinical studies of the neuroses of his time and in accordance with the dominant scientific concepts of his period—find a decisively new access to human motivation by assuming an all-powerful sexual energy (Eros) denied by human consciousness, repressed by the dominant morality, and ignored by science. And the very magnitude, in his time, of the repression of sexuality, aggravated as it was by a massive cultural prohibition, helped to endow the theory of sexual energy first with shocked alarm and then with a glow of liberation. Yet any exhaustive case history, life history, or historical account will lead us to consider the interplay of this hypothesized energy with energies contributed (or withheld!) by the other processes. Freud's own dream reports and case fragments, at any rate, always contain data pointing to such ecological considerations.

The organismic principle which in our work has proven indispensable for the somatic grounding of psychosexual and psychosocial development is *epigenesis*. This term is borrowed from embryology, and, whatever its status today, in the early days of our work it advanced our understanding of the relativity governing human phenomena linked with organismic growth.

When Freud recognized infantile sexuality, sexology stood about where embryology had stood in medieval times. Even as embryology once assumed that a minute but completely formed "homunculus" was ready in the man's semen to be implanted into a woman's uterus, there to expand and from there to step into life, sexology before Freud assumed that sexuality emerged and developed during puberty without any preparatory infantile stages. Eventually, however, embryology came to understand epigenetic development, the step-by-step growth of the fetal organs, even as psychoanalysis discovered the pregenital stages of sexuality. How are the two kinds of stage developments related?

As I now quote what the embryologist has to tell us about the epigenesis of organ systems, I hope that the reader will "hear" the probability that all growth and development follow analogous patterns. In the epigenetic sequence of development each organ has its time or origin—a factor as important as the locus of origin. If the eye, said Stockard (1931), does not arise at the appointed time, "it will never be able to express itself fully, since the moment for the rapid outgrowth of some other part will have arrived." But if it has begun to arise at the right time, still another time factor determines the most critical stage of its development: "A given organ must be interrupted during the early stage of its development in order to be completely suppressed or grossly modified . . ." (Stockard, 1931). If the organ misses its time of ascendance, it is not only doomed as an entity, it endangers at the same time the whole hierarchy of organs. "Not only does the arrest of a rapidly budding part . . . tend to suppress its development temporarily, but the premature loss of supremacy to some other organ renders it impossible for the suppressed part to come again into dominance so that it is permanently modified. . . ." The result of normal development, however, is proper relationship of size and function among all body organs: the liver adjusted in size to the stomach and intestine, the heart and lungs properly balanced, and the capacity of the vascular system accurately proportioned to the body as a whole.

Embryology, too, learned much about normal development from the developmental accidents which cause "monstra in excessu" and "monstra in defectu," even as Freud was led to recognize the laws of normal infantile pregenitality from the clinical observation of the distortion of genitality either by symptoms of "excessive" perversion or of "defective" repression.

How, after birth, the maturing organism continues to unfold, by growing planfully and by developing a prescribed sequence of physical, cognitive, and social capacities—all that is described in the literature of child development.

To us it is first all important to realize that in the sequence of significant experiences the healthy child, if properly guided, can be trusted to conform to the epigenetic laws of development as they now create a succession of potentialities for significant interaction with a growing number of individuals and with the mores that govern them. While such interaction varies widely from culture to culture, all cultures must guarantee some essential "proper rate" and "proper sequence," their propriety corresponding to what Hartmann (1939) referred to as "average expectable," that is, what is manageable for all humans, no matter how they differ in cultural and personal patterns.

Epigenesis, then, by no means signifies a mere succession. It also determines certain laws in the fundamental relations of the growing parts to each other—as the diagram below attempts to formalize:

	Part 1	Part 2	Part 3
Stage III	1_{III}	2_{III}	3_{III}
Stage II	1_{II}	2_{II}	3_{II}
Stage I	1_{I}	2_{I}	3_{I}

The heavily lined boxes along the ascending diagonal demonstrate both a sequence of stages (I, II, III) and a development of component parts (1, 2, 3); in other words, the diagram formalizes a *progression through time of a differentiation of parts*. This indicates that each part (say, 2_{I}) exists (below the diagonal) before "its" decisive and critical time normally arrives (2_{II}) and remains systematically related to all others (1 and 3) so that the whole ensemble depends on the proper development in the proper sequence of each item. Finally, as each part comes to its full ascendance and finds some lasting solution during its stage (on the diagonal) it will also be expected to develop further (2_{III}) under the dominance of subsequent ascendancies (3_{III}) and most of all, to take its place in the integration of the whole ensemble $(1_{III}, 2_{III}, 3_{III})$. Let us now see what implications such a schema may have for pregenitality and, later, for psychosocial development.

Pregenitality is so·pervasive a concept in psychoanalytic literature that it will suffice to summarize here those of its essential features on which a psychoanalytic theory of psychosocial development must be based. The child's erotic experiences are called pregenital because sexuality reaches genital primacy only in puberty. In childhood, sexual development undergoes three phases, each of which marks the strong libidinization of a vital zone of the organism. Therefore, they are usually referred to as the "oral," the "anal," and the "phallic" phases. The far-reaching consequences of their strong libidinal endowment for the vicissitudes of human sexuality have been abundantly demonstrated—that is, the playful variety of pregenital pleasures (if, indeed, they remain "forepleasures"); the ensuing perversions, if one or the other remains demanding enough to upset the genital primacy; and, above all, the neurotic consequences of the undue repression of strong pregenital needs. Obviously, these three stages, too, are linked epigenetically, for anality (2_I) exists during the oral stage (I) and must take its place in the "phallic" stage (III), after its normative crisis in the anal stage (2_{II}).

Granted all this, the question remains: does pregenitality, as an intrinsic part of man's prolonged childhood, only exist for and borrow significance from the development of sexuality?

From a psychobiological viewpoint it is most obvious that these "erotogenic" zones and the stages of their libidinization seem central to a number of other developments basic to survival. There is, first of all, the fundamental fact that they serve functions necessary for the preservation of the organism: the intake of food and the elimination of waste—and, after some delay called sexual latency, the procreative acts preserving the species. The sequence of their erotization, furthermore, is intrinsically related to the contemporaneous growth of other organ systems. In fact, from a developmental as well as a psychosexual point of view one must speak of (1) an *oral res-piratory* and *sensory* stage; (2) an *anal-urethral* and *muscular* stage; and (3) an *infantile-genital* and *locomotor* stage. These stages and all their part aspects must be visualized in the epigenetic order charted in the diagram above. At the same time, it may prove helpful to the reader to localize these stages in column A on Table 1 which lists a survey of all the themes gradually to be related to each other in this essay.

As we now approach the question as to how these organ systems also "acquire" psychosocial significance, we must first of all remember that the stages of prolonged human childhood (with all their instinctual variability) and the structure of human communities (in all their cultural variation) are part of one evolutionary development and must have a built-in potential for serving each other. Communal institutions can in principle be expected to support the developmental potentials of the organ systems, though at the same time they will insist on giving each part function (as well as childhood as a whole) specific connotations which may support cultural norms, communal style, and the dominant world view; they may also cause un-ecological conflict.

But as to the specific question of how the community re-sponds to the erotic experience and expression associated with each stage of pregenitality, we face a dilemma of historical inter-pretation, for the clinical observations of psychoanalysis which led to the discovery of the stages of pregenitality permitted only the conclusion that, by its very nature, "society" as such is so hostile to infantile sexuality that it becomes a matter of more or less strict repression, amounting, at times, to an all-human suppression. Such potential repression, however, can be said to have been uniquely monomanic in the Victorian period of history and specifically pathogenic in creating its prime neu-roses, namely, hysteria and compulsion neurosis. And while psychiatry and psychoanalysis can and must always discover such new aspects of human nature as are reflected in the epi-demiological trends of the times, their interpretation must, at any given time, allow for what we will discuss later as *historical relativity*. Periods not specifically inclined to train children with excessive moralism do permit, up to a point, a direct playing out of infantile sexual trends. And all societies must in principle cultivate an instinctually endowed interplay of adults and children by offering special forms of "dialogue" by which the child's early physical experiences are given deep and lasting cultural connotations. As the maternal person, and then various parental persons, come within the radius of the child's readiness for instinctual attachment and interplay, the child evokes in these adults corresponding patterns of communication of long-range significance for communal as well as individual integration.

Organ Modes and Social Modalities

Pregenital modes. We now nominate for the prime link between pregenital and psychosocial development the *organ modes* dominating the psychosexual zones of the human organism. These organ modes are incorporation, retention, elimination, intrusion, and inclusion; and while various apertures can serve a number of modes, the theory of pregenitality maintains that each of the libidinal zones during "its" stage is dominated both pleasurably and purposefully by a primary mode-configuration of functioning: The mouth primarily *incorporates*, and the anus and the urethra *retain* and *eliminate*, while the phallus is destined to *intrude* and the vagina to *include*. But these modes also comprise basic configurations which dominate the interplay of a mammalian organism and its parts with another organism and its parts, as well as with the world of things. These zones and modes, therefore, are the focus of some prime concerns of any culture's child-training systems, even as they remain, in their further development, central to the culture's "way of life."

On first acquaintance with "primitive" child rearing methods, one cannot help concluding that there is some instinctive wisdom in the way in which they use the instinctual forces of pregenitality not only by making the child sacrifice some strong wishes in a significant way, but also by helping the child to enjoy as well as to perfect adaptive functions from the most minute daily habits to the techniques required by the dominant technology. Our reconstruction of the original Sioux child training made us believe that what we will later describe and discuss as basic trust in early infancy was first established by the almost unrestricted attentiveness and generosity of the nursing mother;

TABLE 1
Epigenetic Stages

Stages	A Psychosexual Stages and Modes	B Psychosocial Crisis	C Radius of Significant Relations	D Basic Strengths	E Core Pathology Basic Antipathies	F Related Principles of Social Order	G Binding Ritualizations	H Ritualisms
I Infancy	Oral-Respiratory, Sensory-Kinesthetic (Incorporative Modes)	Basic Trust vs. Basic Mistrust	Maternal Person	Hope	Withdrawal	Cosmic Order	Numinous	Idolism
II Early Childhood	Anal-Urethral, Muscular (Retentive-Eliminative)	Autonomy vs. Shame, Doubt	Parental Persons	Will	Compulsion	"Law and Order"	Judicious	Legalism
III Play Age	Infantile-Genital, Locomotor (Intrusive, Inclusive)	Initiative vs. Guilt	Basic Family	Purpose	Inhibition	Ideal Prototypes	Dramatic	Moralism

				Competence	Inertia	Technological Order	Formal (Technical)	Formalism
IV School Age	"Latency"	Industry vs. Inferiority	"Neighborhood," School					
V Adolescence	Puberty	Identity vs. Identity Confusion	Peer Groups and Outgroups; Models of Leadership	Fidelity	Repudiation	Ideological Worldview	Ideological	Totalism
VI Young Adulthood	Genitality	Intimacy vs. Isolation	Partners in friendship, sex, competition, cooperation	Love	Exclusivity	Patterns of Cooperation and Competition	Affiliative	Elitism
VII Adulthood	(Procreativity)	Generativity vs. Stagnation	Divided Labor and shared household	Care	Rejectivity	Currents of Education and Tradition	Generational	Authoritism
VIII Old Age	(Generalization of Sensual Modes)	Integrity vs. Despair	"Mankind" "My Kind"	Wisdom	Disdain	Wisdom	Philosophical	Dogmatism

then, still nursing during the teething stage, she would playfully aggravate the infant boy's ready rage in such a way that the greatest possible degree of latent ferocity was provoked — apparently to be channelized later into customary play and then into work: hunting and warring demand competent aggressiveness against prey and enemy. Thus, we concluded, primitive cultures, beyond giving specific meanings to early bodily and interpersonal experience in order to create the "right" emphases on both organ modes and social modalities, appear to channelize carefully and systematically the energies thus provoked and deflected; and they give consistent supernatural meaning to the infantile anxieties which they have exploited by such provocation.

In elaborating on some of the early social modalities related to organ modes, let me resort to basic English, for its spare use of verbs can best convey for us those behaviors which are fundamental to all languages and invite and permit systematic comparison.

The Oral-Sensory Stage is dominated by two modes of incorporation. *To get* means at first to receive and to accept what is given, and there is, of course, a truly fundamental significance in the similarity between the modes of breathing and those of sucking. The "sucking" mode is the first social modality learned in life, and is learned in relation to the maternal person, the "primal other" of first narcissistic mirroring and of loving attachment. Thus, in *getting what is given*, and in learning to *get somebody to give* what is wished for, the infant also develops the necessary ego groundwork to some day *get to be* a giver. But then the teeth develop and with them the pleasure in biting *on* things, in biting *through* them, and in biting bits *off* them. This more active incorporative mode, however, also characterizes the development of other organs. The eyes, first ready to accept impressions as they come along, are learning to focus, to isolate, and to "grasp" objects from the vaguer background—and to follow them. Similarly, the ears learn to discern significant sounds, to localize them, and to guide a searching turn toward them, even as the arms learn to reach out aimfully and the hands to grasp firmly. All these modalities are given widely different connotations in the context of earlier or later weaning and longer or shorter dependence. We are, then, dealing here not with a simple causal effect of training on development but, as we promised, with a mutual assimilation of somatic, mental, and social patterns: an adaptive development which must be guided by a certain inner logic in cultural patterns (a logic later to be discussed as *ethos*) tuned as it must be to the ego's growing capacity to adaptively integrate its "apparatuses."

As to the simple and functional alternative of *holding on* and *letting go*, some cultures—and probably those where possessiveness is central to the cultural ethos—will tend to underscore the *retentive* and *eliminative modes* normatively dominating the anal-muscular stage and may make a battleground of these zones. In their further development, such modes as *to hold* can turn into a destructive and cruel retaining or restraining, or they can support a pattern of care, *to have and to hold*. To *let go*, likewise, can turn into an inimical letting loose of destructive forces, or it can become a relaxed "to let pass" and "to let be." In the meantime, a sense of defeat (from too many conflicting double meanings and too little or too much training) can lead to deep shame and a compulsive doubt whether one will ever be able to feel that one willed what one did—or did what one willed.

The *intrusive* mode, dominating much of the behavior of the third, the infantile-genital stage, characterizes a variety of configurationally "similar" activities, such as the intrusion into space by vigorous locomotion; into other bodies by physical attack; into other people's ears and minds by aggressive sounds; and into the unknown by consuming curiosity. Correspondingly, the *inclusive* mode may express itself in the often surprising alternation of such aggressive behavior with a quiet, if eager, receptivity in regard to imaginative material and a readiness to form tender and protective relations with peers as well as with smaller children. True, the first libidinization of penis and vagina can be manifested in autoerotic play and in oedipal fantasies, although where conditions permit they can also be dramatized in joint sexual play, including a mimicry of adult intercourse. But all this will soon give way to "latency," while the ambulatory and infantile-genital stage adds to that inventory of generalized modalities which lend themselves to basic

English, that of "making,"in the sense of "being on the make." The word suggests initiative, insistence on a goal, and the pleasure of conquest. Again, some cultures are apt to cultivate in the boy a greater emphasis on "making" by intrusive modes and in the girl a "making" by teasing and provoking or by other forms of "catching," i.e., by making herself attractive and endearing. And yet both sexes have a combination of all these modalities at their disposal.

Here a word should be said concerning the fact that, instead of the original phallic phase, I prefer to speak only of an *infantile-genital* stage, and to consider it dominated in both sexes by combinations of intrusive and inclusive modes and modalities. For at the infantile-genital level—and this seems to be one of the (evolutionary) "reasons" for the latency period—a certain bisexual disposition must be assumed in both sexes, while a full differentiation of the genital modes of male intrusion and female inclusion must wait for puberty. True, the girl's observation of the boy's visible and erectible organ will, especially in patriarchal settings, lead to some penis envy, but it will also and more simply introduce the strong wish to eventually include the penis where it seems to belong. The very fact, however, that we are speaking not only of organ modes but also of social modalities of intrusion and inclusion as developmentally essential for both boys and girls demands a shift of theoretical emphasis in regard to female development (1) from the exclusive sense of loss of an external organ to a budding sense of vital inner potential—the "inner space," then—which is by no means at odds with a full expression of vigorous intrusiveness in locomotion and in general patterns of initiative; and (2) from a "passive" renunciation of male activity to the playful pursuit of activities consonant with and expressive of the possession of birth-giving and nuturant organs. Thus, a certain bisexual propensity for the alternate use of both the intrusive and the inclusive modes allows for greater cultural and personal variation in the display of gender differences, while not foreclosing a full genital differentiation in puberty.

The alternation between the inclusive and intrusive modes does, of course, lead to specific conflicts in male childhood. It is true that at this age of great physical concerns, the observation of the female genitals is apt to arouse in boys a castration fear, which may inhibit identifications with female persons. And yet, when permitted expression under enlightened conditions, such identifications can foster the development in boys of caring qualities not incommensurate with vigorous locomotion and eventually intrusive genitality.

A full consideration of the final fate of the genital zones, modes, and modalities must help to clarify certain universal feminine and masculine problems which may have to be understood in their developmental complexity before the now so obvious traditional exploitability of sexual differences becomes fully understandable. There is an undeniable affinity between the mode of inclusion and that of incorporation. Given the obvious absence of a phallic potential for intrusion (and a postponement of breast development), this stage can well aggravate, under given cultural conditions, a repetitive tendency toward taking refuge in dependence. This in turn can lead to a collusion with the exploitative trends of some cultures, and especially so in connection with the dependent states naturally suggested by exclusive and unlimited procreative and generative responsibilities. At least in some cultural schemes, and together with a radical division of the economic function of the two sexes, this tendency may, in human evolution, have contributed to a certain exploitability of the female as one who expects, as she is expected, to remain dependent even while, or especially when, taking effective care of infantile (and adult) dependents.[1] In the male, by contrast, any corresponding need for regressive dependence or, in fact, a nurturant identification with the mother could, under the same cultural conditions, well lead to a militant overcompensation in the direction of intrusive pursuits, such as hunting, warring, competing—or exploiting. What becomes, in either sex, of the countermodes, therefore, deserves comparative study, and this most vigilantly at a time when all theoretical conclusions in such matters are drawn into an acute ideological discord. The main point is that the social ex-

---

[1] While in principle I believe in such an evolutionary potential and the necessity to become aware of it, I must admit that its configurational representation in a chart of modes and zones (Erikson, 1950) can be misleading in its configurational oversimplification.

periments of today and the available insights must eventually lead to a sexual ethos convincing enough to children of both sexes as well as to liberated adults.

Postural modalities. As we review the fate of the organ modes of the erogenous zones and relate them to the modalities of social existence, it becomes important to point more systematically to the psychosocial significance of the sensory, muscular, and locomotor modalities during the very period of pregenitality. For the child undergoing these stages exists, as we have noted in passing, in an *expanding space-time* experience as well as in an expanding *radius of significant social interplay*.

Psychoanalytic theory has not made much of the difference between the changing conditions of being supine or crawling or upright and walking during the stages of psychosexuality, even though the very riddle posed to Oedipus pronounces their fundamental importance: "What walks on four feet in the morning, in midday on two, and on three in the evening?" Let me, then, begin once more with earliest posture and attempt to illustrate the way in which it determines (in consonance with the psychosexual and psychosocial stages) some basic perspectives in space-time existence.

The newborn is prone, gradually looking up and soon searching the inclined and responsive face of the motherly person. Psychopathology teaches that this developing eye-to-eye relationship (J. Erikson, 1966) is a "dialogue" as essential for the psychic development and, indeed, survival of the whole human being as is the mouth-to-breast one for its sustenance: the most radical inability to "get in touch" with the maternal world first betrays itself in the lack of eye-to-eye encounter. But where such contact is established the human being will thereafter always look for somebody to look up to and all through life will feel confirmed by "uplifting" encounters. Thus, in the playful and yet planful dialogue (we will presently call it a "ritualization") which negotiates the first interpersonal encounters, the light of the *eyes*, the features of the *face*, and the sound of the *name* become essential ingredients of a first recognition of and by the primal other. Their lasting existential value is attested to by the way in which these ingredients are said to return in decisive encounters throughout life, be it in that of lovers who "drink to me only with thine eyes," or in that enchantment of the masses which (as in the Indian "darshan") "drink in" the presence of a charismatic figure, or in the lasting search for a divine countenance—as in St. Paul's promise that we shall penetrate the "glass darkly" and shall "know even as we also are known." Modern accounts of the reported experience of individuals who seem to have returned from a certified death appear to confirm the vision of such an ultimate meeting.

As we enlarge here on the significance of· man's initial proneness, we cannot omit mention of the ingenious arrangement of the basic psychoanalytic treatment situation, which paradoxically permits free association under the condition that the patient maintain a supine position that forbids a meeting of the eyes during a most fateful exchange of words. Such mixture of freedom and constriction is indeed bound to lead to passionate and persistent transferences, the most profound (and, to some, disturbing) of which may well be a repetition of the supine infant's deprived search for the caretaking person's responsive face.

Human development is dominated by dramatic shifts in emphasis; and while at first confirmed in its singularly long infantile dependence, the human child soon and with a vengeance must learn to "stand on its own (two!) feet," acquiring a firmness of upright position which creates new perspectives with a number of decisive meanings, as homo ludens also becomes homo erectus.

For the person who stands upright, the head (at first a bit wobbly) is on top, the eyes in front. Our stereoscopic vision thus makes us "face" what is ahead and in front. What is behind is also in back; and there are other significant combinations: ahead and above; ahead and below; behind and above; and behind and below; all of which receive in different languages strong and varied connotations. For what is ahead and above can guide me like a light, and what is below and in front can trip me up, like a snake. Who or what is in back is not visible, although it can see me; wherefore shame is related not only to the consciousness of being exposed in front, when upright, but also of having a back—and especially a "behind." Those who are "behind me" thus fall into such contradictory categories as those who are "backing me up" and guiding me in going ahead; or those who are watching me when I do not know it, and those who are "after me," trying to "get me." Below and behind are those things and people whom I simply may have outgrown, or those that I want to leave behind, forget, discard. Here the eliminative mode can be seen to assume a generalized ejective modality, and there are of course very many other systematic and significant combinations of organ modes and postural perspectives which I must leave the reader to pursue. In regard to all of them, the postural (as well as modal) logic of language is one of the prime guarantors to the growing child that "his individual way of mastering experience (his ego synthesis) is a successful variant of a group identity and is in accord with its space-time and life plan." We shall return to this.

A child, finally, who has just achieved the ability to walk not only seems driven to repeat and to perfect the act of walking with the flair of drivenness and an air of mastery but will also inevitably be led, in line with the intrusiveness of the infantile-genital stage, to a variety of invasions into the sphere of others. Thus in all cultures the child becomes aware of the new status and stature of "one who can walk," with all its often contradictory connotations, be it "he who will go far," or "he who might go too far," or "she who moves nicely," or "she who might tend to 'run around.' " Thus walking, as any other developmental achievement, must contribute to a self-esteem which reflects the conviction that one is learning competent steps toward some shared and productive future and is acquiring a psychosocial identity on the way.

Ritualization

What so far has been called rather vaguely a dialogue or interplay between the growing child and caring adults takes on more psychosocial presence when we describe one of its most significant characteristics, namely, *ritualization*. This term is taken over from ethology, the study of animal behavior. It was coined by Julian Huxley (1966) for certain phylogenetically preformed "ceremonial" acts in the so-called social animals, such as the flamboyant greeting ceremonies of some birds. But here we must take note that the words "ceremonies" and "ceremonial" in this context make sense only in quotation marks—as does the word "ritual," say, when used as a clinical characterization of a handwashing compulsion. Our term ritualization, luckily, is less pretentious, and in a human context is used only for a certain kind of informal and yet prescribed interplay between persons who repeat it at meaningful intervals and in recurring contexts. While such interplay may mean nothing more (at least to the participants) than "this is the way *we* do things," it has, we claim, adaptive value for all participants and for their group living. For it furthers and guides, from the beginning of existence, that stage-wise instinctual investment in the social process which must do for human adaptation what the instinctive fit into a section of nature will do for an animal species.

To choose an everyday analogy to the animal ritualizations described so vividly by Huxley and by Konrad Lorenz (1966), we call to mind the human mother's approach to greeting her infant on awakening or, indeed, the ways in which the same mother feeds or cleans her infant or puts the infant to sleep. It becomes clear, then, that what we call ritualization in the human context can at the same time be highly individual ("typical" for the particular mother and tuned to the particular infant) and yet also, to any outside observer, seem recognizably stereotyped along some traditional lines subject to anthropological comparison. The whole procedure is superimposed on the periodicity of physical and libidinal needs as it responds to the child's growing cognitive capacities and the eagerness to have disparate experiences made coherent by mothering. The mother in her postpartum state is also needful in a complex manner; for whatever instinctual gratification she may seek in being a mother, she also needs to become a mother of a special kind and in a special way. This first human ritualization, then, while fulfilling a series of needs and duties, supports that joint need, already discussed, for a mutuality of recognition, by face and by name. Wherever and whenever this element is repeated, such meetings at their best reconcile seeming paradoxes: they are playful and yet formalized; they become familiar through repetition and yet seem always surprising. Needless to say, such matters, while they can be as simple as they seem "natural," are not altogether deliberate and (like the best things in life) cannot be contrived. And yet they serve the permanent establishment of what in daily usage has unfortunately come to be called the "object" relationship—unfortunately, because here a term technically meaningful for insiders as part of the libido theory is mechanistically generalized, possibly with "unavowed" consequences for the contemporary sexual ethos (Erikson, 1978). At any rate, the psychosexual aspect of the matter is complemented by the capacity to comprehend the existence of a primary other even as one comprehends oneself as a separate person—in the light of that other. At the same time, it counteracts the infant's rage and anxiety, which are so much more complex and fateful than the young animal's upsets and fears. Correspondingly, a lack of such early connection can, in extreme cases, reveal an "autism" on the part of the child which corresponds or, no doubt, is responded to by some maternal withdrawal, in which case we can observe a fruitless exchange, a kind of private ritualism characterized by a lack of eye contact and facial responsiveness and, in the child, an endless and hopeless repetition of stereotyped gestures.

I must now admit that one justification for applying the terms ritualization and ritualisms to such phenomena is, in fact, a correspondence between everyday ritualizations and the grand rituals of the culture in which they take place. My earlier suggestion that the mutual recognition between mother and infant may be a model of some of the most exalted encounters throughout life may now serve to make it plausible that the ritualizations of each of the major stages of life correspond to one of the major institutions in the structure of societies—and to their rituals. I submit that this first and dimmest affirmation of the described polarity of "I" and "Other" is basic to a human being's ritual and esthetic needs for a pervasive quality which we call the *numinous*: the aura of a hallowed presence. The numinous assures us, ever again, of *separateness transcended* and yet also of *distinctiveness confirmed*, and thus of the very basis of a sense of "I." Religion and art are the institutions with the strongest traditional claim on the cultivation of numinosity, as can be discerned in the details of rituals by which the numinous is shared with a congregation of other "I" 's—all sharing one all-embracing "I Am." Monarchies have competed with this claim, and in modern times, of course, political ideologies have taken over the numinous function, with the face of the leader multiplied on a thousand banners. But it is too easy for skeptical observers (including clinicians who, beside a powerful technique, partake in a professional "movement," with a founder's picture on the wall and a heroic prehistory as ideological guide) to consider traditional needs for such inclusive and transcendant experiences a partial regression to what appear to be infantile needs—or forms of mass psychosis. Such needs must be studied in all their historical relativity, including the presence or absence of viable substitutes in periods of radical change.

It is true, however, that every basic ritualization is also related to a form of *ritualism* marked by stereotyped repetition and illusory pretenses which obliterate the integrative value of communal organization. Thus, the need for the numinous under given conditions easily degenerates into adult *idolatry*, a visual form of addiction which, indeed, can become a most dangerous collective delusional system.

To characterize (more briefly) the primary ritualizations of the second (anal-muscular), and third (infantile genital-locomotor) stages: in the second stage the question arises as to how the willful pleasure adhering to the functions of the muscular system (including the sphincters) can be guided into behavior patterns fitting the cultural mores, and this by an adult will that must become the child's own will. In the ritualizations of infancy, cautions and avoidances were the parents' responsibility; now the child himself must be trained to "watch himself" in regard to what is possible and/or permissible and what is not. To this end, parents and other elders compare him (to his face) to what he might become if he (and they) do not watch out, thus creating two opposite self-images: one which characterizes a person on the way toward the kind of expansion and self-assertion desired in his home and in his culture, and one (most fateful) negative image of what one is not supposed to be (or show) and yet what one potentially is. These images may be reinforced by unceasing references to the kind of behavior for which the child is as yet too small, or just the right age, or already too big. All this takes place within a radius of significant attachments which now include both older children and parental persons, with the father figure now being seen as more central. Maybe it is up to the muscular authority figure with the deeper voice to underscore the yeses and nos and yet to balance the threatening and forbidding aspects of his appearance with a benevolent and guiding guardianship.

Clinically, we know the pathological results of a decisive disturbance at this stage. It is again a failure of the ritualizations which define the small individual's leeway in such a manner that some basic choices remain guaranteed even as certain areas of self-will are surrendered. And so the ritualized acceptance of the necessity to differentiate between right and wrong, good and bad, mine and thine, etc. degenerates either into an overly compulsive compliance or, indeed, into a compulsive impulsivity. The elders in turn demonstrate their inability to carry through productive ritualization by indulging in compulsive or impulsive (and often most cruel) ritualisms themselves.

This stage is the arena for the establishment of another great principle of ritualization. I call it the *judicious* one, for it combines "the law" and "the word"; to become ready to accept the spirit of the word conveying lawfulness is an important aspect of this development. Here, then, is the ontogenetic origin of that great human preoccupation with questions of free will and of self-determination, as well as of the lawful definition of guilt and transgression. Correspondingly, the institutions rooted in this phase of life are those which define by law the individual's freedom of action. The corresponding rituals are to be found in the judicial system which makes all visible on the public stage of the courts a drama that is familiar to each individual's inner life—for the law, we must be made to believe, is untiringly watchful, as is, alas, our conscience; and both must declare us free as they condemn the guilty. Thus, the judicious element is another intrinsic element of man's phylogenetic adaptation, as rooted in ontogenetic development. But the danger of ritualism lurks here, too. It is *legalism*, which—now too lenient and now too strict—is the bureaucratic counterpart to individual compulsivity.

The *play age*, finally, is a good stage with which to close the description of the ritualizations of preschool life. Psychosexually speaking, the play age must resolve the oedipal triad governing the basic family, while intensive extrafamilial attachments are postponed to a time after the child has passed the school age, whatever the society's method of first schooling may be. In the meantime, the play age entrusts the vastly increased sphere of *initiative* to the capacity of children to cultivate their own sphere of ritualization, namely, the world of miniature toys and the shared space-time of games. These are apt to absorb in imaginative interplay both excessive dreams of conquest and the severe guilt which can be the result of the ritualized interplay of adults and children during this stage.

The basic element of ritualization contributed by the play age is the infantile form of the *dramatic*. Epigenesis will insist that the dramatic does not replace but rather joins the numinous and the judicial elements, even as it anticipates the elements as yet to be traced ontogenetically, namely, the *formal* and the *ideological*. No adult ritual, rite, or ceremony can dispense with any of these. The institutional equivalents of the child's play sphere, however, are alternately the stage, which specialized in the awe-filled or humorous expression of the dramatic, or other circumscribed arenas (the forum, the temple, the court, the common) in which dramatic events are displayed. As for the element of ritualism rooted in the play age, I think it is a moralistic and inhibitive suppression of initiative in the absence of creatively ritualized ways of channeling guilt. Maybe *moralism* will be the word for this trend.

Having arrived at the connection between play and drama it seems appropriate to say a word about the psychosocial significance of the infantile fate of King Oedipus, who was, of course, the hero of a play. For in charting some aspects of the organismic order, we have so far neglected the increasing number of *counterplayers* with whom the growing child (via the zones, the modes, and the modalities) can enter into meaningful interplay. First there is, of course, the maternal person who in the stage of symbiosis permits the libido to be attached to what in psychosocial terms I would call the *primal other*.[2] This other

[2] The term "other" is taken from Freud's letters to Fliess, where Freud confesses to seek "the Other" ("der Andere") in his correspondent (Freud, 1954; see also Erikson, 1955).

who, as.we saw, also becomes the guarantor of a kind of self-love (for which Narcissus seems, indeed, to be a somewhat special case) and thus provides that *basic trust* which we will presently discuss as the most fundamental syntonic attitude.

It is when this original *dyad* develops into a *triad* including the father(s) that the "conflictuous" conditions for the oedipus complex are given—that is, a strong instinctual wish to possess the parent of the other sex forever and the consequent jealous hate of the (also loved) parent of the same sex. The psychosexual aspects of this early attachment have made up the very *core complex* of psychoanalysis. Here we must add, however, that these passionate wishes are carefully scheduled to be at their height when the somatic chances for their consumption are totally lacking, while playful imagination is flourishing. Thus prime instinctual wishes as well as the corresponding reactions of guilt are scheduled to appear at a period of development which combines the most intense infantile conflict with the greatest advance in playfulness, while whatever fantastic wishes—and guilt feelings—come to flourish are scheduled to be submerged in the next "latency" and school stage. With the advent of genital maturation in adolescence and its direction toward sexual mates, the remnants of infantile fantasies of oedipal conquest and competition are linked with those of others to create idealized heroes and leaders (governing concrete areas and arenas as well as "theaters" and worlds). All these are endowed with instinctual energies on which the social order must count for its generational renewal. In all this the development of psychosocial identity becomes a crucial issue, to which we will return in an overview of the major psychosocial stages.

In passing, however, we must note another essential attribute of all developmental unfolding: as the radius of counterplayers increases, graduating the growing being into ever new roles within wider group formations, certain basic configurations such as the original dyad or triad demand to find a new representation within later contexts. This does not give us the right, without very special proof, to consider such reincarnations a mere sign of fixation or regression to the earliest symbiosis. They may well be instead an epigenetic recapitulation on a higher developmental level and, possibly, attuned to *that* level's governing principles and psychosocial needs. A charismatic or divine image, in the context of the ideological search of adolescence or the generative communality of adulthood, is not "nothing but" a reminder of the first Other. As Blos (1967) has called it, there is a "regression in the service of development," that is, an attempt to resolve, before it is irrevocably too late, what has been bypassed in childhood.

I conclude this section on the generational implications of epigenetic development with some summary remarks on play. The original play theory of psychoanalysis was, in accord with its energy concepts, the "cathartic" theory, according to which play had the function in childhood of working off pent-up emotions and finding imaginary relief for past frustrations. Another plausible explanation was that the child utilized the increasing mastery over toys for playful arrangements which permitted the illusion of also mastering some pressing life predicaments. For Freud, play, above all, turned enforced passivity into imaginary activity. In accord with the developmental viewpoint, I at one time postulated an *autosphere* for play with the sensations of the body; a *microsphere* for toys; and a *macrosphere* for play with others. Of great help in clinical play was the observation that the microsphere of toys can seduce the child into an unguarded expression of dangerous wishes and themes which then arouse anxiety and lead to—most revealing—sudden *play disruption*, the counterpart in waking life of the anxiety dream. And indeed, if thus frightened or disappointed in the microsphere, the child may regress into the autosphere — daydreaming, thumbsucking, masturbating. Developmentally, however, playfulness reaches into the macrosphere, that is, the social arena shared with others, where it must be learned which playful intentions can be shared with others—and forced upon them. Here, soon, the great human invention of formal games, combining aggressive aims with rules of fairness, takes over. Play, then, is a good example of the way in which every major trend of epigenetic development continues to expand and develop throughout life. For the ritualizing power of play is the infantile form of the human ability to deal with experience by creating model situations and to master reality by experiment and planning. It is in crucial phases of his work that the adult, too, plays with past experience and anticipated tasks, beginning with that activity in the autosphere called thinking. But beyond this, in constructing model situations not only in open dramatizations (as in "plays" and in fiction) but also in the laboratory and on the drawing board, we inventively anticipate the future from the vantage point of a corrected and shared past as we redeem our failures and strengthen our hopes. In doing so, we obviously must learn to accept and make do with those materials—be they toys or thought patterns, natural materials or invented techniques — which are put at our disposal by the cultural, scientific, and technological conditions of our moment of history.

And so, epigenesis strongly suggests that we do not make play and work mutually exclusive. There is an early form of serious work in the earliest play, while some mature element of play does not hinder but augments true seriousness in work. But then, adults have the power to use playfulness and planfulness for most destructive purposes: play can become a gamble on a gigantic scale, and to play one's own game can mean to play havoc with that of others.

Having now sketched the succession, up through childhood, of such basic elements of psychosocial developments as modes and modalities, ritualization and play, it is time to take a global view of the generational cycle within which all these elements have their function. So I now turn to the psychosocial gains of each stage of life. But having already enlarged, as usual, on childhood more than on adulthood, I begin with the latter and attempt, for a change, to descend the steps of epigenesis.

On the way, however, I must return once more to the psychosexual theory which ascribes such specific contributions of instinctual energy to the child's pregenital and genital development. Whatever this libido "is," its transformations into psychosocial development could, as we have seen, not be effected without the adults' devoted and at times passionate or driven interaction with the growing child's challenge. Therefore, the logic of a truly complete psychosexual theory may well demand that some instinctual drive toward a generative interplay with offspring be assumed to exist in human nature as a counterpart to the adult animal's instinctive involvement in "parenting." Thus, as we complete column A of Table 1, we add (in parenthesis) a *procreative* stage which represents the instinctual aspect of the psychosocial stage of *generativity* (column B)—the adult investment, then, not only in creating but also in raising and vitalizing the next generation (Benedek, 1959).

Major Stages in Psychosocial Development

About the Terms Used

To restate the sequence of psychosocial stages throughout life means to take responsibility for the terms we[3] have tentatively attached to them—names including such suspect words as *hope, fidelity*, and *care*.

In regard to my terms in general, I will quote the late theoretical arbiter, David Rapaport. Having tried to assign to me a firm place in ego psychology, he cautioned his readers: "Erikson's theory (like most of Freud's) ranges over phenomenological, specifically clinical psychoanalytic–psychological propositions, without systematically differentiating among them. Correspondingly, the conceptual status of this theory's terms is so far unclear" (Rapaport in Erikson, 1959). The readers of this tract will know what he is talking about. But if we accept the proposition that ritualization is one link between developing egos and the ethos of their communality, living languages must be considered one of the most outstanding forms of ritualization in that they express both what is universally human and what is culturally specific in the values conveyed by ritualized interplay. Thus, when we approach the phenomena of human strength, the everyday words of living languages, ripened in the usage of generations, will serve best as a basis of discourse.

More specifically, if developmental considerations lead us to speak of *hope, fidelity*, and *care* as the human strengths or ego qualities emerging from such strategic stages as Infancy, Ad-

[3] The "we" in this chapter includes, above all, Joan Erikson, who collaborated in outlining the life cycle for the Midcentury White House Conference on Children and Youth.

olescence, and Adulthood, it should not surprise us too much that they correspond to such major credal values as *hope, faith,* and *charity.* (Skeptical Vienna-trained readers, of course, will be reminded of the Austrian emperor who, when asked to inspect the model of a new and flamboyant baroque memorial, declared with authority, "You need a bit more faith, hope, and charity in the lower left corner!"). Such proven traditional values, while referring to the highest spiritual aspirations, must in fact have harbored from their dim beginnings some relation to the developmental rudiments of human strength; and it would be most instructive to pursue such parallels in different traditions and languages.[4]

But here, it may be helpful to call to mind the sequence of these stages on the developmental ladder suggested by the epigenetic viewpoint, as indicated in Table 2. Especially since I intend, instead of always "to begin again with the beginning," to start this discussion of the psychosocial stages high up on the level of adulthood, it seems important to take a quick and reassuring look at the whole ladder leading up to it. To point to the strengths, it will be seen that between those of hope and fidelity we postulate (in firm relation to the major developmental rungs) the steps of *will, purpose,* and *competence,* and between fidelity and care, a step of *love.* Beyond care, finally, we claim something called *wisdom.* But the chart also makes clear in its vertical aspects that each step (even wisdom) is grounded in all the previous ones; while in each horizontal, the developmental maturation (and psychosocial crisis) of one of these virtues gives new connotations to all the "lower" and already developed stages as well as to the higher and still developing ones. This can never be said often enough. The epigenetic nature of this ladder, then, can be expected to be reflected in a certain linquistic coherence of all these terms.

And indeed, such words as *hope, fidelity,* and *care* have a linguistic logic which seems to confirm developmental meanings. *Hope* is "expectant desire," a phrase well in accordance

---

[4] One religious system, at any rate, namely, Hindu tradition, is quite specific in regard to the relation of universal values to some major stages of life as we see them today (Kakar, 1977).

TABLE 2
Psychosocial Crises

		1	2	3	4	5	6	7	8
Old Age	VIII								Integrity vs. Despair, Disgust. WISDOM
Adulthood	VII							Generativity vs. Stagnation. CARE	
Young Adulthood	VI						Intimacy vs. Isolation. LOVE		
Adolescence	V					Identity vs. Identity Confusion. FIDELITY			
School Age	IV				Industry vs. Inferiority. COMPETENCE				
Play Age	III			Initiative vs. Guilt. PURPOSE					
Early Childhood	II		Autonomy vs. Shame, Doubt. WILL						
Infancy	I	Basic Trust vs. Basic Mistrust. HOPE							

with a vague instinctual drivenness undergoing experiences which awaken some firm expectations. It is also well in accord with our assumption that this first basic strength and root of ego development emerges from the resolution of the first developmental antithesis, namely, that of *basic trust* vs. *basic mistrust.* And as to suggestive linguistic connotations, hope seems to be related even to "hop," which means to leap; and we have always made the most of the fact that Plato thought the model of all playfulness to be the leap of young animals. At any rate, hope bestows on the anticipated future a sense of leeway inviting expectant leaps, either in preparatory imagination or in small initiating actions. And such daring must count on basic trust in the sense of a trustfulness that must be, literally and figuratively, nourished by maternal care and—when endangered by all too desperate discomfort—must be restored by competent consolation, the German "Trost." Correspondingly, *care* reveals itself as the instinctual impulse to "cherish" and to "caress" that which in its helplessness emits signals of despair. And if, in adolescence, the age mediating between childhood and adulthood, we postulate the emergence of the strength of *fidelity* (fidélité, fedeltà), this is not only a renewal on a higher level of the capacity to trust (and to trust oneself) but also the claim to be trustworthy, and to be able to commit one's loyalty (the German "Treue") to a cause of whatever ideological denomination. A lack of confirmed fidelity, however, will result in such pervasive symptomatic attitudes as diffidence or defiance, and even a faithful attachment to diffident or defiant cliques and causes. Thus, trust and fidelity are linguistically as well as epigenetically related, and we see in our sickest young individuals, in adolescence, semideliberate regression to the earliest developmental stage in order to regain—unless they lose it altogether—some fundamentals of early hope from which to leap forward again.

To point to a developmental logic in such universal values as faith, hope, and charity, however, does not mean to reduce them to their infantile roots. Rather, it forces us to consider how emerging human strengths, step for step, are instrinsically beset not only with severe vulnerabilities which perpetually demand our healing insights, but also with basic evils which call for the redeeming values of universal belief systems.

So, somewhat encouraged, we will present the psychosocial stages. And, as I said, I will begin with adulthood, not only out of some contrariness, but also because it makes certain sense to view adulthood as another beginning for it is the link between the life cycle and the generational cycle.

Adulthood

In our scheme, there are two adult stages: *adulthood* and *young adulthood*. They are not meant to preempt all the possible substages of the period between adolescence and old age; yet, appreciative as we are of the alternative subdivisions suggested by other workers, we repeat our original conclusions here primarily in order to convey the global logic of any such scheme.

As to the ages appropriate to all such stages, it stands to reason that they are circumscribed by the earliest moment at which, considering all the necessary conditions, a developmental quality can come to relative dominance and to a meaningful crisis, and the latest moment at which, for the sake of overall development, it must yield that critical dominance to the next quality. In this, wide ranges are possible; but the sequence of stages remains predetermined.

To adulthood (our seventh stage) we have assigned the critical antithesis of *generativity* vs. *self-absorption and stagnation*. Generativity, as already stated, encompasses procreativity, productivity, and creativity, and thus the generation of new beings as well as of new products and new ideas, including a kind of self-generation concerned with further identity development.

The word "crisis" here simply denotes decisive turning points when integrative development is mandatory; and the "vs." in all the antitheses which mark our life crises means, of course, versus, and even something like vice versa, for the human being, more or less consciously, always needs to be driven on by a contrary tension—which explains that a sense of stagnation is by no means foreign even to those who are most intensely productive and creative, while it can totally overwhelm those who find themselves inactivated in generative matters. The new "virtue" emerging from this antithesis is *care*: a widening commitment to take care of the persons, of the products, and of the ideas one has learned to care for. All the strengths arising from earlier developments in the ascending order from infancy to young adulthood (hope and will, purpose and skill, fidelity and love) prove, on closer study, to be essential for the generational task of cultivating the same strengths in the next generation. For this is, indeed, the job of adulthood, or what the Hindus call the "maintenance of the world"—eventually to be transcended.

Is generativity, then, we ask once more, a final psychosexual stage in its own right, or is procreation merely a by-product of sexuality? Since every genital encounter engages the procreative organs in some arousal and can result in conception, a psychobiological need for procreation can, it seems, be ignored only at a risk comparable to the erstwhile repression of genitality which psychoanalysis undertook to counteract on the Victorian scene. At any rate, young adults' capacity (acquired in the preceding stage of intimacy vs. isolation) to lose themselves so as to find one another in the meeting of bodies and minds, can lead sooner or later to a vigorous expansion of vital interests and a personal as well as libidinal investment in that which is being generated and cared for together. We therefore may well consider procreativity to be the adult stage, transcending genitality, on the psychosexual schedule, which means that if one is forced or chooses to restrict or omit procreation, one must know what one is *not* doing. Where generative enrichment in its various forms fails altogether, stage-wide regressions may occur, either to an obsessive need for pseudointimacy or a kind of preoccupation with identity renewal—and both with a pervading sense of stagnation.

The sense of *self-absorption* and *stagnation*, like the antitheses in other stages, marks the potential core pathology of this stage. Such pathology will, of course, involve some regression to previous core disturbances. Yet it must be understood also in its stage-specific nature. This, as indicated, is especially important today when sexual frustration is recognized as pathogenic, while generative frustration, according to the dominant technological ethos of birth control, is apt to be rationalized and to remain unrecognized. Thus any great and sudden shift in sexual mores demands vigilance: individuals must not be unaware of what they are sacrificing to necessity, convenience, or changing convention, and what compensatory interests are open to them. Thus, today a new generative ethos, while acknowledging a need for fewer births, calls for a universal care concerned with a qualitative improvement in the lives of all children brought planfully into this world. Such new caritas would include (beyond contraceptives and food packages) some joint guarantee of a chance for development as well as survival—to every child born.

But here I must introduce another set of phenomena characteristic of each stage of life. In line with traditional psychoanalytic interests, we have so far begun to enumerate the core pathologies corresponding to the psychosocial crises under discussion. But there is another set of antitheses which are of fateful consequence for group life and for the survival of mankind itself. If care (as all other strengths cited) is the expression of a vital *sympathetic* trend with a high instinctual energy at its disposal, there is also what I would suggest we call an antipathetic trend which, up to a point, is a vital normative counterpart to the first, and endowed with aggressive energy. In the stage of generativity this dystonic counterpart is *rejectivity*, that is, the unwillingness to include specified persons or groups in one's concern: one *does not care to care* for them; they are outsiders. There is, of course, a certain logic to the fact that the instinctual elaboration of instinctive caretaking tends to be highly selective in favor of what is or can be made to be most familiar. In fact, one cannot ever be generative and care-ful without being selective to the point of some distinct rejectivity. It is for this very reason that ethics, law, and insight must guard the bearable measure of rejectivity, even as religious and ideological belief systems must always advocate a more universal principle of care. It is here, in fact, where such spiritual concepts as a universal caritas give their ultimate support to the developmental one of care. And caritas has much to keep in abeyance, for rejectivity can express itself in intrafamilial and communal life as a more or less well rationalized and more or less ruthless suppression of what does not seem to fit some set goals of survival and perfection. This can mean physical or moral cruelty against one's children, and it can turn, as moralistic prejudice, against other segments of family or community. And, of course, it can lump together as "the other side" large groups of foreign peoples. (At any rate, it is a task of every case study to make explicit the way in which some of our young patients are types who have become the focus of the rejectivity of generations—and not merely of a rejecting mother.)

Collective rejectivity, for all kinds of reasons, periodically finds a vast area for collective manifestation—such as in wars against (often neighboring) collectivities who once more appear to be a threat to one's own kind, and this not only by dint of conflicting territorialities or markets, but simply by seeming dangerously different—and who, of course are apt to reciprocate this sentiment. The conflict between generativity and rejection, thus, is the strongest ontogenetic anchor of the universal human propensity which I have called *pseudospeciation*. Lorenz (1973) fittingly translates it as "Quasi-Artenbildung," that is, the conviction (and the impulses and actions based on it) that another type or group of persons are by nature, history, or divine will a species different from one's own—and dangerous to mankind itself.[5] It is a prime human dilemma that pseudospeciation can bring out the truest and best in loyalty and heroism, cooperation and inventiveness, while committing different human kinds to a history of reciprocal enmity and destruction. The problem of human rejectivity, then, has far-reaching implications for the survival of the species as well as for every individual's psychosocial development: where rejectivity is merely inhibited, there can only be self-rejection.

In accordance with our promise, we must now allocate to each stage a specific form of *ritualization*. An adult must be ready to become a numinous model in the next generation's eyes and to act as a judge of evil and a transmitter of ideal values. Therefore adults must and do ritualize being ritualizers; and there is an ancient need and custom to participate in some

[5] The word "pseudo," in its naturalist meaning, does not imply deliberate deception. Rather, it suggests a grandiose, all too human tendency to create more or less playfully appearances which make one's own kind a spectacular and unique sight in creation and in history—a potentially creative tendency, then, which can lead to most dangerous extremes.

rituals which ceremonially sanction and reinforce that role. This whole adult element in ritualization we may simply call the *generative* one. It includes such auxiliary ritualizations as the parental and the didactic, the productive and the curative, and, among others, the literary.

The *ritualism* potentially rampant in adulthood is, I think, *authoritism*—the ungenerous and ungenerative use of sheer power for the regimentation of economic and familial life. Genuine generativity, however, includes a measure of true authority.

Adulthood is preceded by young adulthood, which, psychosexually speaking, depends on a postadolescent genital mutuality. An immense power of verification pervades this meeting of bodies and temperaments after that hazardously long human pre-adulthood.

Young adults emerging from the search for a sense of identity can be eager and willing to fuse their identities in mutual love and to counterpoint them to that of individuals who, in work, sexuality, and friendship promise to prove complementary. One can often be "in love" or engage in intimacies, but the intimacy now at stake is the capacity to commit oneself to concrete affiliations and partnerships and to develop the ethical strength to abide by loyalties which may call for significant sacrifices and compromises.

The psychosocial antithesis to *intimacy* is *isolation*, a sense of being separate and unrecognized—which provides a lasting motivation for seeking and giving in adulthood a mature form of that mutual recognition which is so essential for early childhood. But a sense of isolation is also the potential core pathology of this stage. There are, in fact, affiliations which amount to an isolation à deux, protecting both partners from the necessity to face the next critical development—that of generativity. But the greatest danger of isolation is a regressive and hostile reliving of the identity conflict and, depending on previous fixations, of the earliest conflict with the primal other. From the resolution of the antithesis between intimacy and isolation, however, emerges *love*, that mutuality of mature devotion which promises to resolve the antagonisms inherent in divided function.

The antipathic counterforce to both intimacy and love is *exclusivity*, which in form and function is, of course, closely related to the *rejectivity* emerging in later adulthood. Again, some exclusivity is as essential to intimacy as rejectivity is to generativity; yet both can become vastly destructive—and self-destructive. On the other hand, the incapacity to reject or exclude anything at all can lead only to self-rejection and self-exclusion.

In their ritualizations, too, intimacy and generativity are related, but intimacy employs an *affiliative* kind of ritualization which cultivates styles of in-group living held together by often extremely idiosyncratic ways of behaving and speaking. For intimacy is the guardian of that elusive and yet all-pervasive power in psychosocial evolution, the power of cultural and personal *style* which gives and demands conviction in the shared patterns of living, guarantees individual identity even in joint intimacy, and binds into a way of life the *solidarity* committed to production. These, at least, are the high goals to which development, in principle, is tuned. But then, this is the stage when persons of very different backgrounds must fuse their habitual ways to form a new milieu for themselves and their offspring: an important vehicle of the gradual or radical change of mores and of the shifts in dominant identity patterns brought about by historical change.

The ritualism apt to make an unproductive caricature out of the ritualizations of this stage is *elitism*, which cultivates all sorts of cliques and clans marked more by snobbery (whether higher or lower class) than by a living style.

Adolescence and School Age

The commitments of intimacy, then, depend on a relative resolution of the *identity* crisis, even as, epigenetically speaking, nobody can quite know who he or she is until he or she has met those with whom he can share his being, whereby the identity conflict is apt to persist into the intimacy stage. Identity, in turn, must emerge from the selective affirmation and repudiation of childhood identifications and their absorption in a new configuration codetermined by the way in which society identifies young individuals, at best recognizing them as persons who had to become the way they are and who, being the way they are, can be trusted; and the community, of course, feels recognized by the individual who cares to ask for such recognition. By the same token it can feel deeply and vengefully rejected by the individual who does not seem to care, in which case society thoughtlessly dooms many whose ill-fated search for fidelity (in gang loyalty, for example) it cannot fathom or contain.

The antithesis of identity is *identity confusion*, obviously a normative and necessary experience which, however, can form a core disturbance most severely aggravating and aggravated by pathological regression.

How is the psychosocial concept of identity related to the self—that core concept of individual psychology? A pervasive sense of identity brings into gradual accord the variety of changing self-images which have been experienced during childhood (and which, during adolescence, are often recapitulated) and the role opportunities offering themselves to young persons for selection and commitment. On the other hand, a lasting sense of self cannot exist without a continuous experience of a conscious "I" which is the numinous center of existence: a kind of *existential identity*, then, which sooner or later transcends the psychosocial one. We will return to this.

We have briefly discussed the nature of the strength and ego quality emerging here, namely, *fidelity*, and its relation both to infantile trust and to mature faith. As it transfers the need for guidance from parental figures to instructors and leaders, it eagerly accepts their ideological mediatorship. The antipathic counterpart of fidelity is *role repudiation*, like exclusivity and rejectivity, an active and selective drive dividing that which seems acceptable and workable in identity terms for what must be resisted or fought. Role repudiation can appear in the form of *diffidence* covering a certain weakness in the developmental preparation for identity formation or in the form of a systematic *defiance*—that is, a perverse preference for the (always also present) *negative identity*, especially where the social setting fails to offer any viable alternative. All this can lead to a sudden malignant regression to the conflicts of the earliest experiences, almost as a desperate form of self-rebirth. Yet again, an identity formation is impossible without a degree of role refusal, especially where the available roles endanger the young individual's identity with himself and with some ideal models.

Role refusal, then, helps to delimit one's identity and invokes at least experimental loyalties which can then be "confirmed" and transformed into affiliations by the proper ritualizations or rituals. Nor is role refusal expendable in the social process, for societal adaptation is maintained with the help of loyal rebels who refuse to adjust to "conditions" and who cultivate an indignation in the service of a *renewed wholeness* of ritualization and ritual without which psychosocial evolution would be doomed. Therefore, the adolescent mind is an *ideological* mind: it loves to play with clusters of grand ideas. Where an assured sense of identity is missing, however, even friendships and affairs become desperate attempts at delineating the fuzzy outlines of identity by mutual narcissistic mirroring.

In summary, the process of identity formation emerges as an *evolving configuration*. It is gradually established by successive ego syntheses and resyntheses throughout childhood. It thus is a configuration gradually integrating constitutional givens, idiosyncratic libidinal needs, favored capacities, significant identifications, effective defenses, successful sublimations, and consistent roles.

The ritualizations of this stage can, of course, appear surprising, confusing, and aggravating in the shiftiness of adolescents' first attempts to ritualize their interplay with age mates and create small-group rituals. But they also foster participation in public events on sports fields and in political and religious arenas. In all of these, however, young people can be seen to seek a form of ideological confirmation, and here spontaneous ritualization rites and formal rituals merge. Such search, however, can also lead to fanatic participation in militant ritualisms marked by *totalism*, that is, a totalization of the world image so illusory and indeed "forced" that it lacks the power of renewal and can become nihilistically destructive.

Adolescence and the extending school years can be viewed as a *psychosocial moratorium*—that is, a period of rapid sexual and cognitive maturation and yet of a sanctioned postponement of definitive commitment. It provides a relative leeway for role experimentation, including that with sex roles, all significant for the adaptive self-renewal of society. The earlier school age, in turn, is a *psychosexual moratorium*, for its beginning coincides with what psychoanalysis calls the "latency" period, marked by a postponement of genital maturity. Thus the future mate and parent may first undergo whatever method of schooling is provided for in his society and learn the technical and social rudiments of a work situation. We have ascribed to this period the crisis of *industry* vs. *inferiority*—the first being a basic sense of competent activity adapted both to the laws of the tool world and to the rules of cooperation in planned and scheduled procedures. And again, one can say that a child at this stage learns to love to learn as well as to play—and to learn most eagerly those techniques which are in line with the *ethos of production*. A certain hierarchy of *work roles* has already entered the playing and learning child's imagination by way of ideal examples, real or mythical, which now present themselves in the persons of instructing adults—and in the heroes of history and fiction.

For the antithesis of a sense of industry we have postulated a sense of *inferiority*, again a necessary dystonic sense, which helps drive on the best even as it can (temporarily) paralyze the poorer workers. As the *core pathology* of this stage, however, inferiority is apt to encompass much fateful conflict; it can drive the child to excessive competition or induce it to regress—which can only mean a renewal of infantile-genital and oedipal conflict, and thus a preoccupation with conflictual personages rather than with the helpful ones right at hand. The rudimentary strength developing at this stage, however, is *competence*, a sense which in the growing human being must gradually integrate all the maturing methods of verifying and mastering *factuality* and of sharing the *actuality* of those who cooperate in the same productive situation.

The antipathic counterpart of this sense of competent mastery, however, is that *inertia* which constantly threatens to paralyze an individual's productive life and is, of course, fatefully related to the *inhibition* of the preceding stage.

Preschool Years

This brings us back to the childhood stages which we have in part discussed in connection with epigenesis, pregenitality, and ritualization. It remains for us to add only a summary statement on the antithesis and antipathies of these three stages.

First, then, the play age, in which the antithesis of *initiative* and of *guilt* comes to its crisis. As we can only repeat, it is an essential basis for all the stages to come; just as oedipal implications force a strong limitation of initiative on the child's relation with parental figures, play frees the small individual for an acting out in the microsphere of a vast number of promising identifications and activities. This, furthermore, occurs before the limiting advent of the school age with its defined work roles, and of adolescence and its experimentation with identity possibilities. All this also makes it plausible that *inhibition* is the antipathic counterpart of initiative, a necessary counterpart in so playful and imaginative a creature, and yet potentially also the core pathology in psychoneurotic disturbances (from the hysterias on) which are rooted in this conflicted stage.

Here, then, we have reentered classical psychoanalytic territory. The stage preceding the play age is that "anal" stage of conflict which was first found to be the "fixation" point for compulsion-neurotic disturbances. Psychosocially speaking, we consider it to be the crisis of a sense of *autonomy* vs. *shame* and *doubt* and the emergence of the rudiments of *will*. As we look at the place of this stage between the preceding and the succeeding stages (and, in principle, we should do this for every stage), it stands to reason that what we have just described as initiative could not have developed without a decisive leap from oral sensory dependence to some anal-muscular self-will and to a certain trust in self-control. We have indicated earlier how, alternating between impulsiveness and compulsiveness, the child will try at times to act totally independent, by altogether identifying with his rebellious impulses, or to become once more dependent by making the will of others in his own compulsion. In balancing these two tendencies, the rudiments of will provide an exercise both in free choice and in self-restraint. Man must try early to will what can be, to renounce (as not worth willing) what cannot be, and to believe he has willed what is inevitable by necessity and law. At any rate, in accord with the double (retentive and eliminative) modes dominating this age, *compul-*

sion and *impulsiveness* are the antipathic counterparts of *will* and, when aggravated and interlocked, can paralyze it.

Even in descending order it must have become reasonably clear now that what thus grows in steps is indeed an epigenetic ensemble in which no part must have missed its early rudiments, its original crisis, and its renewal in all later stages. Thus, hope in infancy already can have an element of willfulness which, however, cannot stand being challenged as yet in the way it must be when the crisis of will arrives in early childhood. On the other hand (to take one glance at the first vertical of Table 2), an infant's hope already has some tiny ingredient which will gradually grow to become an aspect of wisdom—that will be harder to defend against all but the most fanatic devotees of infancy. (On the other hand, does not Lao-tse mean "old child"? And did not Christ say, "Unless you become as little children . . . ?") So it remains for us to return to the earliest stage, infancy, and to complete the life cycle by making a leap from this first to the last stage: old age.

Hope, we have said, is the ontogenetic basis of faith, emerging from the conflict of *basic trust* vs. *basic mistrust*. Hope is, so to speak, pure future; and where mistrust prevails early, anticipation, as we know, wanes both cognitively and emotionally. But where hope prevails, it has, as we indicated, the function of carrying out the numinous image of the primal other through the various forms it may take in the intermediate stages, all the way to the confrontation with the ultimate other—in whatever exalted form—and a dim promise of regaining, forever, a paradise almost forfeited. By the same token, autonomy and will, as well as industry and purpose, are oriented toward a future open, in play and in preparatory work, for the choices of one's economic, cultural, and historical era. Identity and fidelity, in turn, must begin to commit themselves to choices involving some finite combinations of activities and values. Youth still can, in alliance with available ideologies, envisage a wide spectrum of possibilities of "salvation" and "damnation"; while the love of young adulthood is inspired by dreams of what one may be able to do and to take care of together. With the love and care of adulthood, however, there arises a most critical midlife factor, namely, the evidence of a narrowing of choices by conditions already irreversibly chosen—by fate or by oneself. Now conditions, circumstances, and associations are one's once-in-a-lifetime reality. Adult care thus must concentrate jointly on the means of taking lifelong care of what one has irrevocably chosen, or, indeed, has been forced to choose by fate, to care for within the technological demands of the historical moment.

Gradually, then, and with every new strength, a new time sense appears along with a sense of irrevocable identity: one gradually becomes what one has caused to be, and eventually one will be what one has been. Lifton (1970) has vastly clarified what it means to be a survivor, but a person in adulthood must also realize (as Laius did) that a generator will be survived by what he has generated. Not that this is all too conscious; on the contrary, it seems that the stage of generativity, as long as a threatening sense of stagnation is kept at bay, is pervasively characterized by a supremely sanctioned disregard of death. Youth, in its own way, is more aware of death than is adulthood, although adults, busy as they are with "maintaining the world," participate in the grand rituals of religion, art, and politics, all of which mythologize and ceremonialize death, giving it a ritual meaning and thus an intensely social presence. It is youth and old age, then, that dream of rebirth, while adulthood is too busy taking care of actual births and is rewarded for it with a unique sense of boisterous and timeless historical reality—a sense of which can seem somewhat unreal to the young and to the old, for it denies the shadow of nonbeing.

Old Age

Integrity vs. despair; wisdom; disdain. There is something, then, in the anatomy even of mature hope which suggests that it is the most childlike of all ego qualities and the most dependent for its verification on the charity of fate.

If, at the end, the life cycle turns back on its own beginnings, so that the very old become again like children, the question is whether the return is to a childlikeness seasoned with wisdom or (and when) to a finite childishness. The old may become (and want to become) too old too fast, or remain too young too long. Here, only some sense of *integrity* can bind things together; and by integrity we do not mean only an occasional outstanding quality of personal character but, above all, a simple proclivity for understanding, or "hearing" those who understand, the integrative ways of human life. It is a comradeship with the ordering ways of distant times and different pursuits, as expressed in their simple products and sayings. For an individual life is the coincidence of but one life cycle with but one segment of history; and all human integrity stands or falls with the one style of integrity of which one partakes. There is an integrating aspect, as there can be a boringly repetitive one, in the ritualistic tendency of the old to reminisce about what events and what persons made up the decisive trends of their lives. But there emerges also a different, a timeless love for those few others who have become the main counterplayers in life's most significant contexts.

And so, all qualities of the past assume new and distinguishing values which we may well study in their own right and not just in their antecedents, be they healthy or pathogenic. For to be relatively freer of neurotic anxiety does not mean to be absolved from existential dread; the most acute understanding of infantile guilt does not do away with the human evil which each life experiences in its own way; and the best defined psychosocial identity does not preempt one's existential identity. In sum, a better functioning ego does not explain away the mystery of the aware "I."

For all these reasons, and more, the dominant antithesis comes to be now *integrity* vs. *despair*—the despair of the knowledge that a limited life is coming to a conclusion; and also the *disgust* (often quite petty) over feeling finished, passed by, and increasingly helpless. The strength arising from these antitheses, however, is *wisdom*, a kind of "detached concern with life itself, in the face of death itself," as expressed both in the sayings of the ages and in those simplest experiences which convey the probability of an ultimate meaning.

Here, at the conclusion of the psychosocial stages, we may well ponder what we will later discuss as the historical relativity of all development and especially also of all developmental theories. Take these stages: it was in our middle years that we formulated them, at a time when we certainly had no intention of (or capacity for) imagining ourselves as old. This was only a few decades ago; and yet our image of old age was then quite different. One could then think, as models of age, of the few wise men and women who quietly lived up to their special assignments in various cultures at a time when long—but not too long—survival seemed a divine gift and a special obligation. But on second thought, our concepts seem to hold as they connote what, in terms of the whole life cycle, old age is meant to be, whether it is represented by exceptional survivors or by a whole, reasonably well-preserved age group. New versions of old age must, at any rate, not be permitted to contradict that distilled knowledge which has lived in folk wit, as well as in folk wisdom, and in the basic crafts and techniques of making daily life meaningful.

The final stage of the life cycle has great significance in the cycle of generations, too. Children in viable cultures are made thoughtful in a specific way by encounters with old people and will renew such thoughtfulness in successive stages, all the more so in a period when old age must become to them an expectable experience to be thoughtfully anticipated. Such historical changes as the lengthening of the average lifespan thus call for viable reritualizations, and these include a finite sense of summary as well as a different, an active concept of dying. For all this, the word wisdom will still do—and so will despair.

But to conclude our survey: the antipathy to wisdom is *disdain*, again a natural and necessary reaction to the lifelong experience of prevailing pettiness and the deadly repetitiveness of human depravity and deceit. Disdain (as rejectivity and exclusivity before) is altogether denied only at the danger of indirect destructiveness, including self-disdain. But wisdom can well contain disdain as a refusal to be fooled in regard to man's antithetical nature.

Oh, yes, what is the ritualization built into the styles of old age? I think it is *philosophical*: in maintaining some integrity in the disintegration of body and mind, it can also advocate durable hope in wisdom. The corresponding ritualistic danger, however (do I need to spell it out?), is *dogmatism*, which, where linked with undue power, can become coercive orthodoxy.

Finally, we have suggested a procreative drive as a further psychosexual stage in adulthood. For (presenile) old age, I can only suggest a *generalization of sensual modes* which can foster an enriched bodily and mental overall experience even as part functions weaken and overall vitality diminishes. (Obviously, such extensions of the libido theory call for discussion and are therefore rendered in parenthesis.)

By way of a summary, I will review the categories listed on Table 1. For each psychosocial stage, "located" as it is between a *psychosexual* one (A) and an expanding *social radius* (C) we list a *core crisis* (B) during which the development of a specific *syntonic* potential (from basic trust [I] to integrity [VIII]) must outbalance that of its *dystonic* antithesis (from *basic mistrust* to senile *despair*). The resolution of each crisis results in the emergence of a *basic strength* or *ego quality*, from *hope* to *wisdom* (D). But such sympathic strength, too, has an antipathic counterpart, from *withdrawal* to *disdain* (E). Both syntonic and dystonic and both sympathic and antipathic potentials are necessary for human adaptation because the human being does not share the animal's fate of developing according to an *instinctive* adaptation to a circumscribed natural environment, which permits a clear-cut and inborn division of positive and negative reactions. Rather, the human being must be guided during a long childhood to develop *instinctual* reaction patterns of love and aggression which can be mustered for a variety of cultural environments vastly different in technology, style, and world view, although each supports what Hartmann (1939) has called certain "average expectable" conditions. But where the dystonic and antipathic trends outweight the syntonic and sympathic, a specific pathology develops (from psychotic withdrawal to senile depression).

Ego synthesis and communal ethos together tend to support a certain measure of syntonic and sympathic trends, while they attempt to accommodate some dystonic and antipathic ones in the great variability of human dynamics. But these dystonic and antipathic trends remain a constant threat to the individual and social order, wherefore, in the course of history, inclusive belief systems (religions, ideologies, cosmic theories) have attempted to universalize the sympathic human trends by making them applicable to a widening combination of worthy "insiders." Such belief systems, in turn, become an essential part of each individual's development in that their ethos (which "actuates manners and customs, moral attitudes and ideals") is conveyed in daily life through age-specific and stage-adequate *ritualizations* (G). These enlist the energy of growth in the renewal of certain all-embracing principles (from the *numinous* to the *philosophical*). Wherever *ego* and *ethos* lose their viable interconnection, however, these ritualizations threaten to disintegrate into deadening *ritualisms*, from *idolism* to *dogmatism* (H). Because of their joint developmental roots, there is a dynamic affinity between individual core disturbances and social ritualisms (E and H).

Thus, each new human being receives and internalizes the logic and the strength of the principles of social order, from the cosmic through the legal and the technological to the productive and beyond (F), and develops the readiness under favorable conditions to convey them to the next generations. All this, at any rate, must be recognized as one of the essential built-in potentials for development and recovery, even if daily clinical experience and general observation are apt to confront us with the symptoms of unresolved crises in individuals and with the social pathology of ritualistic decomposition.

In our two main sections, we have attempted to point up the nexus of some of the instinctual forces and their organismic modes, and we have outlined the way in which the sequence of stages make up a life cycle and the succession of lives a generational cycle. All such attempts at systematization, however, underlie an historical relativity (as yet to be discussed). That is, we have emphasized primarily some principles of development the recognition of which seemed essential at the time of our entrance into the field (epigenesis), although we cannot insist on the final delineation of the exact stages listed or, indeed, on all the terms used. And while we suggest that a psychosocial approach based on psychoanalytic principles must assume that the integrating processes of *ego-synthesis* and *ethos-formation* are complementary and depend on each other, we are, for any final confirmation, dependent on at least two courses of study which in these pages were ignored; on the psychological side there is the verifying power of *cognitive growth* as it refines and expands, with each stage of growth, the capacity for accurate and conceptual interplay with the factual world. This certainly is a most indispensable "ego apparatus" in Hartmann's sense (1939). So it would be most useful to trace in Piaget's sense to infantile trust; of the intuitive-symbolic ones to play and initiative; of concrete-operational performance to the sense of industry; and finally, of formal operations and logical manipulations to identity development (see Greenspan, 1979).

The other complementary study here neglected would include the *institutional structures and mechanisms* which make for the politics of communality. True, we have attempted to account for the ritualizations of everyday life which provide the link between individual development and social structure: Their "politics" can be easily discerned in any record of intimate social interplay. But we must depend on social science for accounts of how, in given systems and periods, leading individuals as well as elites and power groups strive to preserve, to renew, or replace the dominant *ethos* in productive and political life, and how they tend to support the generative potentials in adults and the readiness for growth and development in those growing up. In my work I have only been able to suggest a first approach to the lives and to critical life stages within these lives, of two religious-political leaders (Erikson, 1958; 1969), and to the way in which they could translate their personal crises into methods of spiritual and political renewal in the lives of a large contingent of their contemporaries.

Much corresponding work is in progress. But in the conclusion of this essay it seems best in a few brief notes to ask in what way clinical experience may both gain therapeutically from psychosocial insight and yield observations conducive to it. This brings us back to the very beginning of this essay.

Ego and Ethos: Concluding Notes

Ego Defense and Social Adaptation

In *The Ego and the Mechanisms of Defense*, Anna Freud (1936) "deals exclusively with one particular problem, i.e., with the ways and means by which the ego wards off unpleasure and anxiety, and exercises control over impulsive behavior, affects, and instinctive urges" (p. v). Thus, the various omnipresent defenses such as *repression* and *regression, denial* and *reaction-formation,* are treated exclusively as phenomena of *inner economy*. In February 1973, in Philadelphia, on the occasion of a panel devoted to a review of Anna Freud's book (then in its thirty-seventh year), the opportunity offered itself to discuss in her presence some of the social and communal implications of the mechanisms of defense.[6] Can *defense mechanisms*, we asked, be shared and thus assume an *ecological value* in the lives of inter-related persons and in communal life? I made a point of re-ferring to some passages in Anna Freud's book which clearly imply such a potential.

Most obvious, of course, is the similarity of certain individ-ual defense mechanisms and the grand ritual defenses of com-munities. Take, for example, "identification with the aggressor." There is the little girl who—for whatever acute reasons—is afraid of ghosts and bans them by making peculiar gestures, thus pretending to be the ghost she might meet in the hall. And we may think of "children's games in which through the met-amorphosis of the subject into a dreaded object anxiety is con-verted into pleasurable security" (A. Freud, 1936, p. 111). Correspondingly, there are, throughout cultural history, all the "primitive methods of exorcising spirits" by impersonating them in their most aggressive forms.

Anna Freud also reports observations in a particular school which in pursuit of modernity had reritualized (as we would say) its procedures, putting "less emphasis on class teaching" and more on "self-chosen individual work" (p. 95). Immedi-ately, some new and yet well-circumscribed defensive behavior of an intimidated and inhibited sort appeared in a number of children previously known to be quite able and popular; their very adaptiveness seemed endangered by the changed de-mands. Anna Freud suggests that such a shared defense, though engaged in genuinely by each individual, could quickly disappear again if the school abandoned its wayward rituali-zations. But what are the social mechanisms of such shared

[6] See the *Journal of the Philadelphia Association for Psychoanalysis*, I:1, 1974. This discussion was continued at Hampstead in May 1975.

defense which, in the long run at any rate, might become habitual and thus change some personalities and careers, as well as the ethos of group life?

Finally, we may well ponder again the social implications of such an adolescent defense mechanism as *intellectualization* in puberty—that is, the seemingly excessive preoccupation with *ideas* including (in the Vienna of that day) "the demand for revolution in the outside world." Anna Freud interprets this as a defense on the part of these youths against "the perception of the new instinctual demands of their own id," that is, the inner, instinctual revolution. This, no doubt, is the psychosexual aspect of the matter; but it stands to reason that intellectual defenses appear and are shared in puberty both as a recourse to the cognitive gains of this stage and as an adaptive use of the ritualizations of an existing intellectual ethos typical for the time and the place. The societal process, in fact, must count on such adolescent processes, including their periodical excesses, for its readaptation to changing conditions.

It appears probable, then, that defense mechanisms are not only molded to the individual's instinctual urges which they are to contain but, where they work relatively well, are shared or counterpointed as they become part of the ritualized interplay of individuals and families as well as of larger units. But where they are weak, bizarre, and altogether isolating, defense mechanisms may well amount to *individualized* and *internalized* *ritualisms* such as those which characterize the symptoms of individuals with compulsive defenses. Such individuals, in turn, may become the mainstay, for example, of bureaucracies which count on them for legalistic work.

Anna Freud, "on reflection," consented to this general trend of thought as she recalled some of her own experiences as a teacher as well as "long discussions at her clinic as to whether obsessional children of obsessional parents used obsessional mechanisms out of imitation or identification or whether they shared with their parents the danger arising from strong sadistic tendencies and, independently of their parents, used the appropriate defense mechanism" (*Journal of the Philadelphia Assn. for Psychoanalysis*, 1974).

I and We

The German word *Ich* is used at times by Freud to correspond not so much to the "ego" but to "I," and in the translation
of certain passages must be so rendered. This is particularly
true where Freud (1923) ascribes to the "Ich" an "immediacy"
and "certainty" of experience "on which all consciousness depends." This is by no means a matter of simple double meaning,
but one of decisive-conceptual import. For the unconscious can
become known only to an immediate and certain consciousness—a consciousness, furthermore, which through evolution
and history has reached a decisive state when it must confront
itself with rational methods, thus becoming aware of its own
denial of the unconscious and learning to study the consequences. Nevertheless, this elemental consciousness seems to
have been one of those primal human facts which Freud took
for granted (*selbstverstaendlich*) and on which, for the moment,
he imperiously refused to reflect. Considering the width and
the passion of his own esthetic, moral, and scientific awareness,
one must consider this exclusive concentration on the unconscious and on the id an almost ascetic commitment to the study
of what is most obscure and yet also most elemental in human
motivation. Yet it should be noted that his method, in order to
make the unconscious yield anything, employs playfully configurational means such as "free" association, dream, or play—all
special states of consciousness—while systematic interpretation,
of course, works toward consciousness expansion.

In subjecting the psychoanalytic technique itself to the
stringent and ascetic rules which deprive it of the character of
a social encounter, Freud put the self-observing "I" and the
shared "we" into the exclusive service of the study of the unconscious. This has proven to be a meditative procedure which
can yield unheard-of healing insight for those individuals who
feel disturbed enough to need it, curious enough to want it,
and healthy enough to "take" it—a selection which can make
the psychoanalyzed in some communities feel, indeed, like a
new kind of elite. But a more systematic study of "I" and "we"
would seem to be not only necessary for an understanding of
psychosocial phenomena, it also seems elemental for a truly

comprehensive psychoanalytic psychology. I am, of course, aware of the linguistic difficulty of speaking of the "I" as we do of the ego or the self; and yet, it does take an "I" to be aware of a "myself" or, indeed, of a series of myselves, while all the variations of self-experience have in common (and a saving grace it is) the conscious continuity of the "I" that experienced and can remember them all. The "I," after all, is the ground for the simple verbal assurance that each person is a center of awareness in a universe of communicable experience, a center so numinous that it amounts to a sense of being alive and, more, of being the vital condition of existence. At the same time, only two or more persons sharing a corresponding world image as well as a language can, for moments, merge their "I"s into a "we."

Freud (1921) went so far as to assert that "there is no doubt that the tie which united each individual with Christ is also the cause of the tie which unites them with one another," but then, as we saw, he did so in a discourse on what he called "artificial" groups such as churches or armies. The fact is, however, that all identifications amounting to brotherhoods and sisterhoods depend on such identifications depending, in turn, on charismatic figures, from parents to leaders to gods. Wherefore the God above the Sinai, when asked by Moses who he should tell the people had talked to him, introduced himself as "I AM that I AM" and suggested that the people be told "I AM has sent me unto you." This existential meaning is, no doubt, close to the evolutionary step of monotheism and extends to associated patriarchal and monarchical phenomena.

Here we are again reminded of the lifelong power of the first mutual recognition of the newborn and the *primal* (maternal) *other* and its gradual transfer to the *ultimate other* who will "lift up His countenance upon you and give you peace." From here we could once more follow the stages of development and study the way in which the original "I" and "Thou" are conveyed to the fatherhoods and motherhoods, the sisterhoods and brotherhoods of the "we" who come to share the reality of a joined identity. But here also it is necessary to amend the very concept of a reality which, as I complained at the beginning, is all too often seen as an "outerworld" to be adjusted to.

Threefold Reality

The ego as concept and term was not, of course, invented by Freud. In scholasticism it stood for the *unity* of body and soul, and in philosophy in general for the *permanency* of conscious experience. William James (1920) in his letters speaks not only of an "enveloping ego to make continuous the times and spaces" but also of *"the ego's active tension,"* a term which connotes the very essence of subjective health. Here, it seems, James (who knew German intimately) thought of the subjective sense of "I" as well as the unconscious workings of a built-in "ego." This ego, we would specify further, strives to integrate experience in such a way that the "I" can feel, in the flux of events, as an effective *doer* rather than an impotent sufferer; *active* and *originating* rather than inactivated (a word to be preferred to "passive," for one can, as it were, be active in a passive manner); *central* and *inclusive* rather than shunted to the periphery; *selective* rather than overwhelmed; and *aware* rather than confounded—all of which amounts to a sense of being *at home* in one's time and place, and even, somehow, of feeling *chosen* even as one chooses.

So far, so good. But, as we noticed, when we follow human development through the stages of life, the human problem is that such a basic sense of centrality depends for its renewal from stage to stage on an increasing number of others, some of them close enough to be individually acknowledged as an "other" in some important segment of life, but for the most part a vague number of interrelated others who seek to confirm their sense of reality by sharing it, if not imposing it on ours, even as they also try to delimit theirs against ours. It is for psychosocial reasons, then, that it is not enough to speak of the ego's adjustment to an outer reality. For conflictual as all human adaptation is, by the time the ego can be said to guide adaptation it has already absorbed adaptive experiences and intense introjections. In fact, Freud's German model for *reality*, the word *Wirklichkeit* (related as it is to what "works") has pervasively active and interactive connotations.

Reality, then, must be said to have a number of indispensable components—all dependent, however, in a psychoanalytic context, on *instinctuality* as the source of those affective energies which, during early training, have been put at the ego's disposal and now work for the immersion of maturing capacities in the phenomenal and communal world, in which they help to establish an increasing area of anchorage against the formless demands of the "id" and of the phenomenal world. Thus, the child can be said to learn to "love" even facts that can be named, verified, and shared and which in turn inform such love.

As to the three indispensable components of a maturing sense of reality, *factuality* is the most commonly emphasized in the usual sense of the "thing" world of facts—to be perceived with a minimum of distortion or denial and a maximum of the validation possible at a given stage of cognitive development and at a given state of technology and science.

A second connotation of the word *reality* is a convincing coherence and order which lifts the known facts into a context apt to make us (more or less surprisingly) realize their nature: a truth value that can be shared by all those who partake of a joint language and world image. "Comprehensibility" (*Begreiflichkeit*, as used by Einstein) would seem to be a fitting word for this aspect of reality.[7] For the moment, however, I would choose the more visual *contextuality*, for it is the astounding interwovenness of the facts that gives them a certain revelatory significance.

Finally, what is thus "realized" in the cognitive sense by a group of individuals also invites them to share in joint "realizations" in the sense of actualization and mutual activation; this I have come to refer to as *actuality*.

Only these three meanings of reality together make up the world that the ego can strive to adapt and that each "I" can feel at home in. In defective development (but also in special giftedness) these three aspects of reality experience are variably emphasized; but in healthy (including special) development they must find their balance. And only by maintaining a meaningful correspondence between such reality and the experience

---

[7] Einstein once said that to "comprehend a bodily object" means to attribute "a real existence" to it. And he adds, "the fact that the world of sense experiences is comprehensible is a miracle" (1954).

of the main developmental stages can the communal ethos secure for itself a maximum of energy from a sufficient number
of participants.

Reality is a viable world view, then, even if it is modestly
called a "way of life," is at its best an all-inclusive conception
which focuses disciplined attention on a selection of certifiable
facts, liberates a joint and coherent vision enhancing a sense of
contextuality, and actualizes an ethical fellowship with strong
work commitments. All these are included in and yet also transcended by an enveloping sense of "I," which may indeed grow
out of that early instinctual development which we call narcissistic, but during maturation may lift itself well above the treach-
erous reflections of self-love.

World images, finally, must grow with each individual, even
as they must be renewed in each generation. We could now
review our discussion, from organ modes to postural and sensory modalities, and from the normative crises of life to the
antitheses of psychosocial development, and attempt to indicate
how world images tend to provide a universal context and
meaning for all such experiences from the beginning of life.
Only thus can the individual "I," as it grows out of the earliest
bodily experiences and their cultural connotations, learn to
have and to share a modicum of a central and active, an aware
and selective, sense of orientation in the universe. Any study
of the orientation provided by world images, then, must begin
with the needs of the "I" for a basic space-time orientation and
then proceed to the community's way of providing a network
of corresponding perspectives, beginning with the simplest
communal concepts of the course of the day and the cycle of
the year, to other periodic and ritual events, and extending to
its limits and "boundaries" in K. Erikson's sense (1966), where
communal otherness begins. While I myself have been able to
circumscribe such matters only in an unsystematic manner
(1974, 1977) as I was trying to sketch perspectives of growing
up in the American way of life, I am convinced that clinical
psychoanalytic observation can contribute essential insights into
the deep unconscious and preconscious involvement of each
individual in established and changing world images. For in
their built-in conflicts and destructive antitheses we can study

the potential complementarity of somatic, social, and ego organization. Such study, in different historical settings, will be all the more fruitful as psychoanalysis becomes more aware of its own history and its ideological and ethical implications. But only a new kind of cultural history can show how all the details of individual development dovetail with or come to diverge from the grand schemes suggested in the existential cycles of religious belief systems, in the historical postulates of political and economic ideologies, and in the experiential implications of scientific theories.

Ethos and Ethics

The most comprehensive statement in early psychoanalysis on the dynamic relation of ego and ethos is probably a passage in Freud's *New Introductory Lectures on Psycho-Analysis* (1933):

> As a rule, parents and authorities analogous to them follow the precepts of their own super-egos in educating children. . . . Thus a child's super-ego is in fact constructed on the model not of its parents but of its parents' super-ego; the contents which fill it are the same and it becomes the vehicle of tradition and of all the time-resisting judgments of value which have propagated themselves in this manner from generation to generation.

Here, as we see, Freud locates some aspects of the historical process itself in the individual's superego—that inner agency which, it is true, the ego itself must guard itself against in order to be relatively free from unbearable *inner suppression*. Freud then spars briefly with the "materialistic views of history" which, he says, emphasize *political suppression* by claiming that "human 'ideologies' are nothing other than the product and superstructure of their contemporary economic conditions":

> That is true, but very probably not the whole truth. Mankind never lives entirely in the present. The past, the tradition of the race and of the people, lives on in the ideologies of the super-ego, and yields only slowly to the influences of the present and to new changes; and so long as it operates

through the super-ego it plays a powerful part in human
life, independently of economic conditions.

This statement has far-reaching implications for the psychological study of revolutionary forces and methods; but most
astonishingly it seems to suggest that in reconstructing a person's inner dynamics the psychoanalyst could and should note
also the superego's "ideological orientation" and this especially
in regard to its resistance to change and liberation, a suggestion
which opens major historical trends as reflected in inner conflicts to direct psychoanalytic study. From a developmental
point of view, however, I would like to suggest that what we
detect in the superego as remnants of the childhood years is,
as Freud suggests, not the reflection of living ideologies, but of
old ones which have already become moralities, for the superego, in balancing the imaginative oedipal stage and the infantile
crisis of initiative vs. guilt is apt to emphasize, above all, a network of prohibitions which must fence in an all too playful
initiative and help to establish a basic moral or even moralistic
orientation.

As I have indicated, I would rather consider adolescence
the life stage wide open, both cognitively and emotionally, for
ideological imageries and tenets apt to marshal the fantasies
and energies of youth for some world view. Depending on the
historical moment, this will confirm or protest the existing order
or promise a future one and thus help the young individual to
overcome a sense of identity confusion. Finally, I think there
is good reason to allocate to adulthood—exactly insofar as it
has outgrown its excess of infantile moralism or of adolescent
ideologism—the potentiality of an ethical sense consonant with
the generative engagements of that stage and with the necessity
for a modicum of mature and far-reaching planning within
historical reality. Ideological leaders, too, must develop and
practice their ideologies with a firm moral sense—and with
ethical concern. (As to our developmental insights, generative
ethics would suggest some new version of the Golden Rule such
as: Do to another what will advance the other's growth even as
it advances your own. [Erikson, 1964]).

Here, and in passing, it may be remembered that in outlining the life stages just reserved for the ritualizations of man's moral, ideological, and ethical potentials (namely, childhood, adolescence, and adulthood), we warned of the corresponding dangers of three ritualisms: moralism, totalism, and authoritism. Also, it may be necessary once more to recall the obligation to visualize all developmental factors epigenetically, and this includes the trends just described—to wit:

	1	2	3
III			ethical
II		ideological	
I	moral		

Thus, there are potentials for ethical and ideological traits in all morality, even as there are both moral and ethical traits in ideology. Therefore, continuing moral or ideological modes of thought in the ethical position are by no means "infantile" or "juvenile" leftovers, as long as they retain the potential for becoming integrated parts of a certain generative maturity within the historical relativity of the times.

Developmental and Historical Relativity

In his 1844 manuscripts Karl Marx claims that "just as all things natural must *become*, man, too, has his act of becoming—history" (Tucker, 1961). For "the act of becoming" Marx often uses the word *Entstehungsakt*, which connotes a combination of "growing out of," "standing up," and becoming; and there is the clear implication of the coming adulthood of the species. There is a comparable utopian statement by Freud (1930): "I may now add that civilization is a process in the service of Eros, whose purpose is to combine single human individuals, and after that families, then races, peoples, and nations, into one great unity, the unity of mankind." The implication that such a future demands an all-human adulthood seems to pervade Freud's systematic preoccupation with man's potentially fatal regressive tendencies toward infantile as well as primitive and archaic affects and images; the human being of the future, enlightened about all these prehistorical fixations, will perhaps have a somewhat better chance to act as an adult *and* as a knowing participant in one human specieshood. In our terms, this would imply than an adult mankind would overcome pseudo- (or quasi-) speciation, i.e., that split into imaginary species which has provided adult rejectivity with a most moralistic rationalization of the hate of otherness. Such "speciation" has supported the most cruel and reactionary attributes of the superego where it was used to reinforce the narrowest tribal consciousness, caste exclusiveness, and nationalistic and racist identity, all of which must now be recognized as endangering the very existence of the whole species in a technological civilization.

The word *Eros* in this context once more underscores the fact that a psychoanalytic theory begins with the assumption of all-embracing instinctual forces which at their best contribute to a universal kind of love. But it also underlines the fact that we have entirely neglected that other unifying life principle, *logos*, which masters the cognitive structure of factuality—a theme of such ever-increasing importance today, when technology and science suggest, for the first time in human history, some outlines of a truly universal and jointly planned environment. However, the world suggested in the imagery of universal technology and apt to be dramatized by the media can turn into a vision of a totally fabricated order to be planned according to strictly logical and technological principles—a vision dangerously oblivious of what we are emphasizing in these pages, namely, the dystonic and antipathic trends endangering the organismic existence and the communal order on which the ecology of psychic life depends. An art and science of the human mind, therefore, must be informed by a developmental, or shall we say life-historical, orientation, as well as by a special historical self-awareness. As the philosopher Collingwood (1956) puts it: "History is the life of the mind itself which is not mind except so far as it both lives in the historical process and knows itself as so living." In commemoration of Einstein, let us give in conclusion some consideration to the way in which the psychoanalytic method of investigation, to us so familiar, both permits and demands a systematic awareness of a specific kind of relativity.

As to this very idea of relativity, all revolutionary advances in the natural sciences, of course, have cognitive and ethical implications which at first seem to endanger the previously dominant world image and, with it, the very cosmic reassurances of the basic ego needs we listed. Thus, to give only one example, Copernicus upset man's (as well as the earth's) centrality in the universe. But eventually, the very insight that comes with such a radical change in basic orientation also reaffirms the adaptive power of the human mind, even as it stimulates a new inventive ethos. I have cited Freud's theoretical commitment to an "energy of equal dignity" in a century most cognizant of energy transformations. Relativity, too, at first had unbearably relativistic implications, seemingly undermining the foundations of any absolute human "standpoint"; and yet it opens a new vista in which relative standpoints are "reconciled" to each other by a special insight.

In this sense, the psychoanalytic situation can be reviewed in terms which picture the psychoanalyst's and the patient's minds at work as two "coordinate systems" moving relatively to each other. (This, of course, can at best be an instructive analogy just because time, in human terms, is experienced as developmental and historical change.) At any rate, the seeming repose and impersonality of the psychoanalytic encounter actually permit and intensify in the patient a "free floating" of "associations" which can move about with varying speed through the distant past, to the immediate present, and the feared or wished-for future, and, at the same time, in the spheres of concrete experience, fantasy, and dream life. The patient suffers from symptoms betraying some arrest in the present and yet related to developmental fixations on one or more of the core pathologies characteristic of earlier stages of life. Free association, therefore, can be expected to induce the analysand to remember and to relive, if often in symbolically disguised form, conflicts intrinsic to previous stages and states of development and thus to reveal the unconscious resistances to their clarification. Their whole significance, however, does not become clear until the psychoanalytic situation reveals the patient as unconsciously "transferring" onto the psychoanalyst some of the revived and more or less irrational images and affects of past life periods.

The psychoanalyst, in turn, has been trained in a kind of perpetual but (as its best) disciplined and unobtrusive awareness of his own motion through developmental and historical time. Thus, while viewing the patient's verbalizations in the light of what has been learned of the general direction of his or her life, the psychoanalyst remains consistently ready to become aware of the way in which the patient's present state and past conflicts reverberate in his or her own life situation and evoke feelings and images from the corresponding stages of the past—in brief, the therapist's countertransference. Such complex interplay must be experienced in order to detect (and to learn from) any possible collusion of the listener's own habitual affects and denials with those of the patient.

But while thus moving about in their respective life cycles, relative as they both are to different social and historical trends, the practitioner's interpretive thoughts are also moving with the past and current conceptualizations of psychoanalysis, including, of course, the analyst's own "generational" position between his or her own training analysis and other influential training personalities and schools, as well as his or her own intellectual ruminations, intrinsically related as they are to one's development as a worker and as a person. And each old or new clinical and theoretical model or "map" can, as we saw, be marked by significant shifts in clinical ethos.

Only by remaining potentially aware of the relativity governing all these related movements can the psychoanalyst hope to reach healing and enlightening insights which may lead to interpretations fitting the therapeutic moment—interpretations often equally surprising, both in their utter uniqueness and in their human lawfulness, to the practitioner and to the client. In thus clarifying the patient's course of life in the light of the given therapeutic encounter, interpretation heals through an expansion of developmental and historical awareness.

This whole relativity, we conclude, is an intrinsic part of a new method of observation which makes the age-old human and artistic empathy systematic and establishes a lawful interplay not otherwise accessible. At the same time, however, it is part of a new kind of healing and self-healing orientation and a new form of life-historical and historical awareness which demands to be integrated into the ethos of modern man, whether it is intensely professionalized as in healing procedures; becomes part of the workings of such related fields as history, sociology, or political science; or, indeed, enters general enlightenment and daily life.

These concluding remarks can do no more than suggest that to see what is most familiar in our daily work in terms of relativity (as well as complementarity) may do better justice to some aspects of psychoanalysis than some of the causal and quantitative terms which were of the essence to the theories of the founders. At any rate, it is evident that a psychosocial orientation fuses naturally with such a developmental and historical view, and that clinical observations made with such awareness in dealing with patients of different ages in different areas of the world can in the very process of healing serve to register the fate of the basic human strengths and core disturbances under changing technological and historical conditions. Thus, clinical work can supplement other ways of taking the pulse of changing history.

But we must end with a word of caution. It is obvious that such modes of observation as those described here can only too easily serve a certain analytic relativism, wherever their built-in discipline is diffused and their universal ethos weakened. Even as clinical psychoanalytic observation carries with it an intrinsic obligation to advance psychic wholeness and to avoid habitual fragmenting for mere analysis' sake, so psychosocial or so-called psychohistorical observation calls for a new Hippocratic vigilance, for in today's world of communication, to analyze history can mean to make history. Therefore, our as yet hyphenated studies must make it their business to recognize and to elaborate developmental potentials, even as they diagnose glaring failures or dangers. Only thus can they support a world image dominated by an ecological ethos of communal responsibility for the full development of human beings chosen to be born in a planned future.

References

Benedek, T. (1959), Parenthood as a developmental phase. *J. Amer. Psychoanal. Assn.*, 7:389–417.

Blos, P. (1967), The second individuation process of adolescence. *The Psychoanalytic Study of the Child*, 22:162–186. New York: International Universities Press.

Collingwood, R.G. (1956), *The Idea of History*. New York: Oxford University Press.

Einstein, A. (1954), *Ideas and Opinions*. New York: Crown.

Erikson, E.H. (1931), Bilderbücher. *Zeitschrift für Psychoanalytische Paedagogik*, 5:417–445.

────── (1937), Configurations in play: clinical notes. *Psychoanal. Quart.*, 6:139–214.

────── (1955), Freud's "The Origins of Psychoanalysis." *Internat. J. Psycho-Anal.*, 36:1–15.

────── (1958), *Young Man Luther: A Study in Psychoanalysis and History*. New York: Norton.

────── (1959), *Identity and the Life Cycle*, with Introduction by David Rapaport. New York: International Universities Press.

────── (1950), *Childhood and Society*, Rev. ed., New York: Norton, 1963.

────── (1964), *Insight and Responsibility*. New York: Norton.

────── (1969), *Gandhi's Truth*. New York: Norton.

────── (1974), *Dimensions of a New Identity: The 1973 Jefferson Lectures*. New York: Norton.

────── (1977), *Toys and Reasons: Stages in the Ritualization of Experience*. New York: Norton.

────── (1978), *Life History and the Historical Moment.* New York: Norton.

Erikson, J.M. (1966), Eye to eye. In: *The Man-Made Object*, ed. G. Kepes. New York: Braziller.

Erikson, K.T. (1966), *Wayward Puritans*, New York: Wiley.

Freud, A. (1936), *The Ego and the Mechanisms of Defense*. New York: International Universities Press, 1966.

────── (1965), *Normality and Pathology in Childhood*. New York: International Universities Press.

Freud, S. (1914), On narcissism: An introduction. *Standard Edition*, 14:67–102. London: Hogarth Press, 1957.

────── (1921), Group psychology and the analysis of the ego. *Standard Edition*, 18:69–143. London: Hogarth Press, 1955.

────── (1923), The ego and the id. *Standard Edition*, 19:12–66. London: Hogarth Press, 1961.

────── (1926), To Romain Rolland. *Standard Edition*, 20:279. London: Hogarth Press, 1959.

────── (1930), Civilization and its discontents. *Standard Edition*, 21:59–145. London: Hogarth Press, 1961.

────── (1933), New introductory lectures on psycho-analysis. *Standard Edition*, 22:7–182. London: Hogarth Press, 1964.

────── (1954), *The Origins of Psychoanalysis: Letters to Wilhelm Fliess, Drafts and Notes 1887–1902*, ed. M. Bonaparte, A. Freud, & E. Kris. New York: Basic Books.

Greenspan, S.I. (1979), An integrated approach to intelligence and adaptation: A synthesis of psychoanalytic and Piagetian developmental psychology. *Psychological Issues*, Monograph 3/4. New York: International Universities Press.

Hartmann, H. (1939), *Ego Psychology and the Problem of Adaptation*. New York: International Universities Press, 1958.

—— (1947), On rational and irrational actions. In: *Psychoanalysis and the Social Sciences*, Vol. 1. New York: International Universities Press.

—— (1956), Notes on the reality principle. *The Psychoanalytic Study of the Child*, 11:31–53. New York: International Universities Press.

Huxley, J. (1966), *From An Antique Land: Ancient and Modern in the Middle East*. New York: Harper & Row, 1966.

James, W. (1920), *The Letters of William James*, ed. H. James. Boston: Atlantic Monthly Press.

Jones, E. (1953), *The Life and Work of Sigmund Freud*, Vol. 1. New York: Basic Books.

Kakar, S. (1977), *The Inner World: A Psychoanalytic Study of Hindu Childhood and Society*. New Delhi and New York: Oxford University Press.

Lifton, R.J. (1970), *History and Human Survival*. New York: Random House.

Loewenstein, R.M., Newman, L.M., Schur, M., & Solnit, A., eds. (1966), *Psychoanalysis: A General Psychology*. New York: International Universities Press.

Lorenz, K. (1966), Ritualization in the psychosocial evolution of human culture. *Philosophical Transactions of the Royal Society of London*, Series B, No. 172, Vol. 251.

—— (1973), *Die Ruckseite des Spiegels*. Munich: R. Piper.

Spitz, R.A. (1963), Life and the dialogue. In: *Counterpoint: Libidinal Object and Subject*, ed. H.S. Gaskill. New York: International Universities Press, 1963.

Stockard, C.H. (1931), *The Physical Basis of Personality*. New York: Norton.

Tucker, R.C. (1961), *Philosophy and Myth in Karl Marx*. London and New York: Cambridge University Press.

3

The Development of the Ego: Insights from Clinical Work with Infants and Young Children

STANLEY I. GREENSPAN, M.D.

Psychoanalysis has a defined stage theory for drive development based on both direct observations of children and reconstructions of analyses of adults and children. It does not, however, have a systematic developmental theory of ego development. Global concepts relating to the development of the superego and ego ideal have been discussed, and the sequence of object relationships, and the way in which they set the foundation for intrapsychic structure, is often hotly debated. There are many unanswered questions, however, regarding the development of basic ego functions and the relation between hypothesized stages of ego development and object relationships (in terms of the creation and differentiation of self-object organizations). This chapter will introduce concepts regarding the early organization of experience based on clinical work with infants and young children and their families. It will use these concepts to examine the development of ego structure, self- and object-representations, and the mechanisms of intrapsychic growth and development.

The approach to follow will be based on the fact that much of what has been of interest to psychoanalysis is the development of the ego in relation to intrapsychic challenges. In fact,

This paper was originally published in the *Journal of the American Psychoanalytic Association*, Special Issue on the Ego Structure (Spring 1988). The present version contains additional material on the preschool years.

the history of psychoanalytic theory is marked by insights derived from clinical reconstructive work or direct observation of children and adults struggling with emotional challenges. In this sense, psychoanalytic theory is a model of the mind as it copes with emotional challenges, i.e., of the mind in dynamic flux.

Concepts such as "autonomous ego functions" are rather global attempts to include within depth psychology important aspects of the personality that pertain to normal perceptual, integrative, cognitive, and motor functioning. What is the best way to observe the mind's way of using its autonomous ego functions to organize dynamically relevant experience? One reliable strategy has been to use clinical material. In the clinical context, the mind's capacity is being "stretched" in one way or another to reveal its contours. A clinically informed inquiry into infancy may clarify some of the important questions challenging psychoanalytic developmental theory (e.g., the degree to which early infancy is characterized by autistic and symbiotic-like phenomena; the nature of incorporation, projection, and part-object relationship patterns early in life). A few well-known attempts at clarifying the early aspects of ego functioning from clinical work and direct observation have produced illuminating but still controversial insights into early relationships (e.g., Mahler, Pine, and Bergman, 1975). (They remain controversial in part because of the limited range of disturbances observed and a lack of appropriate adaptive comparisons.)

There are, of course, serious difficulties as well with approaches to understanding ego development that involve generalizing from experimental findings about infants. The difficulties arise from a tendency to overgeneralize from selected experimental findings to psychodynamic domains. For example, Stern (1985, 1987) argues that the infant's ability to discriminate visual designs or sounds means that ego structure is differentiated even in this early period; that the existence of cognitive memory entails the existence, in early infancy, of internal mental representations of drives, affects, and objects; and that experience is the same for both infants and children—both cognitive and emotional (the latter including sexual, aggressive, traumatic, and pathogenic experience)—because infants form mental images based not on single events but on the average of many similar events. This last notion challenges the main body of psychoanalytic observation and theory, which emphasizes the centrality of certain types of organizing fantasies and early experiences related to phase-specific drive-affect and object relationship patterns. This bold challenge, however, is based on a very narrow area of perceptual research and therefore highlights the danger of overgeneralizing from narrow experimental results to psychodynamic domains. The research involved a visual preference task. A small number of presumedly normal infants in a limited age range (i.e., 10 months old) were presented different visual configurations. In showing the expected preference for the novel configuration, they tended to average together the features of the visual configuration they were familiar with in order to determine the novel one. Here an interesting finding on visual perception in 10-month-old infants is taken out of context and, without appropriate research proving its generalizibility, is applied broadly to all aspects of experience at all ages. One cannot, without explicit research, assume that the way the brain functions in something as specific as preference behavior at 10 months of age is the same as the way the brain functions generally in other domains.

In general, the tendency to overgeneralize from narrow experimental findings to psychodynamic domains tends to ignore three facts. One, there is a difference between what an infant is capable of and what is functionally part of his age-expected ego operations. For example, a 20-month-old can conserve the image of inanimate objects but still have great difficulty conserving the image of his libidinal objects under emotional pressure (the problem of object constancy). Two, the types of dynamic experience that are object of depth psychology are quite different from the types of experience that constitute impersonal cognition and in all likelihood have a different organizational timetable. (Greenspan, 1979). Three, each infant organizes experience differently in the context of individual differences and at various stages of ego organization. (Even in terms of sensoriaffective pathways there are differences between the way some infants organize visual and auditory information.) Therefore, one cannot generalize across different modalities, developmental stages, and groups of infants unless there is explicit experimental evidence proving the generalizations. But even more important is the need for reports of work on clinical populations of infants and young children to reveal, through the comparison of distorted and adaptive patterns, the underlying functions and mechanisms of the ego.

This chapter will present a model of early ego development based on both clinical work with disturbed infants and observations of normal infants and their families. It will attempt to clarify some of the controversies by drawing on observations of early ego development in dynamically relevant contexts. It will tease out the range of operations the early ego is capable of and will focus on that aspect of ego functioning that operates in relation to affective and drive challenges, thereby distinguishing those operations that are *characteristic* of the infant's capacities, and that are used functionally, from those the infant is merely "capable of."

The approach to ego functioning will involve defining the ego as that aspect of the mind that organizes experience. Experience is broadly defined to include experience from within the organism (such as drive-affect related sensations) and interactive experience (seemingly in part outside the organism and then internalized into self-object patterns and representations), and experiences of the physical world. The ego will be seen to include the capacity to *organize, integrate, differentiate, elaborate,* and *transform* experience.

Each stage of ego development will be considered from the following perspectives: (a) physical-sensory(motor) aspects of ego development; (b) experiential-thematic aspects of ego development; (c) phase-specific and later deviations in ego functioning; and (d) implications for a theory of ego development including stage of self-object relationship and level of ego organization.

The Developmental Structuralist Approach

In an attempt to understand early development, my colleagues and I undertook a clinical descriptive intervention study of multirisk families as well as normal infants (Greenspan, 1981; Greenspan, Wieder, Lieberman, Nover, Lourie, and Robinson, 1987). The study of each family began prenatally with the anticipated birth of a new infant. Because there were already severe emotional disturbances in the older children in the family, we expected there would be a high likelihood of a range of psychopathology in the newborn infants. Infants and families with expected adaptive patterns were also observed for comparison. In order to understand the patterns we expected to emerge, a broad theoretical perspective was formulated that would accommodate both the cognitive and the affective domains, in both their disturbed and their adaptive aspects (i.e., a developmental structuralist model based on an integration of psychoanalytic and Piagetian developmental psychology, Greenspan, 1979, 1981). This section will present an overview of the developmental structuralist model.

The clinical interest in early ego development and psychopathology in infancy and early childhood rests on an impressive foundation. Perhaps most widely known are Spitz's report (1946) on anaclitic depression in institutionally reared infants, and Bowlby's *Maternal Care and Mental Health* (1952), describing the now well-known "syndromes" of disturbed functioning in infancy. The interest of child psychoanalysts in disturbances in infants, as indicated by the work of Bernfeld (1929), Winnicott (1931), Freud and Burlingham (1945, 1965), and Anna Freud (1965), as well as the work of Erikson (1959), led to an appreciation of the complexity or multidimensional nature of early problems. Important for current approaches was the work relating individual differences in infants (constitutional and maturational patterns) to psychopathological tendencies, work highlighted by the reports of Escalona (1968), Cravioto and DeLicardie (1973), and Murphy (1974).

Several existing developmental frameworks have provided an understanding of individual lines of development in infancy and early childhood (see S. Freud, 1905; Erikson, 1959; Piaget, 1962; A. Freud, 1965; Spitz, 1965; Kohut, 1971; Kernberg, 1975; Mahler, Pine, and Bergman, 1975). In addition, a great deal of empirical research has generated useful developmental constructs (e.g., Sander, 1962; Emde, Gaensbauer, and Harmon, 1976; Sroufe, 1979). These foundations, together with a rapidly growing body of clinical experience with infants and their families (e.g., Fraiberg, 1979; Provence, 1983; Provence and Naylor, 1983) provided impetus and direction for an integrated approach encompassing the various lines of development in the context of adaptive and disordered functioning.

There was a need for a truly integrated developmental theory reconciling our knowledge of development as influenced by "emotional experience" (including the presumed internalization and differentiation of experience based on human relationships), cognition, and various neurophysiological, behavioral, and social factors currently the subject of empirical research. To meet this challenge we developed an approach that focuses on the organizational level of personality in several spheres and on mediating processes or "structures."

Two assumptions are implicit in this approach. One is that the capacity to organize experience is present very early in life and progresses to higher levels as the individual matures. The phase-specific higher levels in this context imply an ability to organize in stable patterns an ever widening and ever more complex range of experience. For example, it is now well documented that the infant is capable, even at birth (or shortly thereafter), of organizing experience in an adaptive fashion. The neonate can respond to pleasure and displeasure (Lipsitt, 1966); change behavior as a function of its consequences (Gewirtz, 1965, 1969); form intimate bonds and make visual discriminations (Klaus and Kennell, 1976; Meltzoff and Moore, 1977); organize cycles and rhythms such as sleep-wake and alertness states (Sander, 1962); evidence a variety of affects or affect proclivities (Tomkins, 1963; Ekman, 1972; Izard, 1978); and demonstrate organized social responses in conjunction with increasing neurophysiological organization (Emde, Gaensbauer, and Harmon, 1976). It is interesting to note that this empirically documented view of the infant is in general consistent with Freud's early hypotheses (1900, 1905, 1911) and with Hartmann's postulation (1939) of an early undifferentiated organizational matrix. That the organization of experience broadens during the early months of life to reflect increases in the capacity to experience and tolerate a range of stimuli, including responding in social interaction in stable and personal configurations, is also consistent with recent empirical data (Sander, 1962; Escalona, 1968; Brazelton, Koslowski, and Main, 1974; Sroufe, Waters, and Matas, 1974; Stern, 1974a, 1974b; Emde, Gaensbauer, and Harmon, 1976; Murphy and Moriarty, 1976). That increasingly complex patterns continue to emerge as the infant further develops is indicated by complex emotional responses such as surprise (Charlesworth, 1969) and affiliation, wariness, and fear (Bowlby, 1969; Ainsworth, Bell, and Stayton, 1974; Sroufe and Waters, 1977) observed between 7 and 12 months; exploration and "refueling" patterns (Mahler, Pine, and Bergman, 1975); behavior suggesting functional understanding of objects (Werner and Kaplan, 1963) observed in the middle to latter part of the second year of life; and the eventual emergence of symbolic capacities (Piaget, 1962; Gouin-Décarie, 1965; Bell, 1970).

The interplay between age-appropriate experience and maturation of the central nervous system ultimately determines the characteristics of this organizational capacity at each phase. The active and experiencing child uses his maturational capacities to engage the world in ever changing and more complex ways. Here is where the second assumption enters. In addition to a characteristic *organizational level* for each phase of development, there are also characteristic *types of experience* (e.g., interests, wishes, fears, curiosities) that "play themselves out," so to speak, at each organizational level.

The organizational level of experience may be evaluated along a number of dimensions, including age- or phase-*appropriateness; range and depth* (i.e., animate and inanimate, full range of affects and themes); *stability* (i.e., response to stress); and *personal uniqueness.*

As regards the types of experience organized, one looks at specific drive-affect derivatives including emotional and behavioral patterns and, later, thoughts, concerns, inclinations, wishes, fears, and so forth. The type of experience is, in a sense, the drama the youngster is experiencing, whereas the organizational level might be viewed metaphorically as the stage upon which this drama is played out. To carry this metaphor a step further, it is possible to imagine some stages that are large and stable and can therefore support a complex and intense drama. By comparison, other stages may be narrow or small, able to contain only a very restricted drama. Still other stages may have cracks in them and may crumble easily under the pressure of an intense, rich, and varied drama.

According to the developmental structuralist approach, at each phase of development there are certain characteristics that define the experiential organizational capacity, that is, the stability and contour of the stage. At the same time, there are certain dramas expectable at a given age, themes characterized by their complexity, richness, depth, and content.

The developmental structuralist approach is unique in an important respect. In focusing on levels and organizations of experience, it alerts the clinician to look not only for what the infant or toddler is evidencing (e.g., psychopathology) but for what he or she is *not* evidencing. For example, the 8-month-old who is calm, alert, and enjoyable, but who has no capacity for discrimination or reciprocal social interchanges, may be of vastly greater concern than an irritable, negativistic, food-refusing, night-awakening 8-month-old who shows the age-appropriate capacities the other lacks. In other words, each stage of development may be characterized according to "expectable" organizational characteristics.

In formulating a model of the stages of early ego development, the following framework will be used. First will be presented a brief overview of the stage-specific characteristics of object relations and ego functions. Then follows a description of the sensori-affective and affective-thematic foundations of the ego. A description of stage-specific ego deficits, distortions, and constrictions will next be presented, followed, finally, by a statement regarding the stage-specific characteristics and functions of the ego.

Homeostasis: Self-Regulation and Interest in the World (0–3 Months)

During this stage one may postulate a self-object relationship characterized by a somatic, preintentional, global self-object. Ego organization, differentiation, and integration are characterized by a lack of differentiation between the physical world, the self, and human objects. Adaptive ego functions include global reactivity, sensori-affective processing, and regulation; disordered ones include sensory hyper- or hypopreactivity and disregulation.

Sensory Organization

The infants' first task in the developmental structuralist sequence is simultaneously to take an interest in the world and regulate himself. In comparing infants able to master this task with those who cannot, it has proved clinically useful to examine each sensory pathway individually, as well as the range of sensory modalities available for phase-specific challenges.

Sensory pathways functioning at less than optimal levels may be characterized as (1) hyperarousable, e.g., the baby who overreacts to normal levels of sound, touch, or brightness; (2) hypoarousable, e.g., the baby who hears and sees but evidences no behavioral or observable affective response to routine sights and sounds (often described as the "floppy" baby with poor muscle tone who is unresponsive and seemingly looks inward); (3) or neither hypo- nor hyperarousable but having a subtle type of early processing disorder (not that babies who are hypo- or hyperarousable may not also have a processing difficulty). A processing disorder may presumably involve perception, modulation, and processing of the stimulus and/or integration of the stimulus with other sensory experiences (cross-sensory integration), with stored experience (action patterns or representations), or with motor proclivities. Although more immature in form, processing difficulties in infants may not be wholly dissimilar from the types of perceptual-motor or auditory-verbal processing problems we see in older children. In this context, as the developmental structuralist approach suggests, the capacity of babies to habituate to and process the various inanimate sights and sounds may carry over into the entire experiential realm of the child, including the affective-laden interpersonal realm.

If a sensory pathway is not functioning optimally, then the range of sensory experience available to the infant is limited.

This limitation in part determines (1) the options or strategies the infant can employ to meet developmental challenges and (2) the type of sensory experience that will be organized at each level of development. Some babies can employ the full range of sensory capacities at each developmental stage. At the stage of homeostasis, for example, one can observe that such babies look at the mother's face or an interesting object and follow it. When this baby is upset, the opportunity to look at the mother helps the baby become calm and happy (evidenced by a calm smile). Similarly, a soothing voice, a gentle touch, rhythmic rocking, or a shift in position (offering vestibular and proprioceptive stimulation) can also help such a baby to relax, organize, and self-regulate. At the other end of the spectrum are babies who functionally employ only one or two sensory modalities. At times these limitations may be subtle, involving the affective but not the impersonal realm. For example, we have observed babies who brighten up, alert, and calm to visual experiences, but who in the presence of auditory stimuli are either relatively unresponsive, become hyperexcitable, or appear to become "confused" (a 2-month-old baby may be operationally defined as confused when, instead of looking toward a normal high-pitched maternal voice and alerting, he makes some random motor movements—suggesting that the stimulus has been taken in—looks past the object repeatedly, and continues his random movements). Other babies appear to use vision and hearing to self-regulate and take an interest in the world but have a more difficult time with touch and movement. They often become irritable even with gentle stroking and are calm only when held horizontally (they become hyperaroused when held upright). Still other babies calm down only when rocked to the rhythm of their own or their mother's heart or respiratory rate. Studies of the role of vestibular and proprioceptive pathways in psychopathology in infancy cannot be underestimated as areas for future research.

As babies use a range of sensory pathways, they also integrate experiences across the senses (Spelke and Owsley, 1979; Lewis and Horowitz, 1977). Yet there are babies who are able to use each sensory pathway but have difficulty, for example, integrating vision and hearing. They can alert to a sound or a visual cue but are not able to turn and look at a stimulus that offers visual and auditory information at the same time. Instead they appear confused and may even evince active gaze aversion or go into a pattern of extensor rigidity and avoidance.

Sensory pathways are usually observed in the context of sensorimotor patterns. Turning toward the stimulus or brightening and alerting involve motor "outputs." There are babies who have difficulties in the way they integrate their sensory experience with motor output. The most obvious case is a baby with cerebral palsy. At a more subtle level, it is possible to observe compromises in such basic abilities as self-consoling or nuzzling in the corner of the mother's neck or relaxing to rhythmic rocking. Escalona's classic descriptions (1968) of babies with multiple sensory hypersensitivities therefore require further study in the context of a broader approach to assessing subtle difficulties in each of the several sensory pathways.

Affective-Thematic Organization

At this first stage it is clear how affective-thematic organizations can support the phase-specific task, and how in turn the phase-specific task can organize discrete affective-thematic inclinations into more integrated organizations. For example, the baby who wants to calm down is at the same time learning a means for achieving comfort and fulfilling dependency needs. The baby who wants to be interested in the world can often, with a certain posture or glance, let his primary caregiver know he is ready for interesting visual, auditory, and tactile sensations.

It is clear also that in the first stages there are babies who cannot organize their affective-thematic proclivities in terms of phase-specific tasks. In addition to maladaptive caregiver patterns and infant-caregiver interactions (Greenspan, 1981), babies who are uncomfortable with dependency, either because of specific sensory hypersensitivities or higher-level integrating problems, often evidence a severe compromise regarding self-regulation. Babies with a tendency toward hyper- or hypoarousal may not be able to organize the affective-thematic domains of joy, pleasure, and exploration. Instead they may evidence apathy and withdrawal or a total disregard for certain sensory realms while overfocusing on others (e.g., babies who state at an inanimate object while ignoring the human world).

Excessive irritability, hypersensitivities, tendencies toward withdrawal, apathy, and gaze aversion are a few of the dramatic, maladaptive patterns in this first stage of development. If there are maladaptive environmental accommodations, these early patterns may form the basis for later disorders, including autistic-like symptoms and defects in such basic personality functions as perception, integration, regulation, and motility.

Ego Deficits, Distortions, and Constrictions

What are the implications of the faulty formation of these capacities in adult and child psychiatric conditions? These are basic regulatory capacities, including the ability to process stimulus input and organize it (without shutting down or becoming hypo- or hyperreactive). In many conditions this capacity is not well established. For example, the child with severe attentional difficulties cannot process information well. In the most severe instances, the child may appear clinically autistic, retarded, or both. Some children who have only mild attentional difficulties, often labeled attentional deficit disorders, actually have more problems in one sensory mode than in another. Some are more distracted by sounds; others by visual stimuli. Others have tactile defensiveness, a pattern which is not described well in the psychiatric literature. In many clinical populations there are individuals who are hyperreactive to light touch. Sensory processing difficulties have also been seen in child and adult schizophrenic populations that have been studied experimentally. Separating and studying each processing capacity in terms of the sensory pathway involved, (auditory, tactile, vestibular, olfactory, proprioceptive etc.), in relation to both impersonal and affective stimuli, is an important research area. We are beginning such studies with infants and hope to extend them to adult and child psychiatric populations.

Sensory processing difficulties may also involve problems in making discriminations. In addition to a sensory system being hypo- or hyperarousable, we have observed infants in the first few months of life who, though not at these extremes, seem unable to tune in to the environment. When their mother talks to them, instead of decoding her rhythmic sound and brightening up (as most infants do), they look almost confused. Clinically, we have observed that this is present in some children with regard to one sensory pathway but not another. For example, an infant with intact hearing but unable to focus on rhythmic sound, may be able to focus on facial gesturing. When an infant looks confused in reaction to vocal stimuli, we may coach a mother to slow down, to talk very distinctly, not to introduce too much novelty too quickly (though most infants love novelty), and to use lots of animated facial expressions, movements (to encourage the use of vision), and tactile sensations. Often such an infant will then respond by coming alert, brightening up, and becoming engaged.

The sad fate of deaf children in the years before they were commonly diagnosed in early infancy is instructive. By 2 years many looked autistic and were functionally retarded as well. The early diagnosis of deafness led to the introduction of sensory input through the intact modes—visual, tactile, olfactory. With these compensatory experiences, deaf children developed well both cognitively and emotionally. In other words, though critical ego functions may well follow a certain required sequence of experiential inputs, these inputs can be made available in many different ways, especially with regard to sensory pathways. In the theory we have developed from our observations of infants and young children, there is a sequence of psychological stages from interest in the world to forming a human attachment, to cause-and-effect interactions, to engaging in complex organized behavioral and affective patterns, to constructing and differentiating representations. Yet in all of this, no single sensory pathway appears critical. For example, auditory input is not required in order to construct symbols. Symbols can be constructed from purely visual or tactile inputs.

What may have happened with many deaf babies, however, was that their mothers did not know their infants could not hear. A concerned mother would understandably become anxious if she was not getting a brightening response from her new infant. She may then have talked even more, even louder, and even faster. Becoming discouraged, she may have become so anxious that she rigidly and repetitively tried the same pattern.

Other sensory modes were not experimented with. Such a mother overwhelms the nonfunctioning auditory mode, and her infant becomes more and more confused. It is not surprising in this context that in the old descriptions autistic children were commonly found not in severely disturbed families but in professionally successful families with obsessive-compulsive patterns. Infants with hypersensitivities or discrimination difficulties may do worse with an anxious, intrusive, and overwhelming stimulus world. On the other hand, the youngster who is hyporeactive, who needs to be revved up, may do very well with a highly energetic caregiver. "The luck of the draw or fit" is always a factor. By profiling individual sensory processing differences in infancy, however, it may become possible to improve the flexibility or intuitive patterns of the caregiver through counseling.

Implications for a Theory of Ego Development

During homeostasis, regulation and a multisensory interest in the world are the infant's two major goals. As indicated, we observe a range of patterns of sensory arousal and reactivity as well as sensory and sensorimotor discrimination and integration in clinical and normal groups of infants and their families, including hyperarousal and hypoarousal (even to the extent of extreme apathy and hypotonicity). And one observes these patterns in reaction to both animate and inanimate stimuli. For the most part the infant is using what may be considered "prewired" rather than learned approaches to his world. In addition to the well-known primitive reflexes, the sensory and sensorimotor abilities referred to earlier allow the infant to cuddle, follow the caregiver's voice and face, copy selected facial expressions including tongue protrusion, show preferences for different vocal patterns (e.g., the mother's), show visual preferences for objects that have been explored orally (cross-sensory integration), and so forth. Yet even though these and other behaviors can come under operant control (e.g., respond to reinforcement) there is no reason to assume that these basic abilities are not part of the functional capacities many infants are born with.

It may therefore be postulated that there are adapted sensorimotor patterns that are part of the "autonomous" ego function present shortly after birth. It is then useful to consider how these capacities (e.g., the autonomous ego functions of perception and discrimination) are used to construct an emerging organization of an experiential world, including drive derivatives, early affects, and emerging organizations of self and of objects. It would be a logical error to assume that these seemingly innate capacities are themselves a product of early interactional learning or structure building, even though they are influenced secondarily by experiences.

One cannot yet postulate differentiated self-object experiential organizations because the infant's main goals appear to be involved in a type of sensory awakening and interest, and in regulation, without evidence of clearly intentional object-seeking or of self-initiated and differentiated affective interactions. In our observations of high-risk and normal infants, it was observed that they responded to the overall stimulus qualities of the environment, especially human handling. Likewise there is little evidence for a notion that the infant is impervious to his emotional surroundings. In fact, in our studies of multirisk families (Greenspan et al., 1987) the quality of self-regulation, attention, and sensoriaffective interest in the world in the first month or two of life was influenced to a great degree by the physical and emotional qualities of the infant-caregiver patterns (i.e., soothing and interesting caregiving patterns rather than hyper- or hypostimulating ones). But this does not mean that Mahler, Pine, and Bergman (1975), and others who suggest a qualitative difference in this early stage (i.e., the autistic phase), may not have an important insight. Even though the mother's voice can be discriminated from other sounds, this does not mean there is a differentiation between the caregiver and items in the physical surround (say, the sound of a car) in terms of abstracting and organizing types of experiences according to general characteristics. (In other words, one must distinguish what the infant is capable of—e.g., complex discriminations—from how the infant is functionally involved in phase-specific tasks and goals. For example, the 3-year-old with separation anxiety associated with fear of loss of the affective object may have excellent capacities for conserving impersonal objects.) As both types of experience may help the infant calm, regulate, and attend to and process sensory information,one could argue that in terms of phase-specific tasks there is at this time a sensory unity embracing both the physical and the human worlds.

One may therefore posit a preintentional stage of object relatedness (i.e., prewired patterns gradually come under interactive control) and a stage in the organization of experience at which self and object are not yet organized as distinct entities. At this stage the experience of "self" and "other" are closely intertwined and are likely not yet separate from other sensory experiences involving the physical world. It is worth repeating that differential infant responses do not necessarily mean differentiated internal experiences, as behaviors can simply be constitutional, reflexive, or conditioned respondent (Pavlovian) or operant.

Therefore, the concept of an experiential organization of a *world object*, including what later will be differentiated as a "self"-"other"-"physical" world, may prove useful. This state of ego organization may be considered to be characterized by two central tendencies: to experience sensory and affective information through each sensory or sensorimotor channel and to form patterns of regulation. Furthermore, these tendencies may be further characterized by the level of sensory pathway arousal (e.g., hyper- or hypoarousal) in each pathway and by emerging sensory and sensorimotor discrimination and integration capacities. Under optimal conditions, the early sensoriaffective processing, discriminating, and integrating capacities—the early functions of the ego—are being used for the gradual organization of experience. Under unfavorable conditions these early ego functions evidence undifferentiated sensory hyper- or hypoarousal, and lack of discrimination and integration in all or some of the sensoriaffective and sensorimotor pathways. Thus, the early stage of a global, undifferentiated self-object world may remain or progress to higher levels of organization depending on innate maturational patterns and early experiences as together they influence each sensoriaffective (motor) pathway in terms of arousal, discrimination,and integration.

In addition, as early drive-affect organizations are now

being harnessed and integrated by the emerging ego functions of sensoriaffective (motor) processing, differentiation, and integration, it is useful to consider drive-affect development from the perspective of the ego. From this perspective, the concept of the oral phase may be considered more broadly as part of a system of "sensoriaffective" pleasure which involves all the sensoriaffective (motor) pathways of which the mouth (in terms of tactile, deep pressure, temperature, pain, and motor — especially smooth muscle—patterns) is certainly dominant because of the highly developed nature of its sensoriaffective and motor pathways. From the perspective of the ego, however, drive-affect derivatives are elaborated throughout the "sensory surface" of the body.

Attachment (2–7 Months)

During this stage one may postulate a self-object relationship characterized by an intentional, part-oriented self-object. Ego organization, differentiation, and integration are characterized by a relative lack of differentiation of self and object. There is, however, differentiation of the physical world and the human object world. Ego functions include, on the adaptive side, part-object seeking and drive-affect elaboration and, on the maladaptive, drive-affect dampening or lability, object withdrawal, and rejection or avoidance.

Sensory Organization

The second stage involves forming a special emotional interest in the primary caregiver. From the perspective of sensory pathways, one can observe babies who are adaptively able to employ all their senses under the orchestration of highly pleasurable affect in relation to the primary caregiver. The baby with a beautiful smile, looking at and listening to its mother, experiencing her gentle touch and rhythmic movement and responding to her voice with synchronous mouth and arm and leg movements, is perhaps the most vivid example. Clinically, however, we observe babies who are not able to employ their senses to form an affective relationship with the human world.

The most extreme case is where a baby actively avoids sensory and, therefore, affective contact with the human world. Human sounds, touch, and even scents are avoided, either with chronic gaze aversion, recoiling, flat affect, or random or nonsynchronous patterns of brightening and alerting. We also observe babies who use one or another sensory pathway in the context of a pleasurable relationship with the human world but cannot orchestrate the full range and depth of sensory experience. The baby who already listens to the mother's voice with a smile but averts its gaze and looks pained at the sight of her face is such an example.

Affective-Thematic Organization

The task of attachment organizes a number of discrete affective proclivities—comfort, dependency, pleasure, and joy, as well as assertiveness and curiosity—in the context of an intense, affective caregiver-infant relationship. In the adaptive baby, protest and anger are organized along with the expected positive affects as part of his emotional interest in the primary caregiver. A healthy 4-month-old can, as part of his repertoire, become negativistic but then quickly return to mother's beautiful smiles, loving glances, and comfort-oriented behavior.

On the other hand, babies can already have major limitations in certain affect proclivities. Rather than evidencing joy, enthusiasm, or pleasure with their caregivers, they may instead evidence a flat affect. Similarly, rather than evidencing assertive, curious, protesting, or angry behavior in relation to their primary caregiver, they may only look very compliant and give shallow smiles. In addition to being constricted in their affective range, babies may also evidence a limitation in their organizational stability. An example is a baby who, after hearing a loud noise, cannot return to its earlier interest in the primary caregiver. Where environmental circumstances are unfavorable or for other reasons development continues to be disordered, early attachment difficulties, if severe enough, may form the basis for an ongoing defect in the baby's capacity to form affective human relationships and to form the basic personality structures and functions that depend on the internal organization of human experience.

Ego Deficits, Distortions, and Constrictions

As indicated, if the early experience of the world is aversive, affective interest in the human world may be compromised. A total failure of the attachment process is seen in autistic patterns, in certain types of withdrawn and regressed schizophrenics, and, intermittently, in children diagnosed as having pervasive developmental disturbances.

We also see shallow attachments. There is some involvement with the human world, but it is without positive affect or emotional depth. We see a compromise in the depth of human connectedness in some of the narcissistic character disorders, illustrating a subtle deficit in the range of emotion incorporated into an attachment pattern. A severe lack of regard for human relationships is seen in what used to be called the chronic psychopathic personality disorder (now the sociopathic or antisocial personality disturbance). Although some individuals engage in sociopathic behavior because of neurotic conflicts or anxiety (i.e., they are acting out), in the primary sociopathic disturbances there is a failure to see the human world as human. Human beings are seen rather as concrete objects, mere means to concrete gratifications. It would be interesting to study hardened repeat offenders with histories of violent crimes to determine the incidence among them of a failure in early attachments. In many of them, one would expect, multiple foster care placements, disturbed and withdrawn parents, or unusual constitutional tendencies could be seen to have interfered with the formation of warm and affectionate relationships.

Implications for a Theory of Ego Development

The attachment stage, characterized in normal development by pleasurable affective inclinations toward the human world, shows enormous variation. Infants who are apathetic or mechanical may prefer the physical world. They may be passively compliant but not joyful, or may actively avoid their caregivers' gaze and vocalizations. They may be undiscriminating or (after 8 months) unselective or even promiscuous in their object ties. Under optimal circumstances, however, all the senses and the motor system become coordinated during this stage toward the aim of pleasurable interaction with a caregiver. Not only pleasure but distress and curiosity also are beginning to emerge in a more organized fashion.

The pleasurable preference for the human world suggests interactive object seeking. Even such tendencies as apathy in reaction to caregiver withdrawal, preference for the physical world, and chronic active aversion in clinically disturbed populations suggest the emergence of organized object relations, however maladaptive.

Yet there is no evidence of the infant's ability to abstract all the features of the object in terms of an organization of the whole object. Infants seek the voice, the smiling mouth, the twinkly eyes, the rhythmic movements, either alone or in combination, but not yet the whole. In addition, the tendency toward global withdrawal, rejection, or avoidance suggests a pattern of global undifferentiated reaction as compared to differentiated patterns whereby the influence of a "me" on a "you" is detectable. The 4-month-old does not evidence the repertoire of the 8-month-old in "wooing" a caregiver into pleasurable interaction. The 4-month-old under optimal conditions evidences synchronous interactive patterns, smiling and vocalizing in rhythm with the caregiver. But when under clinical distress he evidences global reactivity, in contrast to the 8-month-old, who can explore alternative ways of influencing his caregiver. This suggests that not until the attachment stage is there a full behavioral (representational) comprehension of cause and effect or self-object differentiation. Full psychological comprehension does not occur until late in the second year of life.

Most likely, during this stage the infant progresses from the earlier stage of an undifferentiated global object (in which the human and nonhuman worlds are as yet indistinct, as are self and nonself) to a stage of intentional yet still undifferentiated self-object organization. There is a sense of syncrony and connectedness to a human object which suggests that the infant's experiential organization differentiates the human object from other objects in the surround. But even at the behavioral level there is as yet no evidence of self-object differentiation. In this sense the concept of symbiosis (Mahler, Pine, and Bergman, 1975) is not at odds with the clinical observation of a lack of self-object differentiation.

The functioning of the ego at this stage is characterized by intentional part-object seeking, differentiated organizations of experience (human object from nonhuman, but not human self from human object), and global patterns of reactivity to the human object. These patterns of reactivity include pleasure seeking, protest, withdrawal, rejection (with a preference for the nonhuman world based on what appears to be a clear discrimination), hyperaffectivity (diffuse discharge of affects), and active avoidance.

To the degree that later self- and object organization are undifferentiated, aspects of experience may combine or seemingly organize in different ways. This is due not to organized ways of transforming experience but simply to a lack of structure formation (this tendency is perhaps a precursor to condensations, displacements, and projective and incorporative-introjective mechanisms). Projection, incorporation, and introjection in a differentiated sense, where distinct images are transferred across boundaries, are not yet in evidence.

Somatopsychological Differentiation and Purposeful Communication (3–10 Months)

During this stage one may postulate a self-object relationship characterized by a behaviorally differentiated, part-oriented self-object. Ego organization, differentiation, and integration are characterized by a differentiation of aspects (parts) of self and object in terms of drive-affect patterns and behavior. Adaptive ego functions include differentiated, part-oriented self-object interactions (both initiatory and responsive) in a range of drive-affect domains (e.g., pleasure, dependency, assertiveness, and aggression) and means-end relationships between drive-affect patterns and part-oriented self-object patterns. Maladaptive ego functions include undifferentiated self-object interactions, selective drive-affect intensification and inhibition, constriction in the range of intrapsychic experience, and regression to states of withdrawal, avoidance, or rejection (with a preference for the nonhuman world) or to object concretization.

Sensory Organization

Building on a solid attachment, the task is now to develop the capacity for cause-and-effect or means-end communications. Here we observe an even richer differential use of the senses. Some babies do not possess the capacity to orchestrate their sensory experiences in an interactive cause-and-effect pattern. A look and a smile on the mother's part do not lead to a consequential look, smile, vocalization, or gross motor movement on the baby's part. Such babies may perceive the sensory experiences the mother is making available but, seemingly unable to organize these experiences, either look past the mother or evidence random motor patterns. We also observe babies who can operate in a cause-and-effect manner in one sensory pathway but not in another. For example, when presented with an object, they may clearly look at the object in a purposeful way and then examine it. However, when presented with an interesting auditory stimulus, instead of responding vocally, or reaching out toward the person or object emitting it, these infants behave chaotically, with increased motor activity and discharge behavior such as banging and flailing. Similarly with tactile experience: some babies, instead of touching their mother's hand when she is stroking their adbomen, begin evidencing random motor responses apparently unrelated to the gentle stimulus. We observe even more profoundly the differential use of the senses as infants learn to "process" information in each sensory mode, and between modes, in terms of seeing relations between elements in a pattern. For example, some babies learn that a sound leads to a sound or a look to a look. Other infants do not possess the capacity to so orchestrate their sensory experiences. There are intriguing implications here regarding later learning problems possibly consequent on various sensory pathways not becoming incorporated at the cause-and-effect level of behavioral organization (e.g., children whose abstracting and sequencing problems occur in the auditory-verbal sphere can be differentiated from those whose difficulties are of a visual-spatial nature). Motor differences, such as high or low tone or lags, will also obviously influence the infant's ability to signal his wishes. In organizing cause-and-effect communications, therefore, a compromise in a sensory or motor pathway not only limits the strategies available for tackling this new challenge, but may restrict not only the sensory and motor modalities that become organized at this new developmental level but, as will be discussed, the associated drive-affect patterns as well.

As babies learn to orchestrate their senses in the context of cause-and-effect interactions, we observe an interesting clinical phenomenon—the gradually evolving ability to rely on what may be termed "distal" rather than "proximal" modes of communication. Proximal modes may be thought of as direct physical contact such as holding, rocking, touching, and so forth. Distal modes may be thought of as involving communication through vision, auditory cuing, and affect signaling. The distal modes can obviously occur across space, whereas the proximal modes require, as the word implies, physical closeness. The crawling 8-month-old can remain in emotional communication with his primary caregiver through various reciprocal glances, vocalizations, and affect gestures. Some babies, however, seem to rely on proximal modes for a sense of security. Early limitations in negotiating space will be seen later on to affect the capacity to construct internal representations.

Affective-Thematic Organization

At this stage the full range of affective-thematic proclivities, evident in the attachment phase, become organized in the context of cause-and-effect (means-end) interchanges. The baby joyfully smiles or reaches out in response to a motor movement or affective signal, such as a funny look from the mother, in a reciprocal exchange. Where the caregiver does not respond to the baby's signal, as by returning a smile or a glance, we have observed that the baby's affective-thematic inclinations may not evidence this differentiated organization. Instead they may remain either synchronous, as in the attachment phase, or shift from synchrony to a more random quality, where they appear almost hypomanic, evidencing many affect proclivities in quick succession. The expected range may be present but not subordinated to a cause-and-effect interchange.

There are also many babies who, because of a lack of reciprocal response from their caregiver, evidence affective dampening or flatness and a hint of despondency or sadness. This may occur even after the baby has shown a joyfulness and an adaptive attachment. In some cases at least, it seems as though when not offered phase-specific "experiential nutriments" (the cause-and-effect interactions he is now capable of), but only the earlier forms of relatedness, the baby begins a pattern of withdrawal and affective flattening. It is as though he needs to be met at his own level to maintain his affective-thematic range. Most interesting are the subtle cases where the baby can reciprocate certain affects and themes, such as pleasure and dependency, but not others, such as assertiveness, curiosity, and protest. Depending on the baby's own maturational tendencies and the specificity of the consequences in the caregiving environment, one can imagine how this uneven development occurs. For example, caregivers who are uncomfortable with dependency and closeness may not afford opportunities for purposeful reciprocal interactions in this domain but may, by contrast, be quite "causal" in the less intimate domains of assertion and protest.

The baby's own affective-thematic "sending power" and the degree of differential consequences he is able to elicit may have important implications for how he differentiates his internal affective-thematic life and how he organizes these dimensions at the representational or symbolic level later on.

Ego Deficits, Distortions, and Constrictions

As indicated, early in the stage of somato-psychological differentiation, an infant seems capable of almost the full range of human emotional expressions. This capability now sets the stage for more differentiated patterns of ego deficits, distortions, and constrictions. If one divides the emotional terrain into its parts, one can see the full range of emotions. In terms of dependency, the 8-month-old can make overtures to be cuddled or held. He shows pleasure, with beatific smiles and a love of touching (if he does not have a tactile sensitivity). He is already playing with his genitals in a pleasurable manner and is experiencing gratification through sucking (and through putting everything in sight into his mouth, thereby using the mouth as an organ of exploration). Unquestionably there is also curiosity and assertivenss. The 8-month-old is already reaching, exploring, and banging objects, learning about impact and about cause and effect. There is also anger and protest. Try to take away an 8-month-old's favorite food when he does not want to give it up. He may throw the food on the floor in a deliberate manner and look at you as if to say, "What are you gonna do now?" There is protest, even defiance (e.g., biting and banging). These infants may prefer biting, or sometimes butting, as an expression of anger because at 8 months they have better motor control of their mouths, heads, and necks than of their arms and hands.

Although empathy and consistent love will emerge later, one sees a range of emotional inclinations or affective-thematic proclivities at this age. What is it that determines whether these affective inclinations develop and become differentiated from each other or remain undifferentiated (so that eventually pleasure, dependency, and aggression cannot be experienced as separate from one another)? During the 4–8 month phase the differential signaling of the caregiver tells the child that pleasure is different from pain, that hunger for food is different from hunger to be picked up, that assertiveness is different from aggressiveness, and so forth. If each of the infant's feelings and expressions receives a different empathic and overt response from the caregiver, the child experiences each of his own inclinations. Hilde Bruch (1973) anticipated what we now observe directly when she suggested that in some primary eating disturbances the dyadic signal system was not well formed because caregivers were rigid and unresponsive to the child's communications. For example, the child never learned to distinguish basic physical hunger from other sensations, such as dependency needs.

During this stage, therefore, the affect system is differentiated to the degree to which the caregiving environment subtly reads the baby's emotional signals. Some infants do not experience reciprocity at all; others experience selective limitations. Cause-and-effect feedback in one or another thematic or emotional area is missing. No family will be equally sensitive and responsive in all areas. Some families are conflicted around dependency, and others around aggression. Thus, there will be more anxiety in some areas than in others, and children will receive different feedback in different emotional areas. Although this is part of what makes people different, when an entire area like dependency, pleasure, or explóration receives no cause-and-effect feedback whatever, early presymbolic (prerepresentational) differentiations may be limited.

It is useful to think of this stage of development as a first sstep in reality testing. At this time, prerepresentational causality is established. The child is learning that reaching out, smiling, vocalizing, pleasurable affect, and aggressive affect all have their consequences. The sense that one's behavior and emotions have consequences is what a sense of causality is. Cause-and-effect experiences teach a child that the world is a lawful place. When cause-and-effect behavioral patterns do not develop, the most fundamental aspect of the sense of causality may be compromised. Later in development, ideas or representations are also organized according to cause-and-effect patterns. It may prove interesting to separate psychotic patients who have a failure of reality testing at the level of behavioral causality (4–8 months) from those whose reality testing has failed at the later representational level. Some psychotic individuals tend to think and talk crazily (they may have hallucinations, delusions, and thought disorders), but they *behave* realistically. When I was a resident in psychiatry, I was very impressed with a lady who traveled from downtown Manhattan in a totally delusional state and wound up in the Columbia Presbyterian emergency room. She didn't know how she got there. Behaviorally, she was very purposeful, even though her thinking was disorganized. Conversely, there are individuals who talk in an organized way (i.e., they are free of affect storms or fragmentation) but whose behavior seems crazy. Severely psychotic sociopaths may perhaps be found to evince the latter pattern, suggesting a failure at the earlier level. Thus, it may prove useful to consider two levels of reality testing and related disorders.

Therefore, at the stage of somato-psychological differentiation, the fundamental deficit is in reality testing and a basic sense of causality. There are also subtle deficits which may be part of a lack of differentiation along a particular affective-thematic proclivity. In various character disturbances and borderline conditions we observe a lack of differentiation as regards aggression but not dependency, or vice versa. Certain areas of internal life remain relatively undifferentiated, yet in other areas differentiation and reality testing are quite good. This uneven pattern is in fact noted in many definitions of borderline syndromes.

In summary, a variety of symptoms may be seen in relation to disorders of somato-psychological differentiation. These symptoms include developmental delays in sensorimotor functioning, apathy, intense chronic fear, clinging, lack of explorativeness and curiosity, lack of emotional reaction to significant caregivers, biting, chronic crying and irritability, and difficulties with sleeping and eating. Additional symptoms may be evident if, secondary to the lack of differentiated patterns, there are compromises in the infant-caregiver relationship (e.g., the infant becomes frustrated and irritable as his new capacities for contingent interactions are ignored or misread). If the basic comforting and soothing functions that support the baby's sense of security begin to falter, we may then see compromises in attachment and homeostatic patterns leading to physiological disorders and interferences in already achieved rhythms and cycles such as sleep and hunger. Where disorders of differentiation are severe and are not reversed during later development, they may set the foundation for later disorders, including primary personality (ego) defects in reality testing, as well as disturbances in the organization and perception of communication and thought, the perception and regulation of affects, and the integration of affects, action, and thought.

Implications for a Theory of Ego Development

In this phase, which is characterized by cause-and-effect interactions, one observes the infant taking initiative and participating in reciprocal (rather than synchronous) interchanges. These occur across a' range of sensori-motor pathways and affective patterns. Maladaptive options available to the infant include the tendency to constrict or never develop the full range of affective-thematic patterns and, more worrisome, the tendency to never enter into cause-and-effect signaling and to become rejecting or withdrawn. Clinically we have observed infants initiate and reach out repeatedly to a depressed caregiver, sometimes succeeding in communicating their interest and love. At other times we have observed infants deliberately and selectively reject or angrily poke a caregiver who has been away or is preoccupied (e.g., an infant refuses to look at the mother, but eagerly looks at and smiles at the father or grandmother).

The intentionality of the infant in adaptive modes (reaching out, protesting, etc.) and maladaptive modes (rejecting) suggests the behavioral comprehension of a "self" influencing an "other." A fortiori, suggests the differentiation of self and object, at least at the behavioral level. At this level organization involves behavioral patterns or tendencies rather than symbols. Only late in the second year, through a growing capacity for higher-level abstraction, does a child begin to create mental representations. Earlier than that, the "I" is likely the "I" of behavior ("if I do this it causes that") rather than the "I" of a mental representation, ("if I feel or think or *am* a certain way, it will have this or that impact"). The capacity to construct mental representations will allow the growing child to organize and even rearrange different elements of "self" or "other" into mental images. Given the fact of behavioral cause and effect and differentiated interaction, one can think of a behavioral or prerepresentational type of reality testing.

There is no evidence yet of the ability to abstract all aspects of "self" or "other." Experiences are still in fragmented pieces. Temporal and spatial continuity, while rapidly developing, are not yet fully established. Since the "I" is a physical and behavioral "I," since it can make things happen in the behavior pattern of the "other," and since the "I" and the "other" do not yet represent or organize all the aspects of self and other, it is possible to characterize the self-object at this stage as part-oriented and as somatically and behaviorally differentiated. The ego is characterized now by a capacity to differentiate aspects of experience in both the impersonal and the drive-affect domains, though under stress the organized behavioral aspects of "self" and "other" may undergo dedifferentiation. Hence during this stage one may postulate projective or incorporative tendencies with regard to behavioral patterns and accompanying drive-effect dispositions. When the presumably angry infant actively rejects the caregiver (e.g., a 10-month-old refuses to look at mommy after she has been away for a while), one thinks of the tendency to incorporate the behavior of the "other" as part of one's own strategy. With the very angry insecure infant, who for no obvious reason is exceedingly fearful of novel situations or persons, one may wonder whether the expectable cautiousness toward strangers, brought about by improved cognitive discrimination, has been intensified via projective mechanisms. Interestingly, abused infants evidence fear much earlier than do nonabused infants, suggesting that in certain affective-thematic domains precocious differentiation may serve a protective purpose. Now that differentiated islands of behavioral experience can be organized (part-objects), various configurations, including dynamically relevant part-object drive-affect dispositions are possible.

Behavioral Organization, Initiative, Internalization, and a Complex Sense of Self (9–18 Months)

During this stage, one may postulate a self-object relationship characterized by a self-object that is functional (conceptual), integrated, and differentiated. Ego organization, differentiation, and integration are characterized by an integration of drive-affect behavioral patterns into relatively "whole" functional self-objects. Adaptive ego functions include organized whole (in the functional behavioral sense) self-object interactions characterized by interactive chains; mobility in space (i.e., the use of distal communication modes); functional (conceptual) abstractions of self-object properties; and the integration of drive-affect polarities (e.g., a shift from splitting to greater integration). Maladaptive functions include self-object fragmentation, self-object proximal urgency, preconceptual concretization, and polarization (e.g., a negative, aggressive, dependent, or avoidant self-object pattern, and regressive states including withdrawal, avoidance, rejection, somatic dedifferentiation, and object concretization).

Sensory Organization

This stage involves a baby's ability to sequence many cause-and-effect units into a chain or organized behavioral pattern (e.g., a 14-month-old can take the mother's hand, walk her to the refrigerator, bang on the door, and point to the desired food). Here wish and intention are organized under a complex behavioral pattern. This pattern can be viewed as a task that involves coordinated and orchestrated use of the senses. Here the toddler who is capable of using vision and hearing to perceive various vocal and facial gestures, postural cues, and complex affect signals is able to extract relevant information from his objects and organize this information at new levels of cognitive and affective integration. A toddler unable to incorporate certain sensory experiences as part of his early cognitive and affective abstracting abilities (Werner and Kaplan, 1963) may evidence a very early restriction in the way his senses process information.

Balanced reliance on proximal and distal modes becomes even more important during this phase of development. The mobile toddler enjoying his freedom in space presumably can feel secure through his use of distal communication modes (or simply through his knowledge that they are available to him). It is interesting in this context to examine traditional notions of separation anxiety and the conflicts that some toddlers have over separation-individuation (Mahler, Pine, and Bergman, 1975). With the use of the distal modes the toddler can "have his cake and eat it too." If he can bring the caregiving object with him through distal contact with her, he does not have to tolerate a great deal of insecurity. He can "refuel" distally and use proximal contact only when necessary. The youngster who has difficulty in using distal modes to remain in contact with the primary caregiver may need more proximal contact. This difficulty often occurs because of the insecurity generated by an ambivalent primary caregiver, but the limitations of the child's sensory organization may also be an important factor. In addition, motor delays will also compromise the toddler's capacity to gesture or signal and to negotiate physical space, placing an even greater challenge on the toddler and his caregivers in dealing with the tasks of this stage.

Affective-Thematic Organization

The piecing together of many smaller cause-and-effect units of experience into an organized chain involves a range of experiences—pleasure, assertiveness, curiosity, dependency. For instance, it is not common for a healthy toddler to start off in a dependent mood cuddling and kissing his parents, shift to a pleasurable, giggly interchange with them, and then get off their laps and invite them to engage in an assertive chase game in which he runs to a room that is off limits, such as the living room. When the parents say "No, you can't go in there," protest and negativism may come to the fore. Under optimal circumstances, the interaction may come to relative closure, with the toddler back in the playroom, sitting on his parent's lap pleasurably exploring pictures in his favorite book. Here the child has gone full circle, suggesting that he has connected the many affective-thematic areas.

Around 18 months, as children begin to abstract the meaning of objects, their understanding of the functions of the telephone or of a brush may have its counterpart in their experiencing the caregiver as a "functional" being invested with many affective-thematic proclivities (e.g., father is playful and mother is orderly). Between 12 and 18 months, though children are able to integrate many behavioral units, they do not seem able to integrate intense emotions. When angry, for example, they lose sight of the fact, for the moment at least, that this is the same person they love and experience pleasure with. By 18–24 months, this sense of split-off fury seems, at least in clinical observations, to be modified at some level by an awareness of love and dependency. An infant with a motor delay or a sensory processing lag may be compromised in his ability to initiate or process certain affective patterns such as anger or assertiveness.

Ego Deficits, Distortions, and Constrictions

As indicated, as the child moves closer to 18 months, the ability to gradually relate to the object world in a more functional way and to see objects according to their functional properties emerges. Werner and Kaplan (1963) describe how babies can take a comb or a toy telephone and use it purposefully.

This is not yet imaginary play guided by mental representations or ideas; rather, it is semirealistic play with an understanding of the functional use of the object. Children can also understand the emotional proclivities of their parents in a functional sense. They sense either nurturing, warm, supportive patterns or undermining, controlling, intrusive ones. One little girl, though she did not understand her mother's words, was able to see her as a teasing, envious person and would pull away whenever she verbally teased her.

We have observed that toddlers shift from an early stage akin to ego splitting in adults (12–13 months) to a stage of greater integration of different self-object organizations by 18–19 months. When I am involved in therapeutic play with a child 12–13 months old who becomes angry, it feels as though if he had a gun at that moment he would shoot me. The feeling is very much like that experienced with the borderline adult. When you are the bad object, there is no simultaneous connection with you as the object of security and comfort. For that moment, you are all bad. But by the time a toddler is 18 months old, you may feel his anger, but you also sense that he sees you as an object of security, love, and dependency. You feel more like you would with a neurotic adult. There is anger, but the backdrop of security and relatedness is still there.

Thus, during the stage of behavioral organization, initiative, and internalization, we observe a progression from a type of ego splitting or part-object relatedness to a more cohesive sense of the functional and emotional proclivities of the object. Presumably this integration is occurring also in the sense of self. Just as toddlers are sensing their parents as loving or undermining, or both, they are also abstracting their own patterns of feelings and behaviors. They no longer see themselves as islands of discrete behaviors or feelings, aggressive one moment and pleasurable the next. They are abstracting a pattern. These are higher-level abstractions of feelings and behaviors, but still prerepresentational patterns of the object and the self.

One way to think of the second year of life is as involving the development of a conceptual attitude toward the world. In the first year of life, what might be called a somatic attitude is in evidence because events are experienced somatically and physiologically and through sensorimotor and affect patterns. In the second year, the youngster abstracts larger patterns. Concept building occurs. The child understands the world in terms of its functions and can communicate and abstract across space using the distal modes. The ability to abstract time, organized in terms of the creation of representational memory organizations of self and object, will come only in the representational phase of development.

What are the implications of this stage for adult psychopathology? Problems in the early integration of the functional self relate to syndromes where there is ego splitting, or a lack of cohesive sense of self, or a lack of an ability to abstract the range of emotional properties of self and others. The tendency to remain concrete rather than to develop a conceptual and, eventually, a representational self-object organization is also related to limitations at this stage of development. Many adult patients, for example, speak of themselves in terms of discrete behavioral patterns (e.g., "I hit her; she hit me; I went out drinking"). Life is a series of interrelated but somewhat discrete behaviors. There is no sense of, "She is a frustrating person; therefore, I get upset," or "I go out drinking because I can't tolerate the pain and anguish of her frustrating me," or "She's a sweet person who loves me, but I get scared of the closeness, and therefore I can't handle it and I go out and drink."

Often we inadvertently supply the missing representational level in therapy. The patient says, "I hit her." We say, "You must have felt angry." In fact, the patient's problem is that he does not have the capacity for representational labeling of affect states. He experiences the tendency to hit in the representational mode, but not the feeling of anger. For many with severe character disorders and borderline conditions, life is a series of discrete behavior patterns. In normal development, by as early as 18–19 months a more conceptual attitude toward the world is developed. But many patients have never developed this capacity in the emotional sphere. They possess it intellectually; they can do math and other abstract impersonal problems, but when it comes to emotions they are unable to operate at the level of an 18-month-old. Or they may operate at different developmental levels with different emotions (e.g., pleasure and dependency at one level, assertion and anger at another).

At the extreme, the capacity for organizing behavior, emotions, and a conceptual stance toward the world is not formed at all. We see fragmented images of the self and of the object world. These individuals can relate to others, but they are at the mercy of moment-to-moment feelings. There is no integration of discrete experiences. It is not surprising that borderline patients have affect storms and keep shifting their behavioral and emotional inclinations. Their part-self and part-object images are not tied together; they have not made it to the 18-month level where they have a sense of themselves and significant others as operating individuals. Their part-selves are fueled by unconnected drive-affect proclivities.

This is an especially interesting stage of development because most of the severe character and borderline conditions (which are probably the conditions we treat most frequently today) have important normative parallels in the second year of life.

We also see in the second year of life the emergence of an internal signaling system. Affect, as a signal, seems to develop as part of a more general conceptual attitude toward the world. By 18 or 19 months we see a toddler who, when he does not get what he wants, is not necessarily driven to temper tantrums or other driven behavioral patterns. There is now a capacity to pause and make a judgment regarding what to do. The toddler can consider alternative patterns of behavior. Most children of this age, for example, will pester their mother, pull at her leg, and so forth, but with one look from her will go back to their play area and wait for a while longer. Or, a toddler will want to do something, and the mother will look at him and make the finger-wagging gesture, "No, no, no." He may stop in his tracks, challenge her, stop again, and so forth. The signal function is in the process of being developed. To be sure, many toddlers may not use this new capacity at all or may not yet have it.

Nemiah (1977) has suggested that in certain psychosomatic conditions, such as drug abuse and impulse disorders, there is the lack of a signal affect capacity and hence no transitional capacity to elevate dysphoric affect into a conceptual and subsequently representational signal.

It is interesting to consider what helps the child develop a signal function. One component is the capacity to shift from proximal to distal modes of relating. An infant relates to the adult world with proximal modes, through being held and being touched. But by 4 to 8 months, the distal modes are coming into use; vision and hearing are used in reciprocal signaling, and infants stay in touch by vision and hearing with direct touch. By 12 to 18 months, the toddler, though across the room, can stay connected to mother or father through these distal modes. Vocalizations, visual signals, and affect gestures (a grin or smile) are used to remain in emotional contact. The refueling that Mahler, Pine, and Bergman (1975) discuss occurs not only through proximal modes (coming back and hugging the mother), but through the distal modes as well. The youngster, while playing, looks, sees the mother's alert attentiveness, and feels reassured. Studies by Sorce and Emde (1981) on social referencing show that children are more exploratively confident when their mother is looking at them, and taking an interest in their play, than when she is reading a newspaper in the same room. In other words, a child can "have his cake and eat it too." He can explore, have the freedom of space, and still feel connected. He relates across space, but he cannot yet relate across time. He does not possess the ideational or representational mode.

A child may fail to establish this distal communication capacity because a parent is overanxious, overprotective, or oversymbiotic. Or the child may lack optimal use of the distal modes because of a unique maturational pattern. Consider, for example, a child with an auditory processing problem; he may not be able to decode his mother's "that's a good boy." Or a child with a visual-spatial organizing limitation may have difficulty reading facial gestures or interpersonal distance and may need to rely more on the proximal modes. He may have to be held to feel secure.

The use of distal modes may be an important key in the transition to the development of the ideational or representational mode. In this mode, one has mobility not only across space but across time because one can conjure up the object by creating ideas. As Mahler, Pine, and Bergman (1975) suggest, one feels security through the fantasy of the object.

As adults, there is a balance between proximal modes (being held and cuddled by our loved ones) and distal modes (we enjoy warmth and security through the nodding and gesturing of a close friend in a good conversation, or even that of a new acquaintance at a cocktail party). Adults who cannot receive experience through the distal modes often feel deprived and isolated and so resort to proximal modes. This makes adult life very difficult. (As far as I know, this deficit has not been looked at as a significant component of borderline disturbances and severe character disorders in which there is an inordinate sense of isolation, emptiness, and loneliness.) The transition to distal and then to ideational modes creates flexibility. One can carry with one the love object, first over space and eventually over time. One sees a failure at this stage in deficits in the functional (conceptual) self-object, and in limitations in the affective-thematic proclivities of that self-object.

In summary, a severe disorder at this phase affects the basic capacity for organizing behavior and affects. Most worrisome is the toddler who pulls away from emotional relationships in the human world entirely and develops his affective-thematic proclivities only in relation to inanimate objects. These proclivities are often limited to mild interest, curiosity, and subdued forms of pleasure. A less severe disorder at this stage will be reflected in the narrowness of the child's range of organized experience, as seen in extreme character rigidities (e.g., the child who never asserts himself or is always negative, or has difficulties with affiliative behavior, or cannot use imitation in the service of temporary gratification and delay). As such children are tied to concrete and immediate states of need fulfillment, they may never form the intermediary warning and delay capacities that complex internal affects are used for. They often tend to see people only as fulfilling their hunger for physical touch, or for candy, cake, or other concrete satisfactions.

Symptomatic problems at the stage of behavioral organization are chronic temper tantrums, inability to initiate even some self-control, lack of motor or emotional coordination, extreme chronic negativism, sleep disturbance, hyperirritability, withdrawal, delayed language development, and relationships characterized by chronic aggressive behavior. In addition, if basic attachments and comforting functions are secondarily disrupted, one may see attachment and homeostatic disorders.

Implications for a Theory of Ego Development

The new capacities for behavioral organization, affective integration, and behavioral sense of self and object in functional terms (a conceptual stand toward the world) characterizes this stage of ego development. Now there is what may be thought of as a conceptual self-object relationship as different self behaviors and object behaviors are not only differentiated from each other (as in the earlier stage), but are now viewed as part of a whole. Teasing behavior, jokes, the anticipation of emotional reactions, awareness of how to get others to evidence different emotional proclivities—all point to this new conceptual affective ability. But even more important is how the toddler uses his ability to organize in all dimensions of life. This is illustrated by his tendency, under stress, to organize his negativism, become sophisticated in his clinging dependency, develop intricate aggressive patterns, or exploit and manipulate peers and adults in new interpersonal patterns. In worrisome situations the toddler regresses from organized behavioral patterns to highly fragmented patterns or becomes withdrawn or rejecting. Here complex adaptive and maladaptive patterns as well as regressive potential suggest an emerging capacity characterized by conceptually and behaviorally differentiated whole object patterns. The ego now has new capacities; it can integrate behavioral and emotional differences or opposites (i.e., deal with ambivalence). As noted above, relatively early in this stage (12–14 months) ego splitting or lack of integration is characteristic. But by 17–18 months more integrated patterns are possible. The ego abstracts the properties of experiences of the self with others along functional lines rather than by means of stimulus topography. Daddy is not just big or fat or wearing a brown shirt, but is warm or aggressive or supportive or fun, etc. Just as the toy telephone is used to call people, and is not simply a piece of wood to bang, so "Daddy" and "Mommy" as well as "self" are functional, interactive beings. Functional grouping of behavioral experience permits greater awareness, anticipation, and planning. The ego can now organize experience in terms of functional expectencies. This capacity of the ego further facilities integrated functional identifications. Instead of simply copying a behavior, a child can copy or identify with a functional interpersonal pattern. These patterns can also be projected or incorporated. Now not simply an isolated behavior (e.g., hitting) but a "behavioral attitude" (e.g., being controlling) can be projected or incorporated. Perhaps most defenses exist in a hierarchy related to stages in ego functioning.

As has been indicated, organization of experience at this stage occurs through experiencing oneself in relation to significant others. Reciprocal patterns allow one to experience an emotional partnership where elements of "self" and "other" are continually abstracted from a variety of contexts. The tendency to learn through identifications, often considered a primary way of learning, is in fact secondary to learning through reciprocity. The innate tendency to copy (a likely perceptual-motor tendency) can become encouraged as part of feeling admired for one's ability to be like another, or may be used defensively. Defensive, angry, or dysphoric identifications probably occur in an "undigested manner." Metaphorically the child says, "I will copy what I do not like in order to better be able to defeat you at your own game." Hence rejection leads to rejection, abuse to abuse. But this is the child's way of reciprocating or trying to protect himself and get even. In other words, it is part of a reciprocal pattern.

The degree to which the ego experiences conflicts or deficits at this stage is also important to consider. Where the ability to functionally organize self and object behavior patterns is not achieved, or where it is achieved in certain affective-thematic realms but not in others, a deficit or constriction may occur. Dysphoric affects may also be mobilized as the product of a "no win situation" in which two behavioral tendencies oppose one another (e.g., hitting behavior and being punished, or independent behavior and a feeling of isolation or assertive curious behavior) and of a realistic anticipation of being undermined and humiliated. Because by 16–18 months of age "anticipation" is clearly possible, the potential for conflict is clearly in evidence as toddlers search for ways to meet competing needs. For example, they may use avoidance, aggression, or behavioral compromise formations. It would appear that a type of "behavioral pattern" conflict is a feature of ego functioning.

During this stage ego structure formation is undergoing rapid progress. Both deficits of experience and conflicts between behavioral-affectual tendencies will likely undermine structure formation. One therefore does not need to postulate either deficit models or conflict models of the mind. Rather, the two tendencies can be seen to be working together.

For example, Kohut (1971) would suggest that lack of parental empathy leads the toddler to experience a deficit in self-esteem regulation. Kernberg (1975) would suggest that the unadmiring, overcontrolling, or intrusive caregiver creates a condition whereby the toddler experiences rage and conflict and then resorts to primitive splitting defenses in order to cope with this situation. Clinical work and child observation suggest that both tendencies are operative. A lack of empathy and intrusive overcontrol leads to painful humiliation, rage, and fear of object loss as well as deficits in self-object experiences and the formation of structures regulating self-esteem. For example, the 18-month-old experiencing rage and fear, without therapy, usually resorts to passive compliance, indifferent impulsivity, or avoidance. This regressive way of dealing with conflict during this phase leads to a structural deficit because the ability to abstract affective polarities is not learned. Likewise, a lack of empathic admiration and availability seems to leave the toddler feeling too uncertain about his objects to experiment with his behavioral and affective polarities. Reconstructive work with older children and adults must deal with both the reality of the early object relationship and the rage, humiliation, fear, conflict, and primitive strategies experienced or used at the time and subsequently repeated. At this age, therefore, conflict leads to deficits (e.g., lack of capacity to abstract behavioral polarities and deal with ambivalence), and deficits lead to conflicts. Which came first is a "chicken-or-egg" question: appropriate structure is necessary to resolve conflict and conflicts at an early age often lead to structural deficits.

This stage of ego development is characterized by many new capacities and is transitional to the next stages, where mental representations and differentiated self-object representational structures are possible.

Representational Capacity (18–30 Months)

During this stage, one may postulate a self-object relationship characterized by a representational self-object. Ego organization, differentiation, and integration are characterized by an elevation of functional behavioral self-object patterns to multisensory drive- and affect-invested symbols of intrapersonal and interactive experience (mental representations). Ego functions now include (if things go well) representational self-objects characterized by mobility in time and space (e.g., the creation of object representations in the absence of objects), drive-affect elaboration (themes ranging from dependency and pleasure to assertiveness and aggression now elaborated in symbolic form evidenced in pretend play and functional language), and gradual drive-affect stability (self-object representations slowly survive intensification of drive-affect dispositions), or (if development is hindered) behavioral concretization (lack of representation), representational constriction (only one or another emotional theme at a time), drive-affect lability, and regressive states including withdrawal, avoidance, rejection, behavioral dedifferentiation, and object concretization.

Sensory Organization

As a toddler shifts from organizing behavioral patterns to the ability to abstract the functional meaning of objects and then to the ability to construct mental representations of human and inanimate objects, we observe the establishment of the "representational" capacity. A mental representation is multisensory and involves the construction of objects from the perspective of *all* the objects' properties (including levels of meaning abstracted from experiences with the object). Therefore, the range of senses and sensorimotor patterns the youngster employs in relation to his objects is critical, for the object is at once an auditory, visual, tactile, olfactory, vestibular, and proprioceptive object and an object that is involved in various affective and social interchanges. Where the range, depth, and integration of sensory experiences are limited, the very construction of the object will obviously be limited in either its sensory range and depth or its affective investment and meaning. In such a situation, therefore, important limitations in the child's early representational world may result.

Affective-Thematic Organization

As the child learns to construct his own multisensory, affective-thematic image of his experiential world, the child organizes affective-thematic patterns at the level of meanings. This new level of organization may be thought of as operating in two ways. The youngster with a representational capacity now has the tool to interpret and label feelings rather than simply act them out. A verbal child of 2½ can evidence this interpretive process by saying "me mad" or "me happy." Pretend play is perhaps an even more reliable indicator than language of the child's ability to interpret and label. Pretend play is an especially important indicator because many children have language delays. For example, a child who plays out dramas of dependency (two dolls feeding or hugging each other), of excitement and curiosity (one doll looking under the dress of another), or of assertiveness (searching for monsters) soon provides a picture of his representational world.

The representational capacity also provides a higher-level organization with which to integrate affective-thematic domains. Thus, we observe new experiences as the child develops from 2 to 5 years of age. These include empathy, consistent love (object constancy—a love of self and others that is stable over time and survives separations and affect storms such as anger; see Mahler, Pine, and Bergman, 1975), and, later on, loss, sadness, and guilt.

Because of the complexities of representational elaboration, the conceptualization of this stage may be aided by subdividing the representational capacity into a number of levels or subcategories. These subcategories are *the descriptive use of the representational mode* (the child labels pictures and describes objects); *the limited interactive use of the representational mode* (the child elaborates one or two episodes of affective-thematic interaction, i.e., statements like "give me candy" or "me hungry," or a play scene with two dolls feeding, fighting, or nuzzling); *the elaboration of representational, affective-thematic interactions* (often by the age of 2½ or 3, the child sequences a number of representational units into a drama—the doll eats, goes to sleep, awakens, goes to school, spanks the teacher, comes home and has a tea party, begins looking under the dress of another doll, becomes overexcited, is comforted by Mommy, and then goes back to sleep). Initially, the elements in the complex drama may not be logically connected. Over time, along with representational differentiation, to be described in the next section, the causal-logical infrastructure of the child's representational world emerges in his pretend play and use of language. Over time, the child's thematic elaboration can be observed to include a range of themes, including dependency, pleasure, assertiveness, curiosity, aggression, limit-setting for oneself, and eventually empathy and love.

Ego Deficits, Distortions, and Constrictions

If for any reason the child is not getting practice in the interpersonal emotional use of language and pretend play (i.e., elevating these proclivities to the ideational plane), we often see the beginnings of a deficit or constriction in representational capacity. Deficits or constrictions may occur because parents become anxious about using ideas in emotionally relevant contexts (i.e., they are afraid of emotional fantasy, in general, or in such specific affective-thematic areas as separation or rejection, aggression or assertiveness). Many adults are more frightened or conflicted by the representation of a theme such as sexuality or aggression than by the acting out of the theme. Parental anxiety often leads to overcontrolling, undermining, hyperstimulīng, withdrawn, or concrete behavioral patterns (i.e., they say, in effect, "Let's not talk or play; I will feed you"). In addition, because of unique constitutional-maturational patterns or early experiences, the child may become overexcited and thus afraid of his own use of ideas and new feelings (e.g., sexual themes in the play). As a result, he may regress to concrete prerepresentational patterns. If the parent cannot help the child return to the ideational level (i.e., the child is beating the ground and cannot reorganize and get back into the play), the child does not practice affective-thematic proclivities at the ideational mode, and remains at the behavioral action pattern mode ("acting out").

The ideational mode allows for trial action patterns in thought (whereby the child may contemplate alternatives and choose among them). One can reason with ideas better than with actual behaviors. Therefore, an enormous deficit is present if a sensation or series of sensations that are distinctly human do not have access to the ideational plane. Parents often ask about aggression, "Should I take away aggressive toys?" If parents ignore the need to elevate aggression to the representational plane, they leave aggression to the behavioral discharge mode. As children go from the conceptual mode to being able to label affects, they learn to talk about feelings. Adaptive 4-year-olds can label most of the basic feelings and begin to deal with them in their pretend play.

In summary, disorders in this phase include children who remain concrete and never learn to use the representational mode (e.g., only fragments of play or language are produced). Impulsive or withdrawn behavior often accompanies such a limitation. Usually the child's relationship patterns are also fragmented.

At a somewhat less severe level we see children who have developed a representational capacity in both the inanimate and animate spheres but show severe limitations or regressions with even minor stress in certain areas of human experience. For example, they may be able to use symbolic modes only around negativism, dominance, and aggression and consequently look solemn, stubborn, and angry, showing little range of representational elaboration in the pleasurable or intimate domain.

Implications for a Theory of Ego Development

This stage of ego organization is characterized by the capacity to elevate experiences to the representational level. Experience can be organized into sensoriaffective "images" mobile in time and space (i.e., the child can produce images of objects even in their absence). The representational system can also construct multisensory images of sensations or patterns from within the organism which may have occurred in the past. These earlier patterns of somatic sensation and simple and complex chains of behavior and interaction will not be "interpreted" via representation. How well formed, accurate, or distorted these representations of earlier prerepresentational experience will be will depend on the character of the early patterns, their repetition in the present, the abstracting ability of the ego, and the emerging dynamic character of the ego, i.e., its ability to represent some areas of experience better than others.

A slight digression on the kinds of learning that characterize the ego at different stages may prove useful in understanding how somatic, behavioral, and representational patterns relate to each other, and how earlier somatic and behavioral patterns are transformed into representational structures. To understand the relation between prerepresentational learning and representational learning, three types of learning by which the ego organizes information: somatic learning, consequence-behavioral learning, and representational-structural learning.

Somatic learning is learning that occurs in relation to the human body, in particular bodily or biological functioning (including drive-affect patterns) subject to variations in organization within different environmental contexts. Such phenomena as general arousal patterns, overall interest in the world, specific autonomic nervous system patterns, and bodily rhythmic processes (sleep-wake cycles, alert cycles, hormonal variations), as well as early drive-affect and drive-behavior patterns such as object seeking, self-stimulation, self-comforting, and stimulus preferences, are determined in part by this very early type of learning.

Consequence behavioral learning is the learning of new behaviors and discriminatory capacities as a result of behavioral consequences (the contingencies of reinforcement). Consequence learning may be involved at both the somatic and the representational levels. As a concept it is similar to stimulus-response and operant learning paradigms (Skinner, 1938). While the term can be applied to the level of ideas and meanings, its explanatory power is most useful when applied to observable discrete behaviors. In this context it is not surprising that operant approaches, developed from experiments with animals, in which discrete behaviors are easier to observe and control than in humans, help us understand a level of human experience different from experience at the level of meanings. The reorganization of meanings into new meanings differs somewhat in character from the changing of behavior through altering consequences.

Representational-structural learning is "higher-order" learning involving the formation and organization of mental imagery and symbols which ultimately fit into configurations that permit us to think and learn. This level involves "awareness" in the traditional sense (awareness of ideas, or representational awareness).

We must consider in more specific terms how the three levels relate to one another; in particular, how do somatic patterns relate in an ongoing manner to representational patterns?

Somatic and representational patterns. Somatic patterns relate to representational patterns in three crucial ways. First, somatic patterns form part of the basic structure of the representational system. Second, they are a part of the experiences that eventually become organized (internalized) at a representational level. Third, somatic experience is constantly perceived in the context of representational structures and is interpreted and transformed just as external experience is.

Somatic patterns are part of the basic structure of the representational system because of the constitutional and early developmental somatic differences that account for the individual ways in which infants process experience. For example, the early somatic pattern of arousal may form the basis for later intensity of internal representation. The early stimulus threshold (somatic pattern of shutting out stimulation) may form the foundation for later tendencies of the representational system *not* to experience certain noxious sensations. In her work on anorexia nervosa and obseity, Bruch (1973) postulated that because of experiences in early life certain infants, toddlers, and young children do not ever become aware of such basic bodily sensations as hunger; by contrast, there are children who may respond hyperreactively to minimal stimulation. Some adults are acutely aware of sensations such as sexual longing; others may be totally unaware of such longings. In some instances the denial of usually experienced sensations or feelings occurs secondarily, for dynamic reasons. In other instances, because of early patterns where there are no confirmatory parental responses to the infant's expression of internal states such as those described by Bruch, certain bodily feelings and impulses may become changed or distorted at the somatic or behavioral level and never come to be available to representational awareness.

During the latter part of the first year and through the second year, when complex behavioral interactions are becoming organized, somatic patterns involved in these interactions may become organized and associated with these behavioral patterns. The toddler who experiences intense somatic patterns of irritability upon stimulation (based on earlier somatic learning) may come to experience seemingly playful human interactions as "irritating" and overstimulating. A complex behavioral organization becomes formed within which a somatic proclivity is connected to interactions and expectations. Later, at the representational stage, a personal "meaning" may be established (human relationships provoke irritation and therefore "people are mean and I must be mean in order to make them mean") that incorporates the earlier proclivities.

Another example: the somatically very active infant may, in the second year of life, use this activity in the service of expressing both excitement and rage. If as a consequence of this excitement and rage, the mother or father withdraws, the toddler may associate activity, excitement, and rage with loss of human contact. Subsequently, a meaning may be established to the effect that "my longings are bad and lead to loss." First at a behavioral level and then at a level of meaning, a pattern becomes organized that includes both the original somatic proclivity and the later interaction (activity and withdrawal). Similarly, somatic patterns of all kinds—pleasure, curiosity, assertiveness—may become involved in complex human relationships that reach a representational level and are then interpreted and given meanings.

In this regard, it is interesting to consider defects in the transitional experiences leading to a capacity for representation or internal imagery. Work on alexithymia (Nemiah, 1977) suggests that certain borderline patients may have had faulty experiences early in life which account for a special defect in their capacity for experiencing internal states involving imagery and affects. For example, by being intrusive, parents may undermine the toddler's tendency to organize behavior and experience complex emotional interactions. The toddler may turn away from the human emotional world to the inanimate world, where his initiative is not undermined by intrusiveness. Opportunities for experiencing ideational and affective proclivities may thereby be missed.

Even after experience reaches the representational level, it may be further modified. The representation of experience permits the ego to alter, recombine, and later transform internal representations in accord with defensive and adaptive goals. For example, a vague sensation associated with protest behavior may come to be expressed as an angry feeling. An angry feeling may be transformed into a "loving feeling." Fears may be displaced from one object to another. New fantasies may evolve from old ones. Through processes such as these, an early somatic experience may be hardly recognizable and its role in early development obscured.

In summary, then, the relation between the somatic and the representational levels of learning involves the somatic foundation of the representational system, the organization of complex behavioral interpersonal experiences involving somatic proclivities, and distinct styles of perception, interpretation, and transformation of the representational system in relation to somatic experience.

As one considers "learning" one must also consider the maturational capacities of the child. If, for example, a child evidences a lag in processing sensory information in either the auditory-verbal, symbolic, or visual-spatial symbolic pathways (e.g., can't sequence and thereby abstract units of experience), then the ability to abstract large patterns of experience may be compromised. Therefore, organizing early representations will obviously be more challenging in the child with difficulty in perceptual sequencing. Since many children evidence a range of individual differences in sequencing and organizing information, this capacity, as it interacts with interpersonal experiences, must also be considered.

As indicated earlier, the ego at this stage evidences the adaptive capacity for representational elaboration. It also evidences a range of maladaptive options, including a lack of representation where the physical world can be represented but the drive-affect invested interpersonal world is not represented. This global lack of representational capacity is often associated with interpersonal withdrawal and/or regressive behavioral and somatic discharge patterns. Where there is support for representational elaboration in some areas but not others, or where certain child-initiated themes lead to parental anxiety and/or parental undermining behavior, one observes representational constrictions. One observes also that in some instances these constrictions can be accompanied by intense patterns of behavioral and affective expression. These intense patterns may be in the same or the opposite affective-thematic realm as the representational constriction. One may observe also a lack of representation of delineated self-object thematic patterns (e.g., dependency only with intrusive mother figures) rather than entire areas of emotion (e.g., dependency with everyone). This limited access to representational elaboration often stems from more circumscribed conflicts in parent-child interaction patterns (e.g., the parent becomes intrusive or withdraws only when the child behaves like the parent's sister) and sets the stage for neurotic conflicts and circumscribed character pathology. Patterns that remain outside of representational life are denied access to unconscious symbolism or conscious symbolic reasoning and are therefore more likely to seed the formation of unconscious neurotic configurations.

How children remain concrete (i.e., fail to develop a representational capacity), constrict the representation of certain drive-affect realms, form circumscribed areas of inaccessible to representation, and develop compensatory behavioral and affective patterns of a regressive nature reveals the range of functioning available to the ego. The ego organizes current and past experience (behavioral and somatic) in representational configurations. Initially these are descriptive, but quickly they become functional and interactive. The physical, temporal, and spatial properties of experience are the initial organizers. Representational meanings are quickly learned, however. Each "representational" or interpersonal interaction creates a context for abstracting meanings. To the degree there is a less than optimal interactive experience available (the caregiver is concrete or ignores or distorts certain representational themes), we observe a series of ego operations:

1. *Concretization of experience.* Access to representation is never achieved.

2. *Behavioral-representational splitting.* Some areas gain access; others remain at the behavioral level.

3. *Representational constriction.* Global dynamically relevant areas remain outside the representational system.

4. *Representational encapsulation.* Limited dynamically relevant areas remain in more concrete form.

5. *Representational exaggeration or lability.* Domains of experience which are ignored or distorted become exaggerated and/or labile, or their opposites become exaggerated and/or labile, or other "displaced" dynamically related thoughts, affects, or behaviors become exaggerated or labile.

During this stage, as object relationships and the self are being organized at the representational level, they are not yet differentiated, even though the early prerepresentational behavioral and somatic organizations are differentiated. There is a paradox: differentiation at an earlier level alongside emergent but not yet established differentiation at the new, higher level.

At this time we can postulate an undifferentiated *representational self-object* built on a foundation of somatic and behavioral differentiated self-objects. The behaving child is clearly intentional and behaviorally understands that his actions have an impact on others. Yet he is only now learning to give meanings to his behaviors and feelings and only beginning to learn about intentionality and consequences at the level of meanings. In this sense, symbolic awareness is expanding rapidly and is in evidence in the elaboration of pretend play and the functional use of language. Yet we are also observing how symbolic aware-

ness or consciousness may be concretized, constricted, or encapsulated, or selectively exaggerated depending on the
opportunities the child has to engage his new ability in appropriate interpersonal contexts.

From the perspective of the ego's capacity to organize unconscious phenomena, it is possible to consider the different
levels of experience within which drive-affect dispositions express themselves: *somatic sensations, behavioral patterns (including
inhibition), and emerging mental representations.* Early in development somatic and behavioral patterns exist in various degrees
of differentiation (e.g., along the lines of physical vs. human
and self vs. nonself). Now the same is true for emerging mental
representations.

In this context, it is perhaps useful to rethink concepts
often used to understand the organization and dynamics of
organizing primitive experience—e.g., projection, incorporation, condensation, displacement. At each level of organization—somatic sensations, behavioral patterns, and emerging
mental representations—the infant initially does not differentiate experience sufficiently for one to postulate an organized
defense such as projection. As differentiation occurs, however,
self- and object experiences gradually become grouped along
a number of dimensions, including (a) physical properties, (b)
spatial relationships, (c) temporal relationships (e.g., contingencies based on sequencing in time), (d) functional properties
(in the second year of life), and (e) emerging meanings (18–24
months and on). At each level—somatic, behavioral, and representational—a certain point in experiencing is sufficiently
differentiated to consider the various ways in which experiences
can be reorganized to serve the defensive and adaptive needs
of the moment. In other words, it is proper to postulate the
alteration of experience only after some differentiation has occurred. This differentiation defines some boundaries for the
experience. There is a difference between a lack of differentiation and a dynamically motivated alteration, however primitive, of differentiated experience. In earlier sections I
discussed ways in which these mechanisms operate at the prerepresentational level. At the representational level we can

again look at primitive defense mechanisms. What is put out, projected, taken in, incorporated, or combined (condensation) is a mental image that is acquiring meaning (and these images are related to earlier somatic and behavioral organizations). It is appropriate now to consider *displacement* as a defense mechanism. One image can substitute for another as the ability to construct images allows for greater representational mobility in the intrapsychic world. Condensations will also certainly be richer and more economic once mental representations acquire meanings. Symbols with dynanmic meaning provide the basis not only for logical thought but for new drive-affect organizations of experience. As a higher-level organization of experience (than somatic or behavioral patterns), mental representations or symbols change the nature of condensation, displacement, and projective and incorporative phenomena.

With the advent of mental representations, it also becomes possible to consider the beginnings of *sublimation*. Traditionally, sublimations have been considered to occur only later in development (i.e., in the late oedipal and latency periods), when sexual or aggressive drive derivatives are displaced and achieve the aim of subliminated gratification by being integrated with the factors of reality, superego constraints, and emerging ego ideals. These integrations are often associated with symbolic transformations. Yet the very capacity to represent experience and therefore go beyond behavior discharge is an early form of sublimation. For example, an angry, hitting, biting, spitting, and head-banging 2-year-old can learn to put his behavior into pretend play and words. As this occurs and the "soldiers" are hitting each other, etc., the tendency to directly attack the parent or younger siblings may diminish without a sense of inhibition, and with a sense of conscious satisfaction and gratification.

Often at this stage of development representational elaboration is associated with primary process thinking. Because behavioral and somatic differentiation is already occurring, and representational differentiation, as will be discussed shortly, occurs simultaneously with representational elaboration, it may be best to rethink our notions of primary process thinking. This issue will be discussed in the following section.

Representational Differentiation (24–48 Months)

During this stage one may postulate a self-object relationship characterized by a differentiated, integrated representational self-object. Ego organization, differentiation, and integration are characterized by an abstraction of self-object representations and drive-affect dispositions into a higher level representational organization, differentiated along dimensions of self-other, time, and space. Ego functions include representational differentiation characterized by genetic integration (early somatic and behavioral patterns are organized by emerging mental representations) and dynamic integration (current drive-affect proclivities are organized by emerging mental representations), inter-micro structural integration (i.e., affect, impulse, and thought), structure formation (self-object representations are abstracted into stable patterns performing the ongoing ego functions of reality testing, impulse control, mood stabilization, etc.), and beginning self- and object identity formation (a sense of self and object begins to integrate past, current, and changing aspects of fantasy and reality); or, if development is stymied, by representational fragmentation (genetic, dynamic, or both), absent or unstable basic structures (e.g., reality testing, impulse control), and defective, polarized, or constricted (global or encapsulated) self-object identity formation.

Sensory Organization

For the child to meet the challenges of organizing and differentiating his internal world according to "self" and "other," "inside" and "outside," and along the dimensions of time, space, and affective valence, he is in part dependent on the integrity of the sensory organization underlying his experiential world. Now, even more than earlier, the capacity to process sensory information is critical, including the sequencing of auditory-verbal and visual-spatial patterns according to physical, temporal, and spatial qualities in the context of abstracting emergent cognitive and affective meanings. The child is now challenged to understand what he hears, sees, touches, and feels, not only in terms of ideas, but in terms of what is me and not me; what is past, present, and short-term future; what is close and far; etc. These learning tasks depend on the ability to sequence and categorize information. Therefore, if anywhere along the pathway of sensory processing there are difficulties, the subsequent ability to organize even impersonal information will likely be compromised. For example, if sounds are confused, words will not be easily understood. If spatial references are confused, spatial configurations will not easily be negotiated. If short-term memory for either verbal or spatial symbols is vulnerable, information will be lost before it can be combined with, and compared to, other information (to abstract meanings). And if higher-level auditory-verbal symbolic or visual-spatial symbolic abstracting capacities are less than age-appropriate, the very capacity to categorize experience will be limited. And as the challenge is now to process and organize not only impersonal cognitive experiences but highly emotional, interpersonal experiences (which keep moving, so to speak), this challenge to the sensory system can be formidable. Further, categories such as "me," "not me," "real," and "make believe" are high-level constructs. Not surprisingly, learning difficulties or disabilities often are first evidenced in emotional functioning.

Affective-Thematic Organization

In contrast to the earlier views of Freud (1900) and Mahler, Pine, and Bergman (1975), recent clinical observations (Greenspan, 1981; Greenspan et al., 1987) suggest that a parallel path of differentiation exists simultaneously with the onset of the representational capacity and its elaboration. That is, the child appears to use his new representational capacity to simultaneously elaborate and differentiate experience. There does not appear to be a period of magical representational thinking followed by one of reality thinking. The child continually differentiates affective-thematic organizations along lines that pertain to self and other, inner and outer, time, space, and so forth. This differentiation is based on the child's capacity to experience the representational consequences of his representational elaborations with the emotionally relevant people in his world, usually parents, family, and friends. The parent who interacts with the child, comprehending the child's intentions and feelings, who responds with emotionally meaningful words and gestures, and who engages in pretend play in a contingent manner (offering, in other words, logical representational feedback) provides the child with consequences that help him differentiate his representational world. In this view, reality testing—appears to be a gradual process beginning with the onset of the representational capacity proper and stabilizing prior to the child's formal entry into school.

One observes the child's elaborate representational themes along two dimensions. In the horizontal dimension, the child broadens the range of themes to include eventually a variety of emotional domains or drive-affect realms, including closeness or dependency, pleasure and excitement, assertiveness, curiosity, aggression, limit-setting for oneself, the beginnings of empathy, and consistent love. For example, one not infrequently observes repetitive pretend play of a feeding or hugging scene suggesting nurturance and dependency. Over time, however, the dramas the child may initiate (with parental interactive support) will expand to include scenes of separation (one doll going off on a trip and leaving the other behind), competition, assertiveness, aggression, injury, death, recovery (the doctor doll trying to fix the wounded soldier), and so forth. At the same time, the logical infrastructure of the child's pretend play and functional use of language becomes more complex and causally connected. The "He Man" doll is hurt by the "bad guys" and therefore "gets them." After the tea party, the little girl doll goes to the "potty" and then decides it is time to begin cooking dinner. In discussions, the child of 3½ sounds more and more like a lawyer with "buts" and "becauses"—"I don't like that food because it looks yucky and will make me sick." There is, then, both thematic elaboration and differentiation. Even though the themes may be pretend and phantasmagoric, the structure of the drama becomes more and more logical. The rocket ship to the land of "He-Man" uses NASA rocket fuel.

As indicated, representational differentiation depends not only on a child's being representationally engaged in affective-thematic areas but experiencing cause-and-effect feedback at the representational level. Parents have to be able not only to engage but also to interpret experiences correctly. Parents who react to play with a gun as aggression one day, as sexuality another day, and as dependency on a third, or who keep shifting meanings within the same thematic play session, will confuse the child. This child may not develop meanings with a reality orientation. Parents who confuse their own feelings with the child's feelings, or cannot set limits, may also compromise the formation of a reality orientation.

Ego Deficits, Distortions, and Constrictions

The child needs to learn how to shift gears between the make-believe and the real world. Ordinarily this occurs gradually between the ages of 2 and 4. We see, as part of this process, more planning in children's play, as Piaget (1962) noted (e.g., the child goes upstairs to get just the right cup for the tea party). But what happens if there are failures of development during this stage? Earlier it was suggested that if representational elaboration does not occur, the child is left with a preideational or prerepresentational orientation, somatic and behavioral. If there are limitations in representational differentiation (confused meanings), a child's self- and object differentiation at the representational level may be compromised. It is interesting to consider those people who can engage others warmly (i.e., who have mastered attachment) and can organize their behavior, but who have "crazy" thoughts. They often cannot separate their own thoughts from those of someone else. They may have organized delusions, but are extremely warm and can relate to others; they are neither autistic nor schizoid.

One may also see people who suffer from constrictions, that is, who cannot represent or differentiate aggression or sexuality and are left only with the behavior-action mode, or who are confused about their own and others' ideas or feelings in these thematic areas (but not in others).

It is also interesting to discuss psychosexual trends at this stage. The phallic trend is clearly present, beginning at age 3. Kids love to build towers, pretend to be Superman, and undress to show off their bodies. As I have seen no equivalent preoccupation with anal concerns (eliminative or retentive), I question whether the anal body interest is elaborated as much in the representational sphere as is the phallic one.

It may be useful to consider the oral, anal, and phallic stages of psychosexual inclinations in terms of observable affective-thematic inclinations. I suspect there may be a sensory, tactile, or oral mode early in life. In the second year of life, muscle control may predominate (better gross and fine motor coordination, including anal control by the end of the second year). Then, by 2½ years, one sees the phallic inclinations as part of the ever increasing body control and investment in the body and its parts (which begins at 17–18 months). In summary, even though there is fascination with feces, I have not observed the representational derivatives of anal body interest in normal children to the same degree as phallic derivatives. However, where development is not progressing optimally, either exaggerated phallic trends or excessive anal preoccupation is not uncommon.

To return to an earlier discussion, inclinations that do not have access to the representational mode and its differentiation, even in mild degrees, are perhaps sowing the seeds for severe character pathology or neurotic conflicts. What is often referred to as magical thinking is more probable where representational elaboration and differentiation have not fully occurred. Later on, in the triangular oedipal and latency phases of development, earlier patterns obviously are reenacted and reworked.

In summary, it is useful to observe and assess the representational capacity simultaneously along the dimensions of representational elaboration and representational differentiation. Clinically one observes defects and constrictions in both domains. These are evidenced by the child who remains concrete and never learns to use the representational mode to elaborate "inner sensations" to the level of meanings; who is severely constricted and able to represent only a few of the affective-thematic domains characteristic of human functioning; who evidences the full range of representational affective-thematic life but remains undifferentiated along the dimensions of ideas or thoughts (thought disorder), affective proclivities (mood disturbances), self- and object organizations (reality testing and "self" and "other" boundary disturbances), intentionality (impulse disorders), sense of time and space (disorders of learning, concentration, and planning); or who in order to differentiate avoids affective-thematic realms that are potentially disruptive (character disorders). Contributing to these limitations is the caregiver who cannot engage representationally in all domains because he or she is fearful of certain affective-thematic realms and therefore withdraws or becomes disorganized. Another is the caregiver who engages in all realms but has difficulty operating at a representational contingent level. The child's own limitations from earlier, maturationally based processing problems and psychosexual difficulties also contribute to representational disorders.

Implications for a Theory of Ego Development

Parallel with its capacity to create and elaborate mental representations, the ego, as its development progresses, abstracts representational units into groupings leading to representational differentiation. These groupings occur along a number of dimensions including physical, spatial, and temporal aspects of experience. Self-representations are differentiated from the "other," "nonself," or "object" representations along all the relevant dimensions. But, most important, these groupings also occur along the lines of affective *meanings*. Now self-object patterns colored by drive-affect coalesce into representational organizations according to the characteristics of drive-affect dispositions as they both define and are defined by early relationship patterns.

As one observes both healthy and disturbed children it appears that experience can now be categorized and each category of experience can undergo, depending on the appropriateness and adaptiveness of environmental-representational feedback, relative degrees of differentiation. As indicated earlier, the areas of pleasure, dependency, assertion, curiosity, anger, limit-setting for oneself, love, and empathy may be seen as a way to categorize experience (e.g., separation anxiety would be a feature of dependency). Therefore, drive-affect derivatives are now organized by the ego according to the principles of representational differentiation. As realms of experience are defined and differentiated, each affective-thematic domain becomes a basis for further interaction and more refined meanings.

Thus, self-object patterns at this stage of ego development are characterized by *differentiated and elaborated self-object representations*. The range and stability of these organizations, however, may vary considerably. Differentiatèd self-object representations may encompass a broad range of themes or be narrow and constricted. To the degree there are areas where interpersonal feedback is lacking or has been distorted, self-object representations may remain unelaborated and undifferentiated or may undergo dedifferentiation.

The primary ego functions now develop from the ego's ability to abstract patterns along dimensions of self and object meanings, affective tendencies, and the dimensions of time, space, and causality. These include reality testing (a representational "me" separate from a representational "other"); impulse control (a representational me impacting on and illiciting consequences from a representational other); mood stabilization (a representational me and other becomes organized along a dominant mood as affects are abstracted into larger affective patterns); focused attention and a capacity for planning (a representational me causes events to occur in a temporal context); and a more integrated body self-object representation (the parts of "me" and the "object" are abstracted in spatial contexts).

During this stage, ambivalence can be dealt with in a new way, and an integrated representational self can be organized. Alteratively, one may observe a lack of intigration. Different self-object representational units may exist, depending on interpersonal factors or maturational factors, at various degrees of differentiation. The "sexual" self-object, assertive self-object, dependent self-object, etc. may each achieve its own relative degree of differentiation. As indicated earlier, sensory processing difficulties may undermine differentiation in auditory-verbal or visual-spatial modes. Or a lack of representational feedback or distorted or illogical feedback in certain realms of experience will tend to leave those areas of representational life relatively undifferentiated.

As is well known, anxiety and conflict now tend to play a new role, but perhaps earlier than previously thought. With growing representational capacity, anxiety can be interpreted via the emerging representational system. Conflicts between self-object representations can occur in terms of an "internal debate" at the level of ideas (e.g., the good me and you vs. the angry, evil me and you). Conflicts between self-object representations and external expectations can also occur (the "greedy" me and the "strict," limiting other). Therefore, while anxiety and internal conflict have been thought to be dominant only in the late oedipal and postoedipal phases (because of the necessity of internalized prohibitions, i.e., superego formation), clinical observations of young children suggest that representational differentiation alone may be a sufficient condition for the early experience of conflict between different inner inclinations. The types of fears and anxieties both causing and resulting from conflicts, however, will be quite different in oedipal and preoedipal phases.

What operations are now available to the ego to deal with anxiety and conflict? The ego now has new approaches in addition to the primitive mechanisms described earlier. Observations of both normal and disturbed young children suggest that the approaches available to the ego include:

1. *Global lack of differentiation.* Reality and the object ties that provide reality feedback are too disruptive or "scary."

2. *Selective dedifferentiation.* Boundaries are blurred and meanings changed, as with "my anger won't make Mother leave because we are the same person."

3. *Thought–drive-affect dedifferentiation.* "I can think anything, but I won't have feelings so I won't be scared."

4. *Thought–behavior (impulse) dedifferentiation.* "If I do it, it's not me. Only when I think and plan it is it me."

5. *Selective constriction of drive-affect thematic realms.* Areas such as anger or sexual curiosity are avoided and may remain relatively undifferentiated, often because associated with disorganizing interactive experience such as withdrawal, overstimulation, etc.

6. *Affect, behavioral, or thought intensification.* "If I exaggerate it or its opposite, it can't scare me."

7. *Differentiated representational distortions.* Meanings are

changed along lines of drive-affect dispositions ("I am Super-girl, the strongest") while basic reality testing is maintained ("It is only pretend").

8. *Encapsulated distortions.* There are dynamically based, highly selective shifts of meanings, e.g., "I am the cause of Mother's anger."

9. *Transforming differentiational linkages.* This is an early form of rationalization. As the child's capacity to connect rep-resentational units is forming, he or she can elaborate such thoughts as "I like Mommy because she is home all the time and am mad at Daddy because he travels a lot." These logical links can undergo subtle shifts to change meanings for defen-sive purposes ("I like Daddy to travel a lot because he brings me presents. I am mad at Mommy," etc.).

10. *Compromises in representational integration and represen-tational identity.* The integration of somatic, behavioral, and rep-resentational self-object organizations and associated drive affect proclivities are not fully maintained, as evidenced by the irritable-looking 3-year-old who "feels fine" or the hitting 3-year-old who "loves everyone."

Ego functions progress to make possible triangular patterns and higher level transformations of meanings; i.e., new rep-resentations are derived from older ones. While these levels in ego development will not be discussed here, it may prove useful to briefly discuss the ego mechanisms of primary and secondary repression and the role of anxiety.

Primary and secondary repression and the role of anxiety. It is often thought that there are two kinds of "repression" that cause the absence of memory. Primary repression occurs when very young children simply do not retain information about events of an earlier age. At a somewhat later stage secondary repression occurs when children "repress" earlier experiences that invoke feelings that are unpleasant or disruptive to their current functioning. The active jealousy felt at age 3 toward the birth of a brother or sister is "repressed" by age 5 or 6. But what are the mechanisms by which primary and secondary repression occur? Consider the following hypothesis.

The mechanisms for forgetting emotionally meaningful

events may be related to the state of mind in which the child experiences the event. It may be useful to consider how memory functions under altered states of consciousness or under the influence of medication. Although research on the subject is controversial, it may be presumed that at least sometimes learning that takes place during one state of consciousness, during hypnosis for example, can be remembered only when the person is in a similar state. The same is often true for activities learned while people are under medication. A series of names learned when taking drug A may be better remembered when the person is back on drug A.

Consider the different levels of development postulated earlier—the somatic, the behavioral, and the two representational levels—as different states of mind. When a child operates in the somatic or behavioral world, before he uses emotional concepts and ideas, he remembers and can repeat certain behaviors. Once the child becomes aware of emotions and starts using representations or emotional ideas (at 18–30 months) in pretend play and in language, the child can reproduce these ideas and recall emotional events of this state of mind. But in the representational stage he generally does not recall events of the somatic behavioral stages. For example, the 3-year-old does not forget that he wants his candy or that it was promised to him later, although he may not understand the time sequence and demand the candy two minutes after being told he would have to wait three hours. But he does not remember at all that he was left for a week at 11 months of age while his parents went on vacation, even though he might be worried about loss.

It has been observed clinically that, as a child moves from using emotional ideas in an illogical or unconnected manner to using ideas more logically—i.e., representational differentiation (24–48 months)—he, as with earlier shifts, begins to forget what occurred in the previous state. He not only does not remember playing in his crib, but does not remember, at the age of two, bringing his baby sister home from the hospital, or the first words he said to her, or his early pretend play. He does, however, remember new events very well—e.g., a birthday on which he received presents or his pretend-play dramas. These he learned under differentiated representational capacities. Interestingly, he is likely to remember these events years later, because the state of mind (representational differentiation) continues. It is as though the emotionally meaningful memories in these different states of mind were walled off from one another. That prerepresentational memories in fact still exist may be seen when they are at times recovered during hypnosis or psychoanalysis. Perhaps, then, one's ability to remember emotionally meaningful events is related to the states of mind during which learning occurred, and the associated principles of learning during each developmental stage, as well as the emotional coloration of each event.

It would be interesting to see if early talkers (individuals who have shown evidence of early emotional thinking) have greater access to early memories than people who talked later? Or if the proverbial "absent-minded professor," because he exists in a more abstract mental state, has limited access to memories from more concrete states?

Using this model, one could postulate that what is called primary repression is really the natural forgetting that occurs as one progresses from one state of mental organization to another. We tend to remember events that were experienced in differentiated representational states because these are closer to adult states of mind. Secondary repression on this model, would occur when conflicts and anxiety lead to temporary, circumscribed patterns of dedifferentiation. The events or experiences experienced during this state are quickly lost to the differentiated level and are organized at an earlier level as one returns to a more differentiated state of mind. The elusive dream fading rapidly may illustrate this pattern.

It is perhaps of interest to consider the analytic relationship as one that facilitates, via free association and evenly hovering attention, the capacity to shift back and forth among levels of mental organization and their related states of mind. This makes possible the recovery of feelings and aspects of relationships that occurred in early representational states prior to full representational differentiation. Prerepresentational patterns, however, are difficult to reconstruct, perhaps in part because the analytic relationship, for the most part, facilitates representational elaboration in varying degrees of differentiation. Occasionally, prerepresentational somatic and behavioral patterns are "experienced" through empathic reciprocity and then elevated to a representational level. Perhaps understanding more of the state of mind accompanying each developmental phase would facilitate empathic identification and the integration of prerepresentational and representational patterns.

In summary, we have considered how the ego grows in its ability to organize experience (see Table 1). Somatic and behavioral experience is now abstracted to a higher plane, that of representation. In addition, somatic and behavioral patterns are interpreted or labeled. Most importantly, new experience is now organized and elaborated in representational modes. Representational elaboration and differentiation creates the basis for internal life to be symbolized and categorized along dimensions of self and nonself, affective meanings, time, and space. The categorization of experience in turn becomes the basis for basic ego functions, new relationship patterns, higher-level defenses, and psychosexual advances.

Selected Hypotheses* on the Biological Foundations of the Ego

The discussion on stages in ego development has focused on the way in which the infant and the young child organize experience through a series of stages. In each stage, it is seen how both environmental factors and constitutional maturational factors (biologically based developmental factors) contribute to the way in which experience is organized and the way in which it manifests itself. In this section, some specific hypotheses about the biological side of the equation, that is, how constitutional and maturational factors contribute to specific aspects of the ego, will be considered. While the hypotheses are obviously speculative in nature, they are based on clinical observations and have the capacity to be formally tested through experiments using existing technology.

*A more detailed discussion of the concepts in this chapter can be found in Greenspan (1989).

TABLE 1
Stages of Ego Development

Developmental Stage	Self-Object Relationship	Ego Organization Differentiation & Integration	Ego Functions
Homeostasis 0 – 3 mos.	Somatic preintentional world self-object.	Lack of differentiation between physical world, self & object worlds.	Global reactivity; sensory affective processing & regulation; or sensory hyper- or hyporeactivity & disregulation.
Attachment 2 – 7 mos.	Intentional part self-object.	Relative lack of differentiation of self & object; differentiation of physical world & human object world.	Part-object seeking; drive-affect elaboration; or drive-affect dampening or lability; object withdrawal; rejection or avoidance.
Somatopsychological Differentiation 3 – 10 mos.	Differentiated behavioral part self-object.	Differentiation of aspects (part) of self & object in terms of drive-affect patterns & behavior.	Part self-object differentiated interactions in initiation of & in reciprocal response to a range of drive-affect domains (e.g., pleasure dependency, assertiveness, aggression); means-ends relationship between drive-affect patterns & part self-object patterns; or undifferentiated self-object interactions; selective drive affect intensification & inhibition; constrictions of range of intrapsychic experience & regression to states of withdrawal, avoidance, or rejection (with preference for the physical world); object concretization.

Behavioral Organization; Emergence of a complex self 10 – 18 mos.

Functional (conceptual) integrated & differentiated self-object.

Integration of drive-affect behavioral patterns into relative "whole" functional self-objects.

Organized whole (in a functional behavioral sense) self-object interactions characterized by interactive chains; mobility in space (i.e., distal communication modes); functional (conceptual) abstractions of self-object properties; integration of drive-affect polarities (e.g., shift from splitting to greater integration); or self-object integration); or self-object fragmentation; self-object proximal urgency; preconceptual concretization; polarization (e.g., negative, aggressive, dependent, or avoidant, self-object pattern; regressive states including withdrawal, avoidance, rejection, somatic dedifferentiation, & object concretization).

TABLE 1 (continued)

Developmental Stage	Self-Object Relationship	Ego Organization, Differentiation & Integration	Ego Functions
Representational Capacity & Elaboration 1-1/2 – 3 yrs.	Representational self-object.	Elevation of functional behavioral self-object patterns to multisensory drive-affect invested symbols of intrapersonal & interactive experience (mental representations).	Representational self-objects characterized by mobility in time & space (e.g., creation of object representation in absence of object), drive-affect elaboration (themes ranging from dependency & pleasure to assertiveness & aggression now elaborated in symbolic form evidenced in pretend play & functional language); gradual drive-affect stability (self-object representations slowly survive intensification of drive-affect dispositions); or behavioral concretization (lack of representation); 'representational constriction (only one or another emotional theme); drive-affect lability; regressive states including withdrawal, avoidance, rejection, behavioral dedifferentiation, & object concretization.

| Representational Differentiation 2 – 4 yrs. | Differentiated, integrated representational self-object. | Abstraction of self-object representations and drive-affect dispositions into higher-level representational organization; differentiated along dimensions of self-other, time & space. | Representational differentiation characterized by genetic integration (early somatic and behavioral patterns organized by emerging mental representations) & dynamic integration (current drive-affect proclivities organized by emerging mental representations); inter-microstructural integration (i.e., affect, impulse, & thought); basic structure formation (self- & object representations abstracted into stable patterns performing ongoing ego functions of reality testing, impulse control, mood stabilization, etc.); self and object identity formation (i.e., a sense of self and object which begins to integrate past, current, & changing aspects of fantasy and reality; or representational fragmentation (genetic, dynamic, or both); absent or unstable basic structures (e.g., reality testing, impulse control); defective, polarized, or constricted (global or encapsulated) self-object identity formation. |

This section, in a sense, will attempt to amplify Freud's contention that the biological underpinnings of the ego would eventually be discovered. A few selected hypotheses will illustrate how it is now possible to propose specific biological proclivities and specific environmental patterns as a basis for the formation of certain defenses and psychopathological tendencies:

1. Deficits in auditory-verbal (symbolic) processing, coupled with environments that tend to overwhelm and confuse auditory-vocal-verbal meanings, are an important contributor to both thought disorders (when such compromises are extreme) and obsessive-compulsive disorders (when such compromises are mild or moderate).

2. Deficits in visual-spatial processing, coupled with environments that combine a lack of empathy and a lack of limit-setting, contribute to affective disorders (when the compromises are extreme) and hysterical disorders (when the compromises are mild to moderate).

3. Phobic and counterphobic disorders stem from compromises in the ability to integrate one's body in space (possibly related to vestibular functioning), particularly when such constitutional-maturational compromises are coupled with environments that provide inadequate experience, in terms of early relationship patterns, in differentiating the body from the spatial surround.

The first hypothesis proposes that thought disorders stem from two concomitant difficulties. The infant initially has difficulty in sequencing and abstracting patterns in terms of auditory-verbal experience. Such an infant, in the first few months of life, might have difficulty in abstracting the sequence of parental vocal rhythms and become overwhelmed and confused. This infant may be able to decode a rhythm that has a simple two-cadence sequence to it, but not one with a three-cadence sequence. An infant with an auditory processing difficulty therefore cannot hold in mind a sequence of sounds. Since emotional information, or affective information, is communicated in part through the parents' vocalizations, our prototypical infant also has trouble decoding early communications of emotional valence and tone.

The pathological environment for this infant does not slow down and intuitively realize that this infant needs a simple cadence. Instead it anxiously speeds up and perhaps goes to nine- or ten-beat cadences trying to gain this infant's attention. The more "glassy-eyed" this baby looks, the more anxious the parents feel and the harder they try. Conversly the parents may give up and stop vocalizing or may slow down too much. Contrary to their intentions, the parents undermine their infant even further. By 4 months, instead of tuning into the social world, alerting to the sounds of mother and father and enjoying the rhythm of their loving comments, this baby begins feeling more and more confused, finding the affective world distressing because he cannot decode even simple patterns and rhythms. By 8 months, as cause-and-effect communication is becoming dominant, the infant's ability to form cause-and-effect patterns in terms of decoding the vocal intentions of parents and responding either with motor, affective, or vocal gestures is compromised because the incoming rhythms cannot be decoded. Thus, behavior at this stage becomes chaotic and random rather than purposeful. At 15 or 16 months the toddler, rather than forming conceptual attitudes toward his auditory-vocal world, is even more confused. The negotiation of relationships across space in terms of balancing proximal and distal modalities (as discussed earlier), as well as forming a sense of a pre-representational conceptual self, is compromised.

As our prototypical infant advances to the representational stages (18–48 months), he is now struggling to organize mental representations. However, his representations are based on a foundation of disorganized vocal-verbal-affective patterns. To the degree visual-spatial organizations are intact, there may be some ability to construct organized spatial representations. However, to the degree the environment continues to operate in a pathological manner and confuse meanings, the opportunity to make corrections at the representational stage will not be available to this youngster. Assuming the prototypical environment continues to be pathological, at this stage the environment would tend to overwhelm the infant, not simply with confused meanings. Investigators such as Jackson (1960), Lidz (1973), and Wynne, Matthysse, and Cromwell (1978) have discussed faulty communication in families as a basis for thought disorders, but their findings have been ignored by biologically oriented researchers. This developmental model suggests how biology and family patterns operate together. Confused family communications at the symbolic level (i.e., switching rapidly from themes of pleasure or dependency to aggression and so forth) will not provide this youngster the opportunity to comprehend his prerepresentational world using symbolic representational capacities.

We therefore have a youngster who was born with a compromise in his ability to decode simple vocal rhythms. This interferes with the prerepresentational stages of development. At the representational level the compromise continues because the environment, instead of providing clear meanings that may help the child "figure out" the confusion from his somatic and behavioral "underbelly," so to speak, now further confuses him. We now have a thought disorder operating both at the representational, symbolic level and at prerepresentational levels, somatic and behavioral.

It is possible to also consider how an adaptive environment might help a youngster with auditory-vocal-verbal sequencing difficulties to correct this difficulty. A gifted adaptive environment might intuitively sense, as early as 2 or 3 months, that the youngster is not showing an interest in the world when vocal output becomes too complex or too rapid. Our adaptive parents therefore slow-down to a simple cadence. They do this because they are in touch with the "attention" of their infant and are constantly trying to elicit this attention, experimenting with different "input" patterns. They adjust their normal style of relatedness. This infant begins tuning in to the world and finds the human world interesting and pleasurable, much like a youngster with no processing difficulty. Now the auditory-vocal-verbal world is not overwhelming or confusing. Over time, these parents gradually add complexity in line with increasing maturation and the child's ability for decoding auditory-verbal-vocal sequences. By 8 months, therefore, simple cause-and-effect interactions are possible, and by 15 to 16 months the conceptual attitude is developing. Our toddler now integrates relationships across space and begins understanding the functional meanings of the world. The environment has slowly re-mediated this youngster's difficulty in auditory-verbal-vocal af-fective processing. In addition, to the degree that spatial abilities are intact, this adaptive family uses extra gesturing and lots of empathic repetition to help the child compensate.

At the representational level, the environment now is not only extra patient, but is especially clear on meanings, often repeating them. Differences between self and nonself, and among dependency, aggression, and sexuality, are not vague or obscured. Therefore, structural differentiations involved in the self-nonself dimension and in issues of time and space are clear. Similarly, thematic differentiations are also clear. Intact visual-spatial modes are supported to facilitate compensations. Obviously, this requires a rather stable, mature, and emotionally adaptive family structure. In this sense, the infant's potential for adaptation or maladaptation depends in part on the "luck of the draw," so to speak, in terms of the family a youngster with a "processing difficulty" is born into.

It is interesting to consider what happens when the con-stitutional-maturational difficulty is only mild and the environ-mental accommodation, though incomplete, is on the adaptive side. Here we may have a tendency toward obsessive-compulsive types of psychopathology and defenses such as isolation of af-fect. The reasoning is as follows. The infant in a relatively adaptive environment with difficulty in auditory-vocal-verbal affective decoding would tend to use his intact visual-spatial capacities instead. These capacities are usually aligned with ab-stract reasoning, as seen in science and mathematics. The visual-spatial capacity is associated with understanding continuous dimensions of experience, as in abstracting continuous dimen-sions of space in mathematics. Using this intact abstracting abil-ity, the child finds himself in an interesting dilemma. The moment-to-moment sense of what he means and what I feel in response to it is not available to him because this "sense of meaning" is often experienced via auditory-vocal-verbal affec-tive channels, and lacks quick access to the decoding of auditory-verbal affective meanings. Not sure of the moment-to-moment feelings in communication, the child goes to his intact capacity for abstraction to try to "figure out what's going on." Relying on his spatially oriented abstracting abilities, he is always trying to figure out deductively what it is he is feeling. Here we have a child who is gifted at seeing the "forest" but has trouble understanding the "trees." This is not unlike what we encounter in many obsessives. They try to use logic to deduce what for other people may be self-evident and obvious. "I must be angry because I behaved in such and such a way, or because the following circumstances presented themselves and most people would be angry in such circumstances." While such logic appears rather inefficient, for the individual who lacks access to the immediate changes in his feelings, this is the best he can do. In this sense, isolation of affect as a defense may in part be related to a tendency to isolate affect because of a lack of immediate access to moment-to-moment affective shifts. When anxiety arises in relation to underlying conflicts, the obsessive isolates his affect even further as his ability to process vocal-verbal meanings is increasingly compromised.

Another type of sensory processing deficit involves visual-spatial processing. This type of deficit would seem to predispose a person to affective and hysterical disorders. This would occur as follows. The infant with difficulty in abstracting patterns in the visual-spatial domain has trouble organizing what he sees in space rather than in organizing what he hears. This infant, for example, might initially have difficulty decoding the configuration of the face, and later on in decoding relationships as they occur across space (e.g., holding in his mind where his parents are in the house, or the existence of individuals when they are out of sight). Deficits in visual-spatial processing would seem also to be associated with a broader deficit in "putting the pieces together." The visual-spatial dimension is associated with higher levels of abstraction. Just as this dimension is used in mathematics for abstract reasoning, so it is used in everyday interactions for abstracting the "forest" from the "trees." In addition, the visual-spatial dimension very likely is involved in the deciphering of issues of affective *intensity* as opposed to issues of affective *meaning*. Early in development, meanings appear to be communicated more through the auditory-vocal mode (Caron and Caron, 1982). Further research is needed to document the importance of the visual-spatial mode in decoding affect intensity. We thus see our prototypical infant not only as having difficulty "seeing the forest for the trees," but also as having difficulty piecing together his own behaviors and moods. He therefore tends to operate in a more fragmented way. Behavior and affect tend to be labile. This tendency is often coupled with increases in sensory reactivity (e.g., tactile or auditory). Thus, our prototypical infant is an infant who is highly reactive to routine experiences. He is unable to piece these experiences together into a larger pattern, and has trouble gauging his own and other's intensity.

Our highly labile infant living in moment-to-moment affective storms may find himself in a situation in which he wants to call on his considerable abilities in auditory decoding. (It is assumed that our prototypical infant has only one modality compromised.) He tries to compensate with his auditory capacity for his difficulty in visual-spatial abstracting. Our infant has a good immediate sense of each "tree" communicated through the moment-to-moment affective meanings that his fine-tuned ear picks up. However, the more he picks up the nuance of affect from each "tree," the more overwhelmed he feels as a result of his inability to organize the "trees" into a pattern—that is, to see the "forest." We have a situation quite the opposite of what we had with disorders of thought.

The environment that does not compensate for this pattern, or that in fact accentuates it, is an environment that lacks both empathy and limit-setting. Our prototypical infant needs an environment that is empathic with his distress and extreme affective range. At the same time, he needs extraordinarily firm limits, coupled with this empathy, to provide the structure to organize patterns out of chaos. The combination of empathy on the one hand, and structure on the other, provides the infant the extra practice he needs to form visual-spatial patterns in spite of his limitations in this area. In a sense, empathy keeps the infant connected and makes him feel understood, while limit-setting provides the structure within which to organize patterns and find security.

Such an infant, however, is highly challenging to his environment and will often confuse parents and lead them into patterns of vacillation, rather than into patterns of empathy and consistent limit-setting. Parents are often indulgent because they feel bad about the pain their infants are in. But then they may feel angry and become extra punitive, only to return to more indulgent patterns, and so on and on it goes. Even in relatively healthy families, infants will draw parents into such patterns. It takes a gifted family to find the necessary balance between empathy and limit-setting. Thus, children with this pattern often feel a lack of empathy and a sense of not being emotionally connected.

Not infrequently, as with older children and adults, this sense of not being empathized with, and of feeling unconnected, may lead the child to "rev up" even more. It is as though the toddler himself tries to generate the affect necessary to create a feeling of well-being. Initially this hypomanic style is used, at least in part, in the service of reassurance. In a way, the child is saying to himself, "If they can't make me feel good, I'll try to create this good feeling all by myself." A type of denial is operating. The child revs up to create a false sense of bliss and to ignore the lack of appropriate empathy. The parent's deficit in limit-setting with such a child, which is part of the empathic failure, resembles the inconsistency often seen when parents try to discipline a very difficult child. The child's difficulty in comprehending affective intensity and spatial-affective relationships (e.g., dependence and independence) further accentuates the pattern.

Now project this deficient environment into the third and fourth years of life, when the child's representational system is being formed. Assume that this child has enough experience with adequate caregiving to form symbolic and representational capacities. One may observe a developmental sequence in which meanings are sharply demarcated but interpretations of affect intensity are distorted. The child who already tends toward poor control of affect expression (i.e., every minor frustration is a major calamity), when part of a family in which distortions of affect intensity are present, finds his initial difficulty is intensified. In order to feel connected and maintain a sense of well-being, the child may then construct affect states having no basis in reality. At the representational level, the child is able to construct not only new complex feeling states, but to give these feelings meanings. As a result, he may further distort his own affect intensity and that of others.

A limitation will occur in the organization of an affective self and object. Instead of organized, integrated self- and object representations, there may be concrete islands of self- and object representations governed by discrete affect states (e.g., the sad or depressed self, the hypomanic self, etc.), each one with little relational connection to the other. In this situation, the self is fragmented not at the level of meanings, but in terms of affect proclivities. Clinically, one is impressed that adults with affective disorders are concrete when it comes to understanding emotional patterns (both their own and others'), often in spite of their brilliance in other spheres of endeavor.

What is proposed here, therefore, is that in cases of affective disorder the deficit in the infant is a deficit in visual-spatial processing associated with affective lability and difficulty in comprehending affective intensity. When this is coupled with a lack of limit-setting and empathy in the caretaking environment, the tendency toward affective disorder becomes manifest. In contrast, when the child's tendency is coupled with sensitive empathy and limit-setting, corrective experiences can occur and the child, over the course of the first two years of life, forms internal structures that help him construct larger patterns in which to integrate his affective life.

Mild to moderate versions of this pattern produce a tendency to hysterical disorders. The reasoning behind this proposition is as follows. In the hysteric there is often an ability to comprehend moment-to-moment variations in affect, often with great fanfare, but also an inability to construct the larger patterns that allow an understanding of how life works. At times, even self-object differentiation becomes unclear under the storms of moment-to-moment affective shifts. In the hysteric, however, affective shifts do not undermine the internal structures associated with overall mood stability. An affective sense of self is relatively well formed. The prominent defense of repression, however, is based on the inability to connect up the various meanings that govern internal life. This naivete is, in part, an inability to see how the parts form a whole. Concrete fragments of meaning are therfore left to govern internal life, and each fragment appears "repressed" from its potential partner.

Another type of deficit, that in the integration one's body in space, is related to phobic patterns. This is often seen in infants who are unable to tolerate movement, vertical or horizontal, without going into extensor rigidity or evidencing other signs of panic. Such infants have trouble, initially on a physiological level (perhaps related to vestibular functioning), in dealing with movement in space. But there is also the infant who craves movement in space. Either one of these difficulties, I would argue, predisposes to phobic and counterphobic patterns; the phobic and the counterphobic, as part of their physical makeup, have at their core a difficulty in organizing somatic and, later, psychological space. To the degree that this vulnerability is present, aspects of the inanimate environment, which may be viewed as a component of psychological space, become imbued with dynamically relevant meanings. A fragmented sense of the body in space is present early in life. Later, meanings for "space," while dynamically based, occur in relation to this already vulnerable foundation. Because the early fragmentation predisposes one to a lack of differentiation of one's psychological body space, displacements and projections of meanings onto "spaces" is more likely.

One may wonder why, if the disorders discussed above have biological-maturational underpinnings, they manifest themselves only in later childhood, late adolescence, or even adulthood. Why do these disorders not manifest themselves fully in early infancy, when the biological maturational pattern is first manifested? One hypothesis is that the time of onset for most of these disorders is determined, at least in part, by the fact that each stage in ego development is characterized by new capacities for processing information. These new capacities can "overload" the system as well as enhance it. Each stage in ego development has its cognitive as well as its affective components. (To be sure, it also has its neurochemical and neurophysiological components.) For example, consider the period of late adolescence, when hypothetical deductive reasoning is becoming more organized. This is a great boon to figuring out one's emotional life, particularly as regards identity formation. Yet the capacity, cognitively, for hypothetical deductive reasoning (which involves considering the future) and, emotionally, for organizing an identity that integrates past, present, and future, can.overtax a vulnerable structure. It is like a computer that is barely dealing with cross-sectional information now having to deal with future information as well. To the degree that the existing equipment is substantial and flexible, new information and capacities may enhance its functioning. But to the degree that it is marginal to begin with, we may see information overload and therefore regressive solutions. These regressive solutions may be what leads to the onset of manifest psychopathology. Interestingly, we also see certain types of difficulties, such as panic reactions and social withdrawal, evidence themselves at 18 months to 2 years, when the infant is just learning to symbolize and represent his world. Symbols should help the infant organize. But, if the ability to sequence information is already vulnerable, they may simply overload the system.

In summary, this section has advanced several hypotheses related to the biological underpinnings of the ego. They are (1) that auditory-vocal-verbal affective sequencing difficulties, coupled with environments that confuse meaning, contribute to thought disorders; (2) that moderate to mild versions of this disturbance contribute to obsessive-compulsive disorders; (3) that visual-spatial sequencing difficulties, coupled with environments that lack limit-setting and empathy, contribute to affective disorders; (4) that mild to moderate versions of this disorder contribute to hysterical disorders; and (5) that difficulties in integrating body movement in space (perhaps related to vestibular dysfunction) contribute to phobic and counterphobic disorders. These hypotheses provide interesting avenues both for research and for preventive applications.

References

Ainsworth, M., Bell, S.M., & Stayton, D. (1974) Infant-mother attachment and social development: Socialization as a product of reciprocal responsiveness to signals. In: *The Integration of the Child into A Social World*, ed. M. Richards. Cambridge: Cambridge University Press, pp. 99–135.

Bell, S. (1970), The development of the concept of object as related to infant-mother attachment. *Child Development,* 41:219–311.

Bernfeld, S. (1929), *Psychology of the Infant.* London: Routledge.

Bowlby, J. (1952), *Maternal Care and Mental Health.* WHO Monograph Series No. 2. Geneva: World Health Organization.

———— (1969), *Attachment and Loss: Vol. 1. Attachment.* London, Hogarth Press.

Brazelton, T.B., Koslowski, B., & Main, N. (1974), The origins of reciprocity: The early mother-infant interaction. In: *The Effect of the Infant on Its Caregiver,* ed. M. Lewis & L.A. Rosenblum. New York: Wiley, pp. 49–76.

Bruch, H. (1973), *Eating Disorders: Obesity, Anorexia Nervosa and the Person Within.* New York: Basic Books.

Caron, A.J., & Caron, R.F. (1982), Cognitive development in early infancy. In: *Review of Human Development,* ed. T. Fields, A. Huston, H. Quay, L. Troll, & G. Finley. New York: Wiley, pp. 107–147.

Charlesworth, W.R. (1969), The role of surprise in cognitive development. In: *Studies in Cognitive Development: Essays in Honor of Jean Piaget,* ed. E. Elkind & J.H. Flavell. London: Oxford University Press, pp. 257–314.

Cravioto, J., & Delicardie, E. (1973), Environmental correlates of severe clinical malnutrition and language development in survivors from kwashiorkor or marasmus. In: *Nutrition, the Nervous System and Behavior,* PAHO Scientific Publication No. 251. Washington, D.C.

Ekman, P. (1972), Universals and cultural differences in facial expressions of emotion. *Nebraska Symposium on Motivation.* Lincoln: University of Nebraska Press.

Emde, R.N., Gaensbauer, T.J., & Harmon, R.J. (1976), Emotional expression in infancy: A biobehavioral study. *Psychological Issues,* Monograph 37. New York: International Universities Press.

Erikson, E.H. (1959), Identity and the life cycle. *Psychological Issues,* Monograph 1. New York: International Universities Press.

Escalona, S. (1968), *The Roots of Individuality.* Chicago: Aldine.

Fraiberg, S. (1979), Treatment modalities in an infant mental health program. Paper presented at the training institute on "Clinical Approaches to Infants and Their Families" sponsored by The National Center for Clinical Infant Programs, Washington, D.C.

Freud, A. (1965), *Normality and Pathology in Childhood.* New York: International Universities Press.

———— & Burlingham, D. (1945), *Infants Without Families.* New York: International Universities Press.

———— ———— (1965), *War and Children.* New York: International Universities Press.

Freud, S. (1900), The interpretation of dreams. *Standard Edition,* 4/5. London, England: Hogarth Press, 1953.

———— (1905), Three essays on the theory of sexuality. *Standard Edition,* 7:135–242. London:Hogarth Press, 1953.

———— (1911), Formulations on the two principles of mental functioning. *Standard Edition,* 12:218–226. London: Hogarth Press, 1958.

Gewirtz, J.L. (1965), The course of infant smiling in four child rearing environments in Israel. In: *Determinants of Infant Behavior,* ed. B.M. Foss. Vol. 3. London: Methuen, pp. 205–260.

———— (1969), Levels of conceptual analysis in environment-infant interaction research. *Merill-Palmer Quart.*, 15:9–47.

Gouin-Décarie, T. (1965), *Intelligence and Affectivity in Early Childhood: An Experimental Study of Jean Piaget's Object Concept and Object Relations.* New York: International Universities Press.

Greenspan, S.I. (1979), Intelligence and adaptation: An integration of psychoanalytic and Piagetian developmental psychology. *Psychological Issues,* Monograph 47/48. New York: International Universities Press.

———— (1981), *Psychopathology and Adaptation in Infancy and Early Childhood: Principles of Clinical Diagnosis and Preventive Intervention.* New York: International Universities Press.

———— Wieder, S., Lieberman, A.F., Nover, R., Lourie, R., & Robinson, M. (eds.) (1987), Infants in Multirisk Families: Case Studies in Preventive Intervention. In: *Clinical Infant Reports: No. 3.* New York: International Universities Press.

———— (1989), The development of the ego: Biological and environmental specificity in the psychopathological developmental process and the selection and construction of ego defenses. *J. Amer. Psychoanal. Assn.* 37(3).

Hartmann, H. (1939), *Ego Psychology and the Problem of Adaptation.* New York: International Universities Press. 1958.

Izard, C. (1978), On the development of emotions and emotion-cognition relationships in infancy. In: *The Development of Affect,* ed. M. Lewis & L.A. Rosenblum. New York: Plenum.

Jackson, D. (1960), *The Etiology of Schizophrenia.* New York: Basic Books.

Kernberg, O.F. (1975), *Borderline Conditions and Pathological Narcissism.* New York: Aronson.

Klaus, M., & Kennell, J. (1976), *Maternal-Infant Bonding: The Impact of Early Separation or Loss on Family Development.* St. Louis: Mosby.

Kohut, H. (1971), *The Analysis of the Self.* New York: International Universities Press.

Lewis, M., & Horowitz, L., (1977), Intermodal personal Scheme in Infancy: Perception within a common auditory visual space. Paper presented at the Eastern Psychological Association, Boston, April.

Lidz, T. (1973), *Origins and Treatment of Schizophrenic Disorders.* New York: Basic Books.

Lipsitt, L. (1966), Learning processes of newborns. *Merrill-Palmer Quart.,* 12:45–71.

Mahler, M.S., Pine, F., & Bergman, A. (1975), *The Psychological Birth of the Human Infant.* New York: Basic Books.

Meltzoff, A., & Moore, K. (1977), Imitation of facial and manual gestures by human neonates. *Science,* 1977, 198:75–78.

Murphy, L.B. (1974), *The Individual Child.* Washington, D.C.: U.S. Government Printing Office.

———— & Moriarity, A. (1976), *Vulnerability, Coping and Growth.* New Haven: Yale University Press.

Nemiah, J.C. (1977), *Alexithymia: Theories and Models.* Proceedings of the Eleventh European Conference on Psychosomatic Research. Basel: Karger.

Piaget, J. (1962), The stages of the intellectual development of the child. In: *Childhood Psychopathology,* ed. S.I. Harrison and J.F. McDermott. New York: International Universities Press, 1972, pp. 157–166.

Provence, S., ed. (1983), Infants and parents: Clinical case reports. *Clinical Infant Reports No. 2.* New York: International Universities Press.
———— & Naylor, A. (1983), *Working with Disadvantaged Parents and Their Children: Scientific and Practice Issues.* New Haven: Yale University Press.
Sander, L. (1962), Issues in early mother-child interaction. *J. Amer. Acad. Child Psychiat.,* 1:141–166.
Skinner, B.F. (1938), *The Behavior of Organisms.* New York: Appleton.
Sorce, J.F., & Emde, R.N. (1981), Mother's presence is not enough: The effect of emotional availability on infant exploration. *Developmental Psychol.,* 17:737–745.
Spelke, E., & Owsley, C. (1979), Intermodal Exploration and Knowlédge. *Infant Behavior and Development,* 2:13–27.
Spitz, R. (1946), Anaclitic depression: An inquiry into the genesis of psychiatric conditions in early childhood, II. *The Psychoanalytic Study of the Child,* 2:313–342. New York: International Universities Press.
———— (1965), *The First Year of Life (with W. Cobliner).* New York: International Universities Press.
Sroufe, L.A. (1979), Socioemotional development. In: *Handbook of Infant Development,* ed. J. Osofsky. New York: Wiley.
———— & Waters, E. (1977), Attachment as an organizational construct. *Child Development,* 48:1184–1199.
———— ———— & Matas, L. (1974), Contextual determinants of infant affective response. In: *The Origins of Fear,* ed. M. Lewis & L.A. Rosenblum. New York: Wiley, pp. 49–72.
Stern, D. (1974a), The goal and structure of mother-infant play. *J. Amer. Acad. Child Psychiat.,* 13:402–421.
———— (1974b), Mother and infant at play: The dyadic interaction involving facial, vocal and gaze behaviors. In: *The Effect of the Infant on Its Caregiver,* ed. M. Lewis and L.A. Rosenblum. New York, Wiley, pp. 187–213.
———— (1987), Affect in the context of the infant's lived experience: Some considerations. *Internat. J. Psycho-Anal.,* 69(2):233–239.
Tomkins, S. (1963), *Affect, Imagery, Consciousness,* Vol. I. New York: Springer.
Werner, H., & Kaplan, B. (1963), *Symbol Formation.* New York: Wiley.
Winnicott, D.W. (1931), *Clinical Notes on Disorders of Childhood.* London: Heinemann.
Wynne, L., Matthysse, S., & Cromwell, R. (1978), *The Nature of Schizophrenia: New Approaches to Research and Treatment.* New York: Wiley.

4

Toward a Psychoanalytic Theory of Affect: I. The Organizational Model and its Propositions

ROBERT N. EMDE, M.D.

There is virtual unanimity in today's psychoanalytic literature on the point that the theory of affects in psychoanalysis is unsatisfactory (see e.g., Castelnuovo-Tedesco, 1974; Arlow, 1977; Green, 1977; Limentani, 1977). Paradoxically, this state of affairs exists in spite of the following facts: that from its historical beginnings, affects have been a central concern of psychoanalysis; that today affects are acknowledged as central in clinical work; and that affects are even centered in what has been regarded as "the human core" for psychoanalysis (Rangell, 1967). Freud felt that his affect theory was incomplete and unsatisfactory and that it contained contradictions within it (Schur, 1969; Green, 1977). Since Freud there seems to be a consensus that the historical evolution of the psychoanalytic theory of affects has lagged behind its other aspects, and several have hinted that the framework of psychoanalytic metapsychology may have hampered its development (Klein, 1967; Gill, 1976; Schafer, 1976; Green, 1977).

In a penetrating analysis of Freud's theory of sexuality, Klein (1969) pointed out that Freud, in effect, had two theories: a low-level theory which emerged from his increasingly rich clinical experience, and another, more abstract one linked to his metapsychology, involving a quasi-physiological model of energic force seeking discharge, and emerging more out of a need for theoretical consistency than from data. Further, Klein argued that Freud's two theories of sexuality are on different

165

logical planes and are inconsistent with each other in critical ways. He concluded that the clinical theory is the more useful in today's world, partly because it is susceptible to continued empirical testing and growth. This chapter will make a similar argument concerning Freud's theoretical propositions about affects. However, unlike Klein, I will not detail the inconsistencies between "Freud's two theories of affect." The interested reader can do that by consulting several excellent reviews (Rapaport, 1953; Schur, 1969; Arlow, 1977; Green, 1977) and by applying Klein's framework. In addition, rather than downgrading Freud's more abstract theoretical propositions, I argue for considering them as important in a broader historical picture: (1) there was a progressive evolution in Freud's thinking about affects as a consequence of his taking into account increasing amounts of data from the clinical psychoanalytic situation; and (2) there was a general change of scientific zeitgeist which took place over the near half century of Freud's productivity. The latter led to changes in models guiding his more abstract propositions about affects. However, these models were less clearly envisioned, less clearly articulated, and changed more slowly than did his clinical formulations. As a result, many unresolved contradictions remained in his writings.

By selectively citing a number of Freud's later propositions and the clinical psychoanalytic literature since Freud, I attempt to show that psychoanalytic models of affects have continued to evolve in response to the dual aspects of clinical data and contemporary scientific zeitgeist. Further, I argue that a similar evolution has taken place in psychology in general, as part of the same zeitgeist, but with the accumulation of experimental, developmental, and ethological data, as opposed to clinical data. Finally, I consider recent developmental research. There the same historical perspective highlights a changing view of the infant as well as new data and questions relevant to a more comprehensive psychoanalytic theory of affects.

In the interest of showing the elements of continuity in historical change, my summary of changes in Freud's thinking is selective. It picks up threads to the present rather than attempting to be complete, its sole purpose being to provide the historical background for an emerging organizational model of affects. It is my thesis that an organizational model makes the best sense in terms of contemporary biology and psychology and allows an appreciation of evolving continuity in the literature of psychoanalysis. Such a model is bolstered by clinical propositions from the last four decades, can make use of new data from outside the clinical setting, and can raise useful questions for emerging editions of our psychoanalytic theory of affects.

Evolution in Freud's Thinking about Affects

A Changing Zeitgeist

As used in this chapter, the concept of a scientific zeitgeist (roughly translated "spirit of the times") consists of an often unacknowledged common point of view and way of approaching inquiry. In effect, it represents a shared world view, one which incorporates diverging models from many scientific disciplines and one which implicitly operates so as to stimulate, direct, and sustain investigative pursuits. It has been customary among historians and philosophers of science to describe a zeitgeist in terms of the physics of the day, adding chemistry and biology afterward and dealing with psychology and the social sciences little or not at all. Such a custom is not arbitrary since there are hierarchical arrangements among the sciences, as Platt (1964) and Boulding (1956) have asserted, and since there is usually a temporal sequence in which theoretical changes in physics precede those in chemistry and biology and in which changes in psychology come more slowly afterward. Thus, the views of nineteenth-century physics changed markedly in the early and middle twentieth century in terms of moving from certainty and reductionism to relativity, quanta, complementarity, and the complexities of the universe of small particles. Biology (especially via its "bridge" discipline of molecular biology) followed with an array of advances portraying a movement from reductionism to organized complexity. Psychology moved more slowly, as this chapter documents for the theory of affects.

I believe that the psychologist Freud was partly in tune

with this changing zeitgeist and well in advance of the rest of his field. He also moved from models involving mechanistic certainty to those involving organized complexity. However, this was not because of his extensive communications with other disciplines (unfortunately, the historical fact is that he was isolated from the university during his most productive years), but rather because of the data he generated by the psychoanalytic clinical method. It is also an unfortunate historical fact, however, that for reasons of theoretical consistency, much of what was fostered by earlier models remained in Freud's later thinking; this resulted not only in contradictions, not only in two "theories," but in two separate languages, as scholars have pointed out (Holt, 1967; Grossman and Simon, 1969).

Early S-R Models

Freud's earlier models are reviewed here in schematic form solely for the purpose of indicating the magnitude of subsequent change. The influence of his early education in the reductionistic-mechanistic environment of the Helmholtz school fueled by the fervor of *Naturwissenschaft* has been documented in the classic paper of Bernfeld (1944) and the influence of his neurological training in reflexology by Amacher (1965) and Holt (1965). These influences provided a background for what I shall refer to as Freud's two early stimulus-response (S-R) models for affects. Both are mechanistic models in which affects are the passive, predictable resultants of stimuli. Affects are separate from cognition and are apt to be disorganizing of ongoing behavior.

In Variant A, exemplified in his early writings on neurosis (Freud 1895a, 1895b), the stimulus is external, although influenced by internal context.[1] There is a clash between ideas (I)

---

[1] Pribram and Gill (1976) in their contemporary analysis of Freud's 1895 "Project" emphasize that although affect was viewed as initiated by external stimulation, it was augmented by consequent endogenous excitation; in other words, Freud viewed affect as resulting from environmental activation of charged memories. While these authors point out that there have been a variety of interpretations of Freud's early model of affects (e.g., some authors have interpreted that Freud meant affect to be equivalent to excitation, while others have not), their view in no way contradicts the historical view of a primary reflex or S-R model. I believe there is only a difference of emphasis from the view presented here, partly resulting from what one chooses to highlight in constructing a meaningful historical account.

and unacceptable affects (A)—a clash which leads to repression of ideas and "damming up" of affects. This is represented in the diagram below.

Variant A: Stimulus External

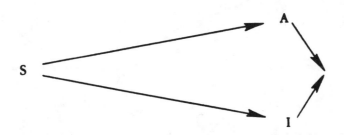

In Variant B, elaborated during the period of flourishing libido theory (roughly 1900–1923), the external S has been replaced by an internal S, or drive (D). In this model, drive discharge channels are conceived of as having relative independence; that is, affects and ideas are not necessarily in opposition or interaction. As this model became elaborated, the main stimulus was considered internal, although influenced by external context. The documentation for this particular schematic has been spelled out best by Rapaport (1953, 1959). The diagram is presented below.

A seductive aspect of the S-R models, perhaps contributing to their longevity, is their promise of simple quantification. From a practical or a theoretical standpoint, an increased S should necessarily lead to an increased R. As is well known, Freud's drive-reduction model of affects persisted in spite of his acknowledgment that differences in qualities of affects could not be accounted for by differences in quantities of drive. As Green (1977) relates so nicely, Freud postulated that the psychic apparatus is supposed to seek pleasure and at the same time avoid tension. This resulted in a dilemma which Freud solved

Variant B: Stimulus Internal

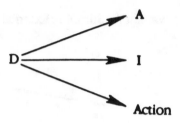

by placing greater emphasis on the avoidance of unpleasure and then envisioning pleasure as a lessening of tension. "Having put the qualitative dimension of affect second to its quantitative variations," Green notes, "Freud conceives of affect above all as a disorganizing factor in the psychic apparatus" (p. 131). But Freud's uncertainty and dissatisfaction with this formulation also persisted. The passage below highlights this fact.

> Pleasure and unpleasure, therefore, cannot be referred to an increase or decrease of a quantity (which we described as 'tension due to stimulus'), although they obviously have a great deal to do with that factor. It appears that they depend, not on this quantitative factor, but on some characteristic of it which we can only describe as a qualitative one. If we were able to say what this qualitative characteristic is, we should be much further advanced in psychology. Perhaps it is the rhythm, the temporal sequence of changes, rises and falls in the quantity of stimulus. We do not know. . . . [Freud, 1923, p. 160]

A Later Organizational Model

As Schur (1969) points out, the early roots of a major change in Freud's thinking can be found in his definition of affects in the *Introductory Lectures* (1916–1917). There he states:

And what is an affect in the dynamic sense? It is in any case something highly composite. An affect includes in the first place particular motor innervations or discharges and secondly certain feelings; the latter are of two kinds—perceptions of the motor actions that have occurred and the direct feelings of pleasure and unpleasure which, as we say, give the affect at the essence of an affect. We seem to see deeper in the case of some affects and to recognize that the core which holds the combination we have described together is the repetition of some particular significant experience . . . placed in the prehistory not of the individual but of the species. [pp. 395–396]

Here we see affects are defined as "highly composite." They are, in other words, complex structures which include motoric perceptions and direct feelings of pleasure and unpleasure. Furthermore, Freud states that "the core which holds the combination . . . together" is rooted in biology ("in the prehistory not of the individual but of the species"). The conceivable implication that affects may be adaptive, not necessarily a resultant of conflict in ontogeny, was not developed further by Freud. However, that this "composite state" could be conscious or unconscious and included cognitive elements was elaborated in later works (Freud, 1923, 1926, 1930, 1933; see also the careful documentation of this point in Shur, 1969).

The elaboration of this line of thinking led to what I would designate Freud's later organizational model of affects. In this model, affects are active principles. Unlike the S-R model, this one is not mechanistic; affects are organizing (involving negentropy instead of entropy), and they are inseparable from cognition. Freud was impressed with two phenomena which led to this virtual sea-change in his thinking. One was *unconscious guilt* as an "agency" (Freud, 1923); the other was *unconscious anxiety* as an "agency" (Freud, 1926). These two affects were thus recognized as "relatively independent factors," as Schafer (1964) later described them, representing active principles which monitor and organize activity, thought, defenses, and symptoms. They were considered signals rather than discharge phenomena, no longer intimately connected with the drives, but located in the ego (or superego), and they were acknowledged as organizing and motivating factors. At the same time, as the structural model of the mind replaced the topographical one, I would say that by implication these affects functioned not only as unconscious monitors, but also as monitors at the preconscious and conscious levels. While it is true that Freud in a number of places stated that affects must be conscious, he clearly stated that anxiety and guilt function unconsciously, making this most explicit in *Inhibitions, Symptoms and Anxiety* (1926) and *Civilization and Its Discontents* (1930).

Because of its complexity and the multiple interactions of its elements, the organizational model does not lend itself to a simple diagramatic representation. Nonetheless, it may be useful to restate its multiple aspects. Affects are composite states including motoric perceptions and direct feelings of pleasure and unpleasure; they are rooted in biology; they include cognition and are evaluative; they function unconsciously as well as consciously; and they organize mental functioning and behavior. All of these properties are included in Freud's formulation that affects are signals, seated in the ego. Although Freud elaborated the signal formulation for anxiety, there is an implied framework for other signal affects, as others have since pointed out (Jacobson, 1953; Engel, 1962a, Schur, 1969; Brenner, 1975). The signal formulation in general describes how affects have a regulatory role, one which often functions automatically. Furthermore, it includes the notion that signal anxiety prevents one from becoming overwhelmed by states of helplessness which in turn are linked to specific, hierarchically arranged early affective structures which have been experienced in development.

Propositions from Psychoanalysis Since Freud

Major propositions about affects from psychoanalytic writers since Freud give a strong impression of the pervasiveness of an organizational model. They can be grouped under five headings.

1. Affects are central in clinical psychoanalysis; they are good

guides for understanding motivation and states of mind (ego states).
The psychoanalytic literature since Freud contains a clear consensus that affects are central in clinical work, that they are
related to unconscious fantasies, and that understanding affects
is a key to therapeutic outcome from the viewpoint of either
analyst or patient (e.g., see Brierley, 1937; Rangell, 1967; Brenner, 1974; Castelnuovo-Tedesco, 1974; Arlow, 1977; Green,
1977; Limentani, 1977). Over the decades, models of the mind
may have shifted and aspects of psychoanalytic metapsychology
may have undergone drastic revision, but what has remained
constant is the professional devotion of analysts to the standard
of maintaining the psychoanalytic clinical situation with a goal
of understanding unconscious fantasy and liberating developmental processes—what Greenacre (1971) has called "emotional
growth." In this endeavor, practicing analysts have developed
the increasing conviction that affects are essential in the day-
to-day search for meaning. Affects have a major role in communication; they engage the listener, allow for transient empathic identifications by the analyst, and are essential for
understanding analytic material (see Landauer, 1938; Schafer,
1964; Rangell, 1967; Schur, 1969). The words of Rangell emphasize this point:

> As dreams are the royal road, so affects are major roads,
> indeed indispensable ones, to the unconscious. They con-
> stitute a language in themselves, both pre-verbal and para-
> verbal. . . . The analysis of affect goes a long way towards
> psychoanalysis. Dreams and free associations add the ac-
> companying ideation. All are necessary for the total product.
> [p. 192]

2. *Affects are adaptive; they are autonomous ego structures as
well as in conflict.* The adaptive point of view in psychoanalysis,
articulated by Hartmann in 1939 and later elaborated by Hartmann, Kris, and Loewenstein in the 1940s and 1950s, led to a
broadening of psychoanalytic theory. Although affects were not
a particular focus of their own writings, it is striking that others
have not used the adaptive point of view to explore seriously
the theory of affects. Freud's formulations that signal affects
are located within the ego (or superego), that they include cog-

nitive aspects, that they organize mental functioning and behavior (both conscious and unconscious), and that they are rooted in biology surely speak of their adaptive functions. As alluded to in the previous section, these propositions about affect have generally been accepted in the clinical writings of psychoanalysis since Freud. Many have written about affects as serving adaptive functions, but there has most often been an assumption that they must be considered derivatives of drive, manifestations of conflict, and analyzed according to the model of symptoms, i.e., as compromise formations (Fenichel, 1941; Lewin, 1965; Arlow, 1977). However, my review of the analytic literature since Freud reveals a seemingly obvious but unstated theme: *Affects are in the conflict-free ego sphere as well as in the conflict sphere; furthermore, they represent apparatuses of primary autonomy as well as of secondary autonomy.*[2]

Many have pointed out that in early infancy the infant must maintain affective contacts with the mother in order to survive. Even Rapaport (1959), so committed to his systematization of Freud's drive discharge model of affects, was forced to admit that "affects seem to start even in human beings to some extent . . . in what Hartmann called states of adaptedness [with] . . . a limited attunement to certain external reality stimuli, such as seen in the startle . . . and smile . . ." (p. 508). The work of Spitz, cited by Rapaport, is well known in both analytic and infancy research circles and will be discussed further in the next chapter, where this point is taken up in greater detail.

A remarkable historical note concerning autonomous affects is provided by considering two European contributions offered independently of Hartmann's work. One was read at the Vienna Psychoanalytic Institute on the occasion of Freud's eightieth birthday (Landauer, 1938); the other was read the same year before the Fourteenth International Psychoanalytic Congress at Marienbad (Brierley, 1937). Paradoxically, although I consider these works to have emerged directly from Freud's later clinical formulations and to have extended them

[2] The only prior direct statements to this effect I have found were by Nathaniel Ross and Edward Joseph, who commented during discussions in a panel on affects at a meeting of the American Psychoanalytic Association reported by Castelnuovo-Tedesco (1974).

with rich new organizational hypotheses about primary affects, they seem to have had little direct or immediate influence on psychoanalytic thinking. In the view which they articulated then and which others have discovered more recently, affects exist as primary structures early in development and represent relatively independent qualities of experience and behavior which are not necessarily derivatives of drive. Implicit in this view has been that there are developmental hierarchies of affect structures with early, simple reflex-like structures and later, more complex structures involving higher forms of representation, with and without conflict. With maturation and development, the number of affects increase. (In addition to these authors, one should see the reviews of Schafer in 1964 and of Schur in 1969.) Needless to say, the early Brierley and Landauer articles provide a rich source of hypotheses for both clinical and developmental research exploration. Some of these will be considered later.

3. *Affects are continuous aspects of our lives.* Another feature of the clinical literature is a growing appreciation that affects are not intermittent, extreme, or disruptive states; they are not generally "traumatic." Rather, they are continuous aspects of our lives, providing interest, engagement, boredom, frustration, and other colorations or states of involvement on the pleasure-unpleasure continuum. This organizational proposition was hinted at in 1953 by Jacobson, who later called moods a "barometer of ego functioning" (Jacobson, 1953, 1957), and subsequently has been made more explicit by others (e.g., Blau, 1955; Novey, 1961; Rangell, 1967; Castelnuovo-Tedesco, 1974).

4. *Affects are vital ingredients for human social relatedness.* In spite of the fact that Freud did not give explicit recognition to this in his organizational model, it is clear from subsequent clinical writers that affects are vital ingredients for human social relatedness. Not only are affects constant factors in our existence but "no human relatedness is conceivable without affective participation," according to Novey (1961, p. 22). Many, including Landauer (1938), Schafer (1964), and Rangell (1967), have pointed to the centrality of affects for object relations. The latter has emphasized their essential functions in the analytic

situation in terms of engaging the listener and stimulating caring and empathy.

From another angle, the very definition of affects may require the inclusion of their social aspects. They are acknowledged as important social communicators in early development (Rapaport, 1953; Schur, 1969; Basch, 1976), and these communicative aspects are often deemed an essential part of the psychoanalytic process (Spitz, 1956; Greenacre, 1971). Schafer (1964) has expressed that early important internalized objects need to be reexperienced affectively for a successful analysis and that many affects express basic identifications. Since affects are considered to be organizing factors in the development of the ego, especially in self-object relations (Brierley, 1937; Spitz, 1959; Schafer, 1964), it is not surprising that they are reactivated in the transference and play an important role in the real relationship with the analyst as well.

Schur (1969), in an extraordinarily rich essay in which he points to the essential link between cognition and affect in Freud's organizational model, provides grounds for considering that affect is linked inseparably with social experience. In a developmental hypothesis, he states that certain cognitive elements and qualities of affect may be linked early in a common fashion throughout our species, thereby ensuring a certain invariance to some aspects of affective experience due to constant factors in human social relatedness, stemming from regularities inherent in the infant-caregiver relationship, and from a reciprocity of adaptation inherent in the human condition. It should be emphasized, however, that neither Schur nor other psychoanalyst-clinicians ignore the rich variety of affective experiences which reflect the uniqueness of individuals, the uniqueness of environments, and the uniqueness of their interactions during development.

5. *There are signal affects other than anxiety.* Are there organized systems for signal affects other than anxiety? Those considering this question since Freud seem to answer in the affirmative. Jacobson (1953), Engel (1962a), Schur (1969), and Brenner (1974) suggest that Freud's formulations about signal functions can be applied usefully to a variety of other affects, pleasant as well as unpleasant, and that there is a need for

theory building in this area. Based on my review I would advance the thesis that we already have a strong beginning for such a formulation regarding another complex affect besides anxiety, namely depression, and that this formulation is likely to be applied more widely. Further, the time seems to have arrived for a more general model for signal affects, one similar to what Engel (1962a) began.

That there is a developmental childhood sequence involving signal depression or "helplessness" which bears analogy to Freud's original developmental sequence involving anxiety, and that this signal anxiety system evolves to regulate self-esteem and avoid depression, has been suggested by a line of thinking which began with Bibring (1953) and has included Engel (1962a), Anthony (1975), Brenner (1975), and Kaufman (1977). To detail the potential richness of this formulation, which involves adaptive considerations not only from clinical psychoanalysis but also from developmental psychology and the study of nonhuman primate behavior, is impossible in this overview. I will illustrate by discussing two of the many contributors.

The work of Engel (1962a, 1962b) and his collaborators (Engel, Reichsman, and Segal, 1956; Engel and Schmale, 1972) is a rich source of developmental and clinical psychoanalytic hypotheses. Engel postulates two basic biological response patterns to stress, reflecting the way the central nervous system is organized. These are the fight-flight pattern and the conservation-withdrawal pattern, the first involving activity and engagement of the environment (serving to avoid or control the stress), and the second involving inactivity and withdrawal from the environment (conserving energy when stress cannot be managed). These reaction patterns are postulated to be biological precursors of later "affect states" of anxiety and depression. Further, in addition to their biological underpinnings, the complex affect states of anxiety and depression each have their own hierarchical developmental histories, their own propensities for sustained mood, and their own signal affect systems. Engel's original observations for this formulation came from an infant, Monica, who had a gastric fistula and who, when approached by a stranger, had a diminished amount of gastric secretion of hydrochloric acid and fell asleep, a pattern of a response which occurred instead of the more expectable one of distress. Subsequent support for Engel's formulation has come from his extensive experience in the practice of psychosomatic medicine as well as in the practice of psychoanalysis. Further discussion of Engel's hypotheses for studying infancy has been presented elsewhere (Emde and Harmon, 1978).

Based on his clinical experience, Brenner (1975) has set forth the view that anxiety is not the only affect which characteristically triggers defenses in psychic conflict; depressive affect does also. Brenner's definition of affect (1974) like that of Schur (1969) emphasizes that there are sensations of pleasure or unpleasure with associated ideas. Anxiety is unpleasure associated with the idea that something bad is about to happen. Depression, by contrast, is unpleasure associated with the idea that something bad has happened. The something bad may be at any stage of psychosexual organization; it may be a narcissistic injury or humiliation, an object loss, a bad deed, or a punishment. It obviously reflects an individual's particular memory and experience. These affects always have ideas associated with them; when there is anxiety or depression and a patient is unaware of its content, the analytic view is that the referents for the affect are unconscious. Signal depression can act much as signal anxiety, as a motive for defense or action. Brenner (1975) states the varying formulae for defense: For anxiety it would be "if I do A, then B will not happen"; for depression it would be "if I do A, then B will change, it will stop happening or will stop making me suffer so or both" (p. 17). In terms of therapy, "one must reconstruct, as far as possible, not only what dangers were, and unconsciously still are, a part of the patient's anxiety, but also what calamities were, and unconsciously still are, a part of his depressive affect" (p. 26).

It should be reemphasized that this area is a lively one for useful theory building. Sandler and Joffe (Sandler, 1960; Joffe and Sandler, 1968) have proposed a "safety principle" whereby a feeling of safety has a regulatory role as a signal affect. Previous suggestions made by Jacobson (1953) and Engel (1962a) that positive affects could also have signal functions are a theoretical territory which remains unexplored.

A Current Controversy Concerning Models for
Psychoanalysis

Recently Freud's "metapsychology" has undergone sharp criticism. Several have pursued Klein's mode of thinking and have documented inconsistencies in the dynamic and economic theories (Holt, 1965, 1976; Schafer, 1970, 1976; Klein, 1967) and in the structural theory as well (Holt, 1975). In agreement with Klein, these authors as well as others (Gill, 1976; Rubenstein, 1976) conclude that there are two kinds of theory in psychoanalysis, and that the clinical theory is increasingly useful while the metapsychological theory is not. Aside from inconsistencies, it is pointed out that the latter is based on an outmoded biological model that has encouraged the reification of concepts and has remained static. A view which has emerged from this criticism is that the metapsychology is a separate universe of discourse, one related to the natural science mode of inquiry, and that it is irrelevant to contemporary psychoanalysis. According to this view, the proper psychology for psychoanalysis is a "pure" or personal "psychology" involving intentions or meanings (Gill, 1976; Klein, 1976) and, according to Schafer (1975, 1976), it should involve an "action language" of verbs and adverbs which eschews nouns and adjectives. Another part of this view is that any metapsychology based on a natural science framework is not useful for a clinical theory based on meaning and sufficient unto itself.

In spite of the cogency of many criticisms leveled at metapsychological theory, I disagree with this conclusion. I believe that a broader historical perspective is enlightening and furthermore that a semantic problem may be clouding the issue. Psychoanalytic metapsychology can be understood in two senses: (1) as referring to an orienting set of propositions and models of mental functioning which are useful for today's psychoanalysts; and (2) as referring to a set of propositions and models delineated by Freud (dynamic, economic, and structural) and later extended by others (adaptive and genetic, as enumerated by Rapaport and Gill in 1959). The second connotation for "metapsychology" is necessarily fixed within a specific historical context whereas the first implies ongoing change—change according to what is useful for contemporary science and clinical practice. When a position is taken that psychoanalytic metapsychology is not relevant in today's world, it is often unclear which connotation is being cited. If models are allowed to remain fixed, they are soon understood to represent limiting cases or instances, the limitations of which were not appreciated at the time of their origin; because increasing knowledge extends what we can see, older models necessarily become viewed as partial, imperfect, and anachronistic. Such is the history of science, traceable in any discipline.

But older models need not be ignored; in fact, an understanding of the historical context for older models is necessary for constructing newer ones. The point is not to discount metapsychology but to strive constantly for models which will explain and predict data from multiple domains—clinical psychoanalysis, developmental and experimental psychology, animal behavior, the neurosciences, and modern biology in general. Restrictions imposed by the exclusiveness of a personal psychology with a phenomenalistic "action language" could inhibit or prevent psychology with a phenomenalistic "action language" could inhibit or prevent multidisciplinary inquiry and perspective. We need models from biology and other sciences for building bridges, for generating novel approaches, and, perhaps most importantly, for understanding disanalogies and distinctions between disciplines. While there is a need for disentangling contradictory elements within psychoanalytic theory, more abstract theory needs to evolve in its own right. Partly because it is more abstract, it relates to models in other disciplines, not only in the neurosciences and biology in general, but also in other sciences (i.e., the scientific zeitgeist, alluded to earlier).

I contend that useful models for psychoanalysis in today's scientific world are organizational ones. Such models can bridge domains which are both personal and public and can incorporate postulates concerning mental processes and interactions among such processes. This view, which has also been articulated by Rubenstein (1976) and Holt (1976), holds that if a model is found to be inconsistent with modern biology or "physiologically implausible," new models must emerge. I agree with these authors that there is nothing necessarily misleading about an abstract, higher-level theory, which can contain useful orienting propositions. Psychoanalytic theory cannot be restricted to a personal psychology of individual meanings and aims, since there will always be a need for generalizing beyond the single case and beyond the clinical psychoanalytic setting. Hypotheses must be generated which can be tested in domains outside that setting. Convergent operations are necessary for progress in any scientific discipline, clinical or otherwise.

Propositions from Outside Psychoanalysis

A Parallel History

In introducing an historical perspective for understanding changing psychoanalytic models for affect, I suggested that changes in models reflected changes in the scientific zeitgeist as well as in the accumulation of specific data and knowledge. Support for this suggestion is found in a similar evolution of models which has taken place in psychology in general. As is well known, S-R models were long dominant in academic psychology. Only recently have organizational models gained prominence. Interestingly, this change has taken place first in the branches of psychology whose data bases are closest to biology (cf. the "Adaptive Point of View" of psychoanalysis) — namely, physiological psychology, comparative psychology (ethology), and developmental psychology (e.g., Piaget, 1936; Lorenz, 1939; Werner, 1948; Hebb, 1949; Harlow, 1953). Furthermore, as in psychoanalysis, the history of psychology is such that affects have held intermittent rather than steady prominence. In the present century there has been a phase of high interest, followed by a phase in which affects were dropped as an area of major concern because of devotion to quantitative factors to the neglect of qualitative ones, and, most recently, a resurgence of interest along with the realization of the practical importance of affects. In the two earliest editions of a classic textbook of experimental psychology (Woodworth, 1938;

Woodworth and Schlosberg, 1954), a major place was given to the study of affects; however, in the third edition (Kling and Riggs, 1971), affects are sparsely dealt with, a lack of interest reflected also in Duffy's conclusion that emotions were no longer a useful construct (Duffy, 1941, 1962). The current resurgence of research interest in affects can be documented by reference to Ekman, Friesen, and Ellsworth (1972); Levi (1975); and Izard (1978a).

Now let us look at these trends in terms of the models I have suggested. The first model, Variant A, discussed under Freud's propositions, was an S-R model in which the emotion was defined in terms of the external stimulus. Watson (1930), who like Freud had a major influence on American psychology, also had a strong initial interest in emotions and attempted to define them in terms of external stimulus conditions. Apparently, the particular stimulus conditions considered were determined more by intuition and theory than by observation and empiricism; therefore, it is not surprising that when responses from identical stimuli proved unreplicable (Sherman, 1927a, 1927b), there was a decline in research on emotions.

As was true for the S-R model in psychoanalysis, the S-R model in academic psychology included assumptions that affects are passive, mechanical responses to stimuli and that they are disorganizing forces, presumably outside of adaptive behavior. In 1946 the standard introductory textbook of Munn stated that "emotions disturb or upset whatever activities are in progress at the time . . ." (p. 263); as in psychoanalysis, more current versions of affects as disorganizing influences can still be found in the literature (Young 1961; Lazarus, 1968).

Academic psychology also had its Variant B of the S-R model. In this, the emphasis was on an internal stimulus instead of an external one although, as with Freud, the external context was still considered important. In this tradition, the "arousal" (Duffy, 1934) or "activation" (Lindsley, 1951, 1957) theories of emotion flourished; some kind of activation, either central or peripheral, was considered the fundamental event, with the quality of effective experience being determined by expectations or by social context. The latter factors were seen to determine the interpretation of the arousal experience. As with

Freud's Variant B, the emphasis on this model is on quantitative factors, on measuring the intensity of activation; qualitative factors are secondary and of lesser interest. More recently Schachter and Singer (1962) and Mandler (1975) have propounded theories of emotion according to this model, in which cognitive content plays a more important role in the secondary qualitative aspects of emotions which follow the arousal.

The reader will not be surprised that an emerging trend in psychology has been concerned with an organizational model of affects. Such a trend can be thought of as spearheaded by Leeper (1948), continuing with Goldstein (1951), and now including Lazarus (1968), Arnold (1970), Pribram (1970), and Izard (1978b). In this model, as with the later Freudian model, affects are viewed as fundamentally active processes and as including adaptive mental functions. They are not extrinsic to behavior, something which characteristically disturbs it, but are intrinsic and biologically organized. They do not necessarily need to be "tamed" or dealt with. They are pervasive and important parts of behavior. In one way or another, these theories encompass major propositions which I have summarized from the psychoanalytic literature with respect to the organizational model of affects. A number of these authors give systematic theoretical statements concering the role of evaluation and cognition in affective functioning. A comprehensive review can be found in Izard (1978a).

The Discrete Emotions; New Data and an Important Theoretical Advance in the Psychobiology of Emotions

A major line of inquiry concerning discrete facial expressions of emotion had its origin in Darwin's classic treatise *The Expression of the Emotions in Man and Animals* (1872) and was revived by Tomkins's later theoretical and empirical work (Tomkins, 1962, 1963; Tomkins and McCarter, 1964). It also had strong roots in clinicians' experience with nonverbal communication. However, it remained for two volumes, published in successive years, to stimulate contemporary interest in this field. The books of Izard (1971) and of Ekman and his colleagues (Ekman, Friesen, and Ellsworth, 1972) critically and masterfully reviewed previous work on the accuracy of judgments of adult facial expressions of emotion and pointed out striking consistencies in the experimental literature which previously had been unappreciated. Ekman and his group found that most investigators who used posed facial expressions had collected evidence for the systematic ability to judge at least seven categories of emotion from them. The list included *happiness, surprise, fear, anger, sadness, disgust/contempt,* and *interest.* Izard developed a similar list which included *distress* and *shame.* Each of these investigators reported the results of independent cross-cultural judgment studies. All such studies included dramatic evidence of regularities. Particularly impressive was Ekman's demonstration of universal agreement about posed still photos of peak emotional expressions in preliterate as well as literate cultures. Such agreement about verbal labeling, even in a forced-choice judgment paradigm such as they used, seemed to imply a universal basis not only for the *expression* of particular emotions but also for their *recognition.* Izard, from his cross-cultural studies and other work, reached similar conclusions: there are discrete patterns of facial expression which represent universal systems of emotional expression. Each of these investigators spelled out specific facial movements involved in each of these patterns of emotion (see Izard 1971, 1972; Ekman and Friesen, 1975). The implication of their work is that such discrete emotional expressions are part of our biological heritage and that members of our species are born with a preprogramed or preadapted readiness to express and recognize these emotions and, finally, that these emotions can be considered in some way fundamental, simple, or primary.

Izard (1972) presents accumulated experimental evidence for anxiety and depression being more complex patterns of emotion which are composed of the primary emotions. His findings fit well with some emerging psychoanalytic views that anxiety is not a simple affect, but one which is structured more complexly in development after the infancy period (see Katan, 1972), as well as with views that anxiety and depression both have organized, and perhaps superordinate, signaling functions (see Brenner, 1975; and for a nonpsychoanalytic formulation in clinical psychology, Costello, 1976).

Conclusion

Clinical and ethological conviction that discrete affect expressions are adaptive and that they represent an early and continuing significant form of communication has received experimental support. It remains for further research and theory to explore the implications of these findings. Further, a host of questions are raised by the organizational model. Among those which are important for a psychoanalytic theory of affects are the following.

When are emotions disorganizing? Under what conditions are they overwhelming, too active, or too prolonged? According to Freud's signal theory of anxiety, trauma or an overload experience with helplessness can occur when danger is evaluated as being too severe or when regulatory activities are overridden. There is now a need for delineating when it is that emotions are organizing and when they are disorganizing, not only for anxiety but also for a variety of discrete emotions, such as anger, fear, sadness, and joy. Further, there is a related question: are there times when emotions are disorganizing because of not enough activity? Are there analogies in real life to what we have learned from sensory isolation experiments? It is known that early emotional deprivation in humans and monkeys results in an overall blunting of emotions: there are fewer expressions of interest and curiosity toward the environment, fewer expressions of pleasure, and fewer specific expressions of fearfulness and other forms of displeasure. This seems to be another form of disorganization. Are there other conditions we could study in which there is not enough emotional activity?

Do emotions need social "nutriment"? This question is related to the previous one. Perhaps if there is not enough social experience to support ongoing emotional activity, something analogous to an "atrophy of disuse," or a diminished organization in emotional systems, would result. Under these conditions, emotions might not be available to serve the usual adaptive functions of social signaling and psychological signaling. If such is the case, what kind of experiences could be regarded as essential "nutriment"? At what stages of development?

When are emotions immersed in conflict, and when are they outside the sphere of conflict? The question of unconscious versus conscious emotions now seems less important, since it is likely that all emotions, especially ones in conflict, have unconscious components. Perhaps the situation with emotions is similar to that with cognition, another complex mental system which is sometimes in conflict but not usually (although clinicians may suspect that functions of feeling are more often engaged in conflict than are functions of thinking). One is reminded of Pribram's model (Pribram and Melges, 1969) in which emotions are "pause points" because of incongruity between new information and ongoing plans for action. Such "pause points" could be organizing (motivating new plans) or disorganizing (interfering with plans), and perhaps it might be productive to think of conflict, and the relation between emotions and cognition, in these terms.[3]

What are the other signal affects besides anxiety, and how do they function? What is their ontogeny?

Finally, there are many developmental questions. How do components of these highly complex affect structures emerge? When do facial expressions, postural expressions, links to predictable incentive situations, and instrumental behavioral responses appear? How do these components become integrated with experience or internal states involving feeling and cognition? What are the relative interactions of biological innate patterning and social learning in the development of complex emotions? How do complexly patterned affects such as signal anxiety, depression, and guilt relate to simpler discrete emotions which may emerge earlier?

How do affect structures develop in relationship to other subsystems in the personality? How do they develop in relationship to moods? (For a review of questions in this area see Emde and Harmon, 1978.) There are still other developmental questions about the relation of emotions to the onset of cognitive capacities, to object relatedness capacities, and to the development of "sentiments," those complex structures which include affective memories and patterned ways of relating such as love, tenderness, hate, and friendship (cf. Shand, 1914).

---

[3] Dr. I. Charles Kaufman reminded me of this possibility.

I believe these are lively questions generated by the organizational model and ones which promise opportunities for useful research and theory building in the future.

References

Amacher, P. (1965), *Freud's Neurological Education and Its Influence on Psychoanalytic Theory*. Psychological Issues Monograph 16. New York: International Universities Press.

Anthony, E.J. (1975), Childhood depression. In: *Depression and Human Existence*,ed. E.J. Anthony & T. Benedek. Boston: Little, Brown, pp. 231–277.

Arlow, J.A. (1977), Affects and the psychoanalytic situation. *Internat. J. Psycho-Anal.*, 58:157–170.

Arnold, M.G. (1970), Perennial problems in the field of emotion. In: *Feelings and Emotions: The Loyola Symposium*, ed. M.B. Arnold. New York: Academic Press, pp. 169–185.

Basch, M.F. (1976), The concept of affect: A re-examination. *J. Amer. Psychoanal. Assn.*, 24:759-777.

Bernfeld, S. (1944), Freud's earliest theories and the school of Helmholtz. *Psychoanal. Quart.*, 13:341–362.

Bibring, E. (1953), The mechanism of depression. In: *Affective Disorders*, ed. P. Greenacre. New York: International Universities Press, pp. 13–48.

Blau, A. (1955), A unitary hypothesis of emotion: I. Anxiety, emotions of displeasure, and affective disorders. *Psychoanal. Quart.*, 24:75–103.

Boulding, K. (1956), General systems theory: The skeleton of science. *Management Sci.*, 2:197–208.

Brenner, C. (1974), On the nature and development of affects: A unified theory. *Psychoanal. Quart.*, 43:532–556.

——— (1975), Affects and psychic conflict. *Psychoanal. Quart.*, 44:5–28.

Brierley, M. (1937), Affects in theory and practice. *Internat. J. Psycho-Anal.*, 18:256–268.

Castelnuovo-Tedesco, P. (1974), Toward a theory of affects. *J. Amer. Psychoanal. Assn.*, 22:612–625.

Costello, C.G., ed. (1976), Anxiety and depression. In: *The Adaptive Emotions*. Montreal: McGill-Queen's University Press, pp. 1–149.

Darwin, C. (1872), *The Expression of the Emotions in Man and Animals*. London: John Murray.

Duffy, E. (1934), Emotion: An example of the need for reorientation in psychology. *Psychol. Rev.*, 41:184–198.

——— (1941), An explanation of "emotional" phenomena without the use of the concept "emotion." *J. Gen. Psychol.*, 25:283–293.

——— (1962), *Activation and Behavior*. New York: Wiley.

Ekman, P., & Friesen, W. (1975), *Unmasking the Face*. Englewood Cliffs, N.J.: Prentice Hall.

——— ——— & Ellsworth, P. (1972), *Emotion in the Human Face: Guidelines for Research and an Integration of Findings*. Elmsford, N.Y.: Pergamon.

——— & Harmon, R.J. (1978), Towards a strategy of studying mood in infants. Presented at NIMH Conference on Affective States in Infants and Young Children (unpublished).

Engel, G. (1962a), Anxiety and depression-withdrawal: The primary affects of unpleasure. *Internat. J. Psycho-Anal.*, 43:89–97.

—— (1962b), *Psychological Development in Health and Disease*. Philadelphia: W.B. Saunders.

—— Reichsman, F., & Segal, H. (1956), A study of an infant with gastric fistula: I. Behavior and the rate of total HC1 secretion. *Psychosom. Med.*, 18:374–398.

—— & Schmale, A. Conservation-withdrawal: A primary regulatory process for organismic homeostasis. In: *Physiology, Emotion and Psychosomatic Illness*. CIBA Foundation Symposium *8*. Amsterdam: Elsevier.

Fenichel, O. (1941), The ego and the affects. *Psychoanal. Rev.*, 28:47–60.

Freud, S. (1895a), On the grounds for detaching a particular syndrome from neurasthenia under the description "anxiety neurosis." *Standard Edition*, 3:87–139. London: Hogarth Press, 1962.

—— (1895b), Studies on hysteria. *Standard Edition*, 2. London: Hogarth Press, 1955.

—— (1916–1917), Introductory lectures on psychoanalysis. *Standard Edition*, 16:320-340. London: Hogarth Press, 1958.

—— (1923), The ego and the id. *Standard Edition*, 19:3–66. London: Hogarth Press, 1961.

—— (1926), Inhibitions, symptoms and anxiety. *Standard Edition*, 20:75–175. London: Hogarth Press, 1959.

—— (1930), Civilization and its discontents. *Standard Edition*, 21:59–145. London: Hogarth Press, 1961.

—— (1933), New introductory lectures. *Standard Edition*, 22:7–182. London: Hogarth Press, 1964.

Gill, M.M. (1976), Psychology versus metapsychology: Psychoanalytic essay's in memory of George S. Klein. *Psychological Issues*, Monograph 36. New York: International Universities Press, pp. 71–105.

Goldstein, K. (1951), On emotions: Considerations from the organismic point of view. *J. Psychol.*, 31:37–49.

Green, A. (1977), Conceptions of affect. *Internat. J. Psycho-Anal.*, 58:129–156.

Greenacre, P. (1971), *Emotional Growth*. New York: International Universities Press.

Grossman, W., & Simon, B. (1969), Anthropomorphism: Motive, meaning and causality in psychoanalytic theory. *The Psychoanalytic Study of the Child*, 24:78–111. New York: International Universities Press.

Harlow, H.F. (1953), Mice, monkeys, men and motives. *Psychol. Rev.*, 60:23–32.

Hartmann, H. (1939), *Ego Psychology and the Problem of Adaptation*. New York: International Universities Press, 1958.

—— Kris, E. & Loewenstein, R.M. (1946), Comments on the formation of psychic structure. *Psychoanalytic Study of the Child*, 2:11–38. New York: International Universities Press.

—— —— —— (1953), The function of theory in psychoanalysis. In: *Drives, Affect, Behavior*, ed. R.M. Loewenstein. Vol. 1. New York: International Universities Press, 1953. pp. 13–37.

Hebb, D.O. (1949), *The Organization of Behavior*. New York: Wiley.

Holt, R.R. (1965), A review of some of Freud's biological assumptions and their influence on his theories. In: *Psychoanalysis and Current Biological Thought*, ed. N.S. Greenfield & W.C. Lewis. Madison: University of Wisconsin Press, pp. 93–124.

——— (1967), Motives and thought: Psychoanalytic essays in honor of David Rapaport. *Psychological Issues* Monograph 18/19. New York: International Universities Press.

——— (1975), The past and future of ego psychology. *Psychoanal. Quart.*, 44:550–576.

——— (1976), Drive or wish? A reconsideration of the psychoanalytic theory of motivation. *Psychological Issues*, Monograph 36. New York: International Universities Press, pp. 158–197.

Izard, C. (1971), *The Face of Emotion*. New York: Meredith, 1971.

——— (1972), *Patterns of Emotions. A New Analysis of Anxiety and Depression*. New York: Academic Press.

——— (1978a), On the development of emotions and emotion-cognition relationships in infancy. In: *Origins of Behavior: Affective Development*, ed. M. Lewis & L. Rosenblum. New York: Plenum.

——— (1978b), The emergence of emotions and the development of consciousness in infancy. In: *Human Consciousness and Its Transformations: A Psychobiological Perspective*, ed. J.M. Davidson, R.J. Davidson, & G.E. Schwartz. New York: Plenum, pp. 193–216.

Jacobson, E. (1953), The affects and their pleasure-unpleasure qualities, in relation to the psychic discharge processes. In: *Drives, Affects, Behavior*, ed. R.M. Loewenstein. Vol. 1. New York: International Universities Press, pp. 38–66.

——— (1957), Normal and pathological moods: Their nature and functions. *Psychoanalytic Study of the Child*, 12:73–126. New York: International Universities Press.

Joffe, W.G., & Sandler, L. (1968), Comments on the psychoanalytic psychology of adaptation, with special reference to the role of affects and the representational world. *Internat. J. Psycho-Anal.*, 49:445–454.

Katan, A. (1972), The infant's first reaction to strangers: Distress or anxiety? *Internat. J. Psycho-Anal.*, 53:501–503.

Kaufman, I.C. (1977), Developmental considerations of anxiety and depression: Psychobiological studies in monkeys. In: *Psychoanalysis and Contemporary Science*. 5:317–363.

Klein, G.S. (1967), Motives and thought: Psychoanalytic essays in honor of David Rapaport. *Psychological Issues*, Monograph 18/19. New York: International Universities Press, pp. 78–174.

——— (1969), Freud's two theories of sexuality. In: *Clinical-Cognitive Psychology: Models and Integrations*, ed. L. Breger. Englewood Cliffs, N.J.: Prentice-Hall, pp. 136–181.

——— (1976), *Psychoanalytic Theory: An Exploration of Essentials*. New York: International Universities Press.

Kling, J.W., & Riggs, L.A. (1971), *Woodworth & Schlosberg's Experimental Psychology*. 3rd ed. New York: Holt, Rinehart and Winston.

Landauer, K. (1938), Affects, passions and temperament. *Internat. J. Psycho-Anal.*, 19:388–415.

Lazarus, R.S. (1968), Emotions and adaptation: Conceptual and empirical relations. In: *Nebraska Symposium on Motivation*, ed. W. Arnold. Lincoln:

University of Nebraska Press, pp. 175–270.

Leeper, R.W. (1948), A motivational theory of emotion to replace "emotion as disorganized response." *Psychol. Rev.*, 55:5–21.

Levi, L. (1975), *Emotions: Their Parameters and Measurement*. New York: Raven Press.

Lewin, B. (1965), Reflections on affect. In: *Drives, Affects, Behavior*, ed. M. Schur. Vol. 2. New York: International Universities Press.

Limentani, A. (1977), Affects and the psychoanalytic situation. *Internat. J. Psycho-Anal.*, 58:171–182.

Lindsley, D. (1951), Emotion. In: *Handbook of Experimental Psychology*, ed. S.S. Stevens. New York: Wiley.

——— (1957), Psychophysiology and motivation. In: *Nebraska Symposium on Motivation*, ed. M.R. Jones. Lincoln: University of Nebraska Press, pp. 44–105.

Lorenz, K. (1939), Comparative study behavior: I. The evolution of instinctive behavior. In: *Instinctive Behavior*, ed. C.H. Schiller. New York: International Universities Press, 1957, pp. 239–263.

Mandler, G. (1975), *Mind and Emotion*. New York: Wiley.

Munn, N.L. (1946), *Psychology: The fundamentals of human adjustment*. Boston: Houghton–Mifflin.

Novey, S. (1961), Further considerations on affect theory in psychoanalysis. *Internat. J. Psycho-Anal.*, 42:21–31.

Piaget, J. (1936), *The Origins of Intelligence in Children*. 2nd ed. New York: International Universities Press, 1952.

Platt, J.R. (1964), Strong inference. *Science*, 146:347–353.

Pribram, K.H. (1970), Feelings as monitors. In: *Feelings and Emotions: The Loyola Symposium*. New York: Academic Press, pp. 41–52.

——— & Gill, M.M. (1976), *Freud's "Project" Re-Assessed*. N.Y.: Basic Books.

——— & Melges, F.T. (1969), Psychophysiological basis of emotion. In: *Handbook of Clinical Neurology*, ed. P.J. Vinken & G.W. Bruyn. Vol. 3. Amsterdam: North-Holland Publishing, pp. 316–342.

Rangell, L. (1967), Psychoanalysis, affects, and the "human core." On the relationship of psychoanalysis to the behavioral sciences. *Psychoanal. Quart.*, 36:172–202.

Rapaport, D. (1953), On the psychoanalytic theory of affect. *Internat. J. Psycho-Anal.*, 34:177–198.

——— (1959), The structure of psychoanalytic theory: A systematizing attempt. *Psychological Issues*, Monograph 6. New York: International Universities Press, 1960.

——— & Gill, M.M. (1959), The points of view and assumption of metapsychology. *Internat. J. Psycho-Anal.*, 40:153–162.

Rubenstein, B.B. (1976), Psychology versus metapsychology: Psychoanalytic essays in memory of George S. Klein. *Psychological Issues*, Monograph 36. New York: International Universities Press, pp. 229–264.

Sandler, J. (1960), The background of safety. *Internat. J. Psycho-Anal.*, 41:353–356.

Schacter, S., & Singer, J.E. (1962), Cognitive, social, and physiological determinants of emotional state. *Psychol. Rev.*, 69:379–399.

Schafer, R. (1964), The clinical analysis of affects. *J. Amer. Psychoanal. Assn.*, 12:275–299.

————— (1970), An overview of Heinz Hartmann's contributions to psychoanalysis. *Internat. J. Psycho-Anal.*, 51:425–446.

————— (1975), Psychoanalysis without psychodynamics. *Internat. J. Psycho-Anal.*, 56:41–55.

————— (1976), Emotion in the language of action. *Psychological Issues*, Monograph 36, ed. M.M. Gill & P. Holzman. New York: International Universities Press, pp. 106–133.

Schur, M. (1969), Affects and cognition. *Internat. J. Psycho-Anal.*, 50:647–653.

Shand, A.F. (1914), *The Foundation of Character*. London: Macmillan.

Sherman, M. (1927a), The differentiation of emotional responses in infants: I. Judgments of emotional responses from motion picture views and from actual observations. *J. Compar. Psychol.*, 7:265–285.

————— (1927b)The differentiation of emotional responses in infants: II. The ability of observers to judge the emotional characteristics of the crying of infants and of the voice of an adult. *J. Compar. Psychol.*, 7:335–351.

Spitz, R. (1956), Transference: The analytical setting. *Internat. J. Psycho-Anal.*, 37:380–385.

————— (1959), *A Genetic Field Theory of Ego Formation*. New York: International Universities Press.

Tomkins, S. (1962), *Affect, Imagery, Consciousness: Vol. I. The Positive Affects*. New York: Springer.

————— (1963), *Affect, Imagery, Consciousness: Vol. II. The Negative Affects*. New York: Springer.

————— & McCarter, R. (1964), What and where are the primary affects? Some evidence for a theory. *Perceptual & Motor Skills*, 18:119–158.

Watson, J. (1930), *Behaviorism*. Chicago: University of Chicago Press.

Werner, H. (1948), *Comparative Psychology of Mental Development*. Rev. ed. New York: International Universities Press, 1957.

Woodworth, R.S. (1938), *Experimental Psychology*. New York: Holt.

————— & Schlosberg, H. (1954), *Experimental Psychology*. New York: Holt.

Young, P.T. (1961), *Motivation and Emotion: A Survey of the Determinants of Human and Animal Activity*. New York: Wiley.

5

Toward a Psychoanalytic Theory of Affect: II. Emotional Development and Signaling in Infancy

ROBERT N. EMDE, M.D.
HELEN K. BUCHSBAUM, PH.D.

The preceding chapter discussed the history of the psychoanalytic theory of affects by highlighting the changing models of mental functioning. An organizational model has replaced an earlier S-R mechanistic model, a change which can be understood both as resulting from a changed scientific zeitgeist and from accumulated knowledge derived from the psychoanalytic clinical situation. It was argued thaht this perspective enabled one to see a compelling continuity in the psychoanalytic clinical literature concerning affects. The organizational model allows for the articulation of an interlocking set of generalizations which include (1) selected propositions from Freud's later writings, (2) overall propositions from psychoanalytic writers since Freud, and (3) new data from experimental psychology.

Freud's organizational model considered affects as complex states rooted in biology, with direct feelings of pleasure and unpleasure, but seated in the ego and involving perceptual, evaluative, and cognitive functions. Affect structures as active

Dr. Emde is supported by NIMH project grant #MH22803, Research Scientist Award #5 KO2 MH36808, and the John D. and Catherine T. MacArthur Foundation Network on the Transition from Infancy to Early Childhood. Dr. Buchsbaum is supported by the Colorado Node of the John D. and Catherine T. MacArthur Foundation Network on the Transition from Infancy to Early Childhood.

agencies have signal functions and therefore have an important role in the regulation of mental functioning and behavior. Subsequent psychoanalytic writers have enriched this model with generalizations added from clinical data. These can be grouped under "the adaptive point of view" (Hartmann, 1939) and include propositions that affects are autonomous structures (as well as in conflict), that they are continuous aspects of our lives (as opposed to intermittent "disruptive" states), that they are vital ingredients for human social relatedness, that their expressions are good guides for understanding motivation and states of mind, and that there are signal affects other than anxiety. Finally, recent experimental data have provided strong evidence for discrete biologically based primary affect systems, evidence hinted at by a number of psychoanalytic writers who have implicitly considered the organizational model.

The previous chapter argued that these propositions were consistent not only with each other but with data from other fields of observation and that they presented new questions for research and theory building. This chapter will examine recent research in infant behavior using this point of view. First, we will summarize changing perspectives in infancy research in which there has been a similar response to a changing scientific zeitgeist along with an increasing appreciation of the usefulness of the organizational model. Second, we will look at several organizational models of emotional development in infancy taken from our own research. These include models dealing with biobehavioral shifts, the affective self, and social referencing. The models are descriptive and will summarize a considerable amount of data relative to the development of affects. One model concerns successive shifts in biobehavioral organization at 2 months, 7–9 months, 12–13 months, and 18–21 months. A second concerns the development of an affective self, and a third describes how social referencing plays an important role in the development of self and early moral internalization. Finally, we will discuss the previously enumerated psychoanalytic propositions about affect in the context of recent infant research and will suggest that they are strengthened considerably.

Changing Perspectives in Infant Research: The Challenge of Conceptualizing Organized Complexity as It Increases

A striking problem facing the clinically oriented researcher is that infants, lacking language, cannot directly tell us how they feel, what they know, or what they want. Yet it can be said that developmental psychology knows a lot more about the infant's internal states and capacity for regulation than was true during the times when William James (1890) spoke of the newborn's "blooming, buzzing confusion"; Watson (1930) of the newborn's love, rage, and fear; and Freud (1930) of the young infant's hallucinatory wish fulfillment in the absence of the breast. In the past two decades, massive amounts of new information have been generated from a computerized technology, from novel methods of observation, and from an international effort to try and understand the world of the infant. While the research enterprise has largely moved away from global theories, insisting that concepts must have operational referents in observed behaviors and that inferences be specific and at low levels of abstraction, it is certain that a number of viewpoints have changed. The overall scientific zeitgeist has changed: just as modern biology has been characterized as the biology of organized complexity, so developmental biology has been characterized as the biology of *increasingly organized complexity*. Three disciplinary influences have added to the changed view. *Ethology* has emphasized a full description of the organism's behavioral repertoire along with the naturalistic context in which it appears; the *neurosciences* have contributed major advances in our understanding systems of brain function; and *multidisciplinary efforts* have proven the advantages of applying multiple techniques and vantage points in solving problems. Rather than proceeding from a point of view of isolation, all of these influences have challenged investigators to consider phenomena under study as part of an array of complex systems—systems which are in continuous interaction, systems which are often at different levels of organization, and systems which can be characterized as having varying degrees of stability or change. The result has been a flourishing research enterprise using an overall organizational model, but with a number of changed perspectives. Let us examine a few of these.

In the past, the human infant was regarded as relatively passive, as an organism who reacts and behaves primarily so as to reduce stimulation. This assumption dominated much of the literature of developmental psychology and psychoanalysis. A multidisciplinary view, however, has given a different picture. Embryology and neurophysiology have highlighted the prominence of early neural activity (Livingston, 1967), and the psychology of Jean Piaget and subsequent research have shown us how much of early cognition and perception can be understood in terms of a sensorimotor theory of action (Piaget, 1936; Wolff, 1960; Haith, 1976). A wide variety of developmental research studies in humans and animals have shown the young infant to have stimulus needs both for soothing and arousal. These needs result in active and complex encounters with a varied environment (for general discussion and data reviews see Kaufman, 1960; White, 1963; Greenberg, 1965; Marler and Hamilton, 1966; Thompson and Grusec, 1970; Jones, 1972).

Related to this, it has become apparent that the young infant is not "undifferentiated" in any simple sense. Naturalistic observations have documented the amount of organization and endogenous control present in the days after birth. The pioneering studies of Wolff (1959, 1966), replicated and extended by others (e.g., Prechtl, 1958; Emde and Koenig, 1969a, 1969b; Korner, 1969) have shown that the newborn's behavioral repertoire includes a multiplicity of clearly circumscribed and highly organized behaviors which are related to internal state. Further, impressive organization is apparent in the rhythmic features of newborn activity cycles (Kleitman and Engelmann, 1953; Sander, 1969; Sterman and Hoppenbrouwers, 1971; Gaensbauer and Emde, 1973; Emde, Swedberg, and Suzuki, 1975). Indeed, the complex regulatory capacities of the newborn serve as a rationale for the widely used Brazelton Neonatal Behavioral Assessment Scale (Brazelton, 1973; Brazelton, Als, Tronick, and Lester, 1979).

Another change in perspective involves an awareness of the limitations of the drive reduction model, which in the past has assumed that infants come to learn about their world primarily through the reduction of drives. Bertalanffy (1968a, 1968b) has cogently shown why this idea runs counter to modern biology; White (1963) has addressed its limitations from the aspect of psychoanalytic developmental psychology and Miller, Galanter, and Pribram (1960) from the point of view of neurophysiology an information theory. Earlier pioneering formulations of Hebb (1949; Heron, Bexton, and Hebb, 1953), deriving from experiments with adults, and of Harlow, deriving from experiments with monkeys (Harlow, 1953; Harlow, Harlow, and Meyer, 1950) must also be mentioned. We now know that the young infant's behavioral organization is of sufficient complexity that it too provides dramatic examples of phenomena not explainable by a drive reduction model. Such a model would assume, for example, that the newborn's wakefulness and interest in the external world are enhanced primarily through their being associated with drive satisfaction from relief of hunger (or thirst). That this is not the case is shown by three observations which were originally made prominent by Wolff (1959, 1965, 1966) but can be replicated simply by anyone. The first is that a newborn will interrupt a feeding (at breast or bottle) in order to look at an interesting novel stimulus; the second is that wakefulness can be prolonged by such a stimulus; and the third is that mild crying can be converted to a state of quiet alertness by the introduction of such a stimulus. These observations are obviously not compatible with the view that the newborn's wakefulness is based exclusively on drive reduction. Nor are they compatible with its corollary that there is a primary organismic tendency to reduce the level of stimulus input. Other observations, indicating that the newborn has an endogenous sleep-wakefulness rhythm whether fed or not (Emde, Swedberg, and Suzuki, 1975), are equally incompatible with the earlier view.

As a result of these changing perspectives, organization has become a central concept in infant developmental research. But demonstrating that the infant is indeed organized is not enough. A multidisciplinary research strategy demands more than the revelation of undiscovered capacities. As difficult as it is, programmatic effort must increasingly be directed toward understanding processes of behavior—that is, relationships which change over time. Up until recently, much research could be characterized as a competition to see who could demonstrate previously undiscovered organizational capacities in early infancy, and there was little concern for naturalistic relevance to the developing infant, to naturalistic surroundings, and ultimately to processes of brain functioning.

But not only must we understand an individual's development in this sense, we must also understand that individual as a part of a developing interactional system. For years researchers were concerned primarily with the caretaker's role in nurturing and shaping the infant's behavior. Interaction was felt to be essentially unidirectional, from mother to baby. Then a small group of clinician researchers, influenced by psychoanalytic theory and an increased understanding of genetics, pioneered the study of early individual differences and infant contributions to development (see Escalona and Heider, 1959; Benjamin, 1961; Thomas, Birch, Chess, Hertzig, and Korn, 1963; Korner, 1964; Escalona, 1968). In addition, an ethological orientation led to a description of the newborn's repertoire of behaviors within the family (e.g., see Wolff 1966, 1969; Richards and Bernal, 1972). As knowledge accumulated concerning the young infant's complex organization, more research attention became devoted to effects of social interaction originating within the newborn (see the reviews of Bell, 1974; Korner, 1974). It is not surprising that such effects are major, especially when one considers infant crying and its potential for initiating caretaking interaction (Moss and Robson, 1968; Bell, 1971). Today researchers are looking at both sides of a developing interactional system, with infant and caretaker being viewed simultaneously. Each partner is viewed as having separate competencies which affect the other's behavior and as initiating and reinforcing the behavior of the other. It is appreciated that the developmental process is *transactional,* with the behavior of each increasing in complexity over time (Sameroff, 1975). Research dealing with developing interactional systems is quite difficult to conceptualize, and computerized statistical techniques for data analysis have only recently become available (see Rosenthal, 1973a, 1973b; Lewis and Lee-Painter, 1974). Nonetheless, it is striking that clinician researchers have been pioneers in advancing this perspective. Most prominent is the early work of Sander, originally arising from his longitudinal study with Pavestedt (Sander, 1962) and continuing with his precise monitoring of long-term rhythms of infant and caretaker activities over the first 2 months (Sander and Julia, 1966; Sander, 1969, 1975). Other current programs in this area are represented by the work of Stern (1971, 1974) and Brazelton (1974; Brazelton, Tronick, Adamson, and Weise, 1975).

In summary, today's researchers have a modified view of human infants which has been influenced by both the contemporary zeitgeist and its concern with organized complexity and by data from multiple disciplines. Such a view holds that infants are fundamentally active, socially interactive, and organized. Infants are stimulus-seeking and participate creatively in their own development. Subsequent experience is not superimposed on a formless beginning. For any behavioral development, including emotional development, experience serves to modulate a preexisting state of endogenous organization.

A Model of Infant Emotions in Biobehavioral Context: Conceptualizing Developmental Shifts in Organization During Infancy

A consideration of infant emotions and when they appear highlights the fact that development is not continuous in any simple way. At certain times there are major shifts in organization, resulting in qualitative transitions in behavior, with emergence of new behaviors and functions. That such shifts occur regularly in development, that the onset of new affect expressions are indicators of these shifts, and that the shifts represent major adaptive changes in ego organization—all are propositions advanced by Spitz (1959) in *A Genetic Field Theory of Ego Formation*. Our own research program was launched by this theory (Emde, Gaensbauer, and Harmon, 1976), and we can now summarize a variety of data, along with a current version of our descriptive model. With each developmental shift, we will demonstrate that a new affective behavior (1) represents a dramatic change in the social life of the infant, (2) has antecedents, and (3) occurs in a nexus of psychobiological change, i.e., change in the organization of other systems. We at first conceptualized these shifts as times of rapid change, but we now realize they are more complex, representing times of creative integration of convergent developmental events. Our current descriptive model not only raises questions about biological underpinnings, but also gives a developmental framework for two additional descriptive models which concern the affective self and the mediating process of social referencing.

A Developmental Shift at 2 Months

As a result of our work and the recent research of many others, we conclude that there is a shift in behavioral organization to a new level of functioning after 2 postnatal months. After this time, behavior cannot easily be accounted for by endogenous rhythms and internal state. There is a shift away from endogenous control; more of life is in wakefulness, and less is in sleep. In fact, "wakefulness becomes used a new way," as Dittrichova and Lapackova (1964) have put it.

For parents the shift from endogenous to exogenous control is most obvious in affective development. There is little in life more quietly dramatic than the onset of their baby's social smile soon after 2 months. Family members are delighted, and the baby is shown off to friends who no longer feel they have to be cautious around a sleeping baby. Instead, the baby smiles at everyone, eyes brightly fixed on those of anyone who looks. About two weeks after the regular social smile makes its appearance, the baby adds a cooing vocalization as another specific accompaniment to the social encounter. Caregivers automatically experience delight and a feeling that their infant is delighted, and an often-heard comment, especially by parents of a firstborn, is that now their baby is human rather than a doll-like object to be protected and taken care of.

This regular social smile, however, is not unheralded. There are antecedents. Prior to it there is a period of irregular smiling followed by an upsurge of smiling to stimuli in a wide variety of modalities (Emde and Harmon, 1972). Moreover, before the social smile becomes predominant, there is another form of smiling, one linked to internal state (Emde and Koenig,

1969a, 1969b; Emde and Metcalf, 1970). It occurs as a concomitant of rapid eye movement state physiology and occurs more often in the premature, where it has a negative correlation with gestational age (Emde, McCartney and Harmon, 1971). We refer to this form of smiling as *endogenous smiling;* it declines during the normal newborn period during the same time that *exogenous smiling,* the form of smiling elicited from outside stimulation, increases. This developmental change is concomitant with a decline in nonhunger (or endogenous) fussiness. The decline in fussiness has been documented by many, including Brazelton (1962), and in two longitudinal studies by our group (Tennes, Emde, Kisley & Metcalf, 1972; Emde, Gaensbauer, and Harmon, 1976). Dittrichova and Lapackova (1964) pointed to the decline of fussiness and the upsurge of babbling and exploratory behaviors during this time of developmental shift.

Our research has also accumulated longitudinal data concerning mean hours of daily wakefulness during the first year. An increase in wakefulness was found to occur during the first postnatal months, followed by a plateau. There then follows a further increase in wakefulness, preceding 7-9 months, which in turn is followed by a second plateau. These data are represented in Figure 1, where they provide the shape for a more general schematization of findings to be discussed below.

Aside from wakefulness there are marked changes in sleep states during this time. Parmelee, Wenner, Akiyama, Schulz, and Stern (1967) and Dittrichova and Lapackova (1969) have reported that quiet sleep increases markedly over the first 3 postnatal months, a phenomenon that has been considered an important correlate of maturation of forebrain inhibitory centers, a correlation we have confirmed (Emde and Walker, 1976). EEG-polygraph studies show a marked decline in "behaviorally undifferentiated" REM states: Before 2 months, REM state physiology can occur during nutritive sucking, fussing, and drowsiness, whereas afterward it is unusual (Emde and Metcalf, 1970). There is a decrease in the large amount of behavioral activity seen during sleep. EEG sleep spindles have their onset during the second month, and an investigator can begin to stage quiet sleep according to EEG criteria after this time but not before. In terms of sleep distribution, there is an increase in

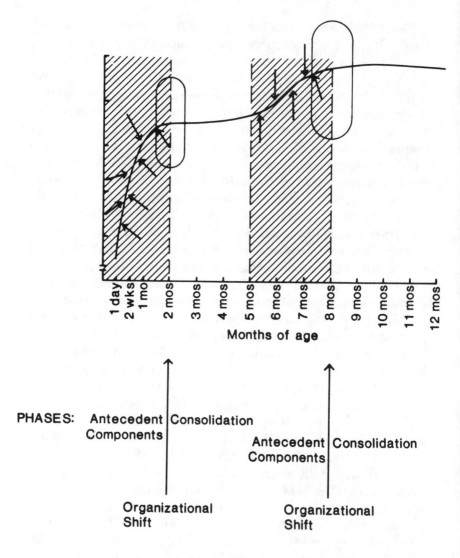

Figure 1. Model of first year shifts.

the ability to sustain long periods of sleep and a shift to a diurnal pattern of nighttime sleep. Two of our longitudinal studies have confirmed this changing distribution, with wakefulness becoming concentrated during the daytime hours, during the period of 6–8 weeks (Emde, Gaensbauer, and Harmon, 1976).

Furthermore, sleep onset shifts from the newborn mode (entry through active-REM sleep) to the "adult" mode (entering sleep through drowsiness and the quiet form of sleep), although this change is not nearly so age locked to 2 postnatal months as we had originally thought (Bernstein, Emde, and Campos, 1973; Kligman, Smyrl, and Emde, 1975).

In terms of perception, such knowledge as we have is also consistent with the notion of a shift in organization. Haith and his coworkers (Bergman, Haith, and Mann, 1971; Haith, 1976) have documented that significant scanning of the face does not occur until around 7 weeks, when there is prominent scanning in the region around the eyes. Such a finding corresponds to the naturalistic observations made by Robson (1967) concerning the time of onset of prominent eye-to-eye contact between mothers and infants. Before this time, in the newborn period, Haith holds there is an endogenous eye-movement activity pattern which is predominant and which is characterized by eye-movement "searching," this becoming inhibited by a "scanning routine" only when an edge is encountered. Haith's findings of a change in visual organization somewhat before 2 months are consistent with the findings of Salapatek (1969), who found the onset of responsiveness to internal aspects of displays at this time, and of Maurer and Salapatek (1976), who found a corresponding shift in infants' fixating faces and in their looking more at facial features, especially eyes.

There also appears to be a change in organization around 2 months with respect to orienting and attentiveness. The literature on heart rate responsiveness demonstrates a difference in the stimulus conditions which are required for predictable decelerations for the first 2 months as opposed to the months afterward. This change in organization also seems consistent with Kagan's point (1970a,b) that discrepancy begins to operate to control infants' attention to external stimuli after 2 months. Before 2 months, discrepancy from the familiar does not account for visual attending, and physical dimensions (such as contour and complexity) are more determining.

Perhaps the most dramatic behavioral evidence for such a qualitative change in development, however, has come from conditioning studies. Here results are different before and after 2 months. That such differences could emerge in a field originally dedicated to demonstrating that the nature of learning does not change (Watson, 1930) is a tribute to the careful methodology and respect for rules of evidence which have characterized recent work. Suffice it to say that before 2 months classical avoidance conditioning is very difficult and operant conditioning effects are short-lived. After 2 months this is not the case. Furthermore, it is difficult to establish habituation before 2 months, whereas experimental habituation can readily be established in auditory and visual modalities after that time. Certainly, learning through active adaptation and from reciprocal interaction takes place before 2 months, but its modes and mechanisms evidence a shift in organization after that time (see reviews in Sameroff, 1971; Emde and Robinson, 1979; Sameroff and Cavanagh, 1979). In Piagetian terms, this time of shift to stage II of sensorimotor development is one yielding the first acquired behavior patterns; this includes the intercoordination of sensory schemes, and it marks the time of going beyond inborn (endogenous) adaptations.

That there is a major qualitative difference between the very young infant and the infant older than 2 months is given further support by the neurosciences. In fact, the notion of a behavioral discontinuity or of a qualitative shift in development becomes much less mysterious when we look at how the brain develops. From every view, whether that of neurology, neurophysiology, or neuroanatomy, an overriding impression emerges: in early infancy growth occurs less by steady accretion and more by irregular stepwise jumps. Our attention is continually drawn more to changes in quality than to changes in quantity.

Pediatric neurology identifies a host of reflexes which are active within the first 2 months and decline thereafter. Among these are the Babkin reflex, the steppage reflex, the palmar grasp, the Moro, and the tonic neck reflex. Because they decline after 2 to 3 months without normally reappearing thereafter, they are often referred to as "transitory reflexes" of the newborn, and their decline is thought to reflect the postnatal maturation of forebrain inhibitory areas (see reviews in Peiper, 1963; Paine, 1965; Parmelee and Michaelis, 1971). Another rapid maturational change involves the cortical visual evoked response. Ellingson (1960) documented that the latency of this response, presumably reflective of information processing in a visual system, shortens markedly between 4 and 8 postnatal weeks. After 8 weeks, changes are relatively small from infancy to adulthood.

Although Conel's classic works (1941, 1947) documented the changes which occur in the human cerebral cortex during the first postnatal months, a precise knowledge of rates of change is lacking. The same could be said for other early rapid postnatal changes which have been documented, changes in (1) dendritic arborization, (2) increased vascularization of the brain, (3) myelinization, (4) glial proliferation, and (5) postnatal neurogenesis in limited areas (Altman, 1967; Bekoff and Fox, 1972).

In passing it should be mentioned that a possible animal model for investigating mechanisms underlying the presumed discontinuity between the behavioral organization of the newborn and that of the postnewborn is found in the kitten. Many changes in sleep-wakefulness organization are similar to the human case. Dramatic shifts with respect to facilitation and inhibition in wakefulness and in active REM sleep are currently under experimental neurophysiological study (e.g., Chase, 1973).

A Developmental Shift at 7–9 Months

Another biobehavioral shift occurs during the age period of 7–9 months. In terms of social-affective development, the differential responsivity to stranger and caregivers, with fearfulness being shown to the stranger, is most prominent. Indeed, the differential affective response to caregivers is such that, whether viewed from its positive or its negative side, it is often regarded as marking the onset of specific attachments. Furthermore, there is some indication from studies of approaching strangers, studies with the visual cliff, and studies using other stimulus conditions (see summaries in Scarr and Salapatek, 1970; Emde, Gaensbauer, and Harmon, 1976) that at this time there occurs the onset of a capacity for fearful responding. We also feel it important that emotional expression now leads to behavior; an infant now can show a fearful expression and then avoid. Evidence of anticipation beyond the motor act now extends to the affective realm. As Sroufe (1977) has pointed out, the infant now laughs in anticipation of the mother's return in a peekaboo game, rather than in response to a completed sequence. However, it is also important to point out that, like smiling, stranger-distress or fearfulness on the approach of a stranger does not emerge without antecedents. Longitudinal study has shown that responses such as comparing faces and sobering at the approach of a stranger regularly occur prior to the onset of stranger distress (Emde, Gaensbauer, and Harmon, 1976). Again, the developmental change seems to involve the integration of preexisting components with newly emergent behaviors. The period of 7 to 9 months is also the time when there is emergence of means-ends relationships in the sense of Piaget's stage IV sensorimotor development (Piaget, 1936). We have also found a prominent change in heart rate organization (Campos, Emde, Gaensbauer, Sorce, and Henderson, 1975). At 9 months there is a cardiac acceleratory response with fearfulness at the approach of a stranger, whereas prior to this shift there is cardiac deceleration (orienting) to both stranger and mother approach.

The increment in wakefulness prior to this developmental shift occurs at a time when K-complexes, EEG waves similar in form to evoked responses but spontaneously occurring, have their onset. As our longitudinal study showed, however, there are no invariant or necessary sequences among the onset of K-complexes, the onset of stage IV object permanence, and the onset of stranger-distress or fearfulness in individual cases (Emde, Gaensbauer, and Harmon, 1976).

A Developmental Shift at 12–13 Months

The shifts that occur during the second year have not been as well studied as have the first-year transformations. Nevertheless, some clear changes have been noted.

Walking usually begins around 12 months. This is accompanied by cognitive, linguistic, and emotional changes. With respect to cognition, the toddler begins to appreciate that entities are independent, with their own individual properties. Linguistically, the toddler is able to understand that a word is agreed on to refer to a specific object, enabling symbolic functioning to achieve a new level (McCall, 1977; see Kagan, 1981). The toddler can imitate new behaviors never before seen. In the realm of affect, many have noted the 1-year-old's frequent mood of elation (Mahler, Pine, and Bergman, 1975; Sroufe, 1977). Social referencing (i.e., the use of others' affect signals to resolve uncertainty) also becomes prominent. Further, the toddler starts to use affect expressions instrumentally (e.g., the smile or pout expression to "get his or her way," as parents have put it). We have also found evidence of pride upon mastery, as well as of positive affect sharing beginning at this age (Emde, Johnson, and Easterbrooks, in press).

A Developmental Shift at 18–21 Months

The 18–21 month age period is a fuzzier time, during which we believe another important shift occurs. This is a time when the child moves from one-word to multi-word utterances, and when self-awareness increases. Cognitive advances include the child's ability to remember and imitate sequences of actions and to understand symbolic relationships between entities. Two-word utterances that contain a subject and a predicate become possible. Affective changes occur, with an increase in "willfulness," the use of the "semantic no," and temper tantrums. Mahler, Pine, and Bergman (1975) have pointed out that mood swings occur, with evidence of sadness and greater subduedness, affects considered related to the rapprochement crisis. Mother-child interactions alter, with more "shadowing and darting away patterns" replacing the earlier patterns associated with "emotional refueling." At this point toddlers appear to be extremely aware of their separateness and of obstacles to mastering the world on their own. They show evidence of this increased self-awareness in a higher frequency of mastery smiles, directives to adults, and self-descriptions (Kagan, 1981). More research is clearly needed to further document the changes that occur with this important shift.

In summary, we have learned that each of these times of developmental shift cannot be conceptualized simply as a time of rapid change. For each there are at least 2 months of preparation during which components of new behaviors appear. These become integrated into a newly emergent organization at nodal times, following which occur periods of developmental consolidation. This is illustrated schematically in Figure 1 with respect to the shifts that take place during the first year of life. The schematic is superimposed on a data graph from our longitudinal study of increments in mean hours of daily wakefulness during the first year (Emde, Gaensbauer, and Harmon, 1976). Component changes, indicated by arrows, appear before the nodal times of shift, which are indicated by circles. The latter represent new fields of emergent organization. Plateaus, representing times of consolidation, follow each shift. Two other investigators found a major qualitative transition in infant behavior at similar age periods. McCall (1977), in reanalyzing data from the Berkeley Growth Study, found qualitative transitions at precisely these two age points. Kagan (1977), in summarizing his research program on cognitive development, presented compelling evidence for a behavioral reorganization at the time of the second shift. At this stage of our knowledge it can be said that our descriptive models seem to give a coherent picture which tantalizes researchers with many unanswered questions concerning biological underpinnings, developmental regulatory principles, and adaptive functioning. But one thing is clear: these organizational shifts are central in affective development and provide the framework for the ontogeny of affect structures during the first year. The next section describes our theory of an affective self and our research on social referencing as it pertains both to self-development and to the beginnings of negotiation, empathy, and moral emotions.

Affective Self

Our theory of an affective self adds a dimension to the adaptive function of emotions described thus far. This theory argues that emotion patterns are present early in life and continue throughout the lifespan. Further, discrete emotions have been shown to be universal, are present early in life (Emde, 1983; Izard, 1971) and persist throughout. That emotions play a central role in development is further supported by findings that the emotional availability of the caregiver is crucial throughout early development (Emde, 1980; Emde and Sorce, 1983; Stern, 1985). Emotions provide us a core of continuity for self-experience throughout development (Emde, 1983), a sense of affective continuity which occurs in two ways. First, because we know our own consistent feelings, we know we are the same in spite of the many ways we change. Second, the biological consistency of an affective core throughout the human species enables us to understand the feelings of others and therefore to be empathic.

An affective self begins in earliest infancy and develops according to three biological principles which permeate development. The first, self-regulation, refers to the young infant's preprogrammed regulation not only of sleep-wakefulness cycles, but also of longer-term developmental functions such as behavioral integrity in the face of environmental change. The notion of self-regulation in development is supported by recent observations of the resilience of important development functions when an adequate environment is restored following deficit or trauma (Clarke and Clarke, 1976; Sameroff and Cavanagh, 1979).

Social fittedness is a second biological principle operating throughout life. This involves the human infant's preadapted capacity to participate in interactions with other humans. Recent research has demonstrated a number of automatic and specialized social capacities present in both the infant and the parent (see Sander, 1975; Stern, 1977; Brazelton, Als, Tronick, and Lester, 1979; Tronick, 1980; Papousek and Papousek, 1982).

Affective monitoring is the third biological principle. From the beginning, the human being monitors experience according to what is pleasurable and unpleasurable. Thus there is a preadapted, organized basis in the central nervous system for guiding behavior. In early infancy this principle is evident in the way the infant's affective expressions guide the caregiver's responses. For example, a mother responds to a cry by trying to relieve the source of the distress. Later on, the infant uses affective experience to guide behavior, regardless of whether the caregiver intervenes.

We regard these three biological principles as separate in theory only; in reality they are intertwined, and in their interrelatedness they allow for both developmental consistency and change.

Social Referencing

We consider social referencing an important mediator in the development of an affective self. Just as there is a sequence in self-regulation that occurs with the development of an affective self, so there is a similar progression for the social referencing process.

The Denver group has defined social referencing in infancy as a form of active emotional communication which occurs when a child encounters a situation of uncertainty and looks to a significant other for an emotional signal to resolve it. Thus, social referencing is thought to mediate behavior when the infant is confronted by a situation of uncertainty, as when seeking emotional information from another (usually by attending to facial cues) and consequently altering behavior. This restrictive definition of social referencing as an aspect of emotional signaling in which an active search occurs is useful for experimental purposes: emotional signals can be manipulated as independent variables, and the infant's search behavior can serve as a clear marker that precedes behavioral regulation.

We have postulated a developmental continuum of social referencing that begins with the caregiver doing most of the referencing and extends to the second and third years of life, when the child uses referencing in the context of negotiation. During the first 6 months maternal social referencing predominates. The infant presents emotional information to the mother in order to direct her behavior to meeting the infant's needs. The latter 6 months of the first year bring the addition of infant social referencing. Now the infant encounters uncertain situations and seeks out clear emotional expressions from the significant other to resolve the uncertainty. Starting in the second year we see social referencing in negotiation. Here social referencing occurs with respect to uncertainty about the other person's response in relation to the child's own needs or intentions. At this point modification of expectations and intentions occurs during the course of social interaction. Preliminary data from a longitudinal study of infants observed at 12, 18, and 24 months provide support for this developmental continuum. We found a significant increase in the amount of positive affect sharing that occurred at 18 months relative to the other two ages, indicating that by the middle of the second year the child actively seeks to exchange emotional signals with significant others.

Social referencing mediates three aspects of the process of self-development: Increased differentiation of the experience of self, of other, and of self-with-other. This occurs as the infant's referencing of the caregiver optimally provides an increased sense of self in relation to this significant other.

The developing sense of the self-with-other, or "we," may require further study to clarify how it develops in the context of social referencing. Social referencing allows for a joint affective understanding about a third event. This communication goes beyond the present situation because, through repetition of this experience, shared memories and expectations develop as well as a shared understanding of aspects of the present experience. These repeated experiences lead eventually to internal working models of the relationship in particular contexts, or shared meaning. This allows for an internal guide for actions and for support based on the internalized sense of the we. Some of our research with 3-year-olds has provided evidence that children rely on an internalized sense of the we in guiding moral behavior. For example, in a temptation situation, many children responded to the temptation to transgress a rule by referring back to their mother's original prohibition with a poignant query, "Didn't you hear my mommy?"

Social Referencing and Early Moral Development

Emergence of Empathy

Social referencing becomes important for early moral development when one reformulates psychoanalytic theory to suggest that the 1–3 year age period is a time when motivational conflict is first internalized and when affectively meaningful rules and standards are developed within the context of specific caregiving relationships. Social referencing can clearly be seen as influential in this early understanding of what rules and standards are important to the caregiver.

However, this psychoanalytic formulation of early moral development does not emphasize the role emotions play. We think there may be at least two streams of early moral development that are centered on emotions—one that pertains to nonconflict areas and one that involves conflict. Again, social referencing is likely to be implicated in this formulation as well.

Empathy has been suggested as an important motivator of prosocial behavior (Hoffman, 1977) and consequently has been implicated in early moral development in nonconflict areas. That comforting responses are evident by the middle of the second year has been demonstrated by the studies of Radke-Yarrow, Zahn-Waxler and their colleagues (e.g., Zahn-Waxler and Radke-Yarrow, 1982; Radke-Yarrow, Zahn-Waxler and Chapman, 1983). Kagan (1984) has also suggested that empathy may serve as a natural constraint for the toddler's aggression against others. Kagan regards empathy as having a strong maturational basis.

The implication of this theory is that some important components of early moral development may have a maturational basis, rather than being dependent on learning or discipline within a conflict situation. Nevertheless, it seems likely that the tendency to be empathic would be influenced by the quality of the empathy experience with primary caregivers and, therefore, by the social referencing experience as well. Also, as discussed with respect to social referencing, during the second half of the first year the child learns a great amount regarding the rules of social interaction, turn-taking, and participating in discourse.

Although such rules do not require empathy per se, they probably do involve affect attunement (Stern, 1985) between the caregiver and the baby.

Early Moral Internalization

We expect that early moral internalization represents another important shift that occurs around the beginning of the third year and await further empirical support for this notion. Whether empathy is necessary for early moral internalization is a question we are currently examining in a longitudinal study of children 18 to 36 months old and their families. That empathy emerges by 18 months is evident in our research as well as in that of Radke-Yarrow, Zahn-Waxler, and Chapman (1983). Our research also shows that during the second year parental prohibitions play an increasingly prominent role in parent-child relationships. These prohibition situations are the most salient ones involving uncertainty to occur during this age period. The child is seen as uncertain about the shared meaning of the prohibition and its consequences, and looks to the parent's face to gain more information. In this manner, social referencing is an important process in the child's internalization of rules. At this stage of development the adaptive purpose of social referencing concerns the facilitation of early moral development, whereas earlier its purpose primarily concerned the development of self-and-other awareness.

Implications for Psychoanalytic Propositions

As we have noted, the organizational model for affects introduced by Freud presented them as complex states rooted in biology, with direct feelings of pleasure and unpleasure as a core aspect. Freud's model linked affect structures with cognition and evaluation, did not restrict them to conscious functioning, and viewed them as motivational, serving to organize mental functioning and behavior. All of this was incorporated into Freud's formulation that affects are signals and that they function as active agents within the ego. That these general propositions are compatible with the contemporary perspective of infant behavior should be clear. Freud's model deals not with a system in isolation but with a complex, active organismic state and its interrelation. As we have seen, there is every reason, because of their early organized appearance and importance, to view infant affects not only as rooted in biology, but in fact as central in biobehavioral development from their onset. Beginning after 2 months (from our point of view, a time in which a biobehavioral shift marks the end of the neonatal period) and, as far as we know, continuing throughout the lifespan, all dimensional studies of emotional expression have revealed that a dimension of "pleasure-unpleasure" is predominant and pervasive. Further, the wisdom of abandoning the drive reduction or "tension" model for pleasure and unpleasure is underscored by these same dimensional studies, in which "activation" emerges as an independent dimension of emotional expression. One can have either high activated or low activated pleasure, and the same is true for unpleasure. Even more directly, that pleasure and unpleasure cannot be equivalent to the increase and decrease of tension is dramatically revealed by considering the social smile of the 3-month-old. When the adult approaches, the infant shows a buildup of behavioral activation. There is a "bicycling" of arms and legs, and the smile continues or broadens as the face seems to "light up" with a sparkling of eyes which engage the adult directly. Consistent with this picture of increasing activity, we have recently shown that infant smiling tends to be associated with increased heart rate, rather than with decreased heart rate as the tension reduction model would predict (Emde, Campos, Reich, and Gaensbauer, 1978).

Other evidence from infancy shows the usefulness of Freud's later model. Affects do indeed serve to organize mental functioning and behavior. They function as motivational signals which are at first predominantly biosocial and then psychological. Psychological signaling emerges in our epigenetic scheme when essential links with cognition (means-end relationships) are established in development.

Later psychoanalytic writers, drawing on a growing clinical experience, supplemented Freud's conviction that affect expressions are good guides for understanding motivation and states of mind (ego states). A consideration of infancy bears this out unequivocally. Affect expressions have been called the language of infancy. Crying, the affect expression which is present immediately after birth, provides a universal and peremptory message to caregivers that the infant is distressed and that something should be changed—as regards feeding, diapering, positioning, or the removal of a particular hurt. Very soon, mothers learn to "read" the meanings of cries of different intensities and pitch occurring in different contexts (Wasz-Hockert, Partanen, Vuorenkoski, Valanne, and Michelsson, 1964; Wolff, 1969). The social smile, on the other hand, connotes a universal message for the continuance of social interaction along with a pleasant feeling state in which change is not required. Similarly, early infant expressions of interest and disgust and later infant expressions of fearfulness, anger, and sadness are read accurately by caretakers as indicating need states and as predictive of certain subsequent infant behaviors. Further, in a larger sense affects do appear to be indicators of major shifts in developmental ego organization. This idea was originally put forth by Spitz (1959) and has since been supported by a considerable number of findings since, as we have detailed in the first descriptive model from our own research.

That affects are adaptive, that they are autonomous structures, and that they are therefore free of conflict as well as in conflict is implied by the very existence of infant emotional expressions which are universal and which connote essential messages to caregivers. Further, that they are rooted in biology, are primarily autonomous, and represent "preadapted" states in the ego is implied as well (Hartmann, 1939; Rapaport, 1953). More than any other work, that of Spitz has contributed directly to this point. Spitz documented the universality of the smiling response and infant distress behaviors along with their crucial importance for early social relations, for early ego development, and for survival itself (Spitz, 1945, 1946, 1965; Spitz and Wolf, 1946). As Novey (1961) and Rangell (1967) have indicated, all meaningful social relationships are affective ones; their point, drawn from clinical experience, is dramatized by the infant-caregiver relationship. In fact, where there is early separation, as in the case of modern intensive care nurseries, and when affective reciprocity is denied between infant and caregiver, the incidence of battering and child neglect is increased (Elmer & Gregg, 1967; Shaheen, Alexander, Truskowsky, and Barbero, 1968). The work of Klaus and Kennell and their coworkers (Klaus, Jerauld, Dreger, McAlpine, Steffa, and Kennell, 1972; Klaus and Kennell, 1976), as well as of deChateau and Wiberg (1977a, 1977b), has shown that there is an enhancement of affective parent-infant relations when mothers and babies are allowed to be together more than the usual hospital postpartum routine permits. Their work implies that many current hospital procedures invoke separation which interferes with this affective interchange. In our own research, the adaptive importance of early infant affect has been highlighted by the case of Down's syndrome infants in whom the initial smiling response is dampened in intensity occasioning their parents extreme disappointment and usually inaugurating another wave of grieving for the normal child who was expected but not born (Emde and Brown, 1978).

Thus, affects are seen to be essential adaptive ingredients for survival and development beginning after birth; they provide a medium for reciprocal and expanding social interactions with the noninfant world. Further, affects in infancy are not intermittent "traumatic" states or disruptive forces. They are continuous factors in the lives of both infant and mother, providing a nurturant medium for their developing relationships as well as for the development of the infant's ego.

Further, from the developmental considerations reviewed in this chapter, it can be concluded that affects do not have to be "tamed." They do not become signals as a consequence of socialization. Rather, they are signals to begin with. In this, we must realize that "socialization" must be considered from other than a drive reduction point of view; affects are active participants in developing social transactions rather than passive, chaotic structures needing to be shaped.

Many questions remain to be answered concerning the development of affect structures. Current evidence suggests that some aspects of affect structures may be so rooted in biology that they will to some extent have invariant qualities for experience and for social expressiveness throughout the lifespan. Other aspects of affect structures will become more complex, subject to social learning, beginning with the earliest reciprocal interchanges and transactions with caregivers. It is conceivable that some might argue that in this sense infant affects are "shaped" by the social environment, but it is equally true that they bring influential preadapted structures to that environment and "shape" it in a major way (Bell, 1971; Sameroff, 1975). Ontogenetically, one could say that affects are social signals before they are psychological signals. They are involved in social reciprocity before they are anticipatory, before they can be mobilized internally and involved in means-end relationships. Also, from the beginning the very process of internalization of social objects is an affective one. For all such cognitive memory schemes prior to the onset of evocative memory capacity, the process is affective, involving reciprocal interchanges between infant and caregivers. What is familiar and recognized as such is embedded in a matrix of positive emotions of joy and interest and intermittent negative emotions related to unpleasure. Thus, for infant as well as mother, affects provide shading, coloration, and important elements of the medium used in making early dynamic memory pictures.

Conclusion

A Biology of Close Connections Between Emotions and Social Life

In considering our four infant models, it is important to emphasize that organizational shifts are biosocial as well as biobehavioral. It has been suggested that these organizational shifts may represent special times when enough components have developed that social learning can have a special organizing impact on experience. In other words, a critical number of components may be required for a shift, not only from an intrinsic point of view but also from the point of view of developing relationships with caretaking adults. Smiling, enhanced eye-to-eye contact, secondary circular reactions, and increased exploratory wakefulness—components which lead up to the first organizational shift—are incentives for social interaction; they are positive reinforcers for parents and necessary ingredients for parental bonding (see Emde, Gaensbauer, and Harmon, 1976; Klaus and Kennell, 1976). The same can be said for affective discrimination of primary caretakers and the capacity for means-end relationships which herald the second organizational shift. Similarly, the elation that accompanies the third shift influences the child's interaction with the caregiver, as do the mood swings of the fourth shift. As incentives and rewards for social interaction, these components necessarily induce a new level of organization in the parent-infant social system. Such a social reorganization in turn stabilizes the internal shift. After the first shift, for example, the baby is seen by parents in a new way, as "more human," as "fun," as "playful." The baby occupies a new position in the family and expectations for interaction are expanded. A valuable overall conceptual scheme for understanding increasing levels of social organization during infancy has been presented by Sander (1962).

From an adaptational point of view, that affects have social signaling functions in infancy, that they are subject to epigenesis and development, and that there are a number of discrete affect systems are evidence for the usefulness of an organizational model of affects in psychoanalytic theory. Our research on social referencing makes a strong argument for a biological connection between social and emotional development. But adaptation refers to phylogenesis as well as ontogenesis. If the model is robust, it should apply to organized affect systems in animals other than man. Evidence for this is not hard to find. One has only to recall that ideas about discrete affect in particular, and ideas for the field of ethology in general, both had their origins in Darwin's classic book of 1872, *The Expression of the Emotions in Man and Animals*. A more current background for thinking about the significance of epigenesis of discrete affect expressions in humans is provided by recent discussions in the ethological literature, where it has been pointed out that there is a functional significance of such sequences in mammals (Fox, 1970; Chevalier-Skolnikoff, 1971; Hinde, 1974). Most recently, Redican (1975), in his review of facial expressions in nonhuman primates, has pointed to an analogous ontogenetic sequence of affect expressions (lip smacking and play face) followed by fearful expressions (grimace) and then by aggressive expressions (threat and yawn).

Further, there is compelling biological evidence in non-human primates for close connections between emotions and social life. Myers (1976), in an extensive research program involving free-ranging and laboratory monkeys (rhesus macaques), has found the regulation of social and emotional behavior to be controlled by the same cortical areas in the forebrain (prefrontal, anterior-temporal, and orbital-frontal cortex). Animals who had these areas surgically ablated could not use facial expressions and vocalizations in emotional behavior or in social communication. Myers concludes that the monkeys' facial expressions and vocalizations have the primary if not the exclusive purpose of expressing emotional states to ensure social communication. From his observations of free-ranging animals he states, "Rhesus monkey facial expressions and vocalizations are used in two settings: they appear either in a context of social interactions with other animals to express aggressiveness or threat or to express submissiveness or aversion; or they are used instead to express such emotions as hunger, or in infants, feelings of anxiety during separation from mother" (p. 21). Ablation studies in adult free-ranging animals gave dramatic results. After removal of the above-noted cortical areas and after release from captivity, these animals passed through their social groups without approaching or interacting with other animals. They were never again seen in the vicinity of their home group, nor did they show any interest in any of the group members, including members of their family and former associates of long standing. Concomitant with a loss of social group affinity was a loss of emotional activity and reactivity. Although operated animals were lost to followup, it was assumed they did not survive in their alone and rather emotionless state.

Evolutionary considerations also highlight the close biological ties between social and emotional development. It would seem that infants' emotions have evolved not only for an expression of need states but also for enhancing social interaction. Certainly the human infant is intricately preprogrammed by genetic heritage for affective social signaling, affective social reciprocity, and social learning in general. Hamburg (1963) has speculated that human emotions evolved because they have had selective advantage in facilitating interindividual bonds and participation in group living. He articulates the principle that individuals seek and find gratifying those situations which have been highly advantageous for survival of the species, and avoid and find distressing those that have been highly disadvantageous in species survival. Applying considerations of interindividual bonds, he views group living as a powerful adaptive mechanism which has operated over the long course of evolution such that the formation of social bonds is experienced as pleasurable for primates and that their disruption is experienced as unpleasurable; the latter, in fact, is associated with profound psychophysiological changes and instrumental behaviors designed to restore close relations. Hamburg concludes his essay with a cogent statement regarding the intimate relations between the emotions and social bonding: "society is not composed of neutral actors but of emotional beings—whether we speak of baboons, chimpanzees, or man, emotion lies at the core of social process . . . the physiology of emotion ensures the fundamental acts for survival: the desire for sex, the extraordinary interest in the infant, the day-to-day reinforcement of inter-individual bonds" (p. 316).

Concluding Questions

At this stage of our knowledge, many questions have been raised and relatively few have been answered concerning the ontogeny of discrete affects, their organization, and the manner in which they lead to more complex affective structures. But the organizational models for biobehavioral shifts, the affective self, and social referencing have fostered a research strategy which offers the promise of answering some of them in the near future. Among those that should be answered soon are those related to knowledge about second-year development shifts and whether or not early moral internalization represents a third such shift. We must also address the question of what factors mediate each developmental shift and how individual differences in temperament or the affective self contribute to the patterning of observed transformations. Finally, we must address questions about the developmental course of preverbal, nonverbal, and preconflict affect structures beyond infancy.

Whatever else, there is unambiguous evidence from infant development, as well as from the clinical psychoanalytic situation, that affect systems are complex adaptive structures. Current thinking and future research will surely lead to useful theory and new horizons.

References

Altman, J. (1967), Postnatal growth and differentiation of the mammalian brain, with implications for a morphological theory of memory. In: *The Neurosciences*, ed. F.O. Schmitt, G.C. Quarton, & T. Melnechuk. New York: Rockefeller University Press, pp. 723–743.

Bekoff, M., & Fox, M. (1972), Postnatal neural ontogeny: Environment-dependent and/or environment-expectant. *Development Psychobiol.*, 5:323–341.

Bell, R.Q. (1971), Stimulus control of parent or caretaker behavior by offspring. *Developmental Psychol.*, 4:61–72.

—— (1974), Contributions of human infants to caregivers and social interaction, In: *The Effect of the Infant on Its Caregiver*, ed. M. Lewis & L.A. Rosenblum. New York: Wiley, pp. 1–19.

Benjamin, J. (1961), Some developmental observations relating to the theory of anxiety. *J. Amer. Psychoanal. Assn.*, 9:652–668.

Bergman, T., Haith, M.J., & Mann, L. (1971), Development of eye contact and facial scanning in infants. Paper presented at the meetings of the Society for Research in Child Development, Minneapolis, April.

Bernstein, P., Emde, R., & Campos, J. (1973), REM sleep in 4-month-old infants under home and laboratory conditions. *Psychosom. Med.*, 35:322–329.

Bertalanffy, L. von (1968a), *General System Theory: Foundations, Development, Applications*. New York: George Braziller.

—— (1968b), *Organismic Psychology Theory*. Barre, Mass.: Clark University Press with Barre Publishers.

Brazelton, T.B. (1962), Crying in infancy. *Pediatrics*, 29:579–588.

—— (1973), *Neonatal Behavioral Assessment Scale*. London: Spastics International Medical Publishers.

—— (1974), The origins of reciprocity: The early mother-infant interaction. In: *The Effect of the Infant on Its Caregiver*, ed. M. Lewis & L.A. Rosenblum. New York: Wiley, pp. 49–76.

—— Als, H., Tronick, E., & Lester, B. (1979), Specific neonatal measures: The Brazelton neonatal behavioral assessment scale. In: *Handbook of Infant Development*, ed. J. Osofsky. New York: Wiley.

—— Tronick, E., Adamson, L., Als, H., & Weise, S. (1975), Early mother-infant reciprocity. In: *Parent-Infant Interaction*. CIBA Foundation Symposium 33. Amsterdam: Elsevier, pp. 137–154.

Campos, J.J., Emde, R.N., Gaensbauer, T., Sorce, J., & Henderson, C. (1975), Cardiac behavioral interrelations in the reactions of infants to strangers. *Developmental Psychol.*, 11:589–601.

Chase; M. (1973), Somatic reflex activity during sleep and wakefulness. In: *Basic Sleep Mechanisms*, ed. O. Petre-Quadens & J. Schlag. New York: Academic Press, pp. 249–267.

Chevalier-Skolnikoff, S. (1971), The ontogeny of communication in Macaca speciosa. Unpublished doctoral dissertation, University of California, Berkeley.

Clarke, A.M., & Clarke, A.D.B. (1976), *Early Experience: Myth and Evidence.* New York: The Free Press.

Conel, J.L. (1941), *The Postnatal Development of the Human Cerebral Cortex: Vol. 2. The Cortex of the One-Month Infant.* Cambridge: Harvard University Press.

——— (1947), *The Postnatal Development of the Human Cerebral Cortex: Vol 3. The Cortex of the Three-Month Infant.* Cambridge: Harvard University Press.

Darwin, C. (1872), *The Expression of Emotion in Man and Animals.* London: John Murray.

deChateau, P., & Wiberg, B. (1977a), Long-term effect on mother-infant behavior of extra contact during the first hour post partum. I. *Acta Pediatrica Scandinavica*, 66:137–143.

——— ——— (1977b), Long-term effect on mother-infant behavior of extra contact during the first hour post partum. II. *Acta Pediatrica Scandinavica*, 66:145–151.

Dittrichova, J., & Lapackova, V. (1964), Development of the waking state in young infants. *Child Development*, 35:365–370.

——— ——— (1969), Development of sleep in infancy. In: *Brain and Early Behavior*, ed. R.J. Robinson. New York: Academic Press, pp. 193–204.

Ellingson, R.J. (1960). Cortical electrical responses to visual stimulation in the human infant. *Electroencephalog. Clin. Neurophysiol.*, 12:663–677.

Elmer, E., & Gregg, G. (1967), Developmental characteristics of abused children. *Pediatrics*, 40:596–602.

Emde, R.N. (1980), Emotional availability: A reciprocal reward system for infants and parents with implications for prevention of psychosocial disorders. In: Parent-Infant Relationships, ed. P.M. Taylor. Orlando: Grune & Stratton, pp. 87–115.

——— (1983), The prerepresentational self and its affective core. *The Psychoanalytic Study of the Child*, 38:165–192. New Haven: Yale University Press.

——— & Brown, C. (1978), Adaptation after the birth of a Down's Syndrome infant: A study of 6 cases, illustrating differences in development and the counter-movement between grieving and maternal attachment. *J. Amer. Acad. Child Psychiat.*, 17:299–323.

——— Campos, J., Reich, J., & Gaensbauer, T. (1978), Infant smiling at five and nine months: Analysis of heartrate and movement. *Infant Behav. & Devel.*, 1:26–35.

——— Gaensbauer, T.J., & Harmon, R.J. (1976), Emotional expression in infancy: A biobehavioral study. *Psychological Issues*, Monograph 37. New York: International Universities Press.

——— & Harmon, R.J. (1972), Endogenous and exogenous smiling systems in early infancy. *J. Amer. Acad. Child Psychiat.*, 11:177–200.

——— Johnson, W.F., & Easterbrooks, M.A. (in press), The do's and don'ts of early moral development: Psychoanalytic tradition and current research. In: *The Emergence of Morality*, ed. J. Kagan & S. Lamb. Chicago: University of Chicago Press.

———— & Koenig, K.L. (1969a), Neonatal smiling and rapid eye movement states. *J. Child Psychiat.*, 8:57–67.

———— ———— (1969b), Neonatal smiling, frowning, and rapid eye movement states. *J. Child Psychiat.*, 8:637–656.

———— McCartney, R.D., & Harmon, R.J. (1971), Neonatal smiling in REM states: IV. Premature study. *Child Development*, 42:1657–1661.

———— & Metcalf, D.R. (1970), An electroencephalographic study of behavioral rapid eye movement states in the human newborn. *J. Nerv. & Ment. Dis.*, 150:376–386.

———— & Robinson, J. (1979), The first two months: Recent research in developmental psychobiology and the changing view of the newborn. In: *Basic Handbook of Child Psychiatry*, ed. J. Call, J. Noshpitz, R. Cohen, & I. Berlin. New York: Basic Books, pp. 72–105.

———— & Sorce, J.F. (1983), The rewards of infancy: Emotional availability and maternal referencing. In: *Frontiers of Infant Psychiatry*, ed. J. Call, E. Galenson, & R. Tyson. New York: Basic Books, pp. 17–30.

———— Swedberg, J., & Suzuki, B. (1975), Human wakefulness and biological rhythms after birth. *Arch. Gen. Psychiat.*, 32:780–783.

———— & Walker, S. (1976), Longitudinal study of infant sleep: A multivariate approach with results of 14 subjects studied at monthly intervals. *Psychophysiol.* 13:456–461.

Escalona, S.K. (1968), *The Roots of Individuality: Normal Patterns of Development in Infancy*. Chicago: Aldine.

———— & Heider, G. (1959), *Prediction and Outcome: A Study of Child Development*. New York: Basic Books.

Fox, M.W. (1970), A comparative study of the development of facial expressions in canids: wolf, coyote and foxes. *Behaviour*, 36:49–73.

Freud, S. (1930), Formulations on the two principles of mental functioning. *Standard Edition*, 12:218–226. London: Hogarth Press, 1958.

Gaensbauer, T., & Emde, R.N. (1973), Wakefulness and feeding in human newborns. *Arch. Gen. Psychiat.*, 28:894–987.

Greenberg, N.H. (1965), Development effects of stimulation during early infancy: Some conceptual and methodological considerations. *Ann. N.Y. Acad. Sci.*, 118:831–859.

Haith, M. (1976), Visual competence in early infancy. In: *Handbook of Sensory Physiology VIII*, ed. R. Held, H. Leibowitz, & H.L. Teuber. New York: Springer-Verlag.

Hamburg, D.A. (1963), Emotions in the perspective of human evolution. In: *Expression of the Emotions in Man*, ed. P.H. Knapp. New York: International Universities Press, pp. 300–315.

Harlow, H.F. (1953), Mice, monkeys, men and motives. *Psychol. Rev.*, 60:23–32.

———— Harlow, M.K., & Meyer, D.R. (1950), Learning motivated by a manipulation drive. *J. Exper. Psychol.*, 40:228–234.

Hartmann, H. (1939), *Ego Psychology and the Problem of Adaptation*. New York: International Universities Press, 1958.

Hebb, D.O. (1949), *The Organization of Behavior*. New York: Wiley.

Heron, W., Bexton, W., & Hebb, D.O. (1953), Cognitive effects of a decreased variation to the sensory environment. *Amer. Psychologist*, 8:366.

Hinde, R.A. (1974), *Biological Bases of Human Behavior*. New York: McGraw-Hill.

Hoffman, M.L. (1977), Moral internalization: Current theory and research. In: *Advances in Experimental Social Psychology: Vol. 10*, ed. L. Berkowitz. New York: Academic Press.

Izard, C. (1971), *The Face of Emotion*. New York: Meredith.

James, W. (1890), *Principles of Psychology*. New York: Holt.

Jones, N.B., ed. (1972), *Ethological Studies of Child Behaviour*. Cambridge: Cambridge University Press.

Kagan, J. (1970a). Attention and psychological change in the young child. *Science*, 170:826–832.

——— (1970b), The distribution of attention in infancy. In: *Perception and Its Disorders*. ed. D.H. Hamburg. Baltimore: Williams & Wilkins, pp. 214–237.

——— (1977), A longitudinal study of development from infancy to age ten. Paper presented at the meetings of the Society for Research in Child Development, New Orleans.

——— (1981), *The Second Year: The Emergence of Self-Awareness*. Cambridge, Mass.: Harvard University Press.

——— (1984), *The Nature of the Child*, New York: Basic Books.

Kaufman, I.C. (1960), Symposium on psycho-analysis and ethology: III. Some theoretical implications from animal behaviour studies for the psychoanalytic concepts of instinct, energy, and drive. *Internat. J. Psycho-Anal.*, 41:318–326.

Klaus, M.H., Jerauld, R., Dreger, N.C., McAlpine, W., Steffa, M., & Kennell, J.H. (1972), Maternal attachment: Importance of the first postpartum days. *N. Engl. J. Med.*, 286:460–463.

——— & Kennell, J.H., eds. (1976), *Maternal-Infant Bonding*. St. Louis: Mosby.

Kleitman, N., & Engelmann, T.G. (1953), Sleep characteristics of infants. *J. Applied Physiol.*, 6:269–282.

Kligman, D., Smyrl, R., & Emde, R.N. (1975), A "non-intrusive" home study of infant sleep. *Psychosom. Med.* 37:448–453.

Korner, A. (1964), Some hypotheses regarding the significance of individual differences at birth for later development. *The Psychoanalytic Study of the Child*, 19:58–72. New York: International Universities Press.

——— (1969), Neonatal startles, smiles, erections and reflex sucks as related to state, sex and individuality. *Child Development*, 40:1039–1053.

——— (1974), The effect of the infant's state, level of arousal, sex and ontogenetic stage on the caregiver. In: *The Effect of the Infant on Its Caregiver*, ed. M. Lewis & L.A. Rosenblum. New York: Wiley, pp. 105–121.

Lewis, M., & Lee-Painter, S. (1974), An interactional approach to the mother-infant dyad. In: *The Effect of the Infant on Its Caregiver*, ed. M. Lewis & L.A. Rosenblum. New York: Wiley, pp. 21–48.

Livingston, R.B. (1967), Brain circuitry relating to complex behavior. In: *The Neurosciences*, ed. F.O. Schmitt, G.C. Quarton, & T. Melnechuk, New York: Rockefeller University Press, pp. 568–576.

Mahler, M.S., Pine, F., & Bergman, A. (1975), *The Psychological Birth of The Human Infant*. New York: Basic Books.

Marler, P., & Hamilton, W.J. (1966), *Mechanisms of Animal Behavior*. New York: Wiley.

Maurer, D., & Salapatek, P. (1976), Developmental changes in the scanning of faces by young infants. *Child Development*, 47:523–527.

McCall, R.B. (1977), Stages in mental development during the first two years. Paper presented at the meetings of the Society for Research in Child Development, New Orleans.

Miller, G.A., Galanter, E., & Pribram, K. (1960), *Plans and the Structures of Behavior*. New York: Holt.

Moss, H.A., & Robson, K. (1968), The role of protest behavior in the development of mother-infant attachment. Paper presented at the meeting of the American Psychological Association, San Francisco.

Myers, R.E. (1976), Cortical localization of emotion control. Paper presented at the meeting of the American Psychological Association, Washington.

Novey, S. (1961), Further considerations on affect theory in psychoanalysis. *Internat. J. Psycho-Anal.*, 42:21–31.

Paine, R.S. (1965), The contribution of development neurology to child psychiatry. *J. Amer. Acad. Child Psychiat.*, 4:353–386.

Papousek, H., & Papousek, M. (1982), Integration into the social world. In: *Psychobiology of the Human Newborn*, ed. P.M. Stratton. New York: Wiley, pp. 367–390.

Parmelee, A., & Michaelis, R. (1971), Neurological examination of the newborn. In: *Exceptional Infant*, ed. J. Hellmuth. New York: Brunner/Mazel, pp. 3–23.

——— Wenner, W., Akiyama, Y., Schulz, M., & Stern, E. (1967), Sleep states in premature infants. *Devel. Med. & Child Neurol.*, 9:70–77.

Peiper, A. (1963), Cerebral function in infancy and childhood. In: The International Behavioral Sciences Series, ed. J. Wortis. New York: Consultants Bureau.

Piaget, J. (1936), *The Origins of Intelligence in Children*. 2nd ed. New York: International Universities Press, 1952.

Prechtl, H.F. (1958), The directed head-turning response and allied movements of the human baby. *Behavior*, 13:212–242.

Radke-Yarrow, M., Zahn-Waxler, C., & Chapman, M. (1983), Children's prosocial dispositions and behavior. In: *Handbook of Child Psychology: Vol. 4, Socialization, Personality and Social Development*, ed. E.M. Hetherington. New York: Wiley, pp. 469–545.

Rangell, L. (1967), Psychoanalysis, affects, and the "human core": On the relationship of psychoanalysis to the behavioral sciences. *Psychoanal. Quart.*, 36:172–202.

Rapaport, D. (1953), On the psychoanalytic theory of affect. *Internat. J. Psycho-Anal.*, 34:177–198.

Redican, W.K. (1975), Facial expressions in nonhuman primates. In: *Primate Behavior*, ed. L. Rosenblum. Vol. 4. New York: Academic Press, pp. 103–194.

Richards, M.P.M., & Bernal, J.F. (1972), An observational study of mother-infant interaction. In: *Ethological Studies of Child Behaviour*, ed. N. Blurton-Jones. Cambridge: Cambridge University Press, pp. 175–197.

Robson, K.S. (1967), The role of eye-to-eye contact in maternal-infant attachment. *J. Child Psychol. & Psychiat.*, 8:13–25.

Rosenthal, M.K. (1973a), Attachment and mother-infant interaction: Some research impasse and suggested change in orientation. *J. Child Psychol. & Psychiat.*, 14:201–207.

—— (1973b), The study of infant-environment interaction: Some comments on trends and methodologies. *J. Child Psychol. & Psychiat.*, 14:301–317.

Salapatek, P. (1969), The visual investigation of geometric patterns by the one- and two-month-old infant. Paper presented at the meetings of the American Association for the Advancement of Science, Boston.

Sameroff, A.J. (1971), Can conditioned response be established in the newborn infant? *Developmental Psychol.*, 5:1–12.

—— (1975), Transactional models in early social relations. Human Development, 18:65–79.

—— & Cavanagh, P.J. (1979), Learning in infancy: A development perspective. In: *Handbook of Infant Development*, ed. J. Osofsky. New York: Wiley, pp. 344–392.

Sander, L. (1962), Issues in early mother-child interaction. *J. Amer. Acad. Child Psychiat.*, 1:141–166.

—— (1969), Regulation and organization in the early infant-caretaker system. In: *Brain and Early Behavior*, ed. R.J. Robinson. London: Academic Press, pp. 311–332.

—— (1975), Infant and caretaking environment: Investigation and conceptualization of adaptive behavior in a system of increasing complexity. In: *Explorations in Child Psychiatry*, ed. E.J. Anthony. New York: Plenum, pp. 129–166.

—— & Julia, H. (1966), Continuous interactional monitoring in the neonate. *Psychosom. Med.*, 28:822–835.

Scarr, S., & Salapatek, P. (1970), Patterns of fear development during infancy. *Merrill-Palmer Quart.*, 16:53–90.

Shaheen, E., Alexander, D., Truskowsky, M., & Barbero, G. (1968), Failure to thrive: A retrospective profile. *Clin. Pediatrics*, 7:255–261.

Spitz, R. (1945), Hospitalism: An inquiry into the genesis of psychiatric conditions in early childhood. *The Psychoanalytic Study of the Child*, 1:53–74. New York: International Universities Press.

—— (1946), Hospitalism: A follow-up report. *The Psychoanalytic Study of the Child*, 2:113–117.

—— (1959), *A Genetic Field Theory of Ego Formation*, New York: International Universities Press.

—— (1965), *The First Year of Life*. New York: International Universities Press.

—— & Wolf, M. (1946), The smiling response. *Genet. Psychol. Monographs*, 34:57–125.

Sroufe, A. (1977), Emotional expression in infancy. Unpublished manuscript.

Sterman, M.B., & Hoppenbrouwers, T. (1971), The development of sleep-waking and rest-activity patterns from fetus to adult in man. In: *Brain Development and Behavior*, ed. M.B. Sterman, D.J. McGinty, & A. Adinolfi. New York: Academic Press, pp. 203–517.

Stern, D. (1971), A micro-analysis of mother-infant interaction: Behavior regulating social contact between a mother and her 3-½-month-old twins. *J. Amer. Acad. Child Psychiat.*, 10:501–517.

——— (1974). Mother and infant at play: The dyadic interaction involving facial, vocal and gaze behaviors. In: *The Effect of the Infant on Its Caregiver*, ed. M. Lewis & L.A. Rosenblum. New York: Wiley, pp. 187–213.

——— (1977), *The First Relationship: Mother and Infant*. Cambridge: Harvard University Press.

——— (1985), *The Interpersonal World of the Infant*. New York: Basic Books.

Tennes, K., Emde, R.N., Kisley, A.J., & Metcalf, D.R. (1972), The stimulus barrier in early infancy: An exploration of some formulations of John Benjamin. *Psychoanal. & Contemp. Sci.*, 1:206–234.

Thomas, A., Birch, H.G., Chess, S., Hertzig, M.E., & Korn, S. (1963), *Behavioral Individuality in Early Childhood*. New York: New York University Press.

Thompson, W., & Grusec, J. (1970), Studies of early experience. In *Carmichael's Manual of Child Psychology*. 3rd ed. Vol. I. New York: Wiley, pp. 565–654.

Tronick, E. (1980), The primacy of social skills in infancy. In: *Exceptional Infant*, ed. D.B. Sarwin, R.C. Hawkins, L.O. Walker, & J.H. Penticuff. New York: Brunner/Mazel, pp. 144–158.

Wasz-Hockert, O., Partanen, T., Vuorenkoski, V., Valanne, E., & Michelsson, K. (1964), Effect of training on ability to identify preverbal vocalizations. *Devel. Med. & Child Neurol.*, 6:393–396.

Watson, J.B. (1930), *Behaviorism*. Chicago: University of Chicago Press.

White, R.W. (1963), Ego and reality in psychoanalytic theory. *Psychological Issues, Monograph 11*. New York: International Universities Press.

Wolff, P.H. (1959), Observations on newborn infants. *Psychosom. Med.*, 21:110–118.

——— (1960), The developmental psychologies of Jean Piaget and psychoanalysis. *Psychological Issues*, Monograph 5. New York: International Universities Press.

——— (1965), The development of attention in young infants. *Ann. N.Y. Acad. Sci.*, 118:815–830.

——— (1966), The causes, controls, and organization of behavior in the neonate. *Psychological Issues*, Monograph 17. New York: International Universities Press.

——— (1969), The natural history of crying and other vocalizations in early infancy. In: *Determinants of Infant Behavior: Vol. IV*, ed. B.M. Foss. Proceedings of the Fourth Tavistock Study Group, at CIBA Foundation. London: Methuen, Barnes and Noble.

Zahn-Waxler, C., & Radke-Yarrow, M. (1982), The development of altruism: Alternative research strategies. In: *The Development of Prosocial Behavior*, ed. N. Eisenburg. New York: Academic Press.

6

The Role of Attachment in Personality
Development and Psychopathology

JOHN BOWLBY

During the first third of this century the two great proponents of developmental psychiatry were Adolf Meyer and
Sigmund Freud. Both believed that the seeds of mental health
and ill health were sown in childhood and that to understand
the present-day functioning of a person it is necessary to know
how he or she has become the man or woman we meet with
today.

In their approaches to the field Meyer and Freud took very
different routes. Initially Freud focused on traumatic family
relationships, including incest, but soon, for reasons that remain
obscure, he claimed that the real-life events he had originally
invoked as pathogenic had in fact never occurred and that the
patient had only imagined them. Thenceforward the emphasis
was on fantasy. Consequently Freud's interests became focused
on a person's internal world of mental processes, especially on
the powerful influence that unconscious processes have on the
way a person feels, thinks, and behaves and, above all, on the
defensive processes that actively keep them unconscious.

Meyer, by contrast, continued to emphasize the part played
by real-life events in shaping personality, but he was never very
specific about the nature of the ones that matter, nor did he

Material in this chapter is reprinted from "Developmental Psychiatry
Comes of Age," *American Journal of Psychiatry*, Vol. 144, 1987; and from
"Attachment and Loss: Retrospect and Prospect," *American Journal of Ortho-
psychiatry*, Vol. 52, 1982. Permission from the Editors to reprint is gratefully
acknowledged.

advance any theory of how being exposed to some event or situation affects a person's mental state. Nonetheless, Meyer's approach played a major part in promoting the mental hygiene movement and child psychiatry. In both these revolutionizing movements the notion that the environment in which a child grows up plays a critical part in determining his future mental health has always been a stubbornly held if ill-defined assumption. Moreover, these are the fields in which Freud's original ideas about the role of childhood trauma have not only persisted but have borne valuable fruit.

We can see now that the tremendous strides being made today in developmental psychiatry owe a great deal to both these pioneers. To Adolf Meyer is due the credit for having continued to emphasize the influential role of the events and situations a person meets with during his development. To Sigmund Freud is due the credit for having emphasized the influence on how a person thinks, feels, and behaves that is exerted by his internal world, namely by the way he perceives, construes and structures the events and situations he encounters. Today we know that the central task of developmental psychiatry is to study the endless interaction of internal and external and how the one is constantly influencing the other, not only during childhood but during adolescence and adult life as well.

Evidence that happenings within the family during childhood and adolescence play a major role in determining whether a person grows up to be mentally healthy is now formidable, and a review of the important epidemiological findings has recently appeared (Rutter, 1985). For that reason, in this chapter I am presenting only a limited amount of data, some epidemiological and retrospective and some ethological and prospective, and am giving most attention to the conceptual framework within which I believe the different sets of findings can best be comprehended.

As an example of retrospective data I draw on the findings of the group led by George Brown and Tirril Harris which has been undertaking sophisticated epidemiological studies to explore the roles of family experience and other social variables as antecedents of depressive and anxiety disorders in adult life.

As an example of prospective data I draw on the work of the developmental psychologists who have been inspired by and are busy expanding the brilliant pioneering studies of Mary Ainsworth into the development of a young child's capacity to make intimate, emotionally mediated relationships with parents. Since the findings from these two quite different approaches are highly compatible, the resulting scientific structure can be likened to a trilithon made up of two stout pillars of evidence and a crosspiece of theory. A major conclusion is that, whatever influence variations in genetic endowment may exert on personality development and psychopathology, an immense influence is unquestionably exerted by environmental variables of the kinds now being systematically explored.

For many years sensitive clinicians with a psychoanalytic orientation have been aware that a person's mental state is deeply influenced by whether his intimate personal relationships are warm and harmonious or tense, angry, and anxious, or else emotionally remote, possibly nonexistent. Among clinicians so oriented a variety of terms are in use: significant other, dependency, symbiosis, object relations. Nevertheless, although a field of manifest importance to psychiatry, there has been no agreement how best to conceptualize it. A number of theoretical systems have been proposed, almost all of them derived in some sort of way from psychoanalysis, and a mountain of jargon has accumulated. Yet none has generated sustained productive research. In scientific quarters the whole field has struggled for recognition.

In recent years a new conceptual framework, known as attachment theory, has been proposed (Bowlby, 1969, 1973, 1980) which is providing explanations for existing data and promoting rapidly expanding research programs in developmental psychology and developmental psychopathology. Whereas Freud in his scientific theorizing felt confined to a conceptual model that explained all phenomena, whether physical or biological, in terms of the disposition of energy, today we have available conceptual models of much greater variety. Many draw on such interrelated concepts as organization, pattern, and information, while the purposeful activities of biological organisms can be conceived in terms of control systems structured in certain ways. The world of science in which we live is radically different from the world Freud lived in at the turn of the century, and the concepts available to us immeasurably better suited to our problems than were the very restricted ones available in his day. Before describing this new conceptual framework, some account of why new concepts have been introduced and how the field has evolved may be of interest.

The Evolution of a New Conceptual Framework

Deprivation of Maternal Care and Its Ill Effects

The origins of the new framework lie in observations made during the late 1930s and early 1940s. At that time a number of clinicians on both sides of the Atlantic, mostly working independently of each other, were making observations of the ill effects on personality development of prolonged institutional care and/or frequent changes of mother-figure during the early years of life. Influential publications followed, including those of Lauretta Bender (Bender and Yarnell, 1941; Bender, 1947), Dorothy Burlingham and Anna Freud (1942, 1944), William Goldfarb (1943a, b, and c; and six papers summarized in Goldfarb, 1955), David Levy (1937), René Spitz (1945, 1946), and myself (Bowlby, 1940, 1944). As each of the authors was a qualified analyst (except Goldfarb, who trained later), it is no surprise that the findings created little stir outside analytic circles.

Then, in late 1949, an imaginative young British psychiatrist, analytically oriented and recently appointed to be Chief of the Mental Health Section of the World Health Organization, stepped in. Requested to contribute to a United Nations study of the needs of homeless children, Ronald Hargreaves[1] decided to appoint a short-term consultant to report on the mental health aspects of the problem and, knowing of my interest in the field, invited me to undertake the task. For me this was a golden opportunity. After five years as an army psychiatrist, I

[1] Ronald Hargreaves's premature death in 1962 when professor of psychiatry at Leeds was a grievous loss to preventive psychiatry.

had returned to child psychiatry determined to explore further the problems I had begun working on before the war at the London Child Guidance Clinic; I had already appointed as my first research assistant James Robertson, a newly qualified psychiatric social worker who had worked with Anna Freud in the Hampstead Nurseries during the war. The six months I spent with the World Health Organization in 1950 gave me the chance not only to read the literature and discuss it with the authors but also to meet many others in Europe and the United States with experience of the field. Soon after the end of my contract I submitted my report, published early in 1951 as a WHO monograph entitled *Maternal Care and Mental Health*. In it I reviewed the far from negligible evidence then available regarding the adverse influences on personality development of inadequate maternal care during early childhood, called attention to the acute distress of young children who find themselves separated from those they know and love, and made recommendations of how best to avoid, or at least mitigate, the short- and long-term ill effects. During the next few years this report was translated into a dozen languages and appeared also in a cheap abridged edition in English (Bowlby, 1965).

Influential though the written word may often be, it has nothing like the emotional impact of a movie. Throughout the 1950s Rene Spitz's early film *Grief: A Peril in Infancy* (1947), followed soon after by James Robertson's *A Two-Year-Old Goes to Hospital* (1952), had an enormous influence. Not only did the two films draw the attention of professional workers to the immediate distress and anxiety of young children in an institutional setting; they also proved powerful instruments for promoting changes in practice. In this field Robertson was to play a lasting part (e.g., Robertson, 1958, 1970).

Although by the end of the 1950s a great many of those working in child psychiatry and psychology and in social work, and some also of those in pediatrics and sick children's nursing, had accepted the research findings and were implementing change, the sharp controversy aroused by the early publications and films continued. Psychiatrists trained in traditional psychiatry and psychologists who adopted a learning theory approach never ceased to point to the deficiencies of the evidence and to the lack of an adequate explanation of how the types of experience implicated could have the effects on personality development that were claimed. In addition, many psychoanalysts, especially those whose theory focuses on the role of fantasy in psychopathology to the relative exclusion of the influence of real-life events, remained unconvinced and sometimes very critical. Meanwhile research continued. For example, at Yale Sally Provence and Rose Lipton (1962) were making a systematic study of institutionalized infants in which they compared their development with that of infants living in a family. At the Tavistock Clinic members of my small research group were active collecting further data on the short-term effects on a young child of being in the care of strange people in a strange place for weeks and sometimes months at a time—see especially the studies by Christoph Heinicke (1956) and Heinicke and Westheimer (1966)—while I addressed myself to the theoretical problems posed by our data.

Meanwhile the field was changing. One important influence was the publication in 1962 by the World Health Organization of a collection of articles in which the manifold effects of the various types of experience covered by the term *deprivation of maternal care* were reassessed. Of the six articles, by far the most comprehensive was by my colleague Mary Ainsworth (1962). In it she not only reviewed the extensive and diverse evidence and considered the many issues that had given rise to controversy but also identified a large number of problems requiring further research.

A second important influence was the publication, beginning during the late fifties, of Harry Harlow's studies of the effects of maternal deprivation on rhesus monkeys; and once again film played a big part. Harlow's work in the United States had been stimulated by Spitz's reports. In the United Kingdom complementary studies by Robert Hinde had been stimulated by our work at the Tavistock. For the next decade a stream of experimental results from those two scientists (see summaries in Harlow and Harlow, 1965; Hinde and Spencer-Booth, 1971), coming on top of the Ainsworth review, undermined the opposition. Thereafter, nothing more was heard of the inherent implausibility of our hypotheses, and criticism became more constructive.

Much of course remained uncertain. Even if the reality of short-term distress and behavioral disturbance is granted, what evidence is there, it was asked, that the ill effects can persist? What features of the experience, or combination of features, are responsible for the distress? And, should it prove true that in some cases ill effects do persist, how is that to be accounted for? How comes it that some children seem to come through very unfavorable experiences relatively unharmed? How important is it that a child should be cared for most of the time by one principal caregiver? In less developed societies, it was claimed (wrongly as it turns out), multiple mothering is not uncommon. In addition to all these legitimate questions, moreover, there were misunderstandings. Some supposed that advocates of the view that a child should be cared for most of the time by a principal mother-figure held that that had to be the child's natural mother—the so-called blood-tie theory. Others supposed that, in advocating that a child experience a warm, intimate, and continuous relationship with his mother (or permanent mother-substitute), proponents were prescribing a regime in which a mother had to care for her child 24 hours a day, day in and day out, with no respite. In a field in which strong feelings are aroused and almost everyone has some sort of vested interest, clear unbiased thinking is not always easy.

The monograph *Maternal Care and Mental Health* has two parts. The first reviews the evidence regarding the adverse effects of maternal deprivation; the second discusses means for preventing it. What was missing, as several reviewers pointed out, was any explanation of how experiences subsumed under the broad heading of maternal deprivation could have the effects on personality development of the kinds claimed. The reason for this omission was simple: the data were not accommodated by any theory then current, and in the brief time of my employment by WHO there was no possibility of developing a new one.

The Child's Lie to His Mother: Attachment

At that time it was widely held that the reason a child develops a close tie to his mother is that she feeds him. Two kinds of drive are postulated, primary and secondary. Food is thought of as primary; the personal-relationship, referred to as "dependency," as secondary. This theory did not seem to me to fit the facts. For example, were it true, an infant of a year or two should take readily to whomever feeds him and this clearly was not the case. An alternative theory, stemming from the Hungarian school of psychoanalysis, postulated a primitive object relation from the beginning. In its best-known version, however, the one advocated by Melanie Klein, the mother's breast is postulated as the first object, and the greatest emphasis is placed on food and orality and on the infantile nature of dependency. None of these features matched my experience of children.

But if the current dependency theories were inadequate, what was the alternative?

During the summer of 1951 a friend mentioned to me the work of Konrad Lorenz on the following responses of ducklings and goslings. Reading about this and related work on instinctive behavior revealed a new world, one in which scientists of high caliber were investigating in nonhuman species many of the problems with which we were grappling in the human, in particular the relatively enduring relationships that develop in many species, first between young and parents and later between mated pairs, and some of the ways in which these developments can go awry. Could this work, I asked myself, cast light on a problem central to psychoanalysis, that of "instinct" in humans?

Next followed a long phase during which I set about trying to master basic principles and to apply them to our problems, starting with the nature of the child's tie to his mother. Here Lorenz's work on the following response of ducklings and goslings (1935) was of special interest. It showed that in some animal species a strong bond to an individual mother-figure could develop without the intermediary of food: for these young birds *are not fed by parents* but feed themselves by catching insects. Here then was an alternative model to the traditional one, and one that had a number of features that seemed possibly to fit the human case. Thereafter, as my grasp of ethological principles increased and I applied them to one clinical problem after another, I became increasingly confident that this was a promising approach. Thus, having adopted this novel point of view, I decided to "follow it up through the material as long as the application of it seems to yield results" (to borrow a phrase from Freud, 1915).

From 1957, when "The Nature of the Child's Tie to His Mother" was first presented (Bowlby, 1958) through 1969, when *Attachment* appeared until 1980 with the publication of *Loss*, I concentrated on this task. The resulting conceptual framework[2] is designed to accommodate all those phenomena to which Freud called attention—for example, love relations, separation anxiety, mourning, defense, anger, guilt, depression, trauma, emotional detachment, sensitive periods in early life—and so to offer an alternative to the traditional metapsychology of psychoanalysis and to add yet another to the many variants of the clinical theory now extant. How successful these ideas will prove only time will tell.

As Kuhn has emphasized, any novel conceptual framework is difficult to grasp, expecially so for those long familiar with a previous one. Of the many difficulties met with in understanding the framework advocated, I describe only a few. One is that, instead of starting with a clinical syndrome of later years and trying to trace its origins retrospectively, I have started with a class of childhood traumata and tried to trace their sequelae prospectively. A second is that, instead of starting with the private thoughts and feelings of a patient, as expressed in free associations or play, and trying to build a theory of personality development from those data, I have started with observations of the behavior of children in certain sorts of defined situation, including records of the feelings and thoughts they express, and have tried to build a theory of personality development from there. Other difficulties arise from my use of concepts such as control system (instead of psychic energy) and developmental pathway (instead of libidinal phase) which, although now firmly established as key concepts in all the biological sci-

---

[2] This is the term Thomas Kuhn (1974) now uses to replace "paradigm," the term he used in his earlier work (1962).

ences, are still foreign to the thinking of a great many psychologists and clinicians.

Having discarded the secondary drive (dependency) theory of the child's tie to his mother, and also the Kleinian alternative, a first task was to formulate a replacement. This led to the concept of attachment behavior as a special class of behavior with its own dynamics distinct from the behavior and dynamics of either feeding or sex, the two sources of human motivation for long widely regarded as the most fundamental. Strong support for this step soon came from Harlow's finding that in another primate species—rhesus macaques—infants show a marked preference for a soft dummy "mother," despite its providing no food, to a hard one that does provide it (Harlow and Zimmermann, 1959).

Attachment behavior is any form of behavior that results in a person attaining or maintaining proximity to some other clearly identified individual who is conceived as better able to cope with the world. It is most obvious whenever the person is frightened, fatigued, or sick, and is assuaged by comforting and caregiving. At other times the behavior is less in evidence. Nevertheless, for a person to know that an attachment figure is available and responsive gives him a strong and pervasive feeling of security, and so encourages him to value and continue the relationship. While attachment behavior is at its most obvious in early childhood, it can be observed throughout the life cycle, especially in emergencies. Since it is seen in virtually all human beings (though in varying patterns), it is regarded as an integral part of human nature and one we share (to a varying extent) with members of other species. The biological function attributed to it is that of protection. To remain within easy access of a familiar individual known to be ready and willing to come to our aid in an emergency is clearly a good insurance policy—whatever our age.

By conceptualizing attachment in this way, as a fundamental form of behavior with its own internal motivation distinct from feeding and sex, and of no less importance for survival, the behavior and motivation are accorded a theoretical status never before given them—though parents and clinicians alike have long been intuitively aware of their importance. Hitherto the terms *dependency* and *dependency need* have been used to refer to them, but these terms have serious disadvantages. In the first place, dependency has a pejorative flavor; in the second, it does nót imply an emotionally charged relationship to one or a very few clearly preferred individuals; and, in the third, no valuable biological function has ever been attributed to it.

It is now thirty years since the notion of attachment was first advanced as a useful way of conceptualizing a form of behavior of central importance not only to clinicians and to developmental psychologists but to every parent as well. During that time attachment theory has been greatly clarified and amplified. The most notable contributors have been Robert Hinde, who in addition to his own publications (e.g., 1974) has constantly guided my own thinking, and Mary Ainsworth, who from the late fifties on has pioneered empirical studies of attachment behavior both in Africa (1963, 1967) and in the U.S. (Ainsworth and Wittig, 1969; Ainsworth, Blehar, Waters, and Wall, 1978) and has also helped greatly to develop theory (e.g., 1969, 1982). Her work, together with that of her students and others influenced by her (e.g., Sroufe and Waters, 1977; Sroufe, 1985; Main, 1985; Bretherton, 1987), has led attachment theory to be widely regarded as probably the best supported theory of socioemotional development yet available (Rajecki, Lamb, and Obmascher, 1978; Rutter, 1980; Parkes and Stevenson-Hinde, 1982).

Because my starting point in developing theory was observations of behavior, some clinicians have assumed that the theory amounts to no more than a version of behaviorism. This mistake is due in large part to the unfamiliarity of the conceptual framework proposed and in part to my own failure in early formulations to make clear the distinction to be drawn between an attachment and attachment behavior. To say of a child or older person that he is attached to, or has an attachment to, someone means that he is strongly disposed to seek proximity to and contact with that individual and to do so especially in certain specified conditions. The disposition to behave in this way is an attribute of the attached person, a persisting attribute which changes only slowly over time and which is unaffected by the situation of the moment. Attachment behavior, by contrast, refers to any of the various forms of behavior the person engages in from time to time to obtain or maintain a desired proximity.

There is abundant evidence that almost every child habitually prefers one person, usually his mother-figure, to go to when distressed but that in her absence he will make do with someone else, preferably someone he knows well. On these occasions most children show a clear hierarchy of preferences so that, in extremity and with no one else available, even a kindly stranger may be approached. Thus, while attachment behavior may in differing circumstances be shown to a variety of individuals, an enduring attachment, or attachment bond, is confined to very few. A child who fails to show such clear discrimination is likely to be severely disturbed.

The theory of attachment is an attempt to explain both attachment behavior, with its episodic appearance and disappearance, and also the enduring attachments that children and other individuals make to particular others. In this theory the key concept is that of behavioral system. As this concept may be unfamiliar to many readers, its full exposition is postponed until after a description is given of how some of the many other phenomena of central concern to clinicians are explained within the new framework.

Old Problems in a New Light

Separation Anxiety

First, new light is thrown on the problem of separation anxiety, namely, anxiety about losing, or becoming separated from, someone loved. Why "mere separation" should cause anxiety has been a mystery. Freud wrestled with the problem and advanced a number of hypotheses (Freud, 1926; Strachey, 1959). Every other leading analyst has done the same. With no means of evaluating these hypotheses, many divergent schools of thought have proliferated.

The problem lies, I believe, in an unexamined assumption, made not only by psychoanalysts but by more traditional psychiatrists as well, that fear is aroused in a mentally healthy person only in situations that everyone would perceive as intrinsically painful or dangerous, or that are perceived so by a person only because of his having become conditioned to them. Since fear of separation and loss does not fit this formula, analysts have concluded that what is feared is really some other situation; and a great variety of hypotheses have been advanced.

The difficulties disappear, however, when an ethological approach is adopted. For it then becomes evident that man, like other animals, responds with fear to certain situations not because they carry a *high* risk of pain or danger but because they signal an *increase* of risk. Thus, just as animals of many species, including man, are disposed to respond with fear to sudden movement or a marked change in level of sound or light because to do so has survival value, so are many species, including man, disposed to respond to separation from a potentially caregiving figure and for the same reasons.

When separation anxiety is seen in this light, as a basic human disposition, it is only a small step to understand why it is that threats to abandon a child, often used as a means of control, are so very terrifying. Such threats, and also threats of suicide by a parent, are, we now know, common causes of intensified separation anxiety. Their extraordinary neglect in traditional clinical theory is due, I suspect, not only to an inadequate theory of separation anxiety but to a failure to give proper weight to the powerful effects, at all ages, of real-life events.

Not only do threats of abandonment create intense anxiety; they also arouse anger, often also of intense degree, especially in older children and adolescents. This anger, the function of which is to dissuade the attachment figure from carrying out the threat, can easily become dysfunctional. It is in this light, I believe, that we can understand such absurdly paradoxical behavior as the adolescent reported by Burnham (1965) who, having murdered his mother, exclaimed, "I couldn't stand to have her leave me."

Other pathogenic family situations are readily understood in terms of attachment theory. One fairly common example is seen when a child has such a close relationship with his mother that he has difficulty in developing a social life outside the family, a relationship sometimes described as symbiotic. In a majority of such cases the cause of the trouble can be traced to the mother, who, having grown up anxiously attached as a result of a difficult childhood, is now seeking to make her own child her attachment figure. Far from the child being overindulged, as is sometimes asserted, he is being burdened with having to care for his own mother. Thus, in these cases, the normal relationship of attached child to caregiving parent is found to be inverted.

Mourning

While separation anxiety is the usual response to a threat or some other risk of loss, mourning is the usual response to a loss after it has occurred. During the early years of psychoanalysis a number of analysts identified losses, occurring during childhood or in later life, as playing a causal role in emotional disturbance, especially in depressive disorders. By 1950 a number of theories about the nature of mourning, and other responses to loss, had been advanced. Moreover, much sharp controversy had already been engendered. This controversy, which began during the thirties, arose from the divergent theories about infant development that had been elaborated in Vienna and London. Representative examples of the different points of view about mourning are those expressed in Helene Deutsch's "Absence of Grief" (1937) and Melanie Klein's "Mourning and Its Relation to Manic-Depressive States" (1940). Whereas Deutsch held that inadequate psychic development renders children unable to mourn, Klein held that they not only can mourn but do. In keeping with her strong emphasis on feeding, however, she held that the object mourned was the lost breast; in addition, she attributed a complex fantasy life to the infant. Opposite though these theoretical positions are, both were constructed using the same methodology, namely, inference about earlier phases of psychological development based on observations made during the analysis of older, emotionally disturbed subjects. Neither theory had been checked by direct observation of how ordinary children of different ages respond to a loss.

Approaching the problem prospectively as I did led me to

different conclusions. During the early 1950s Robertson and I had generalized the sequence of responses seen in young children during temporary separation from the mother as those of protest, despair, and detachment (Robertson and Bowlby, 1952). A few years later, when reading a study by Marris (1958) of how widows respond to the loss of their husband, I was struck by the similarity of the responses he describes to those observed in young children who have suffered a loss or separation. This led me to a systematic study of the literature on mourning, especially the mourning of healthy adults. The sequence of responses that commonly occur, it became clear, was very different from what clinical theorists had been assuming. Not only does mourning in mentally healthy adults last far longer than the six months often suggested in those days, but several component responses widely regarded as pathological were found to be common in healthy mourning. These include anger directed at third parties, the self, and sometimes at the person lost; disbelief that the loss has occurred (misleadingly termed denial); and a tendency, often though not always unconscious, to search for the lost person in the hope of reunion. The clearer the picture of mourning responses in adults became, the clearer became their similarities to those observed in children. This conclusion when first advanced (Bowlby, 1960, 1961) was much criticized, but it has now been amply supported by a number of subsequent studies (e.g., Kliman, 1965; Parkes, 1972; Furman, 1974; Raphael, 1982).

Once an accurate picture of healthy mourning has been obtained it becomes possible to identify features that are truly indicative of pathology. It becomes possible also to discern many of the conditions that promote healthy mourning and those that lead in a pathological direction. The belief that children are unable to mourn can then be seen to derive from generalizations that had been made from the analyses of children whose mourning had followed an atypical course. In many cases this had been due either to the child's never having been given adequate information about what had happened or to there having been no one to sympathize with him and help him gradually come to terms with his loss, his yearning for his lost parent, his anger, and his sorrow.

The next step in this reformulation of theory was to consider how defensive processes could best be conceptualized, a crucial step since defensive processes have always been at the heart of psychoanalytic theory. Before addressing this problem, however, it is necessary to consider some of the other basic features of the new conceptual framework.

Control Systems, Defensive Processes and Internal Working Models

Exploration from a Secure Base

In addition to attachment behavior, and antithetical to it, is the urge to explore the environment, to play, and to take part in varied activities with peers. When an individual of any age is feeling secure he is likely to explore away from his attachment figure. But when alarmed, anxious, tired, or unwell he feels an urge toward proximity. This is the typical pattern of interaction between child and parent known as exploration from a secure base. Provided the parent is known to be accessible and will be responsive when called upon, a healthy child feels secure enough to explore. At first these explorations are limited both in time and space. Around the middle of the third year, however, a secure child begins to become confident enough to increase time and distance away—first to half days and later to whole days. As he grows into adolescence his excursions are extended to weeks or months, but a secure home base remains indispensable nonetheless for optimal functioning and mental health. No concept within the attachment framework is more central to the development of personality than that of the secure base; as shown below, it is when an individual does not have a secure base that development deviates toward pathology.

Control Systems

To explain the behavior described above, attachment theory draws on two concepts which, though hitherto unemployed in the field of personality development, are now in regular use in physiology and cognitive psychology. First, it is postulated that within the central nervous system there exists a special control system, analogous to the physiological control systems that maintain physiological measures, such as blood pressure and body temperature, within set limits. In a way analogous to physiological homeostasis, this attachment control system maintains a person's relation to his attachment figure between certain limits of distance and accessibility. As such it can be regarded as an example of what can usefully be termed *environmental homeostasis* (Bowlby, 1973). Among situations that activate careseeking are anything that frightens a child or signals that he is tired or unwell. Among situations that terminate careseeking and release him for other activities are comfort and reassurance. Since control systems are themselves sources of activity, traditional theories of motivation which invoke a build-up of psychic energy or drive are rendered obsolete.

It is in the nature of a control system that it can operate effectively only within a specified environment. For example, the system regulating body temperature cannot maintain an appropriate temperature when environmental conditions become either too hot or too cold, which means that whenever conditions exceed certain limits the whole organism becomes stressed or dies. Viewed in an evolutionary perspective, it is evident that variation and natural selection have resulted in each organism's physiological systems being so constructed that they operate effectively in the environment to which the species has become adapted and that they will become stressed or fail in others.

An evolutionary perspective is necessary also if we are to understand psychological stress and the environmental conditions that cause it. Like other control systems, the system governing human attachment behavior is constructed so as to promote survival in the environment in which the human species evolved. Since in such an environment it is essential for survival that an infant or older child has an attentive and responsive caregiver to go to in an emergency, it follows that the attachment system will be constructed so as to operate most efficiently in interaction with a person the child believes will respond promptly and effectively when called upon. It is hardly surprising, therefore, that a failure to respond by the familiar caregiver, even if due to physical absence, or a failure to respond appropriately, will always cause stress and sometimes be traumatic.

This leads to consideration of the third major component of human nature relevant to this exposition—namely, caregiving, the prime role of parents and the complement of attachment behavior. When looked at in terms of evolution theory, the occurrence of altruistic care of the young is readily understood, as it serves to promote the survival of offspring (and often of other relatives as well) and thereby the caring individual's own genes. Nevertheless, this form of explanation constitutes a radical shift from most psychological theorizing, including Freud's, which has mistakenly assumed that individuals are by nature essentially selfish and that they consider the interests of others only when constrained to do so by social pressures and sanctions. Nothing, I believe, that stems from an ethological perspective has more far-reaching implications for understanding human nature than this reappraisal of altruism.

Defensive Processes

Although as a clinician I have inevitably been concerned with the whole range of defenses, as a research worker I have directed my attention especially to the way a young child behaves toward his mother after a spell in a hospital or residential nursery unvisited. In such circumstances it is common for a child to begin by treating his mother almost as though she were a stranger; then, after an interval, usually of hours or days, he becomes intensely clinging, anxious lest he lose her again, and angry with her should he think he may. In some way all his feeling for his mother and all the behavior toward her we take for granted, keeping within range of her and most notably turning to her when frightened or hurt, have suddenly vanished—only to reappear again after an interval. That was the condition James Robertson and I termed *detachment* and which we believed was a result of some defensive process operating within the child.

What is so very peculiar about this strange detached behavior is of course the absence of attachment behavior in circumstances in which we would confidently expect to see it. Even when he has hurt himself severely such a child shows no sign of seeking comfort. Thus, signals that would ordinarily activate attachment behavior are failing to do so. This suggests that in some way and for some reason these signals are failing to reach the behavioral system responsible for attachment behavior, that they are being blocked off and the behavioral system itself thereby immobilized. What this means is that a system controlling such crucial behavior as attachment can in certain circumstances be rendered either temporarily or permanently incapable of being activated, and with it the whole range of feeling and desire that normally accompanies it is rendered incapable of being aroused.

In considering how this deactivation might be effected, I turned to the work of the cognitive psychologists (e.g., Dixon, 1971, 1981; Norman, 1976), who during the past twenty years have revolutionized our knowledge of how we perceive the world and how we construe the situations we are in. This revolution in cognitive theory not only gives unconscious mental processes the central place in mental life that analysts have always claimed for them, but presents a picture of the mental apparatus as well able to shut off information of certain specified types and of doing so selectively, without the person being aware of what is happening.

In the emotionally detached children described earlier and also, I believe, in adults who have developed the kind of personality that Winnicott (1960) describes as "false self" and Kohut (1977) as "narcissistic," the information being blocked off is of a very special type. Far from being an instance of the routine exclusion of irrelevant and potentially distracting information that we engage in all the time and that is readily reversible, what is excluded in these pathological conditions are the signals, arising from both inside and outside the person, that would activate their attachment behavior and that would enable them both to love and to experience being loved. In other words, the mental structures responsible for routine selective exclusion are being employed—one might say exploited—for a special and potentially pathological purpose. This form of exclusion I refer to—for obvious reasons—as defensive exclusion, which is, of course, only another way of describing repression. And, just as

Freud regarded repression as the key process in every form of defense, so I see the role of defensive exclusion.[3] A fuller account of this information processing approach to the problem of defense, in which defenses are classified into defensive processes, defensive beliefs, and defensive activities, is given in an early chapter of *Loss* (Bowlby, 1980).

Internal Working Models

Returning now to the attachment control system within the child, it is evident that for it to operate efficiently it must have at its disposal as much information as possible about self and attachment figure, not only in regard to their respective locations and capabilities but in regard also to how each is likely to respond to the other as environmental and other conditions change. Observations lead us to conclude that toward the end of the first year of life a child is acquiring a considerable knowledge of his immediate world and that during subsequent years this knowledge is best regarded as becoming organized in the form of internal working models, including models of self and mother in interaction with each other. The function of these models is to simulate happenings in the real world, thereby enabling the individual to plan his behavior with all the advantages of insight and foresight. The more adequate and accurate the simulation, of course, the better adapted is the behavior based on it likely to be (Johnson-Laird, 1982). Although our knowledge of the rate at which these models develop during the earliest years is still scanty, there is good evidence that by the fifth birthday most children are using a sophisticated working model of mother or mother-substitute which includes knowledge of her interests, moods, and intentions, all of which he can then take into account (Light, 1979). With a complementary model of himself, he is already engaging in a complex intersubjective relationship with his mother, who of course has her own working models both of her child and of herself. Because these models are in constant use, day in and day out, their

[3] As Spiegel (1981) points out, my term *defensive exclusion* carries a meaning very similar to Sullivan's *selective inattention*.

influence on thought, feeling, and behavior becomes routine and operates largely outside of awareness.

Since as clinicians we know that long before a child reaches the age of 5 the patterns of interaction between him and his mother range vastly in diversity, from smooth-running and happy to being filled with friction and distress of every kind and degree, and are also apt to persist, the more we know about how they originate the better. It is here that recent research by developmental psychologists has made huge strides.

Patterns of Attachment and Their Determinants

Three principal patterns of attachment present during the early years are now reliably identified, together with the family conditions that promote them. One of these patterns is consistent with the child's developing healthily and two are predictive of disturbed development. Which pattern any one individual develops during these years is found to be profoundly influenced by the way his parents (or other parent-type figures) treat him. This conclusion, as important as it is controversial, is unpopular in some circles and is constantly challenged. Yet the evidence for it is now weighty and derives from a number of prospective research studies of socioemotional development during the first 5 years. This research tradition, pioneered by Ainsworth during the 1960s (Ainsworth et al., 1978; Ainsworth, 1985), has since been exploited and expanded, notably in the U.S. by Main (Main and Stadtman, 1981; Main and Weston, 1981; Main, Kaplan, and Cassidy, 1985), Sroufe (1983, 1985), and Waters (Waters, Vaughn, and Egeland, 1980; Waters and Deane, 1985) and in Germany by Grossmann (Grossmann, Grossmann, and Schwan, 1986).

The pattern of attachment consistent with healthy development is that of secure attachment, in which the individual is confident that his parent (or parent figure) will be available, responsive, and helpful should he encounter adverse or frightening situations. With this assurance, he feels bold in his explorations of the world and also competent in dealing with it. This pattern is found to be promoted by the ready availability of a parent, in the early years especially the mother, sensitive to the child's signals and lovingly responsive when he seeks protection, comfort, or assistance.

A second pattern is that of anxious resistant attachment in which the individual is uncertain whether a parent will be available, responsive, or helpful when called upon. Because of this uncertainty the individual is always prone to separation anxiety, tends to be clinging, and is anxious about exploring the world. This pattern is promoted by a parent who is available and helpful on some occasions but not on others, by separations, and, later, by threats of abandonment used as a means of control.

A third pattern is that of anxious avoidant attachment in which the individual has no confidence that when he seeks care he will be responded to helpfully; on the contrary, he expects to be rebuffed. Such an individual attempts to live his life without the love and support of others. This pattern is the result of the individual's mother constantly rebuffing him when he approaches her for comfort or protection. The most extreme cases result from repeated rejection and ill treatment, or prolonged institutionalization. Clinical evidence suggests that if it persists this pattern leads to a variety of personality disorders from compulsively self-sufficient individuals to persistently delinquent ones.

There is much evidence that, at least in families where caregiving arrangements continue stable, the pattern of attachment between child and mother, once established, tends to persist. For example, in two different samples (Californian and German) the patterns of attachment to the mother at 12 months were found, with but few exceptions, still to be present at 6 years (Main, Kaplan, and Cassidy, 1985; Wärtner, 1986). Furthermore, prospective studies in Minneapolis (Sroufe, 1983) have shown that the pattern of attachment characteristic of the pair, as assessed when the child is 12 months old, is highly predictive also of behavior outside the home in a nursery group 3½ years later. Thus children who showed a secure pattern with the mother at 12 months are likely to be described by their nursery teachers as cheerful and cooperative, popular with other children, resilient and resourceful. Those who showed an anxious avoidant pattern are likely to be described later as emotionally insulated, hostile or antisocial, and as unduly seek-ing of attention. Those who showed an anxious resistant pattern are also likely to be described as unduly seeking of attention and either as tense, impulsive, and easily frustrated or as passive and helpless.

Ample confirmation of the teacher's descriptions comes from independent observers and laboratory assessments of the same children (Sroufe, 1983; LaFrenier and Sroufe, 1985). Sim-ilarly, an experimental study done in Germany (Lütkenhaus, Grossmann, and Grossmann, 1985) shows that at 3 years of age children earlier assessed as securely attached respond to po-tential failure with increased effort, whereas the insecurely at-tached do the opposite. In other words, the securely attached children respond with confidence and hope that they can suc-ceed, while the insecure are already showing signs of helpless-ness and defeatism.

In a number of these studies detailed observations have been made of the way the children's mothers treated them. Great variability is seen, with high correlations between a mother's style of interaction and the child's pattern of attach-ment to her. For example, in one such study (Matas, Arend, and Sroufe, 1978), made when the children were 2½ years old, mothers were observed while their children were attempting a task they could not manage without a little help. Mothers of secure toddlers enabled their children to focus on the task, respected their attempts to complete it on their own, and re-sponded with the required help when called upon; communi-cation between mother and child was harmonious. Mothers of insecure infants were less sensitive to their toddlers' state of mind, either not giving support and help when appealed to or else intruding when a child was striving to solve the problem himself.

In discussing these and similar findings, Bretherton (1987) emphasizes the easy flow of communication between mother and child in the secure partnerships and concludes that this easy communication is possible only when a mother is intuitively alive to the crucial part she plays in providing her child with a secure base, variously encouraging autonomy, providing necessary help, or giving comfort according to her child's state of mind.

Mothers of insecure infants deviate from this sensitive pattern of mothering in a great variety of ways. One, common among mothers of avoidant infants, is to scoff at a child's bids for comfort and support (Main, Kaplan, and Cassidy, 1985). Another, well-known to clinicians, the effects of which are now being observed by developmentalists (Sroufe, Jacobvitz, Mangelsdorf, DeAngelo, and Ward, 1985; Main and Solomon, 1986), is the failure to respect a child's desire for autonomy, and the discouragement of exploration. This is seen usually in mothers who, not having had a secure home base during their own childhood, consciously or unconsciously seek to invert the relationship by making an attachment figure of the child. In the past this has too often been labeled "overindulgence" or "spoiling," which has led to appalling confusion about what is best for a child.

It is not difficult to understand why patterns of attachment, once developed, tend to persist. One reason is that the way a parent treats a child, for better or worse, tends to continue unchanged; another is that each pattern tends to be self-perpetuating. A secure child is a happier and more rewarding child to care for, and also is less demanding than an anxious one. By contrast, an anxious, ambivalent child is apt to be whiny and clinging, while an anxious, avoidant child keeps his distance and is ill-tempered and prone to bully other children. In each of the latter two cases the child's behavior is likely to elicit an unfavorable response from the parent, encouraging the development of vicious circles.

Although for the reasons given patterns, once formed, are likely to persist, this is by no means necessarily so. Evidence shows that during the first two or three years pattern of attachment is a property of the relationship—for example, pattern of child to mother may differ from pattern to father—and also that if the parent treats the child differently the pattern will change accordingly. These changes are among the evidence reviewed by Sroufe (1985) indicating that stability of pattern, when it occurs, cannot be attributed to the child's inborn temperament, as has often been claimed. On the contrary, the evidence points unmistakably to the conclusion that a host of personal characteristics, traditionally termed temperamental and often ascribed to heredity, are in fact environmentally induced. True, neonates differ from each other in many many ways. Yet the evidence is crystal clear from repeated studies that infants described as difficult during their early days are enabled by sensitive mothering to become happy, easy toddlers. Contrariwise, placid newborns can be turned into anxious, moody, demanding, or awkward toddlers by insensitive or rejecting mothering. Not only did Ainsworth demonstrate this in her original study, but it has been found again and again in subsequent ones. Those who attribute so much to inborn temperament will have to think again.

Thus, during the earliest years features of personality crucial to psychiatry remain relatively open to change because they are still responsive to the environment. As a child grows older, however, clinical evidence shows that both the pattern of attachment and the personality features that go with it become increasingly a property of the child himself and also increasingly resistant to change. This means that he tends to impose it, or some derivative of it, upon new relationships, as that with the teacher in the Minneapolis study. Similarly, experience shows that he tends also to impose it, or some derivative of it, on a foster mother or a therapist.

These tendencies to impose earlier patterns on new relationships, and in some measure to persist in doing so despite absence of fit, are, of course, the phenomena that gave birth to psychoanalysis. They are also the phenomena that during recent decades have led an increasing number of analysts to embrace an interpersonal or object relations version of psychoanalytic theory and, in my own case, to advance the attachment version with its postulate of internal working models of self and attachment figure in interaction. Thus far, therefore, the picture presented can be looked upon as a much modified and updated variant of traditional psychoanalytic thinking in which great emphasis is placed on the particular pattern into which each personality comes to be organized during the early years, with its own distinctive working models or, to use the traditional term, internal world, and on the strong influence thereafter that each individual's models have in shaping his or her life.

An Alternative Framework

During the time it has taken to develop the conceptual framework described here, Margaret Mahler has been concerned with many of the same clinical problems and some of the same features of children's behavior; she has also been developing a revised conceptual framework to account for them, set out fully in *The Psychological Birth of the Human Infant* (Mahler, Pine, and Bergman, 1975). To compare alternative frameworks is never easy, as Kuhn (1962) emphasizes, and no attempt is made to do so here. Elsewhere (Bowlby, 1981) I describe what I believe to be some of the strengths of the framework I favor, including its close relatedness to empirical data, both clinical and developmental, and its compatibility with current ideas in evolutionary biology and neurophysiology; what I see as the shortcomings of Mahler's framework are trenchantly criticized by Peterfreund (1978) and Klein (1981).

In brief, Mahler's theories of normal development, including her postulated normal phases of autism and symbiosis, are shown to rest not on observation but on preconceptions based on traditional psychoanalytic theory, which holds that each nonorganic psychiatric syndrome represents a regression to a phase of development in which features of the syndrome are part of normal development. Adopting that model has the effect of ignoring almost entirely the remarkable body of new information about early infancy that has been built up from careful empirical studies over the past two decades. Although the key concepts with which Mahler's theory is built are very different, some of the clinical implications are not dissimilar; there is in fact one central idea that is shared (Mahler et al., 1975). This is Mahler's concept of a return to base for "emotional refueling," which, as we have seen, is described here as the use of an attachment figure as a secure base from which to explore.

Continuity and Discontinuity: Vulnerability and Resilience

Developmental Pathways

One of the long-running debates between analysts and others in our field turns on the extent to which it is believed that personality, once developed during the early years, is open to change. Analysts have emphasized a strong tendency toward stability and continuity and have explained it as due to the powerful influence of the individual's existing internal world on how he construes and responds to every new situation. Critics have emphasized the extent to which an individual's performance can change given changed conditions of life. Today I hope we can agree that, if we are to do justice to the plethora of data now available, we must abandon simple dichotomies. First, a sharp distinction must be drawn between current functioning, measured in terms of presence or absence of psychiatric disorder, and personality structure, measured in terms of greater or lesser vulnerability to adverse life events and situations. Linked closely to degrees of vulnerability, moreover, are the very different ways that people feel about their lives, either as mostly enjoyable and to be lived to the full or as a burden to be endured; as an emotionally rich and varied experience or an emotional desert.

Second, abandoning the traditional psychoanalytic model of phases of development, fixations, and regressions, we are wise at all times to think in terms of the interactions and transactions that are constantly occurring between an ever developing personality and the environment, especially the people in it. This means that it is necessary to think of each personality as moving through life along some developmental pathway, with the particular pathway followed always being determined by the interaction of the personality as it has so far developed and the environment in which it presently finds itself. If as developmental psychiatrists we adopt these ways of thinking, we need to picture each personality as moving through life along its own unique pathway. So long as family conditions are favorable, the pathway will start and continue within the bounds of healthy and resilient development; but should conditions become sufficiently unfavorable at any time, it may deviate to a lesser or greater extent toward some form of disturbed and vulnerable development. Conversely, should an infant be born into unfavorable conditions, the pathway along which it develops may become deviant very early; yet once again, should there be change, in this case for the better, there is a chance of the deviation diminishing to a greater or lesser extent. Examples of two such deviant pathways are illustrated in Figures 1 and 2.

This leads me back to patterns of attachment, since my hypothesis is that the pathway followed by each developing individual and the extent to which he or she becomes resilient to stressful life events is determined to a very significant degree by the pattern of attachment developed during the early years. Furthermore, this implies that, in identifying the family experiences that result in different children developing different patterns of attachment, my colleagues are identifying also some of the major determinants of each person's future resilience or vulnerability to life's hazards, as well as the extent to which he or she will be able to enjoy life.

So far, unfortunately, the detailed prospective studies described earlier of how some of the different patterns of attachment come into being, and of their relative persistence, have not been carried beyond the sixth year. This means that the hypothesis, however plausible, will be without rigorous testing for some years to come. Meanwhile, however, those who advance the hypothesis point to much supporting evidence coming from the other major school of research referred to earlier, namely, epidemiological studies of adults who are suffering from one or another of a wide range of psychiatric disabilities including anxiety and depressive states, suicidal behavior, borderline conditions, and sociopathic personality.

From among a large array of epidemiological studies I have chosen the work of George Brown and Tirril Harris to illustrate my thesis because it is not only of the highest quality but directs attention to variables of the kind that the prospective research already described is showing to be so very influential. In addition, they use a sophisticated model of developmental pathways for interpreting their findings.

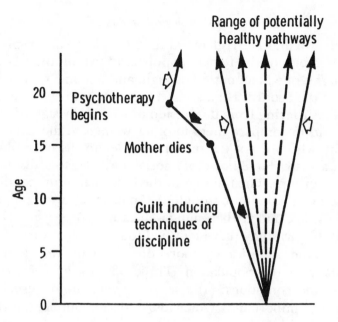

FIGURE 1. Developmental pathway deviating toward anxious attachment and depression.

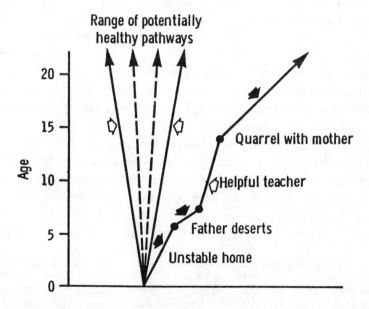

FIGURE 2. Developmental pathway deviating toward hostility and delinquency.

Epidemiological Studies

Brown and Harris have studied four large and representative samples of the female population,[4] two in inner London boroughs, one in an outer borough, and one in a remote rural area of the Scottish Highlands. Their aim has been to identify women suffering from depression of a clinically significant degree and to compare them to other women in the same community who are not depressed in order to discover whether there are any family or other social variables that distinguish the two groups. The findings of the first such study, conducted in the inner London borough of Camberwell, were published ten years ago and are becoming well known (Brown and Harris, 1978). In this study they identified four classes of variable that were found significantly more often among the depressed members of the population. Three of these concern *current* events and conditions: (a) a severe adverse event, usually involving an important personal loss or disappointment, that had occurred within the year prior to onset; (b) the absence of a companion in whom to confide; and (c) chronically difficult living conditions, including extremely bad housing and responsibility for caring for a number of children under the age of 14. The fourth variable associated with current incapacitating depression is an *historical* one, namely, (d) a woman's loss of her mother due to death or prolonged separation before her eleventh birthday. In subsequent studies of two large and mainly working class samples, in Walthamstow and Islington, findings of a similar sort have been the rule (Bifulco, 1985; Brown, Harris, and Bifulco, 1986; Harris, Brown, and Bifulco, 1987; Bifulco, Brown, and Harris, 1987). The annual prevalence of a current affective disorder in women who had lost their mother before their eleventh birthday compared to those who had not were, in the three samples, 43% vs. 14%, 25% vs. 7%, and 34% vs. 17%. Moreover, in the second and third studies it was found

---

[4] Among samples of depressed women there is often also a higher incidence, compared to controls, of loss of father during childhood: in two of these studies the effects of this have been explored. Since the detailed analyses show that loss of father has much less influence on vulnerability than loss of mother, further reference to it is omitted.

that women who had lost their mother during adolescence (between their eleventh and seventeenth birthdays) were also more prone to develop depression than the controls, though less so than those who had lost their mother when they were younger. The consistency of these findings, together with findings from a long-term prospective study reported by Wadsworth (1984), lend strong support to the clinically derived hypothesis that childhood loss of mother is likely to render a person excessively prone to develop psychiatric symptoms, and to do so especially when current personal relationships go wrong.

In their Walthamstow study, members of the Brown-Harris group undertook a prolonged and extensive interview with each woman in order to gain as much information as possible about the family circumstances during her childhood and adolescence and also about her subsequent life course, including, for example, the jobs she had had, her boyfriends, any premarital pregnancy, and her husband and children (if any). With the sample deliberately structured to include a high proportion of women who had suffered a childhood loss or prolonged separation, it became possible to analyze out the extent to which family variables other than loss may have contributed to a woman's current vulnerability.

In keeping with expectations, it was found that both the family circumstances that had led to the childhood loss and the adequacy of care a girl had received afterward were of great consequence. The worse the family circumstances before the loss and the more inadequate the care after it, the more vulnerable to depression the girl had become.

The very detailed analyses of these data carried out by the researchers have led them to explain their findings in terms of developmental pathways that, through the continuing interaction of social and personality factors, eventuate in the plight of a working class London girl who, having lost her mother for any reason, is at appallingly high risk of becoming depressed. In the first place, they found, such a loss carried with it a high likelihood that she would thereafter receive inadequate care; in the Walthamstow study the chances were found to be no better than fifty-fifty. Subsequently, her troubles were likely to snowball. Should the care she received have been poor, risks were high that she would become pregnant before marriage or that she would venture into an early and ill-advised marriage. These two occurrences were found to be strongly associated with later depression, in part because they usually resulted in her living in very unfavorable conditions at high risk of suffering a severe adverse event and with no one in whom to confide. For these reasons a working class girl who had lost her mother was all too likely to find herself on a slippery slope.

Figure 3, adapted from one designed by Brown and Harris, attempts to illustrate these interacting processes. The thick upper line represents the girl's mental state. The middle line represents what may for convenience be described as her family environment. The thin lower line represents her socioeconomic environment, in this case urban working class. The broken lines indicate the endless ways in which mental state and environment interact, with environmental happenings affecting mental state and mental state in turn affecting the way the girl or young woman deals with aspects of her environment.

Two further findings, both from the Islington study, illustrate this interaction (Bifulco, Brown, and Harris, 1987). A girl who received inadequate care, either in or out of her family, is found twice as likely to have developed a negative self-image when compared to a girl who received adequate care. The figures are 54% compared to 27%. Similar differences are reported from Edinburgh (by Ingham, Kreitman, Miller, Sashidharan, and Surtees, 1986). Furthermore, the marriage she enters into is more likely to fail than is that of the more fortunate girl. Here the figures are 36% and 23%. The high risk of this happening is evidently the result of a chain of adverse happenings. For example, when a girl has no caring home base she may become desperate to find a boyfriend who will care for her; that, combined with her negative self-image, makes her all too likely to settle precipitately for some totally unsuitable young man. Premature pregnancy and childbirth are then likely to follow, with all the economic and emotional difficulties that entails. Moreover, in times of trouble, the effects of her previous adverse experiences are apt to lead her to make unduly intense demands on her husband and, should he fail to meet them, to

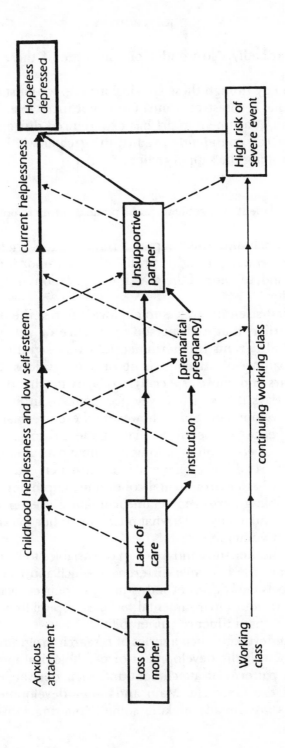

FIGURE 3. Female pathways to depression (adapted from Brown & Harris).

treat him badly. No wonder one in three of these marriages break up.

Gloomy though these conclusions are, we must remember always that a disastrous outcome is not inevitable. The more secure an attachment a girl has experienced during her early years, we can confidently predict, the greater will her chances be of escaping the slippery slope.

Scientific Problems and Practical Implications

In concluding this chapter I refer, all too briefly, first to some of the many scientific problems that clamor for attention and, second, to some of the practical implications of our present knowledge.

A first scientific task is to explore and test the hypothesis, stated earlier, that each person's resilience or vulnerability to stressful life events is determined to a very significant degree by the pattern of attachment he or she develops during the early years and, more especially, to clarify to what degrees and in what ways these early developed patterns influence subsequent development. Since, however, there are many subpatterns of each of the three main patterns, to elucidate the influence of each will be a long and time-consuming task. An integral part of such research is the further examination of precisely what environmental conditions, impinging earlier or later, enable a person to retain or attain a greater degree of resilience and, conversely, what push him or her toward greater degrees of vulnerability.

Yet another substantial group of variables to be taken into account are the heritable differences which must be assumed to exist between different individuals in their capacity to deal with the various environmental hazards, especially inadequate parenting, that influence vulnerability.

In undertaking such a series of research programs an early requirement is the development of psychological methods for assessing patterns of attachment and their derivatives at each phase of the life cycle. Main and other developmental psychologists are already making some promising moves in this direction (see the review by Ainsworth, 1985), while Hansburg's Separation Anxiety Test is proving its worth (Hansburg, 1986). To cast light on problems of continuity and discontinuity, both of patterns of attachment and also of different degrees of resilience and vulnerability, prospective studies following personality development through different phases of the life cycle and in different environments are plainly indispensable, despite their being very costly.

This brief sketch represents what will be an enormous program of research in developmental psychopathology (Sroufe and Rutter, 1984) and one that will clearly require generations of research workers. Both in magnitude and in the biological principles informing it, it can best be compared to the vast program of research which has been undertaken in immunology. Here, as in our own field, research workers are concerned with the extraordinarily complex interactions and transactions that occur between an organism as it develops over the years and the array of hazards present and potentially present in its environment. Concepts analogous to those in our field include the degree to which an organism is immune to a wide variety of hazards and the extent to which an existing state of immunity will persist or change over time.

What then are the practical implications of our present knowledge? For the clinician concerned with the assessment and treatment of a wide range of psychiatric patients of all ages it provides a developmental psychopathology that is biologically based, coherent, and already empirically well-supported. As such it can provide guidance for understanding how a patient's problems and symptoms have evolved in his transactions with the particular environments he has encountered from infancy to the present day. Furthermore, it can provide guidance for planning therapeutic intervention. Though much detailed work is still required in these areas, promising starts have been made (e.g., Heard, 1981, 1982; Belsky and Nezworski, 1988; Lieberman and Pawl, in press). Elsewhere (Bowlby, 1977, 1988) I have outlined the approach to analytic psychotherapy that I believe should be adopted in the light of current knowledge.

What, however, is even more important, is the firm guidance that present knowledge gives for prevention. As I have emphasized throughout, I believe there is already sufficient evidence, coming from diverse and independent sources, that points to the very substantial influence on personality development and mental health of the way an individual's parents (or in some cases parent substitutes) treat him or her. Given affectionate, responsive, and encouraging parents who throughout infancy, childhood, and adolescence provide a boy or girl a secure base from which to explore the world and to which to return when in difficulty, it is more than likely that he or she will grow up to be a cheerful, socially cooperative, and effective citizen, and to be unlikely to break down in adversity. Furthermore, such persons are far more likely than those who come from less stable and supportive homes to make stable marriages and to provide their children the same favorable conditions for healthy development that they enjoyed themselves (Dowdney, Skuse, Rutter, Quinton, and Mrazek, 1985; Quinton and Rutter, 1985). These, of course, are age-old truths, but they are now underpinned by far more solid evidence than ever before.

Unfortunately, as we also know, there is another and less happy side to the picture. Children and adolescents who grow up without their home base providing the necessary support and encouragement are likely to be less cheerful, to find life, especially intimate relationships, difficult, and to be vulnerable in conditions of adversity. In addition, they are likely to have difficulties when they come to marry and have children of their own. It is fortunate, of course, that despite these handicaps some manage to struggle through, though often at a much greater cost to their emotional life than meets the undiscerning eye. Nor must the fortunate exceptions blind us to the rule. Thus, to take an analogy from physiological medicine, the fact that some heavy smokers survive is no argument for tobacco.

If, by exploiting this new knowledge, the burden of mental ill health is to be reduced, Western societies will have to give far more attention to measures that encourage and support stable family life than any do at present. What the social, economic, and political implications of such measures might be, if they are to be effective, will require very serious study and may well be far-reaching. Experts from many fields will be required.

Yet substantial progress in this important area cannot be expected until members of the mental health professions speak with a more united voice than they do at present. Let us hope that we are now within sight of that happening.

References

Ainsworth, M.D. (1962), The effects of maternal deprivation: A review of findings and controversy in the context of research strategy. In: *Deprivation of Maternal Care: A Reassessment of Its Effects.* Public Health Papers 14. Geneva: World Health Organization.

—— (1963), The development of infant-mother interaction among the Ganda. In: *Determinants of Infant Behaviour: Vol. 2*, ed. B.M. Foss. London: Methuen.

—— (1967), Infancy in Uganda: Infant care and the growth of attachment. Baltimore: Johns Hopkins Press.

—— (1969), Object relations, dependency and attachment: A theoretical review of the infant-mother relationship. *Child Development*, 40:969–1025.

—— (1982), Attachment: Retrospect and prospect. In: *The Place of Attachment in Human Behaviour*, ed. C.M. Parkes & J. Stevenson-Hinde. New York: Basic Books.

—— (1985), I. Patterns of infant-mother attachment: Antecedents and effects on development. II. Attachments across the life span. *Bull. N.Y. Acad. Med.*, 6:771–812.

—— Blehar, M.C., Waters, E., & Wall, S. (1978), *Patterns of Attachment: Assessed in the Strange Situation and at Home.* Hillsdale, N.J.: Erlbaum.

—— & Wittig, B.A. (1969), Attachment and exploratory behaviour of one-year-olds in a strange situation. In: *Determinants of infant behaviour: Vol. 4.* ed. B.M. Foss. London: Methuen.

Belsky, J., & Nezworski, T., eds. (1988), *Clinical Implications of Attachment.* Hillsdale, N.J.: Erlbaum.

Bender, L. (1947), Psychopathic behaviour disorders in children. In: *Handbook of Correctional Psychology*, ed. R.M. Lindner & R.V. Seliger. New York: Philosophical Library.

—— & Yarnell, H. (1941), An observation nursery. *Amer. J. Psychiat.*, 97:1158–1174.

Bifulco, A.T.M. (1985), Death of mother in childhood and clinical depression in adult life: A biographical approach to aetiology. Doctoral thesis, University of London.

—— Brown, G.W., & Harris, T.O. (1987), Childhood loss of parent and adult psychiatric disorder: The Islington study. *Journal of Affective Disorders*, 12:115–128.

Bowlby, J. (1940), The influence of early environment in the development of neurosis and neurotic character. *Internat. J. Psycho-Anal.*, 21:154–178.

—— (1944), Forty-four juvenile thieves: Their characters and home life. *Internat. J. Psycho-Anal.*, 25:19–52, 107–127.

—— (1951), *Maternal Care and Mental Health.* Geneva: WHO.

—————— (1958), The nature of the child's tie to his mother. *Internat. J. Psycho-Anal.*, 39:350-373.

—————— (1960), Grief and mourning in infancy and early childhood. *The Psychoanalytic Study of the Child*, 15:9–52. New York: International Universities Press.

—————— (1961), Processes of mourning. *Internat. J. Psycho-Anal.*, 42:317–340.

—————— (1965), *Child Care and the Growth of Love*. Harmondsworth: Penguin.

—————— (1969), *Attachment and Loss: Vol. 1. Attachment*, 2nd ed. New York: Basic Books.

—————— (1973), *Attachment and Loss: Vol. 2. Separation: Anxiety and Anger*. New York: Basic Books.

—————— (1977), The making and breaking of affectional bonds. *Brit. J. Psychiat.*, 130:201–210, 421–431.

—————— (1980), *Attachment and Loss: Vol. 3. Loss: Sadness and Depression*. New York: Basic Books.

—————— (1981), Psychoanalysis as a natural science. *Internat. Rev. Psycho-Anal.*, 8:243–256.

—————— (1988), Attachment, communication and the therapeutic process. In: *The Secure Base*. New York: Basic Books.

Bretherton, I. (1987), New perspectives on attachment relations: security, communication and internal working models. In: *Handbook of Infant Development*, ed. J. Osofsky. 2nd ed. New York: Wiley.

Brown, G.W. & Harris, T. (1978), *The Social Origins of Depression: A Study of Psychiatric Disorder in Women*. London: Tavistock.

—————— —————— & Bifulco, A. (1986), Long-term effects of early loss of parent. In: *Depression in Childhood: Developmental Perspectives*, ed. M. Rutter, C. Izard, & P. Read. New York: Guilford.

Burlingham, D., & Freud, A. (1942), Young children in war-time London. London: Allen & Unwin.

—————— —————— (1944), *Infants Without Families*. London: Allen & Unwin.

Burnham, D.L. (1965), Separation anxiety. *Arch. Gen. Psychiat.*, 13:346–358.

Deutsch, H. (1937), Absence of grief. *Psychoanal. Quart.*, 6:12–22.

Dixon, N.F. (1971), *Subliminal Perception: The Nature of a Controversy*. London: McGraw-Hill.

—————— (1981), Preconscious Processing. New York: Wiley.

Dowdney, L., Skuse, D., Rutter, M., Quinton, D., & Mrazek, D. (1985), The nature and quality of parenting provided by women raised in institutions. *J. Child Psychol. & Psychiat.*, 26:599–625.

Freud, S. (1915), Repression. *Standard Edition*, 14:141–158.

—————— (1926), Inhibitions, symptoms and anxiety. *Standard Edition*, 20:87–174. London: Hogarth Press, 1959.

Furman, E. (1974), *A Child's Parent Dies*. New Haven: Yale University Press.

Goldfarb, W. (1943a), The effect of early institutional care on adolescent personality. *Child Development*, 14:213–223.

—————— (1943b), The effects of early institutional care on adolescent personality. *J. Experimental Education*, 12:106.

—————— (1943c), Infant rearing and problem behavior. *Amer. J. Orthopsychiat.*, 13:249–265.

—————— (1955), Emotional and intellectual consequences of psychologic deprivation in infancy: A revaluation. In: *Psychopathology of Childhood*, ed. P.H. Hoch & J. Zubin. New York: Grune & Stratton, pp. 105–119.

Grossmann, K.E., Grossmann, K., & Schwan, A. (1986), Capturing the wider view of attachment: A reanalysis of Ainsworth's strange situation. In: *Measuring Emotions in Infants and Children: Vol. 2*, ed. C.E. Izard & P.B. Read. New York: Cambridge University Press, pp. 124–171.

Hansburg, H.A. (1986), *Researches in Separation Anxiety*. Malabar, Fla.: Krieger.

Harlow, H.F., & Harlow, M.K. (1965), The affectional systems. In: *Behaviour of Nonhuman Primates: Vol. 2*, ed. A.M. Schrier, H.F. Harlow, & F. Stollnitz. New York: Academic Press.

———— & Zimmermann, R.R. (1959), Affectional responses in the infant monkey. *Science*, 130:421–432.

Harris, T.A., Brown, G.W., & Bifulco, A. (1987), Loss of parent in childhood and adult psychiatric disorder: The role of social class position and premarital pregnancy. *Psychol. Med.*, 17:163–184.

Heard, D.H. (1981), The relevance of attachment theory to child psychiatric practice. *J. Child Psychol. & Psychiat.*, 22:89–96.

———— (1982), Family systems and the attachment dynamic. *J. Fam. Ther.*, 4:99–116.

Heinicke, C. (1956), Some effects of separating two-year-old children from their parents: A comparative study. *Human Relations*, 9:105–176.

———— & Westheimer, I. (1966), *Brief Separations*. New York: International Universities Press.

Hinde, R.A. (1974), Biological Bases of Human Social Behaviour. New York: McGraw-Hill.

———— & Spencer-Booth, Y. (1971), Effects of brief separation from mother on rhesus monkeys. *Science*, 173:111–118.

Ingham, J.G., Kreitman, N.B., Miller, P.M., Sashidharan, S.P., & Surtees, P.G. (1986), Self-esteem, vulnerability and psychiatric disorder in the community. *Brit. J. Psychiat.*, 148:375–385.

Johnson-Laird, P.N. (1983), *Mental Models*. Cambridge: Cambridge University Press.

Klein, Melanie (1940), Mourning and its relation to manic-depressive states. In: *Love, Guilt and Reparation and Other Papers, 1921–1946*. London: Hogarth, 1947.

Klein, Milton (1981), On Mahler's autistic and symbiotic phases: an exposition and evaluation. *Psychoanal. & Contemp. Thought*, 4:69–105.

Kliman, G. (1965), *Psychological Emergencies of Childhood*. New York: Grune & Stratton.

Kohut, H. (1977), *The Restoration of the Self*. New York: International Universities Press.

Kuhn, T.S. (1962), *The Structure of Scientific Revolutions*. 2nd ed. Chicago: University of Chicago Press, 1970.

———— (1974), Second thoughts on paradigms. In: The Structure of Scientific Theory, ed. F. Suppe. Urbana: University of Illinois Press, pp. 459–499.

LaFrenier, P., & Sroufe, L.A. (1985), Profiles of peer competence in the preschool: Interrelations between measures, influence of social ecology and relation to the attachment history. *Development Psychol.*, 21:56–69.

Levy, D. (1937), Primary affect hunger. *Amer. J. Psychiat.*, 94:643–652.

Lieberman, A.F., & Pawl, J.H. (in press), Disorders of attachment and secure base behaviour in the second year: Conceptual issues and clinical intervention. In: *Attachment in the Preschool Years: Theory, Research and Intervention,* ed. M. Greenberg, D. Cicchetti, & M. Cummings. Chicago: University of Chicago Press.

Light, P. (1979), Development of a child's sensitivity to people. London: Cambridge University Press.

Lorenz, K.Z. (1935), Der Kumpan in der Umvelt des Vogels. *J. Orn. Berl., 83.* English trans. in: *Instinctive Behaviour,* ed. C.H. Schiller. New York: International Universities Press, 1957, pp. 83–128.

Lütkenhaus, P., Grossmann, K.E., & Grossmann, K. (1985), Infant-mother attachment at twelve months and style of interaction with a stranger at the age of three years. *Child Development,* 56:1538–1542.

Mahler, M.S., Pine, F., & Bergman, A. (1975), *The Psychological Birth of the Human Infant.* New York: Basic Books.

Main, M., Kaplan, N., & Cassidy, J. (1985), Security in infancy, childhood and adulthood: A move to the level of representation. In: *Growing Points in Attachment: Theory and Research,* ed. I. Bretherton & E. Waters. Chicago: University of Chicago Press, pp. 66–104.

———— & Solomon, J. (1986), Discovery of an insecure-disorganized/disoriented attachment pattern. In: *Affective Development in Infancy,* ed. T.B. Brazelton & M. Yogman. Norwood, N.J.: Ablex.

———— & Stadtman, J. (1981), Infant response to rejection of physical contact by the mother: Aggression, avoidance and conflict. *J. Amer. Acad. Child Psychiat.,* 20:292–307.

———— & Weston, D.R. (1981), The quality of the toddler's relationship to mother and to father: Related to conflict behaviour and the readiness to establish new relationships. *Child Development,* 52:932–940.

Marris, P. (1958), Widows and Their Families. London: Routledge & Kegan Paul.

Matas, L., Arend, R.A., & Sroufe, L.A. (1978), Continuity of adaptation in the second year: The relationship between quality of attachment and later competence. *Child Development,* 49:547–556.

Norman, D.A. (1976), *Memory and attention: Introduction to human information processing.* 2nd ed. New York: Wiley.

Parkes, C.M. (1972), *Bereavement: Studies of Grief in Adult Life.* New York: International Universities Press.

———— & Stevenson-Hinde, J., eds. (1982), *The Place of Attachment in Human Behaviour.* New York: Basic Books.

Peterfreund, E. (1978), Some critical comments on psychoanalytic conceptualizations of infancy. *Internat. J. Psycho-Anal.,* 59:427–441.

Provence, S., & Lipton, R.C. (1962), *Infants in Institutions.* New York: International Universities Press.

Quinton, D., & Rutter, M. (1985), Parenting behaviour of mothers raised in care. In: *Longitudinal Studies in Child Psychology and Psychiatry: Practical Lessons from Research Experience,* ed. A.R. Nicol. New York: Wiley, pp. 157–261.

Rajecki, D.W., Lamb, M.E., & Obmascher, P. (1978), Towards a general theory of infantile attachment: A comparative review of aspects of the social bond. *Behavioural & Brain Sciences,* 3:417–464.

Raphael, B. (1982), The young child and the death of a parent. In: *The Place of Attachment in Human Behavior,* ed. C.M. Parkes and J. Stevenson-Hinde. New York: Basic Books, pp. 131–150.

Robertson, J. (1952), Film: *A Two-Year-Old Goes to Hospital.* New York: New York University Film Library.

────── (1958), Film: *Going to Hospital with Mother.* London: Tavistock Child Development Research Unit; New York: New York University Film Library.

────── (1970), *Young Children in Hospital.* 2nd ed. London: Tavistock.

────── & Bowlby, J. (1952), Responses of young children to separation from their mothers. *Courrier Centre Internationale Enfance,* 2:131–142.

Rutter, M., ed. (1980), *Scientific Foundations of Developmental Psychiatry,* London: Heinemann Medical Books.

────── (1985), Resilience in the face of adversity: Protective factors and resistance to psychiatric disorder. *Brit. J. Psychiat.,* 147:598–611.

Spiegel, R. (1981), Review of *Loss: Sadness and Depression* by John Bowlby. *Amer. J. Psychother.,* 35:598–600.

Spitz, R.A. (1945), Hospitalism: An enquiry into the genesis of psychiatric conditions in early childhood. *The Psychoanalytic Study of the Child,* 1:53–74. New York: International Universities Press.

────── (1946), Anaclitic depression. *The Psychoanalytic Study of the Child,* 2:313–342. New York: International Universities Press.

────── (1947), Film: *Grief: A Peril in Infancy.* New York: New York University Film Library.

Sroufe, L.A. (1983), Infant-caregiver attachment and patterns of adaptation in preschool: The roots of maladaptation and competence. In: *Minnesota Symposium in Child Psychology: Vol. 16,* ed. M. Perlmutter. Minneapolis: University of Minnesota Press, pp. 41–81.

────── (1985), Attachment classification from the perspective of infant-caregiver relationships and infant temperament. *Child Development,* 56:1–14.

────── Jacobvitz, D., Mangelsdorf, S., DeAngelo, E., & Ward, M.J. (1985), Generational boundary dissolution between mothers and their preschool children: A relationship systems approach. *Child Development,* 56:317–325.

────── & Rutter, M. (1984), The domain of developmental psychopathology. *Child Development,* 55:17–29.

────── & Waters, E. (1977), Attachment as an organizational construct. *Child Development,* 48:1184–1199.

Strachey, J. (1959), Editor's introduction to "Inhibitions, symptoms and anxiety." *Standard Edition,* 20:77–86. London: Hogarth Press, 1959.

Wadsworth, M.E.J. (1984), Early stress and associations with adult health, behaviour and parenting. In: *Stress and Disability in Childhood,* ed. N.R. Butler & B. Corner. Bristol: John Wright.

Wärtner, U.G. (1986), Attachment in infancy and at age six, and children's self-concept: A follow-up of a German longitudinal study. Doctoral dissertation, University of Virginia.

Waters, E., & Deane, K.E. (1985), Defining and assessing individual differences in attachment relationships: Q-methodology and the organization of behaviour in infancy and early childhood. In: *Growing Points in Attachment Theory and Research,* ed. I. Bretherton & E. Waters. Chicago: Chicago University Press, pp. 41–65.

────── Vaughn, B.E., & Egeland, B.R. (1980), Individual differences in infant-mother attachment relationships at age one: Antecedents in neonatal behaviour in an urban, economically disadvantaged sample. *Child Development,* 51:208–216.

Winnicott, D.W. (1960), Ego distortion in terms of true and false self. In: *The Maturational Process and the Facilitating Environment.* New York: International Universities Press, pp. 140–152.

7

Psychoanalytic Perspectives on the First Year of Life: The Establishment of the Object in an Affective Field

THEODORE SHAPIRO, M.D.
DANIEL STERN, M.D.

Freud's earliest efforts centered around clinical queries about patients with symptoms. These issues evolved into the founding of psychoanalysis and a new understanding of the meaning and origins of psychological symptoms. Despite the fact that since then psychoanalysis has become a theoretical model that informs many human disciplines, such as anthropology and literature, it still retains its clinical focus.

Queries about the origin of symptoms have pushed analysts to consider experiences during the first year as either pathogenic or paradigmatic for later behavior. Theories built around such postulates must be considered within a frame of reference where retrospection dovetails with direct observation. This review attempts to organize the hypotheses and data of psychoanalysts and baby watchers in order to arrive at a richer set of conclusions about the significance of the first year. The inevitable discrepancies that will be uncovered due to differences in vantage point will be used to readjust our theories so that the models are in better accord with our new data.

In order to understand the impact of psychoanalysis as a clinical science on our grasp of the significance of the first year of life, the origins and emphasis of psychoanalysis must be labored. Patients at bedside or in consultation bring symptoms, attitudes, and a sense of helplessness to therapists. This being so, the psychoanalyst is forced by his position to view behavior in a holistic context of life circumstance, biological substrate, social surround, and affective poignance. Indeed, what is different about the psychoanalytic view of man is the fact that its scientific stance includes affect and other qualities of responsiveness that other sciences find too subjective and difficult to operationalize.

Freud's retrospection began in *Studies on Hysteria* (Breuer and Freud, 1893), in which he reminds us that hysterics "suffer from reminiscences" and that his earliest patients remembered events that he called traumatic as early as age 7. As these events from the past seemed to have a continuing influence on adult behavior, the question arose whether even earlier events could be etiologically significant. His agile mind then pushed our interest further back, into infancy itself. Along with the belief in a dynamic unconscious and psychic determinism, the genetic point of view is central to psychoanalysis as a science. Fixation, regression, infantile sexuality, the import of the first 5 years, and infantile neuroses—all impel us to the view that developmental propositions are at the heart of this science. It would be presumptuous, however, to assert that psychoanalysts alone are interested in development or began the march toward interest in children. Indeed, those who actually observe children might chide analysts (and they do) as "false" developmentalists, "squatters" on alien territory, because by and large analysts do not watch children and do not have the technical skills to carefully observe infants during the first year of life. And yet much clinical theorizing about adult behavior has demanded that we seriously consider this first year as crucial.

Freud (1918) himself ventured into the first year when he tried to reconstruct the Wolf Man's infantile experience, later reflected in the dream whose analysis dominates that case study. He also suggested that the earliest features of biological readiness in interaction with frustration gave rise to the earliest wishes of the infant. *The Interpretation of Dreams* (Freud, 1900) presents a model of mind based on a lens system proposing that the dream appears as percept because of regressions from thought during the state of sleep. This reminds us of the preverbal origins of thought.

The impact of Darwinian embryology is likewise evident

in Abraham's railroad schedule of the steps in libido development (1916), a schema that suggests a preambivalent phase and early oral organizations already present in the first year.

Because psychoanalysis is a dyadic therapy, it focuses especially on the realities and distortions of the relation between patient and analyst. In recent years, the concept of object constancy has risen to theoretical prominence. Freud's early recognition of the distortions within the therapeutic situation led to his discovery of transference resistance and made him pay special attention to the reliving, within the analytic situation, of experiences which were appropriate to earlier times and which he was able to date well into the past. Indeed, as he developed a psychology which rested on fixations and regressions to varying developmental stages, he was forced to view the symptoms of the most severe disorders of development (such as the psychoses) as having their origins even further back than the earliest recognition of objects as the aims of an individual's drive. While he could well find evidence of symbolic themes representing conflicts about oral, anal, and phallic organizations, it was the complexities of the fantasies relating to the oral phase which pushed him back into the first year of life. When challenged by Jung to account for the distortions found in schizophrenia on the basis of libido theory, he resorted to a description of a line of libidinal investment in objects that was complemented by a line of narcissistic libidinal investment (Freud, 1914). Investment in the self, as in megalomania and paranoia, or in one's own body, as in hypochondriasis, became focal. The evanescent stability of objects as experienced by psychotics was analogized as resulting from a state of mind similar to that found in infancy, when object constancy is uncertain.

Ferenczi's imaginative construction of the stages in the appreciation of reality (1913) rounds out the pioneering explorations of the significance of early infant experience in psychoanalysis. The culmination of this view is found in Hartmann's somewhat extravagant suggestion (1950) that the first year remains a most central area for investigation by psychoanalytic researchers.

More recent concentration on the development of self was begun by Jacobson (1964). Her concept of a physiological self as opposed to a psychological self has been expanded and altered by Kohut (1971) and others elaborating the line of narcissistic development. Kernberg's split objects of the borderline and projective identification and splitting as defenses (1975) all bear witness to a terminology which is partially phenomenological but also rests on central genetic propositions concerning the status of objects within the first year of life.

Mahler's line of reasoning in terms of the separation-individuation process (Mahler, Pine, and Bergman, 1975), similarly pushes us into this perioid; she speaks of a normal autism and the gradual cathexis of objects involved in the process of differentiation from others. Clinically, experience even with neurotics or character disorders around themes such as separation again guide us toward some wish to understand how the child develops his contact with, his relation to, and the distortions of experience with people in the world as represented in the theory of object relations.

While the concepts are clinical, they draw heavily on our understanding of development. They have been elaborated within psychoanalysis as follows. The first notion concerns the emergence of a stable object as a developmental line. We are not born with inbuilt representations of people as wholes; rather, they develop only around a matrix of affective, sensory, and perceptual ties to that object which is either fostered or hindered by the way in which the environment responds. Schilder (1950) and Freud (1905) himself led us to believe and understand that in the beginning body parts, body ego representations, and part objects are gradually brought together as wholes which then become separable individual representations. Among the propositions to be considered here is the assumption that in the beginning the object exists only as an extension of need satisfaction (see Anna Freud) with a final emergence of true love after passage through a hierarchy of anxiety signals within the developing ego that are stimulated during the first year of life—the first signal is helplessness, the second separation. All of these processes seem to depend on what Hartmann called autonomous ego functions, e.g., the capacity to perceive and to store mental traces. These mental traces are integrated into wholes which are available to recall when needed, in both affectively loaded and neutral circumstances.

The foregoing notions derive from a view of stable mental representations arising in an affective network, a view based on a variety of models of internalization which include anaclitic identificatory and introjective mechanisms. Psychoanalysis is insistent that objects are brought together in a context of affective as well as sensorimotor matrices. While cognitive psychology may agree that early sensorimotor representations and the like have to be organized into a stable representational reality, it rarely takes into account the affective mode (Piaget, 1973).

Had analysts done no more than indicate the relevance of childhood for adulthood they would have made a significant contribution to developmental psychology, as for many centuries the attitude toward children and infants was one of indifference until they became productive and could be used for economic gain and other social ends. That what one did to an infant in his first year has lasting effects surely was inconceivable—a position as mistaken as the overemphasis currently laid on these early years. Surely a balance will be struck if we know what has been established with certainty and what remains mere speculation and fancy.

Though the direction was pointed by clinical psychoanalysis, the work with infants has been done with nonanalytic techniques—though sometimes by analysts who have learned these techniques. Opinion is divided among psychoanalysts as to whether relevant data useful to analysis itself can be gathered by techniques outside of psychoanalysis. Anna Freud (1953) had referred to the preverbal period as an ice age, while Peter Wolff (1965) has suggested we can find data in the first year that are compatible with psychoanalytic propositions but not corroborative of them. Both believe that discontinuity in method breaks the relevance of the results of one method in relation to those of another.

There are many within psychoanalysis who believe that constructions are reconstructions and that reexperiencing in the transference can be interpreted verbally even though the earliest experiences they derive from were nonverbal. There are a number of recorded cases in which reconstruction was verified by data outside of analysis.

By contrast, there are many who seek to find answers to mentalist propositions even in the first year by relating observed adult behavior and cognition to early bonding or perceptual strategies and knowledge of the stages of cognitive maturation. They try to bridge the preverbal behavior with the verbal, reflexes with later purposefulness, maternal with affective differentiation, etc. One thing is certain: regardless of one's stance regarding the relevance of infancy and the first year of life to later stages, psychoanalysis has asked the right questions. They have emphasized the need for a view of infancy that includes the biological substrate interacting with perceptual strategies to establish a set of stored images in dynamic arrangement. These early organizations include affective registrations that emerge in the growing awareness of an increasingly familiar world which initially focuses on recognizable caretakers.

The maturation of neurodevelopmental structures in dynamic interplay with a patterning environment can be studied and has been studied using a number of techniques. Each technique has revealed new and exciting data regarding the biosocial organizations at each developmental state and their deviations. However, each technique that has been introduced to give us more precision and statistical certainty has of necessity omitted something that psychoanalysis suggests is essential. Indeed, one of the central functions of psychoanalysis in this arena has been that of gadfly, reminding those who are too content with their methods and results of the central role of affect in development. We shall review recent information generated by innovative techniques in infant observation and suggest its deficiencies from the standpoint of psychoanalysis. From this critical review an action plan for continuing investigation should emerge.

Direct psychoanalytic observations of infants by psychoanalysts will be reviewed and their impact on clinical theory considered. Following that, the work of developmental psychologists who have focused on infant perception and cognition will be reviewed in order to determine how psychoanalytic theory must be reformulated to acount for their observations. In addition, we will be able to see the consequence of omitting affective responsiveness in academic formulations. These "reviews" from varied vantage points will focus largely on the establishment of the "object" within an affective field.

Direct Observation of Infants: Object Constancy

Within the psychoanalytic frame of reference, Spitz (1965) is probably the first significant investigator to attempt an observational definition of the developmental stages of stable objects. He adopted nonanalytic methods to answer questions posed by psychoanalysis. While not the first to discover the smile of the infant, he was first to place it in a context of its social significance at around 6 weeks, demonstrating that the baby appears to be responding to the specific Gestalt of an oval with movement and a dark-light gradient for eyes. Spitz (1946) looked at this phenomenon in embryological terms, calling it the first organizer, only later to be supplanted by specific separation anxiety and then stranger anxiety between 6 and 12 months. The second organizer signals the cathexis of a specific object as a whole (i.e., a human caretaker, the mother).

Spitz did not stop at these observations concerning attachment but went on to look at autostimulatory behavior (Spitz and Wolf, 1949) and suggested that the masturbation that naturally occurs at the end of the first year of life occurs in instances where mothering is at least adequate. He places emphasis on the need for contact with the mothering individual associated with reciprocation in the emergence of genetically predisposing maturational sequences.

When marasmic infants or infants in institutions are studied for such behaviors they seem to lack them. Spitz and Wolf (1949) go so far as to state that there is nothing to substitute for the specific care of a specific mother. While this appeals to our humanism, it does not seem universally to be the case; the concept of diffusion of mothering has been looked into by Ainsworth, Andry, Harlow, Lebovici, Prugh, and Wootton (1962) following Bowlby's classic WHO study of maternal care and deprivation (1952). Indeed, if one wished to study the ramification of the study of marasmus in infants in institutions the studies of Provence and Lipton (1962) and Harlow and Harlow's exploration of monkeys reared in varying situations (1962) are landmark observations. One of the striking things that the studies by Provence and Lipton reveal is the fact that children, although reared in an institution for their first year, regain their developmental composure when sent to foster homes, if we take changes in developmental quotient (DQ) as an adequate sign of such gain. The developmental quotients of their subjects show a drop around 4 to 6 months which is similar to Spitz's data. This corresponds to Anna Freud's prediction that a specific form of mothering is required at this juncture different from the need-satisfying caretaking of the prior stage.

Although the developmental tests seem to turn about at 1 year, the nuances of the test data continue to suggest some background of lessened stability of object representation, contrary to what was formerly thought. Similarly, early pathological states such as rumination, bed rocking, and failure to thrive are thought to point to deficiencies in the mother-child interaction which lead to these peculiar variants in adaptation. The symptoms seem to stand for the absent object insofar as that object has been internalized by the child in the form of repeated sensorimotor behavioral patterns. In other words, the clinical syndromes may be looked to as manifestations of an early biobehavioral tendency toward turning passive into active in children reared in disordered matrices.

Both psychoanalysts and nonpsychoanalysts have used nonanalytic techniques to consider the developmental patterns that eventuate in the establishment of object constancy. Whenever possible, they have also tried to infer the process and mechanisms involved in the development of this milestone. Sander's early observations (Sander, Julia, Stechler, and Burns, 1972) led him to suspect that attachment behaviors and stability of representation as evidenced by molding, diminished crying, and soothing capacity are available even within the first weeks of life. He describes the establishment of a kind of "ecological niche" in accord with the kind of caretaking provided within the first 10 days. The patterns established become most visible when there is a disruption because of caretaker change. Similarly, Emde (1976) and his group at the University of Colorado not only echo Spitz's point of view but have demonstrated that at about 2 months of life there is a general "biodevelopmental shift" which involves orienting, attentiveness, reflex changes, and encephalographic alterations that permit increasing time in quiet alert states. They go on to suggest that while endogenous smiling may begin prior to 6 weeks it has continuity with exogenous smiling; the basic physiological beginnings may then be seen as the precursors to psychosocial organizations. Indeed, the biodevelopmental shift is a sign that a new "organizer" has taken hold and signals the fact that affect can serve an increasing role in conscious social regulation.

In the severe pathologies of early childhood, Bender and Freedman (1952) and Fish (1959) have suggested that there are demonstrable distortions and significant pattern variation in the developmental process itself. Fish (1961, 1963) looked at motor behavior, physiological regulation of sleep-wake cycles, and variability of states of consciousness as a way of organizing the data variability in infancy. This approach provides evidence that when endogenous maturational rhythms are unintegrated one with the other or over the maturational sequence of a single function, clinicians ought to be alerted to predisposition to childhood psychoses. The supporting environment should be bolstered for such infants in order to enhance ego support. Mahler (1968) deftly espouses a similar concept in the language of the separation-individuation concept, noting the inability of the autistic child to maintain and utilize the mothering principle. Translated into intrapsychic organizational terms, stable mental representations are not possible because of some intrinsically defective ego variable.

Piaget (1952) is perhaps the most important cognitive psychologist to have explored the sensorimotor development stages of this initial period. He describes a set of careful observations made on his own three children. The conceptual brilliance of his approach guaranteed that his own work and that of others would show them to be valid in larger populations (Gouin-Décarie, 1965). Initially, the infant is thought to register events heterologously in a sensorimotor mental organization called a schema. Gradually, as development proceeds, the motor part of the activity is stripped from the sensory portion, and transient mental representations become built into stable mental organizations. Actions toward things in the world that disappear may continue at stage IV at approximately 8 to 12 months, but searching for recently hidden objects or objects that have long since disappeared attests to stable mental representation not dependent on immediate response to a sensory stimulus. These stabilities await later cognitive achievements included in stage VI at 18 months. It is important to question whether stranger anxiety if it occurs at 8 months is a sign that object constancy (in the Piagetian sense) has been achieved for affective objects earlier than for inanimate objects. (Stated otherwise, why should the child respond differentially to the animate and inanimate world at a point of development when animism is rampant and physiognomic apprehension is the rule and the distinction between things and people is not likely?) This leaves the question on both sides of the psychological fence as to what kind of split functions might accrue in the first year of life which might be the forerunners of such mechanisms as splitting in the psychotic and borderline processes.

As if this were not sufficiently confusing, new data have occasioned uncertainty over whether stable objects are built up over time, as Piaget and others have long theorized. Recent reports suggest that even during the first weeks of life young infants may have strategies available for apprehending objects. For example, 2-month-old infants are reported capable of imitating human facial expressions and tongue thrusts in a probability range better than chance (Meltzoff and Moore, 1977). This suggests that just as the infant may have "prewired" or constitutional perceptual preferences for visual aspects of the object (the eyes), so he may have "prewired" recognitions and imitative responses to specific behaviors of the object (a tongue thrust). Similarly, babies are able to make minor distinctions within one phonetic feature, like /pa/ and /ba/, as has been demonstrated by Eimas, Siqueland, Josczyk, and Vigorito, (1971). Bower (1972) and others have demonstrated that infants of 3 months anticipate the emergence of a hidden object, a performance thought to be possible only with the establishment of a Piagetian stage IV schema. In addition, according to Bower,

1-month-old infants have rudimentary mechanisms for judging size constancy.

If there are inbuilt mechanisms for phonetic analysis and for the perception of wholes even in the earliest months of life, how is this to be reconciled with the psychoanalytic model, which postulates a world gradually built up, layered, and hierarchically organized so as to account for splits and pathological variables in later life on a developmental basis? Much work has yet to be done on the difference between affective and nonaffective objects, a possible distinction at this early stage of development.

In Chapters 4 and 5 of this volume, Emde suggests that inbuilt capacities for emotional expression are gradually mobilized for interpersonal social definition. They are seen as preadapted to shape the caretaker in a role very similar to that Bowlby (1958) ascribes to the earliest inborn response systems which bring the mother halfway to the child. Only later are these affective sets internalized as psychological signals and regulatory adaptors. One can only mention the strong influence of ethology on the thinking of Bowlby and others who look to a revival of Freud's early postulates of component instincts as mediators between the developing infant and the external world.

Psychoanalysis has directed attention to the idea that the development of perception is autonomous (Hartmann, 1939). Even if this were so, the building of the object via perceptual stored data also would be strongly involved in matters of affective states which either overwhelm or understimulate the child—that is, how does the threshold for perception vary with the kind of interaction with the environment as mediated by specific perceptual organizations at each developmental stage? These avenues to holistic approaches to infants are only beginning to be elaborated. Much work has been done already on animal behavior, and distinctions such as that between biosocial and psychosocial organizations have been made by Schneirla and Rosenblatt (1961) to define the specific and limiting roles of mothering as against inbuilt maturational sequences. However, if we now ask what the major organizing features of biosocial development are, the issues must be reformulated to include the initial discussion of object constancy now seen from the complementary perspective of perceptual organization of the early infant. To pursue the matter further, the reader must first be alerted to a number of conceptual confusions.

The progressive differentiation of function and the integration of varying functions during development are undoubtedly modulated by an inner timetable of maturation as well as by a variable set of experiences with the caretaker. This would seem to accord with Freud's position, borrowed from classical thinkers, that all psychopathology is the combined result of accident and necessity. However, this very division of influences into accident and necessity interrupts the holistic vision and tends to deny the global responsiveness of the young infant. Rather, the issues raised coincide with a number of problems that have been studied as aspects of the need for stimulation "versus" the need for protection; the task of creating an object tie versus the task of establishing differentiated self-boundaries; the differentiation of the ego from the id; and the ego's autonomous functions as discrete from its other functions. These are surely all complementary views of the same behaviors that baby watchers may be observing from varying investigative positions. More central to psychoanalytic clinical theorizing is the issue of what later pathology might be determined by these varying perceptual organizations. If indeed the concerns of baby watchers have any relevance for a psychoanalytic theory of development, it most certainly will have to be within the area of regulation of affective states and arousal. These elements are also necessarily integral aspects of the development of object constancy, because objects are above all affectively charged stable constellations which are both stimulating and stimulus-reducing.

Affect is not initially differentiated from arousal within the matrix of infant reactivity, but, as development proceeds, affective states of varying quality emerge from more global arousal states. The earliest stimulus-seeking and barrier-enhancing characteristics of the mother may be construed as the biological prototype of an individual's later defensive operations, which are established at a more advanced stage with the regulation of defined affects. At present there is no longitudinal understanding of the emergence of psychological mechanisms out of biological processes, but there is a formal coherence in the description of the protective function of each that is compelling. We are in the borderlands of our knowledge, then, of how percept evolves into concept and how drives as represented by states of body arousal develop into wishes that serve as a conceptual motivational system in later childhood and adulthood. That questions of precursors of affect and defense ought to be looked for in infant observations in a longitudinal way is not to be gainsaid; that they tend to be ignored by academic psychology is clearly evident. However, while psychoanalysts have pointed the way, we have not, except in rare instances, taken adequate account of what is known already in order to further enrich our theory.

Direct Observation of Infants: Stimulus Barrier

Having alluded to the fact that the infant at birth has at its disposal a number of perceptual strategies by which he comes to recognize that there are persons who are not himself, the natural question emerges as to how these strategies are integrated or emerge in the course of development to establish a mental object that has the representational stability with the characteristic of an end stage of a Piagetian sensorimotor sequence. Within psychoanalytic theory, Freud (1900) himself postulated that the infant discharges excitation by gaining control of the motor apparatus. It is only via delay in motor discharge that hallucinatory wish fulfillment begins. Freud further postulated that there exists a biologically inbuilt barrier to perceptual and other excitation which he called a *Reizschutz*—a stimulus barrier. To judge from the context in which Freud wrote about the stimulus barrier, he was seeking a biological precursor for later defensive operations. He also saw the stimulus barrier as a necessary concept because he was devoted to Fechner's Constancy Principle, which proposes that the organism seeks zero excitation, experienced psychologically as pleasure. How does this concept of a stimulus barrier stand up against the impact of direct careful observation of infants? The fact is that there is a large body of evidence to indicate that from the day of birth the infant is a very active stimulus seeker. At first glance, it would seem difficult to integrate such data into Freud's position.

The stimulus barrier is comprised of two different forms of barrier to or threshold for stimuli. The first is constitutional; Freud proposed that the infant is endowed with a high threshold for all incoming stimuli as a protective mechanism against flooding. The second form of barrier postulates that if the infant's constitutional equipment fails, or does not act as a sufficient barrier, the infant's environment support (usually in the form of its mother) provides protection against a traumatic state. That is to say that by virtue of her appropriate handling of the infant and her capacity to provide moderating stimuli, the mother ensures that her infant is nurtured into a less traumatic early childhood. Only later did Spitz (1965) and his followers suggest that the infant himself might be an active participant in barrier regulation. Bergman and Escalona (1949) invoked a striking extension of Freud's notion of a stimulus barrier and its gradual replacement by early ego structures in their theoretical discussion concerning the origins of autism. In either of two complementary ways—too "thin" an intrinsic barrier to stimuli or "inadequate or overwhelming mothering"—there would be a premature development of ego function. Because of its out-of-phase emergence the ego is "brittle" and "rigid," generating autistic behavior. It is of interest to note this extension of theorizing to a pathological state, because of the features of the autistic child in his affective isolation which again relates excitation and its modulation concretely to the later development of affective responsiveness. Freud's essential point was that excitation within the system is experienced as unpleasure by the infant and that only discharge of that excitation is pleasurable. It was largely on the basis of these energic propositions that the stimulus barrier gained its theoretical importance as the earliest regulator of what is later to become a bevy of affective states classified along the pleasure-unpleasure continuum. The foregoing notwithstanding, direct observation of infants reveals that from day one the infant, when in a state of alert activity, seeks out stimuli rather than wards them off. Even if alert inactivity is infrequent in the earliest months, there is a rapid shift during the first year toward increasing the percentage of time spent in that state.

Observations have been made that during the first phase of life infants do a variety of things in order to ensure stimulation. They show strong preference for both visual and auditory stimulus events and in appropriate experimental situations demonstrate that they will even work to experience a favored stimulus (Kessen, Haith, and Salapatek, 1970). Moreover, there are many experiments on the effect of habituation during the first weeks of life which indicate that some degree of novelty is required to maintain a state of arousal that from the viewer's standpoint appears pleasurable. A general comment on the basis of neurodevelopmental factors is warranted. Since the head end of the organism is the most differentiated, sucking behavior is activated as one of the most focal aspects of the more global tendency of the infant to show arousal by motor excitation. Bridger and Birns (1968) have shown that even a postprandially satisfied infant in a drowsy state (but not in deep sleep) will increase his rate of sucking in response to a general arousing stimulus such as plunging his foot into ice water. This demonstrates that sucking is a sign of general arousal and not simply a feature of nutritive need. Nevertheless, this observation is interesting for psychoanalytic theory because, while nonspecific, generally arousing stimuli increase activity. It is likely that oral activity, being the most differentiated, is the activity that is psychologized as a centrally registered experience in the pleasure-unpleasure continuum. Moreover, it is the response that overlaps with nutritive sucking, from which object representations of the mother may emerge.

Aside from general arousal leading to specific responses, additional facts attest the infant's capacity for an extraordinary array of discriminitive abilities and preferences for different sounds, sights, and tastes (Kessen, Haith, and Salapatek, 1970). All of these imply that infants are stimulus-seeking and do not aim only at tension reduction. Implicit in these facts is the proposition that the seeking of stimulation leads to an increased level of excitation that increases alertness to further stimulation. This body of information also compels us to the proposition that there is an inbuilt autonomous curiosity that is not necessarily a derivative of conflictual determinants—that there is pleasure that is derived from and embedded in stimulus seeking. Indeed, in the earliest organizations available to infants there may be something reinforcing about the very act of seeking stimulation that is not aligned solely with unpleasure. Since stimulus seeking is likely to involve stimulating caretakers in average expectable environments, it should also have its effect on how object representations are formed. The tie is based not only on need gratification but also on the need for stimulation. This finding is relevant to a number of later clinical syndromes in which the seeking of excitement replaces mature object ties, as seen especially in borderline conditions.

Although the psychoanalytic picture of the infant with regard to the stimulus barrier seems to stand opposed to the direct observational picture of the child, this opposition need not be considered absolute. The two views may readily be reconciled if one considers the need to regulate both the amount and the quality of stimulation of the infant within a range that is optimal to his given constitution. It has been noted that the range of excitability befitting the level of "curiosity" suggested may rather easily be exceeded. At such a point the infant acts very much as early analytic theory has proposed; there appears to be a constitutional barrier to further stimulation and a need for protection that is provided by the mothering individual. In fact, we can include both propositions in a single theory and find a complementarity in the development of the child.

If we now recall the auxiliary function of the caretaker as a stimulus modulator, and suggest that in the most naturally occurring circumstances the most likely source of external stimuli comes largely from the mother's behavior itself, we will necessarily arrive at the notion that the need for stimulation and the need to be protected from being overwhelmed relate to the earliest form of self-object interaction. Accordingly, stimulus-seeking behaviors are invariably in the service of creating or further cementing the potential object tie. They ensure the innumerable experiences in perceptual contact which serve to build up an internal representation of the external object in a manner similar to need satisfaction. On the other hand, the stimulus-avoiding or modulating behaviors of the child may not only be in line with future defensive operations but may be utilized in the service of continuing individuation as will later emerge in psychological "hatching" (Mahler, Pine, and Bergman, 1975). In fact, the wide latitude in "good enough mothering" described by Winnicott (1965) may find its dimensions in this model.

Focusing now on the importance of the regulatory functions in early infancy, it is not premature to assume that they will take on increasing importance as the ego takes shape. One of the most interesting developmental observations, even at such an early stage, is observations of behavior in which the infant shows he has direct control over perceptual input; here behavioral regulation may be seen to take on a regular and predictable form of interaction between mother and infant. We know from a variety of studies (Stern, 1976) that the achievement of initiation and interruption of visual gaze at 3 months provides an exquisite paradigm for later regulatory functions. The infant may now regulate visual input by the control of his own gaze and gaze aversion. Similarly, his ability to tune out through changing his focus of attention can be seen as a later form of the earlier changes in state, from high alert inactivity to higher levels of arousal at which he appears to be overwhelmed by input, or to sleepy and drowsy states by withdrawal. Even from earliest infancy the child has the alternatives of sucking and eating or of falling asleep. Piaget has convinced us that sensorimotor registration of these activities must take place in loosely organized mental schemata. This model reminds us of Freud's proposition that the driving force of an analysis is the patient's anxiety. However, Sullivan (1953) reminds us that there is an optimal anxiety which makes an analysis proceed: too little provides no motor, but too much precludes the attention necessary for learning. The foregoing observations of infants, however, suggest that they are already well equipped with a full repertoire of behaviors that will influence their internal state as well as their interest in the external world that is providing new and varied spectacles.

Given this overview of a situation that began with an apparent conflict between psychoanalytic propositions and the data from infant observation, we now are in a position to harness the new observations in a more precise theory linking the origins of psychological regulation in biodevelopmental continuity with later psychological mechanisms having clinical significance. The more consonant our propositions are with the data of direct observation, the more trustworthy will our clinical inferences be.

In summary, then, what may be concluded about the origin of object relations within an affective field, as seen from the separate vantage points of developmental psychology and psychoanalysis? More specifically, at what points has the flow of evidence from one discipline been confluent and mutually enriching with that from other disciplines? At what points have they been in opposition, and with what implications for psychoanalysis?

A first issue involves the growing evidence of developmental psychologists that the infant's perceptual apparatus is prewired or innately present from the moment of birth to form at least attentional ties with part-objects (the mother's face, voice, certain expressions). These perceptual predilections toward the object, which foster object bonding, are present in the absence of any nurturing or drive-reducing experience with the object. They are constitutional. We view this evidence as in no basic way incompatible with psychoanalytic notions regarding the formation of object relations. If anything, it provides a firmer biological basis for the postulate of very early part-objects and in fact gives their early appearance a psychobiological "head start" toward becoming psychological entities rather than solely perceptual tendencies.

A second issue involving the role of tension reduction and drive gratification in the formation of object relations is more problematic. Here the views of psychoanalysis and most developmental psychologies appear to collide head on. To oversimplify, psychoanalysis postulates that object relations are forged by the objects providing the infant with tension reduction for physiological needs; developmental psychology, by contrast, postulates that they are forged by the object providing the infant with adequate stimulation and arousal to meet the "stimulus-seeking" psychobiological drives. As suggested above, these truly opposite views can be conceived of as complementary: the psychoanalytic position best explains the infant's reaction to stimulus events above some optimal level of tension generation, while the "stimulus-seeking" position best explains stimulus events below that level. These two views are complementary in another way. The psychoanalytic view, as outlined by Anna Freud, best accounts in general for physiological drives (hunger, thirst, thermoregulation), while the developmental psychological view best accounts for "drives" related to "ego" drives or the push behind the development of autonomous ego function. The crucial point here is that when the two views are combined, each in its most appropriate context, we begin to see a larger set of events and routes to the formation of object relations.

A third core question involves the relation between affect and arousal (or tension). As stated above, psychoanalysis has postulated that affect is initially a product of the level and trend of arousal; only later do various affective states differentiate from arousal states and state transitions. Until recently, most developmental psychological views of affect have been too phenomenological to relate to the biological bases of psychoanalytic postulates. However, more recently they have been examining infants' affect displays as a function of both the infant's level of arousal and his cognitive evaluation of the stimulus situation responsible for the changes in this level.

It is now believed that in the second half of the first year of life the infant is making such cognitive evaluations (see Chapters 4 and 5; Sroufe, 1976). For example, the infant breaks into a smile at his approaching mother at the moment the tension occasioned by the approach is cognitively resolved through recognition of her as a familiar and "safe" person. This reduction in tension through a successful cognitive operation is experienced as pleasurable.

This line of speculation on the part of developmental psychologists promises to be extremely enriching for psychoanalytic thinking. On this issue the two theoretical frameworks are coming strikingly into line and, in so doing, are reopening the question of the origin of affects within the context of signal affects. Both consider the affective component a sine qua non of the formation of object ties. Under the impact of this ideological confluence, these areas are bound to be more and more interesting and fruitful in the foreseeable future.

A final issue, which brings us back to the beginning of this chapter, concerns the issue of continuity versus discontinuity between the observational methods of the baby watchers and the reconstructive methods of psychoanalysts (and the corresponding question in nature, between preverbal experience and postverbal reconstruction). It is our expectation that now that the two disciplines and methods are largely in agreement on most of the central questions, new data and frameworks will soon emerge that will alter our entire view of where and how the continuity dilemma manifests itself. Moreover, our clinical observations of pathology may be able to be integrated again into a system that includes biological as well as psychological dimensions.

References

Abraham, K. (1916), The first pregenital stage of the libido. In: *Selected Papers on Psycho-Analysis*. New York: Basic Books, 1953, pp. 248–279.

Ainsworth, M., Andry, R.G., Harlow, R.G., Lebovici, S., Mead, M., Prugh, D., & Wootton, B. (1962), *Deprivation of Maternal Care: A Reassessment of Its Effects*. Geneva: World Health Organization, Monograph 14.

Bender, L. & Freedman, A.M. (1952), A study of the first three years in the maturation of schizophrenic children. *Quarterly Child Review*, 4:245–272.

Bergman, P., & Escalona, S.K. (1949), Unusual sensitivities in very young children. *The Psychoanalytic Study of the Child*, 31:333–352. New Haven: Yale University Press.

Bower, T. (1972), Object perception in infants. *Perception*, 1:15–30.

Bowlby, J. (1952), *Maternal Care and Mental Health*. Geneva: World Health Organization, Series 2.

———— (1958), The nature of the child's tie to the mother. *Internat. J. Psycho-Anal.*, 39:350–373.

Breuer, J., & Freud, S. (1893), Studies on hysteria. *Standard Edition*, 2. London: Hogarth Press, 1955.

Bridger, W., & Birns, B., (1968), An analysis of the role of sucking in early infancy. In: *Science and Psychoanalysis*. Vol. 12. New York: Grune & Stratton, pp. 156–165.

Eimas, P.D., Siqueland, E.R., Josczyk, P., & Vigorito, J.M. (1971), Speech perception in infants. Science, 171:303–306.

Emde, R., Gaensbauer, T., & Harmon, R. (1976), *Emotional Expression in Infancy: A Biobehavioral Study*. New York: International Universities Press.

Ferenczi, S. (1913), Stages in the development of the sense of reality. In: *Sex and Psychoanalysis*. New York: Dover, 1956, pp. 181–203.

Fish, B. (1959), Longitudinal observations of biological deviations in a schizophrenic infant. *Amer. J. Psychiat.*, 116:25–31.

——— (1961), The study of motor development in infancy and its relationship
to psychological functioning. *Amer. J. Psychiat.*, 117:1113–1118.

——— (1963), The maturation of arousal and attention in the first months
of life. *J. Amer. Acad. Child Psychiat.*, 2:253–270.

Freud, A. (1953), Some remarks on infant observation. *The Psychoanalytic Study
of the Child*, 8:9–19. New York: International Universities Press.

Freud, S. (1900), The interpretation of dreams. *Standard Edition*, 4/5. London:
Hogarth Press, 1953.

——— (1905), Three essays on the theory of sexuality. *Standard Edition*,
7:135–243. London: Hogarth Press, 1953.

——— (1914), On narcissism. *Standard Edition*, 14:67–104. London: Hogarth
Press, 1957.

——— (1918), From the history of an infantile neurosis. *Standard Edition*,
17:7–122. London: Hogarth Press, 1955.

Gouin-Décarie, T. (1965), *Intelligence and Affectivity in Early Children*. New
York: International Universities Press.

Harlow, H.F., & Harlow, M.K. (1962), Social deprivation in monkeys. *Scientific
American*, 207:136–146.

Hartmann, H. (1939), *Ego Psychology and the Problem of Adaptation*. New York:
International Universities Press, 1958.

——— (1950), Psychoanalysis and developmental psychology. *The Psychoanalytic Study of the Child*, 5:7–17. New York: International Universities
Press.

Jacobson, E. (1964), *The Self and the Object World*. New York: International
Universities Press.

Kernberg, O. (1975), *Borderline Conditions and Pathological Narcissism*. New
York: Aronson.

Kessen, W., Haith, M.A., & Salapatek, P.H. (1970), Human infancy: A bib-
liography and guide. In: *Carmichael's Manual of Child Psychology*, ed. P.H.
Mussen. New York: Wiley.

Kohut, H. (1971), *The Analysis of the Self*. New York: International Universities
Press.

Mahler, M. (1968), *On Human Symbiosis and the Vicissitudes of Individuation: Vol.
1, Infantile Psychosis*. New York: International Universities Press.

——— Pine, F., & Bergman, P. (1975), *The Psychological Birth of the Human
Infant: Symbiosis and Individuation*. New York: Basic Books.

Meltzoff, A.N., & Moore, M.D. (1977), Imitation of facial and manual gestures
by human neonates. *Science*, 198:75–78.

Piaget, J. (1952), *The Origins of Intelligence in Children*. New York: International
Universities Press.

——— (1973), The affective unconscious and the cognitive unconscious. *J.
Amer. Psychoanal. Assn.*, 21:249–261.

Provence, S., & Lipton, R.C. (1962), *Infants in Institutions*. New York: International Universities Press.

Sander, L., Julia, H.L., Stechler, G., & Burns, P. (1972), Continuous 24 hour
interactional monitoring in infants reared in two caretaking environments. *Psychosom. Med.*, 34:270–282.

Schilder, P. (1950), *The Image and Appearance of the Human Body*. New York: International Universities Press.

Schneirla, T.C., & Rosenblatt, J.S. (1961), Behavioral organization and genesis of the social bond in insects and mannals. *Amer. J. Orthopsychiat.*, 31:223–253.

Spitz, R.A. (1946), The smiling response: A contribution to the ontogenesis of social relations (with assistance of K.M. Wolf, Ph.D.) *Genetic Psychology Monographs*, 34:57–125.

——— (1965), *The First Year of Life*. New York: International Universities Press.

——— & Wolf, K.M. (1949), Autoerotism: some empirical findings and hypotheses on three of its manifestations in the first year of life. *The Psychoanalytic Study of the Child*, 3/4:85–120. New York: International Universities Press.

Sroufe, L.A., & Waters, E. (1976), The ontogenesis of smiling and laughter: A perspective on the organization of development in infancy. *Psychol. Rev.*, 83:173–189.

Stern, D. (1976), A microanalysis of mother-infant interaction: Behavior regulating social contact between a mother and her 3½ month old twins. In: *Infant Psychiatry*, ed. E. Rexford, L. Sanders, & T. Shapiro. New Haven: Yale University Press, pp. 113–126.

Sullivan, H.S. (1953), *Interpersonal Theory of Psychiatry*. New York: Norton.

Winnicott, D.W. (1965), *The Maturational Processes and the Facilitating Environment*. New York: International Universities Press.

Wolff, P. (1965), Panel report: Contributions of longitudinal studies to psychoanalytic theories, rep. R. Schafer. *J. Amer. Psychoanal. Assn.*, 13:605–618.

8

Maturational and Developmental Issues in the First Year

DAVID A. FREEDMAN, M.D.

I

Although no serious student of psychoanalysis questions the significance of the first year for later development, the complexities of the processes involved make for considerable difficulty in assessing the importance of specific maturational events and developmental vicissitudes.[1] Broadly speaking, one is confronted with the task of identifying and reconciling the respective roles of the largely gene-determined changes which emerge in the infant's morphology and functional capacity on the one hand, and the impact of the highly individualized environmental pressures to which he is exposed on the other. Both conceptual and technical problems must be addressed and clarified in this regard.

For example, despite the importance accorded infantile experience in psychoanalytic theory, there is no clear specification in our literature of either the ages or the levels of de-

---

[1] In this essay I follow Spitz's usage (1965). He defines maturation and development as follows:

"Maturation: The unfolding of phylogenetically evolved and therefore inborn functions of the species, which emerge in the course of embryonic development or are carried forward after birth as anlagen and become manifest at later stages in life.

Development: The emergence of forms, of functions and of behavior which are the outcome of exchanges between the organism on the one hand and the inner and outer environment on the other. . . ." [p. 5].

velopment to which the term *infantile* properly refers. Freud's own usage appears to have encompassed all of early development up to and perhaps including the oedipal period. In neither his description of the phases of libido development (Freud, 1916–1917) nor his delineation of the egotistical and narcissistic phases of object relatedness (Freud, 1914) did he clarify at what ages he conceived the successive steps of these two parallel series of sequential phenomena to appear. Neither did he state at what ages he assumed the infant to be capable either of the experience of gratification after nursing or of the much more sophisticated experience of hallucinatory gratification (Freud, 1900).

In the past the obfuscating effects of such chronological imprecision have been compounded by the fact that the vast preponderance of the data upon which our hypotheses concerning very early psychological life were based derived from the analytic investigation of older children and adult analysands. Information obtained in this setting is undependable for several reasons. Freud (1899), for example, in discussing infantile amnesia, noted that one's earliest memories date to the second year. Even these are isolated recollections which more often than not serve as screen memories. Their significance lies not in their historicity but in their ability to epitomize conflictual constellations which—at least as they are remembered—are elaborated out of later experience. The fact that such retrospective reworkings are very likely to involve distortions of the past is a second difficulty in the way of the student of psychoanalysis who attempts to relate the clinical phenomena he observes to their presumed primordial roots. A third complicating factor lies in the ubiquity of the propensity to adultomorphize. In the analytic situation this is most clearly seen in the analyst's willingness to accept as historically accurate the analysand's account of his early experience. An analogous problem, however, also confronts the observer of infants and small children. It is seen in the tendency to impute drivelike intentions to behaviors which bear a similarity to the object-directed drive manifestations of later life. Given this assumption, the correlative assumption that the infant has psychological competences analogous to those of the adult follows almost inevitably. The propensity is to attribute to infantile behavior, which is phenomenologically similar to that of adults, the motivational significance that would be appropriate to the adult. On this basis one is led to impute to the.neonate such sophisticated psychological capacities as awareness of self and others, intentionality, and capacity for fantasy. It is a thesis of this chapter that taken together these three complicating factors—infantile amnesia, retrospective falsification, and the propensity to adultomorphize—set a limit on the reliability of the psychoanalytic method as an instrument with which to investigate the earliest phases of psychological development.

A variety of other approaches, taken by investigators who share with psychoanalytic clinicians the common objective of clarifying the processes by which the readily identifiable motivational and structural characteristics of the psychology of older individuals become established, can be understood as efforts to get around these limits. Spitz (1950) and Sylvia Brody (1956), among others, argued for the usefulness of direct observation both of infants and of mother-infant interactions, as well as of experimental psychological methodologies. Such technical approaches make possible the identification of regularities which in turn may give direction to later psychoanalytic investigations. Other sources of information have also provided data of relevance both to the understanding of these earliest phases of human development and as an impetus to more directed research. Perhaps most noteworthy among these, and as yet inadequately integrated into and reconciled with psychoanalytic theory, is the work of Piaget. His studies of the emergence of cognitive competencies during the first 18 months provides a frame of reference against which the significance of infantile behaviors can be assessed. Another, which was also introduced into the psychoanalytic literature by Spitz (1945), involves the exploitation of so-called experiments of nature. In these investigations one studies the developmental progress of infants and children who have been subjected to any of a variety of aberrant experiences or deprivations in the course of their development. To the extent that a systematic relation can be demonstrated between a particular vicissitude and a later behavioral or psychological outcome, such studies also provide a basis for assessing the significance of observations in "average expectable" children, as well as for more explicitly psychoanalytic investigation.

Any attempt to translate data from animal observation to the human situation must of course be undertaken with considerable caution. It is possible, however, to identify certain analogies and even homologies between the situations of developing primates and those of preverbal human infants. Kaufman (1975), in particular, has approached their study from the standpoint of psychoanalysis.

Finally, there is a body of data concerning cerebral development anatomy which may also have considerable relevance for the student of early psychological development. To the extent that we accept the premise that a reasonably intact functioning brain is a necessary though certainly insufficient condition for mental operations, it is obvious that we must be concerned with the maturational status of that organ. While the understanding of cerebral anatomy will certainly not further our comprehension of the complex interrelationships which characterize even infantile psychology, it should provide a limiting floor from which psychological theory building can proceed. That is, to the extent that one can demonstrate the relevance to aspects of psychological functioning of particular anatomical structures, the presence or absence of these structures will determine the limits of what is possible for the individual.

In the following paragraphs I will review data elicited by the use of these various approaches. It is my intention to consider how they affect our understanding both of psychological development during the first year and of such later psychological issues as the vicissitudes of drive organization, the development of the capacity for affect, the formation of object relations and internalized object representations, and the evolution of psychic structure and fixed (characterological) patterns of behavior.

II

Although he may accept the premise that the psychological phenomena with which he deals do in some sense reflect brain function, the psychoanalyst who devotes himself to the problems of older children and adults can ignore the relevance of that organ as he goes about his day-to-day work. That this is the case reflects the fact that the anatomical and physiological substrate upon which the emergence of mental phenomena depends are pretty much fixed by the time the individual becomes old enough to be a candidate for psychoanalytic investigation. By contrast, the worker who is interested in the development of the first year cannot afford to take the constancy of the "organ of mind" for granted. He must reckon with the fact that dramatic changes in its structure and therefore in its functional potentialities occur throughout this period and for some time beyond it. He must also keep in mind the fact that while these changes are to begin with preponderantly gene-determined, as maturation proceeds they are increasingly affected by the ambiance in which the maturation is occurring. Otherwise stated, with the passage of time the role of development becomes more and more important.

The extent of the changes that occur in the maturing brain is illustrated by the following. Figure 1, which is adapted from the work of Conel (1939/1959), demonstrates the dramatic increase in number and complexity of the dendritic arborizations during the first two years. It is the relation of the terminals of dendrites to following neurones—in modern parlance, synapses—to which Freud (1895) referred as "contact barriers" and to which he appealed in his efforts to establish a physiological basis for mental functioning.

Figure 2, from the work of Yakovlev and LeCours (1965), presents yet another aspect of the early maturational process. The bars represent the progress of myelin deposition in various tracts of the central nervous system. While it is not possible to say that a neural system is totally incapable of all functioning in the absence of adequate myelinization, it is well established that lack of this material significantly compromises the transmission of nerve impulses.

These evidences of dramatic alterations in brain anatomy during the first two years call into question the tenability of the assumptions made by some analysts (e.g., Melanie Klein and her school) that the infant is both capable of significant fantasy

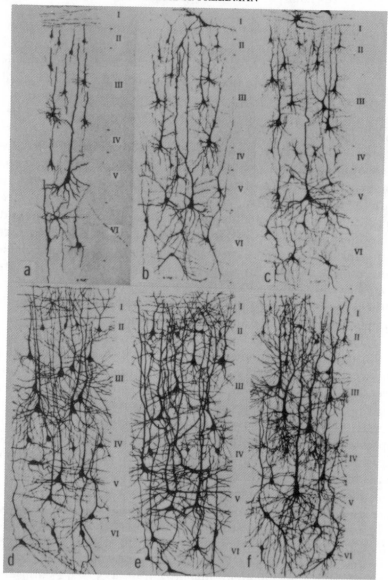

FIGURE 1. Postnatal development of human cerebral cortex around Broca's Area (FCBm); camera lucida drawings from Golgi-Cox preparations. (a) Newborn; (b) 1 month; (c) 3 months; (d) 6 months; (e) 15 months; (f) 24 months (from Conel, 1939/1959. Reprinted with permission of Harvard University Press).

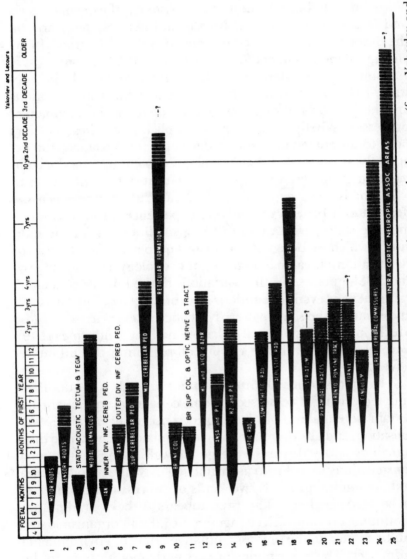

FIGURE 2. The bars indicate the patterns of myelin deposition in the various neural subsystems (from Yakovlev and LeCours, 1965; copyright 1965 by Blackwell Scientific Publications).

life and, from very early in its postnatal existence, in some sense endowed with the awareness of the existence of external objects and of such part-objects as breasts and penises. They are, on the other hand, entirely congruent with those theories of psychological development (e.g., Jacobson, 1954; Brody, 1956; Erikson, 1959; Escalona, 1965; Spitz, 1965; Mahler, 1968; Loewald, 1971) which assume that psychic structures and functions are the products of ongoing maturational and developmental processes. Whether explicitly or implicitly, all these authors hold to an epigenetic view of development. Escalona, for example, has postulated that at any given point in time the combination of the infant's organismic state and the experiences to which he is being exposed yields a transitional state which she designates a pattern of concrete experience. From this intermediate state derive those ongoing modifications of the individual which we designate behavior and personality. By way of clarification, Escalona discusses the etiology of autistic psychosis. She points out that variations in the infant's congenital equipment or even adventitious environmental events can result in essentially the same patterns of concrete experience as those which, in Kanner's original description of the syndrome (1949), were associated with the quality of parenting the infant received.

In Spitz's terms (1959) the infant at birth is an undifferentiated organism possessed of some congenital equipment and certain potentialities but lacking in consciousness, perception, sensation, and all other psychological functions. Over time these functions and structures emerge, as well as the motivational constellations we refer to as instinctual drives. On both clinical and anatomical grounds two kinds of process can be inferred to be involved here. The first appears to be a gradual and continuing one in which changes in the infant's organismic state can be related to the ongoing mutative effect of environmental influences. The descriptions of very early modifications of behavior (e.g., Sander, 1962) on the basis of the exchange between mother and infant will fit this pattern. Stern (1971), for example, made a frame-by-frame motion picture analysis of the visual interchanges between a mother and her fraternal twin sons. The studies, which were carried out between the time the babies were 3½ and 7 months old, revealed consistent differences in her interactions with them. When the children were 15 months old, Stern felt he could demonstrate related differences in their respective behaviors. Presumably such effects are in some way related to the recently established facts that environmental stimulation can influence both the pattern of dendritic arborization (Greenough, 1975) and the internal organization of individual nerve cells (Kandell, 1979).

In addition to such gradual cumulative processes, it has been recognized from very early in the history of psychoanalysis that development also has a discontinuous, saltatory aspect. The zonal phases of libido development, for example, involve the occurrence of relatively abrupt cathectic shifts on the basis of maturational changes. There is also evidence that the maturing youngster undergoes abrupt shifts in susceptibility to various modes of sensory stimulation. Spitz (1945), following Freud (1900), proposed that the neonate is capable of receiving only nonspecific sensory experience in what he called the coenesthetic mode. Unlike diacritic sensation, which predominates later, this is diffuse and poorly localized rather than discrete. The signs and signals to which the infant responds belong to the following categories: equilibrium, tension (muscular or otherwise), posture, temperature, vibration, skin and body contact, rhythm, tempo, duration, pitch, tone, resonance, clang, and probably a number of others of which the adult is hardly aware. I have myself presented evidence (Freedman, 1971) that the special place of coenesthesia is followed by diacritic vision, which becomes the principal medium through which the infant experiences the world at roughly 6 months, and that diacritic hearing becomes preponderant only in the second half of the first year (Figure 3). The data from Yakovlev and LeCours are consistent with this clinical observation. They indicate that discontinuities in the timing of the maturation of neural tracts are very characteristic of the brain during the first year. From them one is justified in inferring that the necessary (but never sufficient) tissue substrata for various behavioral patterns come into maturity independently of one another.

A number of observations involving other altricial mammals have also been consistent with the principle that coenesth-

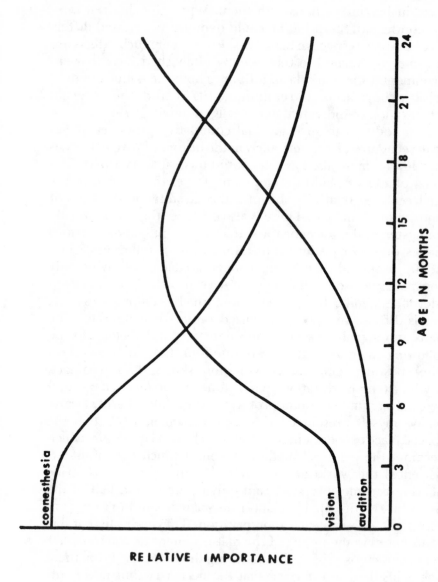

FIGURE 3. Changes in the relative importance of sources of sensory data. Reprinted from American Journal of Psychiatry, vol. 127 (May, 1971).

etic stimulation is crucial if development is to progress normally during the earliest neonatal period. Gustafsson (1948) studied the propensity of rats reared in a germ-free environment to die of megacolon and hydronephrosis. He noted that under normal rearing conditions mother rats will lick their pups' peronei several times a day. When he substituted stroking his animals' peronei with a cotton swab, normal bowel and bladder function was established. More recently, Schanberg and Kuhn (1980) have established that a syndrome analogous to the failure to thrive syndrome of humans develops in rat pups who are separated from their mothers. This can be corrected by stroking the fur on their backs. Schanberg and his coworkers have established that elaboration of the enzyme ornithine decarboxylase, as well as growth hormone, does not occur in isolated pups who do not receive such stimulation. Mason (1968) has shown that the somatic and autistic aspects of the Harlow syndrome in monkeys can be prevented if the animals are reared on a surrogate so constructed that it swings freely and, from the standpoint of the infant monkey, unpredictably in space. Clinically this is reflected in the uneven pace of the infant's overall development. All these observations are congruent with Glover's discussion (1956a) of ego nuclei. He observed that new functional potentialities appear to emerge and become integrated into the infant's behavioral repertoire according to their own timetable. The examination, in this connecion, of any table of developmental norms will make clear that a number of critical new abilities (e.g., hand-eye coordination at 5 months, crawling at 8 months, holding a cup at 9 months, sitting at 10 months) emerge relatively abruptly and become integrated into the complex of developing functional capacities. How such newly emerging abilities will be expressed in terms of behavior and ultimate personality will depend on the experiential ambiance in which they become manifest.

Two such emergences—the social smile response at 2–3 months and stranger anxiety at 7–9 months—have been of particular interest to investigators who approach the study of the first year from a psychoanalytic point of view. It is important to keep in mind, however, that these two are by no means the only newly unfolding behavioral phenomena during this period. Presumably their special importance for psychoanalysis lies in their association with behavioral manifestations of affect. Both are powerful inducers of responsive behavior from care-takers. In the effort to clarify their special importance, Spitz (1959) borrowed the concept of the "organizer" from embryol-ogy. As it is used in that field, the term refers "to the conver-gence of several lines of development at a specific location in the organism. This, in turn, leads to the induction of a set of agents and regulative elements [the organizer] which will influ-ence subsequent developmental processes" (Spitz, 1965, pp. 117–118). To clarify, Spitz offered the following illustration: Before the emergence of the relevant organizer a piece of tissue which is removed from one region of an embryo to another (e.g., from the area out of which the eye will develop to the dorsal skin) will develop identically with the surrounding host tissue. If, however, the tissue is transplanted after the organizer for the eye region has been established, it will retain its original eye characteristics even in the midst of the dorsal epidermis.

A consideration of the vicissitudes which have been ob-served with respect to the emergence of hand-eye coordination will both clarify the usefulness of the concept of organizers and serve as prelude to a consideration of the special importance of the smile and of stranger anxiety for human development. Hand-eye coordination in the form of the ability to execute prehensile movements under the guidance of vision normally emerges when the infant is approximately 5 months old. The following disturbances in its development, which can be seen when maturational readiness occurs in the absence of appro-priate environmental conditions (i.e., a situation *functionally* analogous to the specific location in Spitz's example of the eye anlage) indicate that the emergence of this basic function also involves the confluence of lines of development which lead to the induction of a set of agents and regulators.

Infants who are blinded from birth because of cataracts or retrolental dysplasia will have some ability to discriminate light and dark but have no form vision. They develop blindisms at 5 months. These are characteristic automatisms in which they pass their hands repeatedly in front of their eyes. Needless to say, they are incapable of manual prehension under the guidance of vision, and their subsequent development in this area includes the persistence of automatisms.

An anophthalmic infant who had no light vision never engaged in such blindisms. Neither, obviously, did he ever reach for objects under the guidance of vision (Freedman, Fox-Kolenda, and Brown, 1970).

Anatomically intact infants who are reared under conditions of environmental deprivation which limit the availability of visually stimulating objects may never develop hand/eye coordination. This was true of one such youngster, who died at 23 months. He was the son of a psychotically depressed mother who provided minimal care. At no time did she engage him in play or pay more than perfunctory attention to him. At the time of his death he was unable to use his hands for prehension and instead reached for objects by pursing his lips and craning his neck. Although at autopsy his brain was found to be slightly smaller than those of two normally developing youngsters of the same age who had died accidental deaths, it could not be distinguished from the others by light microscopy. That is, whatever correlation one could assume to obtain between his failure to develop and the state of his nervous system would have to be sought at an ultrastructural, synaptic level (Perry and Freedman, 1973).

The circumstances that result in these deviant outcomes, when considered together with those permitting normal development, underscore the role of what has already been characterized as the cumulative process in establishing the organizer. More formally stated, if the emergence of its necessary (but not sufficient) maturational precursors is to eventuate in the development of the specific ability to prehend objects under the guidance of vision, the youngster must have been exposed to appropriate visually stimulating objects. The effect of this exposure will have been to induce some capacity to organize perceptual experience and thus prepare the child for the new, maturationally determined potential ability. In keeping with Spitz's conception of the role of the organizer, it follows that the consolidation of this ability (or of any distortion of it which may have resulted from deviant circumstances) will profoundly influence the development of those later emerging behaviors of the individual which involve either visually guided manual activity or any of a variety of complex derivative behaviors for which the use of vision and visual representation may have been necessary. This generalization is equally applicable to the social smile and to stranger-separation anxieties. It does not, however, account for their special claim to the interest of psychoanalysis. This question will be considered in the following section.

III

Some form of smiling behavior is observable in the neonate almost literally from birth. At the beginning, however, this appears to be of endogenous origin and is uninfluenced by the environment. There is also no reason to assume that the physical manifestation of the infant's face reflects a subjective experience of pleasure on his part. Emde, Gaensbauer, and Harmon (1976), for example, have shown that neonatal smiling is consistently correlated with REM sleep. They also found it to be present at approximately the same frequency and in the same relation to REM during the two-month survival of an infant whose markedly calcified cerebrum weighed only one-tenth as much as a normal infant's brain. This earliest smile, perhaps better characterized as a "protosmile," would appear to be of endogenous origin and without psychological significance.

Some time during the first or second month this automatic smile begins to give way to a response to exogenous stimuli. The premise that this shift in the evoking agent from endogenous to exogenous sources is dependent on maturational changes in the brain is supported by the observations of Yakovlev and LeCours (1965). Bar 15 in Figure 2 reflects the process of myelin deposition in the optic radiations, i.e., in an element of the optic system which can with considerable confidence be regarded as essential for the psychological representation of visual stimuli. It will be noted that myelinization of this sytem begins at birth and is completed by the fifth month. It is therefore well advanced at 2½–3 months when, according to Emde and his coworkers, maturational readiness for the external induction of the smiling response is present. The effective inducing stimulus at this time appears to be any configuration which roughly simulates the upper portion of the human face. Spitz (1965), for example, has shown that for the 3-month-old a balloon on which two circles approximately in the position of eyes have been painted is a potent inducer. Over time the number of internally established "cognitive" criteria which must be satisfied if the smile is to be elicited increases; i.e., the smiling response becomes increasingly selective. Unlike the inducers of the original endogenous smile, however, these later-established endogenous criteria reflect modifications of the infant's internal functions, which have been established as the result of its earlier ongoing contacts with the environment. From the standpoint of the role of the smile as the nidus around which an organizer will emerge, this has the important consequence that such effective stimuli as the Gestalt of two circles on an oval field are replaced over time by constellations which more and more closely resemble the human face. By this sequence the smile becomes an increasingly important element in a social (or at least protosocial) exchange. To begin with, however, the infant's environmentally induced smile is in response to a stimulus constellation defined by its physical properties. Despite the mothering one's adultomorphic interpretation, its appearance does not justify imputing to the infant that he is smiling at her as a person. Rather, one must infer that he is responding to an aspect of her, i.e., the configuration of her face. Whether or not one considers this a response to a part-object would depend on his definition of objects. It is clear from Piaget's studies of the development of the object concept (1954) that at this age the infant is incapable of conceiving of the human object as having an existence independent of his observation of it. By the same token it is not plausible at this point in the infant's development to conceive of the smile in terms which assume the capacity for such subjective affective discriminations as are implied in the assumption that he can differentiate between good and bad part-objects. How little ability the infant of this age has for making such judgments on the basis of internalized representations is indicated by the following series of observations.

Blind babies have been observed to respond to sound stimuli by smiling when they are as young as several weeks old

(Fraiberg and Freedman, 1964; Fraiberg, 1974). Unlike the obviously generalized smile of the sighted infant, the blind baby's smile *appears* to be highly selective. One anophthalmic infant of 10 weeks, for example, was noted to respond specifically to the sound of its mother's voice. Despite this apparently highly discriminatory response he, like other congenitally blind infants, would not reach for even familiar noisemaking objects until he was approximately 10 months old, i.e., some five months after the sighted child begins to make prehensile movements under the guidance of vision and, at first inspection, also appears to be responding similarly to noisemaking objects. In order to clarify this paradox we investigated the response of sighted babies to noisemaking stimuli (Freedman, Fox-Kolenda, Margileth, and Miller, 1969). We found that until he is roughly 10–11 months old (see Figure 4) the sighted baby does not utilize sound as an indicator of the existence of an external noisemaking object.

Much like a piece of sonar equipment, the younger infant will orient his head to the source of a sound. If, then, he is greeted by an appropriate, visually stimulating object, he will reach and attempt to grasp it. If, however, the object is hidden by a screen, he will lose all interest in the sound. The conclusion seems obvious that the ability to utilize sound to evoke an internalized representation based on earlier experience and thus serve as the indicator of the existence of a noisemaking object emerges following maturational changes occurring at approximately 10–11 months. Presumably the younger infant's inability to establish an internalized object representation on the basis of its acoustical properties is as much in evidence with animate potentially libidinal objects as with inanimate objects. It is of interest in this connection that the observations of Yakovlev and LeCours are consistent with the results of the clinical experiment. Bar 3 in Figure 2 indicates that the process of myelin deposition in the statoacoustical system, i.e., the brain stem, is complete by the time parturition occurs. There is no basis, however, for assuming that the brain stem is competent to support psychological functioning. From that standpoint the data on myelin deposition in the acoustical radiation seem more relevant. Bar 17 indicates that this begins only at birth and is

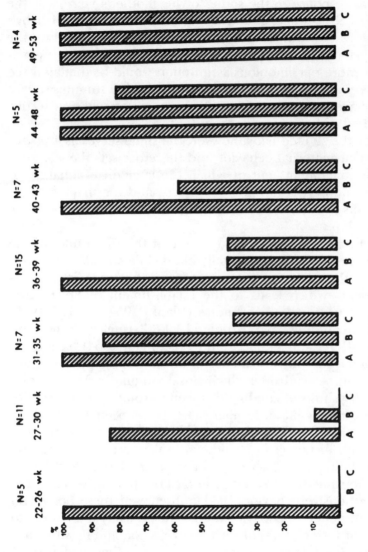

FIGURE 4. For each age (A) indicates percentage of children who recovered a partially hidden object; (B) the percentage of children who recovered a fully hidden object; and (C) the percentage of children who recovered an object on the basis of sound clues alone (from Freedman et al., 1969; copyright 1969 by The Society for Research in Child Development).

not completed until the child is approximately 4 years old. These data suggest that neither the 2½-month-old blind baby's selective response to the sound of his mother's voice, nor the sighted baby's smile, nor the somewhat older sighted baby's turning to the source of a noisemaking object is based on the infant's having established a specific internalized representation. A more parsimonious assumption would be that all three responses are to specific functional aspects of a stimulus source which have yet to acquire specific representational or affective (good/bad) significance for the infant.

For the sighted baby, howver, the smile serves as a potent inducer of maternal behavior and therefore sets the stage for mutual attachments out of which the later differentiation of self and nonself, awareness of objects, and the making of attachments to objects, and internalized representations of them, can develop.

A further consideration of some of the vicissitudes of the development of the congenitally blind child will clarify the relation of the smile to "the convergence of several lines of development" which leads to the establishment of Spitz's first organizer. A number of studies (Blank, 1957; Keeler, 1958; Norris, Spaulding, and Brodie, 1958; Parmelee, Fishe, and Wright, 1959; and Fraiberg and Freedman, 1964) have demonstrated a very high incidence of deviant development in this population. A syndrome which closely simulates the very rare autistic psychosis of childhood is seen in roughly 25 percent of the congenitally blind. Fraiberg (1974) has been able to demonstrate that the process which eventuates in this extraordinarily high incidence of an otherwise very rare syndrome has its origins in the impact on his caretaker of the blind baby's failure to smile and to engage in other expected forms of visually responsive behavior. In the absence of these potent inducers of maternal behavior the mother is likely to respond to her infant with feelings of hurt and rejection and to withdraw. Fraiberg was able to identify at least three other evidences of maturational progress in the infant, i.e., nonvisually induced smiling, hand activity, and spontaneous vocalizing. In a series of nine cases, by helping the mothers to recognize and respond to these cues, she was able to facilitate the development of a mother-infant "dialogue." None of these infants became autistic. "Dialogue" is in quotes in order to emphasize again that it is by no means clear that these blind infants—or, for that matter, comparably aged sighted infants—are able to engage in the kind of mutual activity the word implies. What is certain is that the mothering one assumes such a bilateral exchange is going on and acts accordingly. It is by her behavior that she insures the development of appropriate inner representations when the baby has achieved an adequate level of maturation.

Beginning in the period between his seventh and ninth month, when maturational and developmental changes set the stage for the emergence of Spitz's second organizer, one sees less equivocal evidence of the infant's ability to be aware that the mothering one is in some way unique.[2] Most typically the behavioral manifestations of this newly established "set of agents and regulative elements which will influence subsequent developmental processes" (Spitz, 1965, p. 118) is the relatively abrupt emergence of stranger anxiety. It is important to underscore that this reaction is the *typical* but not invariable expression of the infant's newly established potentialities. Considerations of some of the circumstances under which it does not appear may help clarify the role of this organizer in determining the path of future development.

In the literature the reported incidence of stranger anxiety has ranged from a low of 28 percent (Rheingold and Eckerman, 1973) to a high of 100 percent (Emde, Gaensbauer, and Harmon, 1976). To some extent this discrepancy may be accounted for by differences in experimental design and subject populations. Emde, Gaensbauer, and Harmon (1976) point out, for example, that longitudinal studies in which the same infant is examined repeatedly over time consistently yield a much higher incidence than do cross-sectional studies in which different subjects may be used for each age. That another factor of relevance may be the unique experiences of the population being studied

---

[2] Here I am making a distinction between the evidence of a selective response to functional aspects of the mothering one which, as noted, can be observed as early as 2½ months, and the evidence of a response based on an internalized representation of her which embraces many of her characteristics and serves to distinguish her as an individual.

is suggested by the relatively low incidence of 46 percent reported by Yarrow (1967) in 8-month-old subjects observed in the course of adoption procedures. It is of interest that virtually all of these youngsters managed to differentiate their mothers from strangers in ways other than distress. It is noteworthy also that all had significant reactions to separation. The importance of the infant's earlier experience in determining his reaction is indicated by the frequently reported failure of infants reared under conditions of environmental deprivation, i.e., without the opportunity to make a libidinal attachment or to differentiate strangers from routine caregivers. Provence and Lipton (1963), for example, found such a discrimination to be absent in all but two of their subjects. In the two in whom distress was observed, moreover, the pattern of the reaction was reminiscent of the early smiling response in that it was elicited by the configuration of the examiner's face. When the distressed baby was turned so as to look away from her, the crying stopped at once. When hospitalized at 8 months, Perry and Freedman's baby (1973) also showed no evidence of distress either in relation to the new environment or in response to being handled by strangers. This lack of response is in striking contrast to the inconsolable reaction so often seen in the normal infant. It is in contrast also to the response of Toni, a congenitally blind infant who was developing well (Fraiberg and Freedman, 1964). At 8 months Toni responded with manifestations of intense distress when picked up and held by Mrs. Fraiberg. A month later, merely fingering Mrs. Fraiberg's face while being held by her own mother was sufficient to evoke a similarly intense reaction. It seems justifiable to conclude that Toni, in analogy to normal sighted babies, had developed a libidinally cathected internalized representation of her mother. This was, of course, based on experiences gained through sensory modalities other than vision.

It is not possible to say that at 9 months she, or for that matter any other 9-month-old, had established an inner representation which reflected her mother as a whole object. One is, however, justified in inferring that she had developed a set of inner criteria which served to distinguish aspects of her mother from similar characteristics of Mrs. Fraiberg. These internalized representations were also adequate enough to enable her to make a second intermediate discrimination. Although she clearly preferred her mother and sought her out specifically in times of stress, she was also comfortable with her siblings and a variety of friends and neighbors who visited her home.

The availability of inner criteria for differentiating strange from familiar individuals implies a significant developmental shift—one which can be epitomized by removal of the quotation marks used earlier to enclose the word *dialog*. Spitz (1965) has proposed that this differentiating response is the indicator of the infant's having established "a libidinal object proper." Once established, this object (or part-object) can in his view be mistaken for nothing else. "The child," he says, "has found *the* partner with whom he can establish object relations in the true sense of the word" (p. 161). Spitz also emphasized the importance of idiosyncratic environmental determinants of the behavioral expression of this newly emerging potentiality. Whether the infant will develop an intense and exclusive attachment to a single mother figure or, like Toni, have available a number of individuals to whom the designation familiar may be applied is largely a matter of the ambiance in which he is being reared.

The primate studies of Kaufman (1975) can serve both to illustrate further some of the immediate differences ensuing from contrasting infant-rearing styles and to indicate their implications for later development. Kaufman studied bonnet and pigtailed monkeys. These two closely related species of macaque are characterized by radically different lifestyles and infant-rearing practices. The bonnet is a highly gregarious animal given to considerable physical contact. Although their infants' special relations to their mothers are acknowledged, the babies are handled and played with by all adults. In the pigtailed group, mother and infant form a very close dyadic relation which persists unchallenged until the mother delivers her next offspring. Contact between these infants and other members of the colony is actively discouraged by the mother, who keeps her offspring very close to her. When Kaufman separated pigtailed infants from their mothers, the babies developed intense separation reactions. These consisted of extended periods of agitation followed by depression-withdrawal and gradual restitution. By contrast, when he separated bonnet infants from their mothers, the youngsters simply turned to other members of the colony for nurturance. In a later study, Kaufman and Stynes (1978) succeeded in producing a depressive reaction in a bonnet infant. They accomplished this by raising it in a mixed group of bonnets and pigtails and removing not only the mother but all the other bonnets, leaving the infant in the midst of a group of unresponsive pigtails. After three days of unavailing "pleading" for comfort, he became depressed and curled up in a ball.

Schaffer and Callender (1959) made analogous observations on human infants who were hospitalized during their first year. They found two distinct syndromes, which were related to the ages of the infants. One occurred in youngsters under 28 weeks of age, and the other in those of 29 weeks or more. The older youngsters were fretful. They cried and displayed increased mobility and markedly decreased interest in their environments, both human and nonhuman. The younger group, by contrast accepted the new environment without protest. When the infants were returned home, members of the younger group would, for periods ranging from 20 or 30 minutes to no more than four days, display an unusual interest in their environment. They would scan their surroundings as though totally absorbed by them, but would not focus on any particular feature. The preoccupation was so intense that it was impossible for their mothers to distract them with toys or to make contact with them. The infants 29 weeks and older, by contrast, were markedly overdependent on their mothers. They would refuse to be put down, cried when left alone, and showed fear in the presence of strangers and, occasionally, in that of such familiar people as fathers and siblings. It is also impressive that the mean period of upset after returning home was less than 3 days in the younger and more than 15 days in the older group.

IV

In Mahler's frame of reference, the infant who has developed the capacities to manifest stranger anxiety and to respond to separation with depression-withdrawal has passed from the autistic into the symbiotic phase of development. For the balance of his first and well into his second year, developmental modifications in his capacity for object relatedness will be predicated on the continuation of cumulative changes as opposed to the sequelae of the relatively abrupt emergence of a new organizer. In assessing the child's capacity for object relations during this period, or at least the portion of it which pertains to the first year, it will be useful to refer to the observations of Piaget (1954). According to his timetable, during the last quarter of the first year the infant is most likely to be in the fourth stage of the development of the ability to conceive of an external object as having an existence independent of his perceptions. Although at this time he can retain the notion of its existence when it is moved outside his field of vision, his ability to do so is limited to the actual physical circumstances under which it has disappeared. He is not capable of conceiving of a series of successive displacements such that the object will be found at a place and time remote from where it was last seen. It would seem more than coincidental that this last ability is not consolidated with respect to inanimate objects until the infant is approximately 18 months old. This is approximately the same age that Spitz's third organizer emerges. In Mahler's frame of reference, the baby has emerged from the symbiotic phase and definitively embarked on the processes of separation and individuation. He begins to manifest the capability to enter into a dyadic relation based on his awareness, however limited and tenuous, of his status as a circumscribed entity (a protoself), functioning in relation to a nonself. I choose the designation nonself rather than mother to indicate that others, in addition to the mother, may play a very significant role for the infant and toddler. As I have noted, it is a matter of common observation that even among those with whom he is familiar the older infant and toddler has a hierarchy of preferences. He does not, however, impute to those who constitute his "nonself" that each is, in Kohut's terms, a separate center of initiative—i.e., an individual who can be expected both to enter into relationships and be actuated by motives which have nothing to do with him. I introduce the caveat "however tenuous" because at this age the child will not have established a firm representation of himself as a separately existing entity. Placed in front of a mirror he will give no indication that the reflection he sees has anything to do with him(self). He is also still many months away from the ability to use the first person pronoun. To the extent that he refers to him(self) at all it is with his proper name. The hypothesis that this pattern of development of the use of the first person pronoun is related to the establishment of a sense of self is supported by the observation (Fraiberg, 1977) that among the congenitally blind the use of the first person pronoun can be delayed until the fifth or sixth year or even later. It has already been noted that at least 25 percent of this population does not develop beyond the autistic phase.

During much of the first year, however, the process of individuation has not progressed to the point at which such considerations are relevant. The very young infant is at best only tenuously aware of himself as an entity in his own right. To the extent that he has not yet differentiated himself from others he is lacking as regards at least two of the four criteria—i.e., aim and object—by which Freud (1915) characterized instinctual drives. The others, goal and purpose, can be imputed to him only in the context of here-and-now situations. By the same token, affective behavior is not so much the reflection of subjective experience (the infant, not having fully differentiated himself as an individual, is only marginally capable of subjectivity) as it is, like the 3-month smile, a response to here-and-now evocative stimuli. The differentiation of psychic structures awaits future maturation and development. Lacking established internalized criteria by which to assess his experience, the 1-year-old is limited to global responses. Spitz (1965) characterized the infant as he approaches his first birthday as capable only of identifying with the "external characteristics of behavior on the one hand and with certain global affective states on the other" (p. 258). These latter he epitomized in terms of the attitudes "for" and "against" which he related to the processes of taking in and spitting out—i.e., to primitive peripheral response mechanisms which carry with them only minimal psychological significance.

Since at this age the youngster has not achieved the capacity even for a dyadic relation, the internalizations which occur as a result of his ongoing interactions within the environment cannot, by definition, be elements in intrapsychic conflict. One might, on the contrary, anticipate that like his native language they may be the basis of the conflict-free elements in his personality. In Hartmann's frame of reference (1939) they belong to the realm of autonomous ego functions. That is, they are modes of functioning and character traits which, however adaptive or maladaptive they may prove to be, are regarded by the individual as most typically himself. Glover's analysis of addictive phenomena (1956b), Stoller's hypothesis concerning the etiology of transsexualism (1968), and Steele and Pollock's investigation of the origins of the propensity to batter children (1968) all involve the assumption that such very early preconflictual internalizations have occurred. In each instance it is possible to say that the individual's sense of self, i.e., what Stoller refers to as core identity, includes nonconflictual qualities which result in maladaptive behavior. Unlike the disturbances which occur following the differentiation of psychic structure, these are not the product of intrapsychic conflict. On the contrary, as the individual continues to mature and to develop into the capacity to experience oedipal and postoedipal relations, his experiencing of these new relations and his methods of dealing with them will reflect assumptions about himself and his relation to the world which derive from such early internalization.

References

Blank, H.R. (1957), Psychoanalysis and blindness. *Psychoanal. Quart.*, 26:1–24.
Brody, S. (1956), *Patterns of Mothering*, New York, International Universities Press.
Conel, J.L. (1939/1959), *The Post Natal Development of the Human Cerebral Cortex*, Cambridge: Harvard University Press, 1959.
Emde, R.N., Gaensbauer, T.J., & Harmon, R.J. (1976), Emotional expression in infancy: A biobehavioral study. *Psychological Issues*, Monograph 37. New York: International Universities Press.
Erikson, E.H. (1959), Identity and the life cycle. *Psychological Issues*, Monograph 1. New York: International Universities Press.
Escalona, S. (1965), Some determinants of individual differences. *Transactions N.Y. Acad. Sci.*, 27:802–816.
Fraiberg, S.H. (1974), Blind infants and their mothers: An examination of

the sign system. In: *The Effect of the Infant on Its Caregiver*, ed. M. Lewis & L. Rosenblum. New York: Wiley.

—— (1977), *Insights from the Blind*, New York: Basic Books.

—— & Freedman, D.A. (1964), Studies in ego development of the congenitally blind child. *The Psychoanalytic Study of the Child*, 19:113–169. New York: International Universities Press.

Freedman, D.A. (1971), Congenital and perinatal sensory deprivation: Some studies in early development. *Amer. J. Psychiat.*, 127(11):1539–1545.

—— Fox-Kolenda, B.J., Margileth, D.A., & Miller, D.H. (1969), The development of the use of sound as a guide to affective and cognitive behavior: a two-phase process. *Child Development*, 40:1099–1105.

—— —— & Brown, S.L. (1970), A multihandicapped Rubella baby. *J. Amer. Acad. Child Psychiat.*, 9:298–317.

Freud, S. (1895), Project for a scientific psychology. *Standard Edition*, 1:298–302. London: Hogarth Press, 1966.

—— (1899), Screen memories. *Standard Edition*, 3:303–322. London: Hogarth Press, 1962.

—— (1900), The interpretation of dreams. *Standard Edition*, 5:566–567. London: Hogarth Press, 1953.

—— (1914), On narcissism: An introduction. *Standard Edition*, 14:67–104. London: Hogarth Press, 1957.

—— (1915), Instincts and their vicissitudes. *Standard Edition*, 14:109–140. London: Hogarth Press, 1957.

—— (1916–1917), Introductory lectures on psycho-analysis. *Standard Edition*, 16:320–340. London: Hogarth Press, 1958.

Glover, E. (1956a), A psychoanalytic approach to the classification of mental disorders. In: *On the Early Development of Mind*. New York: International Universities Press, pp. 161–186.

—— (1956b), On the etiology of drug addiction. In: *On the Early Development of Mind*. New York: International Universities Press, pp. 187–215.

Greenough, W.T. (1975), Experiential modification of the developing brain. *Amer. Scientist*, 63:37–46.

Gustafsson, S. (1948), Germ free rearing of rats. *Acta Pathologica et Microbiologica Scandinavica*, 72 (Suppl):12–130.

Hartmann, H. (1939), *Ego Psychology and the Problem of Adaptation*. New York: International University Press, 1958.

Jacobson, E. (1954), The self and the object world: Vicissitudes of their infantile cathexes and their influence on ideational and affective development. *The Psychoanalytic Study of the Child*, 9:75–127. New York: International Universities Press.

Kandell, E.R. (1979), Psychotherapy and the single synapse. *N. Eng. Jour. Med.*, 301:1028–1037.

Kanner, L. (1949), Autistic disturbance of affective contact. *Nervous Child*, 2:217–250.

Kaufman, I.C. (1975), Learning what comes naturally: The role of life experience and the establishment of species behavior. *Ethos*, 3:129–142.

—— & Stynes, A.J. (1978), Depression can be induced in bonnet macaque infants. *Psychosom. Med.*, 40:71–75.

Keeler, W.R. (1958), Autistic patterns and defective communication in blind children with retrolental fibroplasia. In: *Psychopathology of Communication*, ed. P. Hoch & J. Zubin. New York: Grune & Stratton, 1958, pp. 64–83.

Loewald H. (1971), On motivation and instinct theory. *The Psychoanalytic Study of the Child*, 26:91–128. New York: Quadrangle.

Mahler, M. (1968), *On Human Symbiosis and the Vicissitudes of Individuation*. New York: International Universities Press.

Mason, W.A. (1968), Early social deprivation in the nonhuman primates: Implications for human behavior. In: *Biology and Behavior: Environmental Influences*, ed. D.C. Glass. New York: Rockefeller University Press, pp. 70–100.

Norris, M., Spaulding, P., & Brodie, F. (1958), *Blindness in Children*. Chicago: University of Chicago Press.

Parmelee, A.H., Fishe, C., & Wright, R. (1959), The development of ten children with blindness as a result of retrolental fibroplasia, *AMA Journal of Children's Diseases*, 96:198–220.

Perry, J., & Freedman, D.A. (1973), Massive neonatal environmental deprivation: A clinical and neuroanatomical study. *Research Publications Association for Research in Nervous and Mental Disease*, 51:244–268.

Piaget, J. (1954), *The Construction of Reality in the Child*. New York: Basic Books.

Provence, S., & Lipton, R. (1963), *Infants in Institutions*. New York: International Universities Press.

Rheingold, H., & Eckerman, C.O. (1973), Fear of the stranger: A critical examination. In: *Advances in Child Development and Behavior*, ed. H.W. Reese. New York: Academic Press.

Sander, L.W. (1962), Issues in early mother-child interaction, *J. Amer. Acad. Child Psychiat.*, 1:141–166.

Schaffer, H.R., & Callender, W.M. (1959), Psychologic effects of hospitalization in infancy. *Pediatrics*, 24:528–539.

Shanberg, S.M., & Kuhn, C.M. (1980), Maternal deprivation: An animal model of psychosocial deprivation. In: *Enzymes and Neurotransmitters in Mental Disease*, ed. E. Vadin, New York: Wiley, pp. 373–393.

Spitz, R.A. (1945), Hospitalism: An inquiry into the genesis of psychiatric conditions in early childhood. *The Psychoanalytic Study of the Child*, 1:53–74. New York: International Universities Press.

——— (1950), Relevancy of direct infant observation. *The Psychoanalytic Study of the Child*, 5:66–73. New York: International Universities Press.

——— (1959), *A Genetic Field Theory of Ego Formation*. New York: International Universities Press.

——— (1965), *The First Year of Life*. New York: International Universities Press.

Steele, B.F., & Pollock, C.B. (1968), A psychiatric study of parents who abuse infants and small children. In: *The Battered Child*, ed. R.E. Halper & C.B. Kempe. Chicago: University of Chicago, pp. 103–147.

Stern, D.N. (1971), A microanalysis of mother-infant interaction. *J. Amer. Acad. Child Psychiat.*, 10:501–517.

Stoller, R.J. (1968), *Sex and Gender*. New York: Science House.

Yakovlev, P.J., & LeCours, A.R. (1965), The myelogenetic cycles of regional maturation of the brain. In: *Regional Development of the Brain in Early Life*, ed. A. Minkouski. Oxford: Blackwell Scientific Publications.

Yarrow, L.J. (1967), The development of focused relationship during infancy. In: *Exceptional Infant: Volume 1. The Normal Infant*, ed. J. Hellmuth. New York: Brunner/Mazel.

9

The First Year After Birth

MARTIN A. SILVERMAN, M.D.

Reconstruction from the Psychoanalysis of Adults

Psychoanalytic investigation into the human developmental process began with Sigmund Freud's attempts to unravel the meaning of the symptoms brought to him by his adult neurotic and psychotic patients. First using hypnosis, and then via the psychoanalytic method that he devised, he discovered a vast unconscious realm of thoughts and emotions, exploration of which yielded surprising solutions to the mysteries he was investigating. When he analyzed his patients' free associations, dreams, fantasies, and creative productions, and the residues of conflicted relationships with important persons earlier in their lives, which they tended to relive with him in the treatment situation, he realized that the key to understanding their current symptoms resided in their hitherto forgotten past. He was able to trace their difficulties to incompletely resolved intrapsychic conflicts that extended back through their childhoods into the earliest months and years of their lives.

Freud's initial explorations were carried out with hysterical and obsessional patients, in whom dramatic sexual and aggressive conflicts of a startling nature were found to occupy a prominent position in their conscious and, especially, their unconscious emotional life. As he studied his patients' internal emotional struggles and reconstructed their origins in the past, he gradually came to see that a developmental continuum existed between the raw beginnings of physiological and psychological functioning in infancy and the complex, structured existence that characterizes the adult state.

Freud's demonstration of the therapeutic and investigative usefulness of psychoanalysis led an increasing number of other workers interested in relieving human suffering and in exploring the wellsprings of human behavior to join him in his researches. Ferenczi (1913), Horney (1924, 1926), Abraham (1927), and Jones (1948) werre among Freud's most important early coworkers with an interest in mapping out the details of developmental progression during the first few years after birth. Abraham, trained as an embryologist, was particularly interested in tracing the epigenetic sequence of phases of psychic organization and reorganization during early life.

Freud's initial preoccupation with unraveling the neuroses, and his reluctance to recognize the intensity of innate human destructiveness (see Schur, 1972) led to an early concentration upon his monumental discovery, the oedipus complex, and to an emphasis on the role of libidinal drives in human psychic economy. When he turned to paranoia, schizophrenia, and the major affective psychoses, however, his attention was drawn back to the preoedipal period, from birth into the third year, and he could no longer deny the presence in human beings of powerful, innate destructive inclinations.

Throughout his investigative career, however, Freud's clinical and theoretical interests continued to center predominantly on libidinal propositions and the oedipus complex, to the *relative* neglect of the vicissitudes of aggression and preoedipal development. This can be attributed to the fact that Freud worked primarily with adult neurotics, to the ongoing impact of his exciting early discoveries, and to the intense resistance against their recognition and acceptance that he encountered in the scientific community at large. Aggressivity remained less in specific focus than libidinal considerations throughout Freud's writings. Preoedipal development attracted his interest more in terms of preparations for and precursors of the oedipal struggles lying ahead and more in terms of fixation points to which defensive regression might occur in flight from those struggles than in its own right.

Abraham's attention was drawn, by contrast, to aggressivity and the preoedipal period. With his encouragement, his protege, Melanie Klein (1948), was later to develop Freud's observations of innate aggressivity (in its most extreme conceptual form, the "death instinct") and of important drive and ego developments during the first year into a set of clinical and theoretical propositions in which they would be elevated into a position of overwhelmingly primary significance. Klein's controversial views will be considered at a later point in this chapter.

Let us first turn to the way in which Freud and his early coworkers conceptualized development during the first year after birth. Freud concluded from his studies of neuroses, psychoses, perversions, and of the sexual foreplay, character traits, dreams, and artistic works of normal people that the concept of sexuality had to be broadened and extended to include much more than only the genital sexual congress of adults. He concluded that in newborn infants innate pressure to discharge mounting libidinal (and aggressive) drive tension (via action upon external objects) plays a crucial role in organizing experiences of pleasure and unpleasure, in fostering the development of relationships with other human beings, and in promoting the development of the psychic apparatus itself.

He was struck with human infants' protracted helplessness and dependence on outside agents to help them relieve the biological and psychological tensions that arise spontaneously within them and that are aroused by external stimuli. Prior to birth, he observed, placental mechanisms automatically and continuously minimize physiological need tensions, and the fetus is cushioned against the intrusion of stimuli from without. Whatever tensions exist as a concomitant of the anabolic processes of tissue and organ formation and physical growth and maturation, he postulated, must be dispersed and diffused more or less evenly within the internal milieu. The experience of birth disrupts this state of relative equilibrium, divests the infant of the automatic maternal support system within which it has been developing, and floods the organism with stimuli and physiological tensions by which it feels helplessly overwhelmed. Freud postulated that the last must serve as the initial prototype for the experience of anxiety.

Freud believed that the newborn infant is partially protected from excessive distress by the "stimulus barrier" afforded by its initial lack of awareness of sources of tension (internal as well as external). The infant in the process of being born is plunged into a state of shock, and there is a relative absence of perceptual channels primed to recognize the impingement of tension-producing stimuli. It is only with repeated experience of disturbances of its equanimity that its attention is drawn to these sources of tension.

Freud theorized that the infant tries at first to rid itself of these unwanted organismic tensions by declining to recognize their existence, a kind of psychological turning away or "primal repression" (which may be the basis of the negative hallucinatory avoidance of human contact of children with primary infantile autism). He observed that the dream work of adults seems to operate in part to protect their sleep from being disrupted by intrusive internal and external stimuli. It carries this out by denying their existence, transforming their perceptual appearance into forms that are neutral and consonant with continuation of restful sleep, or by representing their demands as already having been met. He also recognized from his clinical work that human beings tend toward the preservation of sameness, defying the need for change, and toward economy in expenditure of energy. Reconstructing backward from these observations, he concluded that the human mental apparatus in the course of evolution has developed a basic aim, acting at cross-purposes to one impelling it toward active life experiences, of ridding itself of stimuli, from whatever source, in order to remain as nearly tension-free as possible. In doing so, he was partly guided by Fechner (see Freud, 1895), who had earlier arrived at the conclusion that living matter strives toward a completely tension-free state. Freud later carried this line of thought ("the principle of constancy") very much further, extrapolating from the clinical observations of negative therapeutic reaction, intense masochism, and suicide to the concept of a death instinct, operating on a biological level in opposition to a libidinal life force, which impelled the organism back toward an inorganic state of zero tension.

The newborn infant is unable to ignore totally the states of tension that disturb its sleep and impel it toward activity to remove the intrusive stimuli, however. Imperative somatic requirements, the most intense of which is that imposed by hunger, periodically disrupt its sleep and forcibly call themselves to its attention. Since the infant's reflex thrashing and crying evoke a maternal ministering response, they bring a perceptual gestalt of the mothering person into view. This consists especially of her face, the breast or bottle, the milk she provides, the sound of her voice, and the feel of her cràdling body. It is registered through sight, hearing, touch, smell, taste, and the kinesthetic sense. The perceptual gestalt brought into registration by the mothering person's arrival becomes associated both with the distress that interrupts the infant's sleep and with the relief from that distress that permits it to return to sleep.

Freud recognized that the infant at first is incapable of integrating the perceptual registration of the mothering person that is associated with discomfort from that which is associated with *relief* from discomfort. It cannot at first recognize that a single entity is being perceived in connection with both. It instead perceives two separate perceptual gestalts, one organized by *bad* feelings and another by *good* feelings, the forerunner, he observed, of the split bad and good mothers found in the fantasies and preoccupations of borderline and psychotic individuals and in the dreams and stories of normal children and adults (e.g., *Hansel and Gretel* and *Cinderella*). The frequent repetition of being awakened from sleep with uncomfortable sensations, being presented by the perceptual gestalt associated with the situation of nursing, and experiencing relief from the discomfort and a return to sleep invokes, via the facilitation of discriminative perceptual and motor neuronal pathways, first recognition memory and then evocative memory of that perceptual gestalt.

There is some evidence that certain individuals are capable of dim recall of this early experience in the form of a hypnopompic experience first described by the psychoanalyst Isakower (1938). While the person, as a child or adult, is falling asleep, he or she becomes aware of a gritty or sandy sensation around the lips and in the mouth and of the presence of something that is not quite inside and not quite outside, or perhaps *both* inside and outside somehow. There is a sensation of movement, or of something or someone that seems to be getting alternately closer and farther away. At times, there is the feeling of an ill-defined female presence that sometimes is described as having a fascinating but foreboding or even witchlike quality. The perception is visually unclear or dimly outlined. Sometimes there is the sensation of convexity or roundedness and/or a mottled textural quality, perhaps like that of orange peel. It is always associated with a combination of pleasurable interest and the wish for the experience to continue, simultaneous with a distinctly unpleasant feeling that approaches dread. There is growing evidence that the Isakower phenomenon may be a complex psychological experience that includes recall of other ambivalently perceived events as well (especially the primal scene), but it is very likely that its primary link is with the infantile experience of nursing at the breast and falling asleep.

Freud theorized, based on his clinical data, that the child's attachment to its mother derives not only from the association of her perceptual registration with repeated relief from hunger, but, even more so, from a gradual shift in the distribution of libidinal drive energy. He defined libido as the psychological reflection of an instinctual life force of biological origin. He inferred from his psychoanalytic observations that from some source within the body, probably chemical in nature, and ultimately related to the forces that originally transformed inorganic matter into active, self-replicating organic life forms, there arises a qualitative and quantitative energic drive tension that builds up periodically to a threshold level that exerts pressure for discharge. In this, he in part predicted the later discovery of hormonal substances. Freud viewed the libido as the psychological representative of that biological pressure that, although initially autoerotic in its expression, in suitable circumstances leads to attachment to love objects and eventually to the reproductive activity that ensures continuation of the species.

He theorized that libidinal pressure before birth is at a low level and is distributed more or less evenly and centripetally. After birth, however, it increases in quantity and presses for discharge. The pathways used by the vital somatic drives after birth present themselves as available channels for attainment of libidinal satisfaction as well. When they are adopted for this purpose, they become "erotogenic zones" for the pleasurable discharge of libidinal tension. The main such zone in the infant, of course, is the mouth, although the perceptual and respiratory apparatuses, the excretory organs, the musculature, and to some extent the genitals serve as subsidiary channels for libidinal discharge. The pleasure that is experienced in the feeding situation, Freud observed, derives largely from the libidinal satisfaction that becomes attached to it. He noticed that sensual sucking of the thumb and fingers is carried out in infancy with intense absorption leading often to sleep or to orgastic-like motor activity (Freud, 1905, 1911). This form of early libidinal satisfaction is carried forward into such adult behaviors as eating for pleasure, smoking, drinking, kissing, oral forms of sexual foreplay, and, in its pathological forms, alcoholism and drug addiction.

The Differentiation Between Self and Objects

The infant in the beginning cannot distinguish between inside and outside. At first, Freud reasoned, it must view all discomfort as coming from outside (it is only later that it comes to realize that external stimuli are avoidable, while internal ones are not). It attempts to escape from the discomfort caused by need tension by ignoring it ("primal repression," the forerunner of the negative hallucinations of psychotics). When this proves insufficient, the infant finds that it can stave off the uncomfortable sensations by evoking the memory of a past experience of relief of tension via discharge through a suitable channel (mainly oral) and investing the memory or fantasy with sufficient cathexis that it feels like a current experience. It is to this early phase of "magical-hallucinatory omnipotence" (Ferenczi, 1913) that Freud and his coworkers assumed that normal adults regress in their dreams and to which psychotics return in their wishful hallucinations and grandiose delusions. They also traced the tendency of some obsessional neurotics to believe in the magical power of thoughts (though they are simultaneously aware of the absurdity of the belief) and the widespread wish among people to find evidence of the parapsychic power to foretell the future or influence objects with the mind, as well as to be fascinated with magic, to the yearning to return to the illusion of magical-hallucinatory power which they once experienced in infancy.

Reality intrudes repeatedly to oppose the infant's illusion of omnipotence. Hallucinatory wish fulfillment does not always occur in close enough temporal proximity to an *actual* experience that relieves somatic and libidinal distress to permit the infant to persist in blissful ignorance of its dependence on outside agencies. It is forced to gradually recognize that hallucinatory evocation of the perception of gratification is by itself insufficient to relieve distress. In fortuitous circumstances (i.e., where the delay interposed between the feeling of needful distress and the arrival of actual relief is short enough to be tolerable, but long enough to call attention to itself), the discrepancy between fantasy and reality spurs the child to exercise and develop the physiological ego nuclei with which it is endowed into executive functions and structures by means of which it can progressively adapt to the demands of reality. The infant becomes increasingly able to remember, discriminate among, and synthesize perceptual data; exercise judgment; test reality; and develop sufficient motor control to act upon the world around it so as to get its needs met. As the child comes to tolerate more and more frustration and drive tension, it moves beyond the "primary process" of automatically seeking immediate and indiscriminate discharge of drive tension according to the "pleasure-unpleasure principle." It becomes increasingly capable of delaying discharge and of not only tolerating increasing amounts of drive tension, but of gaining increasing control over it, harnessing it, and using it to power increasingly efficient ego structures by means of which it can take effective, realistic action. An important part of the "secondary process" (Freud, 1900), which operates according to the "reality principle" (Freud, 1911), is the development of symbolic thought as a highly efficient tool of mastery. Freud emphasized that thought develops out of hallucinatory wish fulfillment as a result of increasing capacity to tolerate drive tension, permitting delay of the discharge of, control over, and transformation of drive energies so that they can be used by the ego for reflective, internal trial action leading to intelligent decisions as to what real action is to be undertaken. In their observations that symbolic thought derives in part from the infant's experiencing and relating to the world at first via its bodily activity and then via the imitative imagery that grows out of it (Ferenczi, 1913), the early psychoanalysts foreshadowed Piaget's later formulation of the evolution of symbolic thought out of sensorimotor activity during the first year and a half. The secondary process, in which thought replaces hallucinatory wish fulfillment, affords the infant the capacity to deal increasingly effectively and realistically both with its own internal impulses and with the outside world. Freud concluded that psychotic regression to primitive, primary process mechanisms takes place when an individual's ego development has been so deficient that he feels overwhelmed by and unable to deal with or coordinate his inner drive pressures with the demands of civilized society.

The infant's illusion of grandiose omnipotence normally is relinquished slowly. It cannot all at once face its relative weakness and dependence on outside forces, but gives up the security provided by its imagined omnipotence only bit by bit (and probably never completely) as it grows more confident in its capacity to tolerate and deal effectively with its inner drive pressures and as it comes to perceive outside objects as reliable and trustworthy.

Freud referred to the infant's initial self-absorption and sense of magical power and importance as its "primary narcissism" (Freud, 1914), after the ancient Greek myth of Narcissus, who fell in love with his own image. Reconstructing from his observations of neurotic and psychotic patients, he concluded that the first step the infant makes in moving beyond this is to incorporate its mother's image into its own narcissistic sphere as an extended part of the self, much as it takes food into its body to relieve hunger. Ongoing experience indicates to the infant, however, that she is not always present, but comes and goes. Only vigorous denial of the infant's own perceptions, as in primary infantile autism, can hide the fact of her separate existence.

As the developing infant becomes increasingly aware of its mother's separateness, important changes take place in its libidinal economy and distribution. First, since the mother's image was initially perceived as part of the self and invested with narcissistic libidinal cathexis, the progressive detachment of her representation from that of the self represents a major shift from narcissistic self-love to the love of others. Second, the infant's ability to recognize its mother's separateness develops *pari passu* with the taming, transformation, and taking over of drive energies by burgeoning ego structures that are strong enough to deal effectively and realistically with the internal and external world. Reality testing and object relatedness, epitomized in the infant by self-object differentiation, continue thereafter throughout life as indicators of general psychological maturity and ego strength.

Recognition of its mother as a separate and powerful being diminishes the infant's primary narcissism, but compensation accrues from the "secondary narcissistic" gain afforded by her love, protection, and maternal care. There is a complex relationship between the child and its mother at this point, with alternating progressive and regressive shifts that make for an overall fluidity in the construction of self- and object representations, libidinal and aggressive expression and distribution, and the functioning of the child's budding ego structures. On the one hand, the infant is still very much under the influence of the pleasure principle, with relatively little frustration tolerance, the tendency to fly into a rage when its needs are not met quickly enough, and intermittent dependence on the primitive mechanisms of denial, introjection, and projection. On the other hand, recognition of the mother as separate introduces a new danger into the infant's life, because someone who is separate can be lost. The fear of being overwhelmed by intolerable levels of need tension (annihilation anxiety due to ego helplessness) is in part replaced and in part supplemented by separation anxiety.

The infant wards off this new danger via the fantasy of omnipotent control of the mother, its primary love object, through magical gestures (Ferenczi, 1913); i.e., it feels that it can make the mother appear at will by opening its eyes, flailing its arms and legs, crying, etc. Although the infant in the latter part of the first year is still utilizing grandiose, omnipotent psychological mechanisms, this is nevertheless a major advance beyond the magical control of tension states via hallucinatory wish fulfillment that had preceded it, since it is moving in the direction of increasing realism and self-control in its relations with its internal and external environment. As the child moves toward the acquisition of symbolic thought, toward the end of the first year or the first half of the second, the gestures by means of which it expresses its desires gradually organize themselves into vocalizations which constitute the rudiments of communicative speech. Wolff (1965) has made the interesting observation that the phonemic units which form the basic units of crying are the same ones, as demonstrated with the use of the oscilloscope, as those utilized later in adult speech.

The danger of loss of the primary love object arises not only from her separate existence and separate will, but also from a source within the child itself. The infant has perceived its mother's image ambivalently from the very beginning, and its capacity to hold her memory image in mind is very limited, especially when it is frustrated and angry. At such times, aggressive cathexis of the mother's mental representation markedly increases, counteracting its libidinal investment and threatening to shatter and destroy it.

Freud (1917) and Abraham (1924b) learned a great deal about infantile ambivalence by examining the condition of melancholia. They pointed out that the infant relates to its mother at first by incorporating or introjecting her libidinally cathected image, the psychological counterpart of its physiological activity of taking in and devouring the nutriment with which she is at first equated. This is the forerunner of identification with loved objects, whereby their values, mannerisms, and other attributes are unconsciously taken over, imitated, and made part of the self, an important basis for learning and cultural transmission of information, attitudes, and values. But the mother's mental representation also is subject to hostile attack, when its association with states of frustration and distress attracts aggressive cathexis to it. As the infant pulls together and integrates its positive and negative images of the mother, it realizes that its sadistic attacks on the mother's image threaten to destroy the person it loves and needs.

Freud observed that early mental mechanisms seem to be

modeled after the infant's biological experiences, i.e., that the ego begins as a body ego. Abraham (1924b), proceeding along this line of thought and noting that infants advance during the first year from sucking to biting as the teeth emerge, divided the oral period into an earlier, simple incorporative phase followed by a highly ambivalent later phase in which the taking in of objects is perceived in terms of biting them to pieces and destroying them. In his 1917 paper on the subject, Freud observed that a central feature of melancholia is an intensely hostile, even murderous attack on an object that has been incorporated into the self via identification. Abraham (1924a) studied this further and concluded that in manic-depressive psychosis there is a regression to intensely ambivalent, hostile incorporation of the primary object, together with vigorous self-punishment to atone for urges to sadistically control, torture, and destroy it, and further regression to self-object dedifferentiation in which self and object are simultaneously attacked and punished.

Freud and his coworkers, in other words, traced the narcissism, omnipotent grandiosity, disturbed reality testing, and primitive defense mechanisms displayed by schizophrenics, as well as the intense oral-ambivalent struggles involving overlapping self- and object representations to be found in the unconscious of manic depressives, back to roots laid down during the first year. (The disturbed object relations, chronic dissatisfaction, feelings of emptiness, insistence on immediate need satisfaction, narcissistic vulnerability, and wide mood swings of borderline and psychopathic individuals lead in the same direction.)

But they saw a great deal more as emanating from events during the first year. Since development is epigenetic in nature, as Abraham in particular pointed out, what takes place in each developmental phase sets the stage for, is carried forward into, and plays a major role in shaping the one that follows it. What transpires during the oral phase is of such vital significance that it imprints itself on all that follows. Basic personality traits, for example, can be traced to variations in experiences during that early period of life. Core mental representations of the self and of external objects in general and basic attitudes toward one's physical and emotional needs and the opportunities available for meeting them are established at that time.

Disturbances in the optimal development of the initial mother-child relationship—and in the development of frustration tolerance, the ability to delay satisfaction, what Erikson (1959) has called "basic trust" (reasonable confidence in oneself and others) or the building up of basic ego apparatuses with which to master the inner and outer world—will impede forward progression. The child can become fixated on the modes and forms of the oral phase, as revealed by prolonged thumb-sucking or nailbiting, eating disturbances, oral perversions, obesity, alcohol or drug addiction, poor impulse control, etc. Abraham (1916, 1924b), pointed out that certain character traits are referable to vicissitudes of experience during the oral phase. Where there are strong oral drives, but significant experiences of deprivation or disappointment involving the taking in of aliment or its emotional correlates during infancy, there may be a lifelong pessimistic attitude, at times associated with chronic demands for redress. Where oral and emotional gratification is readily forthcoming in a highly pleasurable way during the first year, an optimistic expectation that all will go well may persist throughout life. Excessive indulgence and lack of encouragement to tolerate frustration and become self-reliant can lead to a characterological pattern of expecting others to take care of one rather than working and taking care of one's own needs. Abraham traced envy (which was to play an important role in Kleinian theory) to the ambivalent late oral phase and described the emergence of loquaciousness, biting sarcasm, impatience, ambition, intellectual curiosity and thirst for knowledge, and generosity out of seeds that sprout under suitable conditions during the first year.

Freud and Abraham noted that people in general are reluctant to give up oral modes of gratification. This is evident in the ubiquitous importance of food, drink, and tobacco in adult life, both private and social, the prominence in adult sexual behavior of kissing and oral-genital foreplay, and the popularity of oral terms of endearment in which a loved one is likened to food to be eaten up (e.g., honey, sugar, cutie-pie, sweetie, etc.). They emphasized that basic oral modes and yearnings can be discerned throughout higher forms of human experience and activity, however altered and transformed they may become. The ecstasy of orgastic fusion or oneness with one's love object at the climax of the genital sex act, *from which one slips into relaxed and peaceful sleep,* is but one dramatic example of this.

The Psychoanalysis of Children

The early psychoanalysts made sporadic observations of young children. Occasionally they attempted to analyze a phobia which had emerged suddenly and dramatically in a child (Freud, 1909; Ferenczi, 1913), but they did so only indirectly. Not believing that children would submit to analysis conducted by a stranger, they carried out their investigations through a parent on those rare occasions when they directed their analytic skills to the unraveling of children's symptoms. Although Freud and his colleagues were working almost exclusively with adults, they were able to learn an enormous amount about the earliest phases of development. It was inevitable, however, that analysts would become interested in expanding their field of operations so that they could analyze children as well as adults and thereby look more directly at their developmental progression.

It was not until the 1920s that, realizing that children as well as adults can be amenable to the psychoanalytic method so long as it is adjusted to their developmental level, they began to work with children on a full-scale basis. Hug-Hellmuth (1919) was the first to do so, but Melanie Klein and Anna Freud have been the most influential contributors in this regard. Klein (1932, 1948; see Segal, 1964), working with very young and often seriously disturbed children, devised a therapeutic approach in which she used children's play as "equivalent" to the free association of adults as a source of information about the psychological forces at work within them. She was greatly influenced by Freud's prestructural instinct theory, including the "death instinct" hypothesis he elaborated in 1920. She went beyond Freud, in fact, in postulating the instinctual awareness, in the earliest months, of complex, rivalrous, triadic fantasies related to the oedipus complex.

She reconstructed backward from the play material presented to her by her young patients and offered deep sexual and aggressive interpretations that reached back into the very first year after birth. She was encouraged in this regard by Abraham, who offered her unwavering support and served as an early mentor as she pursued her investigations. Klein believed that early development is shaped by the need to contain powerful, destructive impulses which are perceived by the infant as enormously dangerous; the infant gets rid of them by projecting them into the outside world ("projective identification"), following the model of oral expulsion of displeasing, unwanted aliment. She believed that persecutory anxieties typify this period; these arise out of the mechanism of projective identification, and mobilize self-defensive, sadistic attacks against the object in fantasy, from whom the child fears retaliation. Primitive defense mechanisms involving splitting of the object into "good" and "bad" images are posited, with anxiety being warded off via splitting and idealization to preserve the existence of a good object. Klein referred to this as "the paranoid position," which, she theorized, holds sway during the first few months after birth.

Cognitive advance and the experience of being weaned from the bottle or breast lead, according to Klein, to "the depressive position," in which anxiety and guilt develop in relation to the loss of the powerful breast and its contents. The child reacts to loss or unavailability with destructive rage. It tends to blame its destructive fantasies directed against the depriving (and therefore "bad") breast-mother for the loss. Klein emphasized the importance of intense envy of the mother during this period, with urges to "spoil" the breast and its contents. She described "manic" restitutive fantasies to restore good relations with the "good," feeding breast-mother, which the child attempts to dominate and control. It is during the depressive period, in the latter half of the first year, according to Klein, that the oedipus complex and sibling rivalry first make their appearance. They develop, she hypothecated, out of innate awareness of the difference between the sexes, an inborn knowledge of genital sexual activity between the parents, increasing differentiation of objects from one another as a result of cognitive development, and further elaboration of diadic envy into triadic jealousy. The depressive period, according to Klein, is characterized by a combination of persistent anxieties of a paranoid-schizoid and persecuting nature and anxieties associated with depressive mourning for the lost "good" object, which the child hopes to regain. The child uses manic restitutive fantasies and obsessive defenses to control its destructive inclinations and to build a "good" representation of the external object to protect it against the fantasied object (the "bad" maternal internal object) against which its destructive fantasies are directed and from which it fears retaliative, destructive attack. Klein felt that this struggle is never completely resolved but persists throughout life as a basic, overriding psychological force.

Klein's theoretical constructions, which grew out of her contact with Freud's and Abraham's *early* observations on human drives, emphasized the developmental impact of powerful drive pressures (especially destructive urges) emanating from within the child. She paid relatively little attention to the effects on the child of influences impinging from the outside world. Serious objections have been brought against such a one-sided approach to constructing developmental formulations. The question also has been raised as to whether infants in the first year of life are capable of such involved reasoning, complex fantasies, and extensive knowledge of the details of parental sexual activity as are attributed to them by Klein's theories.

Hartmann and Anna Freud, proceeding from very different vantage points, arrived at conclusions about early development that contrasted sharply with those of Klein. Both were very much influenced by Freud's *later* investigations into the psychology of the ego, and they played an important role in developing them further. They emphasized the importance of studying the development of the ego, the executive branch of the mental organization that mediates between the imperative demands of internal drive pressures and the restrictions imposed on their freedom of discharge by the external world.

Freud initially conceived of the ego as developing out of frustration of the drives by an unyielding environment. He reasoned that repeated experiences of relief from tension (feeding) establish pathways of drive discharge which the infant cathects whenever it experiences an increase of drive tension beyond a tolerable level; this creates the hallucinatory fantasy of repetition of the experience of relief. Since hallueinatory wish fulfillment cannot actually remove the inner source of tension, drive energies are taken over and transformed, he concluded, into ego energies serving perception, recall, comprehension, differentiation, reasoning, motor control, language, thought, etc., in order for the organism to distinguish between the wishful *fantasy* of tension reduction and the identification of *real* objects upon which it can act so as to obtain effective drive discharge. He attributed this process in part to the evolution of human beings as a species and in part to structural development taking place in the infant as a result of ongoing experience. In a later paper (1937), he modified his earlier position, in which he had conceived of the ego as growing out of the id, by adding that the anlagen of the individual's ego apparatuses probably are already present at birth.

Hartmann (1964), seizing upon Freud's later conclusions, postulated the existence at birth of an undifferentiated matrix out of which both ego and id emerge, with reciprocal influences one upon the other. He emphasized that the ego emerges not only out of the need to resolve the conflict situations which arise out of the restrictions imposed upon the id by the external world, but also out of the maturation and development of *inborn*, autonomous apparatuses serving adaptation to the world in which we live. He sought to expand psychoanalysis from a method of clinical investigation into a general psychology that might account for human development in its normative as well as pathological aspects, and that would focus upon its conflict-free as well as upon its conflict-derived spheres of activity. Although his own work as a psychoanalyst was with adults, he saw a necessity for direct investigation of the developmental phases of childhood, beginning with infancy, and eventually he entered into collaboration with Kris and others who engaged in the direct observation and psychoanalytic study of child development.

Anna Freud turned to children in the early 1920s with a

dual set of interests: early education and the application of the psychoanalytic method to the emotional problems of children and adolescents. She and her associates studied ego development not only from the point of view of defensive operations, an area to which she made very important contributions, but also from that of the growth of the ego as a structural organization through which the child overcomes its initial helplessness vis-à-vis its internal drive demands and its dependence on the outside world. The holocaust in Europe displaced her from her native Vienna to London, where with Burlingham and others she worked with groups of young children orphaned by the Nazis. A side effect was the opportunity for direct observation of the developmental process, out of which emerged information that could be coordinated with the data arising out of the child analytic work which she carried out first in Vienna and then in London at the Hampstead Child Therapy Clinic (Freud and Burlingham, 1973). She and her colleagues, proceeding slowly and cautiously, amassed a body of data that guided them toward a point of view in which they questioned Klein's conclusions about early development. They expressed doubt about the capacity of infants to carry out the complex thought processes attributed to them by Klein and questioned her emphasis on the inner world and on oral drives in neurosogenesis. Anna Freud in contrast stressed the importance of multiple, intersecting lines of development in which drive forces, ego operations, superego activity, and environmental input play equally important roles in a drawn-out developmental process that progresses through the entirety of childhood and adolescence (A. Freud, 1965).

Despite the differences in the views of Klein on the one hand and of Hartmann and Freud on the other, the net effect of the work of these three psychoanalytic investigators has been to stimulate a new era of research directly into the childhood period itself. Not only has child psychoanalysis acquired respectability as an investigative tool, but a host of psychoanalytically oriented investigators have begun to devote themselves to direct observation into the developmental process during infancy and early childhood.

Direct Observation of Infants

Direct observational research with infants in the first year has naturally centered on ego development and the infant-mother relationship. These are the dimensions most clearly reflected in the infant's overt behavior. With the use of long-range longitudinal studies and the correlation of observational data with those derived reconstructively from clinical investigation, however, it has been possible to draw useful hypotheses and conclusions about internal emotional and ideational processes from this form of investigation. A number of psychoanalysts have also become involved in studies of animal behavior in the hope of learning more about the developmental process.

In summarizing the findings that have come out of direct observational research during the past 30 years or so, it is not possible to give adequate representation to the work of all of the many psychoanalytic or psychoanalytically oriented workers who have been engaged in it. The following is only a partial sampling of the work that has been carried out.

It has become clear, to begin at the beginning, that human infants, although biologically precocial mammals like the other primates, are born in a still embryonic, "secondarily altricial" state of utter helplessness and prolonged dependence on outside forces for their survival. A cogent argument explaining this neotenic reversion is that Homo sapiens has evolved with such a huge brain that it is necessary for the human fetus to end its residence in the womb prematurely, before the cranium has grown so large as to render egress from the maternal pelvis extremely dangerous, if not impossible (Gould, 1976). Human infants are not only born in a state of extreme neurological immaturity, but there is evidence that neurological maturation requires several years thereafter for its completion (Yazmajian, 1967).

Hartmann (see Hartmann, Kris, and Loewenstein, 1946; Hartmann, 1950, 1952), drawing on a late conclusion of Freud's (1937), theorized, with the later agreement of Jacobson (1954, 1964) and of Schur (1966), that the infant enters the world with a structurally and economically undifferentiated matrix of energies, tendencies, and autonomous ego nuclei out of which the drive systems (i.e., the id) and the ego's executive apparatuses become organized as the result of the interaction of innate maturational dispositions and environmental molding. The infant at birth possesses perceptual abilities and motor capacities, some of which are under its active control while others derive from neurological immaturity, without apparent practical value. These include the Babinski reflex, tonic neck reflexes, automatic grasping and walking, and the startle or Moro reflex. The Babinski reflex does not disappear until the long tracts to the lower extremities become myelinated at about a year, but the others fade away by 2 months or so. One can speculate that the startle and grasp reflexes may derive from our relationship to other primates, since neonatal clinging to the mother has obvious survival value, especially in arboreal primates. The rooting and sucking reflexes of the newborn, of course, are essential to survival since they are the means by which the infant takes in aliment. Because the tonic neck reflexes bring the mouth and the thumb or fingers into close apposition as the neonate moves its head from side to side, however, the infant's first experience of sucking is often upon parts of its own body. Observation reveals that such nonnutritive sucking has a calming effect upon a restless infant. Levy (1958) was the first to point out that newborns require a certain (variable) amount of nonnutritive sucking (and of crying) and that it seems to have a tension-reducing effect, without which some infants are unable to go to sleep.

But it is not only the waking activity of infants that has attracted interest. Wolff (1966), in careful studies, has observed that the sleep of the newborn is not entirely quiet but is punctuated by bursts or runs of spontaneous motor activities. These include spontaneous startles, sobbing inspirations, rhythmical mouthing or sucking, penile erections (associated, I have noticed, with testicular retractions), and reflex smiling. From their ability at times to substitute for one another, the variability of their appearance at different stages of sleep, their similarity to behavior induced by external stimulation, and their diminution after externally provoked activity, he was able to conclude that, whatever else is involved, they seem to discharge internally arising tension. Since these motor activities are indistinguishable from ones that later on will be intimately associated with, or are themselves, important mediators of emotional expression, he concluded that they are most likely intrinsic anlagen of those affective modalities.

Neonates tend to drop into deeper stages of sleep after bursts of the spontaneous activities described by Wolff. Eventually, however, they pass through lighter and lighter stages of sleep until they finally wake up. As they do so, they pass briefly through a state of "alert inactivity" (Wolff, 1963, 1966) in which they are quiet motorically but are perceptually alert and receptive in an apparently focused, attentive manner. This is a very transitory state, and they move on quickly to random, diffuse, and perceptually unfocused motor activity that soon evolves into frank crying, the predominant affective behavior of the young infant. When the infant's mother responds by nursing it, the sucking channels and organizes its motor activity so that it becomes quieter and presumably more coherently receptive to perceptual data. The newborn infant processes the oral-tactile-olfactory-gustatory-autonomic-visceral-proprioceptive data of the nursing experience in an apparently diffuse, global, uncritical, and passively receptive fashion. Spitz (1945a) has termed this "coenesthetic reception" as contrasted with the "diacritic organization" characterized by discrete, localized, critical, actively controlled employment of perceptual modalities, with figure-ground discrimination, differentiation of relevant from irrelevant details, etc., that will develop later on.

At first the neonate spends most of its time asleep, and it returns to sleep promptly after it is fed. It is largely self-absorbed, inner-directed, and insulated against intrusion from the outside. The similarity of this picture to that shown by autistically psychotic children led Mahler (1963, 1968; Mahler, Pine, and Bergman, 1975) to refer to the first 3 months or so as an "autistic" phase. The mother during this period is a supportive, holding, and facilitating caretaker (Winnicott 1951, 1965), who after 9 months of emotional investment in the child growing within her, which has fostered a narcissistically regressive, coenesthetic sensitivity toward her child, has become more or less empathically attuned to her child's states and needs (Bibring 1959; Bibring, Dwyer, Huntington, and Valenstein, 1961). The newborn infant, because of its altricial immaturity, requires relatively sensitive handling to protect it from excessive amounts of tension and distress and to provide the appropriately dosed, graduated stimulation it needs for optimal maturation and development. The mother's empathic interest in her relatively unresponsive newborn infant helps to maintain a bond between them during the infant's initial, relatively self-contained distance from her. At first, the still embryonic infant seems to provide its own afferentation, necessary for the maturation of its central nervous system, in the form of the large percentage of its time spent in REM sleep—50 percent of the nearly 24 hours spent each day sleeping, as opposed to the 30 percent of the many fewer daily sleep hours at one year and 20 percent of the still fewer hours spent in sleep each day from adolescence onward (Roffwarg, Muzio, and Dement, 1966).

The newborn infant is not entirely removed from the world around it, however. A finely tuned, reciprocal, bidirectional interaction develops between infant and caretaker in which signals are exchanged between the two participants and each undergoes changes and modifications in response to the other. Spitz referred to this interchange as a "dialogue" (1965, 1966). There is sufficient adaptation between the idiosyncracies of each partner in this interaction as they work together in patterning and regulating the infant's basic biological functions and the caretaker's accommodation to its needs that specific "bonding" becomes established between the two after 10 days or so, as indicated by prompt increase in the baby's crying, the number of distress events, and other signs of perturbation when the caretaker is changed at that point (Sander, 1962, 1964; Sander, Stechler, Burns, and Julia, 1970; Sander, Stechler, Julia, and Burns, 1976).

Visual activity appears to be particularly important in mediating advance in human infants to diacritic perception and object relatedness. Infants can and do attend visually to their surroundings for brief periods, during which they show a preference for patterned, "interesting" sights (Fantz, 1958, 1961; Wolff, 1959; Wolff and White 1965). They are capable of visual pursuit and attention, beginning within hours after birth (Wolff 1965, 1966). During the first few weeks, when awake, they look at anything that moves. During nursing the majority of infants gaze at the mother's face, probably because of the interesting complexity of visual and auditory stimuli it presents to them and because in the first 2 months or so the infant's eyes have a fixed depth of focus at about 13 centimeters, the approximate distance to the mother's face during nursing. Although the infant tends at first to fall asleep at the end of each feeding, after a few weeks it begins to stay awake for longer and longer periods afterward in an alert, attentive, inactive state in which it tends to visually observe the mother's face and listen to her voice. Since a certain amount of learning is possible very early, e.g., limited, short-lived operant conditioning of sucking is observable in the first few weeks, and classical conditioning can be carried out at 3 weeks (Emde, Gaensbauer, and Harmon, 1976), it is probable that the infant begins during the first month to associate its mother's face with the relief from distress during the nursing experience. Brody (1956) has shown that there is a connection between smoothly successful, satisfying nursing experiences and the development of concentration and attention span.

By 6 or 7 weeks the infant no longer looks indiscriminately at everything that moves, but begins to demonstrate a selective scanning response to objects, both animate and inanimate. Even before that, however, animate objects begin to elicit more interest than inanimate ones. Starting between 12 and 18 days, for example, the infant begins to smile more or less systematically at the sound of the human voice. Eye-to-eye contact with another person acquires special significance sometime between 3 and 6 weeks of age, as evidenced by its significantly greater capacity to reduce motor activity than that of other stimuli (Wolff, 1971). Spitz (1965) has described the infant as showing considerable interest in the human face when it is presented to it beginning at a month. Frame-by-frame analysis of videotaped eye-to-eye interchange between mother and infant confirms the special importance of this form of communication by the second month or so (Stern, 1971).

Sightlessness presents an infant with an enormous handicap, in fact. Infants blind from birth encounter enormous problems affecting their relatedness, ego development, and the mobilization and channeling of aggression in the service of mastery and of pleasure in functioning. Even in the best of circumstances, in which unusually sensitive, empathic mothers provide excellent opportunities for interpersonal exchange and for learning about the world to vigorous, persistent, unusually capable infants (an infrequent combination), developmental milestones are reached much more slowly than in sighted infants (Burlingham, 1961, 1965; Fraiberg and Freedman, 1964; Fraiberg, 1971).

At some time between 2 and 3 months, a new development emerges that signals a major shift in the infant's relationship with the world around him. This is the appearance of *social smiling;* i.e., the infant begins to smile regularly in response to the moving face of another person, with his eyes fixed on the eyes of the person looking at him (about two weeks later, the infant adds a cooing vocalization as well). Spitz (1959, 1965) interpreted this as indicating an important reorganization of the psyche in the direction of discriminative, diacritic perception and the beginning of emotional investment in the perceptual gestalt of the human face, which has been extracted from the amalgam of coenesthetic experience of sensations associated with tension relief via feeding.

The appearance of social smiling does not yet denote self-object differentiation or object relationship. Spitz, who made a careful study of social smiling (Spitz, 1965), concluded that the sight of the human face, especially of the region around the eyes and, secondarily, the mouth, at this point acts as a sign stimulus to the child of the memory of pleasurable feeding experiences, which mobilizes recall of all the enjoyable sensations with which they are associated. From this time on, the sight of the human face is enough to indicate to the child that his needs will be met and he will feel good. The social smile is an indicator of the attainment of a number of rudimentary ego functions, including diacritic perception, recognition memory, anticipation, delay, synthesis or integration, patterned affect expression, and recognizable (sensorimotor) intellectual activity.

The sequence from irregular endogenous smiling through irregular, exogenous smiling to regular exogenous, *social* smiling is mediated by a combination of maturational, cognitive, and social interactional factors. It seems clear that maturation of the central nervous system is involved. The bursts of endogenous smiling described by Wolff (1966), for example, occur particularly during REM sleep and REM drowsiness. They are observable mainly during the first 2 months after birth, after which they decrease rapidly over the next 2 months, and fade away by 6 or 7 months (Emde, Gaensbauer, and Harmon, 1976). REM time itself decreases nearly by half over the course of the first year. Spontaneous smiling is apparently mediated and organized by brain stem structures, as indicated by studies carried out with premature and microcephalic neonates by Emde, McCartney, and Harmon (1971) and Harmon and Emde (1972). Maturation of the forebrain appears to be responsible for their suppression from 2 months of age on. Benjamin (1961) some time ago observed that something occurs within the infant's nervous system at about 7 weeks. He described a sudden increase in irritability and vulnerability to external stimuli at that time. Autonomic changes (e.g., a shift from increase to decrease in the heart rate upon presentation of an auditory tone) also have been observed between 6 and 8 weeks (Graham and Jackson, 1970). At 2 months, the inhibitory areas of the maturing forebrain suppress most of the primitive reflexes displayed by the infant until then. The EEG pattern shifts at that time as well. Soon thereafter sleep spindles appear for the first time, and the infant shifts from beginning each sleep period with a REM pattern to doing so instead with a non-REM pattern (Emde, McCartney, and Harmon, 1971). Still other EEG changes appear after a while.

Cognitive development is equally important. We are indebted to the researches of Piaget for our knowledge of this most important dimension of ego development, one which has attracted a great deal of interest among psychoanalytic investigators (see Wolff, 1960; Spitz, 1965; Fraiberg, 1969; Silverman, 1971; Emde, Gaensbauer, and Harmon, 1976; Greenspan, 1979). Piaget (1936, 1947) has demonstrated that during the first few weeks the infant uses its perceptual and motor apparatuses in a reflex manner that, via assimilations and accommodations, leads quickly to the emergence during the next few months of sensorimotor habit patterns, which are performed with increasing efficiency and skill (reproductive assimilation). As these patterns evolve, they expand to embrace new experiential elements (generalizing assimilation) so long as they do not differ too much from ones which are already familiar. Via these partially exploratory actions, in which objects are compared by applying sensorimotor actions to them, objects begin to be disciminated from one another (recognitory assimilation). At this stage the infant is able to recognize objects only via recognitory assimilation, i.e., via its prior sensorimotor actions reflexly accommodating to them.

For example, the infant sucks at first on anything that activates its rooting and sucking reflexes. With repeated experience, however, it comes to recognize the nipple and the multisensory sensations of the feeding experience with which it is associated via adaptive molding of its motor actions to embrace the nipple and suck on it. By a month or so of age, it accepts only the nipple at times of hunger. Soon thereafter the infant begins to coordinate its kinesthetic and visual perception of the breast that is presented with its sucking action schema. It reacts by searching actively for the breast. A little while later it begins to search for the breast when presented with no more than the sight of preliminary, preparatory activities of the mother, such as her opening her blouse (see Wolff, 1960; Emde, Gaensbauer, and Harmon, 1976). It is but a few steps further to coordinating the visual perception of the mother's face with the pleasurable sensations of the nursing experience.

Infantile development proceeds within the matrix of a continual, ongoing exchange between infant and mother, in which there is a wide range of variation in what is contributed by each of the participants. On the infant's side, a number of dimensions have attracted the interest of psychoanalytic and psychoanalytically oriented investigators. These include variations in autonomic functioning (Bridger and Reiser, 1959; Lipton, Steinschneider, and Richmond, 1960; Bridger, 1962); the significance of states (Brazelton, 1962; Korner, 1964); perceptual sensitivity (Bergman and Escalona, 1949); excitability and reactivity (Lustman, 1956; Benjamin, 1961); sensory responsiveness

(Escalona and Heider, 1959); maturational rate (Benjamin, 1961); motor activity level (Fries and Woolf, 1953; Fries, 1954); variations in drive endowment (Alpert, Neubauer, and Weil, 1956); and consistency of patterning (Korner, 1964).

Within a few weeks these various infantile dimensions become organized and patterned by maturation and experience into an identifiable group of general characteristics forming a "basic core" (Weil, 1970) or "psychosomatic matrix" (A. Freud, 1971) of fundamental trends and attributes. Thomas, Birch, Chess, Hertzig, and Korn, (1963) have emphasized the importance of a set of temperamental characteristics in infants that includes mood, reactivity to other human beings, vigor, motor activity, thresholds to stimulation, adaptability, distractibility, attention span, and rhythmicity. Escalona (1968) has found that individual variations in activity level, perceptual sensitivity, motility, bodily self-stimulation, relatedness to animate and inanimate objects, social behavior, behavior while hungry or fatigued, and spontaneous activity during the first 32 weeks reflect a unique pattern of adaptational equipment in each child. Weil (1970) similarly has described variations in mood, activity, sensitivity, excitability, attention, interaction with the environment (especially the human one), ability to communicate, regularity or irregularity of functioning, resilience, vigor, and persistence as the constituents of the basic core which she sees as emerging into identifiable form by 2 or 3 months of age.

There also are differences in what each mother brings to her relationship with her infant. Mothers vary in the extent to which they reach out and activate the baby, their capacity to empathize and read his needs and states, their own activity and that which they require from or tolerate in the child, and the consistency and reliability with which they interact with him. They differ in their feelings about and expectations of the baby as they respond to and impose regulations upon his biological rhythms. Mothers also differ in such dimensions as patience, flexibility, adaptability, confidence, persistence, whether they approach the child in a relaxed or tense manner, and in many other qualities.

As Escalona (1963) and others have demonstrated, it is not only the individual variations in the child and in the mother that are important, but also the particular fit between the two. An oversensitive, excitable, distractible, relatively unadaptive, very active infant with irregular rhythms and low attention span is a child who is very much at risk (Thomas et al., 1963; Weil, 1970). This type of infant is fortunate if his mother is empathic, easygoing, soothing, consistent, and firm but flexible. An infant, on the other hand, who is relatively inactive, low-keyed, and lacking in spontaneity and initiative does best with a mother who reaches out, stirs her child's interest, and provides the external stimulation that such an infant requires to bring it into active contact with the world around it. This type of infant, whose activity expresses itself more via perceptual than motor channels, tends to be jangled by excessive excitement and to withdraw from it. If the mother is too intrusive and offers too much stimulation, she will encourage a tendency toward withdrawal and cautious aloofness in the child. The range of variations within the extremes represented by these two examples, of course, is enormous.

The interaction between the infant's innate dispositions and the molding influence of the mother's interventions leads to the emergence of basic patterns of perceiving and responding to the external world and to internal states and needs (see Escalona, 1968; Mahler and McDevitt, 1968; Weil, 1970; Silverman, Rees, and Neubauer, 1975; Engel and Reichsman, 1979) that tend to persist thereafter and to influence defensive style and adaptational mode as the child develops further. The outcome of the interaction between mother and infant is determined by qualities and characteristics brought to it by each of the participants. Since the infant possesses a very limited range of behaviors compared with the mother's much more extensive repertoire, the mother's empathic ability to read her child's fluctuating states and needs and to synchronize her interventions with him in an optimal fashion that promotes ongoing development is especially important during the first year.

Mahler (1963, 1968) refers to the first 2 or 3 months, during which the infant is unaware of its surroundings except for the brief episodes of interruption of its sleep by peremptory needs that bring it into sensorimotor contact with a responsive mothering person, as the *autistic phase*. During this phase, as described above, progressive maturation and development of rudimentary ego capacities for discrimination, recognition memory, anticipation, delay, synthesis, etc. lead to association of the mother's face with relief from internal distress and with pleasurable sensations. The appearance of social-smiling at 2 or 3 months of age, according to Mahler, signals the advent of a new phase of organization in which the child shifts from the coenesthetic inner-directedness of the autistic phase to a progressively greater interest in the outside world and to the perceptual gestalt of the mother, which is incorporated into its emerging body image and self-representation. Since the infant is not yet at this point capable of distinguishing self from nonself (and only dimly aware of the distinction between what is inside and what is outside), she concluded that it incorporates the mother into its image of itself in an undifferentiated, fused manner, and she refers to this new period as the *symbiotic phase*.

There are a number of major changes in the mother-infant interaction during the symbiotic phase. Although the total amount of wakefulness does not increase much at its outset, the infant begins to use its wakeful time differently. There is a dramatic increase in interest in and interaction with the outside world, animate and inanimate. The infant establishes contact with people via eye-to-eye engagement, smiling, and cooing. The mother and other family members respond with delight to the infant's interest in them and react with actions aimed at keeping the enjoyable interchange going. The infant shows increasing curiosity, exploratory activity, and interest in the new and novel. The use of distance receptors increases markedly.

In contrast with the earlier period, in which crying had predominated as a signal to obtain reduction of stimulation in order to return to sleep, smiling and cooing now predominate as communicative behaviors that are stimulation-seeking rather than stimulation-reducing. The shift seems to derive partly from central nervous system maturation and partly from the stabilization of basic physiological patterns, which frees energies for other purposes (Emde, Gaensbauer, and Harmon, 1976). The balance shifts in the interaction between the mother and the child in the direction of greater activity and initiation of contact by the infant, so that the interaction between them be-

comes more reciprocal and bidirectional (Sander, 1962, 1964).
The activities of caretaking become much less one-sided in their
social dimension. The delight and enjoyment experienced by
the duo makes for an exciting, exuberant, and reciprocal social
exchange between them.

After several months of intense social interaction with the
mother, during which rapid ego development leads to increasing discrimination between real and imagined (i.e., remembered) satisfaction, between self and nonself, and between the
mother and other objects (Jacobson, 1964), the infant "hatches"
(Mahler, 1963, 1968; Mahler, Pine, and Bergman, 1975) from
the symbiotic union and enters the phase of *differentiation*. This
is marked by a shift in the balance between the illusion of permanent, inner-directed, satisfying, symbiotic fusion and out-
ward-directed, differentiating, intense, exploratory interest in
the outside world. The infant actively explores the mother's
face and body and compares her with other people.

When the infant is between 4 and 6 months of age, he not
only achieves enough self-object differentiation to cry and to
reach toward the mother when she leaves the room, but also
enough object-object differentiation to frequently develop an
intense interest in strangers. If left with a stranger, he very
often looks longer at the stranger after the mother's return,
and often visually compares the stranger's face with that of the
mother by looking back and forth between the two. The infant
does this at first with a facial expression reflecting interest, but,
especially in those 5 to 7 months old, this develops after a while
into a "sober" look that combines fascination and an uncertain,
negative quality, which within a month or two generally shifts
to the overt frowning, fussing, and crying of stranger distress
that generally appears between 7 and 9 months (Emde, Gaensbauer, and Harmon, 1976).

Spitz (1965) attributed great importance to the appearance
of stranger anxiety at about 8 months of age. Recognizing that
it reflected the coordination of the emergence of a specific
libidinal object with sufficient self-object differentiation to fear
the mother's loss, he concluded that stranger anxiety is a necessary feature of normal development. We now know that there
is a good deal of variation in the expression of this develop-

mental phenomenon. Infants who have undergone good developmental progression leading to the establishment of adequate basic trust, especially where there has been satisfying exposure to other caretaking persons as well as the mother, do not necessarily develop strong stranger anxiety (Mahler, 1968; Mahler and McDevitt, 1968; Mahler, Pine, and Bergman, 1975).

At first, analytic investigators were puzzled to find that the development of attachment to human objects progresses more rapidly than might have been predicted by Piaget's studies on cognitive development (see Piaget, 1936, 1947; Wolff, 1960; Silverman, 1971). It soon became apparent, however, that the ability to hold the mental representation of an important animate object develops in advance of inanimate object permanence (Wolff, 1971). Stranger anxiety appears at a time when inanimate object permanence is only just beginning to be evident. Fraiberg (1969), in a thoughtful study, came to the conclusion, however, that full evocative memory (Piaget's stage VI of sensorimotor intelligence) is not necessary for the stranger distress shown by infants at 7–9 months, but that the recognition memory and anticipation of pleasing events of sensorimotor stage IV observable at that time suffice to explain the reaction of distress shown by an infant of that age when he expects to recognize his mother's face in the action context of an approaching person, only to see another face instead. Emde, Gaensbauer, and Harmon (1976) have confirmed this experimentally. They also have concluded from their studies of stranger distress and separation distress in the latter part of the first year that stranger anxiety is a complex phenomenon and that Spitz's conclusion (1959, 1965) that it expresses fear of maternal loss is untenable. They explain 8-month stranger anxiety as deriving not only out of developing attachment to the mother, coordinated with cognitive advance, but also out of a maturational shift in emotional differentiation that produces a capacity for fearfulness that had not been possible at a lower level of psychic organization. The fearfulness that appears at that age arises in children in different countries with different child-rearing patterns, is abrupt in its onset, is not influenced by learning, and is directed not only to strangers but also to other unfamiliar, new, or suddenly appearing objects or situations. Although the fearfulness thus appears to be nonspecific, the tendency is for the mother to interpret it as meaning that her infant feels secure only with her and that other caretakers are not acceptable.

The last few months of the first year also are marked by intense curiosity and interest in exploring the world, with the mother as a center of security from whom increasing distance can be tolerated. Infants tend to become more independent and to become increasingly interested in the locomotive capacities, crawling and then walking upright, that appear in the latter third of the first year. Locomotion and interest in exploring the environment and exercising independent ego capacities draw the infant away from the mother, although she has become an intensely important object of the child's interest and devotion. Mahler calls this early period of separation-individuation the *practicing period*, in recognition of the infant's preoccupation with its capacities for independent expression and attainment of pleasurable experiences through its own resources. It is a time of increasing awareness of separation from the mother, representationally as well as actually, and of beginning individuation out of the fused mother-self mental representation into autonomous self-regard and functioning. Awareness of separation from the mother can be painful at times, as evidenced by the struggle shown by many 1-year-olds against going to sleep at night and the need for the mother to stay with them as they are going through this nighttime struggle. As Winnicott (1951, 1965) has pointed out, transitional objects and phenomena, such as a blanket or a favored soft toy, tend to begin to be utilized at times of stress and loneliness to soften the pain and to restore the illusion of union with the mother.

A description of analytic investigation into development in the first year would be incomplete without mention of Spitz's observations of "hospitalism" (Spitz, 1945b) and "anaclitic depression" (Spitz and Wolf, 1946). He observed a group of institutionalized infants who were provided with the best nutritional, sanitary, and health care but very minimal interpersonal contact by the group of nurses who took care of them. The infants not only failed to thrive, but most of them either sickened and died of intercurrent infections, or developed marasmic imbecility within the first year. That infants are in vital need of human attention and handling and are adversely affected by its lack has been confirmed by other investigators since then (see Provence and Lipton, 1962). Infants who are separated for any significant length of time from mothers to whom they have become attached during the second half of the first year become agitated, weepy, withdrawn, and inactive, do not eat or sleep well, and undergo developmental regression from which they recover more or less quickly if they are reunited with the mother before too much time has elapsed. Schaffer and Callender (1959) have described a similar reaction in children of this age group who have been hospitalized without their mothers being permitted to room in with them. The Robertsons (see A. Freud, 1969; Robertson and Robertson, 1971) have studied the problem of separation between young children and their mothers extensively, leading them to produce guidelines applicable to children of different ages. These observations on the need of infants for human contact and attention and on the inability of older infants to tolerate separation from parents to whom they have become attached, unless there is careful provision for suitable substitute care, have greatly influenced societal practices relating to adoption, foster care, hospitalization, and institutional care of infants.

References

Abraham, K. (1916), The first pregenital stage of the libido. In: *Selected Papers of Karl Abraham*. London: Hogarth Press, 1965, pp. 248–279.
——— (1924a), The influence of oral erotism on character formation. In: *Selected Papers of Karl Abraham*. London: Hogarth Press, 1965, pp. 393–406.
——— (1924b), A short study of the development of the libido, viewed in the light of mental disorders. In: *Selected Papers*, London: Hogarth Press, 1965, pp. 418–501.
——— (1927), *Selected Papers of Karl Abraham*. London: Hogarth Press, 1965.
Alpert, A., Neubauer, P.B., & Weil, A.P. (1956), Unusual variations in drive endowment. *The Psychoanalytic Study of the Child*, 11:125–163. New York: International Universities Press.
Benjamin, J.D. (1961), The innate and the experiential in child development. In: *Lectures on Experimental Psychiatry*, ed. J.W. Brosin. Pittsburgh: University of Pittsburgh Press, pp. 19–42.
Bergman, P., & Escalona, S.K. (1949), Unusual sensitivities in very young

children. *The Psychoanalytic Study of the Child*, 3/4:333–352. New York: International Universities Press.

Bibring, G.L. (1959), Some considerations of the psychological processes in pregnancy. *The Psychoanalytic Study of the Child*, 14:113–121. New York: International Universities Press.

—— Dwyer, T.F., Huntington, D.S., & Valenstein, A.F. (1961), A study of the psychological processes in pregnancy and of the earliest mother-child relationship: I. Some propositions and comments; II. Methodological considerations. *The Psychoanalytic Study of the Child*, 16:9–72, New York: International Universities Press.

Brazelton, T.B. (1962), Observations on the neonate. *J. Amer. Acad. Child Psychiat.*, 1:38–58.

Bridger, W.H. (1962), Sensory discrimination and autonomic function. *J. Amer. Acad. Child Psychiat.*, 1:67–82.

—— & Reiser, M.F. (1959), Psychophysiological studies of the neonate: An approach toward the methodological and theoretical problems involved. *Psychosom. Med.*, 21:265–276.

Brody, S. (1956), *Patterns of Mothering*. New York: International Universities Press.

Burlingham, D. (1961), Some notes on the development of the blind. *The Psychoanalytic Study of the Child*, 16:121–145. New York: International Universities Press.

—— (1965), Some problems of ego development in blind children. *The Psychoanalytic Study of the Child*, 20:194–208. New York: International Universities Press.

Emde, R.N., Gaensbauer, T.J., & Harmon, R.J. (1976), Emotional expression in infancy: A biobehavioral study. *Psychological Issues*, Monograph 37. New York: International Universities Press.

—— McCartney, R., & Harmon, R. (1971), Neonatal smiling in REM states: IV. Premature study. *Child Development*, 42:1657–1661.

Engel, G.L., & Reichsman, F.K. (1979), Monica: A 25-year longitudinal study of the consequences of trauma in infancy, reported by Milton Viederman. *J. Amer. Psychoanal. Assn.*, 27:127–144.

Erikson, E.H. (1959), Identity and the life cycle. *Psychological Issues*, Monograph 1. New York: International Universities Press, pp. 50–100.

Escalona, S.K. (1963), Patterns of infantile experience and the developmental process. *The Psychoanalytic Study of the Child*, 18:197–244.

—— (1968), *The Roots of Individuality*. Chicago: Aldine.

—— & Heider, G. (1959), *Prediction and Outcome: A Study of Child Development*. New York: Basic Books.

Fantz, R.L. (1958), Pattern vision in young infants. *Psychological Reports*, 8:43–47.

—— (1961), The origin of form perception. *Scientific American*, 204:66–72.

Ferenczi, S. (1913), Stages in the development of the sense of reality. In: *Sex in Psycho-Analysis (Contributions to Psychoanalysis)*. New York: Dover, 1956, pp. 181–203.

Fraiberg, S. (1969), Libidinal object constancy and mental representation. *The Psychoanalytic Study of the Child*, 24:9–47. New York: International Universities Press.

———— (1971), Separation crisis in two blind children. *The Psychoanalytic Study of the Child,* 26:355–371. New York: Quadrangle.

———— & Freedman, D.A. (1964), Studies in the ego development of the congenitally blind child. *The Psychoanalytic Study of the Child,* 19:113–169. New York: International Universities Press.

Freud, A. (1965), *Normality and Pathology in Childhood.* New York: International Universities Press.

———— (1969), Film review: John seventeen months: Nine days in a residential nursery by James and Joyce Robertson. *The Psychoanalysis Study of the Child,* 24:138–143. New York: International Universities Press.

———— (1971), The infantile neurosis: Genetic and dynamic considerations. *The Psychoanalytic Study of the Child,* 26:79–90. New York: International Universities Press.

———— & Burlingham, D. (1973), *Infants Without Families.* New York: International Universities Press.

Freud, S. (1895), Project for a scientific psychology. *Standard Edition,* 1:281–397. London: Hogarth Press, 1966.

———— (1900), The interpretation of dreams. *Standard Edition,* 4/5. London: Hogarth Press, 1953.

———— (1905), Three essays on the theory of sexuality. *Standard Edition,* 7:3–122. London: Hogarth Press, 1953.

———— (1909), Analysis of a phobia in a five-year-old boy. *Standard Edition,* 10:3–149. London: Hogarth Press, 1955.

———— (1911), Formulation on the two principles of mental functioning. *Standard Edition,* 12:213–226. London: Hogarth Press, 1958.

———— (1914), On narcissism: An introduction. *Standard Edition,* 14:73–102. London: Hogarth Press, 1957.

———— (1917), Mourning and melancholia. *Standard Edition,* 14:237–260. London: Hogarth Press, 1957.

———— (1920), Beyond the pleasure principle. *Standard Edition,* 18:3–66. London: Hogarth Press, 1955.

———— (1937), Analysis terminable and interminable. *Standard Edition,* 23:209–253. London: Hogarth Press, 1964.

Fries, M.E. (1954), Some hypotheses on the role of congenital activity type in personality development. *Internat. J. Psycho-Anal.,* 35:603–608.

———— & Woolf, P.J. (1953), Some hypotheses on the role of congenital activity type in personality development. *The Psychoanalytic Study of the Child,* 8:48–62. New York: International Universities Press.

Gould, S. (1976), Human babies as embryos. *Natural History,* February, pp. 3–4.

Graham, F., & Jackson, J. (1970), Arousal systems and infant heart-rate responses. In: *Advances in Child Development and Behavior: Vol. 5,* ed. H.W. Reese & L.P. Lipsitt. New York: Academic Press, pp. 60–111.

Greenspan, S.I. (1979), Intelligence and adaptation. *Psychological Issues,* Monograph 47/48. New York: International Universities Press.

Harmon, R.J. & Emde, R.N., (1972), Spontaneous REM behaviors in a microcephalic infant. *Perceptual & Motor Skills,* 34:827–833.

Hartmann, H. (1950), Comments on the psychoanalytic theory of the ego. *The Psychoanalytic Study of the Child,* 5:74–96. New York: International Universities Press.

—— (1952), Mutual influences in the development of ego and id. *The Psychoanalytic Study of the Child*, 7:9–30. New York: International Universities Press.

—— (1964), *Essays on Ego Psychology*. London: Hogarth Press.

—— Kris, E., & Loewenstein, R. (1946), Comments on the formation of psychic structure. *The Psychoanalytic Study of the Child*. 2:11–38. New York: International Universities Press.

Horney, K. (1924), On the genesis of the castration complex in women. *Internat. J. Psycho-Anal.*, 5:50–65.

—— (1926), The flight from womanhood: The masculinity complex in women as viewed by men and women. *Internat. J. Psycho-Anal.*, 7:324–339.

Hug-Hellmuth, H.A. von (1919), *Study of the Mental Life of the Child*. Washington, D.C.: Nervous and Mental Disease Publishing.

Isakower, O. (1938), A contribution to the pathopsychology of phenomena associated with falling asleep. *Internat. J. Psycho-Anal.*, 29:340–348.

Jacobson, E. (1954), The self and the object world: Vicissitudes of their infantile cathexes and their influence on ideational and affective development. *The Psychoanalytic Study of the Child*, 9:75–127. New York: International Universities Press.

—— (1964), *The Self and the Object World*. New York: International Universities Press.

Jones, E. (1948), *Papers on Psycho-Analysis*. 5th ed. Boston: Beacon Press, 1964.

Klein, M. (1932), *The Psychoanalysis of Children*. New York: Grove Press, 1960.

—— (1948), *Contributions to Psycho-Analysis 1921–1945*. London: Hogarth Press.

Korner, A.F. (1964), Some hypotheses regarding the significance of individual differences at birth for later development. *The Psychoanalytic Study of the Child*, 19:58–72. New York: International Universities Press.

Levy, D. (1958), *Behavioral Analysis: Analysis of Clinical Observation of Behavior, as Applied to Mother-Newborn Relationships*, Springfield, Ill: Charles C. Thomas.

Lipton, E.L., Steinschneider, A., & Richmond, J.D. (1960), Autonomic function in the neonate. *Psychosom. Med.*, 22:57–65.

Lustman, S.L. (1956), Rudiments of the ego. *The Psychoanalytic Study of the Child*, 11:89–98. New York: International Universities Press.

Mahler, M. (1963), Thoughts about development and individuation. *The Psychoanalytic Study of the Child*, 18:307–324. New York: International Universities Press.

—— (1968), *On Human Symbiosis and the Vicissitudes of Individuation*. New York: International Universities Press.

—— & McDevitt, J.B. (1968), Observations on adaptation and defense in statu nascendi. *Psychoanal. Quart.*, 37:1–21.

—— Pine, F., & Bergman, A. (1975), *The Psychological Birth of the Human Infant*. New York: International Universities Press.

Piaget, J. (1936), *The Origins of Intelligence in Children*. 2nd ed. New York: International Universities Press, 1952.

—— (1947), *The Psychology of Intelligence*. Paterson: Littlefield, Adams, 1960.

Provence, S., & Lipton, R.C. (1962), *Infants in Institutions*. New York: International Universities Press.

Robertson, J., & Robertson, J. (1971), Young children in brief separation: A fresh look. *The Psychoanalytic Study of the Child*, 26:264–315. New York: Quadrangle.

Roffwarg, H.P., Muzio, J.N., & Dement, W.C. (1966), Ontogenetic development of the human sleep-dream cycle. *Science*, 152:604–619.

Sander, L. (1962), Issues in early mother-child interaction. *J. Amer. Acad. Child Psychiat.*, 7:141–165.

—— (1964), Adaptive relationships in early mother-child interaction. *J. Amer. Acad. Child Psychiat.*, 3:231–264.

—— Stechler, G., Burns, P., & Julia, H. (1970), Early mother-infant interactions and 24-hour patterns of activity and sleep. *J. Amer. Acad. Child Psychiat.*, 9:103–123.

—————— Julia, H., & Burns, P. (1976), Primary prevention and some aspects of temporal organization in early infant-caretaker interaction. In: *Infant Psychiatry: A New Synthesis*, ed. E.N. Rexford, C.W. Sander, & T. Shapiro. New Haven: Yale University Press, pp. 187–204.

Schaffer, H., & Callender, W. (1959), Psychological effects of hospitalization in infancy. *Pediatrics*, 24:528–539.

Schur, M. (1966), *The Id and the Regulatory Principles of Mental Functioning*. New York: International Universities Press.

—— (1972), *Freud: Living and Dying*. New York: International Universities Press.

Segal, H. (1964), *Introduction to the Work of Melanie Klein*. New York: Basic Books.

Silverman, M.A. (1971), The growth of logical thinking: Piaget's contribution to ego psychology. *Psychoanal. Quart.*, 40:317–341.

—— Rees, K., & Neubauer, P.B. (1975), On a central psychic constellation. *The Psychoanalytic Study of the Child*, 30:127–157. New Haven: Yale University Press.

Spitz, R. (1945a), Diacritic and coenesthetic organizations. *Psychoanal. Rev.*, 32:262–274.

—— (1945b), Hospitalism: An inquiry into the genesis of psychiatric conditions in early childhood. *The Psychoanalytic Study of the Child*, 1:53–74. New York: International Universities Press.

—— (1959), *A Genetic Field Theory of Ego Formation*. New York: International Universities Press, 1959.

—— (1965), *The First Year of Life: A Psychoanalytic Study of Normal and Deviant Development of Object Relations*. New York: International Universities Press, 1965.

—— (1966), The evolution of dialogue. In: *Drives, Affects, Behavior: Vol. 2*, ed. M. Schur. New York: International Universities Press.

—— & Wolf, K.M. (1946), Anaclitic depression: An inquiry into the genesis of psychiatric conditions in early childhood, II. *The Psychoanalytic Study of the Child*, 2:313–342. New York: International Universities Press.

Stern, D.N. (1971), A micro-analysis of mother-infant interaction: Behavior regulating social contact between a mother and her 3½-month-old twins. *J. Amer. Acad. Child Psychiat.*, 10:501–517.

Thomas, A., Birch, H.G., Chess, S., Hertzig, M.E. & Korn, S. (1963), *Behavioral Individuality in Early Childhood*. New York: New York University Press.

Weil, A. (1970), The basic core. *The Psychoanalytic Study of the Child*, 25:442–460. New York: International Universities Press.

Winnicott, D.W. (1951), Transitional objects and transitional phenomena. In: *Collected Papers: Through Paediatrics to Psycho-Analysis.* New York: Basic Books, 1960, pp. 229–242.

―― (1965), *The Maturational Processes and the Facilitating Environment.* New York: International Universities Press.

Wolff, P.H., (1959), Observations on newborn infants. *Psychosom. Med.,* 21:110–118.

―― (1960), The developmental psychologies of Jean Piaget and psychoanalysis. *Psychological Issues,* Monograph 5. New York: International Universities Press.

―― (1963), The early development of smiling. In: *Determinants of Infant Behavior: Vol. 2,* ed. B.M. Foss. New York: Wiley, pp. 113–134.

―― (1965), The development of attention in young infants. In: *New Issues in Infant Development: Annals of the New York Academy of Science,* 118:815–830.

―― (1966), The causes, controls, and organization of behavior in the neonate. *Psychological Issues,* Monograph 17. New York: International Universities Press.

―― (1971), 'Object permanence' and 'Object relations': Observations on the infant's response to animate and inanimate objects. Presented to the Boston Psychoanalytic Society, May 26. (Reported by L. Vachon in *Bull. Phila. Assn. for Psychoanal.,* 22:235–238, 1972).

―― & White, B.L. (1965), Visual pursuit and attention in young infants. *J. Amer. Acad. Child Psychiat.,* 4:473–484.

Yazmajian, R. (1967), Biological aspects of infantile sexuality and the latency period. *Psychoanal. Quart.,* 36:203–229.

10

Investigation of the Infant and Its Caregiving Environment as a Biological System

LOUIS W. SANDER, M.D.

The Research Problem

The purpose of this chapter is to illustrate a research program designed and carried out as a way to study the infant and its caregiving environment together as a living biological system. There are at least three reasons that this account has relevance to this volume. The first is that psychoanalysis, in its current concern with the argument that a "self-psychology within psychoanalysis" (Kohut, 1977) is needed, is turning once again, as it has from its very outset, to both biology and early develop-

The projects reported in this chapter were carried out while the author was Professor of Psychiatry in the Division of Psychiatry at Boston University Medical Center. Project support was provided by funds from U.S.P.H.S. Project #NICHD 01766 (1965–1969). L. Sander, Principal Investigator, G. Stechler, Co-Principal Investigator in collaboration with P. Burns and H. Julia. Funds from the Grant Foundation, New York, supported work from 1972 to 1974 which was carried out in collaboration with W. Condon (Co-Principal Investigator), P. Chappell, P. Snyder, and J. Gould. Supplemental funds were provided by the University Hospital General Research Support Funds, and Dr. Sander was recipient of NIMH Research Scientist Awards, #K5-MH20-505, between the years 1968–1973, 1973–1978. In addition, Dr. Stechler was recipient of NIMH Career Development Award Level II, #5-K2-MH-18. Reports of the data included in the chapter were presented at the International Society for the Study of Behavioral Development Biennial Conference, July 1975, Surrey, England, and at the annual meeting of the American Academy of Child Psychiatry, October 1975, St. Louis, Missouri. G. Van Melle was responsible for analyzing a major portion of the infant crying data for this report.

ment for light on the matter of the ontogeny of behavioral and psychological organization (e.g., Basch, 1977). Psychoanalysis needs the conceptual and empirical perspective which recent advances in biological systems research are opening up.

The second is that research in the area of early development is currently experiencing a transition in emphasis from the classical experimental approach, which aims at isolating variables, reducing sources of variability, and pursuing a linear concept of causality, toward the study of concurrent and interactive effects of multiple variables, mechanisms of integration, and the formulation of nonlinear concepts of causality. Developmental research itself, then, is looking toward biological models and methods of investigating living processes from the holistic, evolutionary, and systems perspectives of biology.

The third is that intense pressure is being exerted upon clinical facilities to intervene actively now at the earliest pre- and postnatal levels in order to accomplish aims of "primary prevention" of developmental deviations when either the infant or the caregiving environment is considered at risk for them. The pressure is for the predictable manipulation of the developmental process. We have but a meager empirical base of prospective data from which the conceptualization of process can be constructed, or the lawfulness of change, plasticity, or the integration of complex determinants in producing a predictable outcome can be well enough understood to guide "prevention."

It is not clear to many what the differences are between traditional research designs and the study of a living system; this includes the kind of questions that can and cannot be addressed by each, or the relationships between variables which are relevant to either. In what follows, then, certain perspectives drawn from the domain of biology will be introduced, an example of mechanisms of regulation in biological systems given, and an account presented of the design, methodology, and findings of a project aimed at operationalizing some of the implications of a biological systems viewpoint (Sander, 1977).

The first of these perspectives drawn from the biologist's observation of the living system is that time and the temporal organization of events constitute a domain of order that cannot be in any way neglected, avoided, minimized, or bypassed. It remains a central reality around which the significance of other phenomena become assembled. Its importance does not come into view unless one is considering the system, the living organism within its environment of life support.

To begin with, then, and at the most general level, the ecological niche of the newborn is one which must provide at least the essential conditions for the proper negotiation of a profound revision after birth in the temporal organization of the infant's various functions (Sander, Chappell, Gould, and Snyder, 1975). Those who have had the joy of caring for a new baby know what can happen in the wee small hours of the morning. Often, at first, more happens then than during the rest of the 24 hours of the day, until, that is, the baby's rhythms of activity and quiescence tune in to, or synchronize with, the day and night differences within his new environment. At first, in addition to being awake when the rest of the world is asleep, the newborn may be falling asleep himself when he is in the midst of eating or crying and hungry when he should be sleeping. He may swallow when he is in the midst of breathing or bite down on a nipple closing it off, when sucking would allow delivery of milk.

On the basis of present investigations of newborn physiology, it is conceivable now to regard the new baby as a composite of semiindependent physiological subsystems, each with its own rhythm, such as those controlling heart rate, respiration, brain waves, and body movement (Luce, 1970). Infants arrive with varying degrees of coherence or phase-synchrony between these component subsystems. Since they affect such activities as waking, sleeping, and feeding, and, under certain conditions, each has the ability to run on its own time track, they must become harmonized and coordinated within the new baby, and in turn, tuned-up with the regular periodicities of the world and of the people who make up the baby's world.

There are many time levels involved. The rhythms involved may be circadian, that is, arranged in relation to an approximately 24-hour cycle of variation; or ultradian, higher frequency rhythms in relation to timespans less than 24 hours; or infradian, lower frequency rhythms over 24 hours (Sollberger,

1965). Periodic behaviors involved in the interaction between infant and caretaker can be explored at the level of seconds and even microseconds (Stern, 1971; Condon and Sander, 1974; Brazelton, Tronick, Adamson, Als, and Weise, 1975). The orchestration of such a complexity is one of the major accomplishments of the postnatal caretaking task. Its aim is to bring the infant to function as a unified organism in coordinated harmony with an ecology based on a 24-hour cycle, arranged in day-night organization, with the day arranged in subunits such as morning, afternoon, and evening. On the background of harmony at this more macroscopic level, caretaker and infant are engaging in exchanges, cycling at a much higher frequency, in seconds or microseconds, etc. But how does one approach the problem of investigating such complex organization and the mechanisms depending on location of events in time?

We started out trying to conceptualize the lawfulness governing longitudinal changes in the transactions between infant and surround postnatally, in terms of the biological concepts of adaptation and the adaptive process (Sander, 1962). The biologist, however, begins at an even more basic level, namely, with the problem of regulation—the regulation of exchange between the organism and its environment of life support. It is at this most basic point that time plays the fundamental role. I am referring here, again, to the matter of biorhythmicity, a subject which represents one whole discipline of biology, which for more than fifty years has been investigating the adaptive process in terms of mechanisms of temporal organization regulating exchanges in different ecological systems.

The Biological System

An illustration can be given by the way time in the biological system provides the basic organizational structure for a life-support framework by providing for the phase synchronization, or for the co-occurrence of essential periodic encounters between the organism and its niche, such encounters being sparsely distributed, but at precisely the right time (see Figure 1).

In this figure, Enright (1960) illustrates the activity of three batches of synchelidium (amphipods or "sand fleas") collected from three different beaches in Southern California, some 319 in one, 2,100 in another, and 600 in a third. Because of coastal configurations, the time and character of tidal ebb and flood on different beaches vary from one beach to another. The time and configuration of tidal peaks and troughs characteristic for the three beaches from which the samples of amphipods were collected are illustrated in the top line of each of the three sections of Figure 1. It is to be noted that the time between tidal peaks is 14.4 and 11.2 hours for one beach, 16.0 and 9.0 another, etc. The ecology of the amphipod is such that the time for its greatest activity on the beach occurs at the onset of the ebbing tide, estimated for the three populations by the arrow. The meaning of "fitting together," or adaptation, in respect to the organization of the ecological system, is dramatically portrayed by the lower line of the graph for each of the three sections. This represents a count of the numbers of actively swimming amphipods in each sample at a sequence of time points; this line shows peaks of swimming activity in the creatures which correspond to the estimated time of expected peak activity on their respective beaches. However, when being counted, the amphipods now are *not* at the beach at all, but in the laboratory, each group isolated under the same controlled and constant conditions. Regulation of the timing of the recurrent activities essential for its survival from *endogenous* sources within the amphipod adjust it to, or synchronize it with, resources provided by essential recurrent events in its environment being regulated by a separate independent and *exogenous* source of periodicity. The meaning of phase synchrony for the organism as a whole is that of establishing a general *state of readiness* for the encounter. If properly timed, evidently the key exchanges between the interacting components of the system need only be episodic, not continuous.

Much has been learned of the various mechanisms governing phase-control of biorhythms (Aschoff, 1969). Investigators of the role of biological rhythms in different ecological

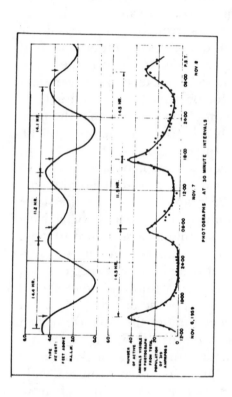

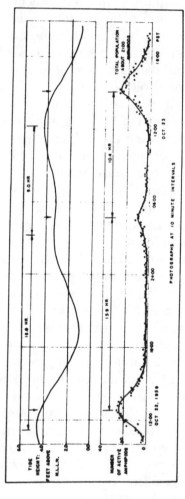

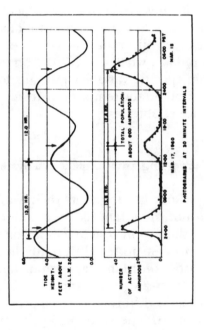

FIGURE 1. Activity rhythms in *Synchelidium* n.sp. isolated in laboratory, compared with, tidal movements (U.S.G.S predictions) on beach from which they were collected. Vertical arrows on tide graph indicate position of estimated maximal activity of amphipods. Note that the time scales differ. (Reprinted from Enright, 1960. Copyright 1960, Waverly Press.)

systems suggest that both the processes of adaptation without and of integration within the organism can be resolved as matters of phase-synchronization of interacting components (Halberg, 1960; Pittendrigh, 1961; Aschoff, 1969).

Each infant arrives with a unique set of regulatory characteristics, and each meets a caretaking environment with its own unique regulatory features, two disparately organized entities at the outset, to say the least. The way they finally adjust themselves to exist together around the clock in some reasonable harmony consequently involves exchanges which must also be uniquely configured. But unique configurations become manageable as with the three different beach configurations of Figure 1, at least conceptually, when one focuses on the timing of recurrence of certain specific variables relevant to each of the interacting partners and on the temporal pattern which the timing of such recurrence establishes.

The Infant and Caregiving Environment as a System

The initial strategy of our investigation, then, was to make the unit of observation not the infant alone, or the caretaker as a separate entity, but the two in concurrent action together around the clock. Systems constituted differently in terms of the particular characteristics of infant or of caretaker provide experiments in nature. The strategy of comparing the 24-hour course of events over time in different systems provides clues to mechanisms of regulation. The second step, then, was to devise methods by which we could chart day by day, the values of multiple variables related to the different functions or subsystems mediating between the participants. Variables would be selected which could be given quantitative values and could be continuously recorded or frequently sampled. The third step, finally, was to compare across the infant-caregiving systems at some outcome point the progress in the development of the functions and the sensorimotor subsystems on which the measurements of variables had been recorded. The effect that having a role in the regulation of essential exchanges has on the developmental process of infant functions provides further clues as to *mechanism* and *process*, especially if such infant functions can be assessed in terms of the specific way they contribute to regulation of the system. This can be carried out, for example, by perturbing the system and charting the course of recovery of variables related to particular subsystems (Cassel and Sander, 1975).

A combination of methods therefore is necessary in order to study the organization of events in the infant-caretaker system and the changes in this organization over the first days and weeks of postnatal life. The scope of the chapter does not permit more than the briefest description of the methods we have used and the three major categories of variables which have been combined to describe the temporal organization of events in the postnatal infant-caregiver system over the first weeks of life.

Methods

It was while working with a stabilimeter to measure the motor activity of the newborn, which we first had constructed in 1958, that the idea emerged of using the infant's bassinet itself to monitor, continuously, automatically, and around the clock, the timing of events in the infant and the way they matched the clock time of occurrence of activities and interventions of the caretaker. It was important that this bassinet be exactly like any infant's ordinary bassinet, both for the mother and for the infant, so that their developing interaction would not be disturbed—no wires on the baby, no special maneuvers by the mother.[1] The present model, almost indistinguishable from an ordinary nursery bassinet, provides unattended a continuous record on a real-time basis, around the clock and day

[1] Over the years the ideas and efforts of a number of engineers and researchers have contributed to the present monitoring bassinet model, especially those of Dr. Don Jackson of Williamson Developmental Co.; Dr. Gerald Stechler, now chairman of the Department of Child Psychiatry, Boston University School of Medicine; Mr. Richard Burwen of Burwen Labs; Dr. Herbert Teager, Director of Biomedical Engineering at Boston University Medical Center; Dr. Jeffrey Gould, Director of the Department of Newborn Medicine at Boston City Hospital; and Mr. Paul Miller of the Department of Neuropsychology, Boston University School of Medicine.

after day, of seven different states[2] of sleep or wakefulness in the infant, its crying, its respirations, its activity, the time when it is removed from and when it is returned to its bassinet, and the presence of its caretaker at the side of the bassinet.

This first set of variables provided by the monitor record was combined for analysis with sets of infant, caretaker, and interactional behavioral variables that had been obtained by event-recorded observations[3] during a feeding or over the entire course of an awake period from transition to awake until the onset of the first subsequent non-REM substage of sleep. These measures were chiefly those of frequency, duration, and sequence, with a rough intensity scale for certain of the variables. In one project, event-recorded observations of feeding interaction were carried out daily for the first month of life and twice weekly over the second month.

A third category of variables was measured by a third set of methods to obtain repeated assessments of specific sensorimotor functions of the infant. These involved: infant behaviors upon presentation of visual stimuli, especially that of the human face (Stechler, Sander, Burns, and Julia, 1973); the use of specific perturbations to the ecological system by altering important visual configurations, such as by masking the mother's face during a feeding (Cassel and Sander, 1975); sucking behavior (Burns, Sander, Stechler, and Julia, 1972); crying behavior (Van Melle, Sander, Stechler, Julia, and Burns, 1973). In more recent independent research by Boston University investigators, substitution of a strange feeder (Chappell and Sander, 1978) and

[2] The research team has accomplished the computer interfacing of the monitor output, giving high agreement between sleep-state distributions obtained by the analysis of monitoring data using computer-state recognition programs and the scoring of concurrent 5-parameter sleep polygraphy (Sander, Gould, Snyder, Lee, Teager, and Burmen, 1976).

[3] Event recording methods were begun by the Boston University group in 1965 by Padraic Burns, M.D., using a Rustrak 4-key event recorder (Burns et al., 1972). The present method has been developed by Dr. Patricia Chappell from her original infant-mother interactional variables and her recording method using a 15-second epoch (Boismier, Chappell, and Meier, 1970). Dr. Chappell's present method utilizes a 60-key computer interfaced keyboard recorder based on the White Recording and Transcription System (White, 1970) as modified by Mr. Paul Miller at Boston University, now of Sunrise Systems, Inc. (Chappell and Sander, 1978).

acoustic stimulation, especially that of the human voice (Condon and Sander, 1974) have been used to further examine avenues of adaptive exchange. It should be self-evident that continuous monitoring entails the generation of huge amounts of data. Upon the heels of the problem of developing relatively non-intrusive methods to obtain such data came the problem of developing procedures and programs to reduce and analyze them, while hard upon the heels of that problem came the problem of display and communication of the data.

Thus far in the chapter certain points have been made: (1) about regarding infant and caretaking environment, taken together, as an interactive regulative ecological system; (2) about the charting of changes over time in the organization of events within the system; (3) about individual uniqueness of the interacting partners who constitute different infant-environment systems (the unique organization of the individual requires unique exchange patterns by which the partners can achieve adapted coordination and maintain mutual regulation); (4) about the specificity of events and exchanges that bond the partners so regulated; (5) about a connection between the role of specific infant functions in the early regulation of exchanges with the caregiver, their course of development, and their adaptive employment at later points in development.

The following examples illustrate the way these points have been operationalized in study of the infant-caregiver system and are not intended as a comprehensive review of the project findings.

Research Findings

Figure 2 provides an illustration of the relationships that come to light as simple variables from infant and caregiver are recorded continuously, around the clock in real time, and are charted for visual display (Sander, 1969). The infant variables were occurrence of crying and of movement; the caregiver variable was removal and return of infant to bassinet. Such simple variables, continuously and automatically recorded, provide an observational window on a two-partner system, illustrating the

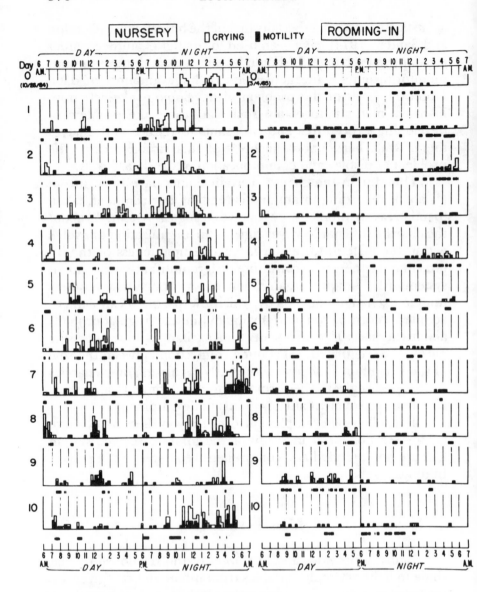

FIGURE 2. Relative frequency, duration, and distribution of motility, crying, and caretaking blips as measured by bassinet monitor for a nursery and a rooming-in baby over the first 10 days of life. Caretaker interventions for each baby and for each day of life are represented by black marks directly below solid lines indicating days of life. (Reprinted from Sander and Julia, 1966. Copyright 1966, American Psychosomatic Society.)

way change over days can be displayed and indicating those features of the adaptive process which distinguish differently constituted systems.

The data were obtained over the first 10 days of life from two ecological systems: an infant boarded in a general hospital newborn nursery, on 4-hourly scheduled feedings given by many different nurse caretakers on frequently changing duty hours; and an infant roomed in on the maternity floor with its own experienced (multiparous) mother providing complete care and breast feeding on an infant-demand regimen. The legend identifies the data displayed. The display shows (a) the gross asynchrony in the nursery in timing between the recurrent caretaking interventions and the recurrent episodes of activity in the infant; (b) the persistence in the nursery of a high degree of activity and crying over the entire 10 days, with the greatest portion of activity and crying produced per 24 hours remaining in the 12 night hours; and (c) in contrast, the baby rooming in with single caretaker showing far less total activity and crying. There is an evenly distributed amount of activity all through Day 2, with a great many frequently repeated responses by the mother. By Day 3, for the rooming-in pair, there is already synchrony emerging between episodes of activity in the infant and episodes of caretaking events, between which there are long periods of no exchange. Not only is there coordination of caretaker with infant at the onset of an infant activity span, but a correspondence of activity of the mother over the total duration of the infant's activity span. Then, between Days 4 and 6, for this pair the 24-hour distribution shifts so that the greatest amount of the activity and crying of the infant begins to settle in the 12 day hours, with long sleep periods and only rare exchange at night.

The essential points presented in Figure 2 have been confirmed in larger samples of normal infants reared in the neonatal nursery and in samples of normal infants roomed in with a single caretaker, receiving a demand feeding regimen (Sander, Julia, Stechler, and Burns, 1972; Sander and Julia, 1966). In the latter group, those receiving infant-demand feeding, predictable organization of the 24-hour day begins during the first 10 days of life. The shift of the major occurrence of motility

and crying from night to day hours occurs for the sample between the fourth and sixth day. By 10 days of life the major
part of the longest sleep period each day has settled within the
12 night hours.

By contrast, for samples of normal infants boarded in the
newborn nursery for 10 days, circadian rhythmicity does not
begin at all during the first 10-day period. Activity and crying
remain greatest during the 12 night hours, as in Figure 2. On
Day 11 we have transferred the infants of such a sample, one
by one, to the individual care of a single foster caretaker who
roomed in with them around the clock as sole caretaker. The
caregiving response shifts at this point from a clock-scheduled
timetable to interventions contingent to the infant's change of
state, i.e., the individual caregiver provides a demand feeding
regimen.

Within 24 hours the motility and crying output of the infants dramatically reverse their day/night distribution and assume the normal pattern. Persistent effects of these very
stressful first 10 days in the 4-hourly scheduled nursery on
circadian rhythmicity are seen when such infants are kept with
the single rooming-in foster surrogate mother over the next 2
weeks while being monitored. During this subsequent 2-week
period, a precocious advance in day/night differentiation takes
place, which during the same days of life significantly exceeds
that of the infant rooming in with single caretaker from birth.
Furthermore, there are clear differences between male and
female infants in this effect, the female infants responding to
the stress with a significantly more advanced degree of day/night
difference. Infant effects, caretaking effects, and age-in-days-
of-life effects thus interact in producing the different courses
which differently constituted systems reveal when we can chart
them day by day.

Figure 3 illustrates the day-by-day distribution over the
first month of life of the total duration per 24 hours of awake-
active states, plotted here in terms of 3-day means for 30 infants.
What we see is a daily duration of awake-active states over the
first 3 days of life which is not reached again until the end of
the first month. This effect is independent of caretaking regimen. The same curve is obtained whether the infants are

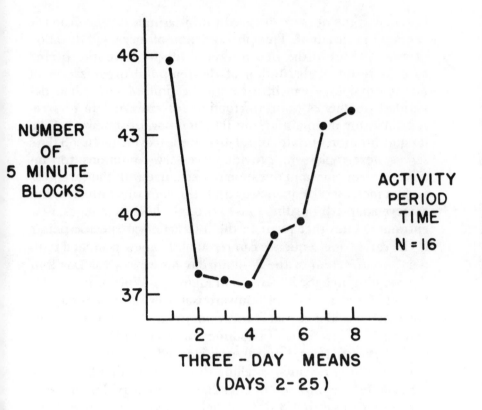

FIGURE 3. Awake-active states per 24 hours. Each point represents a mean for 3 days of number of 15-minute segments of the 24-hour record, which are characterized by activity increase above sleep level or crying or removal from bassinet by caretaker. N = 16 babies, 8 cared for in nursery, and 8 in rooming-in condition. Quadratic F = 27.85; df = 1/84; Cubic F = 7.37; df = 1/84; Linear F = 1.464; df = 1/84. (Reprinted from Sander et al., 1972).

boarded in the nursery or cared for by a single caretaker in the rooming-in situation. This phenomenon of increased duration of awake states in the first 3 days of life we have interpreted to be a result of disruption of the temporal organization of infant physiology which, up until the time of birth, had depended on the 24-hour fluctuations of maternal factors responsible for maintaining the fetal temporal framework. The longer duration of states of relative arousal over the first 3 days serves nevertheless to provide necessary conditions for increased frequency and duration of exchange with the caregiver and an increased frequency of trials through which the two can achieve adapted coordinations. Through these exchanges, new entraining cues that recur in the interaction at specific points in the caregiving sequence can reestablish a new postnatal temporal organization of the 24-hour day (as we saw for Day 2 in the rooming-in baby illustrated in Figure 2). When one couples the finding of greater 24-hour arousal over the first 3 days of life with the evidence that in the rooming-in, demand-fed infant appropriate day/night distributions of sleep and awake states begin between Days 4 and 6, one is faced with the possibility that something essential is jelling during those first 3 days regarding the organization of circadian rhythmicity. Further evidence that these first 3 days of heightened arousal may have a different significance than the ensuing days is provided by the crying record of the nursery-reared group. Although in the nursery there is no change in caregiving regimen, the high level of total 24-hour crying of the first 3 days falls strikingly in this group after the third day. By the end of the first week of life, the clock-scheduled, nursery-reared infant appears to conserve energy. Instead of crying until something happens—an effort early in the week that may go on uninterrupted for 1–2 hours if there is no caregiving response—by the end of the week there is a burst of crying, then a pause during which a drowsy appearance may be present, then another arousal and outburst of vigorous crying and a subsequent pause. We have seen this go on over and over, then, for as long as 2 hours or until the nurse intervenes. Such behavior often can be observed in the night hours, when the nursing staff is reduced and long delays in response to crying are unavoidable, as was pointed out by Aldrich, Sung, and Knop (1945).

Wide differences between nursery and rooming-in groups in motility and/or crying output were shown by infants under these different postnatal caretaking circumstances, as demonstrated by the 24-hour monitoring method (Figure 4).

On the other hand, wide individual infant differences were demonstrated between infants under the same caregiving regimen. Figure 5 shows the length of each sleep period over the first month of life plotted in sequence as it occurred for two infants receiving the same caregiving regimen over the first month of life, namely individual fostering in the rooming-in (demand-fed) situation.

The gradual postnatal appearance of circadian rhythmicity is illustrated for one infant in Figure 6. Here the data were cast in terms of minutes of sleep per hour. One-hour, lagged, autocorrelations were performed for a 210-hour span (second to tenth day) and a consecutive 240-hour (eleventh to twentieth day). The ultradian rhythm which appears clearly in the first 210-hour analysis is replaced by a major 24-hour rhythm in the subsequent 240-hour analysis. It has not been generally recognized that 24-hour sleep-awake organization begins to occur between Days 4 and 6 under optimal circumstances, nor that circadian rhythmicity can be established in the second week of life.

Continuous sleep state data also reveal individual differences related to the rate of achieving circadian rhythmicity. In Figure 7 are shown the autocorrelations obtained over Days 11–20 of life for two infants, both having had the nursery experience of care over the first 10 days, and both having had the same caretaking regimen of individual surrogate mother rooming in over the second 10 days. The first subject is a male and the second a female. The individual difference seen here are consistent with the differences between males and females which we found in comparing males and females for extent of day/night difference in sleep occurrence during the second 2 weeks of life. The effect of the stressful initial 10-day nursery experience seems to *advance* precociously the rate of organization of the 24 hours for females so they sleep significantly

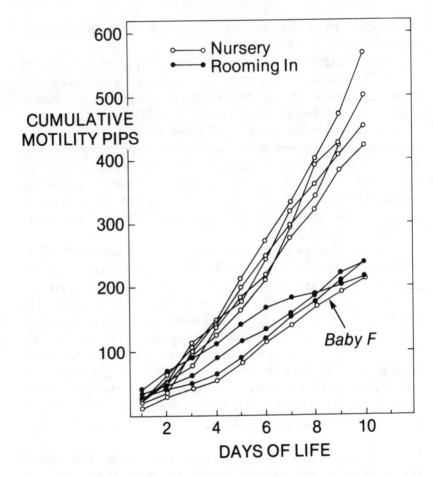

FIGURE 4: Cumulative graph of motility blips (24-hour totals) recorded by monitoring bassinet for 6 nursery and 3 rooming-in infants over the first 10 days of life. By Day 4, the two populations have diverged in activity generated, except for Baby F, who belonged to the sample boarded in the neonatal nursery. (Reprinted from Sander and Julia, 1966. Copyright 1966, American Psychosomatic Society.)

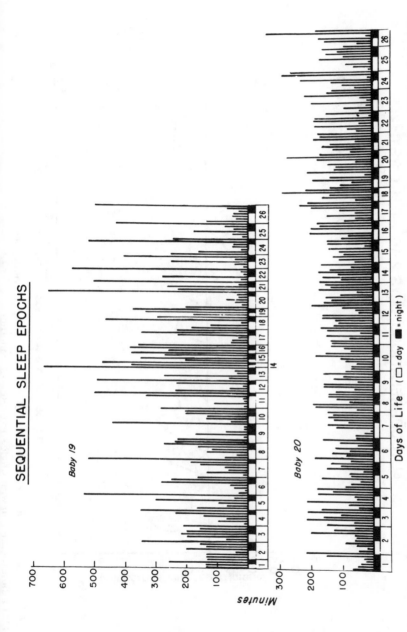

FIGURE 5. Real-time durations of all sleep periods plotted in actual sequence over the first 29 days of life for two infants. Black sections represent hours between 6 p.m. and 6 a.m. each day. (Reprinted from Sander, 1975. Copyright 1975, Plenum Publishing Corp.)

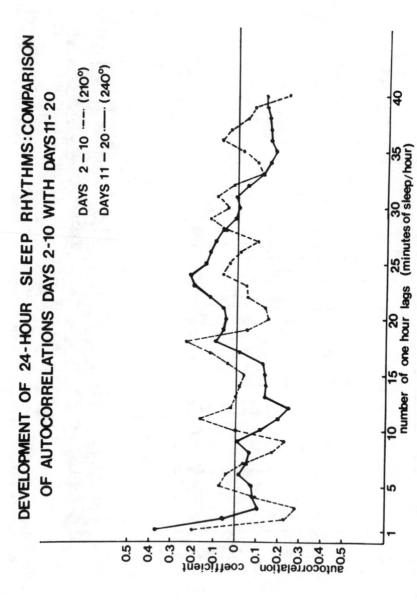

FIGURE 6. One-hour, lagged, autocorrelations of minutes of sleep per hour for sleep, Days 2–10 (210 hours) and Days 10–20 (240 hours) for infant rooming in with single surrogate foster mother.

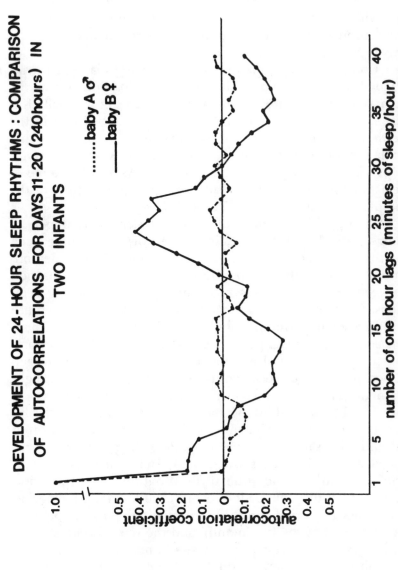

FIGURE 7. One-hour, lagged, autocorrelations of minutes of sleep per hour, over Days 10–20 (240 hours) on two babies, (a) male and (b) female, each having had nursery caretaking during the first 10 days and single surrogate foster mother rooming in over Days 10–20.

more at night and less in the day. The same 10-day nursery experience appears to *retard* the rate of day/night organization during the second 2 weeks of life for the males, who are also receiving the same caregiving regimen as the females during the second 2 weeks, i.e., an individual surrogate mother rooming in (Sander, et al., 1972).

Comparison by Julia (Sander, Stechler, Julia, and Burns, 1970) of autocorrelations calculated over 240 hours during the second 10 days of life, obtained from infants individually fostered in the first 10 days (n = 8) with those boarded in the newborn nursery in the first 10 days (n = 8), indicates that while the former show their circadian peak of sleep occurrence at precisely 24 hours, the latter group shows a wider range of deviations from a 24-hour peak in a significant number of the sample, i.e., peaks at 23 to 25 or 26 hours.

In the differentiation of a longest sleep period per 24 hours, individual differences in 24-hour organization between infants receiving the *same* caregiving regimen can be demonstrated, as well as the group differences in 24-hour organization between *groups* of infants receiving *different* caregiving regimens. In Figure 5, the first baby, Baby 19, shows the presence of an excellent differentiation almost from the outset. There is a clear longest-sleep period per day with a number of clearly shorter periods. After Day 3 the occurrence of the longest-sleep period per 24 hours becomes consistently located in the night segment. This was a responsive, well-organized baby, easy to care for. The second infant, Baby 20, by contrast, though also meeting our rather stringent criteria for normality, and cared for under the same individual demand feeding caregiving, produced a record which showed many more sleep periods of briefer duration, and little differentiation of sleep-period length. It was difficult to identify one clear longest-sleep period per 24 hours. Period-length differentiation appeared only toward the end of the first month, and the stable occurrence of the longest-sleep period per 24 hours within the 12 night hours was only getting under way on the tenth day of life. This infant was reported by both the foster mothers to be the most difficult to care for of all the infants of the sample.

We found, for the babies, n = 27, of this project (three

samples differently constituted as to caretaking system, of 9 infants each) that there was a significant positive correlation between length of longest-sleep period per 24 hours and length of longest-awake period per 24 hours, a "period-length" factor, if you will (as Figure 5 suggests).

There was also an interaction of length of longest-sleep and longest-awake period per 24 hours with the effect of the individual caretaker. Over Days 11–25 of this study, with each nurse fostering 8 babies, we found evidence that one of the two foster nurses produced infants with significantly longer longest-sleep and longest-awake periods per 24 hours than did the other. For any given infant-caretaker ecological system, interactions between infant determinants and caretaking determinants set the stage for individual uniqueness of their exchange patterns.

As one looks more closely at infant differences in sleep and awake behavior, it is evident that the way babies wake up and go to sleep is quite different. For some, crying begins during the last REM period and increases steadily to imperative levels; the last thing to occur in the awakening sequence for such infants may be the opening of the eyes. In other instances, the infant, with but very little increase of movement over that of his last REM period, may open his eyes and lie relatively quiet for 10-15 minutes, until finally the first whimper will be produced.

In addition to the many obvious, as well as subtle, differences between our two principal foster nurses, with which we became familiar in detail, there were striking differences in style of caretaking by our natural mothers also (Group C). Each of these had had experience with at least one previous baby of her own and had developed a measure of confidence in her own way of doing things. For example, one such mother's dictum, apparently handed down from her mother, was that she would not pick up her baby until the infant had cried for five minutes. Our records showed a crying curve for this pair which was just an order of magnitude above that of the other natural mother pairs. However, everything otherwise went well. Another mother, who tended to keep the bassinet with her in the room in which she was working, would respond at the very first sign of arousal, scarcely ever allowing her infant more than a whimper before she responded. We were hard put to locate the few scattered single crying blips that were accumulated on that record.

Time does not permit a review of the data from which we have studied the matter of *specificity* of the synchronization or bonding between the individual infant and the individual caretaker. We have done this by rearing infants with one experienced foster mother rooming with the infant 24 hours a day from birth and then on the eleventh day changing to another experienced foster mother. The change is marked by significant increases in the occurrence of distress events during feeding and in 24-hour crying over hours and days subsequent to the change (Van Melle et al., 1973). Another way of studying specificity by event-recorded interactional observations is to change caretakers for a single feed on Day 7, when only one individual has done all the feeding up to that point; still another is to mask the familiar caretaker during a feeding on Day 7, comparing infant behaviors and state distributions during the awake period, including latency to first non-REM sleep period, with values obtained on Day 6 and before (Cassel and Sander, 1975).

Finally, the repeated assessment of the developmental course of key sensorimotor functions that are involved in transacting the regulatory exchanges between the partners in differently constituted infant caregiving systems indicates important relationships to be understood. We have carried out repeated assessments twice weekly over the first 2 months of life of a variety of infant behaviors related to the visual system, when the infant is presented with the human or drawn face under systematically different stimulus conditions of presentation. These have included "looking" and "looking away" time, peripheral gaze, motility, crying, etc. (Stechler et al., 1973). The course is quite strikingly different in the three different caregiving systems over the first 2 months of life, significant differences appearing, for example, in total looking time and crying during stimulus presentation (Stechler et al., 1973; Sander, Stechler, Burns, and Lee, 1979). It is our conviction that in spite of the more careful individual fostering after the tenth day of life, the effects of those first 10 stressful days of being boarded in the newborn nursery persist over the rest of the first 2 months of life and influence the integration of sensorimotor functions in state and interactional regulation.

Summary

In summary, then, the study of infant and caregiver as an interactive regulative system by continuous monitoring and methods of repeated measurement on infant and caregiver variables centers our attention on the temporal organization of events. We have indicated the following.

1. Birth is a point of profound rupture in mechanisms of temporal organization in the fetal-maternal system.

2. The ecological niche of the newborn must provide for a reestablishment of this temporal organization postnatally in terms of a framework of new exchanges between neonate and environment which constitute the initial processes of regulation and adaptation and represent interactions of infant, caretaker, and age-in-days-of-life determinants.

3. The first 3 days may be a crucial span of time in which the interaction of events responsible for optimal 24-hour temporal organization is established. Events such as the recurrence of maternal entraining cues in consistent relation to state changes in the infant provide the necessary conditions for the array of biorhythms that characterize both the infant and its caregiving environment to gain the organization that will ensure their role in the regulation of the system.

4. Individual infant differences in periodicities and rates of change over the first days of life, interacting with individual differences in caretaking configurations, eventuate in specific patterns of 24-hour exchange between the two. Mechanisms of bonding are based on the way specificity of regulation is established and maintained in the system. Much of this specificity depends on time and the timing relationships between events in critical recurring caregiving situations.

5. This specificity of regulatory fittedness between a particular infant and a particular caregiver can reach an appreciable degree by the tenth day of life.

6. The later adaptive employment of sensorimotor functions upon which the establishment of regulatory coordination in the system has depended is influenced by this earlier role which they have played in establishing that regulation.

Discussion

The material that has been presented of an investigation of the infant and its caregiving environment together as a biological system illustrates the perspective that such an approach provides, directing attention to mechanisms and processes of change in the organization of events in the system, as one goes from fetal to postnatal life. Fundamental to this perspective is the role of time and the central place of temporal organization as a first level in the construction of the behavioral framework of interaction between the participants making up the system. The central role of biorhythmicity in the achievement and maintenance of coherence in the living system cannot be underestimated. Biorhythmicity requires a consideration of 24-hour, around-the-clock time as well as the time structure of events in briefer durations. Events between infant and caregiver assume importance in terms of the exactness of their synchrony, of the temporal characteristics of their phase relationships, and of their characteristics of asynchrony. There is a *background* in the low frequency rhythms (e.g., states of sleep and awake or activity and quiescence) that is necessary for the analysis of characteristics of interaction between the higher frequency rhythms that make up the *foreground* of the interaction (e.g., sucking, linguistic-kinesic, gaze and gaze-aversion rhythms, etc.) Time requires a holistic perspective of different levels in the system as well as providing the framework for studying the precise individual specificity of the process of "fitting together" by which adapted interaction in a given *moment* of time is achieved. The process of fitting together effects connection or bonding between the unique dispositions and behavioral configurations of partners that have behavioral organizations that are highly disparate, i.e., the newborn infant and its caregiver.

The methodological and analytic requirements for the investigation of change in the organization of living systems during the lifespan differ from the more traditional experimental paradigm; the questions one asks are different; the route of discovery is different. For example, from the visual display of continuous and repeated measures, points of change come into focus or the relationships between interacting variables change, differences in rates of change appear, or the "history dependence" of the system becomes evident.

In other publications (Sander et al., 1979) based on the same biological systems perspective, data have been presented as illustration of the way particular sensorimotor systems of the infant (e.g., the visual system) become integrated over the first 2 months of life in relation to their role in the achievement and maintenance of initial regulation. Visual behavior plays an important role in the regulation of the initial feeding interaction, and the feeding interaction is in turn directly related to the regulation of states in the sleep/wake continuum. In other words, the infant's employment of specific sensorimotor systems becomes shaped by the contribution such systems make to more basic state regulation as an around-the-clock adaptive requirement for infant and caregiver. This viewpoint suggests that the "ordering function" proposed by Basch (1975), as being a function central to the ontogeny of self, is itself determined by an interactional ontogeny integrating basic biological processes in a specific adaptive context. The infant's active organization of his world involves the inseparable nature of the endogenously active biological processes which underly our conceptual domains of regulation, adaptation, integration, and organization.

In still other publications (Sander, 1962, 1964, 1969, 1975; Sander et al., 1975), the changing organization of events and interactions over the first 3 years of life in the infant-caregiver system has been described as a sequence of levels of fitting together between infant and caregiver. These extend from a beginning level of coordination concerned with biological issues, such as those related to regulation of states of sleep and waking and the basic functions of feeding, motility, etc., to the levels of adaptation concerned with fitting together between toddler and caregiver on the basis of correct inferences of intentions, goals, feelings, words, and expressions. Each new task of "fitting together" is ushered in by new activities or capabilities that the infant can begin to introduce into the interaction with its caregiver. The preservation of an active role for the infant in the adaptive sequence is the basis for the establishing and maintenance of the infant's or toddler's "sense of agency" (Lewis, 1977) in actively organizing his adaptive repertpry. Such an active role is essential in the widening achievement of effectance in self-regulation. Self-regulatory capability becomes crucial as the complexity of adaptation increases over the second and third years of life. Such increasing complexity calls into play additional newly emerging mechanisms of integration as a means of maintaining the coherence of the individual in his unique adaptive situation. These integrative mechanisms must involve the development of a language and of symbolic representations that have gained common usefulness both to the individual and his caregivers; they must involve also a certain awareness of one's own state, dispositions, intentions, and thought content.

This epigenetic sequence of issues of adaptive coordination constructs an ontogeny of self-regulation, each issue for the infant relating specific caregiving contexts to his own individual adaptive content, and depends on additional increasingly differentiated and, for the infant, newly employed mechanisms of integration. The negotiation of the sequence of issues provides the basis for proposing that the ontogeny of self-regulation is paralleled by an ontogeny of awareness and self-awareness. The latter are functions which increasingly enter the construction of the repertory of adaptive strategies by which infant and caregiver become coordinated, especially in the second and third years of the child's life. From the adaptive perspective, consciousness (or awareness) is not a generally uniform or unitary state, the same for everyone, but involves an individual organization of state and content of awareness in terms of the moment-by-moment configuration of the ongoing process of that individual's adaptive encounter. Here, the static imagery of structures is not adequate to capture the conceptualization of temporally organized process. The necessary conditions for the ontogenetic progression of self-awareness as a mechanism of self-regulation depends, then, on the capacity for changing organization of events and processes *in the system* and not only on the potential of the individual infant.

Obviously, the later steps in the establishing of this sequence of adaptive coordinations, which now involve "secondary process" functions such as representations and their recognition, require a partner also capable of specificity of fittedness in these more subtle levels. Prior to this level of adaptation during the *second* 18 months of life in the infant-mother system there has been the foundation of a long history of regulatory achievements that have been gained by the partners over the *first* 18 months. These coordinations now provide a mutually experienced context in which the "meaning" of each other's behavior is already clear for the most part. This context of mutual familiarity provides the necessary condition to set the stage for precision of fitting together on these next, more subtle levels of thought and inner perception that involve the "reading" of intentionality, feeling states, emotional expression, etc. It is the correct reading of intentionality that is critical for the preservation of initial trust during negotiation of the later issues. Correct and specific recognition by the "significant other" during the second 18 months may be a necessary requirement for a consolidation of the experience of self-recognition and for the establishment of the function of self-recognition in further adaptation. Validation of the toddler's perception of his own state and inner content by the partner's act of recognition is essential for the toddler to learn to depend on his own inner perception to guide his continuing active organizing of his widening repertory of adaptive strategies. Conversely, at this chronological point in development, the invalidation of his own inner percepts in the adaptive encounter requires him to turn to alternative "defenses"—inhibition, compliance, etc. A new level of recognition in the second 18 months of life involving the coordination of mutual awareness, then, is a system achievement, an "emergent property" of the whole, setting the stage for an integration greater than the part properties of either of the partners alone. It is a matching or meeting by which the system comes to be regulated at the level of the spirit, so to speak, a regulation that provides "states" in the system necessary for the successful inclusion of subsequent, even more subtle mechanisms such as those of long-term goals, identifications, values, etc.

There are other conditions as well that are provided by the state of organization in the system. These constitute necessary contextual elements for the progression of changes in organization that mark the ontogeny of self-regulation. Here I am referring not only to the maintenance in the system, as a system's characteristic, of the infant's role as "agent" in organizing his world, but the construction of the "intermediate area" as formulated by Winnicott (1951). From the systems perspective, the context for "the intermediate area" is that of the mother "holding the situation in time"—a condition that allows the infant to experience inner and outer percepts at the same moment in time without his option for the initiation of activity in the service of integrating the inner and outer domains being threatened or preempted by demands for regulation. The "intermediate area" can be viewed as an "emergency property" of the system, an "open space" in regulatory exchanges when these are considered in terms of their temporal organization. The formulation of the "open space" in the postnatal infant-caregiver system has been discussed in more detail elsewhere (Sander, 1977). It is mentioned here only to illustrate the alternative conceptualizations, offered by the systems perspective, from which to consider conditions necessary for change in organization during development.

There is a fundamental polarity of events and directions in the biological system (i.e., attachment and detachment, bonding and isolation, synchrony and asynchrony, combination and differentiation, togetherness and separation, complexity and unity, etc.) that provides the context for organizing processes that allow for unique adaptive and integrative solutions to be arrived at in each system. In formulating a "self psychology" from the perspective of the biological system, the necessary conditions for the emergence of a coherent self as a step in the ontogeny of self-regulation will fall into the domain of emergent properties of the system.

There are new vistas currently in biology which elaborate the properties of open systems, especially those that are far from equilibrium. These formulations are concerned with new concepts such as the difference between information and instruction, that between resilience and stability, the "amplification of adaptation," "order through fluctuation," mechanisms related to "boundary properties," and the role of "attractor surfaces" (Holling, 1976; Prigogine, 1976; Waddington, 1976).

As psychoanalysis now turns again both to biology and to early development to implement the formulation of a self psychology, it is to newer data and newer conceptualizations in both disciplines that we must look for more adequate tools to grapple with the task. Obviously, there is a great distance to go, but what must be done now is to orient our research directions and designs so that the exploration of development in terms of the infant and its environment together as a biological system can begin. Data are needed to provide the empirical base from which to formulate and document the rapid and lawful process of changing organization of the system, as exchanges between its component parts increase in scope and complexity over the first years of life, both within the developing individual and in relation to his larger environment of life support.

References

Aldrich, C., Sung, C., & Knop, C. (1945), The crying of newly born babies: II. The individual phase. *J. Pediatrics*, 27:89–96.

Aschoff, J. (1969), Desynchronization and resynchronization of human circadian rhythms. *Aerospace Med.*, 40:844–849.

Basch, M.F. (1975), Toward a theory that encompasses depression: A revision of existing causal hypotheses in psychoanalysis. In: *Depression and Human Existence*, ed. E. J. Anthony & T. Benedek. Boston: Little, Brown.

———— (1977), Developmental psychology and explanatory theory in psychoanalysis. *Annual of Psychoanalysis*, 5:229–263.

Boismier, J., Chappell, P., & Meier, G. (1970), A behavior inventory for assessing states of arousal in the human newborn. Paper presented at the meeting of the Southeastern Psychological Association, Louisville, Ky.

Brazelton, T.B., Tronick, E., Adamson, L., Als, H., & Wise, S. (1975), Early mother-infant reciprocity. In: *Parent-Infant Interaction*. CIBA Foundation Symposium 33 (new series). Amsterdam: Elsevier, pp. 137–154.

Burns, P., Sander, L., Stechler, G., & Julia, H. (1972), Distress in feeding: Short-term effects of caretaker environment on the first 10 days. *J. Amer. Acad. Child Psychiat.*, 11:427–439.

Cassel, T. Z., & Sander, L. W. (1975), Neonatal recognition processes and attachment: The masking experiment. Paper presented at biennial meeting of the Society for Research in Child Development, Denver, Colo.

Chappell, P., & Sander, L. (1978), Mutual regulation of infant-mother inter-active process: The context for the origin of communication. In: *Before Speech: The Beginnings of Human Communication*, ed. M. Bullowa. Cambridge, England: Cambridge University Press, pp. 89–109.

Condon, W.S., & Sander, L.W. (1974), Neonate movement is synchronized with adult speech: Interactional participation and language acquisition. *Science*, 183:99–101.

Enright, J.T. (1960), Discussion (tidal rhythmicity). *Cold Spring Harbor Symposia on Quantitative Biology*, 25:487–498.

Halberg, F. (1960), Temporal coordination of physiologic function. *Cold Spring Harbor Symposia on Quantitative Biology*, 25:289–310.

Holling, C.S. (1976), Resilience and stability of ecosystems. In: *Evolution and Consciousness*, ed. E. Jantsch & C. Waddington. Reading, Mass.: Addison-Wesley, pp. 73–92.

Kohut, H. (1977), *The Restoration of the Self*. New York: International Universities Press.

Lewis, M. (1977), The search for the origins of self: Implications for social behavior and intervention. Paper presented at Symposium on the Ecology of Care and Education of Children under Three. Berlin, February 23–26.

Luce, G.G. (1970), Public Health Service Publication #2088. Washington, D.C.: U.S. Government Printing Office.

Pittendrigh, C.S. (1961), *Harvey Lecture Series 1960–61*. New York: Academic Press, 56:93–125.

Prigogine, I. (1976), Order through fluctuation: Self-organization and social system. In: *Evolution and Consciousness*, ed. E. Jantsch & C. Waddington. Reading, Mass.: Addison-Wesley, pp. 93–126.

Sander, L.W. (1962), Issues of early mother-child interaction. *J. Amer. Acad. Child Psychiat.*, 1:141–166.

———— (1964), Adaptive relationships in early mother child interaction. *J. Amer. Acad. Child Psychiat.*, 3:231–264.

———— (1969), Regulation and organization in the early infant caretaker system. In: *Brain and Early Behavior*, ed. R. J. Robinson. New York: Academic Press, pp. 311–315.

———— (1975), Infant and caretaking environment: Investigation and conceptualization of adaptive behavior in a system of increasing complexity. In: *Explorations in Child Psychiatry*, ed. E.J. Anthony. New York: Plenum, pp. 129–166.

———— (1977), The regulation of exchange in the infant-caretaker system and some aspects of the context-content relationship. In: *The Origins of Behavior: Vol. 5. Interaction, Conversation, and the Development of Language*, ed. M. Lewis & L. Rosenblum. New York: Wiley, pp. 133–156.

———— Chappell, P., Gould, J., & Snyder, P. (1975), An investigation of change in variables of infant state and infant-caretaker interaction over the first seven days of life. Paper presented at the biennial meeting of the Society for Research in Child Development, Denver, Colo.

———— Gould, J.B., Snyder, P., Lee, A., Teager, H., & Burwen, R. (1976), Continuous non-intrusive bassinet monitoring of neonatal states on the sleep-awake continuum. *Sleep Research*, 5:208 (Abstract, APSS).

———— & Julia, H.L. (1966), Continuous interactional monitoring in the neonate. *Psychosom. Med.*, 28:822–835.

———— ———— Stechler, G., & Burns, P. (1972), Continuous 24-hour interactional monitoring in infants reared in two caretaking environments. *Psychosom. Med.*, 34:270–282.

———— Stechler, G., Burns, P., & Lee, A. (1979), Change in infant and caregiver variables over the first two months of life: Integration of action in early development. In: *Origins of the Infant's Social Responsiveness*, ed. E. Thomas. Hillsdale, N.J.: Erlbaum, pp. 349–407.

———— ———— Julia, H., & Burns, P. (1970), United States Government Public Health Service, National Institute of Child Health and Human Development Project #01766: Terminal Report.

Sollberger, A. (1965), *Biological Rhythm Research*. Amsterdam: Elsevier.

Stechler, G., Sander, L., Burns, P., & Julia, H. (1973), Infant looking and fussing in response to visual stimulation over the first two months of life in different infant-caretaking systems. Paper presented at the biennial meeting of the Society for Search in Child Development, Philadelphia.

Stern, D.N. (1971), A micro-analysis of mother-infant interaction behavior regulating social contact between a mother and her 3½-month-old twins. *J. Amer. Acad. Child Psychiat.*, 10:501–518.

Van Melle, G., Sander, L., Stechler, G., Julia, H., & Burns, P. (1973), In-crib crying over the first month of life in different caretaking systems. Paper presented at the biennial meeting of the Society for Research in Child Development, Philadelphia.

Waddington, C.H. (1976), Evolution in the subhuman world. In: *Evolution and Consciousness*, ed. E. Jantsch & C. Waddington. Reading, Mass.: Addison-Wesley, pp. 11–15.

White, R.L. (1970), WRATS (White Recording and Automatic Transcribing System): A computer system for automatic recording and transcribing date. Unpublished paper prepared at Rutgers University, Institute of Animal Behavior, Newark, N.J.

Winnicott, D.W. (1951), Transitional objects and transitional phenomena. In: *Collected Papers: Through Paediatrics to Psycho-Analysis*. New York: Basic Books, 1958, pp. 229–242.

11

Neonatal Assessment

T. BERRY BRAZELTON, M.D.

As we become aware of the importance of early intervention in optimizing an infant's potential for development, it becomes more and more important that we be able to evaluate infants as early as possible for being at risk, with an eye to more sophisticated preventive and therapeutic approaches. Early intervention may prevent a compounding of problems that occur all too easily when the environment cannot adjust appropriately to an infant at risk. Prematures and minimally brain-damaged infants seem to be less able to compensate in disorganized, depriving environments than do well-equipped neonates, and their problems of organization in development are compounded early (Greenberg, 1971). Quiet, nondemanding infants do not elicit necessary mothering from already overstressed parents and are selected by their neonatal behavior for kwashiorkor and marasmus in poverty-ridden cultures such as are found in Guatemala and Mexico (Brazelton, Tronick, Lechtig, Lasky, and Klein, 1977). Hyperkinetic, hypersensitive neonates may press a mother and father into a kind of desperation and produce child-rearing responses from them that reinforce the problems of the child so that he grows up in an overreactive, hostile environment (Heider, 1966). Parents of children admitted to the wards of Children's Hospital in Boston for clinical syndromes such as failure to thrive, child abuse, repeated accidents and ingestions, and infantile autism often are successful parents of other children. By history, they associate their failure with the one child to an inability to "understand" him from the neonatal period onward, and they claim a difference from the other children in his earliest reactions to them (Brazelton,

Young, and Bullowa, 1971). If we are to improve the outcome for such children, a sensitivity to the risk in early infancy could mobilize preventive efforts and programs for intervention before the neonate's problems are compounded by an environment that cannot understand him without such help.

Children who reach school age with reading disabilities or minimal brain disorders often are suffering from an expectation to fail in their life tasks. Their mild disorder of central nervous system may be far outweighed by the effects of a poor self-image built in over the years by repeated failures at tasks set up for them by an environment that urges them to succeed beyond their capacities. Most often, parents are unconsciously aware of mild disorganization, and in their efforts to compensate they either press such a child or overprotect him. In either case, the message to him is that he is inadequate and unable to compete in the society around him. After years of such patterns of failure, the expectation of failure begins to dominate his personality, and a cycle of passivity and of self-devaluation is added to the mild organic disorder. These problems in personality become more difficult for teachers of learning-disordered children or those with MBD (minimal brain damage) than are the structuring efforts at reorganization in rehabilitation programs. If we as pediatricians could become sensitive to mild disorders and could interfere with the well-intentioned but destructive child-rearing patterns of parents, we might indeed salvage exciting and excited children—even though they must live with CNS (central nervous system) pathology.

But we need more sophisticated methods for assessing neonates and for predicting their contribution to the likelihood of failure in the environment-infant interaction. We also need to be able to assess at-risk environments, for the impracticality of spreading resources too thin points to the necessity for selecting target populations for our efforts at early intervention. With better techniques for assessing strengths and weaknesses in infants and the environments to which they will be exposed, we might come to understand better the mechanisms for failures in development that result in some of the above-mentioned syndromes.

We cannot continue to blame socioeconomic stress alone

for failures in interaction between parents and their children. Of course, the stresses of poverty and hunger make it less likely than an adult can nurture a dependent infant. But desperate socioeconomic conditions produce comparable stresses in many families whose children do not have to be salvaged from the clinical syndrome of child abuse, failure to thrive, or kwashior-kor. Chavez, Martinez, Cravioto, and Yashine (1975) now be-lieve that a predisposition to kwashiorkor among malnourished populations results from poor psychological nurturing as well as protein deprivation. Minimally brain-damaged babies do make remarkable compensatory recoveries in a fostering en-vironment. Understanding the infant early and the problems he will present to his parents may enhance our ability to support them and work to help them understand him as they adjust to a difficult infant.

Perhaps most important of all to clinicians who are trying to assist in this process, an assessment of the normal neonate's behavior might contribute a prediction of his temperament, which would allow for a more incisive approach to assisting the parents as they cope with any newborn at home—either an intense, colicky one, or one who tends to be too quiet. We have found that a demonstration in the neonatal nursery of her infant's complex behaviors and of temperament allows the mother to see him as a personality from the very first, and she can react to him with more objectivity than she might otherwise (Parker, Als, and Brazelton, 1978). If she sees that the pedia-trician is interested in the baby as a person, she will be more likely to turn to him for questions about her baby's develop-ment, and he can play a more significant role from the first in the prevention of psychological and somatic difficulties.

The neonate has been grossly underestimated in the past. Thinking of him as a passive "lump of clay" has shut our eyes to his complexity. He offers many complex responses from the first for generating attachment from his caregivers. Through the early work period of adjusting and learning to attach to him, he continues to offer rich feedback. We have ignored some of the rich signals he can give us at birth to understand him. We can look at his stages of development, his appearance, and his behavior. They can be seen as a predictor of the kind of interaction he will generate around him. Thus at birth the new-born infant offers us a real opportunity for both weighing predictions and offering supports for intervention when indicated.

Intrauterine Experience

Many mothers have reported that their babies, while they are in the uterus, respond to lights, sounds, maternal emotions, or activities. Experimental studies so far have focused on fetal responses to sound. The cochlea is functional by about the fifth month of gestation and already is structurally similar to the adult cochlea (Eisenberg, 1969). Using new noninvasive techniques for monitoring fetal heart rate (FHR) and fetal activity, third-trimester fetuses have been found to respond to sound with FHR changes (Kittner, 1976). There also is evidence that the fetus can have some control over his responses to a sound that is presented to him over and over again. A normal fetus, like a normal newborn, is not totally at the mercy of his environment, but when the same sound is presented repeatedly to the in utero fetus, he can gradually shut down on any response; i.e., he behaves as if he does not hear the noise when one judges this from changes in fetal heart rate. However, if the sound is changed to a new pitch, he again attends to it, showing an ability for sound discrimination. FHR responses to sound thus become clinically relevant. They are absent in anencephalics and deaf babies. They can be used to measure fetal distress, since responses to sound may either diminish or even disappear in a stressed fetus.

Reports have shown that prolonged emotional stress during pregnancy results in infants who weigh less than average and have high activity levels (Sontag, 1944). A positive relationship has been found also between the mother's anxiety levels during pregnancy and the amount of neonatal crying (Rottinger and Simmons, 1954). For the fetus in utero, is maternal emotional distress actually a different experience than other physiological stresses? Is the baby of a woman who is emotionally disturbed actually learning to cope with this stress in utero? We could begin to answer these questions by looking at differential fetal responses to maternal emotional stresses. Since there is evidence to suggest that maternal stress and emotionality during pregnancy can affect neonatal behavior and can shape the extrauterine experience of the baby, we now need to apply our more sophisticated monitoring techniques to explore this dimension of fetal behavior and development.

Prenatal nutrition has been shown to have significant differential effects on the growing fetus. Winick (1973) has pointed out that organ growth occurs as two general phases. The initial phase is cellular division with resultant increase in the number of cells. The subsequent but overlapping phase is an increase in cell size. The number of cells is measured by determining total organ DNA, whereas cell size is reflected in weight/DNA ratio. Cell division ceases at a more or less specific time for each organ system. Significant malnutrition during cell division will irreversibly result in a smaller organ because new cells will not be made regardless of subsequent nutrition. In contrast, malnutrition during the period of increase in cellular size is reversible. The brain is not spared these nutritional insults, but their timing affects it differently. These data suggest strongly that the timing of malnutrition is important to neonatal function. If malnutrition occurs just during the period of increase in cellular size in the CNS, postnatal nutritional supplementation may result in CNS recovery. In order to sort out these varying effects, we need more sensitive measures to reflect the fixed and nonfixed effects on the central nervous system, as well as its capacity to recover when deficits are remedied.

An initial assessment of such a depleted newborn, who demonstrates a decrease in weight with respect to height, slightly decreased head circumference, loss of subcutaneous tissue, and relatively poor behavioral responses, is not adequate to an understanding of the infant's specific in utero nutritional experience and future capacities. But a repeated evaluation of his behavior, which might assess his potential for recovery, would tell us a great deal more.

For example, if the infant's behavioral responses remain poor over repeated assessments, one could postulate early intrauterine depletion with a reduced number of cells in the CNS. If the behavioral responses improved with postnatal supplementation, we could assume that malnutrition occurred relatively late in gestation. The infant's capacity for recovery thus becomes an assessment of the timing of previous stresses and also a measure of his prognosis.

The importance of multiple assessments and the pattern of recovery is dramatically evidenced in a study of Zambian infants (Brazelton, Tronick, and Koslowski, 1976). Twenty Zambian infants were examined on Days 1, 5, and 10 with an earlier version of the Brazelton Scale (Brazelton, 1984). Their mothers were multiparous, had used no birth control measures, and had experienced a series of pregnancies in rapid succession (reportedly at 10–11 month intervals between the onsets of pregnancies). The infants were seen as having suffered from their mothers' protein malnutrition in pregnancy, since histories from the mothers substantiated inadequate intake of eggs, meat, or fish, with low caloric intake.

On Day 1, the infants showed all the signs of dysmaturity, indicating recent intrauterine depletion suggestive of placental dysfunction. Their skin was dry and peeling. Subcutaneous tissue was sparse throughout the body; the neonates' faces were wizened, and their eyes glazed. The cord stumps were yellow, as if this had resulted from intrauterine stress in the last trimester. These depleted babies lacked muscle tone, had poor head control in pull-to-sit maneuvers, did not cuddle when held, and were irritable. They had low scores in all elicited responses, especially in such complex responses as alerting and following an object with their eyes (see Table 1). This pattern of response as well as their depleted appearance certainly would have put them in a high-risk category in a U.S. group, and parents would have responded to them with an anxious, overprotective approach.

By Day 10, breast feeding had rehydrated the depleted infants, and they seemed to have recovered in all observable respects from the intrauterine physiological stress. The infants showed no sign of dehydration or depletion at 10 days, and their performance showed remarkable recovery. They were consolable, alert, and participated actively when cuddled. Their irritability had decreased, and their muscle tone had improved. Most striking was their interest in social stimuli and their ca-

TABLE 1

Mean Scores for Zambians and for Americans on Day 1, 5, and 10 for All
Measures that Distinguished Between Groups on at Least One Day[a]

Measure	Day 1		Day 5		Day 10	
	Zambians	Americans	Zambians	Americans	Zambians	Americans
Motor activity	3.00	4.90	5.89	5.50	4.60	5.90
Tempo at height	3.20	5.77	5.90	5.50	4.40	6.44
Rapidity of buildup	3.22	4.80	5.62	4.50	3.50	5.50
Irritability	2.50	4.40	4.40	4.70	3.80	5.00
Consolability	6.60	5.56	5.00	4.63	6.12	4.75
Social interest	4.20	4.29	6.20	5.22	6.70	4.33
Alertness	3.40	4.20	6.30	5.11	7.40	4.80
Follow with eyes	2.40	4.16	4.60	4.70	4.67	5.11
Reactivity to stimulation	3.35	4.38	5.30	4.71	6.14	4.67
Defensive movements	3.20	4.38	5.11	5.50	4.90	6.11
Cuddliness	3.30	4.40	5.22	5.60	6.30	5.12

[a]Underlined scores indicate that the difference between the groups was significant.

pacity to control interfering motor behaviors. They now were
appropriately active and vigorous.

This dramatic recovery pattern emphasizes the importance
of making multiple assessments for "at-risk" levels during the
neonatal period. Assessment for prediction cannot be made
with any single examination as effectively as with several examinations. Several examinations allow for the dissipation of
transient stresses and allow the infant to manifest his capability
for recovery. At no time did the Zambian mothers treat their
infants as though they were at risk. They took their infants out
of the hospital on Day 1, carrying them upright against their
sides, wrapped in a dashiki that did not even provide support

for the shoulders and head. The mothers placed the limp infants in the dashiki by swinging them over their shoulders while holding the infant by one arm. To arouse the infant, a mother would joggle and bounce her baby. Mothers left these infants out on the bed to be played with by other siblings and visitors. In short, they handled their infants as if they were strong and vigorous on Day 1, when it looked inappropriate to us to do so, but by Day 10 it was perfectly suited to their now vigorous and responsive infants.

We believed that the mother's practices were based more on the expectancies of how their infants would develop than on the neonatal behavior with which they were presented. Assuming that the infants were not atypical of the population, one can infer that the Zambian mothers in our sample had seen other Zambian infants recover shortly after birth. Individually, each mother's expectations were also reinforced by the dramatic change in muscle tone and responsivity that took place in her infant after Day 1. Her knowledge of the recovery pattern thus was based on cultural and historical knowledge and information presented by her own infant.

This example of the recovery of the Zambian infants demonstrates the interaction of the mothers' expectations and the infants' adaptive capacity to stress. This outcome might be different with depleted babies in societies where mothers' expectations of the infants' ability to recover are not so firm or are interfered with by other concerns. Poor, isolated parents stressed with significant socioeconomic factors in urban America have a relatively high proportion of dysmature and depleted infants. Their neonatal behavior is affected as well, and when the infants are quieter, difficult to arouse, and difficult to bring to responsive states for interaction, it is easy to imagine that they will elicit fewer responses and maybe even less nourishment from their stressed mothers. We can see that the beginnings of the cycle of chronic minor undernutrition that is getting much publicity in the United States can start with in utero undernutrition and then be mediated and continued by the effects of resultant neonatal behavior on the environment. Unlike the Zambian mothers, isolated ghetto mothers may not have the same historical or cultural knowledge about recovery or they may be too stressed themselves to feed and energize a relatively lethargic, poorly interacting baby to optimal recovery.

Another factor adversely influencing behavioral recovery in the neonate can be a lack of nutritional resources to maintain adequate nutrition after birth. Chavez, Martinez, Cravioto, and Yashine (1975), in a study of infants during their first 2 years, empirically illustrated the cycle of improved nutrition → increased activity → greater demands → greater interaction. The supplemented child slept less and played more. Not only was the greater interaction seen in more time spent in caretaking activities, but mothers spoke almost twice as much to these infants compared to the nonsupplemented group. They spoke in sentences with adjectives and adverbs and used explanations rather than commands. Fathers became more involved earlier as well. When the infant became a toddler, the greater activity of the nutritionally supplemented group was manifested by increased exploratory behavior and by toddlers who were more mischievous, demanding, and disobedient. The family needed to respond with greater supervision and more limit setting. In general, the nonsupplemented, malnourished child was found "predominantly negative, passive, withdrawn and timid; and at certain ages, especially when signs of evident deficiency [were] shown, an attitude of apathy was manifest, mixed with certain attitudes of anxiety when separated from the mother" (p. 1574).

In summary, we have briefly explored aspects of an interactive process involving nutrition, starting with the in utero environment. The neonate's behavior and recovery are seen as pivotal in that they reflect in utero shaping and predict to prognosis in both terms of CNS depression as well as how the environment may respond to him.

Perinatal Events

Maternal anesthesia and analgesia during labor and delivery are known to have a pharmacological effect on the fetus and subsequently on the newborn with their rapid transport across the placenta. Studying maternal drug effects in an animal model, Moya and Thorndike (1962) concluded that these drugs had a greater effect on the fetus because of increased permeability of the blood-brain barrier, inefficient metabolism in the liver, and the asphyxia and physical trauma of normal deliveries. Specific neurobehavioral responses of these intrapartum drugs have been investigated. Based on observations, Brazelton (1961) has observed and described a 1–2 day prolongation of CNS depression or disorganization following birth in babies of more heavily medicated mothers. Relative CNS disorganization normally is seen in the first 48 hours post partum. Added to this increased and prolonged disorganization, mothers of these babies reported greater difficulty in breast feeding for 48 hours longer than a comparison group in which minimal sedation had been used. Neonatal weight gain was delayed by 24 hours in the heavily premedicated group. By affecting neonatal behaviors, these intrapartum drugs could easily influence the early mother-infant relationship. Mothers who have any postpartum depression might easily see the baby's disorganization around feeding as amounting to a rejection of their efforts to reach them.

Using sucking as a modality to study, Kron (1966) described the effects on nutritive sucking of 200 mg of IV secobarbital given from 10 minutes to 3 hours before delivery. Compared to infants whose mothers received no sedatives, these infants had a significant decreased sucking rate with an associated decrease in consumption over the first 4 days.

Using visual attention as an outcome measure, Stechler and Latz (1966) concluded that the more drugs administered around delivery, the less attentive the infant is likely to be. They measured attention as total time spent starting or scanning a visual stimulus as opposed to nonattention behaviors such as looking away, closing the eyes, or fussing.

Hypoxia is another significant intrapartum event and affects the outcome of the fetal brain, but it may also have a more transient effect on significant behaviors in the newborn baby. These behaviors may in turn affect more or less permanently the mother-child relationship by the mother's distorted image of her infant's future. Even transient and recoverable insults become of importance in this light.

Neonatal Assessments

The preceding discussion has reviewed some of the factors that may place an infant at risk for normal postnatal adaptation and subsequent development. When the effect of these factors results in more obvious sensory, motor, or morphological disabilities, routine pediatric and neurological examinations coupled with the mother's observations should be able to uncover the disability either immediately or at least in the first few months.

Improved perinatal care, including better prenatal nutrition, earlier and more appropriate use of oxygen, maintenance of intravascular volume, recognition of the importance of temperature control, and closer monitoring of blood glucose should improve the chances of recovery from intrauterine stress. We have reason to believe that this will result in fewer catastrophic disabilities, such as seizure disorders, spastic diplegia, or quadriplegia. As we reduce the number of factors that result in significant disabilities, we may be increasing the possibility for more subtle disabilities. Medical care has increased survival and improved outcome, and now we must work to optimize function and the subsequent development of these babies. In order to do this, we should become more adept at identifying behavioral deviances early and in providing appropriate intervention.

Neonatal and infant evaluations should be able to identify neurobehavioral deviations as well as individual differences in normal behavior. To date, neurological evaluations have given us an understanding of the neonate's ability to "cope" with negative stimuli at a midbrain level. What is needed is an assessment of the neonate's behavioral style and capacities to recover from the stress of delivery over time, which not only becomes a sensitive measure of his CNS organization, but also can provide information about his potential contribution to his postnatal environment. This latter assessment provides insight into what it will take for a specific infant to "make it" with a specific set of parents and the specific environment they provide for him. It is only with this kind of assessment that the individuality of the infant becomes clear as an interaction in his in utero and ex utero environment. Only within an interactive framework of looking at the psychological and physiological interaction over time can we begin to estimate the neonate's potential for recovery from the stresses of normal labor and delivery, as well as from prenatal or perinatal stress.

Ponderal Index

A unique and helpful measurement to define the end results of fetal growth and nutrition is the ponderal index, a ratio of birth weight to body length

$$\frac{\text{wt in gm} \times 100}{(\text{length in cm})}$$

Miller and Hassanein (1971, 1973) describe the use of the ponderal index to identify fetal malnutrition, defined as either the relative decrease in soft tissue accumulation or increase in its utilization. Unlike birth weight, the ponderal index was shown in term babies not to be confounded by race, sex, fetal age, or parity when defining malnutrition. By taking length into consideration, babies who are long, with a relatively small amount of soft tissue mass, can be seen as having experienced a late gestation nutritional insult. The ponderal index was not shown to change after 37 weeks' gestation, making an evaluation of chronological age unnecessary. Between 29 and 37 weeks it increases slightly with age, and malnutrition is defined as a ponderal index of 2.00 as opposed to 2.20 at 37 weeks. In a study utilizing the ponderal index, factors associated with fetal malnutrition were poor maternal weight gain, absence of prenatal care, preeclampsia, and major chronic illness.

Gestational Age

Assessment of gestational age is an important adjunct in assessing impaired fetal growth and provides the appropriate context in which one can interpret an infant's behavioral and CNS capacities. Specifically, it provides a way of differentiating premature appropriate-for-gestational-age (AGA) babies from similar weight, full-term, small-for-gestational-age (SGA) babies. This distinction is important in understanding in utero conditions and in planning for appropriate management after delivery. Clinical problems associated with premature infants, based on their immaturity, include jaundice after 4 days, respiratory distress, intracranial hemorrhage, diminished ability to handle solute loads, decreased ability to maintain body temperature, decreased ability to absorb fats, apnea, and susceptibility to retrolental fibroplasia. SGA babies, on the other hand, have an increased frequency of hypoglycemia and a relative increase in oxygen consumption, requiring greater caloric intake on a per-kg basis. Chromosomal abnormalities and fetal infection are more likely to be associated with in utero growth retardation as seen in SGA babies. These babies have a different prognosis. Drillien (1972) has shown that SGA babies did less well on developmental testing when compared to premature AGA babies of the same weight. She concluded that these babies were subjected to mild degrees of hypoxia or malnutrition in the last trimester and that this accounted for their small size and a higher frequency of mental retardation and minor neurological abnormalities.

Neurological Assessment

The neurological examination of the newborn has progressively undergone modification to increase its sensitivity. The newborn was initially believed to function at a brain stem level (Peiper, 1963), and his evaluation was based on observed reflexes, which were also found in anencephalic infants. However, more careful observations showed that these same reflexes were qualitatively different in the anencephalic infant; they tended to be stereotyped, obligatory, or partial. The qualitative aspect of the reflexes thought to represent control by the pyramidal tract and motor cortical areas has become an important aspect of the neurological examination (Parmelee, 1970).

An addition to newborn evaluation has been based on André-Thomas and Ajuriaguerra's work on muscle tone (1949).

Instead of attempting to localize a specific lesion in the nervous system, they believed that variations in muscle tone reflected the general organization of the nervous system. Specifically, they assessed muscle tone in the following three ways: (1) active tone—tone that is seen during spontaneous and voluntary movement; (2) passive tone—tone that is seen by complete extension of an extremity at each joint; and (3) passive tone—tone that can be seen by swinging the extremity at each joint. Not only did they compare the tone on both sides of the body, but they also found it useful to note whether the three types of muscle tone varied in the same direction.

Prechtl and Beintema (1964) have organized many of the previously mentioned observations, including state of arousal, muscle tone, and quantification of reflexes into a comprehensive newborn neurological examination. For this examination, they have described six different behavioral states. They observed that infants with CNS damage had difficulty modulating or controlling their states, that they would go from deep sleep to inconsolable crying and back again.

Using his examination with newborns who had pre- or perinatal complications, Prechtl (1965) was successful in predicting the outcome for at-risk babies.

The classical pediatric neurological assessment of the neonate is based on his responses to painful or intrusive stimuli, and, as such, the resulting reflex behavior seems to be mediated by the midbrain. But such an examination neglects the available organized behavior which the infant can demonstrate as he suppresses reflexive behavior in order to attend to more "interesting" stimuli—the human face or voice, a soft rattle, a light caress.

As a newborn lies undressed and uncovered in the nursery, his color begins to change with mottled uneven acrocyanosis of his extremities as he attempts to control loss of body heat. He begins to shiver, then to cry and flail his limbs in jerky thrusting movements in an effort to raise his own temperature. In the face of such enormous demands, as one speaks gently and insistently into one ear, his movements become smoother, slower, and he gradually quiets completely. His face softens, then brightens, his eyes move smoothly to the side from which the voice is coming. His head follows with a sudden smooth turn toward the voice, and he searches for the face of the speaker. He fixes on the eyes of the examiner and listens intently for several minutes. If the examiner moves his face slowly to the baby's midline and then across to the other side, the newborn will track him, his head and eyes smoothly turning in a 180 degree arc. This complex interaction of visual, auditory, and motor behavior to respond to a human stimulus is managed by the neonate despite the enormous physiological demands of being undressed and unrestrained in a cold, overstimulating nursery. If one ignores the importance of this capacity as he evaluates the neurological and physiological integrity of the neonate, he misses the implication of the powerful effect of the cortex on the autonomic and physiological systems in the neonatal period.

Sensory Capacities

The newborn is equipped with the capacity for processing complex visual stimulation and showing organized motor responses to visual stimuli. When a bright light is flashed into a neonate's eyes, not only do his pupils constrict, but he blinks, his eyelids and whole face contract, he withdraws his head by arching his whole body, often setting off a complete startle as he withdraws, his heart rate and respiration increase, and there is an evoked response registered on his visual occipital EEG. Repeated stimulation of this nature will induce diminishing responses. For example, in a series of 20 bright light stimuli presented at 1-minute intervals, we found that the infant rapidly "habituated" out the behavioral responses, and by the tenth stimulus had decreased not only in his observable motor responses, but in his cardiac and respiratory responses as well. The latency to evoked responses on the occipital cortex as measured by EEG tracings were increasing, and by the fifteenth stimulus his EEG reflected the induction of a quiet, unresponsive state similar to that seen in sleep (Brazelton, 1961). His capacity to shut out repetitious disturbing visual stimuli protects him from having to respond to visual stimulation and at the same time frees him to save his energy to meet physiological demands.

Just as he is equipped with the capacity to shut out certain stimuli, he demonstrates the capacity to alert to, turn his eyes and head to follow and fix upon a stimulus which appeals to him. Fantz (1965) first pointed out the neonatal preference for complex visual stimuli. More recently, Goren (1975) showed that immediately after delivery, a human neonate would not only fix upon a drawing which resembled a human face, but would follow it with eyes and head turning in 180 degree arcs. A scrambled face did not demand the same kind of attention, nor did the infant follow the distorted face with his eyes and head for the same degree of lateral following. We found that the capacity of neonates to fix upon and follow a red ball was a good predictive sign of neurological integrity.

In a noisy, overlighted nursery, the neonate tends to shut down on his capacity to attend, but in a semidarkened room, a normal neonate in an alert state can be brought to respond to the human face as well as to a red or shiny object. For example, the following description indicates the behaviors of which the infant is capable.

The neonate is held or propped up at a 30 degree angle. Vestibular responses enhance eye-opening and tend to bring him to a more alert state (Korner and Thoman, 1970). His eyes begin to scan the environment with a dull look, wide pupils, and saccadic lateral movements of both eyes. As a bright red ball is brought into his line of vision and moved slowly up and down to attract his attention, his pupils contract slightly (Figure 1). As the ball is moved slowly from side to side, his face begins to brighten, his eyes widen, his limbs become still, and he stares fixedly at the object, beginning slowly to track the ball from side to side (Figure 2). He maintains the stilled posture in order to attend to the ball. His eyes first track in small arcs that take him off the target, but as he becomes more invested, the eye movements become smoother. As his eyes move laterally, his head begins to turn, and he begins to move his head from side to side in order to facilitate the tracking of the object. He is able to follow it for as much as 120 degrees, to right and left, and will even make eye and head movements to follow it 30 degrees

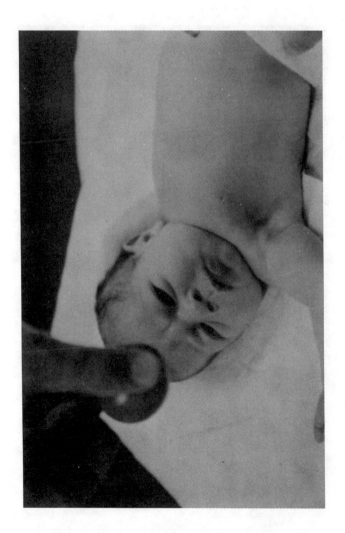

FIGURE 1. Ball attracts attention of neonate.

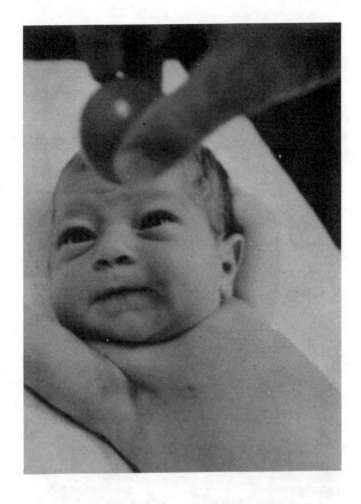

FIGURE 2. Neonate stares at ball, and begins to track its movement.

up or down. Meanwhile, interfering body movement or startles seem to be actively suppressed. We can maintain this intense visual involvement for several minutes before he startles, becomes upset or dull, and loses the alert state necessary for this kind of visual behavior.

The involvement of the neonate's state behavior, as well as the coordination of visual motor and head turning, seems to point to the entrainment of rather complex nervous system pathways. It is difficult not to implicate cortical controls over state, and interfering motor behavior as well as that of the visual and motor cortex in the observed following by the head and eyes.

State

The matrix of state as a concept for organization in the neonate has become important since its use as a background for neurological behavior in Prechtl's and Beintema's assessment (1964). Within the context of optimal state of alertness, Prechtl (1965), demonstrated that the newborn's midbrain reflexive behavior improved, and the neurological exam became a better diagnostic measure.

Sleep states have been recognized and defined since 1937, when Wagner described some of the behaviors seen in deep or regular sleep—jerky startles and relative unresponsiveness to external stimuli and more regulated smooth movements accompanied by responsiveness to stimuli in lighter sleep. Wolff (1966) added his observations of deep sleep—regular, deep respirations with sudden spontaneous motor patterns such as sobs, mouthing, sucking, and erections which occurred at fairly regular intervals in an otherwise inactive baby. He observed that babies were more responsive to stimuli in light sleep. Aserinsky and Kleitman (1955) described cycles of quiet, regular sleep followed by active periods of body movements and rapid eye movements (REMs) under closed lids. Hence, light sleep has come to be designated REM sleep. At term, active sleep (REM) occupies 45–50 percent of total sleep time, indeterminate sleep occupies 10 percent, and quiet sleep 35–45 percent.

The predominance of active sleep has led to the hypothesis that REM sleep mechanisms stimulate the growth of the neural systems by cyclic excitation, and it is in REM sleep that much of the differentiation of neuronal structures and neurophysiological discharge patterns occur (Anders and Roffwarg, 1973). Quiet sleep seems to serve the purpose of inhibiting CNS activity and is truly an habituated state of rest.

The length of sleep cycles (REM active and quiet sleep) changes with age. At term they occur in a periodicity of 45–50 minutes, but immature babies have even shorter, less well-defined cycles. Newborn infants have as much active REM in the first half of the deep period as in the second half. Individual sleep and wake patterns coalesce as the environment presses the neonate to develop diurnal patterns of daytime wakefulness and night-time sleep. Appropriate feeding patterns, diet, absence of excessive anxiety, sufficient nurturing stimulation, a fussing period prior to a long sleep have all been implicated as reinforcing to the CNS maturation necessary for the development of diurnal cycling of sleep and wakefulness. Sleep polygrams, as determined by both EEG and activity monitoring, are proving to be sensitive indicators of neurological maturation and integrity in the neonatal period.

In our behavioral assessment of neonates, we have utilized the two states of deep, regular and active REM sleep described by Wolff (1966) and Prechtl (1965). These states can be reliably determined by observation and without any instrumentation.

Deep sleep (State 1). Regular breathing, eyes closed, spontaneous activity confined to startles and jerky movements at quite regular intervals. Responses to external stimuli are partially inhibited and any response is likely to be delayed. No eye movements, and state changes are less likely after stimuli or startles than in other states.

Active REM sleep (State 2). Irregular breathing, sucking movements, eyes closed but rapid eye movements can be detected beneath the closed lids; low activity level, irregular smooth organized movements of extremities and trunk. Startles or startle equivalents as response to external stimuli often with change of state.

Alert states have been separated into three states for our behavioral assessment:

Drowsy (State 3). Semidozing, eyes may be open or closed, eyelids often fluttering, activity level variable, with interspersed mild startles and slow, smoothly monitored movements of extremities at periodic intervals; reactive to sensory stimuli but with some delay; state change frequently follows stimulation.

Wide awake (State 4). Alert bright look; focuses attention on sources of auditory or visual stimuli; motor activity suppressed in order to attend to stimuli. Impinging stimuli break through with a delayed response.

Active awake (State 5). Eyes open, considerable motor activity, thrusting movements of extremities, occasional startles set off by activity. Reactive to external stimulation with an increase in startles or motor activity, discrete reactions difficult to distinguish because of general high activity level.

Crying (State 6). Intense crying, jerky motor movements, difficult to break through with stimulation.

The waking states are easily influenced by fatigue, hunger, or other organic needs, and may last for variable amounts of time. The neonate lies in his crib looking around for as long as 20–30 minutes at a time. Appropriate stimulation can bring him up to a responsive state 4. Rocking, gently jiggling, crooning, stroking, setting off vestibular responses by bringing him upright or by rotating him, all serve to open his eyes. Then his interest in visual and auditory stimuli helps him to maintain a quiet alert state. In this state his respirations are regular at a rate of 50–60 a minute; his cardiac rate too is regular and fairly slow (around 100–120/minute), his eyes are wide, shiny, and capable of conjugate movements to scan and to follow with head turning to appropriate objects; his limbs, trunk, and face are relaxed and inactive; the skin is pink and uniform in color. Alert inactive states occur in the first 30–60 minutes after delivery but then are likely to decrease in duration and occurrence over the next 48 hours as the infant recovers, but they return after the first 2 days and make up as much as 8–16 percent of total observation time in the first month (Wolff, 1966).

Crying serves many purposes in the neonate, not the least of which is to shut out painful or disturbing stimuli. Hunger and pain are also responded to with crying, which brings the caretaker to him. And there is a kind of fussy crying which occurs periodically throughout the day—usually in a cyclic fashion—which seems to act as a discharge of energy, and an organizer of the states which ensue (Brazelton, 1962). After a period of such fussy crying, the neonate may .be more alert, and he may sleep more deeply.

As a behavior for organizing his day and for reducing disturbance within his CNS, crying seems to be of real importance in the neonatal period. Most parents can distinguish cries of pain, hunger, and fussiness by 2–3 weeks and learn quickly to respond appropriately (Wolff, 1969). So the cry of ethological significance to elicit appropriate caretaking for the infant.

We have found differences in newborns in their use of states. The difficulty in rousing certain infants from sleep states to alert to crying with disturbing stimuli versus the rapidity with which others go from sleep to crying and down again, or the lability which certain newborns demonstrate as they move rapidly from one state to another, or others who console easily from crying, and the self-quieting efforts on the part of other infants in order to maintain alert or quiet states—all suggest differentiating characteristics that will help to predict in neonates their future individualities. Certainly these differences will affect the kind of nuturing they will receive from their environments. We reported an infant whose rapidly labile movement from crying to deep sleep left his mother no opportunity to reach him. She found him such a difficult infant that we correctly predicted profound difficulties in their relationship. Since we had found this difficult state lability and unreachability in the neonatal period, we were able to support the mother with extra advice along with a preventive approach to her anxiety. We supported her in maintaining their relationship until the baby could begin to develop more adequate state controls. As his threshold for sensory input became more adequate, his state behavior became smoother, and he became more reachable by those around him. In this case, neonatal observations served to prevent a serious breakdown in the mother-infant interaction, as we could assure the mother that his lability was not due to her handling of the infant (Brazelton, 1962).

Neonatal Behavioral Assessment Scale (NBAS)

In order to record and evaluate some of the integrative processes evidenced in neonatal behavior, we have developed a behavioral evaluation scale which tests and documents the infant's use of state behavior (state of consciousness) and the response to various kinds of stimulation (Brazelton, Koslowski, and Main, 1974).

Since his reactions to all stimuli are dependent on his ongoing "state," any interpretation of them must be made with this in mind. His use of state to maintain control of his reactions to environmental and internal stimuli is an important mechanism and reflects his potential for organization. State serves to set a dynamic pattern to allow for the full behavioral repertoire of the infant. Specifically, the NBAS tracks changes in the infant's state over the course of the examination and assesses its lability and direction. The variability of state points to the infant's capacities for self-organization. His ability to quiet himself, as well as his need for stimulation, is another measure of this adequacy.

The behavior exam tests for neurological adequacy with 20 reflex measures and for 26 behavioral responses to environmental stimuli, including the kind of interpersonal stimuli which mothers use in their handling of the infant as they attempt to help him adapt to the new world. The examination includes a graded series of procedures—talking, hand on belly, restraint, holding, and rocking—designed to soothe and alert the infant. His responsiveness to animate stimuli, e.g., voice and face, and to inanimate stimuli, e.g., rattle, bell, red ball, white light, temperature change, are assessed. Vigor and attentional excitement are measured, as well as motor activity and tone, and autonomic responsiveness is assessed as the infant changes state. With this examination given on successive days we have been able to outline (1) the initial period of alertness immediately after delivery—presumably the result of stimulation of labor and the new environmental stimuli after delivery; (2) the ensuing period of depression and disorganization, which lasts for 24–48 hours in infants with uncomplicated deliveries and no medication effects, but for longer periods of 3–4 days if they have been compromised from medication given their mothers during labor; and (3) the curve of recovery to "optimal" function after several days. This third period may be the best single predictor of individual potential function and seems to correlate well with the neonate's retest ability at 30 days. The shape of the curve made by several examinations may be the most important assessment of the basic CNS intactness of the neonate's ability to integrate CNS and other physiological recovery mechanisms, and the strength of compensatory capacities when there have been compromising insults during labor and delivery. Test-retest reliability is greater than 8, and interscorer reliability of 90 percent can be achieved with training and maintained for at least a year. The examination takes 20 minutes to administer and 10 minutes to score reliably. The behavioral items are:

Response decrement to repeated visual stimuli
Response decrement to repeated auditory stimuli
Response decrement to pinprick
Orienting responses to inanimate visual and auditory stimuli
Orienting responses to the examiner's face and voice
Quality and duration of alert periods
General muscle tone—in resting and in response to being handled (passive and active)
Motor maturity
Traction responses as he is pulled-to-sit
Responses to being cuddled by the examiner
Defensive reactions to a cloth over his face
Consolability with intervention by examiner
Attempts to console self and control state behavior
Rapidity of buildup to crying state
Peak of excitement and capacity to control self
Irritability during the exam
General assessment of kind and degree of activity
Tremulousness
Amount of startling

Lability of skin color (measuring autonomic lability)
Lability of states during entire exam
Hand-to-mouth activity

In addition to the 26 items of behavior, assessed on a 9-point scale, 20 reflex responses are also assessed.

The neonate's capacity to manage and overcome the physiological demands of this adjustment period in order to attend to, differentiate, and habituate to the complex stimuli of an examiner's maneuvers may be an important predictor of his future central nervous system organization. Certainly the curve of recovery of these responses over the first neonatal week must be of more significance than the midbrain responses detectable in a routine neurological examination.

The Neonate as a Social Being

The newborn infant is obviously not prepared to exist outside a matrix of social supports from a responsive caregiver. But within this matrix he is not passive. On the contrary, the behavior patterns and sensory capabilities discussed elsewhere in this chapter shape the caretaker's behavior. Moreover, the "feelings of efficacy" which are engendered in the infant and his caretakers by the mutuality which is established become a source of energy to each participant (White, 1959).

Bowlby (1969) has stressed the importance of observing the earliest interactions between mother and infant as predictive of the kind of attachment a mother may form for the infant. He suggests that there is a kind of "imprinting" of responses from her which may be triggered by the neonate's behavior. Moss (1975) and Goldberg (1975) point to the triggerlike value of the newborn's small size, helpless appearance, and distress cries in setting off mothering activities. Klaus and Kennell (1970) have described the kinds of initial contacts which mothers make with their newborn infants and the distortions in this behavior when the mother is depressed by abnormalities in the baby, e.g., prematurity, illness in the neonatal period, etc. Eye-to-eye contact, touching, handling, and nursing behavior on the part of the mother may be assessed and judged for predicting her ability to relate to the new baby. Change in these behaviors over time is stressed as indicators of recovery or nonrecovery of maternal capacity to attach to the baby by mothers who have been depressed and unable to function optimally by having produced an infant at risk.

The ability of the baby to precipitate and encourage the mother's attachment and caretaking behavior must be taken into account. With an unresponsive neonate, the feedback mechanisms necessary to fuel mothering behavior are severely impaired. In a series of medicated newborns of normal mother-infant pairs, the effect on neonatal sucking, coupled with the physiological effect of the medication on her milk production, delayed recovery of weight gain by 36–48 hours in a normal group (Brazelton, 1970). Since this is an observation at a rather gross level, interference in the interaction "dyssynchrony" of more subtle "lack of fit" in the earliest mother-infant attachment interaction can be carefully watched for and observed over time. The opportunity for observing the pair together is never again as available, and surely we are missing valuable predictive information when we do not make regular, repeated observations of interactive situations, such as feeding periods, "play" periods after feeding, bathing, etc.

In the normally competent dyad there are preadapted complementary behaviors which guarantee a high level of mutually produced contingency experience (Goldberg, 1975). A competent infant is one who roots and sucks efficiently, alerts to stimulation selectively, modulates states of arousal, cries loudly when uncomfortable, and quiets when he is comforted. Lorenz (1943) pointed out that certain features make up a "kewpie doll" face which elicits parenting responses—the short vertical axis and puffed cheeks of the face, the relatively large head-to-body size, the uncoordinated body movements, the soft fuzzy skin and hair. The fact that the infant prefers and quiets down to human stimuli such as the voice and face is crucial to maternal attachment. Although Klaus and Kennell (1970) speak of a "critical" neonatal period for maternal attachment, there seems to be more leeway in most human relationships for attachment to develop.

In stressed neonates, the responsive behavior which normally provides feedback to the mother may not be present or satisfying, and the relationship may flounder. If the eliciting stimuli the normal baby presents to caregivers are not forthcoming or are distorted, parental behavior in turn becomes distorted. Prechtl and Beintema (1964) report the high incidence of brain-damaged infants who appear normal externally but elicit anger and rejection from their parents even before an official diagnosis of damage has been made. Klein and Stern (1971) report an unexpectedly large number of battered children from a premature population. Klaus and Kennell (1970) attribute this in part to the effects on the parents of early separation from their prematures. We would add the effects of maternal depression after the delivery of a sick neonate. And the syndrome of failure to thrive seems to be a sequel to many infants who are small for gestational age at birth. Many SGA infants are given up for adoption later on (Miller and Hassanein, 1973).

We have found that premature and SGA babies are poorer in interactive behaviors, in alerting responses, in selecting for the female voice and for the human face in auditory and visual responses, in state modulation, and in producing satisfactory motor behavior. Throughout the first year of life these SGA babies evidence a high incidence of hyperactivity, temperamental behavior, and organizational instability. These difficulties are bound to result in parental frustration.

It is thus apparent that in addition to the physiological and neurological problems at-risk newborns have to cope with, they generate, by their distorted behavior, deficient parenting patterns which in turn exacerbate an already compromised start on life. The interactive, cyclical nature of this process cannot be overstressed and must be taken into account whenever one deals with other than healthy normal newborns (Als, Tronick, Adamson, and Brazelton, 1976).

By contrast, the normal newborn offers qualities to his caregiver which enhance the likelihood for positive interaction—predictability, readability of cues and responses, and responsiveness contingent with behavior from the adult. Osofsky and Danzger (1974) present recent data which demonstrate the high consistency of maternal stimulation and infant behavior in corresponding areas. For example, an attentive mother tends to have a responsive infant and vice versa. Moreover, there is a predictable consistency between a baby's behavior with his mother and that during a neonatal behavioral assessment with an examiner.

We have seen that the infant in the first few weeks requires that the mother adapt her behavior to a cyclic attentional cycle which comes from the infant and which is dependent on the homeostatic requirements of the infant's immature physiological systems. When an infant attends to and becomes intensely involved with a familiar adult, he manifests a cyclical pattern of attention—withdrawal and recovery resembling a homeostatic curve—at a rate of 4 cycles per minute in a period of intense interaction (Brazelton, Koslowski, and Main, 1974). Parents who are sensitive to their baby's needs reflect this self-regulatory mechanism and regulates their affective and cognitive information to the infant's requirements. An insensitive parent overloads the neonate, and their interaction becomes stressed.

In an optimal interaction, the reciprocity which is established on these cycles of attention and recovery became the base for affective development, and fuel for learning about his environment. This interdependency of rhythms seems to be at the root of their attachment, as well as of their communication (Chapple, 1970; Brazelton, Koslowski, and Main, 1974). From this interdependency the infant learns rules about his environment and about himself. Thus, the quality of the interaction becomes more important in assessing an at-risk pair than does an evaluation of either participant alone.

Our own model of infant behavior and early infant learning goes like this: The infant is equipped with reflex behavioral responses which are in rather primitive patterns. He organizes them into more complex patterns of behavior which serve his goals for organization at a time when he is still prone to a costly disorganization of neuromotor and physiological systems, and then for attention to and interaction with his world (Als, 1979). In these ways he is set up to learn about himself, for as he achieves each of these goals his feedback systems say to him,

"You've done it again! Now go on." In this way, each time he achieves a state of homeostatic control he is fueled to go on to the next stage of disruption and reconstitution—a familiar model for energizing a developing system. We use White's "sense of competence" (1959) as our idea for fueling the system from within. We also feel that the infant's quest for social stimuli is in response to his need for fueling from without. As he achieves a homeostatic state, and as he reaches out for a disruptive stimulus, the reward for each of these states of homeostasis and disruption is reinforced by social or external cues. Hence, he starts out with the behaviorally identifiable mechanisms of a bimodal fueling system: (1) a state of homeostasis and a sense of achievement from within, and (2) the energy or drive to reach out for and incorporate cues and reinforcing signals from the world around him, fueling him from without. He is set up with behavioral pathways for providing both of these for himself—for adaptation to his new world, even in the neonatal period. Since very little fueling from within or without may be necessary to "set" these patterns and press him onward, they are quickly organized and reproduced over and over until they are efficient, incorporated, and available as a basis for building later patterns. Greenacre's concept (1959) of early pathways for handling the stress and trauma of birth and delivery as precursors for stress patterns later on fits such a model. It is as if patterns or pathways which work are "greased up" for more efficient use under stress later on. Our own concept is that others are available as well, but these are just readied by successful experience.

With this model of available behavioral response systems and their provision for an increased openness to the outside world, one can then incorporate Sander's ideas of early entrainment of biobehavioral rhythms (1977), Condon and Sander's ideas of the infant's movements matching the rhythms of the adult's voice (1974), Meltzoff and Moore's work on imitation of tongue protrusion in a 3-week-old (1977), and Bower's ideas of early reach behavior to an attractive object in the first weeks of life (1966). As each of these models of responsive behavior to external stimuli fuels a feedback system within the baby toward a realization that he's "done it," i.e., controlled himself in order to reach out for and respond appropriately to an external stimulus or toward a whole adult behavioral set, he is energized in such a powerful way that one can easily see the basis for his entrainment. The matching of his responses to those in the external world must feel so rewarding that he quickly becomes available to whole sequential trains of behavioral displays in his environment and begins to entrain with them, and he becomes energized to work toward inner controls and toward states of attention which maintain his availability to these external sequences. In this way, "entrainment" becomes a larger feedback system which adds a regulating and encompassing dimension to the two feedback systems of internalized control and externalized stimulus-response. Hence, entrainment becomes an envelope within which he can test out and learn about both of his fueling systems. Thus, he can learn most about himself by making himself available to entrainment by the world around him. This explains the observable drive on the part of the neonate to capture and interact with an adult, as well as his "need" for social interaction. Figure 3 is a schematic presentation of this mutual fueling process (Als and Brazelton, 1978).

But the infant is not alone in this process of learning about himself in the first few weeks and months. Because of the available energy, disrupted from old pathways in pregnancy—anxiety, if you will—the new parents are just as raw and ready for learning about themselves as is the neonate. Just as they learn about each new stage in their development and find a control system as well as the excitement of being fueled by the adjustment to the baby, the father and mother are forced to learn about themselves. As each new stage in the infant's development presses them to adjust, they learn about the excitement *and the pain* of disruption and the gratification of homeostasis as they hit a plateau. In this way we see mothers and fathers learning as much about themselves as developing people as they do about the new baby. And in this way come both the fueling for nurturance and the fuel for learning about each new stage in the baby's development. Otherwise, nurturing a new infant would be too costly and too painful. In a reciprocal feedback system, the rewards are built in for the parents as well as for the infant.

As Figures 4, 5, 6, and 7 show, we have adapted some of

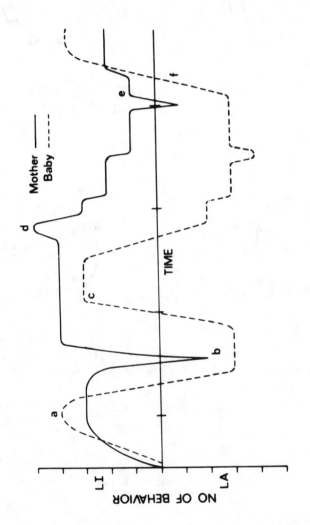

FIGURE 3. Representation of mother–baby mutual feedback interaction.

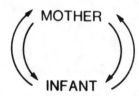

FIGURE 4. Dyadic system in homeostasis.

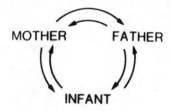

FIGURE 5. Triadic system in homeostasis.

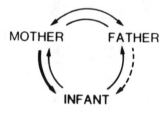

FIGURE 6. Coping system (father not well attached).

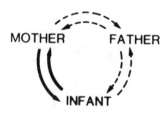

FIGURE 7. Coping system (father absent or out of contact).

the concepts of a cybernetic feedback system to our conceptual base (Tronick, Als, and Brazelton, 1977). This system allows for the feedback rewards of achieving homeostasis as well as the importance of forces for disruption and the subsequent learning to reorganize after each disruption. Thus, it represents a fueling model which fits Erikson's ideas of states of development (1968), McGraw's ideas of spurts in development with periods of regression for reorganization and digestion of newly achieved skills (1945), and Piaget's concepts of assimilation and accommodation (1953).

The provision of organization which takes place in continuous adaptation in response to feedback from the environment potentiates the newborn's increasing differentiation. This differentiation comes from an internalized recognition of his capacity to reach out for and to shut off social stimuli. This in turn results in growing complexity of the interactional channels and structures, thus increasing the opportunities for the individual system's differentiation. Given such a flexible system, his individuality is continuously fitted to and shaped by that of the adult. Our model is that of a feedback system of increasing expansion and potentiation of the developing organism embedded in and catalyzed by the interaction with his parents. (Als and Brazelton, 1978; Als, 1979; Als, Tronick, and Brazelton, 1981; Als, Lester, Tronick, and Brazelton, 1982).

Figure 8 is a schematic presentation of the infant's development within his feedback system (Als and Brazelton, 1978). The first item on a newborn's agenda is control over the physiological system, particularly breathing, heart rate, and temperature control. For preterm and at-risk newborns, this control is more difficult to achieve than it is for healthy full-term newborns. While control over these basic physiological demands is being achieved, the newborn begins to establish organization and differentiation of the motor system, affecting the range, smoothness, and complexity of movement. The next major agendum is achieving a stable organization of his states of consciousness. The goal of this differentiation is to have all six states, from deep sleep to intense crying, available to the infant and to have transitions between states carried out more smoothly. Achieving control over transitions between states de-

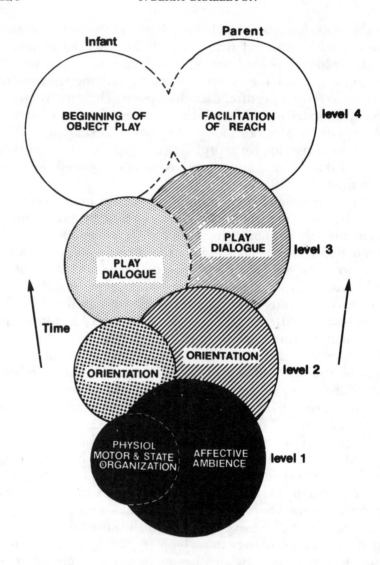

FIGURE 8. Stages of organization of parent-infant interaction.

mands an integration of the control over the physiological and motoric systems and the states of consciousness. The adult caretaker can play the role of organizer and can begin to expand certain states (e.g., the quiet alert state), as well as the duration and quality of sleep states. In addition, the caregiver can help regulate the transitions between states for the infant.

As the state organization becomes differentiated and begins to be regulated, usually in the course of the first month, the next expansion newly emergent, is that of the increasing differentiation of the alert state. The infant's social capacities begin to unfold. His ability to communicate becomes increasingly sophisticated. The repertoire of his facial expressions and their use, as well as the range and use of vocalizations, cries, gestures, and postures in interaction with a social partner, begins to expand. On the basis of well-modulated state organization he can negotiate his new range and regulation of social interaction skills. Figure 9 shows a schematic presentation of parent and infant's mutual feedback system.

We do see these stages as evidence for the first stages of emotional and cognitive awareness in the infant and in the nurturing "other." A baby is learning about himself, developing an ego base. The mother and father who are attached to and intimately involved with this infant are both consciously and unconsciously aware of parallel stages of their own development as nurturers. We, as professionals interested in fostering this early development, must begin to look for these ingredients in the first few months and to recognize the power of real reciprocity as we set up an intervention. I feel we have been stuck for too long in a nonreciprocal "therapeutic" model of judgments, or criticism, of looking for pathology and ignoring strengths in a mother-father-infant triad. If we can visualize the interaction as flexible and our role as supportive to the envelope or within it, perhaps we can begin to utilize the available energy and strengths at a time when we can help the dyad or triad right the interaction. With this model of looking for and expecting recovery, we feel we can more often create a self-fulfilling prophecy, or Rosenthal effect (1966), whereby mother-infant and father-infant pairs are supported toward a rewarding and internalized system assuring success.

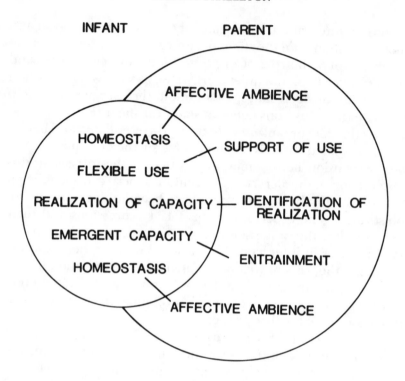

FIGURE 9. Process of interactive negotiation bringing about each stage of organization.

References

Als, H. (1979), Assessing an assessment: Conceptual considerations, methodological issues and a perspective on the future of the Brazelton neonatal behavioral assessment scale (BNSBAS) In: *Organization and Stability of Newborn Behavior: A Commentary on the Brazelton Neonatal Behavioral Assessment Scale*, ed. A. Sameroff. Monograph of the Society for Research in Child Development. Chicago: University of Chicago Press, pp. 1–10.

———— & Brazelton, T.B. (1978), Stages of early infant organization accomplished in the interaction with the caregiver: The study of a multiply handicapped infant and his mother. Paper presented at the meeting of the American Cleft Palate Association, Atlanta, April.

———— Lester, B.M., Tronick, E., & Brazelton, T.B. (1982), Manual for the assessment of the preterm infant behavior (APIB). In: *Theory and Research in Behavioral Pediatrics*, Vol. 1, ed. H.E. Fitzgerald, B.M. Lester, & M.W. Yogman. New York: Plenum.

———— Tronick, E., Adamson, L., and Brazelton, T.B. (1976), The behavior of the full-term but underweight newborn infant. *Developmental Med. & Child Neurol.* 18:590–602.

———— ———— & Brazelton, T.B. (1981), Affective reciprocity and the development of autonomy: The study of a blind infant. *J. Amer. Acad. Child Psychiat.*, 16:194–207.

Anders, T.B., & Roffwarg, H. (1973), The effects of selective interruption and total sleep deprivation in the human newborn. *Developmental Psychobiol.*, 6:79–83.

André-Thomas, A., & Ajuriaguerra, J. (1949), Etude Semiologique du Tonus Musculaire (The semiological study of muscle tone). Paris: Medicales Flammarion.

Aserinsky, E., & Kleitman, N. (1955), A motility cycle in sleeping infants as manifested by ocular and gross motor activity. *J. Applied Psychol.*, 8:11–18.

Bower, T.B. (1966), Visual world of infants. *Scientific American*, 215:80–82.

Bowlby, J. (1969), *Attachment and Loss: Vol. I. Attachment.* New York: Basic Books.

Brazelton, T.B. (1961), Psychophysiologic reaction in the neonate, II. *J. Pediatrics*, 58:513–518.

———— (1962), Observations of the neonate. *J. Acad. Child Psychiat.*, 1:38–52.

———— (1970), Effect of prenatal drugs on the behavior of the neonate. *Amer. J. Psychiat.*, 136:95.

———— (1984), *Neonatal Behavioral Assessment.* National Spastic Society Monographs, Clinics in Developmental Medicine #83. London: Heinemann, pp. 1–123.

———— Koslowski, B., & Main, M. (1974), Origins of reciprocity. In: *Mother Infant Interaction*, ed. M. Lewis & L. Rosenblum. New York: Wiley.

———— Tronick, E., Lechtig, A., Lasky, R.E., & Klein, R.E. (1977), The behavior of nutritionally deprived Guatemalan infants. *Developmental Med. Child. Neurol.*, 19:364–367.

———— ———— & Koslowski, B. (1976), Neonatal behavior among urban Zambians and Americans. *J. Acad. Child Psychol.*, 15:97.

———— Young, G.G., & Bullowa, M. (1971), Inception and resolution of early developmental pathology: A case history. *J. Acad. Child Psychiat.*, 10:124–130.

Chapple, E. (1970), Experimental production of transients in human interactions. *Nature*, 226:630–634.

Chavez, A., Martinez, C., Cravioto, J., & Yashine, T. (1975), Nutrition, behavioral development and mother-child relations in young rural children. *Federation Proceedings*, 34:1574–1580.

Condon, W.S., & Sander, L.W. (1974), Neonate movement is synchronized with adult speech: Interactional participation and language acquisition. *Science.* 183:99–101.

Drillien, C.M. (1972), Aetiology and outcome in low birthweight infants. *Developmental Med. & Child Neurol.*, 14:563–567.

Eisenberg, R. (1969), Auditory behavior in the human neonate: Functional properties of sound and their ontogenic implications. *Internat. Audiol.*, 8:34–42.

Erikson, E. (1968), *Identity: Youth and Crisis.* New York: Norton.

Fantz, R.L. (1965), Visual perception from birth as shown by pattern selectivity. *Ann. N. Y. Acad. Sci.*, 118:793–796.

Goldberg, S. (1975), Competence reconsidered: A model of parent-infant interaction. Personal communication, Brandeis University, Waltham, Mass.

Goren, C. (1975), Form perception, innate form preferences and visually-mediated head-turning in the human neonate. Paper presented at the meeting of the Society for Research in Child Development, Denver, Colo.

Greenacre, P. (1959), On focal symbiosis. In: *Dynamic Psychopathology in Childhood*, ed. L. Jessner & E. Pavenstedt. New York: Grune & Stratton.

Greenberg, N.H. (1971), A comparison of infant-mother interactional behavior in infants with atypical behavior and normal infants. In: *Exceptional Infant*, ed. J. Hellmuth. Vol. 2. New York: Brunner/Mazel.

Heider, G.M. (1966), Vulnerability in infants and young children. *Genetic Psychology Monograph, 73.*

Kittner, S., & Lipsitt, L. (1976), Obstetric history and the heart-rate response of newborns to sound. *Developmental Med. & Child Neurol.*, 18:460–470.

Klaus, M.H., & Kennell, J.H. (1970), Mothers separated from their newborn infants. *Pediat. Clin. N. Amer.*, 17:1015–1025.

Klein, M., & Stern, L. (1971), Low birthweight and the battered child syndrome. *Amer. J. Disabled Children*, 122:15.

Korner, A.F., & Thoman, E.B. (1970), Visual alertness in neonates as evoked by maternal care. *J. Experimental Child Psychol.*, 10:67–71.

Kron, R. (1966), Newborn sucking behavior affected by obstetric sedation, *Pediatrics*, 37:1012.

Lorenz, K.Z. (1943), Die angeborenen Formen möglicher Erfahrungen (The inborn forms of possible experiences). *Zeitschrift der Tierpsychologie*, 5:235–409.

McGraw, M.B. (1945), *The Neuromusculature Maturation of the Human Infant.* New York: Hafner.

Meltzoff, A.N., & Moore, M.K. (1977), Imitation of facial and manual gestures by human neonates. *Science*, 198:75–78.

Miller, H.C., & Hassanein, K. (1971), Diagnosis of impaired fetal growth in newborn infants. *Pediatrics*, 48:4–10.

———— ———— (1973), Fetal malnutrition—white newborn infants: Maternal factors. *Pediatrics*, 52:4–12.

Moss, H.A. (1975), Methodological issues in studying mother-infant interaction. *Amer. J. Orthopsychiat.*, 35:42–48.

Moya, R., & Thorndike, V. (1962), Passage of drugs across the placenta. *Amer. J. Obstet. & Gynecol.*, 84:1778–1780.

Osofsky, J., & Danzger, B. (1974), Relationships between neonatal characteristics and mother-infant interaction. *Developmental Psychol.*, 16:124–142.

Parker, W.B., Als, H., & Brazelton, T.B. (1978), Neonatal behavior and the attachment process between a mother and her infant. (Unpublished data.)

Parmelee, A.H. (1970), Neurological evaluation of the premature infant. *Biologique Neonatal*, 15:65–84.

Peiper, A. (1963), *Cerebral Function in Infancy and Childhood*. Monograph, Consultants Bureau. B. Naglei & H. Naglei.

Piaget, J. (1953), *The Origins of Intelligence in the Child*. London: Routledge.

Prechtl, H.F.R. (1965), Prognostic value of neurological signs and the newborn infant. *Procedures of Research in Social Medicine*, 58:35–48.

———— & Beintema, O. (1964), *The Neurological Examination of the Full Term Newborn Infant*. London: Heinemann.

Rosenthal, R. (1966), *Experimenter Effects in Behavioral Research*. New York: Appleton-Century-Crofts.

Rottinger, D., & Simmons, J.E., (1954), Behavior of human neonates and prenatal maternal anxiety. *Psychol. Report*, 14:391–398.

Sander, L.W. (1977), The regulation of exchange in the infant-caregiver system and some aspects of the context-contest relationship. In: *Interaction, Conversation, and the Development of Language*, ed. M. Lewis & L. Rosenblum. New York: Wiley, pp. 102–110.

Sontag, L.W. (1944), War and fetal maternal relationship. *Marriage & Family Living*, 6:1.

Stechler, G., & Latz, E. (1966), Some observations on attention and arousal in the human infant. *J. Acad. Child Psychol.*, 5:517–528.

Tronick, E., Als, H., & Brazelton, T.B. (1977), Mutuality in mother infant interaction. *J. Communication*, 27:14–26.

White, R.W. (1959), Motivation reconsidered: The concept of competence. *Psychol. Rev.*, 66:297–333.

Winick, M. (1973), Effects of prenatal nutrition upon pregnancy risk. *Clin. Obstet. & Gynecol.*, 16:1.

Wolff, P. (1966), The causes, controls, and organization of behavior in the neonate. *Psychological Issues*, Monograph 17. New York: International Universities Press.

———— (1969), The natural history of crying and other vocalizations in early infancy. In: *Determinants of Infant Behavior, IV*, ed. B.W. Foss. London: Methuen.

12

The Functioning Fetus

PIRKKO L. GRAVES, MAG. PHIL., PH.D.

What, in the course of development, marks the starting point of human experience? Is it found in the infant's first smile directed at the mother? Or in the first gasps for breath at birth, culminating in the dramatic first cry? Or, earlier still, in the parasitic-like existence in the womb where, perhaps not so parasitically, the developing human acts and reacts in ways akin to "human experience"?

Interest in expanding the understanding of human experience before birth has a long history in psychoanalytic literature. Several writers influenced by Rank (1929) have described the event of birth as a catastrophic psychological trauma which forms the prototype for subsequent psychic traumas and incapacitating anxieties. Moreover, birth is said to demarcate an abrupt end to the blissful intrauterine existence characterized by a special "oneness" between fetus and mother. A nostalgic, lingering desire for the return to this intrauterine state of bliss would serve as evidence for the existence of such a state. But it is also postulated, by Klein in particular (1975), that unpleasant experiences of the fetal life foreshadow and pave the way for later "bad" experiences during and after birth. Other sources of evidence for prenatal mental experience, both "good" and "bad," are recurring themes in patients' free associations and dreams (Sadger, 1941; Hall, 1967; Ployé, 1973), including their descriptions in regressed hypnotic states during hypnoanalysis (Kelsey, 1953), or recurring and universal themes in folklore (Darlington, 1945; Menninger, 1953). The reconstructed or recalled prenatal experiences, however, are hardly more than symbolic in nature. Studies on neonatal and infant development, for example, when juxtaposed with psychoanalytic theories of development—based largely on reconstructive methods—have highlighted the need to clarify and explicate several theoretical and clinical assumptions (Lichtenberg, 1983). In the same way, emerging knowledge of fetal development should expose aspects of psychoanalytic notions of prenatal development that are in need of revision and further clarification.

While the reconstructive reports are inconclusive, they are important in signaling a neglected area of human experience. As with the neonatal phase (Spitz, Emde, and Metcalf, 1970), their psychic content may not be existent in the fetal phase. But explorations of fetal development would help delineate the prenatal precedents of psychological functions necessary for psychic life. Such explorations could well expand the conceptual network provided in particular by psychoanalytic ego psychologists. Thus Hartmann (1950, 1958) introduced the notion that the ego, "a cohesive organization of mental processes" (Freud 1923, p. 15), has developmental roots other than conflict alone. One of these roots is found in the inborn apparatuses of the newborn infant, which have a partly independent, autonomous origin and are not entirely traceable to the impact of drives and environment (Hartmann, 1950, p. 12). Accordingly, several components of ego apparatuses—motility, perception, and protective and regulatory mechanisms among them—represent such autonomous factors in ego development (Hartmann, 1958, p. 49). Specifically, such apparatuses are not acquired but represent the constitutional roots of the ego, which develop as a result of maturation (1958, p. 103).

These formulations suggest two main lines of inquiry into fetal development. One is to establish a prenatal maturational timetable of the described functions. Such a normative approach would then lead to determining the nature and range of individual differences in the primary ego apparatuses. The importance of individual differences in later experience and personality formation hardly needs elaboration. As an example let us mention Hartmann's discussion (1950) on ways in which individual differences in the primary ego apparatuses may be linked to later choice of defense and, by implication, to choice of illness. Korner (1964) proposes several ways in which innate differences may actively mold the manner in which later developmental steps are experienced and mastered and contribute to the nature of environmental responses.

The second line of inquiry stems from Hartmann's suggestion of inborn regulatory and protective mechanisms (1958). Besides the need to establish the maturational steps of such mechanisms in the prenatal phase, these concepts raise the provocative question of adaptive processes in fetal life. Thus, processes akin to a "state of adaptiveness," maintained by primitive regulating and protective mechanisms before the intentional processes of adaptation (p. 49), may be suggested between the fetus and its environment. By implication, the fetus may appear functioning relatively independently, rather than leading a passively parasitic existence.

The two lines of inquiry receive added impetus from research done in academic psychology on neonatal development during the past decade. Current knowledge of the newborn infant has led to a reevaluation of its capabilities. This new appraisal suggests that the newborn's first encounter with the world is not, as William James (1890) supposed, "one great blooming, buzzing confusion" (p. 488). Instead the infant enters the world equipped with a readiness for differentiated responses and actions which are mutually organized in relatively complex patterns (for a detailed research review, see Haith and Campos, 1977). It would appear logical to extend studying the development of behavior from the neonate to the fetus as well.

Despite the demonstrated need for systematic knowledge of fetal functioning and development, comparatively little work has been done to promote such knowledge. This chapter aims at gathering together recent findings regarding human fetal development. Specifically, the functional development of the human fetus is explored without the inclusion of neuroanatomical, neurophysiological, or neurochemical correlates.[1] The emphasis on functional events is in accordance with current trends in behavioral embryology. Here, evidence across species dem-

---

[1] An informative description of structural maturation, i.e., neuroanatomical and neurophysiological development, may be found in Barcroft (1973).

onstrates that developing motor and sensory-perceptual systems are capable of functioning before they have completed
neural maturation. This evidence challenges the traditional
view of a unidirectional structure-function relationship in neurobehavioral development according to which "genes give rise
to neural maturation processes that form a structure, which
when fully mature, begins to function in a nonreciprocal way"
(Gottlieb, 1976, p. 218). Instead the evidence has led to a reformulation of the structure-function relationship, which is now
viewed as bidirectional: while genes give rise to structural maturation processes, these processes are susceptible to, even dependent on, the influence of function before complete maturation
is attained (Gottlieb, 1976).[2] As formulated by Gottlieb, function
is viewed in a broad context, including such aspects as the spontaneous or evoked electrical activity of the nerve cells, impulse
conduction, the use of muscles and sense organs, and the behavior of the organism.

The primary aim of this chapter is to review selected research findings on fetal motility and sensory receptivity as functional representatives of two inborn ego apparatuses (motility,
perception) and to highlight certain aspects of prenatal environmental influence. In this latter context, possible regulatory
mechanisms contributing to early adaptiveness are explored.
While the main emphasis is on normal human fetal development, findings from animal studies are included in instances
where relevant information on the human fetus is not available.

Fetal Motility

The first fetal movements are felt by the mother at approximately the sixteenth week of gestation. Initially experienced as quickening, that is, a barely noticeable fluttering
motion, the movements gradually become stronger and form
an important clinical sign of ongoing fetal life. But long before
the movements are experienced, the fetus has been active in

[2] A comparable bidirectional relationship is suggested between genes and
structural maturation as well (Gottlieb, 1976, p. 218).

the uterus. The early fetal motility and its development are discussed in research literature from two basic viewpoints: evoked activity and spontaneous activity. The sequential development of evoked activity helps us chart fetal reflex activity, while spontaneous activity highlights other aspects of behavioral organization.

Evoked Activity

Fetal evoked activity was the focus of intensive studies, especially in the 1930s and 1940s. The theoretical interest was to seek the genesis of human behavior in early exteroceptive responses found during the fetal life. The central question was whether the sequential development of behavior goes from undifferentiated total patterns to individual reflexes, or whether behavior is built up from simple reflexes that secondarily become integrated into larger patterns (Gottlieb, 1976). In this interdisciplinary field, two neurophysiologists, Hooker and Humphrey, have produced notable work on evoked human fetal behavior. They observed 149 human embryos and fetuses that were delivered under local or spinal anesthesia, separated from the placenta, and maintained in a heated water bath. Fetal responses to a light touch (using von Frey hairs) were recorded photographically and analyzed in both slow motion and normal speed. The following summary is based on the findings reported by Hooker (1952) and Humphrey (1969, 1970).[3]

The developing human is capable of reflex movements long before fetal movements are felt by the mother: the earliest evoked motility occurs already in the embryonic state, as early as 7.5 weeks of gestation. The early evoked motility is relatively undifferentiated; however, a sequential pattern can be discerned in the unfolding of the first "total pattern" response. The response starts with the bending of the head away from the stimulus, then spreads to include the hands: they move backward on the shoulder and uncover the mouth. Lastly, trunk and pelvic movements follow. The reaction is called total pattern response since a local stimulation evokes a global, undif-

---

[3] These reports also give a detailed account of the structural differentiation of the nervous system in the development of motility.

ferentiated response. Of interest is the fact that the embryo's first reflex reactions are contralateral, that is, moving away from the stimulus. Ipsilateral reactions moving toward the stimulus occur 2 to 3 weeks later. Since the contralateral avoiding reactions are also more frequent as well as more rapid than the ipsilateral approaching reactions, it appears that potentially protective mechanisms (in the form of withdrawal from the stimulus) are ontogenetically the primary and more effective responses in the approach-withdrawal paradigm.

Reflex activity becomes more differentiated and localized between 10 and 11 weeks of gestation and reaches its peak some 3 weeks later. This peak probably coincides with the height of midbrain regulation, just before higher brain areas start to suppress and regulate the midbrain centers. After about 14 weeks of gestation, reflex activity slows down, until toward the end of the second trimester of gestation a new peak of activity emerges, lasting into postnatal life. Of the numerous documented reflex responses, two are selected for detailed description: fetal hand movement to illustrate a specific sequential pattern, and oral activity because of its implications for the later oral phase.

Fetal hand movements. When the fetus is stimulated in the palm, a reflexive response is evoked as early as 10.5 weeks of gestation. First, the reflex consists of an incomplete finger closure without thumb movement. Also, the individual fingers differ in the amount of flexion. (For example, the index finger is least likely to show flexion.) By 14 weeks, distinct thumb action is included in the reflex, and by 18.5 weeks, thumb and fingers are coordinated into grasp. Grasp becomes increasingly strong, and at 27 weeks it is nearly sufficient to support the weight of the fetus for a brief time. The developmental sequence in hand-movement reflex merits special emphasis: it progresses from uniform finger closure to beginning thumb opposition and independent finger action, and finally shows the characteristic movements of grasp with the thumb lying inside and, by 23.5 weeks, outside the fingers. The same sequence characterizes the postnatal volitional development of grasp.

Fetal oral activity. Although mouth opening occurs as early as 8.5 weeks, the movement is first part of a contralateral total reflex. Stimulus-oriented mouth movements, including rapid snapping of the jaws, occur considerably later, by 11 weeks. At 15.5 weeks the fetus demonstrates a reflex sequence due to oral stimulation akin to the postnatal sucking reflex. When stimulated in the lips and the tongue, it opens the mouth, elevates the tongue to form a groove, and finally closes the lips tightly on the stimulator lifting the lower jaw. Whether actual sucking occurs in utero is still debatable. However, a fetus at 29 weeks ex utero has been noted to suck strongly enough for sucking to be audible. Since, from 18.5 weeks on, the fetus may enter its thumb into the mouth and thus demonstrate prenatal hand-mouth coordination, active sucking in utero is more than likely.

Swallowing becomes an integral part of oral reflex activity, starting as early as 12 weeks of gestation. Fetal swallowing of the amniotic fluid occurs in a phasic pattern and, in the third trimester, may reach the range of 15 to 40 ml per hour (Liley, 1972). Swallowing serves two important functions. First, it serves to regulate the level of amniotic fluid (Humphrey, 1970). Second, it serves an important nutritional function (Pitkin, 1979). Protein ingested in amniotic fluid is about 18 percent of the fetal protein requirements, and about 13 percent of the nitrogen requirement is provided for through the same mode of nutrition (Anon, 1976).

While the individuation of reflex responses appears quite advanced toward the end of fetal life, the actual reflex activity occurring in utero is not well known. The limited range of intrauterine stimulation necessarily limits the range and amount of reflex activity in utero. However, the uterus does not lack entirely in stimuli. The amniotic fluid itself forms one source, as demonstrated by the swallowing reflex. We may also agree with Humphrey (1970) that intraabdominal pressures, due to the mother's coughing, bending, and other motions, may be transmitted through the fluid as well as the uterine wall, affecting fetal reflex responsiveness. Further, the fetus itself may be a source of its own stimulation. With the development of the grasp reflex, it is not unlikely that accidental grasping of various body parts, including the umbilical cord, may occur. The hand-mouth reflex is another example of self-stimulatory activity. Thus, it appears plausible that a great deal of reflex activity may occur as part of normal fetal functioning, and—in accordance with Humphrey (1970)—this "practicing" serves a facilitating function for postnatal reflex readiness necessary for neonatal survival.

We may also consider some implications of fetal reflex activity for later psychological functioning. It may be suggested that the fetal receptivity to stimulation and the potentiality for establishing sensorimotor connections form a necessary anlage for the infant's sensorimotor development. The suggestion implies developmental continuity: reflexes present in the fetal existence and at birth form the building blocks of later sensorimotor intelligence. Such a continuity is also suggested by Flavell (1963), who proposes that "birth reflexes are truly the building blocks of the sensorimotor edifice; intelligence begins with them and is constituted as a function of their adaptation to the environment" (p. 89).

The oral area appears central in the development of reflex activity. It is demonstrably the area of primary sensitivity in that stimulation of the nose-mouth area elicits the first responses. The oral area is also involved in the later important reflex activity of swallowing and—through the hand-mouth reflex—of sucking. We may thus conclude that the fetal phase establishes the functional basis for the oral modality and zonality emerging during the oral phase of epigenetic ascendancy (Erikson, 1950).

Spontaneous Activity

Research interest in spontaneous, that is, nonreflexive motility is old. As early as the 1880s a German psychologist, Preyer (1882) proposed that autonomous motility occurs before reactivity to sensory stimulation. As new technical methods have become available, the proposition of motor primacy in fetal functioning has been amply tested and confirmed. The use of real-time ultrasound equipment as an apparently noninvasive and safe procedure (Scheidt, Stanley, and Bryla, 1978) has permitted detailed observations of fetal motility from early gestation on. The accumulated research may be conveniently grouped into two major categories: studies exploring spontaneous motor patterns in the normal fetus, and studies investigating organizational and integrative patterns in the activities of the fetus.

Motor patterns. The emergence of spontaneous fetal activity has been of special interest for a group of Dutch researchers from the University of Groningen (deVries, Visser, and Prechtl, 1982, 1985). Their reports provide data on fetal motility for the first half of gestation as the present techniques do not permit the visualization of an older fetus as completely as that of a younger fetus. Their findings indicate sixteen specific movement patterns that are clearly demonstrable in the developing fetus. The first identified patterns, between 7 and 8.5 weeks of gestation, are such single events as "just discernible movements"—slow, small shiftings of the fetal contour, lasting from half a second to 2 seconds and disappearing from the repertory of movements after 2 weeks—and "startles," initiated in the limbs and superimposed on, or followed by a general movement. "General movements," i.e., movements of the whole body without, however, any distinctive patterning or sequencing of the body parts, are definitely observed at 10 weeks; they last approximately 1–2 minutes, although bursts of over 4 minutes may occur.

Breathing is another prominent movement pattern, visible from 13 weeks on and frequently seen in combination with jaw opening or swallowing, as well as with general movements. Breathing in utero consists of "inspirations," i.e., fluent movements of the diaphragm spreading to movements of the thorax and abdomen. In contrast to the fluent movements of the diaphragm, connected with breathing, jerky contractions of the diaphragm occur as well, identified as hiccups. It appears that the young fetus has many hiccups: A high incidence of hiccups are observed from 10 weeks on. They frequently occur in bursts and are strong enough to dominate the total movement pattern. The longest continuous episode of hiccups lasted 6 minutes 16 seconds in a 17-week-old fetus!

Other specific patterns are isolated arm or leg movements, the former visible with increasing frequency from 8 weeks on, the latter, in contrast, less frequently and even decreasing after 15 weeks; hand-to-face contact, clearly visible from 12 weeks on; various head movements; stretches, and yawns.

The specific movement patterns are further combined into unique groupings. These groupings appear adaptive in nature in that the fetus employs specific sets of movements to change its position in the uterus. For example, a backward somersault is achieved by a complex general movement including alternating legs, which resembles neonatal stepping. Rotation around the longitudinal axis, on the other hand, is accomplished by leg movements combined with hip rotation, or by the rotation of the head followed by trunk rotation. Fetal positional changes increase in frequency from 10 weeks on, reach a climax at 13–15 weeks, and decrease afterward. It appears that the decrease is not related to a decrease in motor activity (as in several categories of motor activity, the rate increases with maturation) but rather is related to changes in the spatial conditions in the uterus. The increasingly crowded condition makes the positional changes more difficult to perform.

The Dutch researchers rank ordered the different motor patterns according to the patterns' first appearance and found that all fetuses followed a specific sequence or developmental profile. That is, the emergence of each specific motor pattern occurred in a predictable sequence in relation to the rest of the patterns. As mentioned, many motor patterns increased in incidence as the fetus grew older (breathing, head rotation, jaw opening, swallowing). Some patterns, in contrast, showed an initial increase until a plateau was reached and the incidence rate became stabilized (general movements, isolated arm movements), while other patterns, after an initial increase, decreased in their rate of occurrence as the fetus grew older (startles, hiccups, hand-to-face contact, retroflexion of the head). Over the total longitudinal period of observations, the fetus was found inactive only rarely: until 20 weeks of gestation the longest period of quiescence was only 2–6 minutes (median values). In fact, the researchers concluded, periods of fetal quiescence longer than about 13 minutes should alert the obstetrician to further evaluate the fetus's well-being.

Spontaneous motor patterns in the fetus illustrate richness and complexity. Of interest is the notion that there seems to be a specific timetable for each movement, regardless of the assessment method used. For example, the first reflex response, a contralateral flexion of the head, could be elicited in the aborted fetus at the same age (7.5 weeks of gestation) as the first spontaneous ("just discernible") movements were observed in the normal fetus using ultrasound techniques. As another example, swallowing was reported by Hooker (1952) to occur at 12 weeks, which coincides with the age of onset described by the Groningen group. Parallel timetables were further observed in retroflexion and rotation of the head, and in trunk and arm movements. This striking similarity of the findings from two different approaches suggests that reflexes do not occur ontogenetically earlier, as had previously been postulated. Instead, the parallel timetables indicate that there must be underlying generator processes for fetal motility, processes that with further study may be understood.

Another noteworthy aspect of spontaneous fetal motor patterns is their similarity with the postnatal movement patterns identified among neonates and young infants (Prechtl, 1985). With the exception of "just discernible movements," all motor patterns can be observed after birth. Although the fetal patterns naturally lack the intentionality and specificity of function which characterize them in postnatal life, their early existence demonstrates and confirms the primacy of the motor system in human development.

Organization of fetal activity: behavioral states. The Groningen group has demonstrated that as early as in the first 20 weeks of gestation patterns of motility become organized in temporal sequences. For example, body movements first appear irregularly; with increasing maturation, however, they start to occur in bursts of activity and gradually become organized into even longer epochs of fluctuating activity. Other areas of fetal functioning, breathing, heart rate, and eye movements in particular, demonstrate parallel organizational trends. The development of biorhythms in each of these four areas will be described briefly.

The Groningen group has followed the organization of fetal body movements from 8 weeks of gestation on, from scattered, irregular movements to longer periods of activity. By 20 weeks of gestation, these periods may last 1–2 minutes and are followed by periods of inactivity lasting up to 9 minutes. Observations from the latter part of gestation bring forth additional features (Patrick, Campbell, Carmichael, Natale, and

Richardson, 1982). Thus body movements tend to diminish between 20 and 40 weeks of gestation while periods of inactivity increase, in some instances up to one hour during the last 10 weeks of gestation. Body movements are more frequent during the night, perhaps suggestive of a circadian rhythm.

Fetal breathing is demonstrable from 13 weeks on. The incidence rate increases fivefold by 30 weeks and stabilizes at that rate for the rest of gestation (Patrick et al., 1982; deVries, Visser, and Prechtl, 1985). Breathing, too, demonstrates specific rhythmicity (Jansen and Chernick, 1983). Peak incidences in breathing occur in the early morning while the lowest incidences occur in the evening. This circadian rhythm is apparently not related to maternal sleep cycle; contradictory findings exploring other explanatory mechanisms (adrenocorticotropic hormone concentration, maternal plasma glucose concentration) render the cause of the diurnal rhythmicity in breathing unknown.

From early on, the fetal heart rate, like the other behavioral variables, shows periodic fluctuations. These fluctuations become signs of fetal cardiac rhythmicity, which is independent of such external factors as maternal exercise or smoking (Awoust and Levi, 1984). There is also evidence to suggest that fetal heart rate patterns are important precursors of neonatal sleep cycles. Hoppenbrouwers, Ugartechea, Combs, Hodgman, Harper and Sterman(1978) explored fetal and maternal heart rate periodicities during the last trimester of gestation and the first week of neonatal life. They found no correlation between fetal and maternal heart rate rhythms or between neonatal sleep state cycles and maternal measures of heart rate cycles or REM (rapid eye movement)/non-REM sleep states. However, the heart rate periodicities of individual fetuses were significantly correlated with their neonatal REM/non-REM sleep cycles.

With the advance in ultrasound methodology, the documentation of fetal eye movements has become possible. It is now known that eye movements appear at the age of 9–12 weeks of gestation (Prechtl and Nijhuis, 1983). Thus the oculomotor system is active for at least 5 months in utero, although it becomes functional only after birth. Like fetal breathing, this prenatal activity serves an important anticipatory function of postnatal behavioral activity. Birnholz (1981) described four levels of organization in eye movements, emerging in sequential order: single, transient, linear deviations (16–25 weeks); single but prolonged deviations (23–40 weeks); complex sequences of deviations including rotational movements but without periodicity (23–41 weeks); repetitive or nystagmoid deviations (33–41 weeks). As with other areas of functioning, eye movements do not occur all the time but in episodes separated by periods of quiescence. Prechtl and Nijhuis (1983) found that while episodes of eye movement activity were quite stable in duration, the periods of quiescence became longer with age and nearly doubled between 36 and 38 weeks of gestation.

The observation of periodic fluctuations in fetal cardiac rhythmicity paved the way to a special area of research in fetal functioning, namely, the identification of fetal behavioral states. In this burgeoning specialty, another group of Dutch researchers, those from the University of Nijmegen, is perhaps the most prominent. Nijhuis, Prechtl, Martin, and Bots (1982) chose to define a behavioral state based on three independent areas of fetal functioning ("state variables"): heart rate, eye movement, and gross body movement. Although fetal breathing was also recorded, it was not used as a behavioral state criterion. It is however, frequently included as a state variable in other studies. Careful observations suggest that while each of the variables shows cyclic arrangements at 36 weeks of gestation and even earlier, the cycles appear more or less independently of one another, and their simultaneous occurrence is first coincidental. Only when the state variables change at about the same time, and the emerging new state lasts for a certain minimum duration, is a "true" behavioral state identified. Such an identification is possible only from 38 weeks of gestation on. The Nijmegen group identified four discrete behavioral states in the fetus, from the quiescent State 1 (eye movements absent; only occasional brief body movements, mostly startles; stable heart rate with a small oscillation band width, showing isolated acceleration in relation to movement) to State 2 (continual eye movements; frequent and periodic body movements; heart rate with a wider oscillation band width than above and accelerating up to 10–20 beats per minute). In State 3 both gross and small body movements are absent, but eye movements are continually present; heart rate is stable but with a wider oscillation band width than in State 1. State 4, the most active state, is characterized by vigorous, continual activity including many trunk rotations, by continually present eye movements, and by an unstable heart rate with large and long-lasting accelerations, which frequently are fused into a sustained tachycardia. The states thus bear a close resemblance to neonatal states, which, as described by Prechtl (1974) range from a State 1 of quiet (non-REM) sleep, to State 2 with REM or paradoxic sleep, and to awake, alert States 3 to 5 with increasing degrees of arousal and somatic activity. The fetal states demonstrate specific developmental characteristics. Thus the fetus spends more time in States 1 and 4 the closer it is to the end of the fetal period; however, the mean duration of both states is about half of that found in the corresponding states in the newborn infant (Martin, 1981).

The synchronization of the separate activity patterns into behavioral states is perhaps the most intriguing and important area in the study of fetal functioning. The progressive integration and mutual organization of behavioral patterns strongly suggest a general and central controlling principle from very early stages of human life onward. Much remains to be understood about the fetal organizational processes—for example, about the developmental course of transitions (i.e., short epochs during which one state changes into the next) or about an accurate timetable for various synchronizations between the state variables (from coincidence to predictable mutuality). Nonetheless, the available knowledge of fetal behavioral states has important implications. Thus, clinically, it becomes clear that fetal health should no longer be described according to morphological growth criteria or observations of a single component (heart rate, eye movement). Instead, the assessment of fetal behavioral states over long periods of observation is necessary for an adequate appraisal of the fetal neurological condition (Martin, 1981; Awoust and Levi, 1984; Prechtl, 1985). Further, the notion that behavioral states have regulative properties over individual functions has significant research implications. Evidence from early stimulation studies with the newborn illustrates that the neonatal behavioral state needs to be taken into account before the response intensity to a partic- ular stimulus or the dominance of a particular stimulus modality can be adequately assessed (Prechtl and O'Brien, 1982). In a parallel fashion, fetal behavioral states need to be taken into consideration in fetal stimulation experiments. One study (Schmidt, Boos, Gnirs, Auer, and Schulze, 1985) on fetal re- sponses to auditory stimulation found significant differences in fetal response rate in different behavioral states. More fre- quent and consistent responses occurred during "awake" states (States 3 and 4) than in States 1 or 2. The possibility that si- multaneous monitoring of behavioral states is perhaps impor- tant in all studies of fetal life is suggested by a recent report on fetal cardiovascular performance. VanEyck, Wladimiroff, Noordam, Tonge, and Prechtl (1985) showed that blood flow changes in the fetal aorta were related to the behavioral states of the fetus.

In conclusion, fetal motility, whether evoked or sponta- neous, clearly has a manifold significance in prenatal devel- opment. Fetal movements frequently have an anticipatory function for postnatal life. Moreover, they reflect a need to practice and exercise. Such practice is considered a necessary prerequisite to normal functional development and morphol- ogical maturation (Dawes, 1973). There are also indications that fetal activity may predict postnatal functioning in other ways as well. The study by Hoppenbrouwers et al. (1978) on the links between fetal heart rate and the neonate's sleep cycle is one example. Another is a study by Richards and his colleagues (Richards and Newbery, 1938; Richards, Newbery, and Fall- gatter, 1938). They followed 12 fetuses postnatally and found a significant positive correlation between levels of fetal activity and performance at the age of 6 months in the Gesell infant test. Infants more active during their fetal development had higher test scores than those who were less active. The findings have not been duplicated elsewhere; however, they raise the intriguing suggestion that fetal activity scores indicate variability among fetuses which is reflected later in postnatal character- istics. One characteristic that appears most plausibly linked with fetal motility is the newborn infant's congenital activity as de- scribed by Fries and Woolf (1953). These authors' longitudinal studies demonstrate how congenital activity is an important factor in influencing the parent-child relationship, later ego structuring, and character formation. More recently, Weil (1978) has proposed similar formulations regarding the role of motility and its maturational variations on psychic structure formation and structural conflicts from the early years onward. An exploration of the prenatal roots of the newborn's motility and activity levels appears central in clarifying how these initial givens of ego development determine and interact with other ego potentials as well as with the environment in the formation of psychic structure.

Sensory Functioning

Neonatal studies indicate notably differentiated functioning of sensory receptiveness in newborns. Thus an infant 1 to 2 days old is visually able to fixate, scan, discriminate, and follow. He is able to respond discretely to complex auditory stimuli and to organize his auditory world (Eisenberg, 1976). Olfaction functions in a discriminating fashion and promotes differential rooting to the mother's breast, rather than to a strange woman's breast (Macfarlane, 1975). Such response readiness in the newborn suggests that sense receptors are already functional during the fetal life. Considerable experimental evidence confirms the suggestion. A survey of literature reveals, however, that the amount of information varies from one sensory modality to another. Predictably, most is known about fetal responsiveness to auditory stimuli, while olfactory functioning in the human fetus is thus far without documentation. The following is a brief description of human fetal capabilities in four major receptors: audition, vision, taste, and tactile functioning. Again, anatomical or physiological correlates of fetal sensory functioning are not included; the information may be found in the reviews by Carmichael (1970) and Bradley and Mistretta (1975).

Audition

By far the most extensive documentation is about fetal auditory functioning. Rich anecdotal information, summarized by Carmichael (1970), has been verified through experimentally controlled studies. Thus, it is known that cochlear function is demonstrable as early as the fifth fetal month and that the fetus in term has a medullated auditory cortex (Eisenberg, 1976). Functional responsiveness has been documented from the twenty-sixth week on. For example, Tanaka and Arayama (1969), using pure tones generated through the mother's abdominal wall, measured changes in fetal pulse rate and movements occurring during or immediately after the stimulation. No response was evoked on auditory stimulation of younger fetuses.

A review of available studies on human fetal auditory stimulation may be found in Eisenberg (1976). Typically, rates of fetal heart beat and movements are used as measures to record responses to precisely defined auditory stimuli. To eliminate the impact of the mother's reactivity to stimulus, pure tones or music presented to her through earphones, are often used to cover the fetal auditory stimulus. As Bradley and Mistretta (1975) point out, the fetus has no air in the mid-ear cavity. Therefore, stimulation of the fetal cochlea is by bone or perhaps by fluid conduction. Direct comparisons of fetal auditory sensitivity with the newborn's sensitivity may therefore not be possible.

Tactile Functioning

With the exception of auditory functioning, fetal sensory functions are rarely the primary target of investigation. Instead, the information comes as a byproduct and, perhaps for that reason, may not always have the reliability of rigorous experiments. Such is the case with fetal tactile function where studies specific to touch-receptor function do not exist. But interesting information may be extracted from the earlier cited studies by Hooker (1952) and Humphrey (1969, 1970), though their primary interest was on motor development. As noted, they used light tactile stimulation and found the earliest responsiveness to touch toward the end of the eighth week of fetal life. Humphrey further describes the sequential spreading of tactile sensitivity in the fetus. The first area showing sensitivity to touch is the upper or lower lip, from where it spreads soon to include the oral-facial area. The next areas to be included are the palms of the hands (10.5 weeks) and, by 11 weeks, the upper and lower extremities. Lastly, by 14 weeks, tactile sensitivity is demonstrable in the entire body surface.

As mentioned, Hooker and Humphrey studied fetuses whose umbilical circulation was interrupted after removal of the fetus from the amniotic sac. Such factors as progressive fetal asphyxia and increasing concentrations of metabolites may well confound the observations (Bradley and Mistretta, 1975). Also, in the simulated fetal environment such important factors as fluid composition and temperature need to be controlled before we have conclusive evidence on fetal tactile functioning.

Taste

Somewhat less inferential evidence is available about fetal taste function. Fetal swallowing of the amniotic fluid, which was mentioned before, provides a naturalistic condition for the existing studies. Specifically, rates of fetal consumption of the fluid were measured after the taste of the amniotic fluid was modified. For example, De Snoo (quoted in Bradley and Mistretta, 1975) injected saccharin into the amniotic fluid of pregnant women and found an increased consumption of the sweetened fluid by the fetus. In contrast, Liley (1972) reported a marked decrease in swallowing following the injection of a noxious tasting substance (an iodinated poppyseed oil). While the two studies were conducted with fetuses at least 34 weeks old, it is likely that taste receptors function much earlier, as taste buds are already developing between the sixteenth and twentieth weeks of fetal life (Bradley and Mistretta, 1975).

The findings on taste receptivity are particularly intriguing when considered together with the early tactile sensitivity of the oral area and the early oral reflex activity described above. They are suggestive of the ontogenetic dominance of the oral area and functioning in human development.

Vision

Despite the central importance of vision among sensory receptors, little is known about visual functioning in the human fetus. As described earlier, it is now known that the oculomotor system is active from 9–12 weeks of gestation on (Prechtl and Nijhuis, 1983) and that eye movements show increasing levels of organization (Birnholz, 1981). Detailed knowledge of the morphogenesis of the eye is also available and suggests that visual functional *readiness* may exist before birth. Premature infants from 29 weeks of age (Dreyfus-Brisac, 1968) demonstrate eye opening; thus, it is likely that the human fetus may be able to open and close its eyes from the same age onward. If so, Liley's notion of fetal receptivity to varying light intensities in the uterus (1972) becomes more plausible. According to him, "given a naked abdomen in sunshine," light intensities would be high enough to increase intrauterine illumination.

Fetal Environment as a Source of Sensory Stimuli

The review indicates that the fetus is capable of responding to sensory stimulation. But whether the sense organs actually function prenatally depends on the nature of stimuli available in the fetal environment. It appears that the uterus is an unexpectedly varied source of sensory stimuli.

In the early phases of pregnancy the fetus floats in a relative state of weightlessness: the ratio of amniotic fluid volume to fetal volume is about 4 or 5 to 1 (Wood, 1970). Toward the end of pregnancy, the ratio changes so that the volume levels are about equal. Also, a shift in the gravity level occurs, indicating greater levels of gravity for the human fetus than for the amniotic fluid. In contrast to its earlier weightless existence, the fetus now tends to sink to the bottom of the amniotic sac. The new position likely increases contact with the uterine wall, which would then increase the stimulation of touch receptors. It is also possible that changes in the maternal condition due to locomotive, cardiac, or respiratory changes will be communicated more clearly to the fetus.

These positional changes are accompanied by changes in the amount of amniotic fluid. Toward the end of term the human fetus may swallow as much as 210–760 ml daily of the fluid (Minei and Suzuki, 1976) and thus reduce its level. At the same time, the rate of urination is increased, contributing to the level and composition of the amniotic fluid. Minei and Suzuki state that the human fetus at 18 weeks of gestation pro-

duces from one to 17 ml of urine daily. At birth, the fetal
bladder may contain up to 44 ml of dilute urine (the average
being 5.7 ml). It has been suggested that the shifting ratios of
fluid and urine contribute to the stimulation of taste buds in
utero (Bradley and Mistretta, 1975).

The general belief that the uterus is a dark, quiet place is
challenged by Bench (1968) and by Liley (1972). Bench measured the acoustic energy that was transmitted to the fetal ear
through the amniotic fluid and found that the internal noise
generated within the mother was as high as 72 dB. The human
fetus appears to be exposed to such levels of internal auditory
stimulation at least during the last 4 months of intrauterine
existence. Liley, as mentioned earlier, suggests that as the abdominal wall becomes stretched toward the end of pregnancy,
it may allow light to filter through and so may intensify the
fetus's exposure to light.

To summarize, the survey of fetal receptor function leads
us to conclude that peripheral sensory systems are functional
in utero and that the intrauterine environment provides an
adequate source of stimulation for functional development.
Such a degree of sensory maturity raises the question of whether
the human fetus is capable of perceiving stimuli—an assumption inherent in the cited reconstructive studies on prenatal
experience. A conservative reply is negative: considering the
gross immaturity of the human cortex at birth, the fetal nervous
system may not yet respond in a manner comparable to the
situation after birth (Bradley and Mistretta, 1975). However,
the assumption of a bidirectional relationship between structure
and function (Gottlieb, 1976) wherein structural maturation
may be influenced by function (as well as determining it) leads
toward an affirmative reply, since the fetal cortex need not be
structurally fully mature before its functional maturity. Perhaps
a definitive answer will emerge when the receptor development
of the fetus is more fully explored and is linked with neonatal
sensory responses and perceptual development.

Prenatal Environment and Fetal Functioning

The pregnant woman's physical and psychological conditions have long been known to influence the developing fetus.

The various animal and human studies exploring prenatal conditions have been designed primarily to determine the vulnerability of the fetus to such influences. Thus deviations in the psychological and physical development of the newborn infant have been correlated with such macro-events as war, drought, or famine affecting whole populations, and to factors affecting the pregnant woman solely. As examples of the latter, specific viral diseases, drugs, or poor nutrition have been shown to interfere crucially with the infant's healthy development. More recently, the effects of smoking and alcohol on the infant's growth and development have received increased attention. In addition to specifying "toxic" influences, studies have endeavored to determine the mechanisms through which they influence prenatal development. The available literature is vast and will not be reviewed here. (An interested reader may find the books by Ferreira [1969], Joffe [1969], and Stevenson [1977] highly enlightening.) Instead, another prenatal factor, perhaps more elusive than those already mentioned will be discussed: maternal emotional stress.

The pioneering work by Sontag, who since the 1930s has studied fetal responsiveness and behavior, should be mentioned. He was among the first to study systematically the impact of severe maternal emotions on the fetus. During his long-term study on pregnant women (Sontag, 1965), eight mothers suffered a severe emotional trauma late in pregnancy (e.g., husband's serious illness or unexpected death). In all instances, fetal activity showed extreme increases in response to the sudden maternal trauma. Thus, fetal kicking was often described as violent to the point of being painful. Worth adding is that while the children, when born, showed no congenital defects, they were irritable, hyperactive, and showed a tendency to frequent stools or feeding problems.

Sontag and his colleagues (Sontag, Steele, and Lewis, 1969) further demonstrated that even benign pleasurable experiences of the mother altered fetal heart and motility rates. Mothers, reclining comfortably in a quiet room, listened to music they had selected according to their own preference. While maternal heart rate showed no changes in the situation, fetal heart rate first increased significantly, then gradually abated after about a minute. A recent report by Zimmer, Divon, Vilensky, Sarna, Peretz, and Paldi (1982) confirms Sontag's findings.

The possibility that maternal psychological stress may be life-threatening to the fetus has been dramatically demonstrated by Myers (1977). Using rhesus monkeys in the study, he was able to place catheters in both the maternal and the fetal femoral arteries to record blood pressure and heart rate, with additional catheters to record intrauterine pressure. After complete recovery from the operation, the monkey mothers were exposed to a series of stressful stimulation. Some of the stimulus events were quite mild (e.g., a brief incoming telephone call), while others were quite stressful (e.g., a simulated threatening attack by the examiner). In all the stimulus episodes, maternal psychological stress led to changes in both fetal vital signs and blood chemical findings. These alterations in fetal state regularly followed the onset of the episode by 50 seconds and usually remitted 50 seconds following termination of the episode. The most stressful episode of simulated attack upon the mother, which lasted about 2.5 minutes, produced profound changes in the fetal vital signs, so severe that in one instance the recovery of the fetus was in question. Myers concluded that maternal stress increased sympathetic nervous system activity, which in turn impaired the circulation of blood to the uterus, as the maternal blood flow from the abdominal viscera to other organs was stunted.

The cited studies are provocative and raise several questions, in particular about the effect of stress on fetal development. For example, both Sontag and Myers point out that even benign and mild alterations in maternal emotional condition bring forth reactive responsiveness in the fetus. Both authors indicate that in some instances maternal emotional state may change fetal stress into fetal distress, though little is known about the causal links. For example, Myers's study leads us to ask whether the particular nature of a single episode, or the cumulative effect of stressful events, or the preexisting asphyxic condition of the fetus, or all of these factors together contributed to the life-threatening fetal reactions. What becomes clear, however, is that fetal life is not a condition of "oceanic bliss," as suggested by some reconstructive psychoanalytic studies. Perhaps it is as it should be. From the viewpoint of survival, fetal exposure to, and tolerance of, stress may be necessary and an aid in preparing the fetus for the unavoidable stress of birth.

But it also appears that the fetus itself is capable of developing protective mechanisms to adjust to stressful situations imposed by the mother. Assali and Brinkman (1973) offer a model for such mechanisms occurring in fetal vascular structures. They studied changes in utero-placental blood flow and oxygen transfer between sheep mother and fetus during maternal hypotension. Regardless of the causes for blood pressure fall on the maternal side, the alteration led to a fall in fetal oxygen tension. This in turn triggered a chain reaction in various fetal vascular structures. These reactions seemingly acted as "circulatory buffering systems" that enabled the fetus to tolerate maternal stress.

The possibility of lasting consequences from fetal events and environment has already been mentioned. Sontag (1965) provides us some provocative findings suggesting links between fetal and adult patterns of reactivity. He was able to sample heart rates at the age of 20 years of the same individuals whose heart rates were measured at the eighth month of fetal life. Using the standard deviation as a measure of lability, he found a significant correlation between fetal and adult heartbeat variability. In other words, cardiac labiles during fetal life tended to be cardiac labiles in adult life as well. Further, the cardiac response pattern was related to a variety of personality correlates, the low reaction pattern being typical of persons showing much higher degrees of emotional and behavioral control in all situations.

The fact that fetal environment may mold patterns of reactivity in many subtle ways is well demonstrated by Smith and Steinschneider (1975). They selected a group of slow-heartbeat mothers and another group of rapid-heartbeat mothers during their third trimester of pregnancy. When the babies were born, the babies' responsiveness to simulated slow heartbeat (75 b.p.m.), to simulated rapid heartbeat (105 b.p.m.), and to a blank tape was explored. Also, ratings of the state of the baby during the experiments were collected. The findings showed that babies did not universally respond to the rhythmic beat

approximating their own mother's heartbeat, as suggested by
Salk (1962). Instead, the babies quieted to any rhythmic sound
(either of the beat tapes) more frequently than to no sound. In
addition, clear group differences emerged. Babies born to slow-
heartbeat mothers tended to fall asleep faster, sleep more, and
cry less than the babies born to rapid-heartbeat mothers. As
indicated by the investigators, our knowledge of the mediating
mechanisms between maternal and infant sensitivities is at this
point only speculative. Is neonatal behavior the result of a hyperactive fetal autonomous nervous system, as suggested by
Sontag? Or, as Smith and Steinschneider suggest, do prenatally
specified levels of stimulation determine the postnatal arousal
level? According to them, children of rapid-heart-rate mothers
become accustomed to greater levels of stimulation prenatally.
Postnatally, "In the absence of sufficient environmental input,
high-maternal-heart-rate children's arousal levels might rise in
order to meet their need for sensory stimulation, thereby diminishing their soothability" (p. 577).

   Though the mediating mechanisms between maternal and
infant reactivity are not yet known, it becomes clear that individual patterns of arousal and reactivity begin to be established
during prenatal development. A Japanese report (Audo and
Hattori, 1970) raises the provocative suggestion that these patterns may be molded at specific periods of prenatal life critical
for their establishment. Two groups of mothers were studied:
a group who lived near Osaka International Airport (perhaps
the noisiest airport in the world) during their entire pregnancy,
and a group who lived there for only the last 5 months of their
pregnancy. The infants of these mothers showed distinctly different patterns of arousal and reactivity during their first year
of life: Infants who had been exposed to the airport environment for all their fetal life slept more soundly, awakened less,
and cried less on exposure to the environmental noise.

   The presented evidence leads to the conclusion that the
interaction between organism and environment begins in the
prenatal phase, and, more important, that the effects of the
interaction are complex and prolonged. This interaction contains the beginnings of the process of adaptiveness whereby the
fetus is not only molded by the environment but also begins to

buffer and regulate its impact. Most of the early regulatory processes are seemingly biological and neurophysiological, suggesting that the adaptive roots of the first "average expectable environment" are somatic in nature. At the same time, primitive patterns of learning have been demonstrated. Classical conditioning (Ray, 1932; Spelt, 1948; Kolata, 1984) and habituation in the form of response inhibition to a repetitive stimulus (Leader, Baillie, Martin and Vermeulen, 1982) have been shown to occur during fetal life. These diverse processes suggest an inborn readiness for the fetus to monitor its environment and, preparatorily, a functional readiness to monitor the complex stimulus bombardment of the extrauterine world.

Discussion

The research material selected for description here is not exhaustive of fetal functioning. Another area of functioning (one of many) is fetal crying. It appears that the newborn's cry may be its "first" only in its postnatal life. Several clinical reports suggest that fetal crying may be a frequent event and has been shown to occur while the fetus is still in the amniotic sac (Carmichael, 1970). Other experiences of pain and pleasure may similarly be part of fetal life. For example, Humphrey (1970) described a sequence of facial expressions in a 23.5-week-old fetus, reminiscent of the infant's cry of pain, as illustrated by Finnish researchers (Wasz-Höckert, Lind, Vuorenkoski, Partanen, and Valanne, 1968). Thus far, the information on experiences of pain and pleasure is more anecdotal than systematic, prohibiting definitive statements. In particular, it would perhaps be a mistake to attribute psychological significance to fetal emotive expressions. Too little is known about the relationship between emotionally expressive movements possible at the subcortical level and the subjective emotional experience presumably requiring cortical integration.

This survey gives positive support to the initial lines of inquiry. We have seen that the fetus is capable of functioning, both acting and reacting, in a remarkably differentiated way. The functional propensities correspond to the areas postulated

as representative of autonomous ego apparatuses and may be
viewed as the prenatal roots of ego functions emerging later
under cortical domination. Moreover, fetal development, though
maturing according to a generalizable ground plan, is often
influenced by intrauterine environmental factors in a complex
and lasting fashion. This fetal experiential imprint molds later
development in ways that at the present time can only be sur-
mised. Available information suggests that later arousal levels,
indicating a range from hyper- to hyposensitivity, as well as
varying threshold levels, may well be molded during the prenatal experience.

But the conclusion that the roots of human experience are
to be found in prenatal life opens more questions than we are
able to answer today. One important question concerns the
organization of development from pre- to postnatal life. The
prevalent tendency to seek developmental continuities is supported in some areas of functional development. For example,
the reflex activity and spontaneous movements of the neonate
may be readily viewed as gradients of the fetal functional readiness. Such a gradient is explainable in the light of functional
facilitation. In other words, fetal motility may facilitate postnatal
motility and, through it, the later organization of behavior
(Weil, 1978). The facilitating role of fetal functional development may also explain some of the astonishing achievements
of the newborn, such as the capacity for rhythmic synchrony
between the newborn baby's movements and adult speech (Condon and Sander, 1974). Given the level of fetal auditory responsiveness and the repertoire of fetal movements, it is not
impossible that already in utero some synchronization may occur between the movements of the fetus and the intrauterine
sound variations.

But there are other functional organizations in which developmental continuities between pre- and postnatal behavior
are not immediately apparent. To illustrate, let us consider two
studies on notably complex neonatal behavior during the first
2 days of life. One of them (Fantz and Miranda, 1975) demonstrates the newborn infant's readiness not only to scan and
focus visually, but selectively to fixate on patterns with special
characteristics (curved rather than straight contours). The im-

plied degree of visual organization is impressive, especially when compared with fetal visual experience, presumably limited to differences in light intensity.

The second study describes the newborn infant's discriminatory use of olfaction. In an ingenious study, Macfarlane (1975) balanced the mother's breast pads, worn for 3–4 hours, and clean pads, moistened with sterile water for equal weight, on either side of the supine baby's face. The pad location and the baby's tendency to favor one lateral direction were controlled. The babies turned significantly more often to the mother's pad, even as early as the second day of life. Since presumably the fetus does not have olfactory responsiveness, the neonate's selective orientation on the basis of smell suggests not a gradient, but a complex, rapidly occurring sensory organization. In both studies the facilitating role of prenatal functioning is not apparent; instead, they beg for other explanatory concepts. One possible explanation may be found in the optimal arrangement of stimuli which would trigger an innate, although not functionally rehearsed response readiness.

Added challenge to the notion of developmental gradients comes from fetal reflex functioning. As we recall, the developmental steps of fetal grasp are repeated in the same sequence in postnatal life when the volitional grasp develops between 8 and 44 weeks. Such sequences suggest a cyclic process of development wherein skills develop and disappear, to reappear again, but perhaps in more complex levels of integration. This cyclic repetition of development, in contrast to a continuous incremental process, is not new in developmental psychology. Both Bower (1974) and Weil (1978) refer to similar developmental phenomena. Together with the two earlier studies, the finding suggests that a range of organizational trends should be explored between pre- and postnatal life. A challenging task would be to define additional trends and to evaluate their applicability in the organization of psychic phenomena. Such findings may well complement the prevailing trend to view psychic phenomena as occurring in an invariant and orderly unfolding.

Of interest is the finding that avoidance-inhibitory reactions ontogenetically precede the approach-appetitive reactions toward stimulus and surpass the latter in effectiveness. Hum-

phrey (1970) discussed the importance of the inhibitory activity
in the context of overall organization of behavior. Accordingly,
from the very early stages of life, the greater part of neural
activity is geared to suppress most of the potential overt action
so that specific, discrete, purposeful acts may take place (p. 39).
But we may also view the early avoidance reactions as neuro-
biological prototypes of later psychological stimulus barrier or
protective shield. So far, relatively little is known about fetal
protective mechanisms, serving as a "fetal protective shield."
Some research evidence has been cited (Ray, 1932; Spelt, 1948;
Audo and Hattori, 1970; Assali and Brinkman, 1973; Brazelton, chapter 11) suggesting the notion of the fetus as an independent, nonparasitic organism with its own protective
monitoring devices; these devices may be considered a fetal
stimulus barrier. Benjamin (1965), who postulated a "passive
neonatal stimulus barrier" in contrast to the "active stimulus
barrier" of an older infant or young child, cautioned against
the interpretation that the passive neonatal barrier represents
a genetic continuity to the later protective shield. It may well
turn out that fetal and neonatal protective barriers form such
a continuity, but fail to show a genetic correlation with later
psychological barriers. At this point, the issue stands as an appeal to further investigations.

The fetal readiness for stimulus avoidance, in contrast to
its stimulus-seeking readiness, is compatible with the basic psychoanalytic view of the essential noxiousness of stimulation.
"Protection against stimuli," wrote Freud (1920) "is an almost
more important function for the living organism than reception
of stimuli" (p. 27). However, to postulate fetal functioning, as
well as postnatal functioning, as striving to keep stimulation at
a minimum would not be keeping with the known facts. Much
of fetal activity is spontaneous by nature, and, as noted, one of
the functions of this spontaneous activity is to ensure practice
for the developing joints and musculature. The analog of this
function with the young infant's "instinct to mastery," as suggested by Hendrick (1942), is intriguing. If indeed the fetal
need to practice is viewed as a precursor of the young child's
need to function, we may conclude that ontogenetically it is as

old as the oral need, the precursor of which we may find in the early oral activity of the fetus.

In conclusion, this review reveals the fetus as a sentient, active organism capable of regulating and monitoring its environment. This picture of a "competent fetus" forcibly suggests that our search for the origins and early developmental phases of human mental life must begin with the fetus. The search, though barely begun, promises to be exciting and rewarding and may well fulfill the poet Coleridge's prophecy more than 150 years ago. ". . . Yes,—the history of a man for the nine months preceding his birth, would, probably, be far more interesting, and contain events of greater moment, than all the three-score and ten years that follow . . ." (1885, p. 301).

References

Anonymous (1976), Amniotic fluid protein: A nutritional function. *Nutrition Rev.*, 34:431–343.

Assali, N.S., & Brinkman, C.R. (1973), The role of circulatory buffers in fetal tolerance to stress. *Amer. J. Obstet. & Gynecol.*, 117:643–653.

Audo, Y., & Hattori, H. (1970), Effects of intense noise during fetal life upon postnatal adaptability. *J. Acoustical Soc. of Amer.*, 47:1128–1130.

Awoust, J., & Levi, S. (1984), New aspects of fetal dynamics with a special emphasis on eye movements. *Ultrasound in Med. & Biol.*, 10:107–116.

Barcroft, J. (1973), Foetal and neonatal physiology. In: *Proceedings of the Sir Joseph Barcroft Centenary Symposium*. London: Cambridge University Press.

Bench, R.J. (1968), Sound transmission to the human fetus through the maternal abdominal wall. *J. Genetic Psychol.*, 113:85–87.

Benjamin, J.D. (1965), Developmental biology and psychoanalysis. In: *Psychoanalysis and Current Biological Thought*, ed. N. Greenfield & W. Lewis. Madison: University of Wisconsin Press, pp. 57–80.

Birnholz, J.C. (1981), The development of human fetal eye movement patterns. *Science* 213:679–681.

Bower, T.G.R. (1974), Repetition in human behavior. *Merrill-Palmer Quart.*, 20:303–318.

Bradley, R.M., & Mistretta, C.M. (1975), Fetal sensory receptors. *Physiological Rev.*, 55:352–382.

Carmichael, C. (1970), The onset and early development of behavior. In: *Carmichael's Manual of Child Psychology*, ed. P.H. Mussen. Vol. 1. 3rd ed. New York: Wiley, pp. 447–563.

Coleridge, S.T. (1885), *Miscellanies, Aesthetic and Literary: To which is added The Theory of Life*, ed. T. Ashe. London: George Ball and Sons.

Condon, W.S., & Sander, L.W. (1974), Synchrony demonstrated between movements of the neonate and adult speech. *Child Development*, 45:456–462.

Darlington, H.S. (1945), The problem of prenatal mentation. *Psychoanal. Rev.*, 32:319–324.

Dawes, G.S. (1973), Revolutions and cyclical rhythms in prenatal life: Fetal respiratory movements rediscovered. *Pediatrics*, 51:965–971.

deVries, J.I.P., Visser, G.H.A., & Prechtl, H.F.R. (1982), The emergence of fetal behaviour: I. Qualitative aspects. *Early Human Development*, 7:301–322.

————— ————— ————— (1985), The emergence of fetal behaviour: II. Quantitative aspects. *Early Human Development*, 12:99–120.

Dreyfus-Brisac, C. (1968), Sleep ontogenesis in early human prematurity from 24 to 27 weeks of conceptional age. *Developmental Psychobiol.*, 1:162–169.

Eisenberg, R.B. (1976), *Auditory Competence in Early Life*. Baltimore: University Park Press.

Erikson, E.H. (1950), *Childhood and Society*. New York: Norton.

Fantz, R.L., & Miranda, S.B. (1975), Newborn infant attention to form of contour. *Child Development*, 46:224–228.

Ferreira, A.J. (1969), *Prenatal Environment*. Springfield, Ill.: Charles C Thomas.

Flavell, J.H. (1963), *The Developmental Psychology of Jean Piaget*. Princeton, N.J.: Van Nostrand.

Freud, S. (1920), Beyond the pleasure principle, *Standard Edition*, 18:3–64. London: Hogarth Press, 1955.

————— (1923), The ego and the id, *Standard Edition*, 19:3–63. London: Hogarth Press, 1961.

Fries, M.E., & Woolf, P.J. (1953), Some hypotheses on the role of the congenital activity type in personality development. *The Psychoanalytic Study of the Child*, 8:48–62. New York: International Universities Press.

Gottlieb, G. (1976), Conceptions of prenatal development: Behavioral embryology. *Psychological Rev.*, 83:215–234.

Haith, M.M. & Campos, J.J. (1977), Human infancy. *Ann. Rev. Psychol.*, 28:251–293.

Hall, C.S. (1967), Are prenatal and birth experiences represented in dreams? *Psychoanal. Rev.*, 54:157–174.

Hartmann, H. (1950), Psychoanalysis and developmental psychology. *The Psychoanalytic Study of the Child*, 5:7–17. New York: International Universities Press.

————— (1958), *Ego Psychology and the Problem of Adaptation*. New York: International Universities Press.

Hendrick, I. (1942), Instinct and the ego during infancy. *Psychoanal. Quart.*, 11:33–58.

Hooker, D. (1952), *Prenatal Origin of Behavior*. Lawrence: University of Kansas Press.

Hoppenbrouwers, T., Ugartechea, J.C., Combs, D., Hodgman, J.E., Harper, R.M., & Sterman, M.B. (1978), Studies of maternal-fetal interaction during the last trimester of pregnancy: Ontogenesis of the basic rest-activity cycle. *Experimental Neurol.*, 61:136–153.

Humphrey, T. (1969), Postnatal repetition of human prenatal activity sequences with some suggestions of their neuroanatomical basis. In: *Brain and Early Behavior: Development in the Fetus and Infant*, ed. R.J. Robinson. New York Academic Press, pp. 43–71.

————— (1970), The development of human fetal activity and its relation to postnatal behavior. In: *Advances in Child Development and Behavior: Vol. 2*, ed. H.W. Reese & L.P. Lipsitt. New York: Academic Press, pp. 1–57.

James, W. (1890), *The Principles of Psychology: Vol. 1*. New York: Holt.

Jansen, A.H., & Chernick, V. (1983), Development of respiratory control. *Physiological Rev.*, 63:437–483.

Joffe, J.M. (1969), *Prenatal Determinants of Behavior*. New York: Pergamon Press.

Kelsey, D.E.R. (1953), Phantasies of birth and prenatal experiences recovered from patients undergoing hypnoanalysis. *J. Mental Sci.*, 99:216–223.

Klein, M. (1975), *Envy and Gratitude and Other Works, 1946–1963*. New York: Delacorte Press.

Kolata, G. (1984), Studying learning in the womb. *Science*, 225:302–303.

Korner, A.F. (1964), Some hypotheses regarding the significance of individual differences at birth for later development. *The Psychoanalytic Study of the Child*, 19:58–72. New York: International Universities Press.

Leader, L.R., Baillie, P., Martin, B., & Vermeulen, E. (1982), The assessment and significance of habituation to a repeated stimulus by the human fetus. *Early Human Development*, 7:211–219.

Lichtenberg, J.D. (1983), *Psychoanalysis and Infant Research*. Hillsdale, N.J.: Analytic Press.

Liley, A.W. (1972), The foetus as a personality. *Austral. & N. Zeal. J. Psychiat.*, 6:99–105.

Macfarlane, A. (1975), Olfaction in the development of social preferences in the human neonate. In: *Parent-Infant Interaction*. CIBA Foundation Symposium 33. Amsterdam: Elsevier, pp. 103–117.

Martin, Jr., C.B. (1981), Behavioural states in the human fetus. *J. Reproductive Med.*, 26:425–432.

Menninger, K.A. (1953), An anthropological note on the theory of prenatal instinctual conflict. *Internat. J. Psycho-Anal.*, 20:439–442.

Minei, L.J., & Suzuki, K. (1976), Role of fetal deglutition and micturition in the production and turnover of amniotic fluid in the monkey. *Obstet. & Gynecol.*, 48:177–181.

Myers, R.E. (1977), Production of fetal asphyxia by maternal psychological stress. *Pavlovian J. Biol. Sci.*, 12:51–62.

Nijhuis, J.G., Prechtl, H.F.R., Martin, C.B., & Bots, R.S.G.M. (1982), Are there behavioural states in the human fetus? *Early Human Development*, 6:177–195.

Patrick, J., Campbell, K., Carmichael, L., Natale, R., & Richardson, B. (1982), Patterns of gross fetal body movements over 24-hour observation intervals during the last 10 weeks of pregnancy. *Amer. J. Obstet.& Gynecol.*, 142:363–371.

Pitkin, R.M. (1979), Fetal ingestion and metabolism of amniotic fluid protein. In: *Nutrition and Metabolism of the Fetus and Infant: Fifth Nutricia Symposium*, ed. H.K.A. Visser. The Hague: Martinus Nijhoff, pp. 29–41.

Ployé, P.M. (1973), Does prenatal mental life exist? *Internat. J. Psycho-Anal.*, 54:241–246.

Prechtl, H.F.R. (1974), The behavioural states of the newborn infant: A review. *Brain Research*, 76:185–212.

——— (1985), Ultrasound studies of human fetal behaviour. *Early Human Development*, 12:91–98.

———— & Nijhuis, J.G. (1983), Eye movements in the human fetus and newborn. *Behavioural Brain Research*, 10:119–124.

———— & O'Brien, M.J. (1982), Behavioural states of the full-tern newborn: The emergence of a concept. In: *Psychobiology of the Newborn*, ed. P. Stratton. New York: Wiley, pp. 52–73.

Preyer, W. (1882), *The Mind of the Child*. Part I. New York: Appleton, 1888.

Rank, O. (1929), *The Trauma of Birth*. New York: Brunner, 1952.

Ray, W.S. (1932), A preliminary report on a study of fetal conditioning. *Child Development*, 3:175–177.

Richards, T.W., & Newbery, H. (1938), Studies in fetal behavior: III. Can performance on test items at six months postnatally be predicted on the basis of fetal activity? *Child Development*, 9:79–86.

———— ———— & Fallgatter, R. (1938), Studies in fetal behavior: II. Activity of the human fetus in utero and its relation to other prenatal conditions, particularly the mother's basal metabolic rate. *Child Development*, 9:69–78.

Sadger, J. (1941), Preliminary study of the psychic life of the fetus and the primary germ. *Psychoanal. Rev.*, 28:327–358.

Salk, L. (1962), Mothers' heartbeat as an imprinting stimulus. *Transactions N. Y. Acad. Sci.*, 24:753–763.

Scheidt, P.C., Stanley, F., & Bryla, D.A. (1978), One-year follow-up of infants exposed to ultrasound in utero. *Amer. J. Obstet. & Gynecol.*, 131:743–748.

Schmidt, W., Boos, R., Gnirs, J., Auer, L., & Schulze, S. (1985), Fetal behavioral states and controlled sound stimulation. *Early Human Development*, 12:145–153.

Smith, C.R., & Steinschneider, A. (1975), Differential effects of prenatal rhythmic stimulation on neonatal arousal states. *Child Development*, 46:574–578, 1975.

Sontag, L.W. (1965), Implications of fetal behavior and environment for adult personalities. *Annals of the N. Y. Acad. Sci.*, 134:782–786.

———— Steele, W.G., & Lewis, M. (1969), The fetal and maternal cardiac response to environmental stress. *Human Development*, 12:1–9.

Spelt, D.K. (1948), The conditioning of the human fetus in utero. *J. Experimental Psychol.*, 38:338–346.

Spitz, R.A., Emde, R.N., & Metcalf, D.R. (1970), Further prototypes of ego formation: Working paper from a research project on early development. *The Psychoanalytic Study of the Child*, 25:417–441.

Stevenson, R.E. (1977), *The Fetus and Newly Born Infant: Influences of the Prenatal Environment*. 2nd ed. St. Louis: Mosby.

Tanaka, Y., and Arayama, T. (1969), Fetal responses to acoustic stimuli. *Practica oto-rhino-laryngologica*, 31:269–273.

vanEyck, J., Wladimiroff, J.W., Noordam, M.J., Tonge, H.M., & Prechtl, H.F.R. (1985), The blood flow velocity waveform in the fetal descending aorta: Its relationship to fetal behavioral states in normal pregnancy at 37–38 weeks. *Early Human Development*, 12:137–143.

Wasz-Höckert, O., Lind, J., Vuorenkoski, V., Partanen, T., & Valanne, E. (1968), *The Infant Cry. A Spectrographic and Auditory Analysis*. Clinics in Developmental Medicine No. 29. London: Heinemann and Lavenham.

Weil, A.P. (1978), Maturational variations and genetic-dynamic issues. *J. Amer. Psychoanal. Assn.*, 26:461–491.

Wood, C. (1970), Weightlessness: Its implications for the human fetus. *J. Obstet. & Gynecol. Brit. Commonwealth,* 77:333–336.

Zimmer, E.Z., Divon, M.Y., Vilensky, A., Sarna, Z., Peretz, B.A., & Paldi, E. (1982), Maternal exposure to music and fetal activity. *Eur. J. Obstet., Gynecol. & Reproductive Biol.,* 13:209–213.

13

Prenatal Attachment and Bonding

W. ERNEST FREUD, B.A.

As I see it, the challenge of the topic is one of achieving a perspective that is reasonably compatible with the firmly held beliefs of various disciplines—cultural anthropology, obstetrics, gynecology, pediatrics, psychology, child psychiatry, psychoanalysis—and, not least, with the consistently expressed views of the International Study Group for Prenatal Psychology (Graber and Kruse, 1973; Graber, 1974; Hau and Schindler, 1982; Schindler, 1982; Schindler and Zimprich, 1983).

It required a major effort to assemble the various aspects of *The Secret Life of the Unborn Child* (Verny and Kelly, 1981), and pursuing the subject remains an uphill struggle, because one tends to conceptualize prenatal phenomenology in terms of postnatal manifestations. Additionally, there is the lure of adultomorphization (the ascription of adult human modes of behavior to embryo and fetus, neither of which may in any way be equipped or ready to perceive and react like an adult or child).

Bowlby (1969) wrote about the infant's *attachment* to the parents. Klaus and Kennell (1976, 1982) used the term *bonding* in the title of the first book and its second edition. The title of their latest book, *Bonding: The Beginnings of Parent-Infant Attachment* (1983) reflects a loosening of terminology. I myself sometimes use the psychoanalytic term *cathexis* (emotional investment), which lends itself to a richer, more flexible, and

This chapter previously appeared in *Pre- and Peri-natal Psychology: An Introduction*, ed. T.R. Verny, Human Sciences Press, New York, 1987.

467

dynamic view, and in general accounts more easily for fluctuations and changes in mental life.

At the May 1983 conference of the ISPP in Dusseldorf, Petersen reported how some parents had actually experienced the moment of conception—as if the unimpeded strength of their emotional investment (optimal cathexis) of the event had primed their senses to almost uncannily accurate perceptions. Though one might regard this as the very earliest stage of the parents' tie to the infant, the story begins, of course, much earlier, at a time when mother and father were still children themselves. They would play at making and having babies, their creative fantasy life (Freud, 1908) being commensurate with the prevailing stage of their emotional development. Experiences in adult life are colored by early omnipotent fantasies and build on the kind of model one's parents presented. With a multigenerational orientation we think that mothering capacity is closed connected with the mother's own mothering experience. Boys too wish for a baby (Brunswick, 1940), and a good fathering experience will go a long way toward laying the foundations for one's own good fathering (Herzog and Sudia, 1973).

Men play a decisive role in getting the process started, but from then on seem relegated to a backseat existence. They experience envy of the female's creativity—Greenacre (1953) speaks of "exclusion anxiety"—knowing that they can neither grow a baby inside nor give birth or breastfeed. They can nevertheless "corner the market" by having "babies unlimited." In our society the majority of physicians in perinatology are men, and one can hardly escape the impression that the embryo and fetus belong to the gynecologist and obstetrician, while the newborn belongs to the pediatrician (in much the same way as the patient belongs to the hospital and not to his family).

The matter comes to a head around the time of birth, when men are ultimately confronted with their physiological inferiority. In so-called primitive societies even today (and until not long ago in some Western industrialized societies as well) the culturally sanctioned custom of *couvade* allows fathers to simulate a birth (Trethowan and Conlon, 1965). Progressive neonatologists can empathize and provide birthing beds that are wide enough for the father, if he so wishes, to lie by the side or sit right behind his delivery spouse, thus participating in the birth as closely as possible.

Because most fathers are competitive and cannot bear to be left out, their conscious and unconscious motivations can propel them in directions that assume almost grotesque proportions. Liebenberg (1973) observed that the father's envy of the wife's creativity was reflected in 52 percent of her sample engaging in heavy work or class schedules; 65 percent developed "pregnancy symptoms" such as fatigue, nausea, backache, headaches, vomiting, or peptic ulcers. Some of the fathers gained 10–20 pounds in weight, which was lost shortly after the baby's birth. Several stopped smoking, saying it was "for the baby."

At the same time, other forces are at work in the prospective father. His fear of passivity may be countered by reckless and physical daring, reflected in car accidents, heavy drinking, or resorting to other women. After the birth the father my regress, so that the mother has not one baby on her hands but two.

What about other members of the family? Sometimes it looks as if siblings and even pets share the birth trauma. Cats and dogs, who sense that the mother's focus of interest is on the baby (inside or outside), have been known to show signs of jealousy; they refuse food, withdraw, seem "depressed," and sleep more. Similarly, the sibling, if not taken into the parents' confidence, will sense a secret. He feels excluded and rejected, especially if he is boarded out to grandparents or relatives around the time the baby is due. If the parents can let the older child share in the pregnancy he can more positively cathect the fetus and will quickly be jumps ahead of the mother, busily feeding, changing, cleaning, and pramming his baby doll, just as he loved stuffing a pillow into his shirt to pretend being pregnant.

In spite of what he will have been told, he usually expects a playmate his age who can walk and talk and readily respond to him. The sibling's bonding to the fetus is likely to be conflicted between joyful expectation, identification with the mother (naturally, the baby is his, and *he* will give birth to it), and feelings of jealousy. When he realizes that he may have to give up cherished possessions or will have to share favorite foods, he may feel anxious. The more scope he is given for identifying with mother or father in their caring attitude for the expected baby the better he is likely to cope, even though some regression is not unusual once the baby is born. With a high premium placed on "being a baby," recent acquisitions like talking, walking, or self-feeding may temporarily give way to crawling, babbling, and wishes to be fed. Perhaps parents would have an easier time if they realized the power of imitation, present shortly after birth (Meltzoff and Moore, 1977) as helping with adaptation. I recall a little boy walking about the house on all fours, carrying a kitten in his mouth after he had watched the cat retrieving her young.

Does the fetus, on his part, attach to the sibling? A mother tells me that when her older child bursts into her bedroom on a Sunday morning and "makes a row" the baby inside her responds with movement (perhaps because this is the first "noise" of the day).

To appreciate fully the extent and quality of the mother's emotional investment in her pregnancy we would first want to know whether she has sufficiently come to terms with her own femininity (Deutsch, 1944, 1945) or whether it has remained negatively or ambivalently cathected. What were her conscious and unconscious motivations for becoming pregnant? Often the social setting lends a certain prestige to motherhood, or perhaps she just wanted a "live doll" or may be competing with her own mother, sister, a relative, friend, or neighbor. She may merely have wanted to re-create a better infancy than her own, believing also that the only person in the world who would genuinely love her and care for her would be a baby.

One would like to know who the baby represents to her (a brother, sister, parent, or herself?) and to what extent she is identified with it (e.g., by being a firstborn). What expectations does she have of her offspring? A wealth of information can often be gleaned by simply asking parents, those whose religion does not require that the baby be named only after it is born and has survived, whether their unborn child already has a name. If they have not yet made up their minds, this is itself significant. If the chosen name is one that equally fits boys or girls (like Evelyn) they are probably "sitting on the fence." If it is a name like Roberta or Alexandra, the choice may suggest an underlying wish for a boy.

When we have gained the mother's confidence we may catch a fascinating glimpse of the kind of fantasy relationship and often revealing conversations she has with the baby inside. I am indebted to the Frankfurt pediatrician Hans von Lüpke (1980) for example. One mother felt that the "child" does not feel well when she, the mother, lies on her side, and that "it" would feel better if she lay on her back. By contrast, another mother, whose previous baby was born with a prolapse of the cord, felt she could prevent a recurrence of this complication if during her second pregnancy she lay on her side. It is intriguing to see the ease with which mothers can read meaning into the activities of the fetus. Sometimes we can discern a defense mechanism being used. One mother was convinced that when the fetus was gripped too hard by the father it was "offended," while when its head was stroked it was pleased. You will not be surprised to hear that the mother herself had conflicts over being touched, conflicts she projected onto the fetus. Another mother still in her teens, thought that her pronounced tiredness stemmed from the wish of the "child" that the mother rest a lot (another projection?). Once, after running fast, she experienced strong pains in the upper part of her belly and was convinced that this was the result of kicks with which "it" had punished her for not being more considerate. She could distinguish between kicks of pleasure and "punishment kicks." This mother said that the child would "withdraw" in reaction to loud music and could then no longer be felt (not surprisingly, the mother herself has always been sensitive to noise). Other mothers, those who like rock music, will tell you that the fetus kicks with joy in response to loud music.

The emotional involvement of the mother extends to the growing shape of her body. Many women display a well-being exceeding their normal health during pregnancy. Their pride in "being two of us" increases with the size of the fetus (Menninger, 1943). The realization that the fetus changes from being a part of herself to a living baby that will soon be a separate individual is thought to prepare the mother for birth and physical separation from her child. Once the mother can perceive the fetal heartbeat her emotional investment receives fresh impetus. One mother described it to me as "like a shock, like an engine starting up." But there are wide individual differences. Another landmark is the perception of fetal movement (the "quickening"). With new methods of investigation (ultrasound scanning) we may be cheating nature: the fetus can now be perceived before fetal movement is felt or when the mother is still insensitive to it. Michel Odent recalls a mother who proudly got out a photo of the ultrasound picture of her baby to show it to him. I myself remember a mother who at the first scanning could not see the fetus as a whole; it looked more like a collection of separate pieces, "like a jigsaw puzzle" to her. At the next scanning the husband was present and together they could see the whole fetus. From then on the mother cathected the image. She stressed that the support from her husband had been crucial, but a "minimal sign-Gestalt" (Spitz, 1965) may also have been needed in order to give the impression of a "person." Another mother's ultrasound scanning showed three fetuses. She had not expected that, and it came as a shock to her which required considerable readjustment on her part. When a later scan showed four fetuses we expected a further shock. However, the mother felt relieved and told me that four babies were better for her than three, that she actually preferred that. Asked why, she burst out: "At least there won't be any ganging up of two against one. It will always be two versus two!" The enquiry by Campbell, Reading, et al. (1982) into the impact of ultrasound scanning on maternal behavior and attitudes during pregnancy and following delivery deserves close scrutiny.

Let us now look at the fetus. What we will see depends largely on the extent to which we regard him as a sentient "human" being. Albert Liley (1972) ended a delightful paper by stating humbly: "What I have tried to do is to provide a background, so that by asking the right questions in the right way, we might sometime get the right answers" (p. 105). I doubt whether anyone could improve on that. To come to conclusions about the fetus's attachment it may help to remind ourselves what he is actually doing. He floats (is in a "state of neutral buoyancy") but is attached to the umbilical, which Feher (1980) regards as a first "fixation point" in the psychological sense. He is sucking (e.g., his thumb or finger); he is swallowing and voiding the amniotic fluid; he may be holding on to the umbilical and can twist and roll over (26 weeks). He can somersault, kick, and hiccup. Far from being an inert passenger in a pregnant mother, the fetus is seen by Liley as very much in command of the pregnancy: "It is he who guarantees the endocrine success of pregnancy and induces all manner of changes in maternal physiology to make her a suitable host. . . . It is the fetus who determines the duration of pregnancy . . . who decides which way he will lie in pregnancy and which way he will present in labour" (p. 100). Liley also mentions an intriguing detail, i.e., that the fetus has a much larger number and much wider distribution of taste buds in his oral cavity than has the child or adult. Odent (1980) thinks that the sense of smell may phylogenetically play a role as a first "distance receptor" in a liquid environment, and the question arises whether (and if so, how) the fetus currently monitors his surround. Does he taste the amniotic fluid? Is he responsive to fluctuations in its chemical composition, pressure, or temperature? Might he in this way pick up and react to biochemically transmitted mood fluctuations in his mother? The fetal ear matures relatively early (Clauser, 1971; Korner and Thoman, 1972) and he hears the mother's heartbeat either through the ear or by conduction via the more solid structures of his body. He may be aware of "the rhythmical whooshing sound of the mother's bloodflow . . . punctuated by the tummy rumbles of air passing through his mother's stomach" (Macfarlane, 1977, p. 15) and the noise and rhythm of her breathing, just as he may be aware of her wake-sleep patterns and her general style of functioning (lethargic or hectic). To what extent might intrauterine sounds be thought of as forerunners of "transitional objects" (Winnicott, 1951) or "imaginary companions" (Nagera, 1969)? Ruth Rice (1979) quotes Salk (1962) when she wonders about "imprinting" (Lorenz) to intrauterine sound.

In any case, rhythm itself provides a most reassuring "cradle" though its promise of repetition and continuity. If continuity is one of the most important baseline parameters one should not overlook its implications for the care of prematures.

The fetus is in touch not only with his liquid environment but can also touch himself, the umbilical cord, the wall of the uterus, and the placenta. Feher (1980) thinks that touch epitomizes continuity, Odent (1978) speaks of the skin as the primary sense organ from which all others derive, and Rice (1979) quotes Kulka, Fry, and Goldstein (1960), conjecturing that contact needs are probably fully gratified in intrauterine life.

According to Feher (1980) bodily sensation is the medium of expression most accessible to the infant, and body movements in the womb are also significant in that they may affect later emotional states and mental development. "According to Corliss" (1976), she writes, "movements create sensations which have patterns. These patterns are actually imposed on the musculature, and then on the cortex itself, as imprints or memories, which remain like a permanent 'motion picture' to influence our consciousness and future reactions" (p. 26).

Can we then speak of "body memories" when we observe a premature baby pressing hand and feet against the wall of his incubator, or when a colleague tells us of a dream about his hands, pressing against a concave rubber wall, accompanying his account by demonstrating the "feeling" in his fingers? Greenacre (1945) speaks of unique somatic memory traces. Does the fetus cathect his mother in terms of body memories? We might then ask, What is or is not worth remembering? Does the fetus bond to tangibles, to that which he may be "in touch" with, like himself (narcissism), the amniotic fluid, the umbilical cord, the uterine wall, or the placenta? With increasing size, the fetus is ever closer to the uterine wall. We think of a baby's comfort in being held and wrapped, and of swaddling (Richards and Chisholm, 1978). But why are some babies happier unwrapped, left to kick and move their limbs to their heart's delight?

Bonding may also be to intangibles, such as interaction, continuity, regularity, rhythm, movement, and stimulation. If it is assumed that the fetus "expects" interaction, we might ask whether he is capable of initiating it. Should one think of "interaction hunger" in terms of the organism's head for homeostasis alternating with "disturbances"? Interaction implies reciprocal communication (Brazelton, Tronick, Adamson, Als, and Weise, 1975), feedback, and perhaps "dialogue" (Spitz, 1965). At this point we should remind ourselves that in the course of traversing his developmental microstages the fetus is not one but many, just as the pregnant mother does not remain the same but changes all the time. This, incidentally, may have implications for the way we organize antenatal classes, which usually are attended by mothers in all stages of pregnancy. One mother told me that she could fully pay attention only to what corresponded to her prevailing state of pregnancy. In other words, the mother may be programmed to focus optimally only on her state of pregnancy at any given time, and on the corresponding state of development of the fetus.

Is it possible to identify the essential ingredients of mother-fetus interaction? Does the mother's contribution always have to be contingent? Could it be that in the absence of one or more essential part-interactions the fetus reacts over time like Tronick and Adamson's "still-face" infants (1980) whose mothers had been instructed to withhold feedback? Would the fetus after being exposed to a certain amount of a mother's ambivalent cathexis become trapped between contradictory messages, so that eventually his cooperation at the time of labor and birth is impaired?

The question is how much stimulation the fetus needs at any one time in his development around which to organize himself progressively. If it is insufficient, or absent, we might speak with Hau (1973) of "intrauterine hospitalism" (deprivation of basic psychological nurturance).

We know of the newborn infant's "dance" in synchrony with his mother's voice (Condon and Sander, 1974). Henry Truby (quoted by Verny and Kelly, 1981) points to recent studies which seem to indicate a prenatal precursor phenomenon in which the fetus moves his body in rhythm to his mother's speech. Perhaps there is also a prenatal counterpart to Spitz's coenesthetic mode of communication. Spitz (1965) gave the example that "any animal knows as a matter of course when someone is afraid of him and acts without hesitation on this knowledge. Most of us are unable to duplicate this simple feat" (p. 136). Similarly, it is known that a mother remains "in touch" with her infant during her sleep. Unfortunately, no research has been done on the coenesthetic mode of communication.

I need not dwell on the three separate systems of communication between mother and fetus which Verny and Kelly (1981) have described (see also Fedor-Freybergh, 1983). I will simply mention them: behavioral communication (e.g., kicking as a reaction to rock music, or as a sign of distress when anxiety-provoking hormones flood the system of the fetus); communication through dreams; and physiological communication (e.g., the mother's excessive drinking, improper eating, or use of drugs).

Sontag (1941) at the Fels Institute in America found that deeply disturbed emotion produces a marked increase in fetal activity, probably as a result of increased adrenalin level in the maternal and therefore the fetal blood. Severe maternal fatigue has the same effect, probably also through changes in blood chemistry. A sound of proper pitch, intensity, and proximity will produce an instantaneous and convulsive movement of the fetus, probably through auditory nerve stimulation by bone conduction. Sontag instanced the vibration of a washing machine. Violent emotional upsets also increase fetal activity (Sontag observed a more than tenfold increase).

The issue of fetal learning, habituation, and anticipation arises here. Lieberman (quoted in Sontag, 1970, p. 265) took a sample of habituated women smokers who were denied cigarets for 24 hours. They were then offered a cigaret. Even before it had been lit, a significant acceleration in fetal heartbeat could be demonstrated. Lieberman concluded that the effect of the mother's emotional response was mediated through placental interchange, which induced the accelerated fetal heart rate, though there may be other explanations.

Another suggestion that the fetus responds to maternal emotional stress comes from the ultrasonographic observations of Ianniruberto and Tajani (1981), who examined 28 panic-stricken pregnant women (18–36 weeks gestation) during a 1980 Italian earthquake which shook the area near their maternity hospital. Though none of the mothers had suffered any physical trauma, all the fetuses showed intense hyperkinesia lasting 2–8 hours. In 20 cases this was followed by a period of reduced motility lasting 24–72 hours; the remaining 8 fetuses recovered immediately.

There are also instances of prenatal influence in which it is more difficult to establish reliable cause-effect correlations. Ferreira (1960) found in a prospective study that deviant behavior in the newborn (e.g., as regards amount of crying and sleep, degree of irritability, bowel movements, feeding behavior) was associated with negative attitudes in mothers who had shown a higher score on a Fear of Harming the Baby Scale and who had an "either extreme" score on a Rejection of Pregnancy Scale.

Blau, Staff, Eriton, Welkowitz, Springam, and Cohen (1963) conducted a retrospective study at Mt. Sinai Hospital in New York. Their group of 30 mothers of premature infants showed a distinctive clinical picture, including more negative attitudes to pregnancy, greater emotional immaturity, greater body narcissism, and less adequate resolution of familial oedipal problems. Based on these findings, a predictive, self-reporting questionnaire test of prematurity was devised.

Stott (1973) conducted a retrospective study on child morbidity up to 4 years in which he found that ill health, neurological dysfunction, developmental lag, and behavior disturbance were closely associated with stresses involving severe continuing personal tensions, marital discord in particular.

Probably the best known study in this area is that of Rottmann (1974). He distinguished six possibilities of the mother's hostile attitude affecting fetal development: (1) noxious actions (neglect of diet, excessive smoking, drug taking, professional stress); (2) interferences in the process of pregnancy and birth (increased frequency of spontaneous abortions, prematurity, postmaturity, tendencies to reject the fetus psychosomatically); (3) psychotoxic effects; (4) disturbances of physiological rhythm; (5) trauma of fetal unpleasure; and (6) telepathic or Psi effects. Rottmann's "catastrophic" mothers bore children who were significantly lighter or heavier than those of mothers in his other groups ("ideal," "cool," and "ambivalent" mothers). He found that mothers with a negative attitude to pregnancy are more irritable, emotionally more labile, aggressive, etc., which tends to lead to changes in their pulse, breathing, and vascular rhythms. This means interference with the rhythms to which the fetus has become accustomed, causing disharmonic and repeated arythmic discontinuity in his acoustic vibratory environment. As regards the positive influences exerted by Rottmann's mothers, his "ideal" mothers had the shortest and easiest labors and a minimum incidence of prematurity and postmaturity.

Lederman, Lederman, Work, and McCann (1979), in a prospective study, tested the hypothesis that maternal conflict and anxiety affect plasma catecholamine and cortisol production which in turn affect uterine activity and progress in labor. Epinephrine, norepinephrine, and cortisol are related to stress and inhibit uterine motility. The researchers reason that if psychological conflict and anxiety in pregnancy have an effect on progress in labor, they may also have consequences for the well-being of the fetus and neonate and for the mother-infant relationship.

Sosa, Kennell, Klaus et al. (1980), in their study on the effect of a supportive companion on perinatal problems, length of labor, and mother-infant interaction, suggests an association, mediated through similar mechanisms, between acute anxiety and arrest of labor or fetal distress. The concept of the "supportive companion" may be one of the key issues in the field under investigation, beginning ideally with "good enough" mothering (Winnicott, 1965) in the mother's own infancy, continuing throughout her development in the environment of her extended family, and reaching its height with the spouse's support during labor and delivery. Significantly, in England, where most hospitals nowadays allow fathers to be present at delivery, a recent survey by a parents' magazine revealed the gratifying result that in a sample of 4000 families the fathers were present during labor. However, in 54 percent of the cases in which complications arose, they were sent out of the room—ironically, at the very time their wives needed them most!

The importance of a supportive companion is not restricted to the time around labor and delivery, but most likely also has a large share in the success of prenatal bonding enhancement schemes. These may become increasingly in demand in Western industrialized societies where traditional social support systems and family life have disintegrated through urbanization (Lozoff, Brittenham, Trause, Kennell, and Klaus, 1977). It is striking how few of the younger generation have had personal acquaintance with holding, feeding, and cleaning babies when they themselves were children. One cannot help wondering to what extent such lack of experience is a handicap in optimal bonding.

Lind and Hardgrove (1978) stressed the beneficial effect of the pregnant mother's singing to her unborn child ("lullaby bonding"), while Judith Kestenberg (1978) at her Child Development Research Center in New York State developed a program for pregnant women in which she systematically teaches them to notate tension changes occurring in fetal movement. Prospective mothers learn to accommodate the fetus's body by widening, lengthening, or bulging. The idea is to cooperate with the fetus: "Becoming acquainted with, and attuning to, the baby's movement is a preparation for child care in the extra-uterine environment" (p. 2). Working with mothers in this way not only promotes prenatal attachment through a primarily physical approach but also serves to focus on reasons for less than optimal cathexis of the fetus. "Tuning in" to mother and infant has also been one of the essentials in our work at the Hampstead Well-Baby Clinic (W.E. Freud and I. Freud, 1976).

Linda Carter-Jessop (1980) of the University of Rochester systematically studied the effect of specific prenatal "bonding intervention" on the frequency of postnatal maternal attachment behaviors. It serves the two-fold purpose of preparing mothers (1) to optimize the growth and development experience of their children throughout childhood, through being "tuned in" to identifying and acting on the individual child's needs, and (2) to help them weather threats to the relationship, e.g., separation due to prematurity, illness, or handicaps. Her "bonding intervention" included (1) teaching mothers to interact with their infants in utero by talking to, touching, stroking, and locating particular body parts of the infants and (2) raising mothers' awareness of the uniqueness of their infants and their own reactions and interactions. The 5 experimental subjects exhibited significantly greater frequency in overall behaviors and "advanced attachment" behaviors, compared to the 5 con-

trol mothers who did not receive the prenatal "bonding intervention."

Using the mother's voice in a more systematic way, Spence
and De Casper (1982) explored how prenatal experience affects
postnatal auditory perception of the mother's voice. Five weeks
before delivery the mother read aloud a story twice daily until
delivery. After delivery the old story and a new story were read
to the infants by their mothers. Within three days after delivery
the infants showed through the manner of their sucking inter-
burst intervals that they preferred the familiar story by maxi-
mizing input. The authors cautiously conclude that the
preferences shown suggest that prenatal auditory experience
may be important for speech perception.

Franz Veldman (1982) recommends that a 4½ to 5 months
(or more) pregnant woman should gently put her hands on her
abdomen, one on the right side of her womb, the other on her
left. "By leaving them there in the same position and without
exerting pressure, she can cause the child in the womb to move
from one side to the other. Thus she can gently 'rock' the child
from left to right and from right to left. If she wishes to touch
and caress her child she can do so by letting her feeling of love
flow into one of her hands. . . . The child nestles, as it were,
with its back in the hollow of its mother's loving hand."

On this endearing note I am happy to end.

References

Blau, A., Slaff, B., Eriton, K., Welkowitz, J., Springarm, J., & Cohen, J. (1963),
The psychogenic etiology of premature births. *Psychosom. Med.*, 25:201–211.
Bowlby, J. (1969), *Attachment and Loss: Vol. I. Attachment.* Hogarth Press.
Brazelton, T.B., Tronick, E., Adamson, L., Als, H., & Weise, S. (1975), Early
mother-infant reciprocity. In: *Parent-Infant Interaction.* CIBA Foundation
Symposium 33. N.-Holland: Elsevier, pp. 137–154.
Brunswick, R.M. (1940), The preoedipal phase of the libido development.
In: *The Psychoanalytic Reader*, ed. R. Fliess. London: Hogarth Press, pp.
261–285.
Campbell, S., Reading, A.E., et al. (1982), Ultrasound scanning in pregnancy:
The short-term psychological effects of early real-time scans. *J. Psychosom.
Obstet. & Gynecol.*, 1:57–61.
Carter-Jessop, L. (1981), Promoting maternal attachment through parental
intervention. *Amer. J. Maternal Child Nursing*, 2:107–112.

Clauser, G. (1971), *Die vorgeburtliche Entstehung der Sprache als anthropologisches Problem: Der Rhythmus als Organisator der menschlichen Entwicklung.* Stuttgart: Ferdinand Enke Verlag.

Condon, W., & Sander, L.W. (1974), Neonate movement is synchronized with adult speech: Interactional participation and language acquisition. *Science,* 183:99–101.

Corliss, C.E. (1976), *Patten's Human Embriology.* New York: McGraw-Hill.

Deutsch, H. (1944), *The Psychology of Women.* Vol. I. New York: Grune & Stratton.

—— (1945), *The Psychology of Women.* Vol. II. New York: Grune & Stratton.

Fedor-Freybergh, P. (1983), Psychoneurodendkrinologie: Zugang zu einem interaktionistischen Modell der Mutter-Kind-Beziehung während der Schwangerschaft. Paper presented at the Seventh Conference of the International Study Group for Prenatal Psychology, Dusseldorf, May.

Feher, L. (1980), *The Psychology of Birth: The Foundation of Human Personality.* London: Souvenir Press.

Ferreira, A.J. (1960), The pregnant woman's emotional attitude and its reflection on the newborn. *Amer. J. Orthopsychiat.,* 30:553–561.

Freud, S. (1908), On the sexual theories of children. *Standard Edition,* 9:207–226. London: Hogarth Press, 1959.

Freud, W.E., & Freud, I. (1976), The well-baby clinic. *Child Psychiat. & Human Development,* 7:67–84.

Graber, G.H. (1974), *Pränatale Psychologie.* Munich: Kindler Verlag.

—— & Kruse, F. (1973), *Vorgeburtliches Seelenleben.* Munich: Wilhelm Goldmann Verlag.

Greenacre, P. (1945), The biological economy of birth. *The Psychoanalytic Study of the Child,* 1:31–51. New York: International Universities Press.

—— (1953), *Trauma, Growth and Personality.* New York: International Universities Press.

Hau, T.F. (1973), Perinatale und pränatale Faktoren der Neurosenätiologie. In: *Vorgeburtliches Seelenleben,* ed. G.H. Graber & F. Kruse. Munich: Wilhelm Goldmann Verlag.

—— & Schindler, S. (1982), *Pränatale und Perinatale Psychosomatik: Richtungen, Probleme, Ergebnisse.* Stuttgart: Hippokrates Verlag.

Herzog, J.M., & Sudia, C. (1973), Children in fatherless families. In: *Review of Child Development Research,* ed. M. Caldwell. Chicago: University of Chicago Press, pp. 73–79.

Ianniruberto, A., & Tajani, E. (1981), Ultrasonographic study of fetal movements. *Seminars in Perinatol.,* 5:175–181.

Kestenberg, J.S. (1978), Pregnant women—cooperation with the child before it is born and during birth. *Child Devel. Res. News,* 1:2.

—— (1980), Pregnancy as a developmental phase. *J. Biological Experience,* 3:58–66.

Klaus, M.H., & Kennell, J.H. (1976), *Maternal-Infant Bonding: The Impact of Early Separation or Loss on Family Development.* St. Louis: Mosby.

—— —— (1982), *Parent-Infant Bonding.* St. Louis: Mosby.

—— —— (1983), *Bonding: The Beginnings of Parent-Infant Attachment.* St. Louis: Mosby.

Korner, A.F., & Thoman, E.B. (1972), The relative efficacy of contact and vestibular-proprioceptive stimulation in soothing neonates. *Child Development*, 43:443–453.

Kulka, A., Fry, C., & Goldstein, F.J. (1960), Kinesthetic needs in infancy. *Amer. J. Orthopsychiat.*, 30:562–571.

Lederman, R.P., Lederman, E., Work, B.A., Jr., McCann, D.S. (1979), Relationship of psychological factors in pregnancy to progress in labor. *Nursing Research*, 28:94–97.

Liebenberg, B. (1973), Expectant fathers. In: *Aspects of a First Pregnancy*, ed. P.M. Shereshefsky & L.J. Yarrow. New York: Raven Press, 103–114.

Liley, A.W. (1972), The foetus as a personality. *Austral. & N. Zeal. J. Psychiat.*, 6:99–105.

Lind, J., & Hardgrove, C.B. (1978), Lullaby bonding. *Keeping Abreast, J. Human Nurturing*, 3:184–190.

Lozoff, B., Brittenham, G.M., Trause, M.A., Kennell, J.H., & Klaus, M.H. (1977), The mother-newborn relationship: Limits of adaptability. *J. Pediat.* 91:1–12.

Lüpke, H. von (1980), personal communication.

Macfarlane, A. (1977), *The Psychology of Childbirth*. London: Fontana/Open Books.

Meltzoff, A.N., & Moore, M.K. (1977), Imitation of facial and manual gestures by human neonates. *Science*, 198:75–78.

Menninger, W.C. (1943), The emotional factors in pregnancy. *Bull. Menn. Clin.*, 7:15–24.

Nagera, H. (1969), The imaginary companion: Its significance for ego development and conflict solution. *The Psychoanalytic Study of the Child*, 24:165–196. New York: International Universities Press.

Odent, M. (1978), *Die sanfte Geburt: Die Leboyer-Methode in der Praxis*. Munich: Kösel-Verlag.

——— (1980), *Die Geburt des Menschen: Für eine ökologische Wende in der Geburtshilfe*. Munich: Kösel-Verlag.

Petersen, P. (1983), Empfängnis und Zeugung: Phänomene der Kindesankunft. Paper presented at the Seventh Conference of the International Study Group for Prenatal Psychology, Dusseldorf, May.

Rice, R. (1979), The effects of the Rice Infant Sensori-motor Stimulation Treatment on the development of high-risk infants. *The National Foundation, Birth Defects: Original Article Series*, 15:7–26.

Richards, M., & Chisholm, J.S. (1978), Swaddling, cradleboards and the development of children. *Early Human Development*, 2/3:255–275.

Rottmann, G. (1974), Untersuchungen über Einstellungen zur Schwangerschaft und zur fötalen Entwicklung. In: *Pränatale Psychologie*, ed. G.H. Graber, Munich: Kindler Verlag, pp. 68–87.

Salk, L. (1962), Mother's heartbeat as an imprinting stimulus. *Transactions N. Y. Acad. Sci.*, 24:753–763.

Schindler, S. (1982), *Geburt: Eintritt in eine neue Welt*. Hogrefe: Verlag für Psychologie.

——— & Zimprich, H. (1983), *Okologie der Perinalzeit*. Stuttgart: Hippokrates Verlag.

Sontag, L.W. (1941), The significance of fetal environmental differences. *Amer. J. Obstet. & Gynecol.*, 42:996–1003.

—— (1970), Prenatal determinants of postnatal behavior. In: *Fetal Growth and Development*, ed. Waisman & Kerr. New York: McGraw-Hill.

Sosa, R., Kennell, J.H., Klaus, M.H., et al. (1980). The effect of a supportive companion on perinatal problems, length of labor, *N. Engl. J. Med.*, 303:597–600.

Spence, M., & De Casper, A. (1982), Human fetuses perceive maternal speech. Paper presented at the Society for Research in Child Development conference, Austin, Texas.

Spitz, R.A. (1965), *The First Year of Life*. New York: International Universities Press.

Stott, D.H. (1973), Follow-up study from birth of the effects of prenatal stresses. *Developmental Med. & Child Neurol.*, 15:770–787.

Trethowan, W.H., & Conlon, M.F. (1965), The couvade syndrome. *Brit. J. Psychiat.*, 111:57–66.

Tronick, E., & Adamson, L. (1980), *Babies as People: New Findings on Our Social Beginnings*. New York: Collier.

Veldman, F. (1982), Life welcomed and affirmed. *St. Cloud Visitor*, Catholic Diocese of St. Cloud, Minn., November 11.

Verny, T., & Kelly, J. (1981), *The Secret Life of the Unborn Child: A Remarkable and Controversial Look at Life Before Birth*. Summit Books.

Winnicott, D.W. (1951), Transitional objects and transitional phenomena. In: *Collected Papers: Through Paediatrics to Psycho-Analysis*. New York: Basic Books, 1958, pp. 229–242.

—— (1965), *The Maturational Processes and the Facilitating Environment*. New York: International Universities Press.

14

Notes on Some Psychological Aspects of Neonatal Intensive Care

W. ERNEST FREUD, B.A.

> *Infantile experiences . . . call for particular consideration. They are all the more momentous because they occur in times of incomplete development and are for that very reason liable to have traumatic effects.* [Sigmund Freud, 1917, p. 361]

Donald Winnicott once said he wished that John Bowlby had applied his concept of separation to the perinatal period rather than to infancy (Brimblecombe, 1978). I share this view, and after helping to develop the Baby Profile (W.E. Freud, 1967, 1971) and techniques for teaching infant observation to psychoanalytic candidates (W.E. Freud, 1975), I was drawn to observe low birth weight babies. Their physical development is measurably incomplete, and they were routinely separated from their mothers and subjected to massive medical intervention—infantile experiences that are certainly potentially "momentous."

On subsequent visits to neonatal intensive care units in England and the United States, I quickly became aware of the wealth of technical skill and equipment deployed on the babies' behalf. Like other visitors to these units, I was also aware that technical advances had outstripped the psychological side of medical care. It is not surprising that medical staff are troubled, too, by the realization of the iatrogenic risks implicit in the setting and by the question of what impact their care will have on the babies' later development.

I was familiar with the studies of Klaus, Jerauld, Kreger, McAlpine, Steffa, & Kennell, (1972), Kennell, Jerauld, Wolfe, Chesler, Kreger, McAlpine, Steffa, & Klaus, (1974), and De Chateau and Wiberg (1977a, 1977b), which had demonstrated the beneficial effect of early and extended postpartum contact between mother and baby. I then heard the story of a premature baby born in Brazil to American parents a hundred years ago who was successfully incubated and nurtured by being "bound" between the breasts of his Portuguese wetnurse. He thrived to graduate and became a professor at an American university (Lockwood, 1978). Was this an isolated incident, or is such caregiving customary in nonindustrialized societies? It prompted a search for more than anecdotal evidence, but by now the lines of thought had converged: Was it possible that even in Western industrialized societies skin-to-skin nurturing might hold the key to redressing the growing imbalance between technological and psychological care of low birth weight babies? I believe it does, and in the following pages hope to point out some of the challenges and problems connected with this orientation.

As a psychoanalyst, I maintain "evenly suspended attention" in listening to my patients. Analytic students learning to observe mothers and infants are similarly admonished to keep an open mind and not to look for this or for that, as the medical student is. By using the same approach in observing neonatal and postneonatal intensive care units (for convenience, NICU and PNICU). I hope I have been able to empathize and identify temporarily in turn with parents, babies, doctors, and nurses without becoming involved.

Parent-Infant Interaction in the NICU

Conversations with parents and hospital staff confirm the general awareness of imbalance between highly sophisticated mechanical aspects of neonatal intensive care on the one hand and humane considerations on the other. In many cases it would seem that neither the parent's nor the baby's psychological needs are optimally met. Good mental hygiene requires mother and newborn to remain close together, not only immediately after delivery (Leboyer, 1975) but also for some time afterward. By contrast, the infant-at-risk is usually whisked away from his mother to the NICU. From then until the emergency is over, father, mother, and baby will be together only during the family's visits to the unit. If the baby is in an incubator, a particularly high degree of physical separation persists.

Besides being struck by the number of plastic tubes, wires, gadgets, and machines designed to safeguard the lives of these babies, visitors to a NICU are impressed by the activity and unstinted devotion of the nursing staff in feeding, cleaning, and medicating their charges, as well as keeping records and graphs and making sure that machines and monitors are working properly. The doctors' medical competence and mechanical expertise are phenomenal. They repeatedly rally at short notice to any crisis, day or night, and stay until the situation has stabilized. Nor can a visitor fail to be impressed by the number of occasions nursing staff and doctors find time to talk with parents.

Still, to what extent does the intensive care setting successfully meet the parents' psychological needs? Understandably, much of the mother's[1] emotional energy is spent worrying about her baby. When she first visits the unit, she must become accustomed to the strange and often bewildering and frightening surroundings. When she is not there, she never stops wondering in what condition she will find her baby when she sees him next. This sporadic contact between mother and baby necessarily militates against optimal mutual cathexis (emotional investment).

Almost invariably parents long to be in closer contact with their babies. They realize that their wish to have them at home

---

[1] I am aware of the father's role and assume that when appropriate the word "mother" is understood to refer to the father as well. Similarly, though the infant is referred to by the masculine pronouns *he, him*, etc., this is merely for ease of exposition.

is unrealistic, but they question the necessity of being passive onlookers to the doctors' and nurses' caretaking. Even when unrestricted visiting is encouraged (including visits by the baby's siblings), parents cannot help feeling that they are the guests of the hospital and that their presence is a privilege that can easily be withdrawn, especially when their own or other babies require emergency medical intervention. Could parent-baby interaction be improved with no decrease in medical benefits were we to consider their various psychological needs?

The Mother's Psychological Needs

Contact and Continuity

During her pregnancy a woman increasingly cathects the developing fetus (Bibring, 1959; Bibring, Dwyer, Huntington, and Valenstein, 1961). The extent to which she does this in relation to other aspects of her life deserves to be studied systematically, because it may help forestall possible adverse developments. For example, a married student in analysis who wanted to finish her Ph.D. thesis before starting a family was ambivalent about an unexpected pregnancy, but hardly ever talked about it. She was clearly preoccupied with getting her degree; the rucksack on her back in which she carried her papers was prominent, while in front any visible signs of her pregnancy remained conspicuously absent. It came as no surprise when she miscarried at about 18 weeks.

A fetus is known to have an active individual personality (Liley, 1972) which interacts with his mother in many subtle ways (Sontag, 1941; Macfarlane, 1977), so that by the time of delivery mother and baby have shared many experiences and are thoroughly attuned to one another. The mother is therefore usually upset at having her baby taken away immediately and longs to be reunited; the continuum (Liedloff, 1976) has been interrupted at a crucial time. A mother who is not too exhausted wants to remain literally in touch with her newborn. She wants to see and feel him; to hold, smell, and stroke him; to smile, coo, and talk to him; later to rock and carry him. She wants, moreover, to be free to do these things at any time.

Feedback

The growth of the mother's understanding of her baby depends on the feedback she receives from her overtures and ministrations. With the immature, often unattractive, and initially unresponsive low birth weight baby, who may even have difficulty in opening his eyes, she may feel disappointed and frustrated. Her problem can be compounded when her older children, having looked forward to the new arrival as an active playmate, react on the primitive level of experiencing his lack of responsiveness as willful rejection. Especially when the baby is less than 29 weeks of gestational age, the mother needs a great deal of support from the nursing staff and the medical social worker.

*Explanation of the Baby's Appearance and of Medical
Procedures*

The mother wants an explanation for the smallest blemish on her baby. Even a speck of blood or a bruise can distress her. She also wants to know just what is being done by the hospital staff and why. Often she feels the need to observe her baby's reactions to intervention as well. Her labile emotional state and the obvious need of the infant for special care make it more likely than ever that her anxieties will interfere with her ability easily to understand what she is told and what she sees. Perhaps it does not matter so much whether or not the mother grasps the intricacies of medical procedures, but from the very first it is important that she experience the staff as sympathetic and genuinely interested in supporting her. It is difficult enough for her while she is in the unit, but once she leaves, she has no way of testing her fears and fantasies against reality.

Involvement and Active Participation

Expert opinion has begun to favor the parents' involvement with the caretaking team (Steinhausen, 1976; Brimblecombe, Richards and Roberton, 1978; Kitzinger and Davis, 1978). The importance for a mother of active participation as an aid to working through her inevitable (though often unconscious) disappointment and guilt at having produced a less than healthy baby can hardly be overestimated. Active participation is excellent occupational therapy; having close bodily contact with the baby as well makes for even better therapy. Medical and nursing staff should be on the lookout for every opportunity to enlist the parents' help.

Need for Extra Support

Above all, prospective parents look forward to having a healthy baby. When an infant-at-risk is born, the father often suffers a blow to his self-image of virility, and the mother begins immediately to compare herself to mothers who have been delivered of healthy full-term babies.

The mother's sense of failure, especially if there has been a previous miscarriage or neonatal death (Lewis, 1976), is augmented by the baby's being taken from her: Feeling that under the circumstances he must particularly need her, she experiences the separation as especially stressful and disheartening. It has been suggested that the separation from her baby may actually retard a mother's recovery. Seen in this light, the newborn is effectively an important caregiver himself (Anderson, 1977).

On a deeper psychological level, unresolved conflicts from the time of the mother's toilet training may be reactivated: guilt and distress over not having been able to produce "the right thing at the right time" add to her depressive feelings. With her confidence and self-esteem so shaken, anxieties over being and remaining useless may interfere with normal processes of mourning and recovery (Lewis and Page, 1978). Such women can profit from the privacy of a room of their own; certainly they, as well as their spouses, need extra help and understanding (Prugh, 1953).

Education

All in all, modern neonatal intensive care takes too little notice of parents' psychological needs. With a pervasive sense of failure putting their mutual support system in jeopardy, ways must be found to bolster their equilibrium. Everything possible should be done to help them look forward without undue apprehension to their baby's return home, lest, as one mother said, "He'll be a complete stranger."

The mother especially must gain sufficient knowledge and experience of her baby's care in the unit to feel confident in looking after him at home (Miller, 1948). Any aspect of nursing she learns is insurance against failure in home nurturing and reduces the risk of child abuse and neglect.

Let us now turn our attention more directly to the baby and his needs. Has early separation been any less exacting for him than it was for his parents? While some of the newborn's needs are obvious, others, of course, can only be inferred.

The Baby's Psychological Needs

Ongoing Interaction

Intensive postnatal care of low birth weight babies tries on the one hand to simulate intrauterine conditions, and on the other, to provide optimal extrauterine environments. The discrepancy between continuous interactional processes in utero and discontinuous postnatal intensive care is too often ignored as a potential iatrogenic risk in itself.

Awake or asleep, the fetus thrives on ongoing interaction with his mother. After he is born, the baby still needs continuous interaction (albeit of an attenuated kind during sleep), but in the NICU he is largely denied it. A recent study by Marton, Dawson, and Minde (1979), showed that in their units babies had human contact for only 5 to 8 minutes per hour. I do not know what percentage of time a baby born at home is likely to have with members of his family, but certainly it would be more. Lack of continuous contact and sleep deprivation through intervention by medical procedures and continuous overhead lighting are prominent iatrogenic hazards of modern neonatal intensive care.

Primary Nursing and Integration

Because the intrauterine experience has familiarized the fetus with only his mother's rhythms, the newborn's need is for primary care by his biological mother. As a second best, he needs to receive food, comfort, and affection from a single person on whom he can attach his awakening emotions. The creation of such a tie is essential if he is to discriminate between the familiar and the unfamiliar, the known and the unknown, in his environment (A. Freud, 1922–1970).

Minde, Ford, Cellhoffer, and Boukydis (1975) found that during stays of approximately 7 weeks, the prematures in their large unit had to adapt to handling by 70 different nurses. To what extent is the baby's budding capacity for integrating experiences (Sander, 1962; Spitz, 1965; Weil, 1970) overtaxed by so many divergent styles of handling and by so many kinds of mechanical sensory input?

Stimulation Programs

The great number of studies on the effects of stimulation testify to the concern felt about the sensory deprivations suffered particularly by babies who spend many weeks or even months in incubator or cot (Freedman, Boverman, and Freedman, 1960; Smitherman, 1969; Katz, 1971; Kramer, Chamorro, and Green, 1975; Kramer and Pierpont, 1976). Piecemeal stimulation is a poor substitute for the wide range of natural and integrated stimuli which only close bodily contact can provide. All channels of communication, but especially the kinesic (Montagu, 1978), should be available to the infant.

For the baby carried on his mother's body, maternal heartbeat and breathing provide an immediate and continuous background stimulation which may be even more effective than oscillating waterbeds (Korner, 1979) in reducing apnoeic episodes (Kattwinkel, Nearman, Fanaroff, Katona, and Klaus, 1975; Korner, Guilleminault, Van den Hoed, & Baldwin, 1978). Asleep or awake, the mother provides essential vestibular-proprioceptive stimulation (Korner and Thoman, 1972).

Investigators are in agreement that short-term stimulation is beneficial (Richards, 1978)—all the more important then that it is available in the NICU and the PNICU. That the gains level off after some time may no more than reflect nature's requirement that to give long-lasting benefits stimulation must be ongoing. Brown and Helper (1976) stress that each baby needs an individual stimulation program. They believe, moreover, that long-range success depends on its being continued both in hospital and after discharge.

Initiating Contact

All infants, programmed to initiate contact with their environment (Brazelton, Tronick, Adamson, Als, and Weise, 1975), need responses to their attempts to communicate if they are to thrive. The low birth weight baby may often be too ill to make the first move, or we may as yet be too inexperienced to recognize his efforts (Newman, 1981). In addition, medical procedures may prevent him from expressing himself or literally keep us from seeing what he is doing. Andersson, Lagercrantz, Winberg, and Öfverholm (1978) have shown, for instance, that the side effects of putting drops into the newborn's eyes (Credé prophylaxis) affect the expressive mimicry that may be significant for bonding and continued interaction between mother and baby.

Mothers of low birth weight babies may often fail to initiate interaction because of shock or disappointment at the appearance and unresponsiveness of their infants. Grief can further handicap their ability to recognize and understand outgoing moves the baby may make, so that he gets no feedback when he is ready to initiate.

In societies where the infant is carried on his mother's body (Konner, 1977; Lozoff and Brittenham, 1978), both are at an advantage, for the baby can communicate subtle, initiating impulses that are scarcely perceptible except through the mother's skin (Montagu, 1978). For this reason, toilet training is hardly an issue: perceiving her infant's need to urinate or defecate, the mother simply lifts him away from her body.

Some procedures, like CPAP (Continuous Positive Airways Pressure) amount to "initiating by machinery." They create a setting which leaves little scope for spontaneous, reciprocal interaction, and until the baby has been successfully weaned from his attachment to the machine, his opportunities for initiating contact are significantly reduced. Even so, when occasionally a baby extubates himself, one has sometimes the impression that it did not happen entirely by chance, but that the baby was trying to say that he is ready to manage without the tube.

Nonnutritive Sucking and "Holding On"

Nonnutritive sucking probably plays a major role in safeguarding continuity of salient stimuli from intrauterine to extrauterine experiences (Ribble, 1943; Anderson, 1977). Tube-fed babies are denied basic psychological experiences mediated through the oral cavity (Spitz, 1955) and via the tongue (Bonnard 1960), but too little is known about how such deprivation affects later development. For this, one may need longitudinal studies supported by periodic evaluation (see Engel and Reichsman, 1956; Engel, 1967). Exploration of parameters that are clinically meaningful and significant in terms of emotional development (Eissler, Freud, Kris, and Salnit, 1977) may prove useful here.

An infant needs something to hold on to in the widest sense. Brazelton (1973) speaks of maneuvers like holding, cuddling, rocking, and crooning as ways of bringing a baby to more alert states. On several occasions a coobserver (Dr. Averil Earnshaw) and I offered a very sick baby who was in an incubator a finger to suck. More than once he rallied dramatically: he sucked with amazing vigor and became temporarily far more alert and coordinated than he had been before; sometimes this was accompanied by marked changes in the color of his skin. Both of us had the distinct impression that his sucking was in the service of holding on, and we felt that the uninterrupted presence of his mother might have assured sufficient alertness for him not to give up and die.[2]

Psychological Immunity

When infants fail to thrive in spite of excellent physical surroundings through lack or insufficiency of maternal care (Spitz, 1945, 1946; Provence and Lipton, 1962), one can think in terms of "psychological immunity."[3] It is conferred on a baby when his mother is in tune with him and meets his requirements for warmth, comfort, and mutually enjoyable interaction. In breast-feeding it is not only the chemical composition of the

[2] The importance of nonnutritive sucking in terms of "holding on" and survival is supported by studies on the recovery, following nonnutritive sucking, of newborn lambs from severe respiratory distress (Anderson, 1975).

[3] Foundations for psychological immunity are probably laid in utero through the quality of the mother's cathexis of the fetus. A somatic substratum, perhaps in terms of body memories, may be the basis for later pleasurable and satisfying feelings, which in turn promote ego formation.

milk which gives protection but also the intimate emotional interchange that takes place in the feeding process itself (Newton, Peeler, and Rawlins, 1971). Pleasurable experiences build up a fund of resilience which facilitates adaptation and on which the infant can draw in times of stress. Generally, psychological immunity may play a much larger part in the infant's viability and in his resistance to infection and other hazards than has hitherto been assumed.

Psychodynamic Aspects of Mother-Infant Interaction

Of the three psychological inner agencies in the adult—id, ego, superego (conscience)—the ego has the crucial role of mediating among instinctual demands, the pressures of the external world, and the person's conscience. In infancy and childhood the adult precepts and demands represent the superego until they are internalized (taken over and consolidated) through the ongoing structuralization of the inner personality.

For earliest infancy we postulate a gradual development from physiological-biological modes of functioning to psychological ones. In this process of ego building the mother acts as the infant's auxiliary ego: she has the task of finding compromises between his vital needs on the one hand and her own needs and the demands of the environment on the other (W.E. Freud, 1967).

Ideally, a mother is always sufficiently in tune with her infant to anticipate his needs promptly and to held him consolidate gains in his development. She supports him in taking the next steps on the way to independence whenever he is ready for them. Sometimes, however, latent aspects of her personality interfere with optimal mothering; inflexibility of rigid defenses, fixation points, unresolved conflicts, and anxieties can make her less aware of her infant's needs and less responsive to his signals (Kris, 1957). Psychotherapeutic intervention may then be indicated. A well-baby clinic, in the role of "the auxiliary ego's auxiliary ego," can often be helpful here (W.E. Freud and I. Freud, 1976). An enlightened NICU can similarly be supportive, when its staff is sufficiently aware of the parents' and the baby's psychological needs (Klaus and Kennell, 1976; Prince, Firlej, and Harvey, 1978).

Implications for Neonatal Intensive Care: Skin-to-Skin
Nurturing

From a psychoanalytically oriented perspective the inter-
connected hazards of separation, the dearth of the baby's oral
experiences, and the general lack of stimulation are perhaps
the most prominent drawbacks to a smooth development of the
mother-infant relationship. My preliminary impressions suggest a solution which puts the emphasis on greater physical
closeness between mother and baby as a vehicle for promoting
mother-infant interaction. Some of the iatrogenic hazards may
thereby be ameliorated; others may simply not arise.

The biological mother is the obvious person to attend to
the neeeds of her baby. I believe that even in contempoary
industrialized societies many mothers of full-term as well as of
at-risk babies would welcome more skin-to-skin contact if given
the option. When a mother is not willing or able, for whatever
reasons, to take part in such a program, her decision and condition must be respected.

Observation of mother and baby during skin-to-skin caregiving would give more reliable indications of the mother's parenting potential and of the infant's response capacity. Early
spotting of flaws in their interaction patterns would facilitate
earlier planning for psychotherapeutic intervention within the
hospital setting, if necessary (Aradine, Shapiro, and Fraiberg,
1978). In cases when a baby is to be adopted, skin-to-skin caregiving by the prospective substitute mother could provide new
opportunities for assessing compatibility and might offer better
prospects for early bonding and mutual attachment.

Even though seriously ill, babies may be the ones who need
the closeness of their mothers most; their condition may in itself
be a contraindication for too much physical contact. The general attitude of medical and nursing staff, however, is probably
decisive in creating a favorable climate in which such setbacks
are regarded as purely temporary.

To start with, I envisage skin-to-skin caregiving primarily
for babies who have achieved "intermediate" status (i.e., who
are able to breathe room air, are in cots, and have reached a
certain weight) but who now "mark time" in the units to put on

weight and "grow"; clearly, criteria for eligibility will have to be worked out as experience and confidence are gained. To illustrate the feasibility of implementation, I will mention a pilot study which was done to test the temperature of babies in direct contact with their mothers (Cheetham and Garrow, 1978). In one of the first trials, which I observed, the mother was sitting in bed. Her 5-day-old premature girl of 1760 grams was naked, except for some light cotton blankets covering her back. She was placed inside the mother's nightgown, between her breasts. The mother was at ease and delighted; the baby slept peacefully. After 55 minutes, the baby's core temperature had risen by 1.8 degrees centigrade. Controlled trials to explore this further will be carried out elsewhere.

Conclusion

A mother and her baby are intended to fulfill each other. Greater awareness and appreciation of their psychological needs suggest provision of opportunities for more physical closeness between them as a way out of the present impasse in neonatal intensive care (Lozoff, Brittenham, Trause, Kennell, & Klaus, 1977): Extended skin-to-skin caregiving holds the promise of prophylactic and therapeutic gains. It is not just the close bodily contact which is beneficial but equally its potential for initiating and consolidating the mother-infant relationship. Mothers and at-risk babies could profit greatly from a combination of advanced medical technology and the insights of dynamic psychology.

References

Anderson, G.C. (1975), Severe respiratory distress in transitional newborn lambs with recovery following non-nutritive sucking. *J. Nurse-Midwifery,* 20:24–27.
——— (1977), The mother and her newborn: mutual caregivers. *J. Nurses Assn. Amer. College of Obstetricians and Gynecologists,* 6:50–57.
Andersson, Y., Lagercrantz, H., Winberg, J., & Öfverholm, U. (1978), Konjunktivit, mimik-och synbeteende hos nyfödda barn före och efter Credé

profylax (Conjunctivitis, expressive and visual behavior among newborn children before and after Credé prophylaxis). *Lakartidningen*, 75:302–304.

Aradine, C., Shapiro, V., & Fraiberg, S. (1978), Collaborating to foster family attachment. *Amer. J. Maternal Child Nursing*, pp. 92–98.

Bibring, G.L. (1959), Some considerations of the psychological processes in pregnancy. *The Psychoanalytic Study of the Child*, 14:113–121. New York: International Universities Press.

—— Dwyer, T.F., Huntington, D.S., & Valenstein, A.F. (1961), A study of the psychological processes in pregnancy and of the earliest mother-child relationship: I. Some propositions and comments; II. Methodological considerations. *The Psychoanalytic Study of the Child*, 16:9–72. New York: International Universities Press.

Bonnard, A. (1960), The primal significance of the tongue. *Internat. J. Psycho-Anal.*, 41:301–307.

Brazelton, T.B. (1973), *Neonatal Behavioral Assessment Scale*. Spastics International Medical Publications, Clinics in Developmental Medicine, 50. London: William Heinemann Medical Books.

—— Tronick, E., Adamson, L., Als, H., & Weise, S. (1975), Early mother-infant reciprocity. In: *Parent-Infant Interaction*, Ciba Foundation Symposium 33. North Holland: Elsevier, Excerpta Medica, pp. 137–154.

Brimblecombe, F.S.W. (1978), Personal communication.

—— Richards, M.P.M., & Roberton, N.R.C. (1978), *Early Separation and Special Care Baby Units*. Spastics International Medical Publications, Clinics in Developmental Medicine, 68. London: William Heinemann Medical Books.

Brown, J., & Helper, R. (1976), Stimulation—a corollary to physical care. *Amer. J. Nursing*, 76:578–581.

Cheetham, C.H., & Garrow, D.H. (1978), Personal communication.

De Chateau, P., & Wiberg, B. (1977a), Long-term effect on mother-infant behaviour of extra contact during the first hour post partum: I. First observations at 36 hours. *Acta Paediatrica Scandinavia*, 66:137–143.

—— —— (1977b), Long-term effect on mother-infant behaviour of extra contact during the first hour post partum: II. A follow-up at three months. *Acta Paediatrica Scandinavia*, 66:145–151.

Eissler, R., Freud, A., Kris, M., & Solnit, A.J., eds. (1977), *Psychoanalytic Assessment: The Diagnostic Profile*. New Haven: Yale University Press.

Engel, G.L. (1967), Ego development following severe trauma in infancy: A 14 year study of a girl with gastric fistula and depression in infancy. *Bull. Assn. for Psychosom. Research*, 6:57–61.

—— & Reichsman, F. (1956), Spontaneous and experimentally induced depressions in an infant with gastric fistula. *J. Amer. Psychoanal. Assn.*, 4:428–452.

Freedman, D.G., Boverman, H., & Freedman, N. (1960), Effects of kinesthetic simulation on weight gain and smiling in premature infants. Paper presented at the meeting of the American Orthopsychiatric Association, San Francisco, April.

Freud, A. (1922–1970), *The Writings of Anna Freud*. Vols. 1–7. New York: International Universities Press.

Freud, S. (1917), Introductory lectures on psycho-analysis, *Standard Edition*, 16. London: Hogarth Press, 1963.

Freud, W.E. (1967), Assessment of early infancy-problems and considerations. *The Psychoanalytic Study of the Child*, 22:216–238.

—— (1971), The baby profile: Part II. *The Psychoanalytic Study of the Child*, 26:172–194. New York: International Universities Press.

—— (1975), Infant observation: Its relevance to psychoanalytic training. *The Psychoanalytic Study of the Child*, 30:75–94. New York: International Universities Press.

—— & Freud, I. (1976), The well-baby clinic. *Child Psychiat. & Human Development*, 7:67–84.

Kattwinkel, J., Nearman, H.S., Fanaroff, A.A., Katona, P.G., & Klaus, M.H. (1975), Apnea of prematurity: Comparative therapeutic effects of cutaneous stimulation and nasal continuous positive airways pressure. *J. Pediatrics*, 86:588–592, 1975.

Katz, V. (1971), Auditory stimulation and development behavior of the premature infant. *Nursing Research*, 20:196–201.

Kennell, J., Jerauld, R., Wolfe, H., Chesler, D., Kreger, N., McAlpine, W., Steffa, M., & Klaus, M. (1974), Maternal behavior one year after early and extended post-partum contact. *Developments in Medical Child Neurology*, 16:172–179.

Kitzinger, S., & Davis, J.A., eds. (1978), *The Place of Birth*. Oxford: Oxford Medical Publications, Oxford University Press.

Klaus, M.H., Jerauld, R., Kreger, N., McAlpine, W., Steffa, M., & Kennell, J.H. (1972), Maternal attachment: Importance of the first post-partum days. *N. Engl. J. Med.*, 286:460–463.

—— Kennell, J.H. (1976), *Maternal-infant bonding: The impact of Early Separation or Loss on Family Development*. Saint Louis: Mosby.

Konner, M. (1977), Infancy among the Kalahari Desert San. In: *Culture and Infancy*, ed. H. Liederman, S.R. Tulkin, & A. Rosenfeld. New York: Academic Press, pp. 288–328.

Korner, A.F. (1979), Maternal rhythms and waterbeds: A form of intervention with premature infants. In: *Origins of the Infant's Social Responsiveness*, ed. E.B. Thoman. Hillsdale, N.J.: Erlbaum, pp. 95–124.

—— & Thoman, E.B. (1972), The relative efficacy of contact and vestibular-proprioceptive stimulation in soothing neonates. *Child Development*, 43:443–453.

—— Guilleminault, C., Van den Hoed, J., & Baldwin, R.B. (1978), Reduction of sleep apnoea and bradycardia in preterm infants on oscillating water beds: A controlled polygraphic study. *Pediatrics*, 61:528–533.

Kramer, L.I., & Pierpont, M.E. (1976), Rocking waterbeds and auditory stimuli to enhance growth of preterm infants. *Journal of Pediatrics*, 88(2):297–299, February 1976.

Kramer, M., Chamorro, I., Green, D., & Knudtson, F. (1975), Extra tactile stimulation of the premature infant. *Nursing Research*, 24:324–334.

Kris, M. (1957), The use of prediction in a longitudinal study. *The Psychoanalytic Study of the Child*, 12:175–189. New York: International Universities Press.

Leboyer, F. (1975), *Birth Without Violence*. London: Wildwood House.

Lewis, E. (1976), The management of stillbirth—coping with an unreality. *Lancet*, 2:619–620.

—— & Page, A. (1978), Failure to mourn a stillbirth: An overlooked catastrophe. *Brit. J. Med. Psychol.*, 51:237–241.

Liedloff, J. (1976), *The Continuum Concept.* London: Futura Publications.

Liley, A.W. (1972), The foetus as a personality. *Austral. & New Zeal. J. Psychiat.*, 6:99–105.

Lockwood, R. (1978), Personal communication.

Lozoff, B., & Brittenham, G.M. (1978), Infant care: Cache or carry. Presented at the Society for Pediatric Research Spring Meetings, New York.

—— —— Trause, M.A., Kennell, J.H., & Klaus, M.H. (1977), The mother-newborn relationship: Limits of adaptability. *J. Pediatrics*, 91:1–12.

Macfarlane, A. (1977), *The Psychology of Childbirth.* London: Fontana/Open Books.

Marton, P., Dawson, H., & Minde, K. (1980), The interaction of ward personnel with infants in the premature nursery. *Infant Behav. & Development*, 3:307–313.

Miller, F.J.W. (1948), Home nursing of premature babies in Newcastle-on-Tyne. *Lancet*, Oct. 30, pp. 703–705.

Minde, K., Ford, L., Cellhoffer, L., & Boukydis, C. (1975), Interaction of mothers and nurses with premature infants. *Canad. Med. J.*, 113:741–745.

Montagu, A. (1978), *Touching: The Human Significance of the Skin.* 2nd Ed. New York: Harper & Row.

Newman, L.F. (1981), Social and sensory environment of low birth weight infants in a special care nursery: An anthropological investigation. *J. Nervous Mental Dis.*, 169:448–455.

Newton, H., Peeler, D., & Rawlins, C. (1971), Does breastfeeding influence mother love? *Psychosom. Med. Obstet. Gynecol.* Proceedings of the 3rd International Congress. London: Karger. pp. 296–298.

Prince, J., Firlej, M., & Harvey, D. (1978), Contact between babies in incubators and their caretakers. In: *Separation and Special Care Baby Units,* ed. F.S.W. Brimblecombe, M.P.M. Richards, & N.R.C. Roberton. Spastics International Medical Publications, Clinics in Developmental Medicine, 68. London: William Heinemann Medical Books, pp. 55–63.

Provence, S., & Lipton, R.C. (1962), *Infants in Institutions.* New York: International Universities Press.

Prugh, D.G. (1953), Emotional problems of the premature infant's parents. *Nursing Outlook*, 1(8):461–464.

Ribble, M.A. (1943), *The Rights of Infants: Early Psychological Needs and Their Satisfaction.* New York: Columbia University Press.

Richards, M.P.M. (1978), Possible effects of early separation on later development of children: A review. In: *Separation and Special Care Baby Units,* ed. F.S.W. Brimblecombe, M.P.M. Richards, & N.R.C. Roberton. Spastics International Medical Publications, Clinics in Developmental Medicine, 68. London: William Heinemann Medical Books, pp. 12–32.

Sander, L.W. (1962), Issues in early mother-child interaction. *J. Amer. Acad. Child Psychiat.*, 1:141–166.

Smitherman, C. (1969), The vocal behavior of infants as related to the nursing procedure of rocking. *Nursing Research*, 18:256–258.

Sontag, L.W. (1941), The significance of fetal environmental differences. *Amer. J. Obstet. & Gynecol.*, 42:996–1003.

Spitz, R.A. (1945), Hospitalism: An inquiry into the genesis of psychiatric conditions in early childhood. *The Psychoanalytic Study of the Child*, 1:53–74. New York: International Universities Press.

————— (1946), Hospitalism: A follow-up report. *The Psychoanalytic Study of Child*, 2:113–117, New York: International Universities Press.

————— (1955), The primal cavity: A contribution to the genesis of perception and its role for psychoanalytic theory. *The Psychoanalytic Study of the Child*, 10:215–240. New York: International Universities Press.

————— (1965), *The First Year of Life*. New York: International Universities Press.

Steinhausen, H. (1976), Psychologische Aspekte der Neonatologie: Zur Entwicklung von Fruhgeborenen. (Psychological aspects of neonatology: On the development of premature infants.) *Monatsschrift für Kinderbeilkunde*, 124:570–576.

Weil, A.P. (1970), The basic core. *The Psychoanalytic Study of the Child*, 25:442–460. New York: International Universities Press.

15

Infants, Mothers, and Their Interaction: A Quantitative Clinical Approach to Developmental Assessment

STANLEY I. GREENSPAN. M.D.

ALICIA F. LIEBERMAN, PH.D.

It is well documented that infants' spontaneous behavior is richly organized from birth and that this organization becomes progressively more complex during the first few years of life. The accumulated knowledge supporting this view has led to a radical change in the scientific conception of the infant, from a conglomerate of isolated reflexes to an organism born with considerable preadaptation to the social encounters that are an essential feature of the postnatal environment.

This current conception is neither new nor original. Clinicians working within the psychoanalytic tradition have long postulated that the infant's behavior is organized and complex. Freud (1911) attributed to the infant the capacity for hallucinatory wish fulfillment, and while this view was criticized by Piaget (1951) on the grounds that representational thinking does not occur until late in the second year of life, more recent empirical investigations do support the notion of an innate organizational capacity (Sander, 1962; Emde, Gaensbauer, and Harmon, 1976). Similarly, Freud's postulation of the pleasure

Staff of the Clinical Infant Development Program of The Mental Health Study Center conducted the clinical work on which this chapter is based. Clinicians, infant specialists, supervisors, and developmental assessor recorder of the cases reported were Mrs. Euthymia Hibbs, Mrs. Eva Hollingsworth, Dr. Reginald Lourie, Dr. Robert Nover, Mr. Edward Turner, and Miss Martha Esch.

principle (1911) as a governing element in the early organization of behavior is also consistent with recent empirical findings (Lipsitt, 1979). Hartmann's work (1939) is perhaps most clearly in tune with current views. His hypothesis that both psychic structures and drives evolve from an undifferentiated matrix containing the rudiments of ego and id was advanced at a time when it could muster little empirical support. Yet studies by Brazelton, Koslowski, and Main (1974) and Murphy and Moriarty (1976) now make it plausible to assume that certain rudimentary ego functions are already present at birth. These comments are meant to show that the early clinicians had a deep appreciation for the complexity of infant behavior and that their theoretical formulations—while perhaps open to further refinement—reflected nonetheless some basic truths which have become clearer in the last fifteen years.

The evolving conception of the infant's capabilities has in turn influenced thinking on the first human relationship—the infant-mother dyad. As Schaffer (1975) pointed out, it is now apparent that the mother does not create order out of chaos; rather, she accommodates her behavior so that it fits in with a preexisting organization. The exchanges between mother and infant are social encounters in which mutual influence is exerted through each participant's responsiveness to the partner's behavior (Bell, 1968). This view is reflected in current research trends which emphasize the need for a dyadic framework and rely increasingly on microanalytic techniques (Stern 1974a; Kay, 1975; Stern, Beebe, Jaffe, and Bennett, 1975) and the use of sequential analyses that attempt to capture the temporal flow of the interaction (Bakeman and Brown, 1977).

While they are promising, these approaches do not address the question of the meaning of behavior, a central concern for clinicians interested in mother-infant interaction and its implications for the infant's development. The reasons for this are various. Some studies have focused on behaviors whose relevance to a broad picture of the mother-infant relationship is not immediately apparent. Other investigations focus only on a few behavioral dimensions (e.g., vocal interchange, patterns of mutual gazing) which are important vehicles for the social exchanges but do not by themselves exhaustively describe those exchanges. The same may be argued about some of the studies that pioneered the current interest in mother-infant interaction. Ainsworth and her colleagues (Ainsworth and Bell, 1969; Ainsworth, Bell, and Stayton, 1972; Tracy, Lamb, and Ainsworth, 1976;.Blehar, Lieberman, and Ainsworth, 1977), for example, developed very sensitive measures to describe different aspects of the interaction in the home. They then complemented these naturalistic observations with a structured laboratory instrument—the strange situation—that provides a summary glimpse, so to speak, of the quality of infant-mother attachment. These studies illustrate how different aspects of the daily transactions between mother and infant contribute to one dimension of their relationship—the quality of the child's attachment. Yet valuable as they are, they do not provide an instrument to assess simultaneously other parameters of the mother-infant relationship—for example, the infant's range of phase-appropriate affect and capacities for eliciting maternal overtures or the mother's encouragement of the infant's exploration.

In general, the issue of the meaning of behavior has not been thoroughly addressed in current academic research because behavioral units are not interpreted within the total developmental context in which they occur. Two aspects of this developmental context should be highlighted. The first is the level of personality organization as evidenced by structural features, such as the level of differentiation attained by the individual. The second aspect is content-oriented and involves thematic as opposed to structural features. Examples are the styles of pleasure (oral, anal, genital) characteristic of an individual or the specific solutions found to organize polarities of impulse and affect.

Rationale for an Alternative Approach

In developing our method for the study of meaning in infant-mother dyads, we adopted a "clinical" approach. The clinical paradigm teaches us to use the maximum amount of information in an attempt to make sense out of it and to understand how different components fit together. We do not exclude information to improve rating reliability. Instead, we welcome ambiguity and use it with the goal of unraveling its hidden meaning by broadening our constructs.

In developing our approach, we took some guidance from the free-associative method developed early in the history of psychoanalysis. It was found then and is still confirmed that a great deal of information is obtained when an adult seeking clinical assistance is permitted to talk without restrictions, with the therapist or interviewer doing little more than facilitating the flow of associations. These free associations allow the clinician to make reasonably good judgments about the structure of the individual's mental processes, as well as the dynamic trends operating in the context of that structure.

Using the free-associative method in adults as our point of departure, we reasoned backward that it may be possible to look at the "free associations" of the infant and the mother-infant dyad. What, we asked, would be the equivalent of the free-associative approach at this stage of development? Here we took another clue from the history of psychoanalysis. Anna Freud (1922–1970) has repeatedly pointed out that the free play of children resembles the free associations of adults in the access it provides to complex emotional life. Children are different from infants because they have an internalized psychic structure. Infants, on the other hand, function primarily within the context of a dyadic relationship. Nevertheless, we reasoned that the dyadic free play may provide us access to complex emotional phenomena similar to the free play of childhood and the free associations of adulthood.

In order to learn about meaning in infant-mother dyads in the context of structure and content, we have developed a method for the study of mother-infant interaction which employs a seminaturalistic situation (a playroom) in which mother and infant are free to interact as they are accustomed to. We then attempt to understand the behavioral sample obtained by focusing on expected, phase-specific developmental tasks during each stage of infant development. (These tasks are described in the next section.)

The most crucial step was to identify and describe the complex psychic phenomena we wished to assess, leading us to devise a conceptual framework for the sequence of developmental tasks facing the infant. We identified these tasks as involving the capacity to achieve homeostasis, the establishment of attachment relationships, the differentiation of psychological and behavioral patterns, and, finally, the attainment of higher order organizational processes characterized by internalization, initiative, originality, and autonomy in the second year of life (Greenspan, 1979). From this conceptual framework we derived specific measures to assess how these levels of organization are reflected in the mother-infant free play and to investigate the relative incidence of each organizational level at different times in the infant's development. We present first a brief outline of the conceptual framework underlying the measures developed, and will then describe each of them.

The Conceptual Framework

This framework is based on three premises now well supported by empirical evidence. The first is that the infant is capable of adaptive responses to the environment from birth (Gewirtz, 1965, 1969; Lipsitt, 1966; Klaus and Kennell, 1976; Meltzoff and Moore, 1977). The second is that behavior becomes progressively more organized during the first 2 years (Escalona, 1968; Sroufe, Waters, and Matas, 1974; Stern 1974a, 1974b; Emde, Gaensbauer, and Harmon, 1976). The third is that infants show individual differences from the time of birth and that these differences are related to the later development of coping skills, including precursors of a number of basic ego functions (Wolff, 1966; Thomas, Chess, and Birch, 1968; Parmelee, 1972).

The Capacity to Achieve Homeostasis

The capacity to achieve homeostasis can be defined as the first area in which we may observe the newborn infant's strengths and weaknesses. This task involves the ability to regulate states, form basic cycles and rhythms of sleep and wakefulness, organize internal and external experience (e.g., habituate to stimuli, organize patterns), and integrate a number of modalities into more complex patterns such as self-soothing and coping with noxious stimuli. Many factors may contribute to a disorder of homeostasis, among them gross physical and neurological defects, immaturity of the central nervous system, difficulties in early patterns of integration, organ sensitivities, and allergies. The excitable infant who cannot habituate to stimulation, the infant with specific (auditory, tactile) sensitivities, the infant with immature motor responses who cannot orient successfully or use the caregiver to calm down, are all experiencing difficulties of homeostasis. While gross deficits in perceptual apparatuses (e.g., blindness or deafness) make the infant more prone to a disorder of homeostasis, other integrative functions may exert their influence and provide the infant a reasonably good compensatory experience.

It should be emphasized that the capacity for homeostasis is not simply the capacity for a state of calm or rest. Rather, the optimal capacity for homeostasis involves the integration of developmentally facilitating life experiences in the fullest sense. This means reaching a state of organized experience in the context of taking in stimulation through available sensory modalities and organizing internal experience in a developmentally appropriate manner which will foster the initiation of human relationships and interest in the world.

Even in the absence of manifest symptoms (e.g., excessive irritability, withdrawal, etc.) or in the face of stress, we can observe the degree to which an infant organizes a homeostatic experience. For example, the infant who is alert, oriented to, and engaged in the animate and inanimate world in the context of established patterns of feeding and of sleep and waking may be contrasted with the infant who can be calm only at the expense of an optimal state of alertness and engagement. The former might react to a mild stress or illness with a temporary change in sleep pattern, while for the latter a similar stress may trigger intense apathy and lack of engagement with the animate or inanimate environment.

Individual differences are important in determining the homeostatic patterns of the newborn, but it is also well known that the relationship between infant and caregivers plays a crucial role in establishing basic rhythms (Sander, 1962; Lewis and

Rosenblum, 1974). In optimal situations there appears to be an early synchrony between the neonate and its nurturing environment, a "fitting in" described in his own terms by Winnicott (1954, 1956). This "fitting in," in conjunction with the innate behavioral repertoire and neurophysiological equipment, allows the neonate to begin organizing its somatic patterns. In less than optimal conditions, the lack of synchrony leads to a brittle somatic organization, even when the newborn is constitutionally intact. Witness the infant who is maintained in a constant state of drowsiness by a caregiver who finds it more convenient to keep the infant quiet, or the neonate who is kept in a state of heightened excitation by an overstimulating caregiver, or the infant who cannot reorganize after stress because the caregiver declines to intervene in a soothing manner. These examples highlight the importance, as an adaptive tool, of the organism's capacity for establishing rhythmic homeostatic patterns within itself and with the caregiving environment. This capacity provides the infant important protection during the earliest weeks of life and serves as a foundation for later adaptation.

The Capacity for Human Attachment

Whereas in the first few months of life we can observe the flexibility of the infant's capacity for achieving a homeostatic experience, we should see a higher level of organization by age 2 to 4 months, as manifested in the evolving capacity for human attachment.

The capacity for attachment is reflected in the quality of somatic-homeostatic experience achieved between the infant and primary caretakers and in the quality of feeling and reciprocal interaction available to the dyad. The reciprocal use of multiple sensory modalities, the degree of contingency in the interactions, the organization and complexity of the early communication patterns, and the depth and phase appropriateness of feelings experienced and expressed by the dyad are all parameters which may indicate the range and quality of the attachment relationship. The degree to which stress on the part of either partner compromises optimal quality provides a picture of the stability of the early attachment patterns and also indicates the level of organization attained in the earliest learning.

The disorders of this phase illustrate the variability of individual patterns already present at this age. The most severe attachment disorder is that of the autistic youngster who, because of genetic or constitutional difficulties˙ or severe early environmental trauma, never fully achieves homeostasis and does not move on to the second task of human attachment. We also see disorders of human attachment in infants of depressed mothers who cannot reach out to their infants. These infants' attachments seem shallow and insecure. The infant whose constitutional makeup makes physical touch or other kinds of human stimulation painful may also have the basis for a disorder of attachment.

The Capacity for Somato-Psychological Differentiation

Once a secure human attachment is achieved through the mutual cueing and reciprocal responses of infant and primary caregivers, there occurs a process of emotional differentiation similar to the process of means-ends differentiation in sensorimotor development. Through this process basic schemes of causality are established that are the bases for the most fundamental aspects of reality testing. While the infant is having internal "emotional" sensations and experiences, however, these do not exist at an "organized" psychological or mental representational level.[1]

Means-ends differentiation may be observed in the somato-psychological sphere as the infant begins to differentiate one person from another, distinguishes among a variety of somato-psychological states (e.g., hunger and other states such as dependency needs or the need for affection), and differentiates the many moods or communications from primary caregivers. Differentiation is facilitated through social interaction as well as interaction with the inanimate world. Thus, contingent responses help the infant to appreciate his role as a causal agent and thereby to distinguish means from ends in interpersonal

---

[1] The organization of internal representations obviously occurs gradually, and we are therefore speaking in *relative* terms.

relationships. Not only obvious patterns of interaction, but also subtle emotional and empathic interactive patterns undergo a process of differentiation. As a result, an infant may be capable of differentiation in the areas of gross motor responses and general interpersonal causality and yet remain undifferentiated at a subtle empathic emotional level. For example, if there is no empathic emotional interaction between caregiver and infant, the family may not learn to appreciate basic causal relationships between people at the level of feelings as compared to acts (e.g., feeling angry can cause another to feel bad). Or an infant, because of undifferentiated or inappropriate responses from the caregiver, may use psychophysiological patterns of response to situations where a social response would be more adaptive (e.g., responding with gastric distress rather than motor activity to communicate emotional hunger or frustration).

During this stage we can observe the shift from magical causality (as when an infant pulls a string to ring a bell which is no longer there) to consolidation of simple causal links, and later to the beginning of more complicated means-ends differentiation, as in the use of substitutes, detours, or intermediary devices. The foundation for flexibility of coping style is thus initiated.

Somato-psychological differentiation may be studied in the context of phase-appropriate dimensions of differentiation in cognition, human relationships, affects, and the flexibility to deal with phase-appropriate experience and stress without compromising developmentally facilitating behavior.

An extreme defect in differentiation occurs in the infant who fails to develop age-appropriate contingent responses either because of constitutional factors, earlier development, or a withdrawn or overly intrusive primary caregiver. A less severe problem exists when, because of the character of contingent responses, only one aspect of emotional differentiation is compromised; for example, anger is ignored or leads to withdrawal.

Behavioral Organization, Initiative, and Originality
(Internalization)

As the stage of somato-psychological differentiation becomes well organized, and the infant becomes able to differentiate clearly and subtly the significant others in the interpersonal sphere, an increase occurs in the process of internalization or "taking in." This is evidenced by an increase in initiative behavior. As the capacity to internalize becomes more developed, emotional systems like affiliation, fear and wariness, and curiosity and exploration become organized (Bowlby, 1969). The study of attachment (Main, 1973; Ainsworth, Bell, and Stayton, 1974) as a complex "high-order" behavioral organization illustrates the development of constructs that match the infant's greater organization of behavior at this time.

Initiative and exploration are enhanced by the capacity for combining schemes into *new* behavioral organizations that are goal directed (e.g., further use of detours, substitutes, delays, and intermediary devices). The infant's capacity to take initiative and organize behavior and feeling states is enriched by and in part further facilitates his capacity to internalize. For example, we see more initiating behavior after 8 to 10 months of age, which in turn facilitates organized exploratory behavior from the secure base of the primary caregivers. The gradual individuation which occurs is perhaps best described by Mahler's description (1975) of the practicing subphase of the separation-individuation process.

The capacity to engage in original behavior by combining known schemes, complex behavioral patterns (tertiary circular reactions), trial-and-error exploration, enhanced memory, and the gradual shifting from imitation to identification leads to a much greater sense of the toddler as an organized, initiating (e.g., pulling a parent somewhere) human being. There is also evidence for the beginning of a psychological sense of self.

Basic disorders in behavioral organization and internalization may compromise the beginning of internal "psychological" life. Behavior then remains fragmented, related to somatic or external cues. Intentionality and a sense of self are nipped in the bud, so to speak. The capacity to use fantasy and even thought in general may be impaired.

In this regard it is interesting to observe, on the one hand, toddlers who are overprotected and therefore undermined in their initial attempts to take initiative in the human world and, on the other, toddlers who lack access to human support as they attempt to take initiative. In both instances the toddler often shifts from taking initiative in the human world to taking initiative in the inanimate world. Relative overinvestment in the inanimate world—which can be manipulated and controlled, does not undermine initiative, and can be reliably returned to as a base of security—may form the basis of an incapacity for internal experience (fantasies) regarding the human object world.

Rationale for the Development of the Measures

In attempting to develop an empirically valid scoring procedure for mother-infant interaction, we selected "indicator behaviors" that occurred spontaneously and were representative of the developmental level of the mother-infant dyad in the context of the framework outlined above. The term *indicator behaviors* implies that these behaviors are observable and measurable manifestations of the abstract, complex issues that are negotiated at different developmental phases. We were guided in the selection process by a few assumptions.

First, we postulated that all the developmental patterns described earlier are present to some degree during the first 2 years, but that during the ascendancy and dominance of a particular developmental phase we would see relatively more "indicator behaviors" that are representative of either the adaptive or maladaptive characteristics of that phase. The important question is then to define and identify appropriate indicator behaviors that evidence a particular developmental phase and reflect the quality of the mother-infant interaction at that phase.

Our second assumption was that we could select clinically relevant indicator behaviors that would not ignore the harder-to-measure issues of each phase, but rather would capture the richness of clinical meaning in a structural and thematic sense. We should stress that the indicator behaviors to be presented were selected because they appear to be the kinds of behaviors that we and others are using clinically in observing and assessing mother-infant interaction. In other words, we tried to reason backward, starting with an attempt to learn how we make clinical judgments about the quality of mother-infant attachment or the infant's mastery of different developmental phases. Each time we observed a mother-infant dyad directly or watched a tape, we refined the ways in which we developed our clinical judgments. We then tried to clarify our clinical hunches and observations and translated them into categories of indicator behaviors. These categories have undergone a process of continuous modification that is still in progress. In essence the "challenging new case" often challenges us to develop new categories of indicator behaviors. While at some point we will need closure on the instrument to establish norms for various mother-infant populations on the basis of a clinically oriented assessment tool, a readiness for continuing revision should be maintained.

Maternal Behavior

Let us now consider each phase of development in relation to the maternal indicator behaviors we selected for that phase. We predicted that behaviors reflecting somatic patterning would be relevant as indicators of homeostasis. These behaviors involve the mother's relationship with her infant's body and her ability to provide proprioceptive and tactile experiences that might help the baby achieve a balance between internal regulation and interest in the world. Examples include rhythmic behavior, affectionate physical comforting, consoling and soothing behavior, and, in contrast, abrupt handling, physical overstimulation, and direct aversive physical punishment.

In relationship to attachment, our second stage of development, we hypothesized that all the items relevant to homeostasis would be important because behaviors that facilitate homeostasis are also the basis for the formation of an attachment relationship. The mutual engagement between mother and infant helps the latter develop an interest in the world in the context of internal regulation, and this process simultaneously leads to the achievement of homeostasis and forms the building blocks for the formation of attachment. Attachment is obviously taking place during this homeostatic period. For theoretical purposes we distinguished attachment proper as being on the ascendant when the infant's interest in the world acquires a specific quality of interest in the primary caregiver (Bowlby, 1969). Here the focus is more differentiated than the balance between inner harmony and investment in the world: it involves inner harmony in the context of a specific investment in the caregiver. In addition to indicators of homeostasis, other behaviors indicative of attachment are the mother's ability to facilitate interpersonal exchanges and the quality of the pleasure she experiences in interaction with her baby (e.g., overt, guarded, "as if," flat). Other dimensions of attachment are reflected in the mother's behavior, such as nonparticipating but available, nonparticipating and withdrawn, and aversively intrusive.

The developmental phase of somato-psychological differentiation is measured by a number of indicator behaviors selected around the concept of contingency. This concept seemed to us a powerful index of the meaning of behavior because it reflects both structural and thematic personality features. We can assume that at least some minimum level of personality organization underlies an individual's ability to tailor his social responses to his partner's behavior. As personality becomes more differentiated, the ability to respond contingently should become an increasingly prominent feature of social behavior. At the dyadic level, we can assume that two partners who have developed a subtly differentiated relationship tend to respond contingently to each other's cues (Lieberman, 1977). In this sense, contingent behavior is a promising structural index at both the individual and the dyadic levels. Moreover, contingent behavior is an index of thematic features as well, as the incidence may be higher in one thematic area of interaction than in another. For example, an infant may tend to respond contingently to the mother's encouragement of exploration, but protest her attempts to promote physical proximity. Describing such a pattern would do much to convey the flavor of the mother-infant interaction. In summary, contingency is a promising tool for understanding the meaning of behavior, both structurally and thematically.

We identified three basic behavioral manifestations along the contingency dimension: contingent, anticontingent, and noncontingent behaviors. Contingent behaviors involve the mother's (or the caregiver's) ability to read accurately and respond to the infant's signals and communications. Anticontingent behaviors by the mother or caregiver are those that are contradictory to the intended goal of the infant's behaviors and signals as interpreted by the observer. For example, the mother moves away when the infant seeks physical contact with her. Noncontingent behaviors are those that are addressed to the infant but are in no way tailored to the infant's concurrent signals or communications. For instance, the infant may be crawling after a toy and the mother tries to attract his attention by speaking to him.

We sought to describe the thematic context of contingent behavior by identifying areas where contingent behavior might occur (i.e., mother's response to infant's pleasure, displeasure/distress, assertive exploration, aggression, search for interaction or physical contact, or potential for hurt in baby's behavior). We also examined the communication modalities used by the mother (visual, vocal, tactile/motion) and the infant's communication modalities responded to by the mother (visual, auditory/vocal, tactile, movement). The same categories were used to investigate the thematic context of anticontingent and noncontingent behaviors.

In the following phase, labeled organization and initiative (internalization), the infant shifts to more complex organized behavioral patterns in the context of the relationship with the primary caregivers. We also see greater initiative, originality, and independence during this phase. The infant is able to move away from the mother and the mother is able to tolerate this greater independence, at the same time being available as a base of security as the infant organizes his behavior into larger units. Here we postulated that the ability for the infant and the mother to engage in chains of contingent exchanges (Lieberman, 1977) and chains of anticontingent exchanges would partially indicate this capacity for greater organized complexity on the part of the infant and the mother-infant dyad. In addition, we again attempted to capture the thematic context of the interaction by using the same subcategories we developed for contingent and anticontingent behaviors, namely, areas of interaction where chains of contingent and anticontingent exchanges take place, mother's use of communication modalities, and the infant's communication modalities responded to by the mother. We postulated also that the mother's ability to facilitate involvement with the inanimate environment and to encourage developmentally advanced behaviors may be indicators of this capacity for more organized, complex behavior. Finally, the mother's tendency to interfere with or undermine ongoing activities or exploration may be a negative indicator of this capacity for more internalization and organization.

Infant Behavior

The infant behavior measures were developed, following the same format used for the measures of maternal behavior. Somatic patterning refers to the phases of homeostasis and attachment and involves measures of the infant's reaction to his own body and to physical contact with the caregiver: seeking proximity and contact, affectionate behavior, or becoming overstimulated, avoiding or resisting physical proximity and contact, etc. We adapted the measures involving physical contact developed by Ainsworth and her colleagues (e.g., Ainsworth, Bell, and Stayton, 1972). The quality of attachment is also manifested in the initiation or cessation of social interaction, the infant's affect (pleasurable or distressed, flat), and the incidence of aggressive behavior during free play with the caregiver. As was the case with maternal behaviors, the sphere of somatopsychological differentiation is explored through measures of contingent, anticontingent, and noncontingent behavior. Finally, the phase of organization and initiative (internalization) is investigated through measures of orientation to the social and inanimate environment, exploratory manipulation, and roaming. The incidence of chains of exchanges is a dyadic measure, since both mother and infant contribute to it, and the infant's specific contribution in initiating it is reflected in the measure of "initiation of social interaction." Needless to say, the incidence of chains of exchange is considered a measure of the degree of organization of the infant behavior as well as a measure of the organization of dyadic interaction.

The measures of internalization, organization, and initiative developed at the present time address only the more rudimentary initial stages of this process. We anticipate developing new measures to probe the more sophisticated achievements of the infant in this sphere. For example, we are postulating that measures of initiation and of originality are useful in assessing the increasing complexity of behavioral organization and the development of initiative. Similarly, we anticipate that an infant's failure to develop age-appropriate internalization, organization, and initiative may be signaled by a polarity around either extreme negativism or overcompliance, that is, a failure to integrate behavioral polarities. The development of these measures awaits the opportunity to examine carefully the videotaped behavior of our mother-infant dyads when more of the infants move beyond their first birthday and into the second year of life.

In summary, in presenting this approach and some clinical illustrations, we are also offering indirectly a philosophy of empirical research with infants that stems from a developmental structuralist approach to understanding infant development (Greenspan, 1979). This approach attempts to use and benefit from complex clinical insights. In this sense we may think of assessment as a spectrum, comprising at one pole indicator behaviors that are easy to rate because evident and obvious but that perhaps lack clinical relevance, and at the opposite pole undefined behaviors used in unspecified ways to arrive at global clinical judgments. Our goal is a synthesis of empirical clarity and clinical relevance: we tried to specify in empirical, reliable ways those observations that reflect clinical assessments.

Measures of Mother-Infant Interaction and the Observational Setting

The empirical measures we developed are based on the conceptual framework defined above. We conceptualized the free play as a dyadic situation in which the contribution of each participant affects the partner's response (Lewis and Rosenblum, 1974). At the same time, we needed to give proper emphasis to the mother's role in helping the baby achieve age-appropriate developmental goals. Our observational setting and measures were selected to reflect not only the separate contributions of mother and infant to the interaction, but also the fact that each behavior is both determined by, and a response to, the partner's behavior.

The Observational Setting

For the purpose of observing unstructured mother-infant interaction, we developed a seminaturalistic situation which takes place in a playroom and in which mother and infant are free to interact as they are accustomed. The instructions to the mother are: "Can you show me the kinds of things you and your baby like to do together when you are at home?" Mother and infant are then free to interact as they wish for approximately 3 to 5 minutes, after which the observer leaves the room saying that she will return shortly, and mother and infant remain alone for about 5 to 7 minutes. The total interaction is videotaped behind a one-way mirror. The videotapes are automatically timed with a date-time generator in order to facilitate temporal analysis of the data. Behaviors are scored every 15 seconds. The measures are not mutually exclusive: several can be scored simultaneously in the same 15-second interval.

Measures of Materal Behavior

Somatic Patterning/Homeostasis

This dimension involves the mother's relationship with her infant's body, and her provision of proprioceptive and tactile experiences that might be pleasurable, neutral, or aversive to the baby. These measures are described below.

Direct physical punishment: percent of 15-sec. intervals in which the mother slaps, hits, or in other physical ways punishes the infant.

Physical overstimulation leading to infant's distress: percent of 15-sec. intervals in which the mother engages in overly exciting physical interaction with the infant.

Abrupt handling: percent of 15-sec. intervals in which the

mother's holding of the baby is characterized by sudden shifts of position, attempts to force the baby to assume a certain position on mother's lap, or use of jerky movements in handling the infant.

Rough-and-tumble: percent of 15-sec. intervals in which the mother engages in animated but not overly exciting physical games with the infant.

Rhythmic behavior: percent of 15-sec. intervals in which the mother engages in rhythmic games or interactions with the infant (e.g., rocking, or games that have a characteristic and consistent inner rhythm).

Communication modalities used:	Infant's modalities responded to:
visual	visual
vocal	vocal
tactile/motion	tactile
	movement

Affectionate physical behavior: percent of 15-sec. intervals in which the mother cuddles the baby, holds him tenderly, nuzzles him, or kisses him (in the presence or absence of other behaviors, such as vocalizing or smiling).

Communication modalities used:	Infant's modalities responded to:
visual	visual
vocal	vocal
tactile/motion	tactile
	movement

Consoling, soothing: percent of 15-sec. intervals in which the mother resorts to physical contact or vocalization in response to the infant's overt distress.

Communication modalities used:	Infant's modalities responded to:
visual	visual
vocal	vocal
tactile/motion	tactile
	movement

Attachment

Facilitation of interpersonal exchanges: percent of 15-sec. intervals in which the mother actively attempts to engage the baby in a social exchange by speaking to him, encouraging him to coo back at her, smiling, or initiating games with the infant.

Pleasure: percent of 15-sec. intervals in which the mother shows overt pleasure in the infant by laughing or smiling while observing or interacting with the infant.

Guarded, "as if" pleasure: percent of 15-sec. intervals in which the mother's expressions of pleasure seem contrived, as if she were making an effort to enjoy the interaction with the infant.

Flat affect: percent of 15-sec. intervals in which the mother appears to be affectless or depressed while observing the infant or interacting with him.

Nonparticipating but available: percent of 15-sec. intervals in which the mother keeps visually in contact with the baby and seems interested in his activities, but does not engage in any type of interaction.

Nonparticipating withdrawn: percent of 15-sec. intervals in which the mother seems oblivious of and unresponsive to the baby's whereabouts.

Aversively intrusive: percent of 15-sec. intervals in which the mother's attempts to engage the infant in social interaction are markedly out of tune with the baby's current mood and interests as assessed by the observer.

Somato-Psychological Differentiation

Contingent response: percent of 15-sec. intervals in which the mother's behavior is interpreted as a direct and *appropriate* response to her infant's signals and meets the aims of the baby's behavior as evaluated by the observer.

Different Areas of Contingency:

    a.   response to baby's pleasure
    b.   response to baby's displeasure/distress
    c.   response to potential for hurt in baby's behavior
    d.   response to baby's assertive exploration or interest in environment
    e.   response to baby's aggression
    f.   response to baby's seeking interaction or physical contact

Communication modalities used:	Infant's modalities responded to:
visual	visual
vocal	vocal
tactile/motion	tactile
	movement

Noncontingent behavior: percent of 15-sec. intervals in which the mother does not respond to the baby's cues or does not tailor her behavior to them.

Anticontingent behavior: percent of 15-sec. intervals in which the mother's response to the baby's cues is the opposite of what the baby seeks, as interpreted by the observer (e.g., the baby touches the mother's hand in search of physical contact, and the mother responds by withdrawing her hand).

Different Areas of Contingency:

a.   response to baby's pleasure
b.   response to baby's displeasure/pleasure
c.   response to potential for hurt in baby's behavior
d.   response to baby's assertive exploration or interest in environment
e.   response to baby's aggression
f.   response to baby's seeking interaction or physical contact

Communication modalities used:	Infant's modalities responded to:
visual	visual
vocal	vocal
tactile/motion	tactile
	movement

Initiative and Organization

Chains of contingent exchanges: percent of 15-sec. intervals in which there is an uninterrupted succession of two or more exchanges between mother and infant, with a contingent relation linking each exchange pair to the next. An exchange is defined as a dyadic behavior in which either mother or baby clearly responds to the other's signals.

Different Areas of Chains of Contingent Exchanges:

a.   response to baby's pleasure
b.   response to baby's displeasure/distress
c.   response to potential for hurt in baby's behavior
d.   response to baby's assertive exploration or interest in environment
e.   response to baby's aggression
f.   response to baby's seeking interaction or physical contact

Communication modalities used:	Infant's modalities responded to:
visual	visual
vocal	vocal
tactile/motion	tactile
	movement

Chains of anticontingent exchanges: this measure can be considered the obverse of chains of contingent exchanges. Here the mother elicits a behavior from the baby and then responds to it *anticontingently* rather than contingently, forming a chain of two or more exchanges. For example, the mother offers the baby a toy, the baby reaches for it (signaling that he wants it), and the mother withdraws the toy only to offer it again, and so on. The percentage of episodes in which this type of exchange occurs is scored.

Different Areas of Chains of Contingent Exchanges:

    a.   response to baby's pleasure
    b.   response to baby's displeasure/distress
    c.   response to potential for hurt in baby's behavior
    d.   response to baby's assertive exploration or interest in environment
    e.   response to baby's aggression
    f.   response to baby's seeking interaction or physical contact

Communication modalities used:	Infant's modalities responded to:
visual	visual
vocal	vocal
tactile/motion	tactile
	movement

Developmentally facilitating behavior: percent of 15-sec. intervals in which mother attempts to promote behaviors that are not yet completely mastered by the baby, or in which the mother encourages the baby to increase or consolidate mastery (e.g., the mother encourages the baby to reach and grasp by showing him a toy just beyond reach, or holds hands out to him to entice him to walk toward her).

Facilitation of involvement with the inanimate environment: percent of 15-sec. intervals in which the mother encourages the baby to explore the environment or to manipulate toys, or in other ways promotes the infant's interest in the inanimate surroundings.

Interfering or undermining: percent of 15-sec. intervals in which the mother abruptly interrupts the baby's ongoing activity (e.g., the mother draws the infant away from ongoing exploration that takes place independently of the mother). This does not include attempts to protect the baby from danger, such as preventing the baby from poking a finger into the electric outlet.

Measures of Infant Behavior

Somatic Patterning/Homeostasis and Attachment

Resisting physical contact: percent of 15-sec. intervals in which the infant actively struggles to end physical contact with the caregiver by arching backward, pushing away, or attempting to get off the mother's lap.

Physical overstimulation/distress: percent of 15-sec. intervals in which the baby appears to be either overexcited or fussy and distressed.

Seeking proximity: percent of 15-sec. intervals in which the infant approaches the mother but does not establish physical contact with her.

Seeking physical contact: percent of 15-sec. intervals in which the infant clearly signals his desire for physical contact by approaching the mother, clambering up, pulling up to the mother, or in other ways attempting to establish physical contact.

Affectionate physical behavior: percent of 15-sec. intervals in which the infant's behavior culminates in affectionate physical contact. For example, if the infant is already on the mother's lap, he initiates nuzzling or kissing or hugging. If the infant is not physically close to the mother, he approaches and kisses, nuzzles, or hugs her.

Avoidance of physical contact: percent of 15-sec. intervals in which the infant responds to the mother's attempt to initiate physical contact by turning away or crawling/walking away.

Initiation of social interaction: percent of 15-sec. intervals in which the infant makes a social overture toward the mother (scored only if no interaction of any type occurred for at least 15 seconds prior to the infant's behavior).

Interrupts social interaction or physical contact: percent of 15-sec. intervals in which the baby moves away from the mother, thus putting an end to social interaction or physical contact.

Aggressive behavior: percent of 15-sec. intervals in which the infant hits, bites, or kicks the mother.
Pleasure: percent of 15-sec. intervals in which the infant smiles, laughs, and/or bounces.

Distress: percent of 15-sec. intervals in which the infant cries, fusses, or whimpers.

Flat affect: percent of 15-sec. intervals in which the infant appears to be noticeably sober and unresponsive to social stimulation or to the physical environment.

Somato-Psychological Differentiation

Contingent response: percent of 15-sec. intervals in which the infant's behavior is interpreted as a direct and appropriate response to a signal from the mother and meets the mother's intention as evaluated by the observer.

Different Areas of Contingency:

- a.   response to mother's pleasure
- b.   response to mother's facilitation of exploration
- d.   response to mother's seeking interaction or physical contact
- e.   response to mother's commands

Communication modalities used:	Mother's modalities responded to:
visual	visual
auditory/vocal	auditory/vocal
tactile/motion	tactile
	movement

Noncontingent response: percent of 15-sec. intervals in which the infant does not respond to the mother's behavior or does not tailor his responses to the caregiver's cues.

Anticontingent response: percent of 15-sec. intervals in which the infant's response to the mother's signal is the opposite of what the mother seeks as interpreted by the observer (i.e., the caregiver talks and smiles to the infant and the infant averts his face or gaze; or the infant protests caregiver's social initiation).

Different Areas of Contingency:

- a.   response to mother's pleasure
- b.   response to mother's displeasure/anger
- c.   response to mother's facilitation of exploration
- d.   response to mother's seeking interaction or physical contact
- e.   response to mother's commands

Communication modalities used:	Mother's modalities responded to:
visual	visual
auditory/vocal	auditory/vocal
tactile/motion	tactile
	movement

Onlooking behavior: percent of 15-sec. intervals in which the infant observes people or social interactions in his vicinity but does not initiate social contact.

Orientation to inanimate environment: percent of 15-sec. intervals in which the infant observes the inanimate environment or aspects of it without engaging in exploratory manipulation or roaming.

Exploratory manipulation: percent of 15-sec. intervals in which the infant examines an object independently from the mother while remaining in one place.

Exploratory roaming: percent of 15-sec. intervals in which the infant leaves the mother's side and roams or crawls around, either enjoying this activity per se or looking at objects in the environment.

Empirical Application of the Measures

The first step in evaluating the usefulness of the measures was to assess the "goodness of fit" between our clinical impressions of the mother-infant dyads participating in our program and the empirical profiles that emerged when we systematically analyzed videotapes of their free play behavior. To assess this "goodness of it" we selected four cases which had been videotaped on three different occasions, when the infants were 4, 8, and 12 months of age. The videotape analysis was first conducted by one of the authors (A.L.) without systematic reference to the clinical data, although there was some familiarity with the cases. A measure of reliability was then obtained by both authors independently scoring half of the tapes. Reliability was calculated as the sum of the number of agreements, divided by the sum of the number of disagreements (the coders recorded a behavior differently), plus the number of omissions (only one coder recorded a behavior). Intercoder agreement ranged from 70 percent in the case of infant contingent behavior to 100 percent for maternal aversive intrusiveness. The length of the free play periods ranged from 7 to 10 minutes, total (observer in the room and out of the room). In our discussion of the cases, we put particular emphasis on the relationship between the clinical impressions preceding the videotape analysis and the behavioral profile emerging from the data analysis.

Case 1: Mrs. Waters and Eric

Mrs. Waters is black, married, and 32 years old. She and her husband have four children, including the infant who is the focus of our intervention. Clinically, Mrs. Waters presents some obsessive-compulsive personality features which find their most overt expression in her need to plan and control even minor details of the family's daily life. She is engaged in a sadomasochistic relationship with her husband, who has abused her physically and makes no secret of his involvements with other women. Mrs. Waters sees herself in this relationship as a martyr who will endure many indignities for love of her family. There are some indications that the sadistic components of her personality can find expression in her relationship with the older children and in particular with her 11-year-old daughter, whom she often teases or scolds sarcastically. However, Mrs. Waters's personality is, on the whole, well integrated. She has a strong, resilient, and well-functioning ego. When not under severe strain, she is a warm, loving, and empathic mother who works very hard both to support the family financially and to protect her children's psychological welfare.

Mrs. Waters was under severe strain when she agreed to participate in our program. Her husband was on trial for drug-related offenses and eventually was sentenced to a long prison term. Mrs. Waters then found herself alone, pregnant with her fourth child, and forced to support the family on her own. She was overwhelmed by these events and reacted with a pronounced depression, defensive withdrawal from the children, and apathy toward her pregnancy and the new baby's impending birth.

Under these circumstances, the clinician used a crisis-oriented approach. She provided practical help in locating and contacting community agencies that could provide concrete assistance. Listening sympathetically while Mrs. Waters expressed her many worries, the clinician also gave permission to express her grief at being alone and her anger at the husband for leaving her. As she became aware of these feelings and felt it was permissible to articulate them, Mrs. Waters became increasingly able to protect her children from her own conflicts. After an initially difficult period of adjustment to Eric's irritability as a newborn, Mrs. Waters was able to become involved with her infant and to take much pleasure in her interactions with him.

We felt at this point that Mrs. Waters had surmounted a severe situational crisis and that her considerable nurturing capacities were no longer engulfed in her personal conflicts. As a result, we predicted that Mrs. Waters and Eric would engage in phase-appropriate behaviors during the developmental assessments. This prediction was accurate.

Table 1 shows the empirical profile of their interaction at 4, 8, and 12 months. The empirical analysis shows that when Eric was 4 months old, Mrs. Waters engaged in much rhythmic and rough-and-tumble behavior, a pattern that in our conceptual framework serves to facilitate the infant's development of homeostasis. These behaviors declined by 8 and 12 months, although at these two ages there was an increase in physical affection, another indicator of somatic patterning that connotes maternal attachment. Mrs. Waters engaged in very little soothing or consoling behavior, a direct concomitant of the fact that Eric cried or protested only seldom. An important index of attachment—facilitation of interpersonal exchanges—was high at all three ages, as was overt maternal pleasure in exchanges with the infant. The incidence of another index of attachment—her being nonparticipant but available—increased with the infant's age, most probably because the mother, re-

TABLE 1
Case 1 Empirical Analysis Scores[a]

Mother		4 months	8 months	12 months
A.	Somatic patterning/homeostasis			
	1. Direct physical punishment	0%	0%	0%
	2. Physical overstimulation	0	0	0
	3. Abrupt handling	0	0	0
	4. Rough-and-tumble	33.3	21.2	9.1
	5. Rhythmic behavior	66.7	45.5	0
	6. Affectionate physical behavior	0	18.2	14.5
	7. Consoling, soothing	N/A	N/A	1.8
B.	Attachment			
	8. Facilitation of interpersonal exchanges	50.0	39.4	54.4
	9. Nonparticipating, available	8.3	15.2	25.5
	10. Nonparticipating, withdrawn	0	0	0
	11. Aversely intrusive	0	0	0
	12. Pleasure	50.0	65.5	70.0
	13. Guarded, ''as if'' pleasure	0	0	0
	14. Flat affect	0	0	0
C.	Somato-psychological differentiation			
	15. Contingent response.	28.3	29.1	29.1
	Areas:			
	a. Response to baby's pleasure	70.0	60.0	50.0
	b. Response to baby's distress	0	0	10.0
	c. Response to potential for hurt	0	0	0
	d. Response to baby's exploration	0	10.0	15.0
	e. Response to baby's seeking interaction	30.0	30.0	25.0
	16. Noncontingent behavior.	0	0	0
	Areas:			
	a. Response to baby's pleasure	N/A	N/A	N/A
	b. Response to baby's distress	N/A	N/A	N/A
	c. Response to potential for hurt	N/A	N/A	N/A

TABLE 1 (continued)

Mother		4 months	8 months	12 months
	d. Response to baby's exploration	N/A	N/A	N/A
	e. Response to baby's seeking interaction	N/A	N/A	N/A
	17. Anticontingent behavior.	0	0	0
	Areas:			
	a. Response to baby's pleasure	N/A	N/A	N/A
	b. Response to baby's distress	N/A	N/A	N/A
	c. Response to potential for hurt	N/A	N/A	N/A
	d. Response to baby's exploration	N/A	N/A	N/A
	e. Response to baby's seeking interaction	N/A	N/A	N/A
D.	Organization & initiative (internalization)			
	18. Chains of contingent exchanges.	10.0	12.1	23.6
	Areas:			
	a. Baby's pleasure	0	0	0
	b. Baby's distress	N/A	N/A	N/A
	c. Potential for hurt	N/A	N/A	N/A
	d. Baby's exploration	N/A	20.0	10.0
	e. Mutual social interaction	100.0	80.0	90.0
	19. Chains of anticontingent exchanges.	0	0	0
	Areas:			
	a. Baby's pleasure	N/A	N/A	N/A
	b. Baby's distress	N/A	N/A	N/A
	c. Potential for hurt	N/A	N/A	N/A
	d. Baby's exploration	N/A	N/A	N/A
	e. Baby's seeking interaction	N/A	N/A	N/A
	20. Developmentally facilitating behavior	0	3.0	0
	21. Facilitation of involvement with inanimate environment (exploration)	0	12.1	45.5
	22. Interfering or undermining	0	0	0

TABLE 1 (continued)

Infant		4 months	8 months	12 months
A.	Somatic patterning/ homeostasis and attachment			
	1. Resists physical contact	0	3.0	0
	2. Physical overstimulation	0	0	0
	3. Seeks proximity	0	3.0	14.5
	4. Seeks physical contact	0	5.0	3.0
	5. Affectionate physical behavior	0	0	10.0
	6. Avoids physical contact	0	0	0
	7. Initiates social interaction	0	0	7.3
	8. Interrupts social interaction	0	0	0
	9. Aggressive behavior	0	0	0
	10. Pleasure	13.0	30.0	42.0
	11. Distress	0	3.0	14.5
	12. Flat affect	0	0	0
B.	Somato-psychological differentiation			
	13. Contingent response. *Areas:*	50.0	39.0	36.0
	a. Response to mother's pleasure	0	0	0
	b. Response to mother's displeasure	N/A	N/A	N/A
	c. Response to mother's facilitation of exploration	N/A	20.0	12.0
	d. Response to mother's seeking interaction/ physical contact	100.0	80.0	78.0
	e. Response to mother's commands	N/A	N/A	N/A
	14. Noncontingent response. *Areas:*	25.0	18.2	9.1
	a. Response to mother's pleasure	0	0	0
	b. Response to mother's displeasure	N/A	N/A	N/A
	c. Response to mother's facilitation of exploration	N/A	0	0
	d. Response to mother's seeking interaction/ physical contact	100.0	100.0	100.0

TABLE 1 (continued)

Infant		4 months	8 months	12 months
	e. Response to mother's commands	N/A	N/A	N/A
	15. Anticontingent response.	0	3.0	0
	Areas:			
	a. Response to mother's pleasure	N/A	0	N/A
	b. Response to mother's displeasure	N/A	N/A	N/A
	c. Response to mother's facilitation of exploration	N/A	0	N/A
	d. Response to mother's seeking interaction/ physical contact	N/A	100.0	N/A
	e. Response to mother's commands	N/A	N/A	N/A
C.	Organization & initiative (internalization)			
	16. Onlooking behavior	20.0	14.3	10.0
	17. Oriented to inanimate environment	12.5	28.6	5.0
	18. Exploratory manipulation	0	35.7	40.0
	19. Exploratory roaming	0	14.3	30.0

[a]Areas are percentages of the total number of responses.

spectful of the infant's growing capacity for autonomous roaming and exploration, observed his movements without interfering. It is noteworthy that the mother's behavior shows a progressive increase in her attempts to interest the infant in the inanimate environment—a developmentally appropriate occurrence, if we consider that "facilitation of involvement with the inanimate environment" was developed as a measure of the mother's ability to promote internalization and organization of behavior. The mother's appropriate level of contingent responses and the age increase in the incidence of chains of exchanges also reflect this increased behavioral organization. The exchanges centered on reciprocal social interaction between mother and infant.

It is interesting that this otherwise very competent mother seldom encouraged developmentally advanced behaviors in her infant and was content to interact with him without enticing him to attempt unmastered developmental tasks. Also noteworthy is the absence of "negative" behaviors: Mrs. Waters was not observed to engage in anticontingent, interfering, or intrusive behaviors.

Eric's behavior was that of a baby eagerly in love with the world. His contingent responses to the mother were remarkably high at all three age levels. Conversely, the incidence of noncontingent and anticontingent responses was negligible. By 12 months he started to initiate social interaction with the mother, something the other infants we discuss were seldom observed to do. By 12 months he also was busily oriented to the inanimate world, manipulating toys and roaming around the room exploring the environment. There was a moderate incidence of distress.

The dyadic picture that emerges is that of a mother-infant pair in adequate synchrony with each other. The mother, while thoroughly involved with her baby at all ages, shows a structurally appropriate developmental progression from behaviors promoting homeostasis at 4 months to behaviors promoting organization and initiative at 12 months. The baby's own behavior mirrors this change as he engages in progressively more autonomous exploration without a decline in social responsiveness, and indeed with an increase in the ability to initiate social interaction with the mother. Thematically, the interaction focused largely on the pleasure derived from contingent social exchanges and the infant's exploration of the inanimate environment. It is worth emphasizing that pleasurable interactions were occurring in the context of structural differentiation. There was no incidence of behaviors that might interfere with either the growing structural sophistication of the exchanges or with the baby's enjoyment of reciprocal interactions with the mother and autonomous exploration of the surroundings.

Case 2: Mrs. Andrews and Jenny

Mrs. Andrews is a thin, worn-looking, but attractive 27-year-old, divorced woman with two children. She carefully cultivates a "hip" image and wears long hair, faded jeans, and skimpy tops. She often adopts a cool, indifferent air which is at odds with her real-life problems and with her sense of insecurity and rootlessness.

Mrs. Andrews has a borderline personality organization with a history of shallow interpersonal relationships, unstable living arrangements, frequent changes in employment, and extensive use of drugs and alcohol. She maintains herself and her children at the brink of complete poverty and disorganization, and her mothering reflects these characteristics. She professes great love for her children, particularly the infant, but also acknowledges that she wishes they would "go away." The nutritional and hygienic needs of the children are severely neglected. The oldest child, barely 3 years old, was found stranded from home so many times that Protective Services started an investigation of Mrs. Andrews's mothering. At the same time, Mrs. Andrews takes pride in the infant's accomplishments and refuses to acknowledge any areas of concern about her development. This investment in the infant appears to us to be mainly narcissistic in nature, and we see little evidence of genuine intimacy between mother and infant. The infant is cherished only insofar as she reflects positively on Mrs. Andrews's competence. When the infant's needs interfere with the mother's own preoccupation with herself and her social life, Mrs. Andrews becomes angry and impatient. While articulate and seemingly capable of insight, Mrs. Andrews has not translated her intellectual understanding of herself into a consistent nurturant relationship with her children.

We predicted that Mrs. Andrews would show a pattern of shallow, "as-if" pleasure in her interaction with Jenny and that she would fail to promote close physical bonds at the early stages, or interpersonal exchanges or chains of interaction later on. We also hypothesized that any pleasure would be centered on "showing off" the infant's accomplishments rather than on her own interactions with the infant.

The scores appear in Table 2. In the videotape analyses, Mrs. Andrews was the only mother who failed to engage in any affectionate, rhythmic, or rough-and-tumble behaviors during the 4-month assessment. These behaviors were observed for the first time at 8 and again at 12 months, when they were already decreasing for the other mothers we observed. At 4 months, Mrs. Andrews spent most of the free-play period observing the infant lying on the floor (nonparticipant, available); her responses to the baby were predominantly noncontingent to the infant's cues. A pattern of overstimulation and anticontingent interventions with sadistic overtones appeared at 8 months, at a time when Mrs. Andrews was preoccupied by the marriage of Jenny's father to another woman. By 8 and 12 months, Mrs. Andrews interactions with her infant focused on encouraging the infant to crawl and walk. Chains of mutually contingent exchanges occurred only at 12 months. These chains involved sequences in which the infant was responsive to the maternal encouragement to walk and crawl, and the mother, reinforced by this responsiveness, persisted in encouraging the infant's mobility. There was a low overall incidence of maternal attempts to engage the infant in social interaction. Mrs. Andrews was, however, able to express some overt pleasure, although she also showed some "guarded," "as if" pleasure and flat affect in her exchanges with her infant.

Jenny was a constitutionally sturdy baby who initially was able to respond to her mother and to show interest in the inanimate environment. However, at 4 months she spent most of the free-play period watching toys and other aspects of the inanimate environment. She shared no pleasure or affectionate behavior and was often disturbed. At 8 months she managed

TABLE 2
Case 2 Empirical Analysis Scores[a]

Mother		4 months	8 months	12 months
A.	Somatic patterning/homeostasis			
	1. Direct physical punishment	0%	0%	0%
	2. Physical overstimulation	0	10.0	0
	3. Abrupt handling	0	0	0
	4. Rough-and-tumble	0	2.2	17.0
	5. Rhythmic behavior	0	13.0	7.7
	6. Affectionate physical behavior	0	5.5	7.7
	7. Consoling, soothing	9.1	1.1	2.9
B.	Attachment			
	8. Facilitation of interpersonal exchanges	0	6.6	2.9
	9. Nonparticipating, available	72.7	19.8	25.7
	10. Nonparticipating, withdrawn	0	0	0
	11. Aversely intrusive	0	20.0	20.1
	12. Pleasure	9.1	5.5	10.1
	13. Guarded, "as if" pleasure	10.1	15.6	20.1
	14. Flat affect	40.0	13.0	10.1
C.	Somato-psychological differentiation			
	15. Contingent response.	9.1	7.7	2.9
	Areas:			
	a. Response to baby's pleasure	0	0	20.0
	b. Response to baby's distress	60.0	30.0	20.0
	c. Response to potential for hurt	N/A	N/A	N/A
	d. Response to baby's exploration	N/A	60.0	60.0
	e. Response to baby's seeking interaction	40.0	0	0
	16. Noncontingent behavior.	18.2	3.3	0
	Areas:			
	a. Response to baby's pleasure	0	40.0	N/A
	b. Response to baby's distress	0	20.0	N/A
	c. Response to potential for hurt	N/A	N/A	N/A

TABLE 2 (continued)

Mother		4 months	8 months	12 months
	d. Response to baby's exploration	N/A	0	N/A
	e. Response to baby's seeking interaction	100.0	40.0	N/A
	17. Anticontingent behavior.	0	15.6	0
	Areas:			
	a. Response to baby's pleasure	N/A	10.0	N/A
	b. Response to baby's distress	N/A	10.0	N/A
	c. Response to potential for hurt	N/A	N/A	N/A
	d. Response to baby's exploration	N/A	0	N/A
	e. Response to baby's seeking interaction	N/A	80.0	N/A
D.	Organization & initiative (internalization)			
	18. Chains of contingent exchanges.	0	0	22.9
	Areas:			
	a. Baby's pleasure	N/A	N/A	0
	b. Baby's distress	N/A	N/A	0
	c. Potential for hurt	N/A	N/A	N/A
	d. Baby's exploration	N/A	N/A	100.0
	e. Mutual social interaction	N/A	N/A	0
	19. Chains of anticontingent exchanges.	0	0	0
	Areas:			
	a. Baby's pleasure	N/A	N/A	N/A
	b. Baby's distress	N/A	N/A	N/A
	c. Potential for hurt	N/A	N/A	N/A
	d. Baby's exploration	N/A	N/A	N/A
	e. Baby's seeking interaction	N/A	N/A	N/A
	20. Developmentally facilitating behavior	0	28.6	40.0
	21. Facilitation of involvement with inanimate environment (exploration)	0	18.7	5.7
	22. Interfering or undermining	0	0	0

TABLE 2 (continued)

Infant		4 months	8 months	12 months
A.	Somatic patterning/ homeostasis			
	1. Resists physical contact	0%	1.1%	0%
	2. Physical overstimulation	0	13.2	0
	3. Seeks proximity	1.1	1.1	5.7
	4. Seeks physical contact	0	2.2	0
	5. Affectionate physical behavior	0	0	0
	6. Avoids physical contact	0	0	0
	7. Initiates social interaction	0	0	5.7
	8. Interrupts social interaction	0	1.1	2.9
	9. Aggressive behavior	0	0	0
	10. Pleasure	0	17.6	11.4
	11. Distress	18.2	13.2	20.1
	12. Flat affect	0	0	0
B.	Somato-psychological differentiation			
	13. Contingent response.	9.1	18.7	40.0
	Areas:			
	a. Response to mother's pleasure	10.0	0	0
	b. Response to mother's displeasure	N/A	0	0
	c. Response to mother's facilitation of exploration	N/A	20.0	20.0
	d. Response to mother's interaction/physical contact	90.0	80.0	60.0
	e. Response to mother's commands	N/A	N/A	20.0
	14. Noncontingent response.	0	9.9	11.4
	Areas:			
	a. Response to mother's pleasure	N/A	0	0
	b. Response to mother's displeasure	N/A	0	0
	c. Response to mother's facilitation of exploration	N/A	N/A	N/A
	d. Response to mother's interaction/physical contact	N/A	100.0	100.0

TABLE 2 (continued)

Infant		4 months	8 months	12 months
	e. Response to mother's commands	N/A	0	0
	15. Anticontingent response.	0	8.8	14.3
	Areas:			
	a. Response to mother's pleasure	N/A	0	0
	b. Response to mother's displeasure	N/A	N/A	N/A
	c. Response to mother's facilitation of exploration	N/A	30.0	20.0
	d. Response to mother's interaction/physical contact	N/A	70.0	80.0
	e. Response to mother's commands	N/A	0	0
C.	Organization & initiative (internalization)			
	16. Onlooking behavior	0	0	0
	17. Oriented to inanimate environment	72.7	24.2	0
	18. Exploratory manipulation	0	25.3	7.7
	19. Exploratory roaming	0	1.1	14.3

[a]Areas are percentages of the total number of responses.

to respond contingently to the mother's overtures, to engage in manipulation of toys, and to remain oriented to the inanimate world. Her responses to her mother tended to be contingent, but not in the pleasurable domain. Noncontingent and anti-contingent responses were also observed, particularly in re-sponse to the mother's often intrusive attempts to engage her in social exchanges. At 12 months, while largely responsive to her mother's encouragement to crawl, Jenny also showed signs of strain. There was a considerable incidence of distress. She often responded both noncontingently and anticontingently to the mother's overtures, and the contingent exchanges that took place were lacking in mutual pleasure.

The maternal behavior clearly supported our predictions about Mrs. Andrews's distant attitude and her discouragement of intimacy with Jenny, except when the child gratified the mother's narcissism. Physical interaction in the form of rough-and-tumble games often deteriorated into overstimulating ep-isodes that were distressing to the child. Significantly, reci-procity took place only when the infant complied with the maternal demand that she be mobile—an infant skill associated in Mrs. Andrews's mind with her child's growing independence. The infant's behavior showed a constitutionally intact baby whose social responsiveness and interest in the inanimate en-vironment were well developed, but who was experiencing little pleasure and at least moderate strain in her relationship with her mother. The structural features of the interaction show that Jenny was able to progress toward behavioral organization to a greater degree than her mother, as evidenced by her grow-ing ability to respond contingently to the mother, as opposed to Mrs. Andrews's consistently limited ability to read her infant's signals. Mrs. Andrews was capable of organized, integrated, interactive patterns only when she encouraged the child to "perform" in the guise of walking and crawling. Thematically, this dyad thus shows an idiosyncratic concentration on ex-changes involving the mother's narcissistic gratification in the child's achievements, with little affection and pleasure. It is also clear that the infant shows an emergent tendency to shut the mother out by responding noncontingently and anticontingently to a substantial proportion of the mother's intrusive overtures.

Case 3: Ms. Bronson and Yvette

Ms. Bronson is a 23-year-old unmarried black woman with three children. She lives with the children's father but returns periodically to her parents' home. She was the seventh of 13 children reared in rural poverty. Though poor, the family stayed together, but Ms. Bronson left home at 16 because she reportedly could no longer endure the crowded conditions in the home.

Ms. Bronson is secretive, aloof, given to explosions of anger that alternate with periods of dependent neediness. She demands attention and concrete help on her own terms, and when these are not forthcoming she either withdraws emotionally, disappears for weeks at a time, or has outbursts of anger. Our knowledge of her childhood is fragmented because she can reveal only glimpses of her past before closing up again. We have been struck, however, by her sense that she relinquished her childhood to care for siblings younger than herself, that nobody can give her what she needs, and that things will not change for the better for her. In her relationship with her infant, Yvette, Ms. Bronson alternates between tender lovingness and insensitive abruptness. She has been observed to alternate between unresponsiveness to the baby's prolonged, fretful crying, even when the crying is obviously due to hunger, and periods of obvious delight and tender physical interaction with the baby.

We predicted that the behavioral profile would reflect these characteristics and that Ms. Bronson would engage in a wide variety of behaviors, ranging from phase-appropriate and nurturant to rejecting and inappropriate to the infant's needs. We predicted also that the infant would show some phase-appropriate behaviors as a result of both her constitutional soundness and her ability to profit from the periods of harmonious interaction with the mother. However, we anticipated that the child would be sober and apathetic as a result of the unpredictability of the maternal behavior.

The scores appear in Table 3. The most striking aspect of

TABLE 3
Case 3 Empirical Analysis Scores[a]

Mother		4 months	8 months	12 months
A.	Somatic patterning/homeostasis			
	1. Direct physical punishment	0%	0%	0%
	2. Physical overstimulation	0	0	0
	3. Abrupt handling	1.9	4.1	1.9
	4. Rough-and-tumble	0	4.1	0
	5. Rhythmic behavior	22.2	2.0	11.1
	6. Affectionate physical behavior	0	10.2	11.1
	7. Consoling, soothing	0	4.1	0
B.	Attachment			
	8. Facilitation of interpersonal exchanges	66.7	18.4	29.4
	9. Nonparticipating, available	0	24.5	16.7
	10. Nonparticipating, withdrawn	5	10.0	15.0
	11. Aversely intrusive	1.9	0	1.9
	12. Pleasure	0	0	0
	13. Guarded, "as if" pleasure	0	0	0
	14. Flat affect	0	0	0
C.	Somato-psychological differentiation			
	15. Contingent response. *Areas:*	11.1	10.2	14.8
	a. Response to baby's pleasure	N/A	0	0
	b. Response to baby's distress	N/A	25.0	20.0
	c. Response to potential for hurt	N/A	N/A	N/A
	d. Response to baby's exploration	100.0	50.0	80.0
	e. Response to baby's seeking interaction	N/A	25.0	N/A
	16. Noncontingent behavior. *Areas:*	0	14.3	0
	a. Response to baby's pleasure	N/A	12.5	N/A
	b. Response to baby's distress	N/A	12.5	N/A
	c. Response to potential for hurt	N/A	N/A	N/A

TABLE 3 (continued)

Mother		4 months	8 months	12 months
	d. Response to baby's exploration	N/A	50.0	N/A
	e. Response to baby's seeking interaction	N/A	25.0	N/A
	17. Anticontingent behavior.	0	10.2	1.9
	Areas:			
	a. Response to baby's pleasure	N/A	0	0
	b. Response to baby's distress	N/A	25.0	0
	c. Response to potential for hurt	N/A	N/A	N/A
	d. Response to baby's exploration	N/A	50.0	100.0
	e. Response to baby's seeking interaction	N/A	25.0	0
D.	Organization & initiative (internalization)			
	18. Chains of contingent exchanges.	22.2	0	10.0
	Areas:			
	a. Baby's pleasure	0	N/A	0
	b. Baby's distress	0	N/A	0
	c. Potential for hurt	0	N/A	0
	d. Baby's exploration	0	N/A	50.0
	e. Mutual social interaction	100.0	N/A	50.0
	19. Chains of anticontingent exchanges.	0	0	0
	Areas:			
	a. Baby's pleasure	N/A	N/A	N/A
	b. Baby's distress	N/A	N/A	N/A
	c. Potential for hurt	N/A	N/A	N/A
	d. Baby's exploration	N/A	N/A	N/A
	e. Baby's seeking interaction	N/A	N/A	N/A
	20. Developmentally facilitating behavior	11.1	12.2	10.0
	21. Facilitation of involvement with inanimate environment (exploration)	0	40.8	37.0
	22. Interfering or undermining	0	18.4	20.0

TABLE 3 (continued)

Infant		4 months	8 months	12 months
A.	Somatic patterning/ homeostasis & attachment			
	1. Resists physical contact	0	0	5.6
	2. Physical overstimulation	0	0	0
	3. Seeks proximity	0	3.0	0
	4. Seeks physical contact	0	6.1	5.6
	5. Affectionate physical behavior	0	0	0
	6. Avoids physical contact	0	0	0
	7. Initiates social interaction	0	2.0	0
	8. Interrupts social interaction	0	0	3.7
	9. Aggressive behavior	0	0	0
	10. Pleasure	0	4.1	3.7
	11. Distress	0	20.4	13.0
	12. Flat affect	10.0	12.2	20.0
B.	Somato-psychological differentiation			
	13. Contingent response.	22.2	22.4	29.6
	Areas:			
	a. Response to mother's pleasure	0	0	0
	b. Response to mother's displeasure	0	0	0
	c. Response to mother's facilitation of exploration	N/A	75.0	70.0
	d. Response to mother's seeking interaction/ physical contact	100.0	25.0	30.0
	e. Response to mother's commands	N/A	N/A	N/A
	14. Noncontingent response.	0	8.2	0
	Areas:			
	a. Response to mother's pleasure	N/A	N/A	N/A
	b. Response to mother's displeasure	N/A	N/A	N/A
	c. Response to mother's facilitation of exploration	N/A	100.0	N/A
	d. Response to mother's seeking interaction/ physical contact	N/A	N/A	N/A

TABLE 3 (continued)

Infant		4 months	8 months	12 months
	e. Response to mother's commands	N/A	N/A	N/A
	15. Anticontingent response.	44.4	6.1	9.3
	Areas:			
	a. Response to mother's pleasure	N/A	N/A	N/A
	b. Response to mother's displeasure	N/A	N/A	N/A
	c. Response to mother's facilitation of exploration	N/A	40.0	40.0
	d. Response to mother's seeking interaction/ physical contact	100.0	60.0	50.0
	e. Response to mother's commands	N/A	N/A	10.0
C.	Organization & initiative (internalization)			
	16. Onlooking behavior	22.2	8.2	9.3
	17. Oriented to inanimate environment	0	22.4	5.6
	18. Exploratory manipulation	0	28.6	37.0
	19. Exploratory roaming	22.2	8.2	5.6

ªAreas are percentages of the total number of responses.

the empirical profile of Ms. Bronson's behavior is the occurrence, in relatively low percentages, of many different kinds of behaviors, from affectionate to teasing, and from withdrawn to interfering and aversively intrusive. Our impression of inconsistency was thereby supported, as was our concern regarding Ms. Bronson's inability for a truly intimate attachment and a differentiated pattern of interaction. There was little affectionate and pleasurable behavior. Contingent behavior occurred relatively infrequently and focused on impersonal exploratory activities rather than on intimate interpersonal interaction. At the same time, while Ms. Bronson was clearly invested in promoting her child's interest in the inanimate environment, she also tended to interrupt and in other ways interfere with the baby's exploration and roaming. On occasion she teased the baby, usually by pretending to take for herself a toy the baby was trying to reach.

Yvette's behavior is that of an apathetic baby. She started crawling early and used this skill to roam around the room at 4 months, but she barely did so at 8 and 12 months. However, she did manipulate toys at these ages, an activity that had been absent earlier on. Striking features are the very low incidence of pleasure at all ages and the high frequency of anticontingent responses at a very early age—4 months. Her anticontingent responses consisted mainly of turning the head away and averting her gaze when Ms. Bronson attempted to engage her in social exchanges. While this specific pattern was not observed at later ages, we saw little progression to internally organized, reciprocal behavior with the mother, as evidenced by the absence of chains of exchanges at 8 months and their low frequency at 12 months.

The dyadic picture that emerges is that of a mother with an inconsistent pattern of relating to her infant. The infant, in turn, is low-keyed and apathetic, often curtailed by the mother in her attempts to explore. While invested in each other, it is clear that mother and infant cannot experience overt pleasure in their exchanges and that they have not yet established a reciprocal, mutually contingent behavioral pattern. We thus concluded that while some structural features show elements of behavioral organization, these are certainly below optimal expectations, especially in the interpersonal domain. The thematic content also indicates that interactions involve little overt pleasure and relatively little mutual involvement in social exchanges.

Case 4: Ms. Thompson and Albert

Ms. Thompson is an unmarried, 21-year-old black female with two children. She was referred to the project because of suicidal ideation during her pregnancy with her second child. The initial interviews revealed a woman with a psychotic personality organization. She has poor reality testing, is highly suspicious, and has experienced hallucinations from adolescence on. She has a history of violent outbursts—at 16 she was accused of trying to stab her foster mother. She was simultaneously afraid of abusing her as yet unborn infant and of spoiling him by "too much coddling."

Because of these severe emotional impairments we were concerned that while Ms. Thompson might provide adequate mothering in the first months of life, she might thereafter begin to feel overwhelmed by her infant's growing complexity and show a deterioration of caregiving, with potential physical abuse. These predictions were reinforced by our observations of her unrealistic demands from her infant, now 13 months old. She expected him to "do as he is told," "remain quiet," and "obey." We therefore expected a highly erratic mothering pattern, with possible incidence of physical punishment and much controlling, interfering behavior. How the baby would respond was not clear to us. We hypothesized that he might withdraw and become lethargic and apathetic, or that he would behave like his mother and engage in disorganized, intrusive, and aggressive behavior.

The scores appear in Table 4. Ms. Thompson's behavior during the 4-month assessment showed an expectable pattern of affectionate, rhythmic, rough-and-tumble, and contingent behavior. However, by 8 months the picture began to deteriorate. There was a gradual diminution in the incidences of interpersonal exchanges, affectionate behavior, and playful rough-and-tumble, and Ms. Thompson was now showing a relatively high incidence of interfering and teasing behavior.

TABLE 4
Case 4 Empirical Analysis Scores[a]

Mother		4 months	8 months	12 months
A.	Somatic patterning/homeostasis			
	1. Direct physical punishment	0%	1.6%	14.9%
	2. Physical overstimulation	0	4.8	6.0
	3. Abrupt handling	0	0	0
	4. Rough-and-tumble	35.0	9.5	0
	5. Rhythmic behavior	25.0	1.6	0
	6. Affectionate physical behavior	30.6	11.1	1.5
	7. Consoling, soothing	0	1.6	0
B.	Attachment			
	8. Facilitation of interpersonal exchanges	0	20.6	7.5
	9. Nonparticipating, available	25.0	19.0	0
	10. Nonparticipating, withdrawn	0	0	0
	11. Aversely intrusive	0	3.2	26.9
	12. Pleasure	15.0	4.8	1.5
	13. Guarded, "as if" pleasure	0	0	0
	14. Flat affect	0	0	0
C.	Somato-psychological differentiation			
	15. Contingent response.	20.0	6.3	1.5
	Areas:			
	a. Response to baby's pleasure	30.0	10.0	N/A
	b. Response to baby's distress	10.0	20.0	5.0
	c. Response to potential for hurt	N/A	N/A	N/A
	d. Response to baby's exploration	10.0	30.0	90.0
	e. Response to baby's seeking interaction	50.0	40.0	5.0
	16. Noncontingent behavior.	5.0	0	4.5
	Areas:			
	a. Response to baby's pleasure	0	N/A	N/A
	b. Response to baby's distress	0	N/A	0
	c. Response to potential for hurt	N/A	N/A	N/A

TABLE 4 (continued)

Mother	4 months	8 months	12 months
d. Response to baby's exploration	0	N/A	0
e. Response to baby's seeking interaction	0	N/A	100.0
17. Anticontingent behavior.	0	3.2	16.0
Areas:			
a. Response to baby's pleasure	N/A	0	N/A
b. Response to baby's distress	N/A	0	0
c. Response to potential for hurt	N/A	N/A	N/A
d. Response to baby's exploration	N/A	70.0	80.0
e. Response to baby's seeking interaction	N/A	30.0	20.0
D. Organization & initiative (internalization)			
18. Chains of contingent exchanges.	0	12.7	0
Areas:			
a. Baby's pleasure	N/A	5.0	N/A
b. Baby's distress	N/A	0	N/A
c. Potential for hurt	N/A	N/A	N/A
d. Baby's exploration	N/A	55.0	N/A
e. Mutual social interaction	N/A	40.0	N/A
19. Chains of anticontingent exchanges.	0	12.7	16.0
Areas:			
a. Baby's pleasure	N/A	0	N/A
b. Baby's distress	N/A	0	0
c. Potential for hurt	N/A	N/A	N/A
d. Baby's exploration	N/A	90.0	85.0
e. Baby's seeking interaction	N/A	10.0	15.0
20. Developmentally facilitating behavior	0	0	4.5
21. Facilitation of involvement with inanimate environment	5.0	6.3	26.9
22. Interfering or undermining	0	20.0	14.9

TABLE 4 (continued)

Infant		4 months	8 months	12 months
A.	Somatic patterning/ homeostasis & attachment			
	1. Resists physical contact	0	4.8	10.4
	2. Physical overstimulation	0	1.6	0
	3. Seeks proximity	0	0	0
	4. Seeks physical contact	0	0	0
	5. Affectionate physical behavior	0	0	0
	6. Avoids physical contact	0	4.8	4.5
	7. Initiates social interaction	0	1.6	0
	8. Interrupts social interaction	0	1.6	4.5
	9. Aggressive behavior	0	5.0	20.0
	10. Pleasure	30.0	1.6	0
	11. Distress	15.0	28.6	11.9
	12. Flat affect	0	0	0
B.	Somato-psychological differentiation			
	13. Contingent response.	40.0	27.0	4.5
	Areas:			
	a. Response to mother's pleasure	30.0	0	0
	b. Response to mother's displeasure	N/A	N/A	0
	c. Response to mother's facilitation of exploration	0	90.0	80.0
	d. Response to mother's interaction/physical contact	70.0	10.0	20.0
	e. Response to mother's commands	N/A	0	0
	14. Noncontingent response.	0	12.7	16.4
	Areas:			
	a. Response to mother's pleasure	N/A	0	0
	b. Response to mother's displeasure	N/A	0	0
	c. Response to mother's facilitation of exploration	N/A	0	0
	d. Response to mother's interaction/physical contact	N/A	60.0	50.0

TABLE 4 (continued)

Infant		4 months	8 months	12 months
	e. Response to mother's command	N/A	40.0	50.0
	15. Anticontingent response.	0	4.8	3.0
	Areas:			
	a. Response to mother's pleasure	N/A	0	0
	b. Response to mother's displeasure	N/A	0	0
	c. Response to mother's facilitation of exploration	N/A	0	0
	d. Response to mother's interaction/physical contact	N/A	100.0	60.0
	e. Response to mother's command	N/A	0	40.0
C.	Organization & initiative (internalization)			
	16. Onlooking behavior	0	0	0
	17. Oriented to inanimate environment	5.0	6.3	3.0
	18. Exploratory manipulation	10.0	17.5	22.4
	19. Exploratory roaming	0	11.1	31.3

[a]Areas are percentages of the total number of responses.

These behaviors were manifested most explicitly in her tendency to pull the infant back when he attempted to roam around
and in snatching a toy from the infant and pretending to busy
herself with it. When Albert protested, she pointed out how
nasty he was. By 12 months there was a dramatic diminution
in attachment and differentiating behaviors. She now compounded her verbal criticism with physical punishment, particularly by slapping Albert's wrist or threatening him with an
upraised hand for no visible transgression on the infant's part.
We concluded that the pattern of interfering with the infant's
activity had continued unchanged and was now compounded
by aversive intrusiveness: a forceful attempt to engage the baby
in social interaction, often with total indifference to the infant's
own wishes.

Albert's behavior mirrors dramatically this worrisome deterioration of the mother's behavior. At 4 months he showed
pleasure in the interaction with the mother and was able to
respond contingently to her overtures. By 8 months the incidence of pleasurable affect and contingent responses had noticeably declined. He was now distressed in almost a third of
the episodes. He did not seek proximity or contact with the
mother and seldom initiated interaction with her, but he did
to some extent resist and attempt to terminate contact when
she started it. By 12 months he seems to have consolidated an
interest in roaming and manipulation that could in part be a
coping mechanism against maternal intrusion and interference.
He continued to resist and avoid contact and engaged in much
aggressive behavior against the mother. It is as if Ms. Thompson's projections on the baby as aggressive and "mean" had
fulfilled themselves. The baby now fought back, a development
that might hold more promise for developmental progress than
the alternative possibility of infant overcompliance and withdrawal.

In summary, we see in this dyad a mother and baby locked
in battle with each other. Ms. Thompson's suspicions of the
baby and her desire to protect herself by controlling him have
brought about what she feared most—a rebellious, "aggressive"
baby who seems to derive the impetus for continued development more from his explorations of the inanimate environment

than from his interactions with his mother. Structurally, we saw a worrisome lack of progression toward more organized behavior; if anything, dyadic interaction became increasingly more disorganized (less contingent) in the course of the first year. The mother interferes with the infant's exploration in a teasing and sadistic manner, and the infant responds with aggression, with resistance to and avoidance of physical contact, and with consistent rejection of maternal attempts at social interaction.

Discussion

We have pursued an approach to the observation and assessment of infant-mother dyads that combines our clinical understanding of behavior with a quantitative data analysis. We first examined the data from a clinical perspective, using as guidelines our conceptualization of the subphases of infancy, i.e., homeostasis, attachment, somato-psychological differentiation, and organization, initiative, and autonomy (internalization). We then identified indicator behaviors that in our opinion reflected the underlying developmental issues of each subphase, were clinically relevant, and were readily observable in videotaped unstructured interactions between infants and mothers. The videotaped interactions were broken into 15-second intervals, and each interval was scored for presence or absence of indicator behaviors. Percentages were then calculated to obtain a profile of the relative incidence of indicator behavior in individual infant-mother dyads at different subphases of infancy.

We hypothesized that the trend in the first 2 years of life toward greater organization in the context of specific developmental lines would be reflected empirically in the changing incidence of clusters of indicator behaviors observed at different subphases. Accordingly, we expected that a well-functioning mother-infant dyad would show a progression from behaviors indicative of homeostasis and attachment in the first half of the first year to indicator behaviors associated with somato-psychological differentiation and greater organization and initiative later on. We also predicted that the prevailing thematic concerns of the dyad would be reflected in the areas of interaction where the clusters of indicator behaviors tended to appear and that this thematic dimension would enlarge and enrich the picture emerging from the structural features of the interaction. Finally, we expected a growing trend toward the integration of communicative modalities, i.e., the infant's ability simultaneously to use vision, audition, proprioception, and other modalities, and the mother's ability to coordinate these modalities in the service of state-specific interactive tasks. We have not yet scored our data in terms of the communicative modalities used and responded to by mother and infant; this aspect of our approach awaits further analysis.

Our empirical analyses were consistent with our conceptual framework and clinical descriptions. Mrs. Waters (case 1) was evaluated clinically as a reasonably healthy mother with a healthy baby. On this basis, we anticipated a relatively smooth developmental progression, and this prediction was confirmed by the empirical profile. In contrast, cases 2, 3, and 4 showed clinical evidence of psychopathology that led us to predict distortions in the dyadic developmental progression. Indeed, the empirical profiles showed idiosyncratic clusters of indicator behaviors. Structurally, none of the three cases showed a dyadic progression from homeostatic and attachment behaviors to more differentiated and organized patterns, although case 3 was somewhat more organized than the others. Superimposed on the structural features were idiosyncratic thematic preoccupations. For example, in case 2 the mother was preoccupied with aggressive-sadistic concerns and engaged in intrusive and anticontingent behavior rather than in pleasurable interactions with her infant during the stage of somato-psychological differentiation. In case 3 there was an inconsistent interactive pattern whereby periods of smooth contingent exchanges alternated with interfering or abrupt interventions on the mother's part and a lethargic withdrawal on the part of the infant. In case 4 we saw a structural regression and an escalating cycle of maternal punitiveness and intrusiveness, and infant aggression and rejection of social contact.

On the basis of these observations and of our experience

in scoring other cases, we consider our instrument a useful step toward the systematization of clinical impressions through a quantitative approach. Such attempts at systematization and quantification are essential: if not done, research in mother-infant interaction will continue to employ measures with little clinical validity, and the contributions of skilled clinicians will continue to be limited to clinical settings without being incorporated into a larger and more generally available body of research.

We reasoned that the first step in developing a new quantitative approach is to select measures that are consistent with clinical judgments. The second and third steps are to expand and then refine clinical observations and insights. We propose that by following these steps we have developed an instrument that is useful in detecting subtle individual differences, both in structural features and in thematic behavioral content. Moreover, we suggest that quantification has not resulted in any loss of flexible clinical understanding. This was a basic concern in devising the instrument, which was conceived as an adjunct to, rather than a substitute for, meticulous clinical observation and inference. Data yielded by the instrument are to be interpreted not in isolation but in the context of extensive clinical knowledge and understanding of the case. Our concern for clinical flexibility and subtlety also accounts for the large number of measures, a characteristic of the instrument that might be of concern from a purely methodological or statistical perspective.

We must also stress the preliminary character of our endeavor. We have not yet established the predictive validity of the measures by applying the analysis to a large number of cases on a long-term longitudinal basis. While the reliability figures are satisfactory, it must be kept in mind that these figures reflect agreement between highly trained, skilled observers, and we have not yet attempted to train less experienced observers in the scoring procedure. Finally, and at a broader conceptual level, there might be disagreement about the extent to which the behaviors we selected are indeed indicators of the subphases of infancy that guided our thinking. It is quite clear to us that even if the measures are adequate indicators of underlying psychological processes, they are by no means exhaustive. Other measures may turn out to be equally useful, or even more so, than the ones we have presented here. This awareness leads us to advocate a spirit of open enquiry: the instrument is in a process of refinement and revision, as we continue to learn from our clinical data. Nevertheless, we feel that the basic approach is worth pursuing, with the goal of systematizing our understanding of the structural and thematic features of personality development.

References

Ainsworth, M., & Bell, S. (1969), Some contemporary patterns of mother-infant interaction in the feeding situation. In: *Stimulation in Early Infancy*, ed. J. Ambrose. London: Academic Press, pp. 133–170.

Ainsworth, M., Bell, S., & Stayton, D. (1972), Individual differences in the development of some attachment behaviors. *Merrill-Palmer Quart.*, 18:123–143.

——— ——— ——— (1974), Infant-mother attachment and social development: Socialization as a product of reciprocal responsiveness to signals. In: *The Integration of the Child Into a Social World*, ed. M. Richards. Cambridge: Cambridge University Press, pp. 99–135.

Bakeman, R., & Brown, J. (1977), Behavioral dialogues: An approach to the assessment of mother-infant interaction. *Child Development*, 48:195–203.

Bell, R. Q. (1968), A reinterpretation of the direction of effects in studies of socialization. *Psychological Rev.*, 75:81–95.

Blehar, M., Lieberman, A., & Ainsworth, M. (1977), Early face-to-face interaction and its relation to later infant-mother attachment. *Child Development*, 48:182–194.

Bowlby, J. (1969), *Attachment and Loss: Vol. I. Attachment.* New York: Basic Books.

Brazelton, T., Koslowski, B., & Main, M. (1974), The origin of reciprocity: The early mother-infant interaction. In: *The Effect of the Infant on Its Caregiver*, ed. M. Lewis & L. Rosenblum. New York: Wiley, pp. 49–76.

Emde, R., Gaensbauer, T., & Harmon, R. (1976), Emotional expression in infancy: A biobehavioral study. *Psychological Issues*, Monograph 37. New York: International Universities Press.

Escalona, S. (1968), *The Roots of Individuality.* Chicago: Aldine.

Freud, A. (1922–1970), *The Writings of Anna Freud*, Vols. 1–7. New York: International Universities Press.

Freud, S. (1911), Formulations on the two principles of mental functioning. *Standard Edition*, 12:218–226. London: Hogarth Press, 1958.

Gewirtz, J. L. (1965), The course of infant smiling in four child rearing environments in Israel. In: *Determinants of Infant Behavior*, ed. B. M. Foss. Vol. 3, London: Methuen, pp. 205–260.

——— (1969), Levels of conceptual analysis in environment-infant interaction research. *Merrill-Palmer Quart.*, 15:9–47.

Greenspan, S. I. (1979), Intelligence and adaptation: An integration of psychoanalytic and Piagetian developmental psychology. *Psychological Issues,* Monograph 47/48. New York: International Universities Press.

Hartmann, H. (1939), *Ego Psychology and the Problem of Adaptation.* New York: International Universities Press, 1958.

Kaye, K. (1975). Toward the origin of dialogue. In: *Studies in Mother Infant Interaction: Proceedings of the Loch Lomond Symposium,* ed. H. R. Schaffer. London: Academic Press, 1977, pp. 89–177.

Klaus, M., & Kennell J. (1976), *Maternal-Infant Bonding: The Impact of Early Separation or Loss on Family Development.* St. Louis: Mosby.

Lewis, M., & Rosenblum, eds. (1974), *The Effect of the Infant on Its Caregiver.* New York: Wiley.

Lieberman, A. F. (1977), Preschooler's competence with a peer: Relations with attachment and peer experience. *Child Development,* 48:182–194.

Lipsitt, L. (1966), Learning processes of newborns. *Merrill-Palmer Quart.,* 12:45–71.

―――― (1979), The pleasures and annoyances of infants: Approach and avoidance. In: *Origins of the Social Responsiveness of Infants,* ed. E. B. Thoman. Hillsdale, N.J.: Erlbaum.

Mahler, M. S. (1975), On the current status of the infantile neurosis. *J. Amer. Psychoanal. Assn.,* 23:327–333.

Main, M. (1973), Exploration, play, and cognitive functioning as related to child-mother attachment. Unpublished doctoral dissertation, Johns Hopkins University.

Meltzoff, A., & Moore, K. (1977), Imitation of facial and manual gestures by human neonates. *Science,* 198:75–78.

Murphy, L., & Moriarty, A. (1976), *Vulnerability, Coping and Growth.* New Haven: Yale University Press.

Parmelee, A., Jr. (1972), Development of states in infants. In: *Sleep and the Maturing Nervous System,* ed. C. Clement, D. Purpura, & F. Mayer. New York: Academic Press, pp. 199–228.

Piaget, J. (1951), *Play, Dreams and Imitation in Childhood.* New York: Norton.

Sander, L. (1962), Issues in early mother-child interaction. *J. Amer. Acad. Child Psychiat.,* 1:141–166.

Schaffer, H. R. (1975), Early interactive development. In: *Studies in Mother Infant Interaction: Proceedings of the Loch Lomond Symposium,* ed. H. K. Schaffer. London: Academic Press, 1977, pp. 3–16.

Sroufe, L., Waters, E., & Matas, L. (1974), Contextual determinants of infant affective response. *The Origin of Fear,* ed. M. Lewis & L. Rosenblum. New York: Wiley, pp. 49–72.

Stern, D. (1974a), The goal and structure of mother-infant play. *J. Amer. Acad. Child Psychiat.,* 13:402–421.

―――― (1974b), Mother and infant at play: The dyadic interaction involving facial, vocal and gaze behaviors. In: *The Effects of the Infant on Its Caregiver,* ed. M. Lewis & L. Rosenblum. New York: Wiley, pp. 187–213.

―――― Beebe, B., Jaffe, J., & Bennett, S. L. (1975), Infant's stimulus world during social interaction: A study of caregiver behaviors with particular reference to repetition and timing. In: *Studies in Mother Infant Interaction: Proceedings of the Loch Lomond Symposium,* ed. H. R. Schaffer. London: Academic Press, 1977, pp. 177–202.

Thomas, A., Chess, S., & Birch, H. (1968), *Temperament and Behavior Disorders in Children*. New York: New York University Press.

Tracy, R., Lamb, M., & Ainsworth, M. (1976), Infant approach behavior as related to attachment. *Child Development*, 47:571–578.

Winnicott, D. W. (1954), Metapsychological and clinical aspects of regression within the psychoanalytic set-up. In: *Collected Papers: Through Paediatrics to Psycho-Analysis*. New York: Basic Books, 1958, pp. 278–294.

—— (1956), Primary maternal preoccupation. In: *Collected Papers: Through Paediatics to Psycho-Analysis*. New York: Basic Books, 1958, pp. 300–305.

Wolff, P. (1966), The causes, controls, and organization of behavior in the neonate. *Psychological Issues*, Monograph 17. New York: International Universities Press.

16

Psychoanalytic Views of Infancy

LOIS BARCLAY MURPHY, PH.D.
DORIAN MINTZER, PH.D.
LEWIS P. LIPSITT, PH.D.

Basic Principles

Psychoanalytic understanding of infantile psychic development has developed parallel to the development of, and changes in, Freudian theory beginning with a preoccupation with drives, then with ego psychology and with the mother-infant object relationship. With the challenge of observations of infants separated from their mothers during World War II, empirical studies multiplied. With the establishment of the Yale Child Study Center and the National Institute of Mental Health, and with grants from foundations, collaborative research by psychoanalysts working with psychologists, pediatricians, clinical social workers, neurologists, and other scientists led to a refinement of theory and to a closer look at the complex, interwoven processes and individual differences in infants. We now recognize the variety of determinants in psychic development. The mind of the infant is shaped not just by instincts or by predetermined cognitive steps, but rather by many factors interacting with the inborn capacities of the individual infant. The more we recognize the wide range of individual differences

This chapter is a revision of "Psychoanalytic Views of Infancy," L. B. Murphy, in *The Course of Life: Contributions Toward Understanding Personality Development: Vol. 1. Infancy and Early Childhood,* edited by S.I. Greenspan and G.H. Pollock, NIMH, 1980. Dr. Ishak Ramzy has been the consultant for this revision, and Dr. Joy Osofsky generously shared recent writings on infancy, both published and unpublished.

in strengths and weaknesses, and in variations in the pace of development of different functions, the more cautious we must be in our evaluations and predictions.

After Freud's writings on the ego in the 1920s (1921, 1923), the challenge offered by Piaget, and psychoanalysts' observations of their own and other infants, psychoanalytic thought broadened to include a greater concern with the development of ego functions such as perception and motor activity, the development of concepts, and the relationship with the mother or mothering person. Hartmann, Kris, and Loewenstein (1946) and others discussed ego development in terms of its interplay with drives and their mutual influences. In such discussions the "ego" is a global concept, an umbrella covering a wide range of functions.

Both theory and research guided by psychoanalytic concepts have found it difficult to deal with the complexity and the subtlety of the multitude of interacting forces involved in the development of the growing and changing infant. The tendency to deal with one issue at a time often prevents an adequate understanding of the multiple processes involved in every aspect of functioning in the context of the personal and the impersonal environment. Both the organism and the environment undergo change separately and in their interaction; it is when an early patttern is repeatedly reinforced that continuity is seen. Similarly, it is impossible in our discussion here to follow each basic concept separately. For instance, differentiated recognition of the mother or other major caregiver emerges at different ages dependent on the perceptual development of the infant. The latter evolves in turn as an interaction of genetic and environmental factors, and includes affective responses to environmentally generated reinforcements of early signals. Consequently, as we move our focus from one concept to another we must deal with these overlapping processes. No aspect of infant development proceeds in isolation from the rest.

As our scrutiny of infant experience grows more and more detailed, new relationships between physiological and psychological functioning are found; for instance, Katherine Tennes and her collaborators (Tennes and Lampe, 1961; Tennes, Emde, Kisley, and Metcalf, 1972) found that variability in the levels of excretion of cortisol was significantly greater on days on which 1-year-old infants were exposed to stress in laboratory studies than on control days. Moreover, ratings of separation anxiety and levels of cortisol excreted 40–160 minutes after the stress (of separation from mother) were positively correlated. Comprehensive studies of relationships between psychic and physiological responses to the vicissitudes of the baby's life remain to be undertaken. With increasing collaboration between child analysts, psychiatrists, psychologists, and other clinical and academic students of infant pathology has come support for some classical psychoanalytic views of infancy, revision of others, and some additions for psychoanalysis to assimilate.

Historical Sequences

The historical sequence in psychoanalytic thinking about infants was reviewed by Kris (1950) after he began to contribute to the development of empirical psychoanalytic studies of infants at the Yale Child Study Center under the direction of Milton Senn. He saw the first period of psychoanalytic child psychology as outlining the genetic, economic, and dynamic interrelations in sequences of child reactions. The second period involved the development of ego psychology and an interest in early object relations, usually focusing on the infant's relationship to its mother. The third period brought systematic observations to the study of the mother-child relationship with reference to ego autonomy, phase specificity, aggression, and education. Under the leadership of Kris, research at the Yale center made major contributions to the psychoanalytic understanding of infancy.

Just as Hartmann's *Ego Psychology and the Problem of Adaptation* (1939) pointed to the urgency of the need for studies of the infant as an *active* organism with senses programmed to orient to and interact with the world, so Spitz's studies of the devastating effect of the infant's separation from the mother (1946) implied a need for much more intensive studies of the mother-infant relationship. Erikson's *Childhood and Society* (1950) made another giant leap with the concept of the interrelation of the child with the total world of the culture into which he or she was born. The full impact of Erikson's lifespan view has not yet been felt. It requires a much more comprehensive study of the variations in ego development, paths to mastery, and object relations, in different cultures and in different times. It requires in addition a more finely honed study of the impact of social change on the caregiving experiences of infants in contemporary society, with its mobility, its anxieties, and its technological contributions to infants and with caregivers who are no longer, in over half of all families, the married home-maker with full-time availability to her baby.

Until the 1940s most psychoanalytic discussions of infancy were based on inferences from the psychoanalysis of children, adolescents, and adults, and on deductions from libido theory. Few analysts recognized the relevant contributions of psychological research on the first year of life, studies such as those by Charlotte Bühler (1930) and by Mary Shirley (1933). Bernfeld (1929) was an exception, and his book on infancy was for many years the most balanced discussion of infancy among psychoanalytic publications. In the early thirties Melanie Klein's *Psycho-analysis of Children* (1932), based on her treatment of extremely disturbed children, introduced a new dimension with her concepts of the infant's images of the mother—"good and bad mother," "good and bad breast." Early in the next decade Spitz observed variations in the effects of separation of the infant from the mother, as he reported in the articles "Hospitalism" (1945) and "Anaclitic Depression" (1946). Soon he and the psychologist K.M. Wolf undertook direct observation of growing infants, focusing on the evolution of the smiling response as a "contribution to the ontogenesis of social relations" (Spitz and Wolf, 1946). Kris, Spitz, and Anna Freud were all defending the importance of direct observations as a basis for further refinement of theories of infant development. By the late 1940s and early 1950s, psychoanalytically oriented psychologists and psychiatrists (e.g., John Benjamin, Sylvia Brody, Sibylle Escalona, Lois B. Murphy) were engaging in systematic studies of infancy with a focus on individual differences in infants, interactions with mothers, and the infant's own active efforts to deal with the environment. Also in the 1950s, the analyst Winnicott was communicating observations of mother-infant interactions based on his extensive pediatric experience. "There is no such thing as a baby," he wrote, "—there is always a baby and its mother" (or other caregiver). The emerging appeal of systems theory in science gradually led to a view of infant and mother as a system. The whole system—the ecology, the society, as well as the whole family into which a baby is born is involved in the baby's sensory experiences, the atmosphere of the surround, the differing emphases on specific aspects of development.

Due to the tragically early deaths of K.M. Wolf and Ernst Kris at Yale, and to vicissitudes of the work setting in other study centers, detailed and sustained longitudinal studies of individual infants in their home environments are extremely rare. Such studies alone can pursue questions of the influence of different developing aspects of the infant on each other and on the changing relation with the changing mother. The work of Margaret S. Mahler and her collaborators, especially Fred Pine and Anni Bergman (Mahler, Pine, and Bergman, 1975), has made a major contribution to this complex view of infant development. The parallel work of Brody and Axelrad (1978) is the major longitudinal study including the infants' interaction with their fathers.

Psychoanalysts had not paid much attention to early studies of individuality in infants, such as that of Mary Shirley (1933), but in 1949 the analyst Paul Bergman published a paper with Sibylle Escalona at the Menninger Foundation, "Unusual Sensitivities in Very Young Children" (Bergman and Escalona, 1949) and the Yale Child Study Center began intensive studies of constitutional tendencies interacting with the environment (Kris, 1950; Wolf, 1953; Ritvo, McCollum, Omwake, Provence, and Solnit, 1963). Augusta Alpert, Peter Neubauer, and Annamarie Weil meanwhile were studying variations in drive endowment (1956). By 1959 Escalona and Heider's *Prediction and Outcome*, based on data from the first stage of Lois Murphy's Coping Study compared with Escalona and Leitch's infancy data (1952), provided evidence of continuity in such aspects of the infant's equipment as energy, activity, attention, and intensity. And in 1971 Annaliese Korner reported on the implications of individual differences at birth for early experience and later development.

These post–World War II studies by analysts and their psychoanalytically trained colleagues in related disciplines provided data for a refinement of the psychoanalytic view of infancy, and a recognition of different patterns of strength and weakness. Fries and Woolf's study of the role of the congenital activity type (1953) was followed by Escalona's study of most and least active babies (1968) and by other studies of differences in activity level. Escalona noted that active babies evoke more response from their mothers and that quiet babies need more stimulation. Very sensitive babies need sensitive care; very intense babies may need help in modulating their responsivity.

While analysts and psychologists were reporting individual differences in constitution related to behavior, Roger Williams, in *Biochemical Individuality* (1956), documented individual differences in every organ of the body—shapes of hearts, stomachs, livers, intestines, and in patterns of cardiac functioning, needs for vitamins and different nutritional elements. Differences in growth patterns and various aspects of mental functioning were studied by others.

Psychoanalysts no longer ignore the observations of psychologists and other social scientists; they are assimilating some of the results of the careful experimental and natural history studies of the infant—studies stimulated in part by the reports of Bowlby, of Spitz, and of others in the forties, and in part by the burgeoning studies of social development, personality, cognition, and perception in the 1930s and 1940s. The task of integration continues as independent studies of infancy focused on specific variables multiply, and as psychoanalytic hypotheses are enriched by the results of changes in the assumptions and techniques of psychoanalysis—with its contemporary interest in the earliest years and especially in the roots of disturbed relationships with people in the patient's work or personal world.

These studies have demonstrated the wide range of individual differences both in every aspect of infants' equipment, and in the developmental pace of different functions, as well as the interactions of these functions with each other during the sequences of change in the first year of life. An equally wide range of individual differences in mothers, and in their patterns of expectation of their infants at birth and at later stages, interact with the individual patterns of the infants. Empirical studies of normal infants also challenge concepts developed from psychoanalytic findings on disturbed children and adults.

Psychoanalysts who studied infants and young children from the mid-twenties through the rest of the century have been influenced by a zeitgeist expressed in a wide variety of disciplines; it was demonstrated that the individual organism must always be seen in interaction with its environment. The social and mental development of babies and growing children is affected for better or worse by the quantity and quality of stimulation they receive. Studies of subhuman species found that physiological and chemical aspects of the brain, as well as skill in problem solving, are similarly affected by the stimulation provided. Neuropsychological studies of brain and mental development emphasize the importance of social stimulation in the development of cognitive functions and language, and studies of the effect of preschool experience on the development of young children have demonstrated improved mental functioning in young children from superior preschools. Anthropologists have documented differences in personality development in different cultures, while social psychologists have conceptualized the organism-environment interaction. From the 1950s on, pediatricians and other professionals working with premature or defective babies or with those who did not thrive, found that stimulation by caregivers was crucial to normal development. More recently, increasing attention has been accorded the infant's impact on the caregiver.

In the last quarter-century there has been increasing recognition of the need for cooperation between the disciplines and also for psychoanalytic training for pediatricians, psychologists, psychiatrists, and social workers involved in early child care. Early in the 1930s L. K. Frank was initiating interdisciplinary conferences focused on problems of infancy; these included psychoanalysts such as Erik Erikson, Ernst and Marianne Kris, and Margaret Fries, along with psychologists and social scientists. By the 1960s Reginald Lourie and Caroline Chandler initiated an interdisciplinary study group on infancy at the National Institute of Mental Health. This too included psychoanalysts along with other scientists involved in the study of and care of young children; they produced a pioneer volume, *Early Child Care: The New Perspectives* (Chandler, Lourie, and Peters, 1968), with chapters by child analysts, psychologists, and pediatricians. Within the last decade, symposia reporting research by similar interdisciplinary groups have proliferated.

The availability of videotape recordings of infant behavior, and the adaptation of electronic devices for the simultaneous recording of autonomic nervous system reactions and sensory (visual, auditory, tactual, etc.) behavior has greatly increased the precision and range of our knowledge of young infants. And the study of premature, defective, or otherwise vulnerable babies along with those who do not gain weight—that is, fail to thrive—has focused attention both on the adaptive capacities of young infants and on the interactions between infants and caregivers, both of which are necessary for survival. Temporal patterns of processing information, preferences in each modality, the adequacy of defensive efforts in the context of the quality and range of the environmental stimuli—all are studied as they affect interaction with the environment, especially the mother.

It is impossible in the limited scope of this chapter to do justice both to the contemporary development of psychoanalytic views of infancy and to recent temporary studies of infants in which psychoanalysts, psychiatrists, neuropsychologists, social psychologists and others are learning with each other. We can, however, attempt an overview of major contributions from psychoanalysis to the understanding of the infant's experience. We need not duplicate Sylvia Brody's (1982) thoughtful critique of psychoanalytic concepts; our interest is in enduring contributions.

The Early Emphasis on Drives

In the early years of the twentieth century, psychologists and psychoanalysts were discussing the role of instincts or innate dispositions. These had been recognized since Aristotle and were further emphasized after Darwin's focus on the problem of adaptation; for William James, for McDougall, and indeed for many thinkers up until Watson began to promulgate behaviorism, human beings were motivated and guided by instinct.

Working with patients in the persisting Victorian climate of sexual repression, Freud found sexual conflicts at the root of neurosis. Observing the voluptuous sucking of infants, he concluded that sexuality was more than the urge for genital contact, and that infancy, with its strong oral drive, was the first psychosexual stage. This revolutionary concept dominated the psychoanalytic view of infancy for a quarter of a century, and remains fundamental to our thinking about the first year of life. Infants grow more rapidly during the first year than they ever will again, tripling their weight in a mere 12 months. Thus, the urgency of hunger is basic to survival, and the psychoanalytic emphasis on infant orality cannot be challenged. But it deals with only one aspect of the infant's survival task; for instance, the maintenance of breathing is equally basic, as studies of babies who suddenly and inexplicably die in the early months are showing; even the healthy neonate has defense and coping resources to prevent interferences with breathing (Lipsitt, 1986). But that fact has been documented only recently, and its implications for psychoanalytic understanding require recognition of the survival need for those defense and coping maneuvers, which doubtless are precursors of internalized patterns. Between these very recent concepts and the earlier ones we find important discussions of early ego functions, anxiety, aggression, the infant's awareness of self, the development of relationships with familiar persons (especially the mother), the problems when separated from them and when strangers come into view.

More than any other view, however, the focus on the oral stage of psychosexuality has influenced the evolution of psychoanalytic thinking about the infant, leading it from a relatively global concept through extensively differentiated analyses to comprehensive integrations. After Freud's discussion of the oral drive came Abraham's reflections on the residues of different patterns of oral functioning which persist in the developing personality (1916), Hoffer's concept of the mouth-hand ego (1949), Spitz's detailed analysis of the oral zone as the area for early ego development (1965), and Erikson's broad statement of the outcome of the oral phase as it determines the infant's balance of trust and distrust of its environment and lays a foundation for continued development (1950).

Other examples of evolving themes include the progress from Rank's controversial discussion of the trauma of birth (1929) to Greenacre's careful analysis of the relation of difficult birth experiences to predispositions to anxiety (1952). In addition, Melanie Klein's pioneer glimpses (1932) of the infant's difficulties in integrating good and bad experiences with its mother were shared with us a quarter of a century before Mahler's concepts of autistic and symbiotic stages in the infant's development, and her studies of separation-individuation (Mahler, Pine, and Bergman, 1975).

Heinz Hartmann's *Ego Psychology and the Problem of Adaptation* (1939) opened the door wide for intensive consideration of "conflict-free" areas of the infant's functioning. (Actually no area is totally conflict-free, as we are reminded by the Japanese monkey trio who "see no evil, hear no evil, speak no evil"—there are taboos on touching as well.) Despite the fact that in 1929 Bernfeld had given so much attention to mastery, it was not until after the explosion of infant research in the 1960s that psychoanalysts began to reflect on the implications of the fact that all the infant's senses are functional at birth and that very early on active infants initiate efforts to enhance their sensory contact with the world—and that they have definite preferences regarding what they will pay attention to. Equally important is the stimulus to the study of cognitive development provided by Piaget's formulations of the epigenetic sequences in the growth of the infant's understanding (1952).

The Mind of the Newborn

Hartmann believed that at birth the ego and the id are not yet differentiated, and for years people doubted that the newborn infant could see, hear, or respond to anything but a nipple or a thumb. But about 20 years ago this view of the newborn child was jolted by the findings of child development researchers. Until that time it was not at all unusual to hear even delivery room personnel, circumcision nurses, and physicians attending newborns asserting that the newborn cannot see, or cannot hear much of anything, or cannot feel pain "in the real sense of the word." That has all changed now. Not only psychoanalysts and psychologists studying infants, but virtually everyone working around newborns knows now that normal babies come into the world with all their sensory systems capable of functioning (Lipsitt, 1977). This is not to say they see what adults see or that they have the same psychophysical auditory gradients as adolescents. It is true that when they are lying down on their backs they go to sleep and are relatively unresponsive. But if we give them a chance to sit up and catch them in the 10 percent or more of the time they are awake, quiet, and alert, they surprise us. They focus on objects a few inches from their eyes, if appropriate stimuli are offered.

Moreover, young infants have a remarkable capacity for rapid pacification, quietude, and eventually sleep, even in the presence of stimulation that would elicit prolonged discomfort in older persons. This capacity provides a protective barrier that keeps them from being overwhelmed by the enormous flood of stimuli around them. Nonetheless, psychophysiological and behavioral research with the very young reveals ineluctably that they will follow a brightly colored object in its trajectory across the visual field; feel touch; are soothed by stroking; will quiet and turn their heads toward human voices of mid-range loudness and away from loud sounds (this is accompanied by crying); and will cry relentlessly to persistent, ordinarily painful stimuli such as pinching, pressure, or pricking of the skin. All of this is compromised in the child who is born at risk due to prematurity, pregnancy difficulties, or such birth problems as anoxia. Normal babies respond to the mother's voice, and after a few days to that of the father if he has talked to them. When shown objects the size of a head, one of which has a face painted on it while the others have scrambled features, the baby focuses on the face. The baby also gets bored with the same old thing and responds to moderately novel stimuli that are not so strange as to be upsetting.

There are, in fact, hundreds of careful infant studies done on this side of the Atlantic, as well as in Great Britain and on the Continent, which give a rich and precise picture of the perceptual and response capacities of babies from birth on (Stone, Smith, and Murphy, 1972); Wolff's (1966) day-long observations of babies in their homes, are perhaps the most famous. He demonstrated differences in babies' responsiveness during different states such as sleep, drowsiness, awake crying, and awake quietly alert. The quiet alert state is, naturally, the time when the baby pays attention to objects with which he is stimulated. Mothers have known this, but scientists were often oblivious to the importance of these differences.

The baby stares and hears from the earliest days, even raising its head to look at a light, as more sustained and organized functions develop through maturation and practice, becoming consolidated at about 8 weeks. Since not long after this we find evidence of *recognition* and *preference* for certain things we have to assume the *registration of images* which presumably become organized and consolidated, leading to progressive cognitive mastery. In some infants as young as 8 weeks, a disturbed reaction to strange situations implies the presence of an organized impression, or *an image of the familiar*, by comparison with which the strange situation is disturbing. Daniel Stern (Stern, Hofer, Haft, and Dore, 1985) has documented the early development of concepts as these evolve from recurring experiences.

From birth, babies have satisfying (tension-reducing) and frustrating (tension-arousing) experiences; experiences of pleasure and pain contribute to their differentiation of stimuli; there are tastes they like and dislike. They even prefer certain visual and auditory stimuli to others. Babies' feelings about all of these varied experiences gradually help them to sort out the environment, and to build realistic expectations. Pleasurable experiences reinforce interest in the environment, curiosity, and a drive to explore—visually, by touch and by taste, and, when the baby can get around, with motor activity.

While the normal baby has a full complement of functioning sense-organs at birth, discrimination is a little more advanced in touch, smell, taste, and hearing than in vision. Research has already demonstrated the baby's "learning" in the womb by showing that the newborn responds selectively not only to the mother's voice, but also to music. This does not necessarily determine sensory preference during development, as some babies can become more eager for visual stimuli than do others; thresholds for pleasure and displeasure in different sensory modes vary from infant to infant.

In all of this we see that some memory traces do develop in utero; in fact, the baby's cortex is now known to be more mature at birth than was formerly believed. And the baby's ability to recognize a familiar setting for its mother's face forces us to accept the normal process of development of images and the possibility of fantasy elaborated from them. These findings are not entirely new. Winnicott (1957) thought of the psyche as developing along with the body from conception on; Winnicott's babies were capable of experience in the uterus. His was not a voice crying in the wilderness. Sontag (1966) and other medical and psychological investigators have demonstrated the reactivity of the baby in the uterus, and many a mother has been interested in the activity of her unborn baby in response to noise, music, and other loud sounds. There are also sounds from inside the mother's body—heartbeat, bowel sounds, sounds from the lungs. Probably the infant has kinesthetic experiences moving about in the amniotic fluid in tune to the mother's moves. The responsiveness of young infants to being held closely, even to swaddling, may well involve a continuation of the comfort experience in the closeness of the womb.

What the mass of pediatric, psychological, and psychoanalytic research on newborn babies tells us, then, is that some of the basic psychoanalytic concepts need to be modified. The undifferentiated ego-id is characteristic of the earliest months of the fetus, but differentiation of drives and perception is soon under way, and then new integrations emerge (Murphy, 1972). Some unborn babies respond to sounds they hear—music, for instance—with movements expressing excitement and possibly feelings of primitive pleasure. The fact that preferences are evident so soon after birth implies an earlier positive response. The baby is equipped not only to learn about the world into which it is born—it is learning even in the uterus. Babies who have experienced difficulties during pregnancy and delivery often have troubles afterward—due partly, of course, to physiological and neurological effects but doubtless also to the untoward effects of learning. Some newborns trust the world far more than others do.

But has the actively responsive baby any picture of its mother in its mind? Spitz (1965), in discussing the "objectless" stage, assumes not. Certainly the newborn has not *seen* its mother before it is born. But it has heard a great deal while in the womb and has learned something about her, about her voice and the sounds of her heartbeat; for instance, when in the prenatal period she has repeatedly read Dr. Suess's *Cat in the Hat,* it remembers enough as a neonate to prefer hearing that story to any other (Kolata, 1984).

How can we judge the importance of the earliest intrauterine impressions? If it is true that a newborn responds more vividly to the voice, the music, the story that he has heard while still in the womb, does that mean that these preferences are permanent? Learning continues, with overlays, additions, losses, and replacements. The baby who loved Mozart may become the man who loves Shostakovich. The organism is flexible, capable of ever new responses and investments.

Moreover, gradual canalization, familiarizing, or imprinting goes on from birth. But it takes weeks or months of many caring experiences and stimulation before the baby can be sure that the person he sees at a distance of ten feet is his mother. Of course, here, as in other functions, there is a wide range of individual differences. Perceptual acuity—not vision alone, but the complex processing of visual stimuli with memory and recall—varies from infant to infant and contributes accordingly to the pace at which a child comes to differentiate his mother.

Beyond the level of sensory experience and elementary goal-oriented effort, we find that the newborn develops preferences within the first few days. The mother's voice soon has top priority, and the baby recognizes the smell of the mother's bra, confusing it with no other.

Granted that it is now clear that the unborn baby hears, is sensitive to touch, moves in response to stimulation, and re-members—in short, that some sensory and motor processes are active—when can an active selecting ego be said to emerge? How much intentionality or control is available to the newborn? When the baby a few hours old turns his eyes and then his head to follow a red cube dangling six inches in front of his face, is this purely reflex action? Turning his head at a touch near his mouth and beginning to suck is a reflex; but when a baby girl 5 days old made ten consecutive efforts to get her thumb into her mouth, this persistence goes beyond the initial reflex. Per-haps we can speak of a primitive ego, or an ego nucleus in the newborn.

Early Defense Capacities

Of special interest in the behavioral repertoire of the infant, and important for psychoanalytic theory, is the capacity of the neonate to defend itself against threats. Brazelton (1969) has pictured the remarkable way in which the newborn moves its arms around its head, seemingly to suppress an overabundance of stimulation. An infant in the first two weeks of life will on occasion appropriately move its arms to cover its eyes in a sud-denly brightened room, or to cover its ears when there is ex-cessively raucous noise, even while being tested for adequacy of hearing.

That respiratory defense behavior seems present even from the earliest moments after birth, and after the clearing of the respiratory passages and the cutting of the umbilicus, is all the more remarkable in view of the fact that the fetus has been ensconced in a "potentially smothering" environment until virtually that very moment. Just as the oral stage of development serves to set the stage for the unfolding of various pleasure-seeking functions, so this defensive behavior in the newborn may set the stage for the emergence of later defensive and coping mechanisms.

Wolff (1966) reported rhythms in the baby's functioning which organize early behavior, and detailed the contributions of both endogenous and external stimuli. He did not dismiss the earliest smiles as of no consequence but followed their causes and sequences from the very beginning to the emergence of a full social smile.

It cannot be said, then, that drives dominate the baby's earliest perceptual responses. The baby looks because eyes are to see with, and listens because ears are to hear with; getting acquainted with the interesting world all around is its own drive. Still, it certainly is true that orally loaded stimuli—the breast, the bottle—evoke a more intense, eager, and excited response than most of the other objects to which the baby is exposed.

The developmental task of fulfilling the potentialities of a life involves using the resources of the environment to meet all of the needs of the growth. These needs include nutrition required for growth of the organism, as well as stimulation required for development of the sensory, motor, and cognitive equipment that will be used in independent efforts to meet needs for nutrition, comfort and relief from pain, and pleasurable interaction with the environment. Even before the newborn infant is offered the breast or the bottle, it begins to orient itself to the environment in its brief waking moments—turning eyes and head toward a colorful stimulating object within six or eight inches of its eyes. And if a kerchief is placed over its face it will defensively push it off. Newborns also have some capacity to help themselves—as when a baby moves its head or even pushes at the breast to improve its grasp on the nipple, as well as to push away anything that interferes with breathing. In other words, newborn babies are equipped both to get acquainted with the world, to obtain the nutriment required for growth, and to cope with the basic threat to survival caused by an obstruction to breathing. The fact that many a fetus in utero responds to external loud sounds with vigorous kicks, and also moves to change its position, implies that sensory and defense or coping responses are already developing before birth—indeed, before the emergence of an oral drive. We must therefore consider the oral drive as but one aspect of the total adaptational equipment.

Brazelton's measures of newborns (1973) included not only such items as activity level, lability of state, irritability, consolability, and cuddliness, but also orientation to objects, face, and voice, alertness, and habituation to the stimuli of light, rattle, and pinprick. The first group of qualities is quickly noticed by the mother who finds the baby "easy" or "difficult" to handle and comfort, while the second group often surprises a mother with a sense that her child has a mind and is responding to the world, especially to her. Osofsky and Danzger (1974) found that the baby's eye contact with the mother, in the first days of life, was positively related to the Brazelton assessment of the infant's state, alertness, and orientation to objects, face, and voice, and also to consolability, irritability, and the baby's success in bringing its hand to its mouth. Moreover, the attentiveness and sensitivity of the mother toward the infant were related to the infant's visual and tactile behavior and its response to sound.

In other words, research is demonstrating the complex processes within the mother-infant dyadic system and the fact that each is equipped to respond to the other, and to evoke from the other responses important both for the baby's development and for the mother's investment in her baby. The mother's care helps the baby achieve a sufficient level of homeostasis to continue developmental differentiation and integration, and the baby's response is gratifying to the mother.

The Newborn's Relation to Caregivers

The first weeks are marked by an important revelation to the infant's caregivers and to any others who happen to be watching. The capacity of the very young infant to express its pleasure at sensation, particularly oral stimulation, is easily seen; the child virtually forces its companions to understand that the promotion of pleasure and the cessation of annoyance are at the top of its list of priorities. Pleasurable eating events are soon accompanied by gurgling, cooing, responsive vocalizations, and smacking of the lips. Obliging caregivers reward such behavior by continuing to provide the milk that is so satisfying.

Annoying events are equally important for stimulation within a responsive environment. Many mothers are exceptionally keen in assessing, within the first few days of their infants' lives, when the infant is "in pleasure" and when "in pain" (struggling with an annoyance). Any physical stimulation in an adult's environment that tends to annoy will annoy the baby, and the mother's own appreciation of a sweet taste is, not surprisingly, perpetuated in her infant. These opportunities for attaining synchrony and sympathy with one's progeny are gifts of the species; other mammals are also attentive to their young, and the young are well equipped to reciprocate with responses that mothers recognize as signals either that all is well or that it is not.

Anxiety, Pain, and Fear

Freud's "Inhibition, Symptoms and Anxiety" was published in 1926, but many years passed before anxiety, stress, and distress in infants came to be studied. Babies cry at birth, and they cry when they are hungry, of course. It was as if there was nothing to study; mothers knew how to soothe babies, although some were not easy to comfort. Not for half a century did comprehensive studies of distress and comfort emerge. However, Levy's discussion of affect hunger (1937), the studies of separation from the mother by Anna Freud (1942), Spitz (1946), and Bowlby (1969), and Spitz's discussion of anxious reactions to strangers (1965) eventually opened the eyes of some infant observers to the suffering that babies can experience. In 1945 Levy described the traumatic effects of surgery on many very young children and in 1960 he reported his study of the infant's earliest memory of inoculation. Meanwhile, in 1949 Leitch and Escalona had published a pioneer study of the reactions of infants to stress. Ramzy and Wallerstein (1958) studied the interrelation of anxiety, pain, and fear in the young baby, and in 1973 L.B. Murphy reported on differences in the reactions of 3-month-old infants' to the pain of inoculation; while one baby screamed for two hours, another refused feeding, another was hyperactive for an extended period, and still another became depressed for several days.

The Birth Experience and Anxiety

Rank's *The Trauma of Birth* (1929) evoked bitter contro-versy. But empirical studies of large samples of children by Pasamanick and Knobloch (1956) showed correlations between pregnancy and birth difficulties and learning, behavior, and emotional problems. These correlations, however, are not ex-tremely high; they leave room for those who suffered difficult pregnancies and births but were spared serious problems later on; the correlations do not permit us to predict the fate of individuals. The fact that some traumatized infants develop these problems and others don't has led to the more conserv-ative concept of "babies at risk"—that is, they are more likely than others to experience developmental difficulties. While a more vigorous, even violent, experience of birth may shape a pattern of the expression of anxiety, equally important is the shaping of the sense of deep security, serenity, bliss, unity with the universe, which begins for the comfortable baby in utero. Winnicott (1949) followed Freud in distinguishing between birth experience and birth trauma. The present authors have seen babies within minutes of birth who have had an easy time of it with a very relaxed mother. Having negotiated the birth canal without problems, such babies, not wrinkled or even red (as more pressured babies often are), seem doll-like and un-troubled. However, empirical data support the need for more systematic study of difficult births and their impact on the de-veloping psyche.

Most important are the contributions of Greenacre (1952, 1960), especially with regard to the effects of the specific birth experience on the patterning of the individual infant's func-tioning; her insights were developed in the course of psychoan-alytic treatment of anxious patients. The emphasis by Greenacre is on the permanent programming of anxiety reactions; a pre-disposition to anxiety may result from upheavals during and after birth which tend to be repeated in the experience of the infant and under later stress conditions. Ribble (1949) empha-sized the role of the mother and the need for her soothing efforts in contributing to equilibrium, which is often hard for a young infant to achieve. Breathing, circulation, and all vegetative functioning are unstable, and this instability is easily aggravated by disturbances in the baby's experience in the environment. Aldrich and Aldrich (1938) and Jackson and Klatskin (1950) were particularly concerned with the importance of the reduction of neonatal stress expressed in crying and screaming; they observed the comforting effects of keeping the newborn baby close to the mother, where it can have her individual and immediate attention whenever it is uncomfortable. This was Jackson's basic point in the development of her concept of "rooming in"—that is, placing newborn babies with their mothers. Here psychoanalytic influences have been instrumental in producing major changes in infant care.

Perhaps it is natural that as a woman Greenacre would be especially perceptive about the processes of birth and its impact on the infant psyche. With our present evidence of the infant's memory of in utero events we cannot ignore her suggestions about the influences of the birth experience on the psychic and physical development of the child. She focused on the painful birth; the sensorimotor balance of stimulation and response possible in the infant just before, during, and after birth; the possible relation of this balance to patterns of normal tension potential established at birth; and the effect of these patterns on the primary narcissism of the infant and its energy distribution.

In this discussion Greenacre noted that pain, like anxiety, is one of the organism's self-protective devices; both are the opposite of pleasure. The birth process involves "rhythmic pounding" of the infant's head by the periodic uterine contraction and severe pressure on the head as it passes through the birth canal. Difficult or prolonged births may produce a state of excessive chronic tension, or a susceptibility to excitation. Greenacre (1952) held that since "anxiety as such cannot exist until there is some dawning ego sense and therefore some individual psychological content, the forerunner of anxiety exists in a condition of irritable responsiveness of the organism" (p. 7). She added that birth is the period of organization and patterning of the somatic components of the anxiety response, and it marks the time of the more definite participation of the respiratory and cardiovascular systems in the defense activities of the infant—components of the somatic pattern of anxiety responses later in life. A tension level arising from a persistent disproportion between increased sensory stimulation and a limited motor discharge may become characteristic of an individual's makeup; then a sudden change in the tension level contributes to anxiety. Greenacre's concept, and Freud's, of the contribution of the birth experience to anxiety adds depth to empirical findings of correlations between birth difficulties and later problems.

At issue here are basic problems in ego development, control of impulses, and integration of drives. We have to assume that such a predisposition to anxiety would be likely to influence sensory awareness in the direction of vigilance, and to contribute to both separation anxiety and stranger anxiety, and indeed to *strangeness* anxiety—a phenomenon which has not been given the attention it deserves. A predisposition to anxiety would be expected to decrease trust and to add to the dependence of the infant on caregivers, thereby contributing to "insecure" attachment. The predisposition might also influence adaptive efforts and defense mechanisms in the direction of strategic withdrawal patterns, the inhibition of exploratory activity and affect expression, or the use of denial, displacement, projection, etc. In short, in an evaluation of the ontogenetic level of anxiety in the infant, such characteristic patterns as hyperactivity, restlessness, and contrasting patterns in the "quiet infant" might well be found to have their basis in a predisposition to anxiety. Infants with such a predisposition are likely to have a low threshold for anxious reactions to a wide range of new stimuli and situations, as well as to frustrations and deprivations. Brazelton's vivid descriptions of babies observed in his pediatric practice (1969) provide many examples of experiences that evoke crying, and also of ways in which babies can be soothed. In view of Freud's interest in anxiety, it is puzzling that psychoanalysis has not paid more attention to the stimuli that arouse it, and the developmental problems it creates. Infantile anxiety, when it has not been reduced and a sense of comfort and trust been established in its place, is likely to contribute to psychosomatic problems and childhood timidity.

Greenacre's theory of the persistent predisposition to anxiety is based on her analysis of anxious *patients*. It does not allow room for the reduction of tension and anxiety in infants who have had restitutive mothering which promoted normal development. Longitudinal studies of such infants (Heider, 1966; Murphy and Moriarty, 1976) have demonstrated resilience and developmental progress not only in cognitive functions but in broader aspects of personality. Flexibility, new learning, and improved stimulation and support all contribute to positive developmental changes, just as cumulative, repeated, or severe trauma may damage the resources of the individual.

The success of a baby's efforts to cope with stress, and the effectiveness of the caregiver's efforts depend not only on defensive, compensatory, and distracting experiences but on the severity, frequency, and persistence of the stress, and the baby's capacity to achieve homeostasis and comfort. When physiological and neurological problems are so disturbing to the baby's equilibrium that comfort is not achieved, affective and cognitive development is compromised along with the development of trustful relationships with caregivers. Both internal and external factors contribute to successful coping with stress and to the achievement of the equilibrium necessary for normal psychic development.

All healthy babies in our culture cry for help when pain, frustration, or hunger require a response from the caregiver. Developing ways to evoke this response proceeds together with the development of ways to provide relief for oneself. These coping systems contribute both to trust in the environment and to confidence in one's ability to meet one's needs. Both are precursors of intentional coping patterns seen at later ages (e.g., strategic withdrawal, resistance, protest, active self-protection), and also of intrapsychic defense mechanisms (Murphy and Moriarty, 1976).

Cognitive and Motor Development

A comprehensive view of the infant's cognitive development must include Stern's integration of inborn capacities, Piaget's concepts of processes of assimilation and accommodation, and Spitz's view of infant and mother, as well as our knowledge of the advances in differentiation and integration made possible by maturation of the central nervous system.

Psychoanalysts are interested in Piaget's emphasis (1936) on the assimilative aspect of perceptual processes and on the accommodating processes and inner adjustments that underlie activities. Touching, banging, throwing, manipulating, combining, and otherwise exploring objects are activities which increase from the age of 3 months on, although of course the infant has had many contact experiences with his hands already, and may even have been able to accomplish some goal-directed actions on objects, in addition to getting his thumb into his mouth. In the early reaching and touching movements, the baby goes through endless practice efforts, with incredible patience in some cases.

Learning to manage one's body usually begins with adjustments to the handling of the mother, incipient movements intended to initiate a change in posture, as in getting the mother to hold the baby so the baby can see better; some babies can wiggle their bodies into comfortable positions even in the first month. But real body control develops especially between 4 and 10 months. Practice and trial-and-error efforts are again visible in the baby's stages of learning to walk. Thus we see the gradual integration of the body ego.

Observing, Organizing, and Internalizing the Environment

If we follow the gaze of an infant watching people within his visual range, we have to credit him with a long period of observing, absorbing, and internalizing images of the behavior of others. Imitation of tongue-thrusting and vocalizing begins very early (Friedrich, 1983). We can hypothesize that much of the integrated sensory-motor-affective behavior of the baby profits from this internalizing of the behavior of people he observes. The failure of "wolf children" to walk upright, to talk, to be able to learn, must, we believe, be the result of this deprivation. The "fundamental education" outlined by Spitz (1965) involves this internalizing of what the baby observes as well as the adaptational processes learned in active interaction with the mother.

Spitz observed that distance perception progresses more slowly than contact perception. This is partly due to the fact that maturation is at different levels; a baby of 3 or 4 months recognizes its mother sooner at two feet than he does at eight, but in all cases perception and recognition, which involve memory, are dependent on learning. As distance perception develops, the baby can perceive his mother going and coming, and he gradually realizes that the mother who comes and goes is the same mother who is with him. He remembers her even when she is not present, and calls her to come.

As distance perception increases, the range of the environment to which the baby tries to become oriented, to become familiar with, increases; home is not just mother's lap and the crib—it is the whole room, and in time, when he has learned to crawl further and to climb upstairs, it becomes the whole house. Aided by distance perception, which evokes curiosity about what is over there, these explorations develop at different ages in different babies, but a baby of 9 or 10 months is usually "all over the place." Distance perception combined with motor integration enlarges the scope of autonomous ego functions, and the baby's knowledge of his environment or reality. Observation leads to discovery, satisfying and even exciting, though in a different way from eating.

The Contributions of Oral Experience to Learning and Ego Development

Important as vision and hearing are, they are not the only avenues to discovery. Spitz (1965) contended that the oral cavity is the first surface in life to be used for exploration and for the development of perception by touch. As he pointed out, the mouth, with its complex cavity equipped with lips, tongue, gums, the inside of cheeks, soft palate, and teeth is an organ for exploring tastes, tactile sensations, and biting experiences—long past the early months of infancy. Even the year-òld infant may explore a new object with his mouth before he tries to see what he can do with it. Some babies have evidently begun thumbsucking before birth, as we can infer from their reddened thumbs. Of course, taste and smell are also provided by thumbsucking and finger-exploration. The satisfaction available in this may be far greater than that afforded by the first visual stimuli, or by the satisfaction provided by touching blankets or other external stimuli—although some babies, though not all, "love to be cuddled." There are great differences among babies in their determination to suck their thumbs or fingers; some are very persistent, while others are easily distracted by their favorite music, stimulating play, or conversation by the caregiver. But with most babies, the early integration of an exploring, selecting, and controlling ego develops in the oral zone. Hoffer (1949) spoke of the mouth-hand ego.

Thus, the integration of a judging, controlling, and guiding ego function is a gradual process probably beginning in the baby's determined and repeated efforts to get his thumb into his mouth. In the next 2 months he begins to reach and swipe at dangling figures in the cradle-gym stretching across his crib, and to change his response as he recognizes the face of someone who, he has learned, brings pleasure or relief. Intentional, directed, sustained motor efforts, as when he struggles to turn over or get up on all fours, reflect a strong little person determined on mastery. Such efforts, along with defensive activities, involve complicated integrations of body muscles under what Hartmann called the organizing function of the ego. Defensive efforts include turning away from overstimulating features of the environment such as a bright light, pushing disliked foods out of his mouth, and pulling off any covering obstructing his breathing.

As we discussed above, when the baby is not sleeping or nursing—when he is in a quiet alert state—he looks, listens, tactually explores his surround. When he is nursing, he looks at his mother's face, hears her voice, pats her breast—in some instances enfolds her arms with his legs—and all of these experiences are colored with the satisfaction from his good feeding. All of his sensory intake is both directly satisfying and additionally reinforced by the simultaneous good feelings from feeding. Conversely, if his feeding "disagrees with him" and arouses discomfort or pain, these feelings too color all the other sensory experiences, and his feelings about the world.

Restating Spitz's view (1965) of the baby's ego at the age of 3 months, we can say that perceiving, recognizing, and responding to the need-gratifying gestalt (the mother's face) with a smile is extremely important; still, most infants cannot yet discriminate between friend and stranger. The rudimentary ego cannot protect the child from serious dangers other than threats to breathing. But when the baby is left after a feeding or after playing, we find that he turns to other stimuli; he gazes at pictures on the wall, or at his colorful mobile, or he swipes at figures on his cradle-gym, or at the balloon hanging from the crib-railing. In short, he directs activity to satisfying the need for stimulation. The baby is more resourceful in its coping than Spitz thought.

At 7½ months, according to Spitz, the baby's ego is no longer "barely capable of coordinating a perception with some memory traces, and of responding with an expression of some positive affect"; the ego "now mediates between the child's instinctual drives . . . which are expressed in the form of affectively colored needs, desires, strivings and avoidances. These are channeled into motor action and affective expression" (p. 114). Actually, by 4 to 6 months, many a baby succeeds in developing signals to evoke responses from his caregiver, and soon he maintains a sitting position, then persistently struggles to creep. All of these goal-directed actions are under central control. After some weeks the baby gets ideas of interesting possibilities such as ways of making noises by banging small blocks together or by pounding on the high chair tray with a spoon. He delights in making things happen as well as in achieving new body skills: being able to stand up or even walk around holding on to furniture; being able to feed himself. Timing, preference for different skills, and inventiveness differ from baby to baby, but in general we see, as Spitz did, an increasing scope of deliberate activity. The ego mediates between the inside (needs and wishes and feelings) and the outside (opportunities, challenges, and obstacles presented by the environment). In this Spitz saw operating a "variety of psychic systems and apparatuses with ego serving mastery and defense"—getting what the baby wants, shutting out what it dislikes, adapting to the caregiver and others in the environment. We can say that the baby is learning how to get along in the world.

Stern (1985) has integrated recent research related to the cognitive development of infants; he discusses various issues in the relation between perception, cognition, drive, and affect. One of these is the implication of new research on stimulus seeking for the concepts of the stimulus barrier and the "normal autistic phase." He points out that the former notion is challenged by Wolff's description of the "alert inactive state," in which the infant does not move but avidly takes in the world through eyes and ears. Moreover, the infant will work hard to obtain stimulation; he will, for example, suck vigorously on a pacifier electronically hooked to a slide projector that shows new slides as long as he sucks. Still, the infant has an optimal level below which he will seek more stimulation, and above which he will avoid it. This active seeking and regulating of stimulation, Stern argues, requires that we abandon both the notion of the stimulus barrier and that of the "normal autistic phase." Around 2 months, to be sure, the infant tolerates more stimulation and seems more social, but this is a quantitative change, not a new development. Further, we can no longer speak clinically of regression to an autistic phase.

Another issue raised by Stern concerns learning and knowledge. Even in the newborn period the infant is a very fast learner, as we see in the week-old's preferential response to his mother's bra and in the nonnutritive sucking pattern he evinces upon hearing his mother's voice as distinct from all others; by a month or so he can differentiate his mother's face from that of another woman. By turning his head, by gazing, and by a sucking pattern, he shows what he has learned.

A third issue is the crucial importance of the infant's "pre-wired" knowledge of colors, evident in a preference for the best example of a color—"the reddest red."

Even more impressive is the infant's ability to transfer knowledge from one modality to another, as when a 3-week-old infant looks more at a nipple previously mouthed than at one not previously mouthed and with a different shape. (Perhaps a related instance is the young infant's attempts to copy the tongue-thrusting play of its parents.) Cross-model equivalences between auditory and visual domains have also been studied; the infant "knows" that sounds belong in synchrony with the visually experienced events that cause them. (And as soon as he can manipulate objects he delights in making sounds himself.) More surprising is the evidence that the cognitive apparatus has a "tendency to make and to test hypotheses from the beginning of life" (Stern, 1985). The illustration provided, in which infants abstracted an average face from a set of many variations, was seen as an inherent tendency to generate knowledge of the world. (Perhaps we should look at this tendency along with the tendency, posited by Lewin (1935), for the human mind to respond to good forms, or even to prefer grace and order to confusion and disarray.)

Stern infers that the capacities just reviewed make it unlikely that self and other will be confused cognitively. The infant "simultaneously forms schemes of self with others, self alone in the presence of other, and self alone. . . . The infant need not individuate from an initial symbiotic position."

In all these varieties of learning which occur as sensory and motor apparatuses mature, both stimulus and reinforcement are provided by the environment as well as by the baby's own trial-and-error and successes; but maturation occurs without specific training, and the activities in the repertory of a baby do not have to be initiated by the adult, however important, gratifying, and even necessary are the opportunities and reinforcement offered by the environment.

Ego-Id Relationships

The fact that early anxiety, rage, and excitement are expressed in such relatively undifferentiated, haphazard motor activity and emotional explosions probably contributed to Hartmann's concept of the "undifferentiated ego-id" in the early weeks of infancy, and to the question being posed whether the ego develops out of the id or whether the two simply separate out. That is, is it a question of the transformation of id into ego or a question of emergence? Actually, when we observe young babies closely, this seems a rather academic question, since, as we have just seen, coordinated motor responses serve the drive for satisfaction of hunger. When a baby persists in efforts to get its hand to its mouth even when not hungry, or when it pushes away confining bed coverings, we see the primitive beginnings of ego function. As soon as the requisite neurological maturation occurs, these responses become more smooth.

This is not to say that such autonomous functions, to use Hartmann's term (1952), develop independently of other aspects of the baby's equipment and experience. The infant is looking at his mother's face while being fed, is listening to her voice if she is a social and warmly responsive mother, and, if he is an active baby, may be patting her breast with his hand while hugging her arm with his feet. As we have seen, ego functions and instinctual activities do not go on in isolation from each other. This is increasingly true as the baby is better able to focus at a distance and to listen, so that by the time he is 2, 3, or 4 months old he is looking at, listening to, and kicking at his mother as part of feeding, bathing, diapering, dressing, and other activities. In the happy instances in which the mother enjoys anything and everything she does with her baby, every function will be participating in the gratifying atmosphere of a mutually happy and playful relationship. As hunger becomes less urgent and the baby eats less often and sleeps less, the other sensory, motor, and social functions loom increasingly large and have more time devoted to them. However, even after feeding is no longer the setting for a major share of the contact between the caregiver and the baby, sensory and motor experiences of all kinds overlap in varying clusters. The deep emotional meaning of music and the stirring potentialities of auditory experiences throughout life doubtless have their roots in this overlapping and clustering of sensory, instinctual, and interpersonal experiences in early infancy. If the rhythms and sounds of the mother's voice are associated with every kind of basic gratification in infancy, her voice carries an emotional evocativeness far beyond any inherently esthetic quality it may have. We may say that the tone, the warmth, the color, the richness, the rootedness, the meaningfulness of each autonomous area of functioning will develop in the setting of the baby's experience in each area, as if it were dyed with the colors of the relationship between the mother (and father) and infant. Basic richness of personality and perhaps richness of thought may have a source in this early complexity of sensory, motor, and interpersonal experience.

At the same time, progress in myelinization and other aspects of neurological, muscular, and skeletal development, as well as glandular changes, go on under the control of genes. In other words, as Hartmann, Kris, and Loewenstein discussed (1946), there are roots for the autonomy of functions and a basis for the mutual influence of ego and instinctual functions and the influence of both in the context of the mother-infant relationship.

Ego Development Related to Drives

We saw that Kris (1950) emphasized that we cannot deal with the development of the ego, of object relationships, or of the libidinal and aggressive drives separately, but that each must be seen in relation to the others. The development of the ego is profoundly influenced by the relationships in which it participates, and both are deeply influenced by the interplay of the infant's drive intensity with the stimuli and responses of those in the environment. Perceptual thresholds and alertness in different modalities, as well as executive skills, both manipulative skills and gross motor skills used in exploring and discovering the environment, are given a greater or lesser degree of exercise, depending on the relative intensities and strengths of different drives involving use of the child's perceptual and motor equipment. These drives fall into several different categories.

With Erikson (1950) we can consider the *intake drives* together. All of these involve taking in, being given to, receiving stimulation. We find that oral, visual, auditory, and tactile interests differ in their relative intensity in different infants and children, as reflected in the expression and feeling tone of the child when motivated in each of these areas, and also by the persistence of the child's interests in each of them.

Contact drives involve the experience of contact for its emotional value and the gratification it provides, along with its informational aspects. The increasingly intense sexual drives can be distinguished from the more global and diffuse tactile interests, and each of these can be distinguished from a more comprehensive and inclusive social drive expressed in the infant's responsiveness to faces in preference to impersonal objects.

Motor or action drives include both the constructive and aggressive potentials of manual manipulation and gross motor activity, as well as biting and even angry hostile expressions. A very strong tactile interest may reinforce and augment some of the dangers involved in the infant's activity drive. For example, Sally, a preschooler, told the candid tale of a child who touched things in the house and then got spanked, only to touch them again; this appeared to be a realistic statement of her knowledge of herself as an active child who could not restrain herself beyond a certain point from exploring, touching, and manipulating objects around the house. When she was a young baby, her mother ruefully said that "she might as well have been a boy."[1]

As another example, we can look at a child with a very strong oral drive combined with great motor skill and energy, which has led to interests in manipulating toys, motor exploration, and thence to early skill in self-help. Despite the strong oral drive in such an infant, the counter-balancing interest in

[1] The case illustrations of infant and child behavior are drawn from (1) unpublished primary data from the Escalona-Leitch study in Topeka (1948–1952), analyzed by L.B. Murphy; (2) Heider's analysis (1966) of Escalona-Leitch records; (3) unpublished data from the records of children in the Sarah Lawrence College Nursery School, Bronxville, N.Y. (1937–1944); (4) examples of behavior and remarks of the children taken from L.B. Murphy's study of the Escalona-Leitch group at the preschool stage (1954–1957); and (5) unpublished photographic documents (1930–1965) and other unpublished records of infants observed by L.B. Murphy outside of any study. Later sequelae of infant behavior are drawn from unpublished records of the longitudinal study of some of the children originally in the Escalona-Leitch study. The subsequent studies were carried on by L.B. Murphy and her staff from 1953 to 1969.

the external world and the satisfactions gained in manipulating it, together with the self-confidence arising from skill in self-help, can lead to an experience of weaning as a comfortable process of shifting. Thus, such a child has a weaning experience vastly different from that of a child with strong oral drive combined with very little motor drive, interest, or skill, for whom weaning may constitute a far greater deprivation. This deprivation in the second child would tend to reinforce dependency trends which were already hard to outgrow because the lack of a strong motor drive prevented the development of the self-help resources acquired by the first child. If the second child does not get sensitive help in developing interests in the environment outside of those contributing to oral satisfaction, weaning is likely to be more disturbing than it is for the first child, even if it comes rather late. In other words, it is not the timing as such, so much as the range of resources the child has developed for himself at a time when a new orientation to the world is demanded.

The Drive to Mastery

What is the instinct to master, the drive for competence? Wolff (1966) draws on Piaget's thinking and that of Rapaport (1960) in search of an answer to this question, noting that the sucking reflex repeats itself with increasing smoothness until it is perfected. It acts when the lips encounter a touch that stimulates the sucking response. We saw that some babies have sucked their thumbs before birth. Is there a preformed hand-to-mouth drive? Or does the hand accidentally encounter the mouth so that the sucking reflex is then started? Some analysts believe this is the case. Probably there are two origins. In any event, when sucking brings milk, it brings not only nourishment but a taste, a smell, a tactile experience—simultaneous pleasures. Later the baby reaches for objects to explore via sucking—objects with different tastes and smells, different tactile experiences. He ignores or rejects those he does not find pleasant. Efforts toward mastery are reinforced by the pleasurable accompaniments of success.

Sucking is rhythmical; the rhythm is relaxing, soothing, pleasurable. The baby presumably initiates this rhythm for more pleasure. If there is nothing to suck on, some babies engage in sucking their own lips, or mouthing. Important here is the soothing, discomfort-reducing, or even pain-reducing effect of rhythmical sucking, one of the first sources of pleasure of the baby. Also important here is the fact that reflexes are programmed to food intake, and they integrate into patterns that reduce discomfort and provide pleasure without the presence of food. Thus, the baby has a resource for coping with stress and to some degree mastering it.

While all normal babies spontaneously look at available patterns, some babies scan more actively than others, energetically turning from one side to the other, even stretching their heads back to try to see what is behind them. It is as if they want to see everything, to visually master the environment. In general, babies pay more attention to relatively complex, moving, or three-dimensional objects than to plain surfaces, and they are more fascinated by faces, especially eyes, than by anything else. Selection as well as scanning contributes to visual mastery.

Within the first week, babies not only discriminate sounds but try to locate where they come from, and again the baby responds to the sounds of human speech more than to any others. Mothers in the Escalona-Leitch study often volunteered what their babies "liked" to respond to and in turn they responded to the babies' active cues. Recent psychoanalytically oriented studies focus on details of the interaction between mother and baby (Stern, Hofer, Haft, and Dore, 1985), and the mother's sensitivity to the baby's state, which largely determines its readiness for and response to stimulation, and affects both the smoothness of the dyadic exchange and the baby's mastery of social responses.

The fact that some learning occurs in the womb, and that at birth all of the senses are functional to a degree does not mean that we can forget all that has been seen about the limitations of early responsiveness to stimulation. Brazelton's newborn babies who are responding to a brightly colored ball dangled several inches in front of their eyes do not see Brazelton

20 feet away, although they do hear and respond to the crying of nearby babies. Benjamin (1961b) commented that Freud's concept of the early "stimulus barrier" probably refers to the passive effect of the relative lack of functional connections in the period when the baby's active resources for protecting itself are limited. As myelinization proceeds, the baby is better able to do something in order to reduce unwanted stimulation; for instance, one of the babies in the Escalona-Leitch study closed her eyes and went to sleep when three observers hovered over her crib at the same time.

Escalona, in *The Roots of Individuality* (1968), demonstrates differences between infants in terms of strong and weak boundaries and also in terms of variations within the same infant in the strength of boundaries in different sensory zones. Some babies are especially sensitive to lights, others to certain qualities or intensities of sound, still others to skin contact. Cuddly and uncuddly babies have been studied by others.

The instability of ego boundaries is documented by Sontag's data (1966) on "high cardiac reactors" among normal males and their tendency to be more emotional. Autonomy of cognitive functioning is variable from infant to infant and child to child and is vulnerable—in some infants and children—to variations in drive, maturation, affect, or stress in the context of experience with caregivers.

Mastery, then, starts with the rewarding experience of equipment, and with reflexes which are refined and gradually integrated into behavior patterns that are useful both in restoring equilibrium and in coping with the environment. All this involves drives and ego functions, accompanied by affects. These vary in intensity from infant to infant. Just as eagerness and gratification in feeding vary from one infant to another, so do needs for bodily comfort in kinesthetic and contact activities, and responses to visual and auditory stimuli, along with less observable responses to olfactory stimuli. At the early stage the baby, with its limited motor capacities, is a creature of complex sensory experience and also strong reactions to discomfort, with a capacity to become very disorganized under frustration, as when very hungry or in distress.

Still, the early functions that contribute to the capacity for mastery include, in addition to primitive learning and memory, the intentionality seen in persistent efforts; the selectivity of visual, auditory, olfactory, and oral responses; and the active protection of breathing, by head-turning when prone and by flailing arms to remove an obstructing covering, as well as protection from overstimulation. The drive to mastery is the drive to maximize effectiveness of efforts to satisfy the many adaptational needs of the infant.

Mothers' and Caregivers' Reinforcement

The expression of glee in infancy, often in association with mastery, as when an infant reaches for and attains an attractive object, shows us how the initial fascination of the baby with the physical pleasures of sensation is soon followed by other—at times complex—reinforcing events, such as the smile of the caregiver. By the same token, the infant in the first few months of life will express displeasure with an annoying situation, such as a sudden change in noise level, the removal of an attractive object with which he was attentively involved, or (alas) the mother's disappearing smile.

At around 2 to 4 months of age the infant is equipped with manual and other psychomotor resources to reach for, grab, and reciprocate the movements of inanimate objects. Mothers and other interested baby watchers are fascinated with the achievements of the child at this time, perhaps in part because of the rapid acquisition of new psychomotor "tactics" and the experimenting activities of the infant. Feature an infant reaching for a sunbeam passing over its crib, seeming to capture it and hold it in his hand, perhaps in an attempt to move it around. (Of course, the sunbeam reciprocates, at least illusorily.) In all likelihood the watching adult's delight will not go unnoticed by the infant. The behavior of the child did not emerge full-blown from an unprepared psyche, nor did the reaction of the proud parent. Both are demonstrating "prepared" patterns of reaction.

An infant nursing at the breast does not necessarily have an easy experience—the nipple may be inverted or not very erect; the milk may come slowly or give out altogether. Weaning may be sudden, as when a mother becomes ill or decides to wean the baby because of some family emergency. In sudden weaning some mothers smear the nipple with a distasteful substance from which the baby will withdraw. When weaning is to be gradual, a mother prepares the baby by developing pleasure in solid foods, and by using a bottle first for orange juice or water, and then for milk, so that there is no sudden transition.

Since some degree of delay as well as frustration is a frequent part of the feeding experience, the oral zone is an important area in which tolerance of delay and the ability to cope with it is developed—when the baby learns that food will come soon.

The mouth, along with the eyes, is the earliest social tool. With smiles, babbling, cooing, and squeals of delight the baby responds to the smiles, care, and playful activity provided by the caregiver who discovers "how much fun the baby is." The sober, unsmiling baby may be considered unresponsive and "not much fun." And perhaps the earliest imitation occurs via the mouth, as when the baby imitates more or less adequately the playful parent who provocatively sticks out his or her tongue. With some babies playful imitative vocalizing occurs as well, when the adult provides a simple Ah-boo! noise. Equal in importance is the baby's communication of needs and distress with an array of cries which now can be electronically differentiated. Screams of pain or terror, begging cries or whimpers, "fussing" in mild discomfort or boredom, and other qualities are recognized by mothers as communications, although some psychoanalysts may regard them as forms of tension discharge, as they are initially.

Moreover, babies differ widely in sensitivity, tolerance for stimulation or its lack, and the ability to meet their own needs and to entertain themselves, as well as in resourcefulness in evoking responses from others, soberness or gaiety, equanimity and smoothness of physiological functioning, vigor or frailness, and stability or predisposition to anxiety. To an inexperienced mother these and other differences may not be noticed or understood: a baby is just a baby—fussy or cheerful, easy or difficult. The connection between a baby's behavior and its relationship with its caregiver may also not be understood.

In addition, the mother's handling of the baby may include behavior which the baby experiences as painful, intrusive, interfering, or neglectful, as well as behavior that comforts, entertains, or responds to the baby's signals. The more complex the overall demands of the family on the mother, the less possible it is for her to respond to the baby's needs for stimulation, play, affection, or even frequent physical care. Or she may be conscientious in physical care but lack playfulness, affection, or the capacity for attunement. Thus, good and bad experiences may contribute to good and bad images of the mother, and it may be very difficult for the baby to integrate these contradictions into a whole image. It was Melanie Klein who first reflected on the consequences for psychic development of good and bad experiences at the breast and with the mother.

Stern et al. (1985) imply that the sensitive, flexible response of the mother to the baby's tempo, intensity and style of behavior is fundamental to smooth integration of the baby's functioning. *Affect attunement* is his term for that response to an infant's exuberant achievement or play pattern in which the caregiver matches the level of intensity, the timing, and the shape of the infant's expressive behavior. Generally, attunements occur across sensory modes. If the infant expressed himself vocally, the mother was likely to attune in gestures or with a facial expression or with a combination of the infant's pattern and another in a different mode. Mothers or other caregivers who respond to infants this way explain their wish to share, to join in, to be with the infant—in other words, to *commune*. If a mother's response is out of synchrony in intensity or timing, the infant is perturbed and his response may be interrupted; with attunement, his activity continues to flow.

Early Patterns of Change and Development

Development from the newborn period onward is very rapid indeed. Close observations of the child in the first 2 or 3 months of life suggest that a major transitional period of development occurs at around 2 to 4 months of age, as Benjamin (1961b) discussed, but that prior to this time there are gradual accretions not only of the basic physiological substrate, including rapid growth of myelin tissue and proliferation of dendrites, but in behavioral capacities as well. One of the most striking aspects of development in those first few weeks relates to the gradual "awakening" of the sensory capacities, each day's advances capitalizing upon those of the previous days.

Unless one is observing one's own child daily at home, it appears that there are quantum leaps in integration which suggest Mahler's term *hatching* (Mahler, Pine, and Bergman, 1975). But in our observation, just as a baby gradually doubles and then triples his weight in the first year, so he gradually develops the capacity for more sustained alertness, more meaningful smiles, greater integration of visual-mother-affective response, more freedom in motility, more differentiation of the familiar with the strange, and greater tolerance of separation from the mother. Even when the baby succeeds in pulling up to stand at the playpen railing and lets out a yelp of triumph, this is the result of cumulative efforts that finally reach their goal. And when some babies appear to suddenly "take off" and begin to walk alone, this has usually come about after walking with the aid of a walker or holding an adult's hand. This is not to deny that the moment of integration that potentiates the new achievement is itself a developmental step. But there are many such moments in the series of integrations that continue from birth through the next several months. The first social smile; the first success in swiping at an interesting object; the first triumph in turning from prone to supine, or in "getting up on all fours"; the first "word" that integrates some fragment of adult speech into the baby's effort to communicate—all are examples of integrative climaxes.

At about 8 weeks the baby's staring changes to a "more human kind of looking," as some people have described it. Certainly processes, both of differentiation and of integration, have been going on which indicate that the baby shows recognition and is perceiving what he sees in a more organized way. Visual and auditory stimuli become increasingly important to him, to the point that it is not uncommon for a baby around this age to be restless and to wiggle in order to be held in a posture in which he can see more.

As Benjamin (1961b) has pointed out, this is a critical phase for stimulus deprivation and overstimulation. The mother is needed in order to protect the baby from excessive stimulation, to which it is now increasingly exposed, precisely by virtue of its increased responsiveness. At the same time, it needs adequate stimulation to support the development of these new behaviors. (Stimulus deprivation has been discussed at so many age levels and from so many different points of view that we do not need to pay attention to it now other than to point out its basic importance for ego development at this stage.)

Another aspect of this critical phase of stimulus interest has been pointed out by Escalona (1952) and by Heider (1966)—the tendency for some babies to respond very intensely to certain stimuli up to a point and then to feel extreme distress when the stimulus becomes too strong. This contributes to the development of ambivalence, which may be seen as broader than the ambivalence that develops out of the alternating gratification and deprivation given by the mother.

Mahler's pioneering longitudinal study of babies (Mahler, Pine, and Bergman, 1975) focused on infants 4 months old; thus she did not observe the active visual and tactile explorations now seen much earlier. It is correct to emphasize the gradual evolution of attention and its increased duration; but we cannot say, as she does, that outwardly directed attention "comes into being" only in the latter part of the first half year. Moreover, with observations focused on mothers with their babies, she failed to see that when mothers are elsewhere—busy with chores about the house—babies' attention is often attracted to a range of stimuli available to them in the environment. We need more detailed records of babies in their early months—like those of Wolff in the 1950s, or of Spitz and Wolf in the 1940s—if we are to have an adequate view of the infant's earliest responses to his entire environment, and of the adaptational importance of those responses from birth.

Individual Differences in Oral Drives and Experience

Contemporary studies document the complexity of expressions of the oral drives. There are individual differences in level of intensity, frequency, and regularity of hunger, and in the consequent demand and activity in expressing that demand, as well as differences in taste preferences leading to eager acceptance or decisive rejection of solid foods. At the beginning there are differences in the efficiency of sucking and swallowing, in their speed or slowness, in persistence in sucking, and in the intensity of pleasure taken in nursing and eating.

There is a contrast between the data in the Escalona-Leitch records of infants and much of the psychoanalytic literature where the young infant is often referred to as "greedy," "avid," or "totally absorbed" as regards the sucking and feeding experience. There are, of course, infants who can be described this way. However, other infants are passive, lackadaisical, not very interested in sucking, or rather bored with it. Mothers respond to this in different ways: by patiently keeping at it, by trying to stimulate the infant actively, or by getting anxious and irritated at the infant's "ungrateful" lack of interest in what the mother has to offer. One baby relaxes with contentment; another smacks his lips or purrs and coos in sensuous delight. Termination and rejection patterns range from a passive letting go of the nipple to closing the lips, pushing out the nipple or the food, letting it dribble, or spitting.

The baby's nursing experience also differs with the degree of autonomy permitted by the mother as regards timing of the feeding. The baby's experience also varies with the mother's adaptation to the baby's sucking tempo and rhythm. Frustration may result when the mother is insistent and pushes beyond satiation, as well as when her supply is inadequate, or when she interrupts sucking in order to burp the baby when he does not want to be burped. When solid food is first introduced, the baby's puzzlement, ineptness, and inexperience in managing it may be ignored by a mother who keeps pushing food into the baby's mouth regardless of the time needed to become acquainted with it, to get used to the new swallowing experience.

Babies who feed well, with apparent vigor and eagerness, are "good babies," whereas the passive, lazy, uninterested babies are frustrating to their mothers. This, of course, is partly because mothers recognize the enormous need for food intake in the early months, in order to make possible the rapid rate of growth typical of this period. The fact that a baby is not very interested in food, however, does not necessarily indicate a lack of drive in general, as some babies develop much greater enthusiasm about other activities.

In this context, experiences of gratifying cooperation—as opposed to frustration and the passive or active protest or resistance it engenders—along with experiences of successful mastery of the problems arising with nipples (too slow or too fast flow) or solid food (too hard to swallow) lay down basic patterns of feeling that may color a child's attitude toward food, or be displaced or extended to feelings about the mother or the world in general. The level of trust, confidence, and optimism is influenced by the quality of this basic experience as well as by the many other successes and failures the baby experiences in the first year.

Feeding is not the only use of the mouth. Playful bubbling, mouthing, and vocalizing give babies experiences that they can do things with their mouths that are fun, and sucking a thumb or pacifier is a reliable method of self-comforting, of screening out disturbing stimuli, and of maintaining a balance of pleasure. Pleasurable sucking early attracted the attention of psychoanalytically oriented observers and is well discussed by Bernfeld (1929). But there are great differences in the intensity and persistence of thumbsucking. One baby is born with a red thumb, and the pediatrician remarks that it probably has been sucking in utero; at any rate it has no trouble getting its thumb into its mouth immediately after birth and continues through the early months. Another baby makes 10 or 15 attempts before it succeeds at first, and then gradually reduces the number necessary. Others suck their thumbs very little or for only a short time. Some babies give up thumbsucking as soon as grasping and playing with objects become a new source of pleasure at 3 or 4 months.

Sucking is, then, one libidinal satisfaction in early infancy which contributes to the development of adequate investment in the environment. However, for some babies, kinesthetic experiences of being carried and rocked, and other experiences of contact with the warmth and softness of the mother's body, are at least as important. The body comfort is satisfying both in its own right and as offsetting the discomforts of the early weeks, in which the infant can do little about its own body. The importance of tactile experience and the infant's need for it have been emphasized in recent years (Frank, 1957).

Just as the oral zone is a major area for the establishment of trust in the world, it is also a zone in which profound disturbance of the baby's equilibrium may be experienced—when gastrointestinal troubles are chronic, when colic is persistent, when the baby is so miserable that pleasure and trust are not experienced. Such a baby suffers angrily and fearfully, and the bad start may be difficult to overcome.

While sensory and motor capacities are also developing from before birth, the importance of the baby's oral experience during this year (a period in which birth weight must be tripled) is of such great importance that we can continue to speak of the first year as the oral stage of development.

Expressions of Autonomy in the Oral Phase

When Erikson (1950) emphasizes the second year of life as the stage of autonomy, he does not imply that the baby suddenly develops autonomy and control with no previous hints of this development. We have already implied initiative in our account of the activity of the newborn baby. Among the partial or separate expressions seen in longitudinal studies are the young baby's ability to move to a comfortable position; the baby's insistence on a position where there is something interesting to look at or protest against; and the baby's struggle to turn over. In these and many other instances, we see the baby's autonomous efforts to manage both the environment and a still intractable body. The child does not yet say, "Want to do it myself," as will occur so frequently around the age of 2.

Early Development of Affects

As early as 1895 Freud reflected on the survival value of the neonate's red-faced screaming and random flailing movements, which both discharge the tension arising from hunger and evoke the response of the caregiver. Spitz (1965) quotes Freud's comment: "The original helplessness of human beings is thus the primal source of all moral motives" (p. 73fn). Whether or not such a broad contribution to human morality can in fact be attributed to the effect of a baby's screams, we have to admit that they make most of us uncomfortable and eager to reduce his distress.

And when a baby learns that cries succeed in bringing relief, communication at other levels is encouraged; according to Ainsworth and Bell (1972), the baby whose cries are respected does less crying after speech develops than babies whose crying is ignored. From this it may be inferred that early cries are a means of communication, of sending a message. Moreover, it is not long before the baby's cries are expressive at simple differentiated levels—from mild fussing, to staccato cries of pain, to long-drawn-out wails and other patterns which mothers recognize and to which they respond.

Psychologists are on solid ground when dealing with ego functioning, which is easily observed in the goal-directed behavior of infancy; the early interpretation of subtle affects, however, is more difficult. A 4-week-old baby who until then had been nursed at the breast frowned as she began to suck on the nipple of a bottle, so very different from the nipple on her mother's breast. Was that baby frustrated, disappointed, or simply puzzled? This is an example of the difficulty of identifying the quality of a baby's feeling. Despite this, however, many mothers feel sure they can at least distinguish the baby's hunger cry from a cry of pain.

Some babies begin to smile at the mother very early, and in some experimental studies babies have been observed to give a definitely social smile before the age of 4 weeks (Jones, 1926); a large proportion of babies seen in their homes are smiling by the age of 8 weeks in response to the smile of an adult. Along with the development of the smile, increasing differentiation of affects has been reported. As the baby shows more explicit delight or irritation in being bathed, changed, or powdered, the mother is given more feedback. These expressions and the range of sources of pleasures multiply rapidly between 8 and

16 weeks; they are closely allied with increasing perceptual development, as the baby becomes able to recognize the bottle and to listen attentively to the caregiver's talking, to lullabies, and to music.

The recognition that the infant is a responsive social being—responding more to faces, especially eyes, than to impersonal stimuli—has generated interest in the expressiveness of infants' faces and in the dyadic interaction of eye-to-eye contact, smiles, and other facial expressions passing between mother and child. In recent years, smiling and crying, as well as "sobering," frowning, "wariness," and various more nuanced expressions of surprise and pleasure, have been studied in relation to the cognitive and social developments that provide a context for their emergence. Fraiberg's observation (1968) of the restricted range of facial expression in blind infants points to the importance of visual responses to other persons in the development of facial expressions.

Pain, Soothing, and Preventing Traumas

It is intriguing to reflect on the fact that mothers often spend more time soothing a young baby and making it comfortable than they spend on feeding it. Yet the baby's urgent sucking has made a stronger impression on analysts than has its distress and its cries for relief. As we have noted, it has often been thought that very young babies do not feel pain; their heels are pricked for blood samples, and inoculations are given by doctors who imagine the babies are not hurt. However, the child analyst David Levy (1960) long ago reported evidence of distress when a baby is taken again to the hospital or doctor's office where inoculations were administered, or when the baby sees the doctor in a white coat. The anxiety-provoking memory is global in the early period; the baby does not differentiate the needle as the threatening object before the age of 6 months. Individual differences in babies' reactions to the pain of inoculation give important clues to ranges of reactivity to pain.

Doubtless inspired by Harlow's demonstration (1958) of the baby monkey's preference for the soft comforting mothers, in contrast to the feeding mother, clinicians and researchers are paying greater attention to the maternal soothing role. Soothing processes implicitly involve the principle that strong enough pleasure drives out unpleasure.

Adaptation, Mutual Regulation, and Coping

Although Hartmann's concept of adaptation (1939) included active dealing with the environment, the terms *adaptation* and *adjustment* tend to be used with the connotation of fitting in, as if the environment were something static out there and the infant a pliable thing to be somehow squeezed into it. Erikson (1950) used the phrase *mutual regulation,* which implies that mother and infant are not a couple, one of whom fits into the patterns of the other, as the programmatic philosophy of infant care during the 1930s seemed to expect, nor that the mother is capable of infinite adaptability and extension of herself, as the demand approach of the 1940s seemed to imply. Rather, mother and baby together find a way of living which meets, to a sufficient degree, the baby's needs, tempo, and approach to life, while at the same time the baby fits to some extent into the patterns of its mother. Mutual regulation has to include the mother's respect for the active, self-initiated responses to the environment made by the baby practically from birth.

Thus we see the baby not only as an organism fitting into the environment, but as a self-propelling being, able to stimulate others, especially the mother, and able to initiate changes in the environment. We refer to the infant's capacity for expending effort, initiating change, and dealing creatively with the environment as *coping.* We heard the analyst-pediatrician Benjamin Spock use this term in the late 1930s, and Freud and Burlingham (1942) used it to describe the various ways their English charges at the Hampstead nurseries dealt with bombs, separation from mother, and other threats posed by World War II.

Influences and Contributions of the Early Oral Phase

Traditionally in psychoanalysis, the oral phase has been divided into two parts—the early oral phase, that is, the oral receptive phase, before teeth begin to influence oral functioning, and the later oral phase, influenced by, though not wholly dominated by, the acquisition of teeth. This second phase is generally referred to as the oral-aggressive phase.

We have already touched on some of the many interacting aspects of the baby's experience in the early oral phase, which lasts approximately the first 6 months. Following Freud, Abraham, in writing the 1916 article on the contribution of orality to character formation, laid a foundation for the work of analysts of very different emphases—e.g., Klein (1932) on the one hand, and Erikson (1950) on the other. Abraham pointed to two types of sequelae: (1) specific oral habits which persist or are revived, either under stress or in later life when genital gratification becomes less available; and (2) "character traits" derived from oral experience—e.g., greediness, holding on, or a tendency to renounce all expectation of gratification in one's life.

Bernfeld (1929), following Freud's thinking (1911, 1914, 1920, 1923), made a contribution of enormous importance in integrating a step-by-step study of the infant's psychic development with inferences from the behavior and associations of adults in analysis. He also used the diaries of early writers and data made available by experimentalists such as Canestrini (1913). While he considered these observations in the light of his own rich psychoanalytic experience (he was a member of the group close to Freud and was analyzed by him), the material suffers from the natural limitation that individual differences cannot be specified in detail, as he did not have intensive observations on a wide sample of children. However, this was compensated by his sensitivity to cultural differences and his use of anthropological knowledge to place the data in perspective. This allowed him to recognize the differences in character development which must result from the long nursing and very gradual weaning typical of many cultures other than the Western European. He considered early and abrupt weaning an important factor in the strong ego development characteristic in Western European society.

Research on infants has led to a more detailed picture of the infants' oral experience. Among the babies evaluated by Escalona and Leitch (1952) as in general free from defect, some were either so inefficient in their early sucking and managing of the milk, or had such difficulty in grasping and handling the nipple, that it took heroic and persistent efforts by the mother to help the baby learn to nurse well. We can assume here that the results of such learning may be the achievement not only of satisfaction but perhaps also, at a very deep unconscious level, of the lesson that the effort to make something work better can succeed. Greenacre (1960) and others speak of the baby's nursing activities as his way of "working for a living"; beyond this, the effort of conquering the difficulties involved in early nursing provides the first experience of mastery.

At least 20 percent of the babies in our Topeka sample (Murphy and Moriarty, 1976) had considerable colic. In the very first weeks of life the baby is not able to manage his body very well or to do much to change its position in a way which could facilitate the movement of internal contents so as to obtain relief (as is possible at a later age). Assistance from the mother is necessary. She pats or rocks the baby, and in other ways tries to help him "get up the air" or alleviate the distress of colicky pain. To be sure, a certain number of cases of colic are probably the result of, or are at least made worse by, tension in the mother which induces cramplike tensions in the baby, interfering with gastrointestinal functioning. Whatever the cause of the trouble, some mothers are endlessly patient and do succeed in alleviating the colic, inducing good feelings to displace the pain. The mother of Susan, one of the children in the Topeka study, said, "I rocked her and rocked her and rocked her" when asked what she did about the colic. Susan was a child with an extraordinary drive to master distress and pain.

Gratification is reflected in a baby's relaxed comfort, cooing, and smile while looking at the mother during a good nursing period. Reinforcement of the earliest recognition of the mother makes it possible for the baby to anticipate gratification and to wait in the expectation that it will come. This sequence is not only a prerequisite for later impulse control; it is also a foundation for the ability to plan ahead at later stages of development.

Residues of this earliest part of the first oral phase are assumed, then, to include early trust in the possibility of relief of tension, along with the achievement of healthy narcissism, comfort in bodily functioning, and the beginnings of cathexis of the environment—the taste of milk, the feel of warm enfolding arms, the acceptance of mothering persons. We assume also that the baby has been "learning to learn" and that the practicing activities seen in the baby's struggles with the nipple and with its thumb contribute to a foundation for autonomous efforts and a capacity to deal with the environment.

By contrast to this optimal picture, we find variations all along the line; we see the baby whose physiological equilibrium is easily upset, who screams in anger at severe hunger, and who is doubtless forming an anlage for distrustful or hostile reactions to self and the environment, reactions which become more clear as the baby gets older. Severe frustration or failure in sucking, or failure to evoke a response from the mother, can lead either to the extinction of early drives, to marasmic tendencies, or to compulsive drives. In another scenario, inconsistency in the caregiver's responsiveness, and a resulting insecurity about gratification, can lead either to diffuse anxiety or to greed and compulsive efforts to obtain gratification. Or again, frustration in self-help activities may lead to a disinclination to continue these efforts. Contagious reactions or, as Anna Freud calls them, infectious responses to an extremely anxious or depressed mother may interfere with these very early learnings and may contribute to distress, increased crying, or depression.

The difference between the serenity or peacefulness of the comfortable baby and the massive distress and disorganization that accompany inner pain, frustration, or overstimulation is dramatic. Feeding experiences and gastrointestinal functioning are only a part of what determines the clinical picture; while adequate gratification in feeding is important as a prerequisite for the establishment of basic "healthy narcissism" in the young infant, so are adequate vegetative functioning and bodily comfort in every zone. What is at stake here is the establishment of comfort as a basis for the narcissism that must be present before the baby can develop the confidence to which Benedek (1938) refers, or the trust that Erikson (1950) describes. The failure to establish basic healthy narcissism—a failure which cannot be attributed to the mother alone, but which is a matter also of the equipment of the individual infant and the ease with which he can be cared for and comforted—interferes with early ego development and healthy libidinal development. Without a comfortable and satisfied body, the infant is unable to develop stable expectations of gratification.

The Early Beginnings of A Sense of Self

The long sequence of experiences that contribute to a baby's sense of being an independent object, separate from all the environment, involves all of the senses. The baby hears himself cry or babble, looks at his hand as he intentionally holds it up in a sunbeam, tastes his thumb or his toe, and feels the discomfort of his wetness and the effort of evacuating his bowels. He has a multitude of proprioceptive sensations: swallowing, pressure from gas, the movement of muscles. Gradually these self-observations and inner feelings accumulate and integrate into a self-image. The same hand held up in the sunlight holds the thumb that is now being sucked; it is *his* hand. Interesting babbling sounds that have been discovered are now practiced deliberately; sounds can even be used—squealing, whimpering, screaming—to bring someone to relieve pain or boredom, or to provide a special gratification. Not all vocalization is instrumental, but the baby does find that voice, as well as hands and smiles, can make things happen.

The sense of self includes not only the observed self but also the intentionally active, goal-oriented self. Winnicott (1958) emphasized the experience—and the experiencing—of the infant in the uterus as well as through the months following its entrance into the world. *Everything* the baby does contributes to a subjective sense of self. Pushing the nipple into place, and getting that milk through it, wriggling into a comfortable spot, straining to see as much as possible, turning away from a loud noise—all are ways of experiencing *effectiveness*.

At the same time, increased motility, that is, the capacity to grasp and manipulate objects and to change postures and manage the body, produces much richer experience of contact with the environment. As Greenacre (1960) pointed out, these contribute to a beginning of differentiation of the self from the environment, including the mother. The baby learns the difference between visible body parts which can be directed and visible parts of the environment which can not be. There is a danger that when the baby bounces or pushes against the mother she will react in anger and abruptly slap the child, or in some other painful way inhibit activities which are important in the development of body management and differentiation of self from mother. Greenacre points out also that the baby's expanding motility, and the forceful movements which soon become possible, lead to these bouncing and pushing movements against the mother; these help the baby differentiate from the mother and further enrich the self of self. Along with the baby's differentiation of self from the environment, particularly the mother, there is an increased cathexis of the environment.

Attitudes and orientation toward the world and self, and interactions between them, probably take their tone from the experiences of the early oral phase. Residues of disappointment, indifference, or renunciation vis-à-vis gratification, dependency and inability to take care of oneself, and other character tendencies were classically viewed as rooted in the oral phase. Moreover, gratification and pleasure in the oral zone, with its consequent reduction of tension, as well as a serenity of the organism resulting from adequate vegetative functioning in every area, are probably necessary for the maintenance of autonomy in the emerging ego functions, and for the development of a stable sense of self. If the baby is in a chronic state of tension, discomfort, anxiety, or disturbance when ego functions emerge, they are likely to be contaminated. An example within the normal range is the negative conditioning to newness of a bright, sensitive girl baby who experienced newness during a period of colicky distress. This hypothesis is not new; Erikson (1950) and others have noted that trauma threatens any functions that happen to be emerging as it occurs. This has ordinarily been seen to apply to later stages of development, as in the effect of trauma on emergent speech in the second year of life. However, severe anxiety or disequilibrium during the second to fourth months may have a similar effect on functions emerging at that time; the differentiation of experiences stimulated from the outside from those stimulated from the inside may be interfered with, thereby hindering the emerging sense of self.

Aggression and Motor Development

In psychoanalysis, the last half of the first year marks the beginning of the oral aggressive phase during which teeth bring the possibility of biting, chewing, chomping, and other activities which can, in contrast to the sucking and swallowing of the early oral phase, reduce the object or "destroy" it. Hard foods can be chewed up; plastic rattles or dolls may be chewed on. The nursing baby may bite the nipple, causing pain to the mother, who naturally protests, takes the baby off the breast abruptly, slaps, or in some other way reacts to the pain. The perceptive baby finds that he can produce pain.

At the same time the baby experiences the continuing pain of teething: extraordinary amounts of comforting may be needed if this distress is extreme or prolonged. A new factor in ambivalence now emerges, in addition to the early alternation of frustration and gratification, and the pleasure and pain of stimulation which at times is just enough and at other times too much. The mouth, which has been the source of so much satisfaction, has now become a source of pain. Some babies seem visibly bewildered by this experience and act as if their "feelings were hurt" more than their gums. This fretful or angry disillusionment may occur especially with babies who have made a very serene integration up to this point.

Along with the puzzlements of teething and the strange new pleasures of biting, the baby's capacity for mouth-play increases. With sitting up and creeping, many more things are reachable and can be mouthed by way of exploration. Often the infant learns to bubble at this stage and engages in lip-play. In other words, this is a phase of more complex mouth experiences, with both positive and negative qualities. Biting and chomping on small toys, rattles, or anything else at hand may destroy these objects in the absence of any destructive intention on the infant's part.

More dramatic is the new ability to sit up and, later, to creep or to hitch along in a sitting position; this provides new activity and interests, but, when tired, the baby still wants to be picked up; the capacity for pleasure from skin contact and being held, rocked, or played with still exists. The pleasure of playing with toes, which began toward the end of the preceding period, increases as the toes become more reachable; the baby can now bend over as he sits. He may even get his toe into his mouth, something which was harder to do when he was lying down.

During this period of further exploration of objects, including his own body, a little boy is likely to find his penis and begin to play with it in a very simple way—pushing it or pulling it, usually quite gently and without any evidence of climax. The baby playing with his penis in this way seldom approaches the voluptuousness of the avid baby sucking on bottle or thumb. The penis is there, but the child is still in a predominantly oral phase.

Sitting up is primarily an instrumental achievement, according to Bernfeld (1929), but this may not be correct; one often sees a baby smiling in satisfaction when assisted into a sitting position, and not necessarily just because more can be seen. The pleasure in motility is obvious in such activities as creeping, pulling oneself into a standing position, walking with support, dancing or being danced up and down on the mother's lap or on the floor, bouncing, or pushing against things. Observing the pleasure and the drive toward such activities, Mittelmann (1954) speaks of a *motor urge* on the same basis with other drives. Certainly all the motor achievements introduce new possibilities of kinesthetic pleasure and also a wider range of kinds of contact.

The drive to motor activity and the pleasures it entails have many sources. One is simply the development of the motor apparatus, which creates its own need to be used as other autonomous ego functions develop from maturational processes. Other sources include the wider range of kinesthetic, tactual, visual, auditory and other experiences made possible by locomotion, and a sense of achievement that introduces a new affect of triumph into the child's range of expression. Here we have ego functions, libidinal factors, and aspects of aggression all intermingled, with varying emphases in the activities which increased motility now makes possible.

While we have been speaking here of large muscle activities, the fine muscle coordination of fingers and hands, is developing apace; the bottle-fed baby now prefers to hold the bottle. Babies also combine objects, bang blocks on the high chair tray, and discover the delights of making a clatter by throwing things onto the floor. This capacity for combining objects, doing things with them, making a noise with them, making them go away and come back, is accompanied by increased delight in the handling of objects. This increased investment in impersonal objects, toys, and in exploring the environment led Spitz (1965) to comment that this is the period in which weaning can best be accomplished. In fact, some babies spontaneously wean themselves, preferring the cup or bottle to the constraint of sitting on the lap and being held for nursing. Mastery has to precede separation. Certainly when they are gradually prepared for weaning by the preliminary use of bottle or cup, and by being fed solid foods with a spoon, many babies easily make a gradual transition from the breast by the elimination of one nursing session a day. By the time the last breast-feeding is eliminated, the baby has derived so much satisfaction from the other feeding methods that it may hardly be noticed.

Not enough attention has been paid to the fact that when babies are weaned mothers no longer have to hold them for long periods. If another baby, ill health, fatigue, housework, or other factors make it difficult for her to hold the baby, weaning means the loss not only of the breast but of the lap, the mother's body, the cuddling, and the closeness associated with nursing. When weaning occurs after the baby has developed a strong response to the mother as a whole, as a love object, the loss may be overwhelming and unmanageable. Mothers do not always recognize this loss, because the baby is developing so many resources at such a rapid rate that they may attend primarily to these new capacities. If a mother is interested in the words her baby begins to make or in the imitative capacities brought about by the combination of widening motor resources and a growing awareness of self and object, she may feel a vivid and active contact with the baby through verbal and imitative communication, not realizing that the baby has continuing need for primitive skin contact and body-to-body experiences.

Aspects of the Mother-Infant Interaction

A mother is experienced in many different roles and contexts. She may be a very interesting visual stimulus, especially if she has red or golden hair and bright blue eyes, or dresses colorfully. Her voice may be soothing or staccato, abrupt or harsh. Her touch may be gentle or rough. All of this is part of the mother as an *object*, part of the environment, and later a model for identification. The mother as *caregiver*—reliable or unreliable, satisfying or frustrating, devoted (like Winnicott's "ordinary devoted mother") or casual—also provides experiences of pleasure or frustration, or of some combination of the two.

Mothers vary greatly in their attitudes toward their babies and toward their behavior. Even when a mother loves her baby she may not have much empathy; she may have unrealistic expectations of babies; she may anxiously overprotect the baby and not allow the freedom to explore and experiment that is needed for adequate development. The level of attunement will depend both on the mother's feelings about babies in general, and the degree of *fit* between a given mother and this specific baby. An active mother may not enjoy a quiet baby; a fragile mother may have a difficult time with a vigorous, energetic baby of whom she is at the same time proud.

The mother's affects both toward the baby and toward the rest of the environment are experienced by the baby as well. She may be unambivalently loving, delighted, joyful, and totally accepting; or she may be—even when she is a responsible care-giver, disappointed that this baby is not what she had hoped for. Such specific factors are likely to have an effect on emotional development and how the baby feels about the self, the mother, and the world. For example, the mother who is a vivid object, and a reliable caregiver, but whose hopes and self-esteem are not gratified by a quiet, solemn, or otherwise disappointing baby may be deeply admired by the growing child, who nonetheless forever longs to be truly loved and accepted by the mother.

Moreover, in every family the quality of the mother-infant relationship is different for each successive baby. All during her childhood Mrs. S. had looked forward to having babies, and each one was another fulfillment; but the "last baby" was special, and another one was "like me." Mrs. B. had hoped to travel with her husband and was intensely frustrated when this was impossible because the first baby arrived too soon. But she was delighted with the next baby, a handsome little son. Mrs. H. had lost "a beautiful little boy" in infancy and the "odd" baby girl she produced within a year was no comfort. Mrs. P. had enjoyed three attractive babies and thought that was enough, when another arrived to her great annoyance. Tiny Mrs. T. could not cope with the large energetic baby who came after the quiet and easily manageable first one. Mrs. R., who had been a vigorous mother of four little boys, was surprisingly tender with her fifth baby, a girl. With her second baby Mrs. N. was more relaxed because "now I know how to take care of a baby; I didn't at first."

In short, each baby in the family has in essence a different mother; the babies come at different stages of the mother's experience, at different levels of adjustment in her marriage. Differences in the mother-infant relationship are seen in which one baby is viewed as being "like *my* family," while another seems strange or does not fit the mother's fantasies of her dream baby. In addition, first babies, large ones, and breech presentations are apt to have more difficult deliveries with consequent "predispositions to anxiety" or other effects of birth trauma. The helpfulness of fathers or older siblings who enjoy babies can ease an otherwise tense mother-infant relationship, whereas, by contrast, indifferent fathers or rivalrous younger siblings can increase tension.

Aside from the effects of the mother's feelings about the baby, the quality of the care she provides will be affected by her previous experience with infants; her health and energy; the level of her maternal drive (Levy, 1966); the stress of pressures and demands upon her; and the quality of support she receives from her husband—(if she has one), her family (if they are available), or her husband's family (who may be a source of either support or stress).

Aside from environmental and cultural influences, we see a range of mothers with their own constitutional strengths and weaknesses; areas of understanding and ignorance; anxieties, gratifications, and frustrations; tolerances and breaking-points; readiness or unreadiness for motherhood; and positive or negative feelings about having a baby. The mother's pregnancy may have been a time of blooming, of delight in the life developing within, or a time of physical discomfort, with nausea or kidney problems, and the delivery may have been an experience of triumph or one of overwhelming pain or disappointment. After the delivery she may be in good health or suffer a postpartum depression. The baby may be "perfect" in every way, or it may have minor or even conspicuous defects. The mother may feel proud, disappointed, or ashamed and guilty. And the baby may grow more satisfying or more difficult as time goes by. The mother may want to be "a perfect mother," but may find that with housework and cooking, caring for others in her family, and worrying about finances, she cannot meet all of her baby's needs.

Mothers of Babies with Physical Defects

While the baby who differs from the parents' expectations or constitutional type may be disappointing, the delivery of a baby with defects is a shock that can erode self-esteem and confidence, and brings grief, guilt, feelings of failure, anger, anxiety, and even despair or hopelessness and confusion about how to cope with the baby's problems (Mintzer, Als, Tronick, and Brazelton, 1984). These feelings inhibit empathy, pleasure, and spontaneity in interactions with the baby; the mother may withdraw, or hover over the baby as Deidre's mother did (Murphy and Moriarty, 1976). The bonding and attachment on the parents' side as well as the intuitive response to the baby's cues that a "good enough mother" usually provides may be compromised. The mother's injured pride or self-esteem (Mintzer et al., 1984), the loss of hopes and ideals for the mother-infant relationship may estrange her from the task of mothering at first, especially when the child represents negative or defective parts of herself. Uncertainty and anxiety about the child's development, about how to help the child, difficulty in recognizing and responding to the normal aspects and strengths of the child all compromise the quality of the mother's response. She may avoid showing the baby or even hide it, like a mother observed in a rural parent-child center, or may compensate by dressing up the baby to distract the observer's attention; she may be intrusive, abrupt, or aggressive, calling the baby "Monster" or other derogatory names. But when, for example, surgical repair reduces disfiguration, as the mother begins to restore her self-esteem in other areas of her life, and as she begins to view the infant as a separate individual and not as a negative extension of herself, she may relax, feel more confident, and see more positive potential in the baby; gradually the hurt is healed, however sad she may continue to feel, quite realistically, about the baby's situation.

If in addition to specific defects the baby is easily disorganized, sensitive and upset by overstimulation, and poorly coordinated, the mother may find it hard to calm the baby and restore its equilibrium. If it does not respond with eye-to-eye contact, smiles, reaching out, cooing, or other pleasurable vocalizing, the mother may feel rejected. On the other hand, a baby with a local defect may actively try to engage the mother, stimulating a response by cycling feet and hands, vocalizing, making tongue motions, and later bouncing; such activity becomes irresistible, evoking affectionate, hopeful feelings in the mother. With support from the environment—extended family or neighbors as well as medical staff—attachment and mutuality develop and the baby makes progress, in time catching up to normal developmental expectations, or compensating with high achievement in an area unaffected by the defect.

Social Change and Mother-Infant Relationships

Despite two world wars and a major economic depression, psychoanalytic thinking about infants assumed an "average expectable environment" (Hartmann, 1939) and "a good enough mother" (Winnicott, 1960). But in the last quarter of the twentieth century cumulative social change has compelled attention to many different conditions affecting families and babies. Teenage mothers, unmarried mothers, divorced mothers, working mothers, mothers who smoke and drink, mothers living in poverty, mothers who are depressed—these groups include many who cannot provide an "average expectable environment," who have difficulty being "good enough mothers."

A foundation for understanding what these conditions may mean for infants was laid by Levy (1966), who wrote about different kinds of mothers: rejecting mothers; those who were overprotective; mothers who are more and those who are less naturally maternal; mothers who give responsible physical and intellectual care without enough basic love—whose affect-hungry children seek affection wherever they can find it.

Babies too differ: in their perceptiveness, their empathy, their tendencies to imitate, to identify with their mothers. There is much that we cannot know directly. But just as the mother learns what pleases, soothes, and stimulates her baby, so the baby learns what evokes from the mother a desired response. The baby remembers both pleasant and unpleasant experiences, and the task of integrating an image of the whole mother requires that the mother perceived as a colorful, stimulating object be combined with the mother who feeds, bathes, and diapers the baby—and also with the mother who plays, smiles, and tunes in to the baby's moods. In addition, the mother who is irritable, who delays her responses, or who punishes (slaps, spanks, scolds) the baby for crying or making a mess must also be integrated into the whole image. Melanie Klein distilled this problem into her concept of the "good mother" and the "bad mother." Actually a baby may find delight in a glamorous colorful mother, and satisfaction in her responsible caregiving, while being hurt by her angry expressions or depressed by her unsmiling disappointment in the kind of baby she has produced (or in its timing). If there is a failure of integration—if the baby can never develop an image of adequate complexity—one of several results may ensue: the baby may scotomatize the angry mother and idealize the good mother; may more or less withdraw, never developing an intense attachment; or may look for another mother who can be accepted as a whole person.

Dependency and Symbiosis

Psychoanalysis has long recognized that the infant is dependent on the care of a mother who meets its survival needs. Mahler, Pine, and Bergman (1975) believed for a time that the newborn infant was autistic and that a symbiotic relation with the mother evolved after the first 2 months.

The baby's needs require the assistance of a caregiver, but they do not imply a true symbiosis with the mother. The activity we described earlier reflects the capacities of the baby as an individual in its own right, with preferences and energetic drives to get along in the world. The great differences in the activity level of different babies from birth influence the degree of dependency, but all normal babies are programmed to respond to and use the environment.

At the same time, with a "cuddly baby" there are periods of relaxing and molding to the mother's body. When nursing—mouth on mother's nipple, face close to her breast—the boundary between the mother's body and the infant's body may seem to disappear. But even with feeding at 3-hour instead of 4-hour intervals, this merging is experienced for a fraction of the American baby's time—the rest of the time an American baby is in a crib, stroller, playpen, high chair, or other device with contact sensations very different from being bonded to the mother's body. Her attention is still needed—her attunement, her availability—but this is not symbiosis. Rather, it is the infant's dependence upon the mother or other caregiver to meet needs that cannot be managed alone.

The concepts of symbiosis and individuation need to be considered cross-culturally. The baby in India on the mother's hip with easy access to her breast, and the African baby on the mother's back may well feel that they are one with their mothers. The American baby, however, held in the mother's arms or on her lap only at intervals, sleeping in a crib, and spending much time in other kinds of furniture—carriage or high chair or swing—has a very different experience. Togetherness and separateness are experienced alternately, with separateness occupying the largest share of the time from birth. The affective quality of togetherness times and separate times differs; togetherness times are occupied with feeding, cleaning, relieving discomfort, and perhaps play—though not all parents are playful. Separate times are occupied not only with sleep, but with looking, listening, touching, stretching, kicking, thumbsucking, toesucking, swiping at objects dangling nearby, and other motor, sensory, and cognitive activities. When awake in the morning before the parent appears, many babies babble to themselves as if interested in the sound of their own voices. Processes of individuation need to be studied from birth—the first separation.

Mahler, Pine, and Bergman (1975) discussed the process of separation-individuation and emphasized the contribution of evolving intrapsychic autonomy, perception, memory, cognition, and reality testing which they saw as "the track of *individuation*." They viewed the intrapsychic developmental track of *separation* as involving differentiation, distancing, boundary formation, and disengagement from the mother. The pace of motor development—crawling, paddling, climbing, and walking—influences the relative pace of distancing, and the baby's sense of independence.

Fathers and Babies

World War II, which found many young fathers far away from home, stimulated sociological investigations of the effect of the father's absence on children. These studies, however, did not focus on infants. Nor were there studies in child development or in psychoanalysis at that time that considered the interaction of the infant with the father. Only in the last quarter-century have empirical studies of the relationships of fathers and babies began to multiply. The large number of fatherless families today, and the emergence of "house-husbands" who care for home and baby while the mother earns the family living, have added to the need to study father-infant relationships.

Research by Brazelton, Yogman, Als, and Tronick (1978) has shown that mothers and fathers tend to play differently with their infants; fathers provide more vigorous play. For some babies this energetic play may be more exciting; with boy babies it can assist the process of identification with the father. Findings from psychoanalyses of children, adolescents, and adults have led Blos (1985) to emphasize the infant boy's dyadic relation with his supportive father and the recurrent importance of this relationship, especially in the transition from adolescence to adult male identity. The safe, supportive, loving father is also important to the baby girl and to her development of a feminine identity.

In the 1960s and 1970s awareness of the increasing number of babies developing without the presence of fathers led to an appraisal of the consequences; fatherless babies were found to be relatively deficient in certain cognitive functions when compared to babies who had fathers present in the home (Pederson and Robson, 1969). Moreover, where fathers were involved, infants were seen to be more socially responsive and better able to withstand stress. (Parke and Sawin, 1977).

These reports led to the study of the interactions of fathers and babies; it was observed that fathers were more actively stimulating and playful—roughhousing and evoking babies' laughter with clowning routines. Fathers have been observed to encourage a baby's curiosity and to provide cognitive or motor challenges, fostering a sense of mastery and independence (Pruett, 1984). Important changes in the medical management of pregnancy and delivery have brought fathers into roles of support of the mother and even care of infants. As fathers have come under the observing eyes of investigators of infant development, it has become obvious that the concept of an exclusive mother-infant attachment is unrealistic.

It took still longer to include siblings and the extended family in studies of infant development. Again the Yale group initiated a much-needed pioneer study. Marianne Kris and Ritvo (1983) investigated the influence of parent-child relationships on sibling experiences—mutual attachments, identifications, empathic resonances. A second pregnancy diminishes attention to the firstborn, and that one, especially if incompletely individuated and autonomous, feels left out, replaced, lonely, and sad at the loss of closeness with the mother; the child may withdraw or, like Chester in our Topeka records, may develop precocious independence. Some firstborns suggest giving the new baby back to the hospital; 18-month-old Susan identified with the mother at first, caring for her own doll baby. Outcomes are affected by the mother's ability to include the first child in her care of the second, by the first child's relation with the father and other family members, and by the first child's security or insecurity in its previous relationship with the mother. The stimulation of siblings to a baby is as important in some instances as parental care, and sometimes provides a foundation for later sibling intimacy and support. Babies also respond to other children.

Temeles (1983) noted that while a baby observed over two years responded eagerly to a large number of relatives and visitors (including the observer), she preferred the mother first and the father second. Yet the amount of time the father spent with the baby was less than half that spent by the observer; it was not a matter of the quantity of time but of the quality of the relationship.

Babies and Objects

Babies become attached to things as well as people. "He loves his green frog," a mother of a baby in the Topeka study said. With different babies an object's attractiveness may lie in its action possibilities, as in a favorite toy hammer, or in the sounds it makes, or in its texture. The qualities of the baby's favorite things tell us something about the baby's thresholds for pleasure in different sensory zones. Losing or not being able to find the favorite toy is upsetting to the baby; he will cry for it and look for it, just as he will hunt for his mother when she disappears. The loss of a beloved object—thing or person—is grievous indeed.

Obviously, the pleasure provided by the favorite object reinforces the child's mental image of it—he can remember it. Out of sight is not out of mind when the object is associated with pleasurable possibilities. This does not mean that the baby should be totally protected from the loss of his favorite things. It is important for him to learn that things go and come—he needs to learn that being out of sight does not mean ceasing to exist. Only by experiencing the going and the returning can the child understand the permanence of things. In addition, learning that what is lost can be found is a necessary step in coping with frustration.

The Quality of the Infant's Attachments

All through our discussion of the psychic life of infants we have kept in mind the wide range of individual differences in every aspect of their functioning. Freud's recognition of constitutional factors and his emphases on overdetermination provide an orientation to the issue of the infants' attachment to the mother, to other persons, and to objects. An oversimplified explanation that the baby's attachment is instinctive will not be adequate.

On a visit to the Menninger Foundation, the ethologist Konrad Lorenz remarked that we should not make direct applications to human beings of principles which explain animal behavior. A baby is not imprinted by contact with the obstetrician, who is the first person he sees, as the little goose is imprinted by its contact with the first object it encounters. The human infant follows visually every bright moving object; babies cannot cling to their mothers but must be held. Their smiles appear at first in response to every smiling person; only with time does the mother receive a broader smile than others. In short, the baby *learns* that the mother—or the mothering person—is special and is needed more than anyone else.

The quality of the learned attachment depends on the baby's experience as it is shaped by the interaction of the baby's individual needs, temperament, and capacities with the mother's responses as these are influenced by the factors we have reviewed. An equable smooth-functioning baby with a happy mother relatively free from stress is likely to have a "secure attachment" (Ainsworth, 1969). A baby with a predisposition to anxiety, who is hard to soothe, and easily frustrated or frightened, may have more difficulty in developing the trust that accompanies a secure attachment, despite the best efforts of a caring mother. Illnesses of the baby, traumatic experiences, or deprivations due to the mother's illness or her own stress may disturb the integration of the baby's attachment. In the Topeka study about 20 percent of the mothers in the sample had a shorter or longer postpartum depression; in certain instances, the child's primary attachment was to the supportive father.

When we speak of primary attachment we are referring to the baby's choice or preference. To which person does the baby reach out, smile most broadly, respond with greatest eagerness or excitement? By whom is the baby most easily comforted and soothed? In some cases, a sibling is the favorite.

When we judge the security of attachment by the baby's response to being left by the mother as she moves to another room, we confront the question of the baby's capacity to remember her, to know that she still exists, that he can count on her to return. These aspects of attachment develop over time. Yarrow (1963) found that by 1 month 38 percent of the babies responded positively to the mother but not to a stranger. Still, in the early months most babies will respond to a smiling visitor when the mother has left, while a few months later the baby will miss the mother and reject the person who tries to comfort the baby, who feels deserted.

Responses to Extended Separation

Child analysts, psychologists, pediatricians, and social workers have studied variations in conditions contributing to the wide range of differences in the responses of individual infants to separation from the mother. Yarrow (1963) studied the adaptation to adoptive families of babies who had previously been cared for in different types of foster families. Babies who had initially been cared for in large families, where they were stimulated by several people, adapted more readily to the adoptive mother. We have to assume not only different qualities of attachment of babies in larger families but also differences in their experience of strangeness and separation. In addition to the degree of discrepancy between the familiar and the strange, the baby's experience is influenced by a perception of differences in demands made, the kind of stimulation and care, intensity of attachment, and the degree of interest in newness.

Spitz (1946) observed that the best-mothered babies experienced the most severe anaclitic depression in response to separation. Other students of separation have found that babies in group day care, who have had routine experiences of separation and reunion, as well as experiences of good care by others, are less disturbed by separation from the mother than babies who have been in the constant care of their mothers—and who therefore find separations strange and threatening experiences. Security is also supported by the degree of independence of the infant, especially in motor skills, which permit problem solving, obtaining what he wants, and extricating himself from discomfort. In addition, wide differences in infants' capacity to "reach out and touch someone" are visible in foundling hospitals, where some babies pound on the glass to attract the attention of a passerby and then engage in exchanges of smiles, while others give up, retreating into isolation. Just as there are differences in sensory acuity, motor drive, and motor skills, so there are differences in social initiative among babies, and all of these may influence the response to separation.

Response to Strangers

There are many questions we cannot answer with regard to the fear of strangers shown in varying degrees by different babies. Some sensitive babies are also uneasy in strange places as if only the familiar is safe. Is this related to the painful experience of inoculation in a doctor's office—another strange place? Has the baby learned that he might be hurt in a strange place? We have to assume that the baby develops internal images not only of the mother but of other familiar people as well, and also of the places and things—toys, bottle, crib—with which he is familiar. As Levy (1960) has shown, infants remember and cry at the sight of global aspects of the experience of inoculation—the hospital or the doctor's office, or the doctor in the white coat, long before they clearly associate the pain of inoculation with the needle at the age of 6 months or later. The more sensitive to pain the baby is, the more clearly differentiated are the various aspects of the experience—i.e., the more vivid the memory. By the age of 4 to 8 months, a baby who has been repeatedly hurt may have learned to fear strange people. In the Coping study a baby of 3 months was frightened by the approach of a woman with a loud voice, and in the Yale study, Wolf (1953) reported on a young baby's fear aroused by the approach of a woman with a strikingly different appearance from that of her mother. With more pleasurable encounters and internal images of them, the baby learns to distinguish the potentially harmful from the potentially pleasant. The "paranoid position" is thus not an inborn developmental condition; rather, it is learned, and in favorable situations it is modified. Differences in experience as well as differences in perceptual acuity help to account for differences between babies who are fearful of strangers and those who are merely wary (Schaffer, Greenwood, and Parry, 1972) or curious.

Stages in Development

As babies progress, the effort to define their progress has been expressed by different authors in different concepts of stages, which can sometimes give the impression that development proceeds by quantum leaps from one stage to another. This is especially true when progress involves gradual internal processing that continues to the point at which a baby feels confident enough to take a new step. It appears to be a sudden achievement, but a great deal of orienting and internal rehearsing has preceded it.

Mahler's early thinking, like that of Melanie Klein, grew out of her work with disturbed children, and like Melanie Klein she extended to normal development terms generally used to describe developmental disturbances. In Melanie Klein's case we have in mind the "paranoid" and the "depressive" positions; in Mahler's, the autistic and the symbiotic stages. Both analysts made important observations, but we need to distinguish these from the distorted conception of infancy to which these terms may lead.

"Hatching" is Mahler's metaphor, with its image of a chick pecking at its shell until it breaks and the chick tumbles out, soon to raise itself and scuttle around its mother. The description of the *process* by Mahler, Pine, and Bergman (1975, p. 53) is reasonable, although not entirely accurate in terms of present knowledge: it is, they believe, a gradual genetic evolution of the sensorium—the perceptual-conscious system—which enables the infant to have a more permanently alert sensorium when awake. They add that the infant's attention, which during the first months of "symbiosis" was in large part inwardly directed, gradually expands through a "coming into being" of outwardly directed perceptual activity during the child's increasing periods of wakefulness. But we know now that the infant's sensory responses have begun to develop even before birth and that they develop steadily after birth.

Edward Glover (1945) discussed Melanie Klein's theories in detail, both in terms of the contradictions and confusions in her statements and also in relation to her deviations from accepted Freudian theory, while Sylvia Brody (1982) has criticized her work from the perspective of research on infancy. Without defending the Kleinian system, we can recognize nonetheless that she provided a major impetus to thinking about the psychic consequences of the baby's response to the mother, at a time when the infant's psychic life was seen chiefly in terms of the desire for instinctual gratification. Melanie Klein's *Psycho-Analysis of Children*—based on work with neurotic and psychotic children from 3 years old to latency age—was published in 1932. It is only after this that we find a stream of papers by other analysts dealing with the infant-mother relationship. Moreover, despite her questionable generalizations to normal infants of inferences from the psychoanalyses of these extremely disturbed children, her theories regarding the precursors of oedipal conflicts and the superego directed attention to aspects of infant development that previously were ignored.

As Glover (1945) summarized her views, Melanie Klein believed that from the middle of the first year onward the oral frustrations of the infant together with the increase of oral sadism released oedipal impulses. The consequence of oral frustration, she thought, is the desire to incorporate the father's penis; at the same time the baby believes that the mother incorporates and possesses the father's penis. The baby then wants to destroy the mother's body and its contents. The existence of such fantasies was inferred from her analysis of severely disturbed young children.

That very young infants have mental images, memories, and doubtless primitive fantasies cannot be disputed in view of current evidence, but the images and fantasies come from the infant's experience; babies in cribs in separate nurseries are not likely to see either the father's penis or the intercourse of the parents. We are told nothing about the life setting or the actual prenatal and infancy experience of the children Melanie Klein analyzed. Some vulnerable babies who have come through difficult pregnancy and birth experiences, who have persistent colicky pain and frustration from their inability to be consoled, and who scream endlessly, probably have proprioceptive and enteroceptive images of pain, and an undifferentiated sense of "bad-painful self-in-world" in the period before the self is clearly differentiated from the world outside. Insofar as the affect felt by the screaming infant can be labeled, it may be a precursor of rage, and insofar as impulses are accompaniments of the screaming, they may be primitive aggressive impulses, as Flügel (1945) suggests.

We are offering a biologically based pattern of psychic development at this point. Insofar as a loving parent or other caregiver can succeed in comforting the baby to the point of reducing pain, the baby's experience could be that the sequence pain-anger-aggression brings love. But this is a simple biosocial assumption, a far cry from Melanie Klein's generalization that universal infantile hate ushers in the libidinal stages. What we can gratefully use of her formulations is her emphasis on the seriousness of the infant's frustrations and feelings, and the fact that they contribute to the psychic development of the baby. Her inclusion of anxiety in the pattern she describes is not unsound, but it needs to be supplemented by Greenacre's eminently reasonable discussion of infant anxiety (1952).

The foundation for paranoid fantasies is laid when some combination of frustration in feeding (the "bad breast"), chronic gastrointestinal distress, misery due to other sources of integrative difficulty, and failure to achieve homeostasis contribute to expectations of pain. Inside hurting is not differentiated—bad mother, bad everybody, bad everything are involved in the endless woe. "I never was able to comfort him," mothers say. These integrative failures may need to be considered in relation to other problems—stuttering, hyperactivity, learning difficulties, etc.—which appear much more frequently in male children along with a higher mortality rate. The concept of a paranoid position or a paranoid tendency, then, makes sense in infants who do not outgrow their integrative failures and who appear at the preschool stage as psychotic children.

By contrast, some babies have an outstanding capacity to cope with stress by mobilizing available satisfactions. The infantile experiences which are imprinted very early vary enormously from one baby to another. Melanie Klein pushed us to look at them, and we see more variety than she did, basing her views on an extreme sample of disturbed children. Differences in resilience do not depend on the direct help of the mother alone; studies of depressed but "enabling" mothers document the developmental difference between the infants of depressed mothers who can support the caregiving of good maternal substitutes and the infants of depressed mothers who are possessive and cannot share their babies. Moreover, we do not yet know enough about differences in babies' capacity to reach out and draw supplementary nutrients from the environment—as Pavenstedt has remarked, "Some babies do well on crumbs" (private communication).

As for the "depressive position" Melanie Klein postulated

for the latter part of the first year, we can relate the baby's experience to Spitz's observations of stranger anxiety and separation anxiety without adopting Klein's elaborate theories of guilt and infantile oedipal conflict. Glover (1945) commented that she was evidently "caught up in the swing of the analytic pendulum from purely libidinal etiologies and soon landed herself in theories that aggression causes anxiety" which in turn calls forth different libidinal phases (p. 82). He added that Klein's theory runs counter to psychobiological probability. He recognized that infants show "larval" genital reactions but felt that this fact justifies neither generalizations about the universality of an oedipus complex existing from the sixth month of life, nor her statement that fantasies concerning the father's penis inside the mother develop in the wake of oral frustration.

The work of Melanie Klein has been both the subject of endless controversy and a stimulus to the development of object relations theory. As one of the earliest analysts to work with disturbed children, she was stimulated to speculate on the infantile origins of their wildly hostile fantasies and behavior. She believed that their paranoid reactions had roots in a deeply ingrained expectation of being hurt, and in their projections of the causes of their pain onto their mothers, who were felt to be "bad mothers." And she overgeneralized her inference of early infantile sadistic fantasies of destroying the mother's body and its contents. But whether or not it makes sense to believe that 6-month-old babies have elaborate fantasies, it does make sense to believe that the fantastically destructive tendencies of extremely disturbed 4-year-olds have their roots in the infantile rage they felt as babies with a severely bad start in life, with endless pain and frustration due to gastrointestinal difficulties and other problems in the early months. The infant is a complex system; in the period around 3 and 4 months, when in normal development realistic images of the environment and of the mother are being formed, the existence of chronic pain and the pollution of the brain by the biochemical products of intense rage can be understood to interfere with the process of developing a differentiated concept of reality. The baby is full of pain, and he feels the world is the source of his pain. Such a developmental experience contrasts with that of the serene "easy" baby who has no colic, no feeding or sleeping disturbances, and whose fantasies, if they exist, are likely to deal with trusting wishes for even more of the good feelings she has already had. We say "she" here because statistically more boy babies are vulnerable to the various developmental difficulties.

Bender's essentially organic approach (1955) is in dramatic contrast to Melanie Klein's view of the infant in terms of universal oral sadism. Bender, a child psychiatrist and wife of the analyst Paul Schilder, saw many children with patterns of deficiency and emotional disturbance when she was Principal Research Scientist in Child Psychiatry for the New York State Department of Mental Hygiene. She saw schizophrenic children from families with other schizophrenic members, children with mutism and withdrawal who in later childhood were speaking and had developed pseudoneurotic defenses, while others had become psychotic. She developed a theory that schizophrenia is a maturational lag suggesting an embryonic stage of development. She also noted autistic withdrawn behavior in all types of brain damaged children and also in those emotionally deprived, such as the institutionalized infant. She was acutely aware of differences related to the uniqueness of individuals and to their different life experiences, such as anoxia at birth or encephalitis.

A persistent integrative problem is experienced by the infant from birth, namely, the good and the bad aspects of the same or similar experiences. As we mentioned earlier, psychoanalysts saw this in the experience of the "good breast" and the "bad breast," and in the "good mother" and the "bad mother," but good and bad—that is, gratification or pleasure, frustration and discomfort—are experienced in relation to many different stimuli. Sounds are interesting, but if they are too loud they may be unpleasant; lights are attractive, but if too bright they are stressful. Being bounced or played with is enjoyable, but if it goes on too long or too vigorously it can be exhausting and unpleasant. New solid foods like apple sauce are usually appealing, while others like pureed meat are distasteful to some infants. Splashing water in the baby bath may be fun, but if the same water gets into baby's eyes, it stings a little.

So in dozens of early situations the baby has to come to terms with, and somehow deal with, these ambivalent experiences of stimulation. In addition to "good breast" and "bad breast," there is a good world and a bad world. The baby may deal with the resulting conflict by coping selectively, rejecting what feels uncomfortable or painful, while retaining and demanding the experiences that are just right. Remembering the experiences that are felt to be good helps to resolve the ambivalence as long as the baby is able to select or otherwise deal with the kind and amount of stimulation to which he is exposed.

But either too much deprivation or too much attention can lead to disappointment, resentment, anger, clinging, insatiable demandingness, or too great a distrust of a world in which "bad" overshadows "good." The most hostile child in the Topeka sample had been hovered over more in early infancy than any other infant in the group. A child needs to be let alone enough of the time—although, to be sure, it is not always easy to know what is enough.

When an infant has had enough of the good and has developed some control over the bad, he may, like Helen in the Topeka study (Murphy and Moriarty, 1976) come to believe that the "bad things can turn into good things" or, like others dedicated as adults to making the world better, devote themselves to increasing the balance of the good.

Effects of Variations in the Developmental Sequence

Babies, whether full-term or premature, normal or defective, bring their own levels of energy, activity, responsiveness, sensitivity, alertness, coordination, and charm, which will contribute to their capacity to cope with the environment, to evoke a response from the mother and other caregivers. Some babies with severe problems—e.g., deafness, cerebral palsy, or spina bifida—are nevertheless irresistibly appealing. If their parents are healthy enough to view them as separate individuals with strengths and limitations, and not just negative extensions of themselves, these babies may develop beyond expectation.

In short, every aspect of the physical and psychological equipment of each baby is unique. Averages which cancel out deviations from a midpoint in a range produce misleading expectations of individual children, and an unrealistic concept of what is normal. Expectations rigidly tied to age schedules can blind caregivers to the needs of an individual infant, especially needs during critical phases, which vary from baby to baby; each infant needs support at times of loss of equilibrium.

Individual differences in the pattern of growth and rate of maturation affect the dominance or priority of different systems. One baby who responded intensely to music was able to imitate his parents' habit of blowing on a photograph record to remove any bit of dust before placing it on the player. Soon, his first word was "muz" to ask for another record. His interests in music and communication were far stronger than his interest in locomotion, in contrast to many another 8-month-old baby for whom creeping, crawling, kicking, or toddling are the most exciting parts of life.

Unevenness of growth in different systems may cause frustrations which lead to special efforts or defensive measures. Not many babies, as a matter of fact, are equally advanced in all areas. Social responsiveness or vocalizing and speech may blossom far ahead of motor skill, or the reverse can be seen in the first year of life. Yet, among normal children a good deal of catching up occurs in the first 6 to 8 years. Quiet babies (Murphy and Moriarty, 1976) may become lively later on, after the wealth of perceptions and thoughts that occupied their apparently passive years turns into action—often very creative.

Thus, while retrospective studies by analysts working backward to infancy from adulthood focus on continuities of patterns, longitudinal studies beginning in infancy are replete with records of change in behavior. At a deeper level, the sequences of experiences provided by different patterns of development leave their mark on the psychic economy of the baby and the growing child. The balance within the baby's psychic structure will vary with the relation between the stimulation to which he is exposed and how he deals with it mentally and in activity.

Dynamic and defensive patterns will differ. A very social baby who responds vividly to people and prefers them to other stimuli probably has a different calendar for the development of identification and empathy from that of a baby fascinated with toys and his expanding ways of manipulating things. Similarly, the quiet baby who is chiefly occupied with looking and listening is less likely to come into conflict with an environment concerned with the protection of precious objects.

Vulnerability and Problems of Integration and Mastery

The baby who struggles unsuccessfully to control simple coordinations cannot readily initiate resourceful solutions to basic problems of dealing with the world. This suggests that we have to recognize two major sources of vulnerability in infancy: (1) primary difficulties in achieving integration in motor responses to the environment; and (2) sources of vulnerability in the ego as an organizing, centrally controlling, initiating, selecting, and problem-solving center. Vulnerability in specific ego functions such as perception can interfere with the functioning of the central organizing ego, but vulnerability in the sense of lability and instability of emotional and physiological functioning can be more deeply disorganizing. The former is directly tied to constitutional aspects of motor functioning; the latter has a complex origin. In order to get a firmer grip on possible sources of vulnerability of the integrating ego, let us consider various aspects of development in early infancy.

A first source of cohesion—as opposed to vulnerability in the sense of labile or insecure integration—is found at the basic level of vegetative functioning of the infant; contrast the smoothly breathing, efficiently nursing, rhythmically sleeping, autonomically stable infant with the baby whose functioning is unstable in one or more of these zones, or all of them. The well-functioning, well-integrated baby has a biological foundation for a well-integrated psyche at its deepest roots. He is relatively free of the toxic biochemical flooding stimulated by upheavals of the autonomic nervous system—a flooding which fills the bloodstream, and hence the brain, during the early months during which the central ego is in the process of being integrated. The well-functioning body provides the ego the conditions necessary both for the development of autonomous ego functions, such as perception and active interaction with the environment, and for a cohesive, organizing and directing ego. The inner sense of stability and the clarity of interactions with the environment contribute a deeper level of confidence and trust. A sense of dependability of the self, as well as a sense of competence and of being able to cope with the environment, is necessary in order to become independent enough to stand the separation from the mother.

While psychoanalysis has focused on tension reduction by allaying hunger pangs, removing sources of discomfort, and soothing, the baby needs to sustain an adequate level of tension in the form of interest and investment in the environment. While helping in a hospital ward for foundlings, one of us (L.B.M.) found the widest differences in babies' capacities to do this. She watched the response of each baby as she put him down after playing. One baby turned to gaze at interesting pictures on the wall; another played with a toy; another began to suck his thumb; another seemed to withdraw totally, responding to nothing, his gaze becoming empty and vacuous, his body limp and flaccid. In other words, the active babies turned to visual, manipulative, and autoerotic satisfactions when deprived of the temporary mothering.

When do we see a lack of such efforts? Some premature, frail or ill, or very passive babies may lack the energy and drive to do much for themselves. They are less able to reduce or to maintain tension by using their sensorimotor apparatus. In foundling homes we have seen babies who cannot even cry for attention. Then, evidently, life is not worthwhile, and the mortality rate is extremely high.

At a less severe level, the baby can communicate his needs and is deeply dependent. If his need for mother is responded to by almost constant holding, the primitive sense of oneness is reinforced, and separation is intolerable.

Changes in Experience

The organism-environment system is not static—changes in all aspects of both parts interacting with each other contribute to a changing and evolving system. In thinking about infants in their environments we have then to think of the changing instinctual, cognitive, affective, and motor aspects of the infant interacting with the entire range of stimuli offered by the environment, especially the mother or other major caregiver. It is not only the person and the caregiving of the mother that is important: the physical and personal environment she selects and creates is constantly involved in the interactions within the system. Seen in these terms, the classical oral phase of development is extremely complex and unique for each infant.

Conclusion

We see that over this century many views of infancy have contributed to useful hypotheses about the development of the mind, the feelings, and the behavior of the infant in his relationship with the social and the impersonal environment. The infant cannot be fully understood in terms of any one view, nor can he be validly understood by lining up different aspects of functioning in separate parallel lines—because cognitive, affective, motor, and social aspects of inner and outer experience are constantly influencing each other. An adequate comprehensive psychoanalytic view of infancy remains to be formulated.

References

Abraham, K. (1916), The first pregenital stage of the libido. In: *Selected Papers of Karl Abraham*. London: Hogarth Press, 1927, pp. 248–279.

Ainsworth, M.D.S. (1969), Object relations, dependency, and attachment: A theoretical review of the infant-mother relationship. *Child Development*, 40:969–1025.

——— & Bell, S.M. (1972), Mother-infant interaction and the development of competence. Unpublished manuscript.

Aldrich, C.A., & Aldrich, M. (1938), *Babies Are Human Beings*. New York: Macmillan.

Alpert, A., Neubauer, P., & Weil, A.P. (1956), Unusual variations in drive endowment. *The Psychoanalytic Study of the Child*, 11:125–163. New York: International Universities Press.

Bender, L. (1955), Twenty years of clinical research on schizophrenic children with special reference to those under six years of age. In: *Emotional Problems of Early Childhood,* ed. G. Caplan. New York: Basic Books, pp. 503–515.

Benedek, T. (1938), Adaptation to reality in early infancy. *Psychoanal. Quart.,* 7:200–215.

Benjamin, J.D. (1961a), The innate and the experiential in child development. In: *Lectures on Experimental Psychiatry,* ed. H.W. Brosin. Pittsburgh: University of Pittsburgh Press, pp. 19–42.

——— (1961b), Some developmental observations relating to the theory of anxiety. *J. Amer. Psychoanal. Assn.,* 9:652–688.

Bernfeld, S. (1929), *Psychology of the Infant.* London: Routledge.

Bergman, P. & Escalona, S.K. (1949), Unusual sensitivities in very young children. *The Psychoanalytic Study of the Child.* 3/4:333–352. New York: International Universities Press.

Blos, P. (1985), *Son and Father: Before and Beyond the Oedipus Complex.* New York: The Free Press.

Bowlby, J. (1969), *Attachment and Loss: Vol. 1. Attachment.* New York: Basic Books.

Brazelton, T.B. (1969), *Infants and Mothers: Differences in Development.* Rev. ed. New York: Delacourt, 1983.

——— (1973), *Neonatal Behavioral Assessment Scale.* Philadelphia: Lippincott.

——— Yogman, M., Als, H., & Tronick, E. (1978), The infant as a focus for family reciprocity. In: *Social Network of the Developing Child,* ed. M. Lewis & L. Rosenblum. New York: Plenum, pp. 29–43.

Brody, S. (1956), *Patterns of Mothering.* New York: International Universities Press.

——— (1982), Psychoanalytic theories of infant development and its disturbances: A critical evaluation. *Psychoanal. Quart.,* 51:526–597.

——— & Axelrad, S. (1978), *Mothers, Fathers and Children.* New York: International Universities Press.

Bühler, C. (1930), *The First Year of Life.* New York: Day.

Canestrini, S. (1913), *Uber Das Sinnelsleben des Neugeborenen (The Mental Life of the Newborn).* Monographie Gesamtgab Neurologische Psychiatrie 5. Berlin: Springer.

Chandler, C.A., Lourie, R.S., & Peters, A.D. (1968), *Early Child Care: The New Perspectives,* ed. L.D. Dittman. New York: Atherton.

Erikson, E.H. (1950), *Childhood and Society.* 2nd ed. New York: Norton, 1963.

Escalona, S.K. (1952), Emotional development in the first year of life. In: *Problems of Infancy and Childhood,* ed. M.J.E. Senn. New York: Josiah Macy Foundation.

——— (1968), *Roots of Individuality.* Chicago: Aldine.

——— & Heider, G. (1959), *Prediction and Outcome.* New York: Basic Books.

——— & Leitch, M. (1952), *Early Phases of Personality Development: A Nonnormative Study of Infant Behavior.* Monograph, Society for Research in Child Development 17.

Flügel, J.C. (1945), *Man, Morals and Society.* New York: International Universities Press.

Fraiberg, S. (1968), Parallel and divergent patterns in blind and sighted infants. *The Psychoanalytic Study of the Child,* 23:264–300. New York: International Universities Press.

Frank, L.K. (1957), *Tactile Communication*. Genetic Psychology Monographs, 56.

Freud, A., & Burlingham, D. (1942), *Young Children in Wartime: A Year's Work in a Residential War Nursery*. London: Allen & Unwin.

Freud, S.(1911), Formulations on the two principles of mental functioning. *Standard Edition*, 12:218–226. London: Hogarth Press, 1958.

—— (1914), On narcissism. *Standard Edition*, 14:67–102. London: Hogarth Press, 1957.

—— (1920), Beyond the pleasure principle. *Standard Edition*, 18:1–64. London: Hogarth Press, 1955.

—— (1921), Group psychology and the analysis of the ego. *Standard Edition*, 18:65–143. London: Hogarth Press, 1955.

—— (1923), The ego and the id. *Standard Edition*, 19:3–66. London: Hogarth Press, 1961.

Friedrich, O. (1983), What do babies know? *Time*, August 15.

Fries, M.E. & Woolf, P.J. (1953), Some hypotheses on the role of the congenital activity type in personality development. *The Psychoanalytic Study of the Child*, 8:48–62. New York: International Universities Press.

Glover, E. (1945), Examination of the Klein system of child psychology. *The Psychoanalytic Study of the Child*, 1:75–118. New York: International Universities Press.

Greenacre, P. (1952), *Trauma, Growth, and Personality*. New York: Norton.

—— (1960), Considerations regarding the parent-infant relationship. *Internat. J. Psycho-Anal.*, 41:571–584.

Harlow, H.F. (1958), The nature of love. *Amer. Psychologist*, 13:673–685.

Hartmann, H. (1939), *Ego Psychology and the Problem of Adaptation*. New York: International Universities Press, 1958.

—— (1952), The mutual influences in the development of ego and id. *The Psychoanalytic Study of the Child*, 7:9–30. New York: International Universities Press.

—— Kris, E., & Loewenstein, R.M. (1946), Comments on the formation of psychic structure. *The Psychoanalytic Study of the Child*, 2:11–38. New York: International Universities Press.

Heider, G. (1966), *Vulnerability in Infants and Young Children: A Pilot Study*. Genetic Psychology Monographs, 73.

Hoffer, W. (1949), Mouth, hand, and ego integration. *The Psychoanalytic Study of the Child*, 3/4:49–56. New York: International Universities Press.

Jackson, E.B., & Klatskin, E.H. (1950), Rooming-in Research Project: Development of methodology of parent-child relationship in a clinical setting. *The Psychoanalytic Study of the Child*, 5:236–274. New York: International Universities Press.

Jones, M.C. (1926), The development of early behavior patterns in young children. *J. Genetic Psychol.*, 33:537–585.

Klein, M. (1932), *The Psycho-Analysis of Children*. London: Hogarth Press.

Kolata, G. (1984), Studying learning in the womb. *Science*, July 20.

Korner, A. (1971), Individual differences at birth: Implications for early experience and later development. *Amer. J. Orthopsychiat.*, 41:608–619.

—— (1974), The effect of the infant's state, level of arousal, sex and ontogenetic stage on the caregiver. In:*The Effect of the Infant on Its Caregiver*, ed. M. Lewis & L. Rosenblum. New York: Wiley, pp. 105–121.

Kris, E. (1950), Notes on the development and on some current problems of psychoanalytic child psychology. *The Psychoanalytic Study of the Child,* 5:24–46. New York: International Universities Press.

Kris, M., & Ritvo, S. (1983), Parents and siblings: Their mutual influence. *The Psychoanalytic Study of the Child,* 37:311–324.

Leitch, M., & Escalona, S.K. (1949), The reaction of infants to stress: A report on clinical findings. *The Psychoanalytical Study of the Child,* 3/4:121–140. New York: International Universities Press.

Levy, D.M. (1937), Primary affect hunger. *Amer. J. Psychiat.,* 94:643–651.

——— (1945), Psychic trauma of operations in children. *Amer. J. Diseases of Children,* 69:7–25.

——— (1960), The infant's earliest memory of inoculation. *J. Genetic Psychol.,* 96:3–46.

——— (1966), *Maternal Overprotection.* 2nd ed. New York: Norton.

Lewin, K. (1935), *A Dynamic Theory of Personality.* New York: McGraw-Hill.

Lipsitt, L.P. (1977), The study of sensory and learning processes of the newborn. *Clinics in Perinatol.,* 4:163–186.

——— (1986), Cognition and behavior of the newborn. In: *Neonatal Medicine,* ed. L. Stern & P. Vert. Quebec: Eidisem, pp. 64–77.

Macfarlane, J.W. (1938), The Guidance Study Institute of Child Welfare, University of California, Berkeley, December 1, 1938.

Mintzer, D., Als, H., Tronick, E.Z., & Brazelton, T.B. (1984), Parenting an infant with a birth defect: The regulation of self-esteem. *The Psychoanalytic Study of the Child,* 39:561–589. New Haven: Yale University Press.

Mittelmann, B. (1954), Motility in infants, children, and adults. *The Psychoanalytic Study of the Child,* 9:142–177. New York: International Universities Press.

Moss, H.Q., & Robson, K.S. (1968), Maternal influences in early social visual behavior. *Child Development,* 39:401–408.

Murphy, G. (1947), *Personality: A Bio-Social Approach.* New York: Basic Books.

Murphy, L.B. (1962), *The Widening World of Childhood.* New York: Basic Books.

——— (1964), Some aspects of the first relationship. *Internat. J. Psycho-Anal.,* 45:31–44.

——— (1972), Developmental integration in childhood. *Annals N.Y. Acad. Sci.,* 193:253–259.

——— (1973), The variability of infants' reactions to pain. *Clinical Proceedings Children's Hospital, Nate Medical Center,* 29:3–7.

——— (1983), Issues in the development of emotion in infancy. In: *Emotion: Research and Experience,* ed. Plutchik. Academic Press, pp. 1–34.

——— & Hirschberg, C. (1982), *Robin,* New York: Basic Books.

——— & Moriarty, A.E. (1976), *Vulnerability, Coping and Growth.* New Haven: Yale University Press.

Osofsky, J., & Danzger, B. (1974), Relationships between neonatal characteristics and mother-infant interaction. *Developmental Psychol.,* 10:124–130.

Parke, R.D., & Sawin, D.B. (1975), Father-infant interaction in the newborn period: A re-evaluation of some current myths. In: *Contemporary Readings in Child Psychology,* ed. M. Hetherington & R.D. Parke. New York: McGraw-Hill, 1977, pp. 290–295.

Pasamanick, B., & Knobloch, H. (1956), Pregnancy experience and the development of behavior disorder in children. *Amer. J. Psychiat.,* 112:613–618.

Pedersen, F.A., & Robson, R.S. (1969), Father participation in infancy. *Amer. J. Orthopsychiat.*, 39:466–472.

Piaget, J. (1936), *The Origins of Intelligence in Children.* New York: International Universities Press, 1952.

Provence, S. (1983), *Infants and parents: Clinical Case Reports.* New York: International Universities Press.

Pruett, K.D. (1984), Infants of primary nurturing fathers. *The Psychoanalytic Study of the Child*, 38: 257–277. New Haven: Yale University Press.

Ramzy, I., & Wallerstein, R. S. (1958), Pain, fear and anxiety. *The Psychoanalytic Study of the Child*, 13:147–189. New York: International Universities Press.

Rank, O. (1929), *Trauma of Birth.* New York: Harcourt Brace.

Rapaport, D. (1960), On the psychoanalytic theory of motivation. In: *Nebraska Symposium on Motivation.* Lincoln: University of Nebraska Press, pp. 173–247.

Ribble, M.A. (1949), *The Rights of Infants.* New York: Columbia University Press.

Ritvo, S., McCollum, A.T., Omwake, E., Provence, S.A., & Solnit, A.J. (1963), Some relations of constitution, environment and personality as observed in a longitudinal study of child development. In: *Modern Perspectives in Child Development*, ed. A.J. Solnit & S.A. Provence. New York: International Universities Press, pp. 107–143.

Schaffer, H.R., Greenwood, A., & Parry, M.H. (1972), The onset of wariness. *Child Development*, 43:165–175.

Shirley, M. (1933), *The First Two Years: A Study of Twenty-five Babies.* Minneapolis: University of Minnesota Press.

Sontag, L.W. (1966), Implications of fetal behavior and environment for adult personality. *Ann. N.Y. Acad. Sci.*, 134:782–786.

Spitz, R.A. (1945), Hospitalism: An inquiry into the genesis of psychiatric conditions in early childhood. *The Psychoanalytic Study of the Child*, 1:53–74. New York: International Universities Press.

——— (1946), Anaclitic depression. *The Psychoanalytic Study of the Child*, 2:313–342. New York: International Universities Press.

——— (1965), *The First Year of Life.* New York: International Universities Press.

——— & Wolf, K.M. (1946), The smiling response. A contribution to the ontogenesis of social relations. *Genetic Psychology Monographs*, 34:57–125.

Stern, D.N.(1985), *The Interpersonal World of the Infant.* New York: Basic Books.

——— Hofer, L., Haft, W., & Dore, J. (1985), Affect attunement: A descriptive account of the intermodal communication between mothers and infants. In: *Social Perception in Infants*, ed. T.M. Field & N.A. Fox. Norwood, N.J.: Ablex.

Stone, L.J., Smith, H., & Murphy, L.B. (1972), *The Competent Infant.* New York: Basic Books.

Temeles, M.E. (1983), The infant: A socially competent individual. In: *Frontiers of Infant Psychiatry*, ed. E. Galenson & R.L. Tyson. New York: Basic Books, pp. 178–187.

Tennes, K., Emde, R.N., Kisley, A.J., & Metcalf, D.R. (1972), The stimulus barrier in early infancy: An exploration of some formulations by John Benjamin. *Psychoanal. & Contemp. Sci.*, 1:206–234.

——— & Lampe, E. (1961), *Stranger and Separation Anxiety in Infancy.* Denver:

Child Development Research Council, University of Colorado School of Medicine.

Williams, R.J. (1956), *Biochemical Individuality*. New York: Wiley.

Winnicott, D.W.(1949), Birth memories, birth trauma, and anxiety. In: *Collected Papers: Through Paediatrics to Psycho-Analysis*. London: Tavistock, 1958, pp. 174–193.

——— (1957), *Mother and Child: A Primer of First Relationships*. New York: Basic Books.

——— (1958), *Collected Papers: Through Paediatrics to Psycho-Analysis*. London: Tavistock.

——— (1960), The theory of the parent-infant relationship. In: *The Maturational Processes and the Facilitating Environment*. New York: International Universities Press, 1965, pp. 37–55.

Wolf, K.M. (1953), Observations of individual tendencies in the first year of life. In: *Problems of Infancy and Childhood*, ed. M.J.E. Senn. New York: Josiah Macy Foundation, pp. 97–137.

Wolff, P.H. (1966), *The Causes, Controls, and Organization of Behavior in the Neonate*. New York: International Universities Press.

Yarrow, L.J. (1963), Research in dimensions of early maternal care. *Merrill-Palmer Quart.*, 9:101–114.

17

Assessment of Psychopathology in the First Year of Life

REGINALD S. LOURIE, M.D., MED.SC.D.
ROBERT A. NOVER, M.D.

Psychoanalysts and others trained in psychoanalytic theory have in recent years increasingly turned their attention to the first years of life as the basis for understanding both the earliest manifestations of maladjustment and the foundations for later psychopathology. The pioneering efforts of Buhler (1935) and Anna Freud and Dorothy Burlingham (1943, 1944) with infants and families were the beginning of an evolving body of knowledge regarding personality development in the first year of life. This knowledge, derived from basic clinical research from the psychoanalytic perspective, is the basis for a proliferating variety of interventions with infants and families.

The following sections describe issues in diagnostic assessment, the psychopathological syndromes commonly seen in infancy, and a developmental approach to the classification of psychopathology in infancy.

Constitutional Considerations in Diagnostic Assessment

Psychopathological manifestations in the first year of life rarely have their roots in only one of the forms of disorders to be outlined here. Most often they have their origins in one of the constitutionally based disorders, such as problems related to homeostasis, somato-psychological differentiation, or patterns of internalization (Greenspan, Lourie, and Nover, 1979). Transitory changes and malfunctioning, such as illness or a new developmental phase, may begin on an internal basis. It is their handling and interaction with the external world that usually determine whether they will be only transitory manifestations related to specific developmental conditions, or whether they will become consolidated into a syndrome and acquire secondary values that are then perpetuated (Lourie, 1971).

The first step in evaluating internal factors is taking stock of physical states, especially of chronic depleting conditions. This is particularly important, considering the close relationship of body and mind in the first year of life and the role illness plays in interfering with and disrupting aspects of development. A second logical step is cataloging constitutional characteristics of the infant, i.e., the autonomous functions of the ego. Here one deals with individual differences, beginning with evaluation of the intactness of the infant's neurophysiological makeup, for which assessment measures are available (e.g., Brazelton, 1973). Any clinical examination of a baby should evaluate intact capacities as well as individual differences leading to imbalances between the strengths of the drives and the regulatory apparatus, one of the prime bases for difficulties in achieving homeostasis and in establishing rhythms and distortions in habituation (Sander, 1962). Some infants show difficulty early in calming themselves when anxious (Yorke, Kennedy, and Wiseberg, 1980). Thus, babies with more or less hyperkinetic patterns, for which they need outside controls when their own patterns are overwhelmed, are more or less prone to hyperactivity syndromes. At the opposite pole are babies with little innate energy, who need more than usual outside intervention and stimulation to overcome passivity if they are to deal with developmental tasks. Some of these infants are basically passive, while the low energy in others is related to nervous system irregularities, as in the "floppy infant." A basis on which babies make their needs known is the use of aggressive energy in what Murphy (1968) calls "sending power." The low-energy baby usually has little such capacity to alert the environment to its needs. Another important but not usually explored constitutional aspect to consider in evaluating these imbalances is the individual's ability to integrate responses to both inner and outer anxiety-producing stimuli and conditions. Failures in integration leading to disorganization of thinking and acting under stress are a prime basis for psychopathological responses. As Anna Freud and Shapiro and Stern point out in their contributions to this volume, the earlier such evaluations take place, the better the chance that corrective strategies will be effective, as the nervous system remains relatively plastic in the first 18 months of life.

In evaluating the somatic patterns in the individual, one looks for vulnerable organ systems which can acquire psychological significance or become the means of expressing or responding to stress or anxiety if not handled appropriately (Freedman, chapter 8). To some this may seem related to Adler's concept (1921) of organ inferiority as a prime basis for later psychosomatic pathology involving the gastrointestinal or genitourinary tracts, the respiratory system, the skin, or the immune or autoimmune systems. A fortunately rare, potentially interfering type of such distortion is found in sensory hypersensitivity (e.g., auditory sensitivity at certain tonal ranges only) and sensitivity to intensities of light). These are usually compensated for by 1 year of age, but if not recognized and treated, persistent discomfort can continue. In addition, when any system or function is not used, a distortion of failure to develop can follow as a result of "atrophy of disuse."

When an organ system responds adversely to specific stimuli or conditions, such a response is considered clinically to be psychologically significant.

Developmental Considerations

As we attempt, in diagnostic formulations, to apply knowledge about developmental issues in the first year of life, particularly that generated by Anna Freud and her Hempstead colleagues, Mahler and McDevitt, W.E. Freud, Freedman, and Murphy, we find the more detailed approaches of Anna Freud's Diagnostic Profile (1965) are the most comprehensive. We suggest that the assessment of developmental tasks be performed in two distinct steps as a basis for devising preventive or corrective strategies: the status of emerging ego functions and developmental lines should first be determined, and only then whatever is happening that interferes with expectable developmental progression.

The second area begins with patterns of stimulation and their appropriateness for the developmental phase of the infant. Here an underlying principle is that lack of stimulation can lead to extinction or at least less than optimal development of an emerging new function. Precocity and overstimulation, before or during the critical (optimal) time for development of specific functions, can interfere with their necessary regulation, as well as with the roles of earlier developmental functions as organizers of later developmental lines.

Here the "imprinting" of earliest experiences should be kept in mind in light of the repetition compulsion. Babies whose development in a specific area is delayed should not automatically be labeled retarded. At the same time, the often misleading or destructive phrase, "they'll grow out of it," should be avoided. Also to be kept in mind are individual differences in rates of development, genetic determinants, and, not necessarily optimistically, the concept of "late bloomers" which increasingly is being annotated.

The Psychopathological Syndromes in Infancy

The psychopathological syndromes of infancy should logically be described in terms of primary basis rather than secondary consequences, as is more usual. For this reason we have attempted to integrate biological etiological factors with clinical symptom constellations. We shall begin with the more traditional approach to psychopathology in infancy and early childhood, by describing symptoms (secondary consequences), and then show how these can be integrated within a developmental (primary) approach. The following clinical entities are among those most frequently found in, or rooted in, the first year of life. The entities chosen, and their descriptions, are drawn from the authors' personal experience and are not intended as an exhaustive review of the literature. It is our impression, however, that thus far there has been no presentation of the psychopathological syndromes of infancy and early childhood (from a symptom cluster perspective) as comprehensive as that attempted here.

Autism

Autism includes disturbances of developmental rates or sequences; responses to sensory stimuli; speech, language, and cognitive capacities; and the capacity to relate to people, events, and objects (Ritvo and Freedman, 1978). This condition is considered by some (Mahler, Pine, and Bergman, 1975) to be a regression of fixation to the autisic phase of earliest infancy, in which the child does not perceive the mother as representative of the outside world. Most researchers consider the symptoms as an expression of central nervous system (CNS) dysfunction, whose exact nature has not yet been determined. These children may later manifest extreme forms of self-injurious and aggressive behavior, often requiring vigorous behavioral management. Autism was first described by Kanner (1943) as a syndrome of early infantile autism, but the concept has been expanded to include older children who "live in a world of their own."

Symbiotic Psychosis

Symbiotic psychosis, described by Mahler, Pine, and Bergman (1975), is the result of a severe disturbance in the normal intrapsychic separation-individuation process. The child is emotionally unready to function separately from the mother. Any threat of a break in this tie can lead to organismic panic and ego fragmentation, resulting in a symbiotic infantile psychosis. Without therapy involving both child and mother, developmental progression beyond the separation-individuation phase is not thought possible.

Anaclitic Depression

Anaclitic depression, first described by Spitz (1946), and seen in the second half of the first year of life, is precipitated by a prolonged separation from the mother or caretaking figure. Often seen fully developed in institutionalized infants, it is characterized by crying, withdrawal, and, finally, a frozen rigidity of expression and affect accompanied by autoerotic behavior. It is thought to be caused by loss of the original love object, with an inhibition of attempted restitution. Some infants may have a constitutional susceptibility. The syndrome has also been described in infants reared in a "depriving" atmosphere at home. Recovery is facilitated by restoring the mother or mother substitute to the baby.

Metabolic Depression (Marasmus)

Marasmus is due to both protein and caloric malnutrition and presents a clinical picture of general starvation. Marasmic infants are grossly underweight, with little or no subcutaneous fat and atrophied muscle tissue. The nutritional deficiency, where no physical depleting process is involved, may develop, as in failure-to-thrive babies, from a disturbed mother-infant relationship, leading to the absence of adequate physical care, institutionalization of the infant, or lack of adequate food supply. These infants, even when restored to nutritional adequacy, often manifest seriously disturbed object relations. The kwashiorkor syndrome, which ends in a form of marasmus, has been classified by recent studies as a form of anorexia nervosa in the first years of life.

Failure to Thrive

Failure-to-thrive infants have temperaments and personalities that have displeased or disappointed the mother, who will then respond with displeasure, rejection, or neglect. These babies usually exhibit developmental delays in activities such as smiling and vocalization, lack a capacity for cuddliness, and develop a heightened wariness. There is usually a disturbance in the mother's relationship with her own mother, often involving experiences of deprivation early in her own childhood. The fathers of these infants are often relatively uninvolved with the baby and the family. The most seriously ill of these infants fall below the third percentile in weight during the first 6 months of life. After organic factors are ruled out, this condition is often diagnosed in the hospital as having an emotional basis, particularly when the staff has the opportunity to observe the parents interacting with the baby. It is not reversed, even through adequate feeding, until the baby has been provided with the consistent contact and nurturing that "sells the human race back to it." Though the infant may be kept alive, this condition may result in serious psychopathology if allowed to continue, with the child unable to form attachments or to trust self or others.

Hyperactivity (Hyperkinesis)

The type of hyperactivity seen in the first year of life usually represents a discrepancy between a high level of motor impulses and actions and the emerging regulatory capacity of the infant. Not infrequently it can be traced to the prenatal period. Where there is already a family history of hyperactivity, the condition may indicate defects in the autonomous ego capacities with which an infant is born. When the baby's needs for better control from the outside (as with swaddling or the avoidance of overstimulation from without) are not recognized, the resulting irritability can interfere with homeostasis, attachment, and the emergence in the infant of trust that its dependency needs will be met. Later in the first year, the poorly controlled motor patterns can influence the beginning self-image and the picture others have of it. For example, the baby's poorly controlled pat may become a slap, or a grasp may become a push. The baby may then be cast in the role of aggressor, hurtful, or destructive. In some cases such misunderstandings of the baby's functioning in the environment can lead to compromised solutions whereby, in order to avoid a feeling of helplessness, the baby decides in fact to be hurtful or destructive. This can be the beginning of character patterns which become the basis for the later syndrome of the hyperactive, impulsive, destructive, and aggressive child who is difficult to deal with in the preschool years.

Colic and/or Diarrhea

Colic usually appears in the first 3 months of life and is often an indicator of gastrointestinal instability. Its persistence past the age of 3 months is thought to be the result of anxiety and states of tension, in the mother or in the family, which is then transmitted to the baby. Crying, irritability, and physical depletion may lead to a vicious cycle in which the mother, feeling helpless or rejected, may become even more irritable and disquieted by the baby's behavior. If not interrupted, colic or psychosomatically based diarrhea may lead to a hostile, negative-dependent relationship between baby and mother, with impairment in attachment and subsequent stages of development. This is often treated by counseling the mother in alternative methods for handling the baby, accompanied by efforts to reduce family stress and tension. It is thought by some to "imprint" gastrointestinal responses to stress and anxiety at a later age, an instance of the repetition compulsion.

Hypersensitivities

Some babies are born with unusual sensitivities (Bergman and Escalona, 1949) in one or more modalities (visual, auditory, tactile, gustatory, olfactory, temperature-sensing). Constitutionally determined, these sensitivities, if not recognized and accommodated to in the first months of infancy, can lead to serious disturbance in later stages of development. Protection from overstimulation or too much handling will strengthen the infant's emerging capacity to filter stimulation from within and without. In some of these babies, pain or discomfort may be of sufficient degree to interfere with attachment. In others it may perpetuate primary masochism with the expectation that closeness will involve pain. In still others it becomes a "hunger" for a sensory stimulus which is at the same time avoided. Most often the actual hypersensitivity is compensated neurophysiologically by the end of the first year, but the threat of unrealistically expected pain and discomfort can continue. Primary tactile hypersensitivity (pain on being touched) can later be complicated or perpetuated by skin problems such as eczema.

Cyclic Vomiting

Cyclic vomiting is an example of the compliance of the metabolic process with emotional needs even in the first year of life. This condition often begins in the first year and is characterized by irregularly occurring attacks of vomiting leading to ketosis. Thought to be constitutional (sometimes allergic) in origin, the vomiting becomes erotized and assumes secondary meaning for the child, particularly in relation to issues of dependency or dealing with anxiety. The vomiting is usually controlled by sedation, and attacks become less frequent in later childhood. Some of the babies who suffer from cyclic vomiting are those who build up a high level of excitement in anticipation of impending experiences.

Autoerotic Rumination

Autoerotic rumination is a symptom pattern, usually seen in the second half of the first year, in which babies who are unattached and unrelated continually bring back food from the stomach to remouth it as an autoerotic substitute for closeness to the mother and object availability. Of babies in whom the condition continues uninterrupted, 75 percent die of starvation, as each time the food is brought back to the mouth some is lost. Properly diagnosed and treated, the symptom is given up.

Overprotection and the Vulnerable Child Syndrome

The vulnerable child syndrome is seen in babies born with physical conditions which either were life threatening or required prolonged neonatal hospital care. Some mothers, viewing such babies as vulnerable and easily damaged, overprotect them (Green and Solnit, 1964). Unless the overprotection is halted, these babies are likely to do poorly in developing independent identities and the necessary coping skills to deal with expectable sources of anxiety.

Maladaptive Role Assignments

In some families, the parents view the baby as having specific characteristics which determine the patterns of care that will be given. Thus, mothers who have had a difficult pregnancy or delivery may see the baby as a hurtful individual. Others identify a baby as destructive or even as a potential murderer. In some cases this has been the basis for child abuse. Other variations of inappropriate role assignment include treating a girl as if she were a more desired male infant, or vice versa.

Anorexia and Feeding Problems (Kwashiorkor)

The most extreme of the feeding difficulties is marasmus, which can also take the form of kwashiorkor. In some anorexic babies a constitutional basis exists for the problem, such as marked food allergies or pyloric stenosis. Defects in attachment patterns resulting from such conditions are more often caused not by the baby turning away from caretakers but by caretakers turning away from the baby in frustration over not being able to meet its needs. Some babies, however, stop eating in the second half of the first year, particularly if there has been no significant attachment or if dependency needs have not been recognized or met, as described under anaclitic depression. An unusual condition has been described in which excess secretion of uropepsinogen in the infant's stomach creates sensations of insatiable hunger. Not being able to be satisfied creates distortions in the baby's sense of trustful dependency.

Separation Anxiety

Separation anxiety appears when the infant can begin to be on its own for a while, for example, when it is learning to crawl and can distinguish familiar objects from strange ones. Another factor involved here is that the baby functions as if what it does not see does not exist, so that the ultimate fear is of object loss, abandonment, and even nonexistence. One of the major effects of separation anxiety as it proceeds through the stages of separation-individuation stems from its role as the prototype of later, more partialized fears, such as those which are part of later castration anxiety.

A variety of symptoms can manifest themselves during this expectable stage of development. The more common clinical symptoms, which can become consolidated into psychopathological manifestations, are sleeping problems, eating problems, trichotillomania, new aggressive patterns, and anxiety about the unfamiliar, including fear of new experiences and fear of strangers.

It is important to distinguish the sleeping problems that originate in this stage from earlier ones which may have a constitutional base. However, earlier sleeping problems may be locked into place when separation concerns are added to them.

Eating problems stemming from this developmental phase may take the form of severe anorexia and sometimes have their beginnings in the refusal of new foods. If forced, the baby may refuse all food, accept only liquids, or refuse to chew. Other variations are the result of abrupt changes, such as sudden weaning or removal from the familiar home or caretakers, when anxiety level is high. Sometimes with abrupt weaning all liquids, including mild ones, are refused. These eating problems, like sleeping problems, should be looked at from the perspective of earlier difficulties of a similar sort.

A very few babies, whose separation problems are not recognized and whose changing dependency needs are not met, will begin to pull out hair (trichotillomania) at this stage. From observations it has been postulated that these babies played with or were touched by the mother's long hair during feeding and cuddling.

Stranger anxiety, which often begins months before the height of the "8-month anxiety," has its earliest manifestation when a stranger appears and immediately looks intently at, or reaches out for, the baby. Within a minute or two the baby will cry. If the stranger avoids looking at the baby for a while until the baby, who by now has crawled back to its mother, has the assurance that the stranger is "safe," it is then all right for the stranger to interact with the baby. If, however, the mother is herself uneasy about the stranger or about the baby's initial response, stranger anxiety in the infant may be perpetuated; this is particularly likely in babies who have had difficulties in achieving homeostasis or have developed a poor sense of trust.

It is expected that the baby will experiment with the expression of aggression in every developmental phase, and that stage of separation anxiety is no exception. One such expression that can become the basis for later psychopathology is seen when the mother returns to a baby who had become anxious and had protested when she left. Here the baby often turns away upon her return, as if to say, "You didn't leave or get rid of me—I got rid of you." If the mother then becomes upset the baby has learned an important lesson: "by my leaving I can hurt others." Left unmodified, this pattern of thinking and defense has been found to be a factor in later suicide attempts: "I hurt you by leaving." Very few suicides are undertaken without thought of how others will feel. The defensive pattern of turning away in this stage of development is also considered a basis for later feelings of aloneness (Adler and Buie, 1979).

A Developmental Approach to the Classification of Infant Psychopathology

In the next section we describe a way of looking at primary developmental problems according to the specific stage of development the infant uses to cope with internal and external experience (or stimuli). This approach is based on the developmental structuralist model of the stages of infancy and early childhood developed by Greenspan (1979) and subsequently applied to the delineation of psychopathology in infancy and early childhood (Greenspan, Lourie, and Nover, 1979). The following discussion summarizes these earlier works to set the stage for the ensuing integration of the symptom-oriented (secondary consequence) approach with the developmental (primary disorder) approach to psychopathology.

Disorders of Homeostasis

These disorders, which can be identified very early, involve deficits in the ability to regulate, form basic cycles and rhythms, organize internal and external experience (e.g., implement certain stimulus thresholds, habituate to stimuli, organize initial response patterns, motor integrity, gaze, etc.), and integrate a number of modalities into more complex patterns, such as consoling oneself and coping with noxious stimuli. Gross physical or neurological defects, subtle physical differences (e.g., floppiness), immaturity of the central nervous system, difficulties in early patterns of integration (Sander, 1962; Brazelton, 1973), certain environmental conditions, organ sensitivities (e.g., gastrointestinal problems), and allergies are but a few of the factors that may contribute to a homeostatic disorder. For example, there is the excitable infant who cannot habituate to stimulation; the infant with specific sensitivities (auditory, tactile); the infant with immature motor responses who cannot orient or use the caregiver to calm down; and the hyperstimulating caregiver who keeps the infant aroused. While gross deficits in perceptual apparatuses (e.g., blindness or deafness) make an infant more prone to a disorder of homeostasis, integrative capacities may nevertheless predominate, allowing a homeostatic experience nearer the optimal (Fraiberg, 1977).

Disorders of Human Attachment

The capacity for attachment is shown in the quality of homeostatic experience achieved between the infant and primary caretakers and in the quality of feeling and reciprocal interactions characterizing this human attachment.

The most severe attachment disorders result from genetic or constitutional difficulties or severe early environmental trauma. The infant never fully achieves homeostasis and therefore does not move on to the second task, human attachment. We also see disorders of human attachment with depressed mothers who cannot reach out to their infants and whose attachment seems shallow and insecure. Constitutional differences that make physical touch or other kinds of human stimulation painful may also lay the basis for a disorder of attachment.

Disorders of Somato-Psychological Differentiation

Somato-psychological differentiation reaches a noticeable level at 8 months, around the time of what Spitz (1965) has called stranger anxiety. Now different somato-psychological states (e.g., hunger and other states such as dependency needs or the need for affection) and different moods and communications from primary caregivers are distinguished by the infant. Less dependent now on internal states, no longer simply a victim of its own hunger or tiredness), the infant becomes a more social, interactive being (Emde, Gaensbauer, and Harmon, 1976; Sroufe and Waters, 1976).

It is possible for an infant to undergo differentiation in the areas of gross motor responses and general interpersonal causality and yet remain undifferentiated as regards subtle emotional and empathic experience.

Problems of somato-psychological differentiation can result in failures of phase-appropriate differentiation as regards cognition, human relationships, and affects, and in a lack of the flexibility needed to deal with phase-appropriate experience and stress without compromising developmentally facilitating behavior.

Symptoms include sensorimotor developmental delays, apathy, intense chronic fear (stranger anxiety), clinging, lack of exploration and curiosity, flat emotional reactions to significant caregivers, specific and maladaptive patterns of relatedness such as biting, chronic crying, and irritability. These disorders involve the organization of certain emotional systems, e.g., affiliation, separation, fear and wariness, curiosity and explorativeness (Ainsworth, Andry, Harlow, Lebovici, Mead, Prugh, and Wootton, 1962).

Disorders of Internalization (Behavior Organization and Initiative)

These are developmental failures in the capacity for combining schemes into new, goal-directed behavioral organizations. These failures may show themselves in the continued use of detours, substitutes, delays, and intermediary devices. Behavior remains fragmented in relation to somatic or external cues. Intentionality and sense of self are delayed, thereby negatively affecting, in instances of severe disorder at this phase, the basic capacity for forming mental representations.

Specific disorders of this sort range in severity from compromise in the internalization, organization, and originality of behavior (as evidenced by a complete lack of imitation, intentionality, and organized emotional and behavior systems) to circumscribed limitations in one or another of these systems, e.g., a lack of assertive or affiliative behavior.

Failure by the end of the second year of life to establish an internal sense of self and object, (e.g., the ability to conserve internal representations of animate and inanimate objects) is evidenced by a diminished behavioral, emotional, cognitive, and interpersonal repertoire. Deficits are seen in the age-appropriate ability to establish a sense of person. These deficits are manifest in the behavioral, emotional, cognitive, and interpersonal repertoire of the 2-year-old (e.g., the ability to say no; the development of personal pronouns; the ability to recall and organize mental images and to search for inanimate and animate objects; the ability to remember emotional experience; the locating of experiences as regards self and nonself; the beginning of cognitive insight combining internalized schemes; the ability to identify the various parts of self; the ability to relate in a manner less tied to the fulfillment of needs; and cooperation and concern for others).

Disorders of this phase are evidenced by the lack of psychological life (internal representations) and may be observed in symptoms involving severe regressive behavior (disorganized emotional and motor responses); chronic, unrelenting clinging, with complete disruption of explorative behavior; chronic primitive aggressive behavior (biting, scratching, throwing things); chronic fearfulness; and either interpersonal promiscuity or withdrawal.

Disorders of Psychological Differentiation

These disorders center on the failure to achieve a further differentiation at the level of mental representation (e.g., symbol formation and the corresponding capacity for language development).

Lack of differentiation of self from nonself and a failure to move toward a level of various feeling states and behavior result in the failure to establish libidinal object constancy (Mahler, Pine, and Bergman, 1975). Thus there is no delineated self- and object representation to serve as the foundation for basic ego functions such as reality testing, organization and regulation of impulses, organization and regulation of thought, integration of thought and affect, and ongoing delineation and sense of self. There may be a capacity for some organized internal psychological life, but it is extremely vulnerable to vicissitudes of stress (separation, strong feeling states), and primary process and magical thinking predominates.

At a less severe level, basic differentiation occurs, but at a cost that includes major distortions in personality or character formation, i.e., an overall inflexibility of the personality precluding full engagement in life's major endeavors. Here we see the severe personality disorders, youngsters who are very negativistic, withdrawn, schizoid, paranoid, or very depressed and apathetic.

Disorders of Consolidation in Basic Personality Functions

When consolidation of object constancy fails to occur at ages 3½ or 4, basic personality functions (e.g., reality testing, impulse regulation, integration and organization of affect and thought) do not develop properly. There is vulnerability to regression, states of anxiety and depression, and moderate to mild characterological constrictions. Self-object differentiation occurs but cannot withstand the stress of separation or strong affect states. Instead of regressions, we may see phase-specific symptom formations in terms of certain developmental conflicts or moderate distortions of character—e.g., moderate obsessive-compulsive behavior or patterns of externalization. The final crystalization of character distortions or symptoms usually reflects a condensation of oedipal and preoedipal determinants.

Psychopathological Syndromes of Infancy and Early Childhood in the Context of a Developmental Approach

Table 1 combines the expectable stages of development (A) at which the primary basis for the psychopathology is usually seen, and the stages of development (B) at which the secondary consequences usually appear. As such, it represents a comprehensive, integrated diagnostic system for assessing infant psychopathology. The syndromes are coded as shown below in terms of the classification system used in this chapter.

1. Disorders of Homeostasis
2. Disorders of Human Attachment
3. Disorders of Somato-Psychological Differentiation
4. Disorders of Internalization (Behavioral Organization and Initiative)
5. Disorders of Psychological Differentiation
6. Disorders of Consolidation of Basic Personality Functions

TABLE 1
Stages of Development of Psychopathology

Syndromes	Primary Pathology (A)	Secondary Consequence (B)
Autism	A-1	B-2, 4, 5
Symbiotic Psychosis		
Anaclitic Depression		
Metabolic Depression	A-2	B-3, 4, 5
(Marasmus)		
Failure to Thrive	A-1	B-2, 3
Hyperactivity (Hyperkinesis)	A-1, 3	B-3, 4, 5
Colic and/or Diarrhea	A-1 and/or	B-2, 5
Hypersensitivities	A-1, 3	B-2, 4, 5
Cyclic Vomiting	A-1, 3	B-2
Autoerotic Rumination	A-2	B-1, 4, 5
Overprotection	A-2	B-4, 6
(Vulnerable Child		
Syndrome)		
Maladaptive Role	A-2	B-1
Assignments		
Anorexia and Feeding	A-2	B-1, 3, 4
Problems		
Separation Anxiety	A-1 or 2	B-2, 4, 5
(Manifested by sleeping		
problems, stranger anxiety,		
eating problems, and		
forms of aggression)		

Summary

We have described the application of psychoanalytic studies of infant development to an understanding of psychopathological syndromes commonly seen by clinicians during the first 18 months of life. We have presented a picture of these syndromes and a developmental approach to their understanding. We have attempted to integrate the symptom-oriented and developmental approaches in a manner that facilitates developmentally specific, dynamically oriented treatment plans. It has also been our goal to dispel the understandable reluctance of many health and mental health professionals to believe that an infant less than a year old can develop life-threatening or disabling emotional problems.

References

Adler, A. (1921), *The Neurotic Constitution*. New York: Moffat, Yard.

Adler, G., & Buie, D. (1979), Aloneness and borderline psychopathology: The possible relevance of child development issues. *Internat. J. Psycho-Anal.*, 60:83–96.

Ainsworth, M., Andry, R.G., Harlow, R.G., Lebovici, S., Mead, M., Prugh, D., & Wootton, B. (1962), *Deprivation of Maternal Care: A Reassessment of Its Effects*. Geneva: World Health Organization.

Bergman, P., & Escalona, S. (1949), Unusual sensitivities in very young children. *The Psychoanalytic Study of the Child*. 3/4:333–352. New York: International Universities Press.

Brazelton, T.B. (1973), *Neonatal Behavior Assessment Scale*. Philadelphia: Lippincott.

Buhler, C. (1935), *From Birth to Maturity*. London: Routledge.

Emde, R., Gaensbauer, T., & Harmon, R. (1976), Emotional expression in infancy: A biobehavioral study. *Psychological Issues*, Monograph 37. New York: International Universities Press.

Fraiberg, S. (1977), *Insights from the Blind: Comparative Studies and Sighted Infants*. New York: Basic Books.

Freud, A. (1965), *Normality and Pathology in Childhood*. New York: International Universities Press.

────── & Burlingham, D. (1943), *War and Children*. New York: International Universities Press.

────── ────── (1944), *Infants Without Families*. New York: International Universities Press.

Green, M., & Solnit, A.J. (1964), Reactions to the threatened loss of a child: A vulnerable child syndrome. Pediatric management of the dying child. Part 3. *Pediatrics*, 34:58–66.

Greenspan, S.I. (1979), Intelligence and adaptation: An integration of psychoanalytic and Piagetian developmental psychology. *Psychological Issues*, Monograph 47/48. New York: International Universities Press.

────── Lourie, R., & Nover, R. (1979), A developmental approach to the classification of psychopathology of infancy and early childhood. In: *Handbook of Child Psychiatry*, ed. J. Noshpitz. Vol. II. New York: Basic Books.

Kanner, L. (1943), Autistic disturbances of affective contact. *Nervous Child*, 2:217–250.

Lourie, R. (1971), The first three years of life. *Amer. J. Psychiat.*, 127:1457–1463.

Mahler, M.S., Pine, F., & Bergman, A. (1975), *The Psychological Birth of the Human Infant*. New York: Basic Books.

Murphy, L. (1968), Assessment of infants and young children. In: *Early Child Care: The New Perspectives*, ed. C. Chandler, R. Lourie, & A. Peters. New York: Atherton.

Ritvo, E.R., & Freedman, B.J. (1978), Introduction: The National Society for Autistic Children's definition of the syndrome of autism. *J. Amer. Acad. Child Psychiat.*, 17:565–575.

Sander, L. (1962), Issues in early mother-child interaction. *J. Amer. Acad. Child Psychiat.*, 1:141–166.

Spitz, R. (1946), Anaclitic depression. *The Psychoanalytic Study of the Child,* 2:313–342. New York: International Universities Press.

———— (1965), *The First Year of Life: A Psychoanalytic Study of Normal and Deviant Development of Object Relations.* New York: International Universities Press.

Sroufe, L.A., & Waters, E. (1976), The ontogenesis of smiling and laughter: A perspective on the organization of development in infancy. *Psychological Review,* 83:173–189.

Yorke, C., Kennedy, H., & Wiseberg, S. (1980), Some clinical and theoretical aspects of two developmental lines. In: *The Course of Life: Psychoanalytic Contributions Toward Understanding Personality Development. Vol. I: Infancy and Early Childhood,* ed. S.I. Greenspan & G.H. Pollock. Washington: Government Printing Office.

Name Index

Subject Index

Abandonment, threats of, 241
Abstraction, 115, 121
  patterns of, 117
Action drives, 591
Action language, 180
Activation, in emotional expression, 214
Active awake state, 413
Active REM sleep, 412
Actuality, 73
  sharing of, 59
Adaptation processes, 366, 605
  epigenetic sequence of issues in, 386–387
  focus on, 569
Adolescence, psychosocial development during, 56–59
Adulthood stage, psychosocial development during, 51–56
Affect(s)
  adaptive nature of, 173–175, 185, 194, 215, 216
  arousal and, 282–283, 289
  changing zeitgeist on, 167–168
  in clinical psychoanalysis, 172–173
  conflict and, 186
  continuity of, 175
  current controversy concerning psychoanalytic models of, 179–181
  damming up of, 169
  defenses in psychic conflict and, 178
  definition of, 171
  development of structures of, 186
  early development of, 602–604
  evolution in Freud's theory on, 167–172
  Freud's organizational model of, 193–194
  in human social relatedness, 175–176

  in interpersonal social definition, 281
  as language of infancy, 214–215
  organizational model for, 165–172, 193–194
    implications of, 213–214
  propositions about from outside psychoanalysis, 181–183
  psychoanalytic theory of, 165–187
    based on emotional development and signaling in infancy, 193–221
  signal, 176–178, 186
  social signaling functions of, 218–219
  S–R model of, 193
  structures of, 216–217
Affect attunement, 597
Affect hunger, 578
Affect intensification, 143
Affectionate physical behavior, 520–521, 526
Affective disorders, with visual-spatial processing deficit, 156–160
Affective field, establishment of object in, 271–290
Affective meaning, 141
Affective monitoring, 209–210
Affective relationships, 101
  formation of, 102
Affective self, 208–210
Affective-thematic organization, 95–96
  in attachment stage, 102
  in behavioral organization stage, 115
  in representational capacity stage, 125–126
  of representational differentiation stage, 137–139
  in somatopsychological differentiation stage, 107–108

673